THE
ENGLISH
NATION
THE GREAT MYTH

E D W I N   J O N E S

SUTTON PUBLISHING

This book was first published in 1998 by Sutton Publishing Limited

First published in paperback by Sutton Publishing Limited in 2000

This new paperback edition first published in 2003 by
Sutton Publishing Limited · Phoenix Mill
Thrupp · Stroud · Gloucestershire · GL5 2BU

British Library Cataloguing in Publication Data
A catalogue record for this book is available from the British Library

ISBN 0 7509 3207 4

Typeset in 10/11pt Photina.
Typesetting and origination by
Sutton Publishing Limited.
Printed and bound in Great Britain by
J.H. Haynes & Co. Ltd, Sparkford.

Contents

'national passions are rooted in images which run back through hundreds of years. Memories of this sort are no part of our biology, yet they dominate our lives. . . . These collective memories, whether imposed from above as ruling ideologies or forged from below by the struggle of emerging social movements, are the means whereby we remember the past, our history, and therefore they both guide our present actions and shape our futures.'

Steven Rose, *The Making of Memory* (1992)

'It is important to reaffirm the possibility of discovering the truth about the past. . . . Without a knowledge of our history we could not understand our present society, or plan intelligently for the future.'

C. Behan McCullagh, *The Truth of History* (1998)

Foreword

No-one can fairly doubt the depth and brilliance of Britain's history-writing tradition. If the Prussian School developed the academic approach to history, and the French Annales School pioneered the multidisciplinary marriage of history with the social sciences, the British have long excelled in the propagation of history as a branch of high literature. The names of Gibbon, Macaulay and Trevelyan are unsurpassed both in the quality of their style and their influence on the public at large. Scotland, Ireland and Wales, as well as England, have their own distinguished schools. In addition there are old-established and flourishing traditions of archival services, of documentary publication, of historical journals and of history teaching at every level. Whatever critics may say, Britain is not a backward country in the historical field.

Nonetheless, numerous failings have made themselves apparent in recent decades. History has lost much of its popular appeal with the reading public. Trevelyan's last great work, his *English Social History*, was written in 1941. Not only does it not have a successor of similar stature, it is not read by modern students and scholars, who think they have more important things to do. The historical profession has increasingly fallen foul of obscurantist ultra-specialisation. Universities do not encourage broad historical horizons. In schools, history has lost its place as a fixed component of the curriculum. Worst of all, the pernicious blight of Anglocentrism is spreading. Despite the widespread adoption of the label of 'British' as opposed to 'English' history, very little attention is paid to the non-English elements in the story. Indeed, in popular usage, as in the organisation of libraries, 'British' and 'English' history are frequently taken to be synonymous, thereby eliminating any recognition of the long centuries when Ireland, Wales and Scotland, no less than England, were independent nations. Inexorably, English people have come to rely more on the myths about their past than on solid information, and the English represent a crushing majority of the UK population.

Concerted efforts to stem the tide of Anglocentrism were slow to develop. For years, historians were more concerned with the new perspectives provided by social, economic or gender studies than with the general framework of their subject. Scottish, Welsh and Irish historians tended to cultivate their own separate gardens. When it was first published in 1992, therefore, Linda Colley's *Britons* delivered a considerable shock. It demonstrated that British identity, far from being an emanation of England's seamless continuity, was the product of a particular period following the creation of the United Kingdom in 1707. It was equally the product of less than admirable attitudes connected with Protestant suprematism, war, imperialism and xenophobia. Similarly, Conrad Russell's work on the mid-seventeenth century has amply shown that the 'English Civil War' is a grand misnomer, no proper understanding of conflicts in the pre-Union isles being possible without a full consideration of the Scottish and Irish kingdoms. Rees Davies, as President of the Royal Historical Society, has shifted attention in the medieval era to the agenda of peoples and identities, at a time long preceding any sense of common Britishness.

These historians and their supporters have undoubtedly caused a groundswell of unease, and have shaken the reigning complacency. But the contributions have been chronologically limited and thematically fragmented, and few general conclusions have been drawn. To date, little attention has been paid to the ideological roots of the English historical mind-set, which is coming increasingly under attack from these various directions.

At which point, enter Dr Edwin Jones. Jones is particularly well qualified to ask the most searching questions. As a Welsh-speaking Catholic, he is free from both the English and the Protestant bias by which conventional history has been fuelled. As a distinguished educator, he is very conscious of changing attitudes to history in the public at large. Most importantly perhaps, as a pupil of the late Sir Herbert Butterfield, author of the classic *The Whig Interpretation of History* (1931), he was introduced at an early stage not only to the importance of historiography but also to the most rigorous criticisms of the reigning conventions. In consequence, he has been able to construct a broad and coherent view of a subject where too many of his predecessors have failed to see the wood for the trees.

The English Nation, therefore, presents a grand panorama spanning almost two millennia from the coming of Christianity to the historiography of the 1990s. But two topics are given special emphasis. The first topic, the building of the 'Official Version' by Thomas Cromwell and his successors in the Tudor period, is supported by a detailed examination of the historical preambles to the Reformation statutes. It shows how the legacy of pre-Reformation England, with its strong European and Catholic connections, was systematically distorted, downgraded and denigrated and how the new construct of Protestant English nationalism was established with virtually monopoly status. It also explains how the official version, once installed, was encrusted with layer after layer of historical writing in the same vein. The formidable tradition of English constitutional history, for example, which is based on reverence for the Common Law and for the Westminster Parliament, could never have developed if the older respect for the Canon Law had not been suppressed.

The second topic to be treated in detail is the remarkable career of Revd John Lingard (1771–1851), a Catholic historian whose considerable achievements never found their way into the established historical canon. Lingard's opinions are important not only because they provide a highly professional and detailed counterpoint to the official version but also because they expose the prejudices of so much English history-writing. Once the Tudors had sown the idea that the English were a self-sufficient people with a superior character and a providential mission, it was very hard to challenge it until widespread doubts arose following the collapse of the British Empire more than four hundred years later.

Edwin Jones, however, has a further agenda. He is deeply committed to the European ideal and to the promotion of a supranational community where ancient national rivalries are forgotten. To this end, he inevitably sees nationalistic myths as ammunition for Euroscepticism and as a barrier to the international understanding which is essential to our safety in a globalised age. In this sense, the measured tones and careful scholarship of *The English Nation* cannot change the fact that it is a committed political work. And it is none the worse for that. Edwin Jones is arguing a case which is of burning relevance to the choices of today. His arguments are likely to meet instinctive resistance in some quarters. But they deserve to be read and pondered far beyond the narrow confines of historical circles. They are a brilliant and thought-provoking contribution to a growing debate which concerns the future of the United Kingdom no less than England's past.

Norman Davies
Oxford
February 2000

Prologue

It is certainly arguable that there is a no more quintessentially English area than the Cotswolds. G.M. Trevelyan described Chipping Camden's High Street as the best example of its kind in England, while William Morris said that Bibury was the most beautiful village in the country. Ralph Vaughan Williams, whose music, especially his folk music, reflects the spirit of 'Englishry' so evocatively, was born in Down Ampney where his father was vicar. He edited the *English Hymnal* which includes his own 'Down Ampney'. This whole area is rightly an essential part of the itinerary for visitors from abroad who wish to breathe the atmosphere of genuine 'Englishry'. Some delightful villages, like Broadwell or Upper and Lower Oddington (with its ancient Anglo-Saxon church), hidden away behind Stow-on-the-Wold still remain for the most part outside the normal tourist track.

On New Year's Day, 1997, my wife and I travelled from Wales along the M4 motorway, before turning onto the straight old Roman road – the Fosse Way – over the southern Cotswolds, to visit the ancient town of Cirencester, with its beautiful medieval parish church of St John the Baptist. This is the greatest of England's famous 'wool' churches, built from the wealth of the medieval trade with Flanders. As we approached, St John's twelve bells, the oldest in England, were echoing across the town and surrounding countryside to welcome in the New Year, as they have been doing for centuries past. The soaring west tower dominates the landscape and can be seen for miles around as one approaches across the wolds. The first snowflakes of 1997 were beginning to fall as we arrived.

We stayed at the King's Head, of medieval origin, which overlooks the lively market place across from the church. The town's narrow streets speak eloquently of the past. There is the Spitalgate with its medieval almshouse, the remains of the old hospital of St John; a row of wool merchants' houses and workers' dwellings; the Weaver's Hall founded in 1425; the Bear, another old coaching inn dating from the medieval period. Cirencester, or Corinium, has been an important centre for roads crossing the Cotswolds and the old Fosse Way since Roman times when the town was second in size only to London (Londinium), also a Roman foundation.

The Corinium Museum contains one of England's best collections of Roman remains, including some exquisite mosaics taken from local Roman residences. One of the best examples of a Roman villa can still be visited a little to the north, near the other very old town of Northleach, while one of the largest villa sites in England, Woodchester, between Stroud and Nailsworth, was built in AD 117 and excavated in 1796. We noticed later that an exact replica of one of these mosaics, depicting a hare as its centrepiece, had been built into one of the new shopping malls in Cirencester, so connecting a section of new building with the town's Roman origins.

By now the snow had arrived and it was bitterly cold as the sun set, giving pink, crimson and purple hues to the darkening scene. We turned into the snow-covered grounds of the medieval Abbey of St Mary. Here the old River Churn winds its way into a small lake, inhabited by wild duck and swans. Two sites were indicated on a signpost in the Abbey grounds as being of particular interest to visitors. One was a section of the old Roman wall of Cirencester, built in the second century AD. The other was the only remaining section – the great Norman arched gatehouse – of the Augustinian Abbey of St Mary, built in the twelfth century. I became very conscious of the continuity of history, as well as of a certain timeless quality, as we stood there, touching the old stones, carefully and expertly placed by other hands so long ago. The Norman was separated from the Roman by the same span of time – a thousand years – as we are separated from the Norman. He or she may well have touched the Roman stones with the same kind of thoughts which came to us. Now we are at the beginning of the third millennium after the birth of Christ. How will people look back at us at the end of this new millennium? For what shall we, as people of our time, be famous or infamous, praised or blamed?

History in one sense can be described as the continuous relationship and interaction between elements in the human condition and environment, some of which change, and others which are unchanging. These historical remains in one of England's oldest towns tell their own story of the nature of England's past. They are replicated in many other English towns and villages, like nearby Fairford where the Church of St Mary the Virgin has the only complete set of medieval stained glass windows in England, setting out the Christian faith in pictorial form.[1] Later we visited the county city of Gloucester, dominated by its superb cathedral which has been a site of community and worship for 1300 years, bespeaking stability, continuity and permanence to the human mind. Here again is a soaring Norman tower which is regarded as one of the finest in western Europe, and the harmony of design, light and colour of the Lady Chapel is crowned by the magnificent medieval stained glass of the great east window.

One of the most obvious signs of some drastic change in the past is the disappearance of the old abbey at Cirencester and the monastery at Gloucester. The elegance of the ruined remnant of the Augustinian gatehouse and the still beautiful Benedictine cloisters reminded us – as did the broken, defaced reredos in the superb Lady Chapel at Gloucester – of the countless treasures of art and achitecture which were destroyed during Henry VIII's 'Reformation' and are now much lamented by cultural historians.[2] It gives some perspective to the scene when we remember that, just as in so many other places in England, the great cathedral itself was just the monastic church of the Benedictine community at Gloucester, until the monastery was destroyed in 1540.

Apart from being such obvious and drastic signs of change, these remains also contain strong impressions of other, changeless factors which seem to be closely connected with people's deepest needs and aspirations. The beauty of the church at Cirencester, for example, and its wonderfully evocative atmosphere, the glorious stained glass windows, the remains of the earlier abbey, even the sound of the bells across the snow – all speak of those instinctive needs to worship, to belong in community and to seek human expressions of, responses to, and celebrations of the deeper meanings which lie behind the changing pageantry of life around us. What are those meanings and values which lie at the historical and cultural roots of English identity and which produced the ethereal beauty of such art and architecture? What sort of community did they create in the English past?

As modern architects know, historical remains can be foci of continuity, timelessness and perspective, which put us in touch with our ancestral 'roots' or 'identity' or sense of 'belonging', all of which are necessary to our human well-being. These elements can play a very important part in the building of psychological stability in individuals and in communities. Such factors become particularly influential when these individuals or communities are faced with crises, such as having to make important and life-changing decisions. In making such decisions, people are revealed as truly themselves.[3] Some individuals deliberately return to their familiar surroundings in order to make such important decisions.[4]

People grow and develop their humanity in community, in relationship with others. Culture is the community's way of expressing and celebrating its sense of meaning in life. 'Culture' derives from *cultus*, meaning worship. Religion was at the heart of both community and culture[5] in Christian Europe, including England. This truth is central to the historian's understanding of this community of peoples. In this situation any radical religious change will affect all aspects of a community's life, thought and culture. This is why the Reformation is such a central turning-point in the history of England. One enormous implication was that it changed the English people's allegiance from a universal to a national Church, which affected their ways of thinking in many other directions. A proper understanding of this change, within the perspective of the whole of the English past, is essential to any meaningful understanding of English history and the growth of the modern English outlook on the rest of Europe.

Knowledge of the past can act, like the experience of an individual, as a very important element of guidance for the future. The people of England and of Britain are faced now with a very important decision concerning their future. Should they see their identity now as European, as well as English or British? Or should they see themselves still as exclusively English or British and remain isolated within that independent and sovereign nation-state which has defined their identity since the sixteenth century? This decision is likely to be influenced greatly, if not always consciously, by their knowledge of their past which is the basis for identity. Therefore this past needs to be examined carefully and closely in its widest and deepest perspective, so that it can provide a valid basis for true identity. The English and the British will be better prepared for their place in the world of the new millennium, with all its challenges, problems and opportunities, if they can rediscover and apply those spiritual values which lie at the roots of their own civilization and culture and which played the greatest part in shaping them over most of their history. They must, in fact, lose their false identity and discover their true one, as part of the European community of peoples. These people share the same values which lie at the very root of their common civilization.

Preface

We are all affected greatly by our history, which may be regarded as the unique memory of an individual or the collective memory of a nation. This is what gives us a sense of identity in relation to a community. In doing so, it relates to some of our most important basic needs which we usually take for granted until we are deprived of them. Our memory is also one of the most important influences acting upon our thinking and psychology. It plays a very important part in shaping our attitudes, values, assumptions of thought and general outlook. This is perhaps the sense in which the past can most influence the present and the future. This process occurs, of course, whether or not the knowledge of our past is true. People can be misled by a false version of the past.

The theme of this study is the way in which such a false view of the English past was created deliberately by government in the sixteenth century, so as to fabricate an erroneous collective memory for the English people.[1] This national memory became so deeply embedded in the mind of most English people that it became part of English folklore and one of the most powerful assumptions of thought operating on the behaviour and outlook of the English people for over four centuries. It represents one of the earliest and most successful attempts by a national state to shape the thinking of its own people. The techniques involved in this mass deception are themselves very intriguing. Only very recently have we been shown in detail how a new national and political theology, with obedience to the king – representing 'God's word' – at its centre, was borrowed for political purposes and then used as government propaganda by Thomas Cromwell.[2] Similarly, a new view of the whole English past, based on this same political theology, was created as propaganda by the Henrician government to justify the revolution which we call the Reformation.

It is because of this deliberately conceived misunderstanding of their history that the English were to forget that they were Europeans.[3] They were to become increasingly nationalistic and insular in outlook, despite the acquisition of a great empire overseas. They developed other qualities which were inspired by this view of their past, including a sense of 'specialness', self-sufficiency, superiority and separation from all the other peoples of the world. This false memory influenced their psychology and their outlook on the world. This goes a long way to explain the particular difficulties encountered when England finally lost its empire and was struggling to find a new role in the world and when the forces of political and economic change made it necessary for it to become part of Europe again. In the middle of the twentieth century very few English voices supported such a prospect and there are still many people, at the end of this century, who find it very difficult to accept.

The historian seeks to understand past assumptions of thought in order to understand past peoples. This may lead him or her to look more closely at the assumptions of thought which are the essential commonplaces of our own day, those things which we take for granted without always knowing why we do so. These can be among the most important factors conditioning our thinking and behaviour and they are also the most difficult to discern. We tend not to discuss or write down what we take for granted.[4] The unearthing of these hidden springs of our thinking and behaviour is one of the prime objectives of the historian who wishes to understand a particular society. The student of historiography considers how each generation reflects upon the past, looks at it in a certain way and is in turn influenced by it. He or she is also concerned to discover the various factors which lie behind the way in which history is written, and assumptions of thought loom large in this area.

Attitudes towards nationalism form one of the most powerful bases of our own assumptions of thought. S. Woolf, a contemporary observer, writes:

> Nationalism has become so integral a part of life in Europe today that it is virtually impossible not to identify oneself with a nation-state . . . we have been prepared to fight wars to affirm the independence or rights of our nation against what we regard as the threat of other states, or tragically, other 'ethnically' different peoples. . . . To belong to a nation-state has become so natural that, on the one hand, almost any people capable of articulating its identity and its case of persecution by the existing state demands the right to independence and territory, while on the other hand nation-states build political and legal barriers to exclude all but their own citizens. The passport – in

origin a *passe-partout* issued to protect the traveller – has become an obligatory document of legal existence, symbol of the dependence of the individual on the nation-state, so inconceivable is the concept of statelessness. Yet nationalism, in its identification of a people with the territorial nation-state, is a historically modern phenomenon. . . .[5]

He attributes the blame for the national pride and political aggressiveness of the modern nation-state to historians of the nineteenth century, such as Ranke in Germany and J.R. Green and John Seeley in England, who followed Hegel's ideology of 'destiny' and 'inevitability' in the concept of the nation-state as the embodiment of the 'spirit' or life-force of a people. The assumption that a 'national spirit' could be followed like a thread through the centuries was 'laid down with academic authority to a lay audience' and it became 'through endless simplification and repetition in school and family, an uncritical dogma'. The 'destiny' of the nation-state both explained its past history and justified its aggressively imperialistic designs in the modern world. In spite of the catastrophic effects of such thinking in the twentieth century and after two world wars, the supreme importance of the nation-state still exists as an assumption of thought at the end of this century. The claim is for the existence of a 'primordial instinct, like the family, inherently superior to other loyalties, and that the "nation" as a "natural unit" has always existed, albeit for long in a passive and dormant state'.[6]

This false assumption goes some way towards explaining the apparent need among many twentieth-century historians to seek evidence of 'nationalism' in medieval England; there is grave danger of misreading medieval evidence in order to make it fit in with this modern idea of nationalism.[7] The modern view on the history of nationalism is perhaps best expressed by E.J. Hobsbawm, who sees its origins in the eighteenth century. This view has been contested recently by Adrian Hastings, who argues for a medieval origin, stemming from biblical religion and vernacular literature.[8] In this study I draw the main distinction between *patriotism*, that sense of Englishry which dates back to Bede in the seventh century, and modern *nationalism*, which regards other peoples as inferior aliens and which I see as emerging in England as a result of the Reformation.

This particular assumption of thought relates closely to the theme of this book and, in particular, to the context of the contemporary debate concerning the proper attitude which should be taken in England and Britain towards the question of European unity.

I shall be concerned particularly with the history of the 'official version' of the past, which was created originally in the preambles to the statutes of the Reformation Parliament in the period 1532–6. The subject is strategically important in English historiography because it contains certain seminal ideas which were used then and later to interpret not only the Reformation in England but also the whole of English history before and after that event. As such, it has exercised an extraordinary influence on the thinking of the English people up to the present day. Its critical drawback is that it is not true. We need to know more about it in order to understand the English people. They need to know more about it in order to understand themselves. At the present time this knowledge may help to indicate the best way forward for their country in relation to Europe at this critical stage. England's history needs to be seen in a much wider and deeper perspective than is customary. The truth lies in perspective.

In the light of recent discussion among Tudor historians,[9] I should state that in this work the word 'Reformation' will be used to refer to the revolutionary changes introduced into England by Henry VIII, through the statutes (1532–6) of his Reformation Parliament. The phrase 'official version' will mean that view of the English past, introduced in the preambles to these statutes, which was built on the fundamental notion that English life had always been firstly nationalistic and secondly erastian (Church controlled by the State) in character, using these words in their sixteenth-century sense.[10] From these two notions, other important concepts developed, such as the idea of an early national Church of apostolic origin[11] and the image of 'the elect Nation', which were both to become fully incorporated into the official version.

Another matter which has been debated among historians recently is the use that can be made of the word 'English'. I will use it in the wide sense, which was the normal usage given it by the English themselves, as being synonymous with 'British'. The various Acts of Union with Wales, Ireland and Scotland were meant to assimilate these Celtic countries into the English hegemony of culture and power and they were to a great extent effective.[12] The situation is now changing, but we must look at things as people, particularly the English people, saw them during the period with which we are concerned.

Reference to 'modern' historians will mean historians of the twentieth century whose works are of such professional stature as to be still in use among writers of today. These will include obviously contemporary scholars, but also those, such as F.W. Maitland (1850–1906),[13] whose historical insights and understanding were of such quality as to ensure that their works remain important today. As this study will show, the insights of historians are not always synonymous with their places in the chronology of historiography or indeed with the importance given them in conventional histories of historiography.

Any reference to John Lingard's *History of England* will mean the sixth edition of this work, in ten volumes, published in 1854–5 and reprinted in 1883, unless otherwise stated. This study will show the unexpected significance of the Non-Jurors and the central importance of John Lingard in the history and development of English historical writing.

The term 'Christian humanism' will refer to the tradition of Christian thought in which the aspiration is to become, by the grace of God, fully human in Christ. It is inspired by the Gospel teaching: 'I have come so that they may have life and have it to the full.'[14] It was expressed by St Irenaeus of Lyons in the second century: 'The glory of God is man fully alive.' It was the inspiration of scholastic teaching in the medieval period, as shown in Sir Richard Southern's recent *Scholastic Humanism and the Unification of Europe* (1995). It was embodied by scholars like St Thomas More and Erasmus during the Renaissance and in the educational ideas of Cardinal Newman in nineteenth-century England. Newman's thinking is an important influence in the modern world, particularly because of its bearing on the Second Vatican Council (1964–5). It was reflected again in the incarnationist theology of the great twentieth-century German theologian, Karl Rahner, whose ideas were also influential on the work of that Council. Its teaching that, in the incarnation, humanity has been renewed in the immortal image of God makes clear the innate dignity of all human beings and is the basis for Christian statements on human rights and responsibilities in the modern world.[15] As well as self-expression, Christian humanism also teaches the need for penance and self-denial, which, working within the law of love, can assist in achieving freedom from selfishness and ultimately prepares the way for death, seen as the entry to a new life of complete fulfilment for the whole person. This explains the seeming paradox of Thomas More, the great Christian humanist who loved life, secretly wearing a very painful hair shirt beneath his finery when he was Lord Chancellor of England, and why he was able to face martyrdom cheerfully when he could no longer avoid it without betraying his beliefs.

One reflection of this Christian humanism is a belief in the human capability, within certain limitations, of achieving knowledge of the truth. I mention this, which might seem obvious to many readers, because I am well aware of a sceptical view among certain contemporary theorists of historiography – who are not, however, historians themselves – that it is not possible to achieve historical truth.[16] Recently religion and science have united in their commitment to objective truth against the attacks on this position by certain 'post-modernist' sceptics.[17] I do not wish to enter this debate at this particular time, except to make three observations. Firstly, there is nothing new about the sceptical viewpoint. It is as old as the Greek philosopher, Pyrro (c. 360–270 BC), whose scepticism was expressed in the doctrine of universal nescience. Secondly, the great advances in historical writing and understanding have been made by practising historians who have eschewed this scepticism and attempted to find the truth, self-consciously aware of the interaction of opinion and evidence in themselves and using rigorously the best methods and techniques available to exercise a professional and objective judgment.[18] Thirdly, my own position is that we can look at the past much as we can look at the present. Indeed we can often have better evidence available for an event in the past than in the present. There is certainly a great deal which we cannot know, or of which we cannot be certain. There is also a body of knowledge, however, about which we can be certain, which is accepted among reputable scholars of differing general viewpoints and which is continually increasing as a result of further historical research. It is to this type of knowledge that I refer when I write of certain historians of the past 'getting history right', because of their superior insights, when all others were getting it wrong.

Again, when I write of historians who 'got it wrong', I am not making a personal criticism of them. One has to see them in their historical context, accept what they were able to contribute and recognize that they worked within the constraints of their own time and place. One of the fascinating features of historiography, however, is to discover why certain exceptional individuals – sometimes virtually unknown in the conventional histories – were able to break through these constraints and achieve an understanding which was far above that of the age in which they lived. This can happen when certain environmental factors combine with personal qualities which are so imaginative, sensitive and creative in terms of historical insight that they enable a 'jump' to be made in historical understanding, anticipating the findings of more prosaic research a century or more later.

I have tried to write in a way which will make the results of academic work accessible to a wider audience.[19] I have made extensive use of notes so that the reader can have a better knowledge of the sources behind the textual statement and be better able, therefore, to exercise an independent judgment. Having shown the evidence for certain statements, I have not hesitated to include my own personal views on various matters which are contingent to the subject and have a bearing on the contempoary world. The reader will have no difficulty, I think, in distinguishing between my own factual research findings (especially in chapters 3–6), my use of facts derived from the work of other historians (mostly in chapters 2 and 7) and my expressions of a personal viewpoint on how the history and historiography of the English past can perhaps give some guidance on the way forward in the new millennium (mainly in the Introduction and Epilogue). Opinions are dangerous only when they are hidden or disguised. When everything is displayed, the adult reader is able to become engaged, participate in the discussion and exercise his or her own final judgment on matters which will be important to us all in the future. History, after all, belongs to all of us, not only to professional historians. Like life itself, it never repeats itself exactly, but it does provide valuable experience of the human condition and its requirements. We are all part of the process of making the story of the present and the future. We need the experience of the past to help us in this.

The 'Whig interpretation' of history involved a special definition of progress which assumed that everything had changed for the better in the history of England, and that this better future was anticipated by the people whose actions seemed to produce the changes. In opposing this view, I am not of course denying the concept of progress. There are many categories of life, such as knowledge, information, understanding and skills, where there is continuing progress which we can record and monitor – as in the history of historiography. This does not, however, apply to everything in life. Some changes in the areas of beliefs, principles and values may not represent real progress, if the criterion we use is the general quality of human life for the individual and society. In some vitally important respects there can actually be a 'fallback' in standards and quality of life. This is why we can still learn from people of the past, while enjoying much better material conditions in the present. We can do this, however, only if we make efforts to understand them, are sufficiently respectful to them and receptive to what they had to say. Some of them were better people than some of us. In any given cross-section of society through the ages, it is probable that the same curve of innate ability and moral stature would be found, when related to contemporary conditions. This is what the Whig interpretors of the past could never allow; and this is why they had such a profound disrespect for the past and its peoples.

This work has grown out of a thesis entitled 'A Study of John Lingard's Historical Work, with special reference to his treatment of the reign of Elizabeth I' (1956), which was approved for an M.A. degree of the University of Wales, and a thesis entitled 'English Historical Writing on the Reformation in England, 1680–1730' (1958), which was approved for the Ph.D. degree of the University of Cambridge. I must record my thanks to the University of Wales for granting me a research studentship, followed by a fellowship, which enabled me to pursue these researches over four years. It is a particular pleasure to acknowledge my debt to the late Professor Sir Herbert Butterfield, Master of Peterhouse, Cambridge, who invited me to pursue my researches under his supervision. I count it a real privilege, as well as a pleasure, to have worked with such a distinguished figure in the field of historiography. Indeed this study is partly a belated response to his request that this research should be 'given to the world' because 'your main thesis is so important and the purely historiographical revelations are so interesting . . . that I hope very much that you will have the time to take the matter in hand'.[20] At that time I was involved in a busy and demanding career as Head of a comprehensive school, from which I learned a great deal. Now in retirement, I have tried to meet this request. It also seems to me that the main thesis of this study has something to contribute to the general debate now taking place, as we look forward to the beginning of the new millennium, on Britain's proper attitude towards European unity and the part which it has to play in that important process. I hope, too, that the study will have some original and interesting contributions to make to the history of historical writing as a subject in its own right.

I would also like to record my thanks to the Professor D.B. Quinn and Mr N. Masterman for their help during my early research at Swansea. I am grateful to all my colleagues and pupils in the world of education, who taught me much. Mr Roger Thorp of Sutton Publishing has helped and encouraged me from the start in this, my first venture into publishing a book and I am indebted also to the professional expertise of my editors, Jane Crompton, Sue Thomas and Sarah Flight.

The main manuscript collections used in my researches are in the Library of the British Museum, London, the Bodleian Library, Oxford, Cambridge University Library and the Library of Ushaw College, near Durham, which contains a fine collection of the letters and papers of John Lingard. Other useful manuscript material was found in Lancaster Library and the libraries of St John's College and Corpus Christi College, Cambridge. I am indebted to the librarians at all these institutions and to those of University College, Swansea, for their unfailing help and courtesy.

Finally, my deepest thanks to my parents who encouraged my early interest in history, to my wife Andrea for her care, help and invaluable advice, and to our family for their help and support always, but especially over the time when I have been cogitating over this book.

Edwin Jones
Swansea
1998

Preface to the First Paperback Edition

Since the first edition of this book, we have crossed the threshold of the third millennium. It is a time, particularly, when communities can benefit from reflecting on past mistakes, a process which should and can make people wiser. I hope that this second edition in paperback will introduce it to a new and wider group of readers. It is based on certain assumptions. One is that history matters, and that a proper knowledge of the past plays an essential part in understanding the present and in making intelligent decisions about the future. Another is that proper historical understanding places each individual in a position to play a fuller and more informed part in the decision-making processes of a democratic society. These in turn help to shape the future.

In this edition I have made some slight changes, correcting a few printing errors and altering the emphasis of certain statements in the light of new information. I am grateful to those readers from Britain and abroad who have expressed their appreciation and made their own helpful comments about the book.

Since the first edition in 1998, its main themes have received the considerable support of Professor Norman Davies. He is unique in having followed up his massively ground-breaking work on *Europe* in 1996 with his recently published and equally innovatory treatment of *The Isles* in November 1999. I am grateful for the foreword which he has written for this new edition of *The English Nation: the Great Myth*.

Edwin Jones
Swansea
2000

Preface to the Second Paperback Edition

The first paperback edition of *The English Nation: The Great Myth* has sold out. I have taken the opportunity in this new second edition of 2003, to bring it up to date with contemporary history as it has unfolded since 1998, up to November 2002.

The increase in globalisation and the growing awareness of inter-dependence, inter-connection and inter-responsibility of all nations on the world stage have underlined the inadequacy of purely nationalistic approaches or solutions to contemporary religious, political, social and economic problems. The importance of the European movement for peace and unity, with its underlying and unified value system covering democracy, justice, freedom and human rights, has become increasingly and unprecedently significant as an effective model for world peace and unity. The central importance of religion as a prime motivator of human feeling and action in the world has been made very clear; and it has become vitally important, in the words of Kofi Annan, Secretary General of the United Nations, 'to restore religion to its rightful role as peacemaker and pacifier' in the world. There is, too, the challenge of harnessing the immense and unprecedented power of the United States of America, as the one world 'super-state', for purposes good in the world – for the benefit of the USA as well as the world at large. It is essential that this phenomenon should become part of the solution rather than the problem of achieving world peace. The unprecedented threat of terrorism as a world problem challenging the security of all peoples, has appeared. Its deepest causes need to be analysed and its threat properly addressed. All these features have come together to present mankind with a 'Challenge and Response' situation of Toynbeeian dimension.

I have tried in the new Afterword at the end of this book, to analyse the central, strategic and pivotal role which Britain could play in the present world of this new millennium, in response to these global issues.

Edwin Jones
Swansea
November 2002

Introduction

From the time of the Roman occupation in the second century up to the sixteenth century, that part of Britain which we term England was increasingly and consciously part of continental Europe.[1] Religion played a central part in the culture and public life of the nation as well as in the private life of the individual, to an extent which is now difficult to imagine.[2] It was primarily as part of the Catholic Church, centred in Rome, that England was brought increasingly into the life of Europe during this time.[3]

Christianity first came to Britain with Roman merchants and soldiers who were themselves Christian. By the beginning of the third century there is evidence of a hierarchical organization on the same lines as that in other parts of the Church on the Continent. At the Council of Arles in Gaul in 314 British bishops from York, Lincoln and London attended this general meeting of bishops. In 429 it was in answer to an appeal from the British Christians that Pope Celestine sent Germanus, Bishop of Arles and Lupus, Bishop of Troyes, to help them against the Pelagian heresy. Germanus returned in 446, with Serverus of Treves, on the same mission and also to help them against the invading Saxons and Picts.[4] This was after the Roman legions had left Britain and the British Christians had retreated into the west country and what we now call Wales.

The arrival of Augustine in 597, sent by Pope Gregory the Great, marked the beginning of the conversion of the English people proper to Christianity. We celebrated in May 1997 the 1,400th anniversary of his landing at Ebbsfleet in Kent. At the celebration in Canterbury there was an extraordinary gathering of Christians from all parts of Europe. These included the Pope's Apostolic Nuncio, the Greek Orthodox Archbishop of Thateira, Cardinal Hume and the Archbishop of Canterbury, with other clergy from various other European Churches, and lay pilgrims from all over Europe.[5] It was truly a great ecumenical and European gathering to commemorate this great historical event.

Augustine and his fellow monks had been overcome by anxiety and fear – as Bede tells us – at the prospect of facing the wild and barbarous English. Indeed they had wanted to turn back during their year-long journey from Rome, but Gregory encouraged them to continue. He had wanted to come himself, but was unable to leave Rome. Gregory is described by Bede as 'the apostle of the English'. There was a very close relationship, like that of father and son, between this great Pope, whose wise letters are still extant, and Augustine; and this was reflected from the start in a particularly close link between Rome and the new Church in England.[6]

England now became very firmly part of European Christendom, with frequent communication and travel between England and the Continent, especially to and from the centre of Church government in Rome. Later, important figures in English Church life, appointed by the Papacy, were to be, for example, the Italian Paulinus, the Burgundian Felix, the Frank Angilbert, the African Hadrian and the extremely able Greek Theodore of Tarsus, who became the seventh Archbishop of Canterbury (668–90) and did much to build up the Church on the parochial system. Within England itself the more immediate result was the development of a rich Christian culture. In the words of Gregory's successor 1,400 years later:

> Augustine's mission meant the consolidation of Christianity in Britain, giving it strong links with the See of Rome. He and his companions sowed the seed of a Christian people remarkably gifted from the beginning with saintly men and women who spread civilisation and learning, provided schools, established libraries and produced a wonderful array of literary and artistic works.[7]

But 'quite soon that healthy tree bore fruits beyond England, in the rise of major missionary ventures to other countries of Europe'.[8] The five centuries following Augustine's arrival saw the English play a vitally important part in the creation of European culture and civilization. The conversion of the Germanic lands to Christianity and their assimilation into European civilization was mainly the work of a great English missionary, the Benedictine monk, St Boniface (680–755), who came from Crediton in Devon and 'had a deeper influence on the history of Europe than any other Englishman who ever lived'.[9] Boniface, originally called Winfrith, was given his new name by Pope Gregory II and sent by him on the mission to the vast Germanic lands in 719.

Boniface's extraordinary achievement was to take the lead in bringing vast areas of the Teutonic world (including Frisia, Hesse,

Thuringia, Bavaria, Saxony, the land of the Picts and Scots, and later Norway and Sweden) into the Catholic Church and European civilization. He became Archbishop of Mainz, supervising the organization of the Church in southern and central Germany, and finally died a martyr's death in Frisia. His work prepared the ground for the unification of these lands under Charles the Great (Charlemagne) who, from being simply King of the Franks, was to become Emperor of the Romans, governing Gaul, Italy and large parts of Spain and Germany. Boniface contributed largely therefore to the future civilization and unification of western Europe. Other missionaries from England who helped on similar missions in other parts of the Continent were Walburga, who helped Boniface in Germany, Wilfrid of York, who worked for some time in Frisia, Chadd of the English Midlands, who became the first bishop of Utrecht, Willibrord, who evangelized the Low Countries, and Henrik, who later went to Finland.

Meanwhile England had already produced a European scholar of great distinction in the Venerable Bede (637–735) from Northumbria who, though he never left his own country, 'took all knowledge for his province' and 'retained for at least four centuries a pre-eminent place in the Latin literature of Europe'.[10] Benedict Biscop (628–89), abbot of Wearmouth and Jarrow, had made pilgrimages to Rome, bringing back Mediterranean ideas. Insisting that the spacious monastery should include a library to contain the great writings of the known world, he provided the instrument with which Bede accomplished his achievements. Bede was the first great English European. Sections of his Gospel commentaries passed into the Roman breviary and have been used by priests throughout the world ever since. He is the only Englishman who has been honoured by western Christendom with the title 'Doctor of the Church'. His writings on chronology were used throughout Europe, and it is from him that the world inherited the system of dating: BC and AD. Apart from all this, Bede is most famous for his wonderful learning and accuracy as a historian.

Englishmen also contributed to the success of the Carolingian renaissance on the Continent in the eighth century. Alcuin from York (735–804) was one of the scholar-monks sent for by Charlemagne to assist in the establishment of a standardized Latin language to be used for official purposes throughout his empire. Alcuin became Bishop of Tours, produced the standardized version of the Bible used in medieval Europe and played an important role in the coronation of Charlemagne as Emperor of the West in 800.

Alfred the Great (848–99) was the first great ruler of most of England, arguably the greatest of English kings and also a great European. He is famous for his defence of England against the Danes and for his encouragement of learning and quality of life in England. He adopted Bede's concept of a *single* English people and created a cultural self-image for the English, placing Christian values at its centre, as the basis for its future survival.[11] This built up English morale and provided a united front against the pagan Danish invaders. By 890 his authority was recognized over all England except for the Danelaw in the east. He revealed qualities 'which have come to seem typical of the better aspects of England . . . and he fought and worked for civilized objectives . . . not for blood lust and glory'.[12] He was a fine example of Englishry at its best.

Alfred's life and work illustrates, too, the way in which Englishry was allied *naturally* with the continental dimension: 'behind him was the continental Carolingian "renaissance" . . . which had itself owed much to Northumbrian Anglo-Saxon influence.'[13] He encouraged both the Latin and the vernacular cultures. He was a scholar steeped in both and he 'tried to bring England more into line with continental civilization'.[14] He translated Pope Gregory the Great's *Cura Pastoralis* to help his clergy and a copy was sent to every English bishop. He translated Boethius' *De Consolatione Philosophiae*, adding explanatory extracts from other authors such as Remigius of Auxerre. The West Saxon version of Augustine's *Soliloquia* was also probably Alfred's own work. He translated, or arranged for the translation, of Orosius' *Historia Adversus Paganos*, adding the most recent available geographical information, with interesting detail of events like the voyages of Wulfstan in the Baltic and the Norwegian, Ohthere, to the White Sea. He had a translation made of Bede's *Historia Ecclesiastica gentis Anglorum* and Caedmon's *Hymn*. The systematic compilation of the *Anglo-Saxon Chronicle* probably includes some of his own work and he set out the code of laws which were based on Mosaic and early English precedents.[15] England was the first bulwark of western and Christian Europe to be attacked by the Viking invaders and Alfred became the English counterpart of Charlemagne, representing and defending the Christian civilization and culture of Europe against their onslaughts. He was a figure of European importance as well as being a great Englishman.

The Norman Conquest in 1066 simply reinforced England's position as part of Europe, bringing it still more closely into contact with the French and the (common) Latin culture of the mainland. This was not a break in the continuity of English history, for in religion, law and culture, the old systems and traditions continued, except for the added incursion of a strong French influence into English culture. Very influential figures in English history, such as Anselm and Lanfranc, were appointed by the Papacy and came to England as already eminent Europeans, to be very distinguished archbishops of Canterbury. Lanfranc, born in Pavia, was a noted theologian and teacher. On his death in 1089, he was succeeded at Canterbury by the future saint, Anselm, a Benedictine monk and scholar who had been Abbot of Bec in Normandy. England gained the benefits which flowed from the great revival of learning on the Continent in the twelfth and thirteenth centuries. English scholars and writers now became tri-lingual in culture. All this was to be the seed-bed for the development of the English genius, Geoffrey Chaucer, and for the birth of the great centres of learning at Oxford and Cambridge.

English people of the medieval period, like their ancestors, never thought other than of belonging to the Catholic Church which covered the whole of western Europe. They were self-consciously part of European Christendom and showed this, for example, by answering the call of the Crusades, in company with the rest of Europe, for its defence. So, too, did the English combine with fellow Christians from Normandy, the Low Countries and Portugal to help the Portuguese to regain Lisbon from the Muslim forces in 1147.[16] This action was to prepare the ground for Portugal's prominent role in the history and culture of Europe, from which emerged the significant genius of Luís de Camões in the sixteenth century.[17] The Angevin and Plantagenet kings of England from the twelfth century up to and including most of the fifteenth century were strongly Eurocentric in outlook, having their cultural centre on the Continent, to which they were closely linked by religion, marriage, lands and trade.

One of the most telling differences between medieval England and its post-Reformation counterpart is in the basically important area of language. This, the usual form of human communication, is another of the great centrifugal forces in making and shaping community. A very recent scholar observes: 'Twentieth-century scholarship has reminded us just how fundamental is the structure of language to the way in which we construct our lives and culture.'[18] The existence in medieval England of Latin, the 'universal' language and the common language of Europe, alongside the vernacular English, was an essential expression of the

European nature of pre-Reformation England. This was regarded as a perfectly natural and acceptable part of society, not something alien which had been inflicted upon it. The addition of French to English culture in the twelfth and thirteenth centuries was more the result of the dominance of French culture in Europe at that time than of the Norman Conquest which had simply made its reception easier. Welsh and German culture were affected in the same way.[19] This is another area in which later historians were to read history backwards and mistakenly, because they misunderstood the nature of pre-Reformation England. Ann Williams has pointed out that:

> even before 1066 the volume of works in Latin exceeded that in English. . . . Before 1066 when Englishmen lived in a bi-lingual culture, which became tri-lingual after the settlement of a French-speaking élite in the twelfth century, English scholars, many of whom were trained in the schools of continental Europe and the university of Paris, were competent in Latin, French and English. . . . The monolingual culture of modern Britain has led to neglect of the Anglo-Latin writers. English Literature has been defined as works written in English, rather than by English authors. This definition may hold true today, but is inadequate for the medieval period. Bede's *Historia Ecclesiastica gentis Anglorum* is no less 'English' because its author chose to write in Latin, the common tongue of Christendom; indeed it is a landmark in the development of English nationality.[20]

The English, then, until the Reformation can be described as European as well as English, in terms of religion, language and culture. Nothing, perhaps, better indicates the narrowing of the minds of most English people in the last four centuries than the development of a 'monolingual' culture. The English are now famous, or infamous, for their inability to speak any other language but their own. This was, until recently, and as a result of their extraordinary achievements in trade and colonization, almost a matter of pride, as if it were up to other peoples in the world to learn the English language if they wanted to communicate. Only now, at the end of the millennium, is the linguistic position in England being perceived as a real disadvantage in political and economic as well as cultural terms; there are now attempts to change the educational system to meet the need for greater linguistic flexibility.

INTRODUCTION

This Latin – and later French – influence on English culture was a very important factor in transforming it into a European experience and enabling the English genius to become of universal significance. Any isolated culture will atrophy. Each culture needs the stimulation of contact with others in order to grow and blossom. Historians of English culture now lament the artistic and architectural losses suffered at the Reformation, and English historiography was to be severely diminished by its isolation from continental developments. The dominant tradition in English historical writing from the sixteenth century up to and including our own time[21] has been to deny the significance of the Latin dimension of English experience in the medieval period, regarding it as something alien. The 'official' view of the English past was to regard English institutions as of purely indigenous origin. The only variant, but minor theme was an emphasis on the Germanic origin and teutonic nature of the English people, dismissing a millennium of cultural development as simply an alien intrusion associated with the 'Dark Ages'.

During this first thousand years of England's history, there was, of course, and very importantly, a distinctive quality of 'Englishry' in English culture. This was expressed quite naturally in Latin and in the vernacular, just as in Wales their 'Welshness' was expressed in both languages.[22] One might well ask, 'Where did this concept of Englishry or Englishness come from?' The surprising answer is that it can be attributed in the first place to Pope Gregory the Great who sent Augustine to England in 597. Until this time the inhabitants of this area were always known as 'Saxons', but after Gregory's time they were universally known as *Angli* (English). The story of Pope Gregory's description of the slaves from this area, in a Roman market, as 'non Angli sed angelii' was told in the most famous book of the time, Bede's *History*, which received very wide circulation and acclaim. Also, the see of Canterbury, established by Augustine, was concerned to bring the Saxon and old English peoples together in the unity of ecclesiastical obedience under the name of 'the English' and Bede gained much of the material for his work from Canterbury. Hence the chosen title of his influential book, *The Ecclesiastical History of the English People* (731),[23] which visualized the English as a *single* people for the first time.

The quality of Englishry is indeed very evident from the first in the work of this Northumbrian monk. As one of our distinguished medievalists has written:

He is an Englishman, and the first Englishman to declare himself a lover of England, not by patriotic phrases, but in his desire to tell how England became Christian and of the cloud of witnesses that had so quickly made this island an island of saints.[24]

Bede displays 'a certain blend of qualities that is peculiarly English'. There is 'no brilliance in Bede, but much steady clarity'. He lacks the 'overtones and undertones', the 'subtle intuition . . . twilight mystery . . . flash of genius' of the Celt, but he is 'simple, sane, loyal, trusting, warm-hearted, serious, with that sense of pathos which has always been a mark of English literature'. Again, 'falsehood and vanity of any kind was quite foreign to him . . . because Bede was a good man who, as he himself said, could live without shame and die without fear'[25] – a fitting tribute to Englishry at its best. And he wrote in Latin.

During the later medieval period, the outstanding expression of Englishry must be in the works of Geoffrey Chaucer (?1340–1400). He is a universal figure whose work combines the influence of several languages and cultures – Latin, French (both of England and of the Continent) and Italian. His work shows familiarity with the English dialects used in the East Midlands, Kent and Northumbria.[26] He had spent some time, in fact, in both France and Italy. Chaucer describes for us his idea of the gentle qualities of the real man:

> Loke who that is most vertuous alway
> Prive and apart, and most entendeth ay
> To do the gentil dedes that he can
> And tak him for the grettest gentil man.

This gentleness comes from the example of Christ, not from any rich human ancestry:

> Crist wol, we clayme of him our gentillesse
> Nat of our eldres for hir old richesse.

He goes on quite naturally to quote Dante, 'the wyse poet of Florence', who also says that 'we clayme our gentillesse' from the goodness of God.[27] This helps us to understand the medieval background to the development of the idea of the English 'gentleman' which is so familiar to us. It exists in Chaucer together with his belief in the value of purity in womanhood and his love of nature, alongside the earthy realism, quiet irony, tolerance, understanding and good humour which make him typically English.[28] Like Shakespeare, he was a figure of European status. His great knowledge of European literature was reinterpreted and coloured by the particular lens of his English genius. He is unsurpassed as a narrative poet; his insight and brilliant characterization are reminiscent of Dickens' depiction of the human condition, just as Honoré de Balzac's *Comédie Humaine* is a description of the same condition, but from an unmistakably French viewpoint.

Knowing well the ancient and graceful Malvern Hills which look out over Herefordshire to the Welsh mountains in the west and over Worcestershire in the Vale of Severn to the Cotswolds in the east, I personally take great pleasure in the splendid evocation of Englishry – with its love of history, associated with rural landscape and the sense of time, place, religion, community and culture – revealed in the *Vision of Piers Plowman*, a poem of 'compelling sincerity and power, its sombre landscape lit with gleams of beauty'.[29] On a lovely May morning, William Langland (*c.* 1300–86) had climbed to the Worcestershire Beacon, the highest point on the Malverns. From here he had looked out towards the Cotswolds, over the great plain of Severn with its patchwork of fields, cultivated by generations of Englishmen. He sat down, wrapped in his cloak and his thoughts, and fell asleep:

> In a somere seyson when softe was the sonne
> I shop me in-to shrobbis as I a shepherd were . . .
> Ac on a may morwening on Malverne hulles
> Me byfel for to slepe for weyrynesse of wandryng.[30]

In his sleep there came to him a vision of the English community, past and present, inspired perhaps by the distant views. The central figure in the poem, Piers Plowman, is very English and belongs very obviously to the greater community of the Catholic Church. As Langland's poem continues, we realize that Piers comes to represent the Church and later Christ Himself, under whose invisible care and watchful providence the generations of English people working the land have 'lived and moved and had their being' in community.

Like so many of the craftsmen who built the great English cathedrals, hardly anything is known of Langland, to whom no other poem is ascribed. He has however left us a valuable glimpse of medieval Englishry, where the essential commonplaces of thought and feeling – like the love of Christ and His Church – are revealed more openly and unselfconsciously than in the historical records and documents. Here we can actually feel the importance of the Church as the greatest centrifugal force in creating community for ordinary people at all levels, from the small local parish to western Christendom. This, too, was a community which transcended time, for it included people of the past, present and future, all 'belonging' within the Body or family of Christ and all able to communicate with one another through Him. This created a sense of belonging, of continuity, of stability and security. It tells us of a truth, an 'essential commonplace' of the medieval world, which historians often fail to discern – that before the Reformation Christianity in the West meant a unified body or community of people rather than a body of differing 'isms'.[31]

Like Thomas More later, Langland was severely critical of any abuses which demeaned 'Holy Church', and this has led some Protestant writers to claim him as a 'precursor of the Reformation'.[32] However, this is to misunderstand completely his assumptions of thought. Again like More, Langland was in no sense a revolutionary.[33] His personality is perhaps expressed best in his beautiful stanzas on Christian charity:

> He is gladde with alle gladde and good tyl alle wykked
> And leueth and loueth all that oure lorde made.
> Curseth he no creature ne can bere no wrathe
> He no lykynge hath to lye ne laughe men to scorne
> Al that me seith, he let it soth and in solace taketh,
> And alle manere meschiefs in myldenesse he suffreth;
> Coueiteth he none erthly good but heuene-riche blisse
> That lyuen azens holy loue and the loue of charitie.[34]

The craftsmen, artists and glass painters who worked on the medieval churches and cathedrals which cover the countryside of England were content to make their anonymous contributions towards the community's expression and celebration of its religious faith. A similar anonymity was actively sought by the group of great English mystics who contributed a uniquely English insight to the mystical tradition of the Church. There was, for example, the unknown author of *The Cloud of Unknowing*, written probably late in the fourteenth century, the Yorkshireman, Richard Rolle (*c.* 1300–49) who wrote *The Fire of Love*, and Walter Hilton (d. 1396) whose well-known work is *The Scale of Perfection*.

Outstanding, in my view, among these masterpieces of spiritual writing is the *Revelation of Divine Love*, written in the late fourteenth century by Julian of Norwich. We know almost nothing about her, not even her name, for 'Julian' is simply taken from the name of the church in Norwich to which her cell was attached. This was the first book written in English by a woman and it contains what I would regard as the essential spirit of Englishry at its very best: the very practical and common-sense outlook of an 'unlettered woman', as she describes herself. She was very concerned to keep herself out of the picture, for her task was to point people to Christ. In fact she wrote with keen intellect, brilliant imagination and profound spiritual insight. She was a mystic approached by people from all walks of life for advice, a woman of courage who had obviously suffered, a counsellor who was completely down-to-earth. She knew well that God is concerned with people's physical, emotional and psychological, as well as spiritual needs. A realist who looked at the world through the eyes of God's compassion, Julian wrote with complete understanding of the life and intelligence of the feelings as well as the intellect. This woman, who revealed the insights of mystic, artist and psychologist, has also been ranked in the twentieth century as one of the greatest of all theologians,[35] who brought a feminine intuition to her understanding of God. Well acquainted with the evils of the world, she believed in the ultimate triumph of love through that great power by which God can subdue all things to Himself. She is consequently the least neurotic of writers: 'All will be well, and all manner of things will be well.' Almost unknown for six centuries, Julian has become very well known to thousands of people from all parts of the world in our own day, for whom her teaching seems to be completely relevant to their own times and conditions. She is concerned with true penitence rather than guilt feelings which can be another form of concentrating on self. For true penitence means looking outwards in joyful recognition of God's infinite power, mercy, love and forgiveness:

> Would you know your Lord's meaning in this? Learn it well. Love was His meaning. . . . Our failing is fearful, our falling is full of shame . . . but the sweet eye of pity and mercy never looks away from us, nor does the working of mercy ever cease. . . . All will be well . . . live merrily and gladly because of His love.[36]

Hers is an unmistakably English voice among the world's great mystics, but she is speaking to the whole Christian family of peoples with this English voice. Her central vision is of the love and compassion of God, and consequently of the great hope which exists for us all. She insists that her revelations must come within the framework of 'Holy Church',[37] which is how Julian describes the Catholic Church, but she was quite prepared to push and extend outwards the boundaries of theological knowledge.[38] No such voice of English mysticism has been heard since.

The sense of 'Englishry' and patriotic self-consciousness as a people has been illustrated recently with examples taken from literary rather than historical sources of the first half of the fourteenth century.[39] This sense of Englishry in medieval England, though affected by the dynastic conflict with France, was something quite different from the aggressive nationalism, tainted with chauvinism and xenophobia, of later times.[40] The medieval world was subject to the usual range of human weaknesses, but its assumptions of thought were quite different from those of modern times. Any question of 'national identity' would have to be placed in a completely different context and interpreted within a different historical perspective. Medieval English people lived fruitfully and unself-consciously in harmony with the sense of belonging to the wider family of Christendom, in spite of their Norman kings' policy of 'conquest and domination' in the bordering Celtic regions[41] and the dynastic, 'family' ambitions of their Plantagenet kings, leading to the conflicts in France in the fourteenth and fifteenth centuries. This was the situation right up to the time of the Reformation. At the beginning of the sixteenth century, 'Pilgrims still made their way to the Holy City and lodged in the English College there – over a thousand in the Holy year of 1500, some four hundred in April alone in the next Holy year, 1525':

It is clear that while heresy revived in the late fourteenth century, so too did the orthodox church itself in the vitality of its spiritual life, the vigour of its self criticism and the recruitment of clergy. Moreover, on the very eve of the Reformation, the Pope still enjoyed wide popular support and extensive powers in England . . . the orthodox still sought in Rome, and in great numbers, licences and dispensations from the law of the church.[42]

So it was that on the eve of that great revolution in English life,

> as the children of one mother that Peter Giles the Fleming, Raphael Hytholdaye the Portuguese and Thomas More the Englishman met together in the garden at Antwerp, understanding each other fully, as members of a common civilization.[43]

Similarly, it was as brothers in the wider family of Christendom that Thomas More and Desiderius Erasmus, the great Dutch scholar and More's 'great humanist soul-mate',[44] met, talked at length in the garden of More's Chelsea house alongside the Thames and exchanged ideas, visits and letters during that same period in the early sixteenth century. We still have the letters in which Erasmus records the enjoyment of his stay with that happy family and how More believed that his daughters should be as well-educated as any young male.

These were the two leading representatives of the Renaissance in northern Europe. Their outlook was extraordinarily sane and balanced in their Christian humanism, in their care for the unity and peace of Christian Europe, and in their very positive hatred of war as something barbaric and inhuman. However, the world around them was beginning to move headlong in the opposite direction, with the Reformation beginning to break up that unity and fuelling the emergent political ambitions of the state princes in Germany, and, a little later, in England itself. It was to be the beginning of a new era in the life of Europe, which was to last for over four centuries, see the breakup of Christendom in Europe, the emergence of a new stage in the development of nationalism, and, later, the secularization of thought and society. All this reached its culmination in the colossal and unprecedented tragedies of the two world wars of the twentieth century.

The trial of Thomas More in 1533 was the dramatic centre-point in the clash between the two great forces in English and European history. The new nationalism and the absolute power of the new sovereign state were brought to bear against an extraordinary representative of the qualities of old Englishry and of the European Renaissance. Writer, scholar, religious and social reformer, wit, theologian, Speaker of the House of Commons, Lord Chancellor of England, historian, critic, patron of the arts, happy family man and future saint, Sir Thomas More made his peculiarly English contribution to the Christian humanism of Europe in the early sixteenth century. As an English European, he was bi-lingual and used to great effect both the English language and Latin, as the common language of Christian Europe in which he had many friends. He was the Englishman with the greatest European reputation of his day and the individual most able to express those beliefs and values to which England had adhered since its early conversion to Christianity. Four centuries exactly after his martyrdom in 1535, he was pronounced a saint of the Catholic Church which lay at the heart of the English and European civilization of Christian humanism.

Having been charged and found guilty of treason on perjured evidence,[45] More spoke of that unity of Christendom and European culture, of which the English people had been an integral part for a thousand years until the momentous events resulting from the Divorce Question in the reign of Henry VIII. He referred in his final speech to 'this Realm, being but one member and small part of the Church'[46] and answered the charge of high treason by widening the whole perspective within the introspectively narrow and emotionally charged atmosphere of that English Court held under the hammer-beamed roof of Westminster Hall. It was a moment of high drama, pregnant with implication and consequences for the future history of the English people whose life, memory and identity were going to be changed radically by the ensuing events. More spoke:

> My Lord Chancellor, for one Bishop whom you may produce for your side, I will bring forward a hundred saintly and orthodox prelates who subscribe to my opinion: for your one Parliament, and God knows of what sort it is, I have on my side all the councils that have been held in the whole Christian world for more than a thousand years: and for your one kingdom of England I have with me all the kingdoms of Christianity . . . for in this realm you stand alone, in opposition to the unanimous consent of Christendom. Your law has dissolved the unity, the peace and the concord of the Church, although the Church is, as you all know, a body which is one, universal, whole and undivided.[47]

The intensity was only relieved by More's own charity and unfailing optimism, stemming from the widest of all perspectives: his faith in God and the eternal life.

In this world there will be ever discord, and variety of opinion . . . I trust . . . so we too are now at variance in this world and differ in our opinions, may be one in heart and mind for ever in the world to come. In this hope I pray God to preserve you all, and especially my lord the King and to deign always to send him faithful counsellors.[48]

More's words are of great significance for the history of historiography since they represent a view of the English past which was an assumption of thought in England up to the time of the Reformation. He believed that he could be a patriotic Englishman and a loyal member of the Catholic Church, covering the whole of Europe, at the same time. This idea was unrecognizable to later English people who had been taught a nationalistic set of assumptions of thought in which the central and exclusive loyalty was to their own nation and its ruler. On the scaffold More died 'the faithful servant of the King, and, *in the first place*, of God'. He called the crowd 'to bear witness with him that he should now there suffer death, in and for the faith of the Holy Catholic Church'.[49]

More was a great European as well as a great Englishman. He stood out as a thinker of his own generation who could foresee the effects of the breakup of the ideal of European and Christian unity, based on a common Christian identity and adherence to the values of Christian humanism. He, like Erasmus, hated corruption or abuse wherever it appeared in the Church. They also hated heresy because this could shatter the community of Europe, as well as posing a spiritual danger to the individual.[50] They both had a loathing for war and its effects. In his famous *Utopia* (1516) More described it 'as a thing very beastly, and yet to no kind of beast in so much use as man', and the inhabitants of Utopia 'do detest and abhor it'.[51] Disputes and conflicts, caused by human pride and selfishness, had occurred, of course, in the medieval world. More, as a practising lawyer, knew all about evil in the world. As Lord Chancellor of England, he was no idle or acdemic dreamer. His *Utopia* was a deliberately idealized picture. The real question was how to arrange the affairs of the world in order to control and limit these evils, while allowing the good to emerge. Medieval conflicts happened in spite of the community ideals, but modern wars would occur as a positive result of the new philosophy of aggressive and independent nationalisms in which there would be no greater allegiance than to one's own state. More had the vision to see where this was leading. Both Erasmus and More felt keenly that it was not the common people, on any side, who caused wars, but they were 'driven and enforced to war aginst their wills by the furious madness of their princes and heads'.[52]

Indeed the whole section 'Of Warfare' in the *Utopia* has an extraordinary feeling to it which strikes one as very modern now at the end of the twentieth century. It is difficult to recall any piece of English writing, from the sixteenth century to the era of the Peace Movement in the second half of our century, which so vividly brings out the utter absurdity and horror of war. Certainly it strikes a discordant note when sounded against the utterances concerning the glories of war and conquest which characterized so much of English writing up to the First World War – as if war was a romantic and glorious venture of some sort.

More's view of the past was confronted in 1535 by the new and official version which had just been concocted by Thomas Cromwell in the preambles to the Reformation statutes. More's voice was silenced by the brute force of the new nation-state. In future the heroes of English history books were to be the national war leaders and generals who achieved spectacular victories over other European countries in the spate of internecine wars in Europe and the colonies over the next four centuries. The glory of the nation was achieved often at the expense of the misery of many ordinary people. In contrast, the name of St Boniface, for example, was largely forgotten.[53]

Some voices, however, can never be finally silenced. More's was prophetic in more than one sense. He anticipated in an extraordinary way, and in a number of different areas – such as universal education and social reform[54] – the achievements of the modern age, while fully aware of the dangers ensuing from disunity and war. He proclaimed certain truths which are of permanent importance to mankind and for which he is remembered in our own day. More insisted that, ultimately, the conscience, informed by the teachings of the Universal Church was sacrosanct in deciding the individual's actions. The importance of individual conscience against the power of the state is something which we all recognize in the aftermath of the experience of totalitarian states and two world wars. This was expressed with great skill in the modern play by Robert Bolt, *A Man for All Seasons* (1960), which was also made into a very

INTRODUCTION

successful film. Now at the very end of the millennium, as we look
with hope to the future, I think that we might be attracted
particularly by More's stand for peace and by his belief that the
pursuit of narrowly nationalist aims by European countries can
never lead to peace or stability in that great society of peoples, or
indeed in the world at large. In this I believe that he has something
important to tell English people of today. Some 461 years after
More's trial, another seminal figure in history stood in that same
Westminster Hall and asked the assembled parliamentarians of
Britain to leave behind the colonialist past and the 'clangour of
arms'. Nelson Mandela was ready to forgive the sins of the past,
including his own long imprisonment. His plea to them was to
work in partnership with his own country, to achieve human
rights and a new 'universal order in which we shall all be our
brother's keeper'.[55] The kindred spirit of Thomas More must, I
think, have been present there again on this great occasion.

The Reformation was the greatest revolution in English history.[56]
It meant that England was suddenly separated from the Europe of
western Christendom, of which it had formed an important part for
more than a millennium. The momentous Act in Restraint of
Appeals (1533) made it treasonable for anyone to make an appeal
to the Papal Court, or to any other outside court, against a decision
of the King's Courts. For the first time in 1,500 years England was
being separated from Europe. This was the first great element in the
Revolution, the establishment of an independent nation-state which
was to be isolated from Europe until 1973.

The Act of Supremacy (1534) made the king supreme head of
the Church of England for the first time in English history. This was
the second great element in the Revolution – the establishment of
an erastian structure within the new nation-state. The State was
now in control of the Church as of everything else. A modern
scholar has dated the secularization of society in England as
commencing with these events.[57] Centralized action was taken by
the Tudor governments to ensure that everyone, particularly
preachers and teachers, obeyed the government line as stated in the
Reformation statutes.[58] It became treasonable to oppose them.

These two Acts of Parliament formed the pincers which was to
hold English historiography in a tight grip from the time of the
Reformation until well into the twentieth century. The preambles to
these Acts created what we shall term the 'national–erastian'
dualism of thought in English historical writing which has

conditioned the thinking of English people up to the present. These two concepts – nationalism and erastianism – formed the two great pillars on which the official view of the 'Reformation' and the English past rested. They were to create a peculiarly insular and narrow outlook in the mentality of most English people. This outlook took root quickly for, only some twenty-five years later, Mary Tudor failed because she provoked the opposition of the politically powerful 'insular erastians'[59] in the Establishment. The birth of modern English nationalism is to be found in the preambles to these two statutes, which were to separate the English from western Christendom and provide them with a new identity, derived from a new view of their past.

The Act of Supremacy gave legal force to the Tudor glorification and exaltation of monarchy. Henry was now supreme ruler of Church and State in England. Thomas Cromwell, the pioneer of state propaganda in England, took the matter much further. Richard Rex has recently explored thoroughly, for the first time, 'the new prominence henceforth accorded to obedience by the Henrician regime'.[60] He shows that the enactments of 1533–4 led to the adoption of the 'obedience' theology of William Tyndale's *The Obedience of a Christian Man* (1527), and that the introduction of this Protestant theology into government policy and propaganda was the work of Thomas Cromwell and his followers, for political purposes. He shows, also, that this theology produced a distinctive expression in the new English Church, culminating in the identification of 'the word of God' with obedience to the king, and the belief that such obedience was the primary and paramount claim in religion. Finally, we are shown that it was Cromwell who orchestrated the flow of government propaganda, in the form of tracts, sermons and plays, which was meant to stamp this new belief on the nation as a whole. Some notable agents in this propaganda were Thomas Starkey, Richard Sampson and John Bale. Bale 'gave obedience its most dramatic expression' in his propagandist play on the life of *King John*, which is a 'prolonged dramatic meditation on the theme'.[61] Indeed, 'the ideological enterprise on which the Henrician regime embarked in the course of the 1530s was ambitious and wide-ranging and led to the introduction of what was little less than a version of divine right of kingship.'[62] This identification of God's will with obedience to Henry explains much of that submission to the will of monarchy which was to characterize the English people under the Tudors.

The English people were now going to be taught by government to give absolute allegiance, spiritual and temporal, to one authority, that of the state ruler, the king. It was taught as the first claim on their conscience.[63] All this reinforced the isolationism produced by the Act against Appeals. It took away the old flexibility of mind which had existed in the independent and sacrosanct area of informed conscience.[64] Thomas More had been able to follow his own conscience by his own intelligent understanding of the traditional distinction between matters spiritual and temporal. He was loyal to the king, but owed an even greater loyalty to God. This possibility was now assailed for English people by Cromwell's clever political move. The individual was now firmly in the control of the State. The rigidity and servility of mind which grew in those who lived under the new national-erastianism led to various peculiar phenomena such as the false 'confessions' which were to appear in Tudor state trials.[65] Various forms of 'persuasion' were now available to the nation-state government, which have become familiar to us in other countries in modern history.

The English were also encouraged by the government at this period to be xenophobic. In the Henrician statutes the Pope was depicted as the hatred foreign enemy of the English people, and this learned reaction was soon applied to other Catholic countries in Europe. From now on it was to be a strong force in the psychology of the English people,[66] strongly influencing their attitude towards English politics and religion, as well as their outlook on the outside world. Catholics were now to be regarded as traitors for not giving absolute and exclusive obedience to the king in all things. The very fact that Britain is an island must have played its part originally in investing its inhabitants with a tendency towards insularity of mind.[67] This was countered during the first millennium of its history by England's assimilation into the Europe of western Christendom.[68] The Reformation brought a separation and isolation from the mainland, creating the conditions within which the old and patriotic love of their own country – their sense of Englishry – was turned into an ugly and aggressive xenophobia. This was not helped by the fact that people from the Continent no longer came to settle in England after the Reformation, except as refugees.[69] Xenophobia has been an unfortunate feature of English life ever since, typical examples being irrational outbursts in sections of the tabloid press against the continental 'foreigners' during the BSE crisis in 1996[70] and during the 1997 General Election.[71]

Henry VIII was determined to disguise the revolutionary nature of these proceedings under the Reformation Paliament. In the preamble to the Reformation statutes we find, therefore, the first presentation of the official version of English history, which was to condition the thinking of most English people up to the present time. This version described the English past as having been always and essentially nationalist, erastian and self-sufficient, independent and exceptional in character, vitally different and separate from the rest of Europe and the rest of Christendom. It said that the events covered by these statutes constituted a *reformation*, not a revolution in English life and history. They provided the means for the return to a golden past of English Protestantism and freedom. I think it useful at this stage to note the observations of a distinguished and authoritative legal historian of the present century, Sir William Holdsworth:

> The preamble to this Statute of Appeals is remarkable, partly because it manufactures history upon an unprecedented scale, but chiefly because it has operated from that day to this as a powerful incentive to its manufacture by others upon similar lines. The Tudor Settlement of the relations of Church and State was a characteristically skilful instance of the Tudor genius for creating a modern institution with a medieval form. But, in order to create the illusion that the new Anglican Church was indeed the same institution as the medieval Church, it was necessary to prove the historical continuity of these two very different institutions; and obviously this could only be done by an historical argument. When this argument had been put forward in statutory form it became a good statutory root of title for the continuity and catholicity of this essentially modern institution. But a merely statutory title gave an obvious handle to its opponents, and could hardly be expected to satisfy its supporters. It is not therefore surprising that lawyers, theologians, and ecclesiastical historians soon began, from their different points of view to amplify and illustrate this historical argument, in order to prove that it rested upon a solid basis of truth. Two great professions thus have had and still have a direct professional interest in maintaining this thesis. The lawyers are tied up with it by their statutes and cases; the ecclesiatics by the tradition and authoritative declarations of their Church. Naturally, therefore, its truth is still believed and maintained by a long array of imposing names.[72]

This operation was successful initially because the statutes themselves contained savage penalties against anyone who later spoke or wrote in opposition to what they contained. The new and official version of the English past was to be repeated so often by chroniclers, historians and by all the official agencies of State, now including the Church, that soon people at large came to believe it. This is a procedure familiar enough to us in the twentieth century, but 'before 1530 England had seen very little in the way of organised propaganda'.[73] Nothing was allowed to be published in Tudor England which conflicted with these statutes. After constant repetition over centuries, their message became one of the accepted assumptions of thought in England.

Moreover, various important sections of society became committed to it. The common lawyers, tied to it by statutory process, were also pleased to support a view of the past which ousted the rival and international system of Church (or 'Canon') Law from England, prevented appeals to higher courts outside and left the legal field completely to them and their interests. They were to play a leading role in historical writing in the seventeenth century when they stressed the importance of Common Law as 'the ancient custom of England', and identified it with the English Constitution, as opposed to both the Canon and Feudal Law of Europe.[74] Most of the clergy had initially been forced into acquiescence. Having accepted control by the king, in spite of the loss of their status and authority, they eventually acquired an interest in supporting the new view of the past on which their position now depended for its validity. Most importantly of all, the leading gentry, main influences and law enforcers in the localities and in parliament had a strong vested interest in defending a version of the past which had justified their initial acquisition of monastic lands and had consolidated their important positions in society. 'Enthusiastic supporters' of the Henrician Reformation were 'probably a small minority'.[75] Some Protestants had fled the country after 1525 to escape Henry's wrath against heretics.

We now know that the Reformation in Henry's reign was not popularly supported by the people at large.[76] It was enacted and imposed from above by the State. The popular northern risings – the 'Pilgrimage of Grace' (1536) – were 'essentially a protest in defence of the old religion' and were strong enough to have overthrown the regime if its leaders had not trusted in the king's treacherous promises.[77] Some 216 'rebels' were put to death. Any clergy, monks and lay people who opposed were summarily imprisoned or executed. Most people were disinclined to risk their necks by opposing events which must have seemed to them to be transient in character. Thomas More understood that most people were faced with 'weathering the storm' and making 'shift to do as they could under the prince'.[78] Few had More's vision to understand the huge significance of what was happening or his heroic courage to resist. More, incidentally, did not want to persuade anyone else to share his fate.

All this was accompanied by a new campaign of government propaganda, at the centre of which was its 'official' view of the past.[79] English history was newly interpreted entirely according to nationalist and erastian criteria. It was a new view of the past constructed to meet the needs of the new nation-state. The 'Reformation' was depicted as freeing the English nation from the 'slavery' inflicted upon it by the Papacy in medieval times, and restoring it to its original imperial state in which the English king had reigned supreme over all aspects of national life. All proper English institutions had been created in England itself. The heroes of the past were those who had supported the kings; the villains were those who had opposed them in any way or who represented some outside authority, especially the Papacy. Later, after 1688, the famous 'Whig Interpretation', so well described by Herbert Butterfield,[80] was going to add the Revolution of 1688 as the next great stepping-stone in the inevitable progress of the English people towards world empire and glory. Again, a ready-made criterion was supplied by which English readers could distinguish good from bad, national heroes from traitors, in terms of those who had supported or opposed these two great stepping-stones to freedom and success.

The mentality which characterized the writing of history in England from the sixteenth century onward reflected also the rise of the nation-state, fighting for supremacy over other nation-states. The discovery of America placed England at the maritime centre of the newly expanded world, instead of being an island on the very edge of the old Mediterranean world. England was to become the foremost among the competing trading and colonizing nations. Conquests in the new colonies overseas were to make the British Empire supreme. All this added a sense of reality to the notion of English history as a continuous and unique story of national success achieved by a special people. It is hardly surprising that the English people were tempted into the dangerous view that they represented a superior species of mankind – the 'elect nation' – whose destined role in history was exalted above that of others.

Concomitant with the rise of the nation-states was their perceived need to subjugate any local or fringe cultures, both to secure order and defences at home and to provide a greater power base for any advances abroad. This was a part of the strategy inspired by four centuries of internecine warfare between the stronger states of Europe. The English government set out to bring the regional cultures of Wales, Ireland and Scotland within its own system of political uniformity. This led, after the respective Acts of Union in 1536, 1541 and 1707, to the concepts of 'Great Britain' and the 'British Empire', both of which were generally regarded as being led by England. They represented the pursuit of political uniformity rather than a true unity of cultures.[81] This uniformity or coherence was defined and held together in terms of Protestantism, Empire-building and wars against 'outsiders' – neighbouring continental states.[82]

There was, however, another and deeper factor underlying English nationalism and the political and cultural uniformity of Great Britain which followed from it. It concerns a 'folk memory' which was deliberately and consciously created by the Henrician government in the sixteenth century and was spread to other regions as part of the 'acts of union'. Part of this process was the development of an impression of the superiority of the English, their language and institutions, based on their history as described by the official version. There also developed a spirit of inferiority in the people of Wales who had become 'anglicized' to a greater or lesser extent after the Act of Union (1536).

At the beginning of the twenty-first century, we are now at a stage of historical development when the centrifugal forces of Protestantism, Empire and War are no longer there to hold together the uniformity underlying the concept of 'Great Britain' as a political unit in which both England and its Celtic neighbours remained isolated from continental Europe. This old concept is coming under pressure, too, from the re-emergence of the regional cultures. We seem to be at a stage when the peoples of these cultures are beginning to take stock of their positions in another new world arising around them which might offer prospects of less uniformity and more diversity within a larger unity encompassing the whole of Europe. One purpose of this study is to look at the creation and history of this folk memory in the English people, which had a powerful effect on their national psychology and general outlook. It also affected the history and outlook of the neighbouring Celtic countries of Wales, Ireland and Scotland.[83] It would seem appropriate, as we near the beginning of a new millennium, to look at the past in ways which enable us to see more clearly the realities of the present as well, possibly, as the best way forward in the future. Uniformity, not unity, is the opposite of diversity in regional and cultural expression.

English chroniclers and historians have been expected since the sixteenth century to demonstrate the continuity of English institutions and the steady ascent of the English nation. In knitting together the fabric of the English past, they became experts in invisible mending. The Reformation, being a sudden and dramatic break in continuity, with significant and long-lasting results, might have been expected to have offered the greatest challenge in this respect. The fundamental misinterpretation of this movement was great enough, however, and repeated often enough, for the whole of English history to be rewritten so as to be brought into line with it. The theme which gave unity to this view of the past was the idea of a totally independent England which had developed its own culture, religion and national institutions from the beginning and was destined to lead the post-Reformation world against Catholic Europe.

This kind of historical writing became one of the essential commonplaces of English thought for four centuries. It was an assumption of thought, something taken for granted, which was considered to be so important for the life of the nation that no one was allowed to contract out of accepting it. It therefore supplies an intriguing chapter in the history of persecution. From the sixteenth to the nineteenth century, persecution in the form of legal, political or social pressure was much too intense in England to allow any view of the past other than that of the official version. The English, normally tolerant with perhaps more than the average amount of common sense, developed an abnormal antipathy towards Catholics and Catholicism. This persecution over several centuries of people who simply believed what virtually the whole of the English people had believed for most of their history has been examined recently[84] as an aberration which was extraordinary in its intensity and durability. Rarely have the English people been persuaded to follow such personalities as Titus Oates, Israel Tonge or Lord George Gordon, whom we now know to have been completely unbalanced. Such behaviour can occur when a nation or individual is victim of a small circle of logical but false argument which excludes perspective and reality, especially when it is conducted in isolation. In this sense the phenomenon can be explained as a by-product of that official view of the past, created by the Henrician government in the 1530s and elaborated later by the Whig interpretation.

Various revolutions in modern times have been characterized by the rewriting of the past in order to justify newly established arrangements. Another characteristic is the assertion of the absolute power of the State over individual conscience. Certainly the statutory punishments for 'deviants' were sufficiently draconian in Tudor England, including public hanging, drawing and quartering as a means of dissuading other potential 'rebels'. What distinguishes anti-Catholic persecution in England is its extraordinary durability. It lasted formally for three centuries, until 1829,[85] and continued as an informal phenomenon of social pressure into the twentieth century.

The first significantly deviationist line of historical thought in England developed towards the end of the seventeenth century, in an 'underground' form.[86] This occurred among a group of scholars who had contracted out of the Whiggish and 'low-church' values of the society in which they found themselves after the 1688 Revolution. They refused to take the oath to the new monarchy of William and Mary and thus became known as 'Non-Jurors'. They were consequently disowned, persecuted and outlawed by the Whig regime which took power in State and Church after the Revolution.

These Non-Jurors were High Anglicans who accepted happily the nationalist part of the official version of the past, but rejected strongly the erastian element which asserted the rightful supremacy of the State over the Church. Among these were a group of scholars and antiquarians who loved the past for its own sake and because they believed that their Church was directly continuous with that of medieval England. They delved deeply into original documents and discovered many facts about medieval England and the Reformation which contravened quite drastically the official version. Their researches on the medieval period remained mostly underground in their private papers. Two important exceptions were a very scholarly but anonymous publication though only one man could have written it and we know the author, and the *Ecclesiastical History* (1708–14) of Jeremy Collier. We shall be concerned with both in this study. Their researches on the Reformation remained entirely underground in their private manuscript papers, because political and social pressure did not allow their publication. These important materials, which have never been published, anticipated the findings of modern research and will form the subject of another study.

The importance of these scholars in the history of historiography in England is that they were a group who shared high standards of scholarship and published documents with an accuracy which equalled modern requirements.[87] There is evidence that they were influenced by the remarkable advances being made in technical scholarship on the Continent, led by the great scholar-monk Jean Mabillon.[88] This contact with continental scholarship is itself an important and exceptional feature of their work. After the dissolution of the monasteries, England was denied the advantages of this type of group scholarship which flourished on the Continent.[89] The Non-Jurors, though not living in community, kept in close mutual contact and may be regarded as the nearest imitation in England of the Bollandist monks working in France.

It was lack of will rather than scholarship which prevented the Non-Jurors from challenging the other, nationalist element of the official version. This would have affected their own religious stance and they had been taught to think that it would have been an act of betrayal of their own Church. Even the most courageous of them could not do this.[90] The historical scholarship associated particularly with this group came to an end in about 1730 when historical writing in general came under the influence of the new age of the 'enlightenment' and 'reason'. The official version continued to hold the field, as we shall see, during the eighteenth century because its two main principles (nationalism and erastianism) proved capable of assimilating quite easily the philosophy of life propounded by the men of the 'enlightenment'.

It was only in the nineteenth century that this conventional account of the English past could be openly challenged and the perpetrator would have to proceed very carefully even then, in the face of a still hostile audience. It was significant that the undermining of the old view occurred in the same decade as the Act which emancipated Catholics in England (1829), giving them the vote for the first time. This was also a decade of strong opposition to the Act and feelings were running high in anti-Popery meetings.[91] It is as if there is an optimum point in the relationship between persecution and historiography when political and social pressure is no longer great enough to suppress completely the unpopular statement, or to keep it entirely underground, but is still sharp enough to ensure that only the best substantiated and most balanced expression of that statement will be heard.

This was certainly the case in the work of John Lingard, a Catholic priest, who was very conscious of audience reaction, but also had extraordinary qualities of scholarship and ability as a historian of exceptional stature. He produced his ten-volume *History of England* between 1819 and 1830 and this marked a turning-point in English historiography so great that it can be claimed as the beginning of modern historical writing in England. From a purely technical point of view, his work represents a completely new stage in the development of historiography. Lingard applied a set of rules of source criticism, which enabled him to get behind the source, to determine its weight and value. This has been the subject of research,[92] the importance of which has been recognized, and will be the subject of another study. Our present concern is to look at other aspects of Lingard's work which were new. These included his determination to base his work on original sources only, to write as 'a citizen of the world'[93] and consequently to explore foreign archives. In these ways, he changed the viewing mechanism, so to speak, in English historical writing and looked at the English past within a new and much wider perspective. For these reasons he was able to undermine the official account of the past and produce the 'first modern narrative of the two critical centuries of English history'.[94]

By Lingard's day, however, the old official version had long since become part of English folklore and so its power and influence continued after him in the various more popular histories published during the nineteenth and twentieth centuries. Scholarship can take a long time to filter through to the level of popular knowledge, especially when it is contending with views and attitudes which are fuelled by very strong emotions and deeply rooted prejudices. Indeed some eminent scholars were themselves still affected by the spell of the official version a century and more after Lingard had destroyed it. Lord Macaulay's celebrated *History of England* was a hugely popular best-seller which has never gone out of print. He was 'the great representative English historian of his day'[95] and his book was a literary masterpiece of Whig historical writing. Macaulay's outlook on the world exhibited a sense of superiority. His book was popular because he was telling people what they wanted to hear. Lingard's conclusions had to be rediscovered by scholars in the twentieth century, when the academic world was able to accept them, often without knowing that Lingard had been there before. It takes longer still for new knowledge to reach society as a whole and the time lapse can depend on the depth of feeling attached to the previous premiss of thought. It is very difficult to get people to listen to something which they do not want to hear.

Even today the common outlook and assumptions of thought derived from the official view of the past are still characteristic, at a conscious or subconscious level, of an English sense of separation and 'otherness'. Over four centuries the English became nationalistic and insular in outlook, contemplating their achievements at home and overseas and stressing the differences between themselves and the peoples of continental Europe, the colonies and even the Celtic fringe. This nationalism was something quite different from the spirit of 'Englishry' in the medieval period. From its beginning it was connected with a type of xenophobia which had a warping influence on their outlook.

In terms of national psychology, it was extraordinary that during these four centuries, the people of this island, just off the coast of northern Europe, came to believe that their nation had been always separate from Europe and independent of it, apart from some aberrations in the medieval period. This explains the reaction of an Englishman as intelligent as the Labour leader, Hugh Gaitskell, to Britain's bid to enter the Common Market in 1962: 'the end of Britain as an independent nation . . . the end of a thousand years of history'.[96] Similarly, the Tory Prime Minister, John Major, said in 1996, 'The Labour Party would, in a thousand days, vandalize a thousand years of British history' by seeking closer integration with Europe.[97] From opposite ends of the political spectrum, both were making political judgments based on a historical myth;[98] and both knew that they were tapping a very powerful source of emotional feeling in the English people.

As we begin the new millennium, the world has changed greatly, as has England's position in the world. The English need to understand now that the last four centuries have constituted the real aberration or deviation from the norm in England's natural development in historical and geographical terms over the last 2,000 years. They will need to develop a new sense of perspective which will make them more open-minded in their attitude towards the world outside.[99] Then they can discover the merits of sharing ordinary things like the same time of day, the same currency, even driving on the same side of the road, as their fellow Europeans who live only twenty-five miles away. The Channel Tunnel is a symbolic artefact which points the way to the natural development for England, as an important part of Europe, in the next millennium. There was a similar symbolism to Britain vacating Hong Kong in June 1997. Recognition of the realities of the world in which we live is understandably difficult for a people who once seemed to rule the world but for China this was the erasure of a painful memory.

It is necessary not to cling on to the 'recent' past, however 'glorious' it may have seemed. This can only mean a hindrance to life in the present and the future. The English will need to think differently in order to prepare for this future.[100] A proper understanding of the historical and historiographical forces which have conditioned their thinking in the past could be an important part of that process. No people is in fact superior to all the others, but each identifiable culture has its own unique quality, its own genius, to contribute to the world. These qualities are meant for the good of all. Nor is any culture able to flourish in isolation. Cultures develop and blossom in relationship with one another and it is from the inter-marriage of cultures that the best fruits are obtained.

Europe, too, must change to meet the needs of the new millennium. The medieval world had all the shortcomings and failings associated with a cross-section of any human society. It had its saints and its sinners. It was in pursuit, however, of the vision of a communal ideal for Europe as a partnership of peoples, sharing the same sense of identity and having a common set of fundamental values. These people went a long way towards achieving their aims, particularly in the twelfth and thirteenth centuries.[101]

Since the sixteenth century, in spite of all their achievements, particularly in the fields of science and technology, European nation-states, competing for supremacy, have lost this vision in their constant competitive struggle for individual dominance. The bankruptcy of the values underlying such power politics has become apparent in the twentieth century, with the ultimate failure of two totalitarian systems, the cataclysm of two world wars starting in Europe and the accompanying miseries for millions of people.[102] Even more recently we have seen the horrors of unfettered nationalism displayed once again in the sub-human behaviour which has taken place within the old Yugoslavia. Even our great technical achievements have been turned into self-destructive forms of weaponry.[103]

The great challenge facing the peoples of Europe now is that of learning from this human experience by seeking again to rediscover and implement the vision of a united Europe. It will require a great effort of the human spirit, intelligence, will and moral fibre. It is a difficult but not impossible task to work for a partnership of peoples, in which all would learn to live and work together, within a social, political and economic framework, underpinned by agreed basic values. There would be no question of any country, great or small, losing its historical identity. As a recent observer has remarked, 'Europe is both a region and an idea', yet 'societies and cultures that have existed in this northern extremity of the Euroasian land-mass have always been highly diverse'.[104] Each people would need, of course, to retain its own parliament, to ensure democratic control over its own government. The European Parliament itself would need to be much strengthened so as to retain democratic control over its own bodies like the European Commission. The old concept of Europe could be extended to other countries who were willing to accept basic values such as human rights and democracy, which underpin the common sense of identity. Indeed, the next great challenge would be to extend these principles to a united world, for as Toynbee observed after completing his monumental survey of the rise and fall of the world's civilizations, 'Mankind is simply going to destroy itself unless it succeeds in growing together into something like a single family'.[105]

For historical and historiographical reasons, the challenge has presented particular problems for the English people. Having been part of the mainstream of European life until the sixteenth century, they were isolated from it thereafter and consequently 'British perceptions reliably failed to realise that the world actually contained and accommodated other norms than their own'.[106] Ireland, in contrast, remained a European country, which accounts partly for modern Anglo-Irish problems, but also for Eire's great success as a member of the European Community.

A precondition of successful groupings of peoples is that they have a sense of common identity as well as common interests. The Catholic Church had been a great unifying force in medieval Europe. The Reformation occurred concurrently with the rise of the new nation-states.[107] The particular circumstances of the Reformation in England meant that it was going to take a particularly nationalist and isolationist character, together with a sense of mission as a great Protestant power in the world. The official version of English history played a very significant part in the construction of an extraordinarily persistent isolationist myth of English exceptionalism. Its interpretation of the past was both Protestant and very insular.[108]

It was well into the second half of the twentieth century before powerful political and economic forces pushed the British government into a somewhat grudging acceptance of the need to become members of the European Community, but it all seemed rather half-hearted. English politicians knew that 'it is easier to win votes by posing as the defender of national interests from a supposed "foreign intruder"' and the English tabloid press has found it easier to sell newspapers with this theme. The result is that England 'lies on the periphery of the Continent in more than a geographical sense', while England's European policy was largely dictated by a small group at Westminster and Whitehall.[109] The people have been taught in the past, initially by government and latterly by a long line of popular historians, to regard other peoples of the Continent as aliens, and there is a great and pressing need for a new process of education in the matter at a popular level.

Meanwhile, the situation in Europe has been changing at a religious, cultural and social level. Christian churches have recognized and learned from their past mistakes. The ecumenical movement, involving the search for Christian unity, has become a primary feature of Christian life and thought. In the face of increasing disorder, amorality and a modern philosophy of meaninglessness, Christians have learned the great importance of what they hold in common. At the same time respect for the religious freedom of all people has led to a greater sense of acceptance, toleration and respect. The Second Vatican Council (1962–5), for example, laid the guidelines for a positively outward-looking stance for the Catholic Church in its relationship with all other Christian bodies, other religions, and indeed with 'all people of good will' in a spirit of service to the whole of mankind. There is a greater recognition, too, of the fact that God's grace can blow where it wills and can be found in the most unusual and unexpected people and places. Among many peoples there is now a discernible search for a new framework of peace, order and meaningfulness, to supersede the period of terrible disorder caused by the internecine, nationalist conflicts of modern history.

Sir Richard Southern is arguably – in his combination of imaginative insight with meticulous scholarship – the greatest of living English medievalists. His first book, *The Making of the Middle*

Ages (1953), placed him immediately in the first rank of historians. His recent work on *Scholastic Humanism and the Unification of Europe* (1995) promises to be as epoch-making in English historiography as was that of F.W. Maitland a century earlier. In this latter work Southern shows that the great and successful movement for the unification of Europe in the twelfth and thirteenth centuries arose in reaction to the increasing threat of disorder in the tenth and eleventh centuries, partly caused by the Viking attacks on Christendom. It is possible that the unprecedented disorder of the twentieth century will be a precondition for the same great thrust of the human spirit in the new millennium. Certainly we know that,

> the requirements that conduct should be based on theological principles continued to be generally accepted as a necessary basis for peace and prosperity . . . a large part of the teaching of the medieval schools combined to influence the thought and conduct of the majority of people in Europe on both sides of the great divide between Roman Catholic and Protestant until the twentieth century. . . . It is only as a result of the vast secularisation of the twentieth century that the principles laid down for the communities of western Christendom in the twelfth and thirteenth centuries ceased to provide rules of conduct for their descendants.[110]

We also know now that it was the 'great systematic boldness and desire to extend human powers to the utmost' in Christian humanism, together with the belief that the 'whole created order' was being held together 'in an intelligible union', which provided the tap-root not only for the Renaissance of the sixteenth century, but also for the later advances in experimental science from the seventeenth to the twentieth centuries. These movements formed the basis of the modern world of science and technology. The one great difference characterizing the scientific humanism of the twentieth century was its omission of the spiritual dimension; Christian humanism had regarded that 'as the final, however imperfectly knowable, end and good of all intellectual inquiry'.[111] The great perspective and balance of thought enshrined in Christian humanism was broken by this omission. The taking away of the 'corner stone' was responsible for the collapse of the foundations on which European culture and civilization were based. There is now at last a discernible awareness (as at the Kyoto

Summit, 1997) of the sensitivity and interdependence of the various elements which hold the universe and its life together in a 'mysterious balance'. Similarly we are beginning to recognize the fundamental interdependence of human beings, on a personal, national and global scale. Such recognition has brought with it a certain humility in those who are facing the present problems of the world. Twentieth-century history has taught us that great technical knowledge cannot exist safely in a moral or spiritual vacuum. Some of the greatest inhumanities in human history took place in the twentieth century in one of the most technically advanced countries in the world. The greatest achievements of modern science and technology are too dangerous to handle, unless they find proper perspective within commonly accepted spiritual and moral values.

Southern notes, too, that 'the *study* of scholastic Christian humanism emerged as a model of order at a time of increasing disorder on a world-wide scale in the late nineteenth and twentieth centuries. With what results time alone will show'.[112] It is certainly not clear that there is any other credible alternative as a basic value system for European unity in the new millennium than the same Christian values which sustained the earlier unification of Europe. The qualities of life which the world is seeking now – peace, order, meaning, vision and hopefulness – are precisely those which were the fruits of that earlier form of Christian humanism. This humanism used the Bible as its main textbook,[113] thus basing itself on the spiritual and moral teaching of the great Judaeo-Christian tradition which is at the root of European civilization. It expressed the sacrosanct importance of each individual human being and the 'first fundamental characteristic' of its schools 'is a strong sense of the dignity of human nature. Without this there can be no humanism of any description'.[114]

Southern has contributed two important insights which have completely changed our historical understanding. One is that 'Christian' and 'humanist' are not mutually opposed – a mistake which has arisen from the exclusively secular humanism in modern times. In fact, humanism is derived from Christian teaching on the innate dignity and eternal value of all human beings. Secondly, Southern shows, in opposition to a mistaken understanding going back to the Reformation, that not only did medieval scholastic humanism work with the Scriptures, in fact they formed the chief 'textbook' for its teachings.

This Christian humanism has grown organically, developing in the sense conveyed by Cardinal Newman's seminal *Essay on the Development of Christian Doctrine* (1845), assimilating new knowledge and drawing new insights and understandings from, though consistent with, the original and essential teachings. Catholic Christians have developed a deeper and clearer understanding of their own faith and its application to the modern world in the light of the teachings of the Second Vatican Council. This encouraged, for example, an increased openness and appreciative attitude towards other faiths, together with a great respect for religious freedom and the sanctity of the informed conscience. It proclaimed the important role of the Christian in the modern pluralist society, of acting with all people of good will to serve the needs and human rights of the family of mankind.[115] It is significant that when the Catholic bishops in Britain published in 1996, in preparation for the General Election, their statement on *The Common Good*, this exposition of Catholic social teaching received a high level of support and approval from other Christian bodies and from the trade unions. Moreover, it now seems that this support may extend to 'embrace Muslims, Jews, and all those with a general sense of society as something to which we all have to contribute'. One commentator believes that, as a result 'we now have the beginnings of an ethical system for a pluralist society with which we can all do business'.[116]

A people, like an individual, looks to its memory to find its identity, and a false memory can lead to a mistaken sense of identity. The great contemporary debate revolves round the question of whether England should retain its post-sixteenth-century mentality of 'our sovereign and independent nation-state above all things', or is prepared to play a very different and truly important role in the creation of a new and united society of peoples in Europe. To play this part England will need to rediscover its historical identification with Europe, which was an assumption of thought for English people up to the sixteenth century. If the movement to unite Europe again is successful, then the next great challenge will be for Europeans to learn to give their 'loyalty, not to old divisive nationalisms, but to shared tasks and common citizenship in the City of Man', for now 'our planetary interdependence is as great as that of earlier states'.[117] Within this unity, local cultures, languages, traditions and patriotisms will be re-affirmed, for there will be much greater freedom of expression at this level. Historically, it is the enforced uniformity of the nation-state which has been the great enemy of local cultures.

In this great debate it is very important for the British people to discover their true identity. The weaknesses of their present concept are observable:

> What is clear are the ways in which a dominant sense of Britishness is a manufactured product, engineered to appeal to something far more powerful and deep-seated than much of the parliamentary rhetoric and party frothings. The retreat in the 1990s to a vision of England and Englishness, which is in many senses mythological, is an indication not merely of the barrenness of contemporary discourse in dealing with concepts of National Identity but of the powerfulness of the historical making of what passes for National Identity'.[118]

They can discover their true identity by looking at their past again, this time through the viewing mechanism provided by the history of historiography. This can be a process, albeit sometimes painful, of better self-understanding and self-guidance. Discovering the truth about themselves can set people free to face the realities of the present and the future with greater confidence, hope and motivating sense of purpose. It has been said of the English in the second half of the twentieth century that 'they have lost an Empire and have failed to find a role'. There is in fact an extremely important and creative role for them in the new millennium, giving the opportunity for a constructive and creative achievement. It is to bring their own proven qualities, together with their great sense and experience of democracy and commonwealth, to bear in helping to solve some of the most crucial problems facing the new Europe. They could thus exercise a leading influence in its development – which is what Jean Monnet had originally wanted from England when he founded the Community.[119] If the new Europe is to be influential for good in the world, it will have to learn how to organize itself in a truly democratic manner, so that its own freedoms are preserved; it will also have to look outwards and apply its traditional value system, with its considerable experience and status in the world, in working to establish and preserve the human rights of all other peoples in the world. This way will lie true peace and true progress in this new millennium.

Without a vision the people perish and the British need a sense of purpose now which can motivate them and bring out all that is best in the British character and spirit. To achieve this they will need to abandon their learnt, insular introspection and look outside themselves again to participate in a noble venture which will be for their good as well as that of Europe and the world at large. J. Northcott, in a publication of the independent Institute of Policy Studies, has written recently:

> it seems that the underlying longest-term factors are making for a larger, closer European Union, and that the only realistic future for Britain is within that Union. The challenge will be to take a positive rôle in helping *shape* the future, so that we have a better Europe and a better place for Britain within it.[120]

It is hoped that this study, though written as a piece of scholarship in the first place, may have some part to play in setting the perspective for the great debate which is taking place around us as we near the end of the present millennium. It is written in a spirit of hopefulness for the new millennium and with a great respect, affection and admiration for the English people with whom I have worked, played and made many friends.

ONE
Building the Official Version of the English Past

Henry VIII, as a result of his failure to gain a divorce from Catherine of Aragon, decided to break from the authority of the Papacy and establish a Church over which he would have complete control. Thomas Cromwell, Henry's chief minister, was commissioned as the chief architect of the move. The tools for the task were provided by the famous statutes enacted by the Reformation Parliament between 1532 and 1536.

The king had been a very conservative and orthodox Catholic until the question of the divorce arose. He had been awarded the title of 'Defender of the Faith' by Pope Leo X for his vigorous defence of Catholic orthodoxy against Luther.[1] In 1527 he had referred to the Pope as 'our most holy Lord, the true and only Vicar of Jesus Christ upon earth'[2] and he had acted initially as a perfectly orthodox Catholic in taking the question of his divorce to the Papacy for a decision. Moreover, England was a very Catholic country.[3] When he decided to break with Rome it was therefore very important to Henry that he should justify his actions by making it seem that he was doing nothing unorthodox or revolutionary. So, in the earlier drafts of the Act against Appeals, for example, we find 'apologies and explanations' and defences against anticipated attacks on the score of heresy from 'evyll Interpretours . . . of the laws insuying'.[4]

Thomas Cromwell was much more secular in outlook.[5] While Henry had dabbled in theology, music and literature, Cromwell, son of a Surrey tradesman, had spent part of an obscure early career in Italy during the Italian wars. He had then moved into the world of business and commerce in Italy and the Netherlands where he learnt the importance of efficiency in administration and sharpened his opportunistic outlook. Having returned to England, he entered Parliament in 1523 and in the following year started an important apprenticeship for political power by entering the service of

Cardinal Wolsey, the king's chief minister. His main work for Wolsey was concerned with the dissolution of twenty-nine of the smaller monasteries. He somewhat surprisingly survived his patron's downfall in 1530 and went into the king's service in which he rapidly gained power and influence. In 1530 he was sworn into membership of the King's Council and from then on quickly asserted his position as chief power in that Council, becoming the King's Secretary in 1534 and adding a new dimension and authority to that office.

From 1532 Henry seemed to recognize in Cromwell the man most capable of implementing a break with Rome, for his attributes were just those required for such a move. His opportunistic outlook, ruthless concern for administrative efficiency and his sheer ability in government and 'management' of Parliament were to make him a central figure in the implementation of the break with Rome (1533), taking control of the Church (1534), the Dissolution of the Monasteries (1536), the Act of Union with Wales (1536) and the strengthening of the machinery of government, which was a necessary concomitant of the newly independent 'Nation-State' or 'Sovereign State' of England.[6]

Cromwell had seen power politics at work in Italy. He had read Marsilio of Padua's *Defensor Pacis* (1324),[7] an idealization of the authority and power of the State as opposed to the Church, translated into English by William Marshall in 1535 at Cromwell's expense and used by him to justify the royal supremacy. Another important work of the same sort was the *Exhortation to Unity and Obedience* (1536), written by Thomas Starkey, who worked for Cromwell. These are examples of erastian-minded works and pamphlets which were distributed in England under Cromwell's guidance.

Cromwell in fact was the first man in English history who consciously worked as a minister of propaganda for the State, and it is arguably true that he was the ablest. His was a Machiavellian mind. His every move was preceded by a careful preparation of the ground. The Universities were pressurized to give favourable opinions on the divorce question. The notorious 'visitors' were sent around monasteries to provide an appropriate report on their condition, before the Dissolution. Recently, we have been informed in more detail of his use of William Tyndale's 'obedience-to-State' theology (*The Obedience of a Christian Man*, 1527) to provide powerful propaganda for the Act of Supremacy.[8] Tyndale, as a Protestant, had fled abroad in 1525 to escape Henry's wrath against heretics. It was Cromwell, not Henry, who now made this move. Tyndale's theology was a great propagandist coup for Cromwell in formulating his plans for the all-powerful State. He made great use of it, planning a campaign in which his agents were busy conscripting writers to publish pamphlets and other works along these lines. One of these agents was John Bale. A by-product of this was that there developed in the new Anglican Church a distinctive theology in which 'obedience' to the king was equated with 'God's will', as a centrally important feature of the Christian's life.[9]

The use of these erastian sources, together with the new theology, produced the idea which helps to explain much of sixteenth-century politics and religion in Tudor England. It was the idea of complete obedience in conscience to the king who was God's chosen representative, ruling over Church and State in England. Once the authority of the Pope had been dismissed from England, the door was open for the full implementation of these ideas.

Cromwell was also imbued with the common-law concept of sovereignty. A student of the Common Law himself, Cromwell was closely associated with Rich, Chancellor of Augmentations, and Audley, Lord Chancellor, both common lawyers. So, although Henry VIII came to exercise in practice a power more closely approximating to despotism than that acquired by any other English ruler, Cromwell saw to it that the king's supreme will was exercised through statute in Parliament. In Cromwell's mind the highest concept of theoretical power and authority was that of 'King-in-Parliament'; and it was on this basis that he used his great skill to fashion the statutes of the Henrician Parliament as the major instruments of governmental policy in Church and State. Henry's will was undoubtedly supreme in everything, but it was exercised through a compliant Parliament.[10]

Cromwell was astute enough to realize the importance of religious and political propaganda and of the essential connection between these factors at this time. The English nation had been one of the most religiously orthodox in Europe. It was necessary to take this into account. Cromwell was perhaps the first, but by no means the last, to see that the use of history, representing the memory and identity of a nation, is the most powerful weapon in the armoury of the propagandist. Cromwell determined to write into the preambles of the Reformation statutes a new version of the English past, which would give the movement the required precedents and justifications for its actions. This 'national-erastian' outlook, born in Cromwell's mind, was to become the viewing-instrument, so to speak, for the interpretation of the English past from its very beginnings.

With Cromwell's intervention there emerged a new tone to the proceedings. As opposed to Henry's anxious pursuit of theological justifications, Cromwell was now allowed full play to introduce an unequivocal assertion and unhesitating statement of Henry's regal supremacy in England, based on a categorically stated and confidently assumed historical background. The successful exercise of unprecedented power was making Henry more confident in its use. The new tone to proceedings was typical of Cromwell's character and of that brusquely efficient approach, brooking no opposition, which was typical of the dramatic changes which took place in English history in the decade 1530–40. It was with Cromwell that the preambles to the Henrician statutes 'achieve their full force of expounding policy'.[11] But whether acting through Wolsey or Cromwell, or through Privy Council, Henry was always in control of policy. He made or allowed things to happen when it suited his objective.

So the Act in Restraint of Appeals (1533) forbade anyone to appeal to any court outside England, and its preamble proclaimed proudly:

> Where by divers sundry old authentic histories and chronicles it is manifestly declared and expressed that this realm of England is an empire, and hath been accepted in the world, governed by one supreme head and king having the dignity and royal estate of the imperial crown of the same, unto whom a body politic, compact of all sorts and degrees of people, divided in terms and by names of spiritualty and temporalty, be bounden and ought to bear, next to God, a natural and humble obedience.[12]

The Ecclesiastical Appointments Act (1534) gave Henry the right to appoint archbishops and bishops without reference to any other authority 'as of old time has been accustomed'.[13] The epoch-making Act of Supremacy (1534), in which Cromwell was most typically 'the executant of the King's designs' while leaving 'his own imprint' on it,[14] begins again with the confident reference to the past:

Albeit the King's majesty justly and rightfully is and ought to be the supreme head of the Church of England, and so is recognized . . . yet nevertheless for corroboration and confirmation thereof, and for increase of virtue in Christ's religion within this realm of England, and to repress and extirp all errors, heresies and other enormities and abuses . . . be it enacted . . . that the King, our Sovereign Lord, his heirs and successors . . . shall be taken, accepted, and reputed the only Supreme Head on earth of the Church of England, called Anglicana Ecclesia.[15]

In these preambles, too, we see the ousting of the Canon Law of the Universal Church, which is replaced by the 'King's Ecclesiastical Supremacy'. In the view of the great legal historian, F.W. Maitland, no step was more 'momentous' than this prohibition of the Canon Law in England.[16] England was to be cut off completely in legal terms from the rest of Europe and the outside world and the law was a matter of life and death for Englishmen in the sixteenth century.[17]

The official version of virtually all the great issues of the Reformation in England can be seen to have been rooted in the preambles to these statutes. We shall find the beginnings, for example, of the historiography of the medieval Statutes of Provisors and Praemunire in the preamble to the Act in Restraint of Appeals, that of the great Divorce Question, which was central to everything else which happened,[18] in the preambles to the Acts of Succession and Supremacy, and that of the Dissolution of the Monasteries in the Acts which implemented the Dissolution in 1536 and 1539.

The same imprint is found in the Act of Union with Wales (1536) which was the first move to extend the power of the centralized English State over neighbouring regions and cultures in the British Isles. The exact relationship between this Act and the Henrician Reformation has been a matter of debate among historians, but 'there is no denying the concern with which the Privy Council viewed Welsh reaction to the Reformation changes'.[19] It began the history of 'internal colonialism'[20] which was to be a very familiar feature of the policy of English governments. The Act begins in the usual manner:

Albeit the Dominion, Principality and Country of Wales, justly and righteously is, and ever hath been incorporated, annexed, united, and subject to and under the imperial crown of this realm as a very member and joint of the same . . . yet notwithstanding, because that in the same country . . . divers rights, usages, laws, and customs be far discrepant from the laws and customs of this realm, and also because that the people . . . have and do daily use a speech nothing like nor consonant to the natural mother tongue used within this realm, some rude and ignorant people have made distinction . . . his highness therefore, of a singular zeal, love and favour that he beareth his subjects of . . . Wales minding and intending to reduce them to the perfect order, notice and knowledge of his laws . . . and utterly to extirp all and singular the sinister uses and customs differing from the same . . . established that this said country . . . of Wales shall be . . . incorporated, united, and annexed to and with his realm of England. . . . Also be it enacted . . . that all justices . . . and other officers . . . shall proclaim and keep the . . . courts in the English tongue . . . and also that from henceforth no person or persons that use the Welsh speech or language shall have or enjoy any manner of office or fees . . . upon pain of forfeiting the same office or fees, unless he or they use and exercise the speech or language of English.[21]

From the preambles to these statutes, then, we find that England is, and has always been, an 'empire',[22] subject to no earthly power other than its own king. The authority of the Pope in England is denied and his ecclesiastical powers there attacked as encroachments and usurpations. The fact that these powers existed at all was due only to the laxity and weakness of some of Henry's less capable predecessors who had allowed such encroachments upon their rightful authority by a grasping foreign potentate intent on expanding his power as far as possible and by every expedient. The characterization of the Papacy as a 'foreign power' is one of the most insistent notes in the preambles. When Cromwell changed a reference to the Papacy in one of the earlier drafts of the Act against Appeals, from the 'See Apostolike' to the 'See of Rome'[23] he was sounding a note that was to be taken up and used incessantly by later English historians. The Dispensations Act (1534) accused the Pope of abusing and beguiling the king's subjects.[24] Later in 1534 the Pope had become 'the pestilent idol, the enemy of all truth and usurpator of princes'.[25]

Another feature of the preambles which became a distinct characteristic of later English historiography was the reference to statutes of the medieval period which had 'sought to free English kings from the bondage of the Papacy'. So the Act in Restraint of Appeals states:

> the King, his most noble progenitors, and the nobility and commons of this said realm, at divers and sundry Parliaments as well in the time of King Edward I (1272–1317), Edward III (1327–77), Richard II (1377–99), Henry IV (1399–1413), and other noble kings of this realm made sundry ordinances, laws, statutes and provisions for the entire and sure conservation of the prerogatives, liberties and pre-eminences of the said imperial crown of this realm, and of the Jurisdiction spiritual and temporal of the same, to keep it from the annoyance as well of the see of Rome as from the authority of other foreign potentates, attempting the diminution or violation thereof, as often, and from time to time, as any such annoyance or attempt be known or espied.[26]

Later English historians all followed the historiographical framework of the English past set out in these statutes of the Reformation Parliament. They became what we would call primary original sources. Some, especially the legal and ecclesiastical historians, would refer to these statutes themselves as their main primary authorities. So, nearly two centuries later, Bishop Gibson, in his *Codex Iuris Ecclesiastici* (1713), based his argument for the independence of Church Law in England from the jurisdiction of the Papacy in the medieval period on the Reformation statute concerning Peter's Pence and Dispensations (1534):

> Here we have a plain Declaration that Foreign Laws become part of the Law of *England* by long use and custom. And the Church of *England*, in many cases both of Voluntary and Contentious Jurisidiction had no other Rule by which to proceed: so in admitting and practising the Rules which they found there, they had no Restraints upon them, save these two, that they were adapted to the Constitution of this Church, and so were *proper* Rules; and were not contradicted by the Laws of the Land, and so were *legal* Rules. Which last was the *Condition* of their being received and practised here, as well *before* the Reformation as since.[27]

43

Similarly a more modern historian comments that the theory of an independent English ecclesiastical jurisdiction in the medieval period – as claimed by the common lawyers and church historians in the seventeenth century – had

> no better warrant than some statements which were inserted by Henry VIII or his draftsmen, in certain Acts of the Reformation Parliament to the effect that the Pope's laws have never been recognised in England save by 'usage, sufferance and custom'.[28]

The usual pattern, however, was that the statutes determined the writing of history in the contemporary generation of chroniclers and historians. From then on English historians simply relied on their predecessors for their accounts, which became more amplified as time went on. The statutes, however, always determined the main framework and the main principles of the official view.

In these statutes, too, we find continual reminders of what would happen to anyone who defied them or spoke or wrote against anything they contained. The statutes therefore contained the weapon with which the historiography proclaimed in its preamble was enforced. The clergy had already been forced into submission (1529–30) by the threats of what could happen to them under the government's interpretation of the old medieval Statutes of Provisors and Praemunire, for having accepted Wolsey as papal legate, unless they acquiesced to the king's new title as 'supreme head of the Church'.[29] The same terror tactics were now used against all and sundry who disagreed with government policy. The Treasons Act (1534) stated that anyone who did 'slanderously and maliciously publish and pronounce, by express writing or words, that the king our sovereign lord should be heretic, schismatic, . . . shall be adjudged traitors' and 'the offenders, therin and their aiders, consenters, counsellors and abettors . . . shall have and suffer such pains of death and other penalties, as is limited and accustomed in cased of high treason'.[30] Everyone knew that the highest and most respected layman in the country had died in this way, even without speaking or writing against the king, and it would all the more easily happen to others too.[31]

We see in these statutes the typically Cromwellian approach, backed by the power and resolve of the sovereign king. A bold revolutionary statement was based on some vague 'precedent' which

44

was taken for granted and backed up by terror tactics. The king's chief minister had stamped his imprint on this approach, though he was never ultimately responsible for main policy. The role of Thomas Cromwell in creating the English people's view of their past has never been measured, but it was considerable. It was Cromwell's task, in serving the king's designs, 'to convert them into statutory form, to give them precision and draw out their full meaning', to 'show what was possible and what was not, what was necessary and what was not', and he 'intervened with decisive suggestions'.[32] Cromwell was also in charge of the propaganda campaign, needed to stamp these changes on the mind of the nation.

The detailed character of Cromwell's interventions in the drafting of statutes, rather than the making of policy, was shown in the preparation of the Statute in Restraint of Appeals, where Henry's more anxious pursuit of self-justification is replaced by bolder assertions. So, in the early drafts of this Act, there were 'apologies' and defences against anticipated attacks on the score of heresy from 'evyll Interpretours . . . of the laws insuying'. It is significant that certain of these passages were later omitted, probably by the intervention of Cromwell and his advisers. One such passage had asserted that the kings of England had been called vicars of God in papal epistles. Another passage, which had been previously cancelled, then re-inserted by Henry and finally excluded altogether, stated that spiritual and temporal authority and jurisdiction 'are deryved and dependeth frome and of the same Imperiall crowne of this Realme . . . and in this manner of wise precedeth the Iurisdiccion spirituall and temporall of this realm and from the said Imperiall Crowne and none otherwise'.[33] Cromwell may have realized the weaknesses involved in the excessive use of such words and claims.

It was Cromwell's imprint and approach which became the greatest inherited feature of the later historiography of the Reformation in England. It did more towards the building of a conventional attitude of mind, never contested because taken for granted, becoming ever more rigid and unyielding as it sank deeper into the subconscious mind of the nation than the weak arguments of Henry VIII could ever have done. It gave, from the start, that *a priori* approach which initially acted as an obstruction to historical research at all, defying historians even to think of testing its premises, and later absorbed the early research into its own structure.

During the medieval period, one book had dominated the English people's view of the origins of their nation. Geoffrey of Monmouth's *Historia Regum Britanniae* (1136) was based, he claimed, on an ancient book in the British tongue, by which he probably meant early Welsh; this book has never been discovered and is not mentioned by any other chronicler. He seems to have relied for the most part on a romantic imagination, but his work enjoyed a great and durable popularity. Two factors lay behind the success of Geoffrey's ruminations. One was sheer ignorance of early history before the coming of the Romans; and the other was the obviously popular appeal to the English people of his attempt to seek prestigious origins for their country. He claimed that Brutus, grandson of the heroic Aeneas of Troy who had founded Rome, had sailed to Albion, colonized it with Trojans and renamed it Britain, after his own name. The Roman period of British history was presented not as an occupation, but as an overlordship. English kings still ruled, owing allegiance to Rome.[34] These legends, known as 'Bruts', were very influential and Henry VII, after Bosworth, named his eldest son Arthur, hoping to gain popular support from his own Welsh ancestry which could be linked with the early British and Trojan myth.[35]

The significance of Geoffrey's fables, and their great influence during the medieval period and in the sixteenth century, is that all this demonstrated a psychology which seemed to operate naturally with a world picture in which Britain was not an isolated and independent island, but very much an influential and important part of Europe. As a recent writer has observed,

> Geoffrey of Monmouth showed that England had never been an isolated and backward island; on the contrary, her links with Rome through the Trojan house put her in the van of European civilization from the beginning. . . . In the person of Constantine the Great, born at York, she had even given the world its first Christian Emperor.[36]

Geoffrey was on firmer ground when he wrote of the coming of St Augustine in 597, sent by the Pope in Rome, to bring Christianity to England, which of course had been narrated already by the Venerable Bede in his great work five centuries earlier. In the fables, and their reception, there is a reflection of an awareness and pride in being part of a much greater civilization, which was the truth about medieval England. This mentality was going to be changed radically by the Henrician statutes.

Patriotism, in its various forms, has always been present in groups of people. Individual loyalty to the group and self-sacrifice for it have also been perennial characteristics. During the medieval period there were signs of self-identification in various European peoples, which were often later to be misunderstood by modern historians as signs of emergent modern nationalism. In fact that self-identification was more in the sense of a regional feeling of people who were always aware at the same time that they belonged to the more important international community of a united Christendom. In the sixteenth century, with the appearance of the early modern dynastic states and the breakup of the Christian unity of Europe, there were attempts to categorize the 'national characteristics' by which one could identify and distinguish between these newly formed and powerful groups. There developed a 'well-established and distinguished literary rhetoric' in which the word 'nation' and 'national characteristics' were used as a common way of expressing such identities and distinctions. This is the literary context in which we should interpret, for example, many such passages in Shakespeare's plays.

Alongside this, there emerged a significant activity on the part of historians, antiquaries, topographers and others, which expressed a feeling of national identity. Evidence was sought everywhere to reveal, or imaginatively concoct, an ancient past for the people, with as many 'glorious' adjuncts as possible: 'History, language, folklore, territory, culture or religion could be used to demonstrate the past traditions of a nation, symbolic evidence of its historical continuity and hence of its authenticity'[37]

In England, however, particular circumstances produced the condition within which the modern nation-state made its entry on the scene, earlier than in most other parts of Europe. To begin with, 'Late medieval England was the most centralist and unified monarchy in Europe', with London as its only great urban centre, the unifying factor of its Common Law which had been 'harnessed . . . to the king's purposes', and a central feudal structure which had largely overcome the problems of seigneurial rights.[38] However, until the Divorce Question, English kings could not be absolute rulers, because they recognized the law of the Universal Church and the supremacy in spiritual and ecclesiastical matters of the

Pope to whom appeals could be made from England as from elsewhere in Europe.

The Act against Appeals (1533) and the Act of Supremacy (1534) changed all this. Henry VIII became the most absolute monarch in Europe,[39] though still theoretically expressing his will through Parliament. Moreover, Cromwell had supplied him with the necessary governmental machinery to control and administer a modern-type nation-state.[40] All this meant that the rhetorical sentiment and proud expressions of the English people's ancient past and its glories took on a centrally directed, controlled and purposefully political character which turned them into something which has been a prominent feature of the modern world. Organized goverment propaganda began in England as a concomitant of the Henrician 'Reformation'. It was used to subdue internal protest as well as to activate in its people a xenophobic spirit against 'foreign enemies', especially the Papacy and any Catholic countries. There followed the purposeful harnessing not only of contemporary historical writing, but of culture as a whole, to support the cause of centralist propaganda. This became a very marked feature during the reign of Elizabeth I.

The first post-medieval historian of England was not English, but a fellow European whose career marks the dividing line between medieval and post-Reformation England. Polydore Vergil, a native of Urbino in Italy, came to England in 1502 as a sub-collector of Peter's Pence, a form of annual tax (about £200 from the nation as a whole) which went towards the upkeep of the Papacy as the centre of Church government for the whole of Christendom. A scholarly man, made Archdeacon of Wells in 1508, he became a friend of Thomas More and other English humanists. In 1515 he completed in manuscript form his *Anglicae Historiae* in Latin and probably presented a copy to Henry VIII. He rejected the Trojan fables of Geoffrey of Monmouth and his book was regarded as a product of European humanism, for although he used no new sources, 'those he used he used exactly and as accurately as he could, with some attempt to assess their comparative value'.[41] His work was built very much, in chronology and otherwise, around the line of kings whose importance he emphasized. He described the Tudors as beginning a period of stability and peace after the disturbance of the Wars of the Roses. Wishing to give the king an exalted pedigree, he stated that the imperial crown had come down to Henry VIII in direct succession from the Emperor Constantine and his mother, Helena (who was alleged to have been British), through the legendary Arthur.[42] The main section, up to 1509, was published in 1534, but by now great changes were taking place in England and Vergil delayed the publication of the last section (1509–37) 'until he was safely back in Italy'.[43] His work was going to be 'shamelessly plundered by chroniclers of the next generation, who were safe in the knowledge that few of their readers would have tackled it in the Latin'.[44]

From the time of this book's publication in 1534, the claim to imperial status on Henry's part was consistently pressed in a series of preambles to the Reformation statutes. Before the end of the century 'the term Empire began also to be applied to the overseas expansion of the English State'.[45] We have been reminded, however, that we ought not to attach too much importance to it in relation to the English Reformation:

> It is true that during the drafting of the Act of Appeals, the King for a time suggested that he should claim to derive his spiritual jurisdiction from this imperial authority, but he found that the claim could not be substantiated by reference to the Holy Roman Empire or to any other precedents. He thus ultimately refrained from pressing this emotive but historically circumscribed term, and instead he based his spiritual jurisdiction upon a special claim to a Royal Supremacy over the English Church.[46]

The Henrician statutes of 1533–4 established the twin pillars of the official versions – the nationalist and the erastian interpretations of the English past – from the very beginning of English history. The official version was immediately used by Cromwell for propaganda purposes. A spate of official pamphlets appeared, sponsored *cum privilegio* by the king's printer, from 1534 onwards. Stephen Gardiner's *De Vera Obedientia* (1534) was a classic defence of the royal supremacy by one who later claimed that he had written under duress. We have already noticed the strongly erastian *Exhortation to Unity and Obedience* (1534) written by Cromwell's publicist, Thomas Starkey, who also produced *An Exhortation to the People* (1535). This was the beginning in England of the power of the press, used as a propagandist instrument by government. The same technique was employed again to justify the 'Glorious Revolution' of 1688–9 when William of Orange brought his own press with him for the purpose.[47] Thomas Cromwell was propagandist-in-chief for the Reformation and Gilbert Burnet was going to be his counterpart for the 1688 Revolution. Cromwell created the 'national-erastian' interpretation; Burnet created the Whig interpretation which was built upon the former. Both together made up the immensely powerful official version, covering the whole of English history and lasting in some senses until the present day. A contemporary historian has pointed out, for example, that 'outside the academic community', the old version of English history, in some respects, still 'has kept its potency'.[48] Government has become involved in this, from time to time, because it is well aware of the power of history over the minds of its people.

Another work which appeared just after the middle of the sixteenth century is significant because it expressed the vested interest of the common lawyers in defending the new establishment which had ousted the Canon Law. The composite work, which had common lawyers among its promoters, was entitled *A Mirror for Magistrates*. Its first edition in 1555, during Mary Tudor's reign, was suppressed, but it re-appeared quickly in 1559, after Elizabeth came to the throne, and during her reign five editions appeared, with a sixth in 1609. It was one of the most influential works of the period, postulating clearly the theory of the divine right of kings and helping considerably in the Tudor exaltation of monarchy and the royal supremacy.

Equally apparent was the immediate 'hijacking' of contemporary historiography to serve the purposes of propaganda – another prominent feature of the later Revolution of 1688.[49] The Tudor chroniclers fell into line with the official version with almost amusing rapidity. Robert Fabyan's *The Concordance of Chronicles*, originally published in 1516, was a typical compilation of various medieval sources which described the history of England from the arrival of Brutus to the death of Richard III. The pre-Reformation 1516 edition had been uncomplimentary to King John in his conflict with the Papacy, and had also praised the stand taken by Archbishop Thomas Becket against Henry II. The Reformation statutes, followed by Henry VIII's attack on Becket's shrine in 1538, taught a different historical lesson which had to be learned pretty quickly. All the old references to such matters were omitted in the later, post-Reformation editions of 1542 and 1549. The new heroic depiction of John appeared again in a chronicle play printed much later, in 1591, entitled *The Troublesome Reigne of John*, in which the events of John's reign are mirrored in that of Henry VIII who is the real hero of the piece.[50]

The chroniclers of the Elizabethan period continued to illustrate this subservience of historical writing to the needs of the State. Edward Hall's compilations were completed by Richard Grafton whose *Chronicle* (1568) stated that its intention was that the 'Ecclesiastical State' should learn to 'abhorre trayterous practices and indignities done against Kings' and its anti-Catholic message is plainly propagandist. John Speed, who was a much better cartographer than historian, later published his *Historie of Great Britain* (1611) which was equally predictable in its propagandist use of historical precedents.[51] Ralph Holinshed's *Chronicles of England, Scotland and Ireland* (1577) was a great agglomeration of historical instances purporting to show that any civil or political disturbance was harmful to the proper development of the nation. It is significant in showing how careful these chroniclers had to be in pleasing the government that when, after Holinshed's death, his publishers commissioned a group of less experienced writers to revise and complete his work, their new publication in 1583 provoked the displeasure of the Privy Council which ordered all sections dealing with present government ministers to be removed. When, in 1599, Sir John Hayward produced a historical work dedicated to his patron, the Earl of Essex, which included the deposition and murder of Richard II, he brought so much suspicion on himself that he was sent to the Tower for two years, until Essex had been tried and executed.[52]

Indeed this close government interest in historical work continued throughout the seventeenth century. James I opposed the activities of the Society of Antiquaries, though they pledged 'to decline all matters of State', and in 1627 Sir Robert Cotton was closely interrogated by the Council which suspected some criticism of the present government in his *Short View of the Long Life and Reign of Henry the Third*.[52] Sir Henry Spelman dared not publish his *History and Fate of Sacrilege*, concerning the Dissolution of the Monasteries, during his own lifetime, and a second attempt to publish it in 1663 failed because of opposition by those gentry who had benefited from the Dissolution. Likewise Sir William Dugdale's scholarly *Monasticon* (1655), containing monastic charters, frightened certain Protestants, who feared that it represented a Catholic plot, and the gentry, who feared that their title deeds to monastic lands might be called into question.[53] Most of the manuscript works on the Reformation written by the non-juring scholars could not be published at the end of the century because of Establishment opposition, and indeed have never been published since.[54]

John Stowe (1525–1605), author of *A Summary of English Chronicles* (1565) and *The Annals or General Chronicle of England* (1580), was potentially the ablest of the Elizabethan chroniclers. He could use record material, weigh up contemporary evidence and above all, 'he was really concerned to establish the truth of events – unlike most of his rivals, who merely made pious noises to this effect . . . he had a dawning sense of anachronism . . . and he had a vague understanding, at least, of the fact that institutions and political habits changed over the centuries'.[55]

Unfortunately, 'in competition with Holinshed' who 'set the tone of sixteenth-century English history',[56] he was unable to get his planned History of England published and its manuscript was lost. We can only guess now at its possible importance. Stowe was suspected of being a Catholic. He was charged on two occasions (1569–70) with 'possessing popish and dangerous materials' and appeared before the Ecclesiastical Commission, a body set up by the government to oversee and exercise discipline in such matters. He is significant in English historiography as being the first to attempt to base his work on a systematic study of public records.[57] Having turned to the safer area of topography, he is now best remembered for his great *Survey of London* (1598).

Stowe's pupil was the celebrated William Camden (1551–1623), who was fortunate enough to enjoy the patronage of Lord Burleigh, the queen's chief minister, and the friendship of that great collector of rare books and old documents, Sir Robert Cotton. Camden's famous *Britannia* (1586) was a nationwide survey of the antiquities of Britain, arranged on a topographical basis. This was the first fruition of the debate about the origins of Britain and the antiquarianism which contributed so much to the English sense of national identity in the sixteenth century. Lord Burleigh asked Camden to write about Queen Elizabeth and this resulted in the *Annales Rerum Anglicarum et Hibernicorum Regnante Elizabethae* (1616) which was the basis of so many later descriptions of the national glories of the Elizabethan age – in the arts, trade and exploration, as well as warfare. All the chroniclers were expected to demonstrate 'the politic historian's central message of undeviating support for the government', but Camden's *Annales* was the first to view Elizabeth's reign 'as a great explosion of the national genius, controlled and orchestrated by the great queen'.[58] As H. Trevor-Roper observes, 'It is thanks to Camden that we ascribe to Queen Elizabeth a consistent policy of *via media* rather than an inconsequent series of unresolved conflicts and paralysed indecisions'.[59] This interpretation has dominated English historiography up to the present day, apart from Lingard's account of the reign.[60]

During Elizabeth's reign there developed another form of historical activity associated with antiquarianism, which again was going to be manipulated for State purposes. The new Archbishop of Canterbury, established by Elizabeth after her new Acts of Supremacy and Uniformity (1559), was Matthew Parker who had lost his position as Master of Corpus Christi College, Cambridge and gone into exile during Mary's reign. He was an antiquarian who led the way, in association with John Bale and others, in the collection and publication of editions of some medieval sources. It was from the time of Parker's editions of his works, that Matthew Paris' *Chronicles* began its dubious career as a prominent anti-papal witness in Protestant writings.[61]

Parker also extended his printed editions into the Anglo-Saxon period and we are indebted to him for the earliest editions of Ælfric and Asser. His main motive, however, was to defend the Anglican Church, which he served, and to give it a historical basis. This activity fitted conveniently into the broad framework supplied by the Henrician statutes and gave it a more detailed extension into Anglo-Saxon history where the additional myth of an early national Church, completely independent of Rome, began to take a more elaborate shape.[62] We must, of course, place this antiquarianism in the context of its own time. It was characterized by 'its service of and servility towards . . . English nationalism'. It was confined to English subjects and was based on English sources in ecclesiastical history, while 'their conscientious provincialism sometimes coloured the interpretation of unimpeachable data'.[63] Nevertheless much valuable work was done.

The work of the Society of Antiquaries became more important in the seventeenth century when notable scholars such as Sir Henry Spelman, Camden, Ussher and Selden became associated with its activities. Indeed Sir Robert Brady and Sir Henry Spelman both made notable discoveries about the European feudal law in the medieval period, which included England within its framework.[64] However, eminent though Spelman and Brady were in the field of feudal studies, they had nothing to contribute towards a better understanding of ecclesiastical law and institutions in the medieval period, to which they retained the isolationist and nationalist approach which always characterized the official version.

A notable example of the way in which propagandist motives interfered with development in historical understanding was the treatment of Bede's *Historia Ecclesiastici Gentis Anglorum* (731). As a recent writer has put it, 'Ignorance of the Anglo-Saxons was almost total'[65] in the sixteenth century, and Richard Harvey was pleased to say in 1593, 'What have I to do with the Saxons? Let them lie in dead forgetfulness'.[66] Yet one of the best and most important sources for knowing about them had been written by an Englishman over eight centuries before and this source is still of fundamental importance. In sixteenth-century England, however, the Venerable Bede was 'tarred with the papist brush'[67] and therefore not to be considered. The first popular edition of his great work was published abroad at Antwerp in 1550, the editor hoping that 'this proof of the antiquity of Christianity in England will discomfort those who hope that they can reform it'.[68] The first translation from the original Latin into English was by the Catholic-in-exile, Thomas Stapleton, at Antwerp in 1565, and it was reprinted by the Jesuits at St Omer in 1622 and 1626. In 1658 an anonymous paraphrase of it appeared in Antwerp, entitled, 'England's old Religion faithfully gathered out of the History of the Church of England as it was written almost a thousand years ago'.

Finally, in 1643, an edition of Bede's *History* appeared in England, but significantly it was 'by a scholar for other scholars'.[69] It was not meant for a wide readership. It was produced by Abraham Whelock, the first holder of the Sir Henry Spelman lectureship at Cambridge and was a fine edition, with the Latin and Old English (or Anglo-Saxon) on facing pages. This was an example of the specialized work which relied mostly on the Universities. Indeed, only they supplied the finances for the special typeface needed for such editions. It exemplified too a trend which has continued in English historical writing down to the present day. I refer to the gap between scholarly works, containing the results of the most recent research, which are usually produced as 'scholarly monographs' for the small community of trained historians, and other works intended for the more popular market. The latter obviously have the greater influence on public opinion, and they are frequently the vehicle for the maintenance of popular myths which do not challenge what people want to hear. These have appealed to and fuelled national myths and prejudices, and the historians who have purveyed them have frequently been accounted the great historians because of their eloquent exposition and popular acclaim. Thus the 'official' version of the English past has been maintained up to the end of the twentieth century in such works in spite of detailed scholarship which has effectively undermined it.[70] Sometimes the gap separates two types of historian – the scholar from the popular writer. Sometimes it can exist within the mind of one man, so that the scholar presents his research for the experts in scholarly works, usually confined to small areas, but then succumbs to the siren voice of the old myth-makers when he or she writes a more general book for the more popular market.

Certainly there was a gap between the scholarly editions of Anglo-Saxon texts produced by Wheloc or William Sumner, the second Spelman lecturer at Cambridge, who produced an Anglo-Saxon Dictionary (1659), and the general writings in which people like James Ussher (Archbishop of Armagh) and Edward Stillingfleet (Bishop of Worcester) were concerned to describe the existence of an early British Protestant Church, independent of Rome but having an episcopal form.[71] Strangely enough, it was Ussher, eager to prove the antiquity of the Church of England, who induced Sir Henry Spelman, in 1640, to endow the lectureship at Cambridge in the first place. The same gap between their own detailed research and their general statements about the English past will be seen in the work of the non-juring scholars – sometimes expressed in separate works, sometimes even found within the same work.[72] This dualism of thought is one of the intriguing sub-themes running through the history of the official version of the English past.

The poets and playwrights of the Elizabethan period likewise usually took their cue from government policy. In the Tudor period English culture was dominated by themes such as the glorification of monarchy, the Reformation and the new nation-state. These themes are found in all branches of the arts in the Elizabethan period. The link between government propaganda and contemporary culture is exemplified perfectly in the work of the finest poet of the age. Edmund Spenser dedicated his *Faerie Queene* (1589–90) to Queen Elizabeth, in the style of adulation customary at this time. This work is very definitely propagandist in character and introverted in a nationalist sense. The chief characters represent historical personages. The Faerie Queene herself is 'Glory' personified, representing Queen Elizabeth. Prince Arthur, son of Uther Pendragon, is the Protestant hero, representing the Earl of Leicester who was Captain-General of the English forces in the Netherlands, fighting against Catholic Spain. The Redcrosse Knight is 'Holiness', or the Anglican Church. Duessa represents 'Deceit', or the Church of Rome, or later Mary Queen of Scots.[73] Spenser was very much an Establishment figure. He had worked as secretary to the Bishop of Rochester, before entering Leicester's household, was a friend of the Earl of Essex and went to Ireland as lord deputy. In his work we find the finest poetry of the age being suborned directly for the State's propagandist purpose: culture serving a nationalist interest. Spenser was the finest, and the most typical, of Elizabethan poets.

The greatest English writer of all, however, presents an interesting and rather mysterious exception. William Shakespeare was a 'free spirit', described by his contemporary Ben Jonson as 'not of an age, but for all time'. Cultural change does not, of course, take place within precise boundaries of time, though we use these for our own convenience. Shakespeare was born just before the time that most of us would describe as the birth of Protestant England. He was certainly in no sense an Establishment figure and was opposed to tyranny, cruelty, or torture of any sort. His pride in country is more reminiscent of medieval patriotism than later xenophobic nationalism. No one has more eloquently expressed the feeling of 'Englishry' and patriotism – as in the famous speech from *Richard II* describing 'This blessed plot, this earth, this realm, this England'.[74]

Shakespeare combines this feeling with a wealth of religious references which seem, to several critics, to contain a sympathy with 'recusants' or even a hidden 'pro-Catholic agenda'.[75] This would have been made easier during a time of governmental 'censorship' by the fact that none of his plays was written for the press, but simply to be performed. His native genius was combined with great breadth and universality of mind. He took the plots for his historical plays from the Chroniclers, especially Ralph Holinshed, who, as we have seen, were certainly involved in the anti-Catholic propagandist cause. These plots are however transmuted into plays which are quite different in their ethos. For example, King John and his conflict with the Papacy was one of the chief historical precedents used by the propagandists. Shakespeare's *King John* (1596–7) was based, according to one critic, 'pretty closely, with regard to historical events, the selection of scenes, and even the logical run of many of the dialogues'[76] on an anonymous play entitled *The Troublesome Reigne of John, King of England* (1591) which was very strongly propagandist and anti-papist.[77] Yet in Shakespeare's entirely rewritten play, these elements have almost entirely disappeared. Also intriguing is the fact that at least part of the play *Sir Thomas More*, which has been traditionally placed among the 'Shakespeare Apocrypha', is claimed by several critics to have been written in Shakespeare's own hand, as identified by the paleographer, Edward Maude Thompson.[78] This is also the only extant piece of Shakespeare's authorial manuscript.

There is some evidence, too, that Shakespeare seemed to question the ideological basis of the Tudor dynasty;[79] and a recent student has argued strongly that there is plenty of internal evidence in the plays that Shakespeare's beliefs, sympathies and general outlook were Catholic. We know that *King Lear* and *Pericles* were produced by a group of recusant actors for an audience of Catholics in Yorkshire in 1609–10, because of their 'hidden messages' of sympathy for the Catholic cause. Certainly there is much evidence in his family background of Catholic belief and sympathies.[80] Most interesting of all is the recent comment by Adrian Hastings on Shakespeare's 'last testimony' on nationalism. *Cymbeline* (1613):

> is the story of an irrational and nationalist Britain, set upon being 'a world by itself', where refusal to pay formal tribute to Rome and the disruption of domestic harmony have been produced by the machinations of a thoroughly evil queen [Elizabeth I?]. . . . The destructive blindness of nationalism falls from British eyes. Through Wales the true *Romanitas* of Britain is revealed once more . . . an exaggerated nationalism is overthrown and peace re-established between Caesar and Cymbeline, Brussels and London, Wales and England, the international community and the nation-state, perhaps even Catholicism and the national Church. But it is the British, rather than the English, dimensions of our identity which have made that possible. The path from Rome lies via Milford Haven. The symbolism in this, Shakespeare's final testimony to his fellow countrymen in regard to the matter of nationhood, is mysteriously emphatic, woefully overlooked as it mostly is . . .[81]

I think it fair to say that the difference in ethos between the work of Shakespeare (1564–1616) and John Milton (1608–74), whose best-known work is *Paradise Lost* (1657), reflects in several ways the change in cultural ethos from the sixteenth to the seventeenth century, and from Catholic to Protestant England.

However, if literature in general was influenced by the government's propagandist purposes, there is no doubt that historical writing, in particular, came most directly under its ambit. The misuse of history for such purposes has been a feature of the modern world and the Tudors provided one of the earliest instances of this manoeuvre. The most important and influential expression of the English past to appear in the sixteenth century was undoubtedly John Foxe's *Acts and Monuments of the English Church* (1563), known popularly and famously ever since as Foxe's 'Book of Martyrs'. This work, perhaps more than any other, affected the English people's view of their past and contributed in a quite extraordinary way to the creation of an English attitude of mind over the following four centuries, engendering an intense hatred of Catholics and foreigners. The book itself was the result of intense activity in historical propaganda, which went back to the very beginning of the Reformation in England, and the shadow of Thomas Cromwell's influence was there from the start.

John Bale (1495–1563) was an ex-Carmelite friar who became one of the most bitter critics of his old religion. He was the leading figure among a group of antiquaries who sought to preserve the books and manuscripts of the monastic libraries after the Dissolution of the Monasteries. He pursued this work assiduously for his own anti-Catholic purposes. His talents as a cataloguer and compiler of documents were going to be of great service to John Foxe, but Bale was very much more than this when he entered the service of Thomas Cromwell.

Bale soon attracted attention in England because of his Protestant views. He seemed to have a particular and personal resentment against the Catholic Church. He had renounced his Carmelite vows by taking a wife. It was not long before Cromwell recognized in him 'a man who could strike hard',[82] and took him under his patronage. In this capacity Bale was commissioned to write plays as propaganda for the policies his patron was implementing for the king. These were morality plays on the medieval model, including stories from Scripture and from the medieval Chronicles. For example, Cromwell, as we have seen, was invoking the Tyndalian theology of obedience to the King as representing 'God's word', as political propaganda to support the Act of Supremacy.[83] Bale produced for Cromwell a play on *King*

John, in which 'Everyman' was King John, faced with the temptation to surrender the inalienable authority vested in the royal supremacy to the evil machinations of the Papacy and its agents who were plotting against the English people's interests. Bale gave obedience to the king 'its most dramatic expression' and the play 'is a prolonged dramatic meditation on the theme'.[84] In this way Bale was 'making a start at turning national legends to the use of propaganda in the national cause'.[85] In 1536 Bale wrote a play for Cromwell called the *Impostures of Thomas Becket*, the publication of which preceded the attack by Cromwell on Becket's shrine in 1538. We know that Cromwell paid close attention to preparing the ground for his actions by suitable propaganda[86] and it seems clear that he was using Bale in this way during this episode.

The partnership between Cromwell and his protégé continued until the former's downfall and execution in 1540, which reminds us that Henry as 'sovereign prince' was always the master who pulled the strings in spite of his servant's great ability. This event, too, marked the increasing influence of Stephen Gardiner and his 'conservative' party in the King's Council. Bale fled into exile on the Continent. In choosing Bale as one of his purveyors of government propaganda, Cromwell had shown his usual acumen. It was in fact Bale's main aim in preserving the books and manuscripts of the monastic libraries to use this as propaganda against the Church which they had served. Bale seems to have been one of the first to see that the overthrow of Papal authority in England would require the complete rewriting of English history in a more detailed way, as an elaboration and filling-out of the seminal ideas contained in Cromwell's preambles to the Reformation statutes. An essential part of the rewriting was the creation of a new martyrology in which the old Lollard heretics would become the new Protestant 'martyrs and heroes'. Manuscripts and books which had been compiled by Catholics as records of their actions against heresy could now be used in an entirely new way – as Protestant polemic and propaganda against Catholicism. Bale, and later Foxe, understood that it was essential to find a continuous ancestry for the sixteenth-century 'reformers'.[87] This was the beginning of that reading of post-Reformation attitudes and assumptions of thought into the minds of pre-Reformation English people which was to be a constant feature of English historical writing on the medieval period until well into the twentieth century. As a very recent authority has reminded us, 'the fifteenth century diminished to the status of a set on which the real drama of the Reformation was to take place'.[88]

Bale collected materials for the rewriting of English history along the lines indicated above and one of his main sources was a Carmelite collection of writings on Wycliffe and the Lollards called the *Fasciculi Zizaniorum*. Bale wrote in 1544 that it was necessary that some learned Englishman should emerge 'to set forth the Englyshe chronycles in theyr ryght shappe'.[89] There is some evidence that Bale intended performing the task himself, but in fact the man who eventually became celebrated for this role was John Foxe.

From the time of his return to England in 1548 we know that Bale, now in his early fifties, and John Foxe, then thirty-one, became close friends and lived together in London. Later, during Mary Tudor's reign and the brief return to a Catholic monarchy, they spent part of their exile together in Basle. Their friendship continued until Bale's death in 1563. The first version of the *Acts and Monuments* appeared in a Latin work entitled *Commentarii rerum in ecclesia gestarum*, published at Strasbourg in 1554. It is evident that this work was a cooperative achievement by Bale and Foxe, based on Bale's text of the *Fasciculi* and written probably during their stay together in London. Bale was only too glad to find someone who could undertake the task for which he had prepared the way. When the *Acts and Monuments* appeared in its final form in 1563 it incorporated the preparatory work of other Protestant antiquaries as well, so that it 'can be seen as the culmination of a process, the completion of a generation's efforts'.[90] But if Foxe was the man who finally produced the work, there is no doubt that Bale supplied the initial impetus, and behind Bale there lay the shadow of his patron, Thomas Cromwell.

The main framework for this gigantic piece of historical reconstruction was still that originally supplied by Cromwell in his Reformation statutes. The 'national-erastian' dualism of thought predominated throughout. Bale had certainly looked at English history through the viewing mechanism supplied by Cromwell, but he filled in the details of future folklore. He claimed that Christianity had been brought to England by Joseph of Arimathea and the followers of St Philip. It had come straight from the early Apostles and not via any other country – certainly not from Rome. The English Church had been established by King Lucius, an English counterpart of the Emperor Constantine. From then onwards the history of England was the story of the heroic struggle of its native kings and people, valiantly defending true Christianity against alien invaders who in various guises represented the forces of 'Anti-Christ'. The first attack came from the heathen Saxon invaders from Germany. Then came the corrupting influence of Augustine as an agent from Rome and the Papacy. The Norman Conquest, followed by monks and friars, was another incursion by the forces of evil. Through all this the native kings had fought strenuously against 'foreign' enemies and the corruption of the true Faith of which they were the guardians. They were helped by such true native teachers as John Wycliffe and the Lollards who had suffered persecution in order to preserve the true faith of the Gospel and keep it alive.

Bale had also applied a kind of apocalyptic vision to this history. He saw this struggle by the English kings and their people against the foreign invader in terms of the age-long conflict between Christ and Anti-Christ, described by St John in Scripture. The Popes were regarded as 'agents of Anti-Christ, encroaching upon the authority of kings'.[91] This historical outlook was a concomitant of the ideas of the divine right of kings as God's representatives and of 'obedience to the king' representing 'God's will', as the central duty for the Christian, which ensued from the Reformation in England during the 1530s, under Cromwell's guidance. These ideas were introduced into Cromwell's political propaganda 'as a way of rationalising the consolidation of the nation-state under the Crown and the liberation of the Crown from subjection to the papacy or any other outside authority'.[92]

John Foxe followed Bale faithfully. His massive work was written within the same 'national-erastian' framework of thought. There is the familiar description of the Papacy as a tyrannical power, representing the force of 'Anti-Christ' and threatening the independence, freedom and true religion of the English people.[93] There is also the erastian statement of the supremacy of the king as God's vice-regent, over Church and State.[94] These were the old pillars of Cromwell's original structure.

Now, however, under Bale and Foxe a new and essential element had been added to the myth. Cromwell's presentation of the official version of the English past in the preambles to the Reformation statutes had reflected something of the man himself – a cold[95] statement of certain concepts which buttressed one another in a small but logical circle of argument. It was sufficient for the lawyers and churchmen, but not for the ordinary people. It had lacked emotional appeal, without which it could never have become part of English folklore. Foxe supplied this in a most extraordinary manner. His emotionally charged and imaginative account, accompanied by graphic pictorial images, of the sufferings of the Protestant victims in Mary Tudor's reign became the greatest single piece of anti-Catholic propaganda in English, and perhaps European, history. Foxe succeeded in his intention 'to burn his dreadful history into the minds of his countrymen, both high and low'.[96] Although it was published during Elizabeth's reign when many Catholics died on the gallows, including some who were hanged, drawn and quartered, there was no Catholic work in England to fulfil the same function. Five editions of the 'Book of Martyrs' were published before 1600. Foxe filled his story with a wealth of historical materials culled from episcopal registers, royal archives, parliamentary rolls and from collections such as those of Bale and Matthew Parker, all suitably interpreted to fit into his preconceived picture of the past. He continually appealed to these materials as evidence for the historical authenticity of his story. It was the strong emotionalism of Foxe's book, however, which turned the original ideas, created in Cromwell's legal mind, into a folk myth in England.

Foxe's 'Book of Martyrs' became one of the great and, arguably, the most successful of the world's works of propaganda. It was not history as we have come to know it. Even in the nineteenth century S.R. Maitland objected to Foxe's 'deplorable use of his authorities and his crudely anti-Catholic prejudices'.[97] In 1940 J.F. Mozley, in his *John Foxe and His Book*, wrote that 'Foxe is temperamentally incapable of writing what is now called scientific history'.[98] W. Haller, in *Foxe's Book of Martyrs and the Elect nation* (1963), said that, 'No one, of course, would now think of turning to Foxe for information concerning the history of the Christian Church or the English nation before his own time'.[99] G.A. Williamson, in *Foxe's Book of Martyrs* (1965), referred to the book's 'prolixity, desultoriness and imbalance'.[100] In 1987 C. Haigh commented that the 'perspective' and 'method' of Foxe's approach 'have been undermined by the impact of modern "revisionism"'.[101] To J. Scarisbrick Foxe is 'the most fulsome exponent' of 'a powerful new national epic, indeed, theology of History'.[102] For Katherine Firth, Foxe's book is essentially part of the apocalyptic tradition, the Protestant interpretation of the Apocalypse of St John (Book of

Revelations) as applied to English history'.[103] Penry William has referred recently to its 'absorption . . . into popular mythology'.[104]

Yet, its publication in 1563 was a major historical and historiographical event because its influence on England history and on Protestant historical writing in England has been immense. It would be a complete distortion of Foxe's aim to describe his work as simply a description of the Marian persecution. In the 1570 edition 500 pages were concerned with the reconstruction of the English past to suit the eyes of the Protestant present. At the centre of Protestant historiography was the desire to find some kind of past tradition from which the reformers could claim continuity:

> if they could demonstrate their possession of brave English ancestry, the way of truth and justice could be pushed backwards as well as forwards, and they might be regarded as continuators of those who through a long persecuted past had been defending the cause of the true primitive church in England.[105]

Foxe provided exactly what they wanted. He gave the new Church a tradition and a line of spiritual ancestry which went back to the first arrival of Christianity in these islands. In this he was repeating in different guise what Matthew Parker was attempting to show in his 'antiquarian' findings. But there is more to it again.

The idea of the apocalyptic tradition had started among British Protestants with John Bale, but Foxe was 'the first British author to write a Protestant apocalyptic history that attempted to explain changes in terms of an unfolding pattern of events'.[106] He had brought back with him from exile in Zurich a knowledge of the Protestant apocalyptic writings which he was to use as the framework to give structure and coherence to his 'Book of Martyrs'. The whole of English history had led providentially to the reigns of Henry VIII and Elizabeth who had been appointed by God to lead the English people out of the land of bondage (foreign papal control) into freedom and national success. Henry VIII had completed the work of earlier English rulers and 'martyrs' like Wycliffe and the Lollards who had fought to keep the Protestant faith pure against the corrupting forces from abroad, led by the papal 'Anti-Christ'. This incorporation of the Protestant interpretation of English history, to serve the needs of his apocalyptic vision, turned Foxe's book into a philosophy of history. This gave a crusading appeal to the folk myth of the English past. English Protestants could now become part of that apocalyptic vision in the present and the future. Again, it contained at its centre that logical but inadequately small circle of argument associated with the Calvinist doctrine of the elect people, with its own narrow and particular definition of predestination, which had a great appeal to those who believed that they were of this 'elect'.

This apocalyptic tradition was destined to become ever more important to English nationalism. Foxe himself viewed the 'elect' as a universal people or Church, invisible and mystical. He was one of those Protestants who were international in this sense, and indeed there were several who argued that England had a duty consequently to help Protestants abroad who were in difficulties, especially when, during the Thirty Years War in the next century, Protestants came to England for refuge. Milton was to write a sonnet, expressing passionate indignation at the expulsion of the Protestant Vaudois by orders of the Prince of Savoy in 1657.

Foxe placed England, together with Protestants from other nations, in a context of the 'elect' supplied by his interpretation of the Book of Revelation. W. Haller, in his *Foxe's Book of Martyrs and the Elect Nation* (1963), mistakenly assumed that Foxe had identified England as the 'elect nation';[107] in fact this was left to other people who, following Foxe's line of thought, took it further. Thomas Brightman published in 1615 his *A Revelation of the Revelation . . . Wherein the sense is declared out of the scripture . . . also of things fore told out of Church Histories*, which was written for the Protestants of England, Germany and Switzerland. He gave special respect to the Calvinistic form of church at Geneva, but otherwise 'his sources and exposition were explicitly English' and his highest praise was reserved for Foxe 'our countryman of blessed memory'.[108] This pamphlet contained the first reference to a special place being given to the reformed English Church in the apocalyptic scheme, for there was no 'Parallele to match her, as being a peerless Paragon'.[109] Then Joseph Meade in a later pamphlet verified that in the apocalyptic scheme *one* nation was meant to lead the others during the new millennium ushered in by the reformers.

This Protestant apocalyptic tradition in England finally found its culmination in another of England's famous writers, John Milton, who expressed the conclusion reached by many of his contemporaries during the time of Cromwell's interregnum, that the prophecies of the millennium pointed exclusively to England as the one nation chosen by God to fulfil His purposes in the world and to lead the other Protestant nations. Milton expressed this idea very forcibly in two pamphlets: *Of Reformation* (1641) and *Animadversis* (1642). Relying heavily on Foxe's work for his earlier historical references, he proclaimed that such happenings as the birth of Wycliffe in England and the miraculous scattering of the Spanish Armada in 1588 proved that England itself was indeed the 'Elect Nation'. In *Of Reformation*, Milton exalted England's role in the divine scheme by arguing that it was here that the full Reformation was to be achieved, for God had begun 'to build up this Britannick Empire to a glorious and enviable height'.[110]

Interestingly, Milton changed his own view on the 'elect' according to circumstances. As we have seen, he regarded England as the 'elect nation' in his writings between 1641 and 1644. In 1649, however, when he wrote his *History of Britain* (published later, in 1670), from legendary times up to the Norman Conquest, he was incensed because the Republican government was making attempts to include the Presbyterians in a consensus style of government. In this angry state of mind he deplored the weaknesses of the English national character and, in a 'Digression' within the *History*, sought to reveal these weaknesses in their early history. This forced him to the conclusion that the 'elect' were really a select group of superior and right-minded people within the nation, rather than the nation itself. However, when he came to write his *Defences of the People of England* (1651–4), he felt the need to defend his country against a hostile Europe and therefore returned to the view that the English nation itself was the 'elect nation'.[111] The appeal to this view was to become a constant feature of English historical writing whenever England was either at war with, or at odds with, other European countries on the Continent. It continued to play a part in English morale-building up to and including the Second World War.[112]

By this time, in any case, Milton was pushing at an open door, for many other English Protestants had come to the same conclusion: that England was the elect nation. Other pamphlets followed which spread the certainty of this belief. A great war had been waging in Germany (1618–48) between the forces of the Reformation and the Counter-Reformation and, as a modern writer has observed,

During the Thirty Years War Britain became a refuge of hope for many foreign Protestants. Both at home and abroad, the conviction grew that Britain had a special role to play in the defence of the Protestant faith. On her soil the New Reformation might come to pass. A utopian vision nurtured abroad and set in a millennium context, found its way into Britain and there worked upon the native apocalyptic tradition, giving it a new life and direction.[113]

The dynamic power generated by the idea of the elect nation was to be one element behind England's extraordinary expansion as an imperial power in the world up to and into the twentieth century. It supplied the confidence and morale which such enterprises require, but also led to that sense of pride and superiority which was to bring its own problems. To execute properly that leadership in the world's affairs ordained for it, England needed to be united. Foxe had made a special appeal for the unity of the national Church and State under the royal supremacy. This call for unity, required by England's special identity and role, was to be another feature of English history in times of conflict down to the middle of the twentieth century. During the two world wars of the twentieth century, there were 'formal attempts by the State to create a propaganda of unity to better implement the war effort', and again during the Suez Crisis in 1956 there was a significant call for unity, related to 'a reconstruction and restatement of British identity'.[114]

Although we have now gone ahead of Foxe, so to speak, there is no doubt that it was his book which exercised a 'monumental influence'[115] on the English psychology. Foxe's work became accepted 'as an expression of the national faith . . . and as an unanswerable defence of England's ideological position in the contemporary struggle for national independence and power'.[116] A recent authority has observed that, as a result of the Book of Martyrs and of thousands of 'No-Popery' sermons based on it,

By the end of the 1570s, whatever the instincts and nostalgia of their seniors, a generation was growing up which had known nothing else, which believed the Pope to be Anti-Christ, the Mass a mummery, which did not look back to the Catholic past as their own, but another country, another world.[117]

Nothing did more to inspire the Elizabethan concern with nationhood than the idea that the cause of true religion was identified with the rise of the English sovereign state under its queen, appointed by God to protect the Protestant nation against the evils of Catholic powers such as France and Spain who were in the grip of 'Anti-Christ' – the Papacy. One Elizabethan bishop, John Aylmer, felt confident enough to announce that 'God is English'.[118]

The government understood the importance of all this to its purposes. In 1571 it ordered that every cathedral church must be supplied with a copy of Foxe's 'Book of Martyrs', to be chained alongside the Bible for common reading. Indeed it became a second Bible to the English people and a formative influence on their thinking. In the seventeenth century Archbishop Tillotson reflected that 'Catechising and the history of the Martyrs have been the two great Pillars of the Reformation'.[119]

Foxe managed to link Catholicism firmly in the minds of the English people with two factors which were to colour their view of it for centuries. One was brutal religious persecution and the other was foreign interference. He insisted that it was while Mary Tudor had been married to Philip of Spain that the terrible persecution had taken place,[120] though we now know, since Lingard, that Philip had opposed it.[121] This emphasis by Foxe reinforced and augmented the xenophobic attitude of the English, which had been first aroused by the propaganda of Cromwell and Henry VIII, thirty years before.

Foxe also made the Marian victims stand for 'Everyman'. His 'grisly fables' with 'horribly graphic illustrations', which kept readers 'glued to the book', were chosen to show the fate of men and women of every class, like the readers themselves. It was all meant to convince generations of readers that these people were victims bearing witness 'to their countrymen's Protestant destiny', so that out of their witness would come a 'common steadfastness and triumphant confirmation that their land was blessed'.[122] Nearly three centuries later, that *enfant terrible* among Anglican clergymen, Sydney Smith, reflected on the fierce opposition to Catholic Emancipation in England in his own time:

I have often endeavoured to reflect upon the causes which from time to time, raised such clamour against the Catholics, and I think the following are among the most conspicuous: i. Historical recollections of the cruelties inflicted upon the

Protestants. . . . The great object of men who love party better than truth is to have it believed that the Catholics alone have been persecutors.[123]

It is sometimes asked how we can speak of something like the 'English attitude of mind', and of course we can never use that term in an absolute sense – there will always be exceptions. However, we are now more aware than ever of the influences that can be brought to bear very effectively on group mentality, even that of a nation. Even before the modern means of mass communication were available, even before the majority of people were literate, there existed means of exercising such influence. Before the introduction of compulsory education for all, with Forster's Education Act of 1870, there was the great influence of certain literature on those who could read; and these were appointed to all the important positions in Church and State, from which they could influence others, both in the localities and in the nation as a whole. In considering the influence of the 'Book of Martyrs' in shaping the 'English mind', one has to consider that four editions appeared in the author's lifetime – in 1563, 1570, 1576 and 1583 – and nine editions by 1684. During the eighteenth century it appeared in various editions as 'The Book of Martyrs', and four editions of the *Acts and Monuments* appeared in the nineteenth century. As well as this, there were thousands of sermons given in parishes throughout the land based on Foxe's book. The profuse and luridly sensational illustrations would have an immediate and direct impact, even on the illiterate. The Elizabethan government's order that it should be kept in every cathedral church for common reading was a continuation of that attempt to shape the thinking of its people – and especially to shape the people's memory of their past – which had been started in the preambles to the Henrician statues.

In the eighteenth century the book was 'interpreted in a far more aggressively patriotic fashion' again. In 1732 it was reprinted in a way calculated to meet the demands of a 'very different and much wider reading public'. Since the price of the huge work was beyond the means of most, the printer published a 'certain number of sheets weekly, by subscription, so that the common people might be also enabled, by degrees to procure it'. This was very successful, so in 1761 and 1776 other editions appeared, this time in sixty cheap instalments and the editions of 1784 and 1795 were sold by '"all . . .

booksellers and newsmen" in eighty even cheaper instalments'. So it came about that Foxe's book 'came to be one of the few books that one might plausibly expect to find in even a working-class household'.[124] Another observer writes in 1997 that this book is 'One of the three most influential publications in the English language' with the Bible and 'perhaps Bunyan's *Pilgrim's Progress*'.[125] The dissemination of Foxe's book in England represents the most effective use of mass propaganda ever witnessed before the coming of radio, television and the tabloid press in the twentieth century.

The concept of the English as the 'chosen people' or 'the elect nation', who had had to suffer pain and adversity before reaching their final triumphant victory, sank deeply into the English mind and remained there, helping to sustain national morale in times of conflict through the eighteenth and nineteenth centuries and into the twentieth century. It had a great part to play in the series of wars against France and Spain in the eighteenth century, in the enormous colonial and commercial expansionism which continued through the nineteenth century, and even in the two world wars of the twentieth century. The effect of the Protestant apocalyptic tradition on the English psyche was very enduring: 'Even after the religious power of Protestantism dwindled, its grip on the British imagination remained'.[126] As a recent historian has commented, 'the Protestant world-view was so ingrained in this culture that it influenced people's thinking irrespective of whether they went to church or not, whether they read the Bible or not, or whether, indeed, they were capable of reading anything at all.'[127] It left two great impressions on the English psychology. One was a deeply anti-Catholic and anti-foreign prejudice, distrust and hostility. The other was an abiding belief that Britain was better than other countries:

the conviction that Great Britain was peculiarly blessed was not confined to the prosperous. Nor was it confined to the inhabitants of England. Nor, emphatically, was it confined to Whigs. Like all sustaining national myths, the idea that Britain was a chosen land and therefore fruitful, did not depend for its effectiveness upon its being true. Poor or not, large numbers of Protestant Britons believed – believed precisely because they *were* Protestants, and because it was comforting to believe it, – that they were richer in every sense than other peoples, particularly Catholic peoples, and particularly the French.[128]

It has also been shown that English culture in the eighteenth century was pervaded with this same theme of England's specially chosen role in the world, as the 'promised land', the new 'Israel'. It appears in the apocalyptic vision of Blake's *Jerusalem*, the 'powerful transmission' of Britain as Israel in Handel's anthems and oratorios, and in the 'savage complacency' and anti-Catholic prejudice of Hogarth's brilliant painting of *Calais Gate*, or the *Roast Beef of Old England*.[129] It was a culture which continued through the nineteenth and into the twentieth century, producing 'a profoundly Protestant patriotism and complacency':

> this enormous conceit has to be recognised and taken seriously. It was not just ignorant insularity, though some of it certainly was. It was bound up with a Protestant world-view which helped men and women make sense of their lives and gave comfort and dignity in the face of difficulty and dangers.[130]

This helped to sustain them during the twentieth century, up to and during the Second World War.

Linda Colley concludes her valuable analysis of Britain's Protestant identity in the modern world from 1707 thus:

> Protestantism meant much more in this society than just bombast, intolerance and chauvinism. It gave the majority of men and women a sense of their place in history and a sense of worth. . . . It gave them identity. . . . And as long as a sense of mission and providential destiny could be kept alive, by means of maintaining prosperity at home, by means of recurrent wars with the Catholic states of Europe, and by means of a frenetic and for a long time highly successful pursuit of empire, the Union flourished, sustained not just by convenience and profit but by belief as well. Protestantism was the foundation that made the invention of Great Britain possible.[131]

Interestingly enough, the idea of England as the 'elect nation' was ascribed to Foxe by people who looked retrospectively at the enormous and enduring impact of his work. It was perhaps a logical outcome of the context in which Foxe launched his apocalyptic framework for English history. It is significant in itself that the eminent authority on Foxe and his book, William Haller, assumed this idea in his work which is actually entitled *Foxe's Book of Martyrs and the Elect Nation* (1963). Only later and very careful research by Katherine Firth showed that this was not the case, in her *The Apocalyptic Tradition in Reformation Britain* (1979). Facts can easily become victim of assumptions of thought when we are dealing with such a powerful 'folk myth' – even among professional historians.

With certain exceptions the nation-state can hardly be said to have arrived in Europe in its mature political form until the seventeenth century. England was an exception because the particular circumstances of the Divorce Question bound together the mutual interests of the State and Protestantism at an early stage. Having failed to gain his divorce by attempting to manipulate the old Canon Law and pressurizing the Papacy, Henry tried a new method: 'he called in a new type of minister, one ready to pass far beyond the divorce into new concepts of political organisation, one who possessed a fully professional knowledge of legal instruments and the apparatus of propaganda. This virtuoso of statecraft was Thomas Cromwell.'[132]

It was Thomas Cromwell, acting with the support or consent of the king, who in the 1530s seized the opportunity to build appropriate legal and political forms for the creation of the nation-state of England, complete with its own national Church and a professional-type propaganda campaign to support it. It was Henry who supplied the will and purpose behind the Reformation. Cromwell established, with the king's consent, the necessary machinery required to achieve it.

Cromwell's skilful use of historical propaganda as an instrument of revolution was one of the first and most successful examples of this technique in modern history. Of course this was not the normal revolution by which a new government takes over from the last. This was a revolution in the Church and in the life of the nation organized by the existing government for its own purposes. For Henry it was simply to gain his objective over the Divorce. For Cromwell, it seems that, apart from pleasing the king, he may well have had in his sights the creation of the new nation-state; and he may well have been applying consciously the principles prescribed in Machiavelli's *The Prince* (1513)[133] to achieve this in England. The use of systematic propaganda was to become one of the most effective weapons in the armoury of modern nation-states, reaching its apogee in the hands of the totalitarian systems in the twentieth century.[134] If Cromwell would not have been particularly impressed by the later apocalyptic arguments used by Bale and Foxe, it is probable that he would not have been displeased with their effects on the unity and destiny of that nation-state to the building of which he contributed so much. Strangely enough, he met his end over another matrimonial adventure. He displeased his master by persuading him, for political reasons, to marry Anne of Cleves whom Henry found unattractive. Like Thomas More before him, Cromwell was executed in 1540 on a trumped-up charge of treason.[135] Cromwell had taken his eye, for a moment, off the most important part of his job – pleasing the king. His execution was the act of a 'capricious king', showing that he was 'master' and that his ministers, however powerful or successful, were 'creatures to be ennobled or destroyed at will'.[136]

TWO
England's Past in the Seventeenth Century

THE HISTORICAL BACKGROUND

During the sixteenth century there had been a certain unity of purpose in English Protestantism. Although from the time of the Reformation itself there had been seeds of latent disunity in the mentality of different groups within Protestantism, they had all shared one common outlook – opposition to 'Popery'. This, together with the growing concern for national unity, became a dominant feature of English life as the country became more conformist to the Protestant settlement. This was particularly so in Elizabeth's reign when there developed a real threat of invasion from Catholic Spain. The central division caused by the Reformation had settled down after about 1580 into the difference between a minority who had been converted to Protestantism and those who simply conformed to the new arrangements in Church and State.[1] People who retained their Catholic faith went into exile or remained as 'recusants' to suffer under the various penal laws which outlawed them. The glorification of, and allegiance to the Tudor monarchy expressed, among other things, a sense of the need for national unity which was implicit in the monarchy. During this period there was comparatively little room for Protestants to express their own differences among themselves.

Even in Elizabeth's reign, from about 1580 onwards, the situation was beginning to change. In religious matters several discordant voices began to sound against the State-established Church and its policies. Some genuine Protestants felt that it still retained too much Catholicism and these people became known as 'Puritans', a convenient but rather dangerous term because it suggests a neat theoretical categorization of people who are often much more difficult to place in practice, as historical researchers have discovered. This situation developed particularly after the defeat of the Spanish Armada in 1588, which meant that the threat of foreign invasion was virtually removed. Elizabeth's own personality and the length of her long and spectacular reign played some part in slowing down the process; and even more important was the skill of her ministers, particularly Cecil, Lord Burleigh, in 'managing' Parliament. All this combined to retain the *status quo* in State and religion during her reign.

As the seventeenth century arrived, bringing with it the new Stuart line of monarchs to the English throne, many of the factors which had given Reformation historiography a united front in the previous century were no longer operating to the same extent. The old Whig interpretation of this period, enshrined particularly in the work of historians such as Burnet, Macaulay and S.R. Gardiner,[2] pictured the religious and civil conflicts of the Stuart age as the battle between two distinctly opposite sides: one standing for a dominant monarchy ('arbitrary government') and high Anglicanism (retaining some Catholic practices); the other representing parliamentary government and a more definitely Protestant type of religion. This view saw the Civil War and the Revolution of 1688 as the important landmarks in the success of the latter side, which laid the foundation for England's future greatness. This view dominated English historical writing until the second half of the twentieth century.

During the 1970s there emerged a 'revisionist' interpretation of the seventeenth-century conflicts in Church and State, based upon detailed research in the composition of individual parliaments and local affiliations, together with an attempt to get to grips with the essential commonplaces or assumptions of thought which really guided the thinking of seventeenth-century English people. Historians such as Conrad Russell regard the old view as just another example of the way in which Whig historians of later times read history backwards, attributing later ideas to people of the seventeenth century who simply did not think in that way, and detecting anticipations of later events where it did not exist in earlier times. There were no great and idealistic issues at stake. Russell, for example, argues convincingly that Pym and Strafford, on opposite sides of the conflict, really shared the same premiss of thought on the eve of the Civil War: that the important end was to achieve national unity. Their real disagreement was that each thought that the other was going about it in the wrong way.

There were two underlying causes of the troubles in Church and

State. One was the European-wide inflation which made it impossible for the monarchy, the sole source of real political power, to discharge its functions with an antiquated system of revenue-raising. So the monarch had to devise new and controversial ways of raising money in order to govern the country properly. Contemporaries did not understand this and it led to conflict. The other cause resulted from the clash of two phenomena in the field of religious history. Increasingly, divisions within Protestantism, from the late sixteenth century onwards, made it impossible for government to destroy completely religious opinions of which it did not approve. On the other hand, the essential assumption of thought of the age was that the State should tolerate only one religion, since the important cause of national unity could only be achieved in this way. This thinking stemmed from the age-old reality that the main centrifugal force in creating community and unity was the Church. These fundamental causes of conflict were much more important in seventeenth-century England than the social, religious, or political categorizations into which earlier historians had tried to place the supporters of each side.[3] All sides wanted national unity, on their own terms, and all saw religious policy as the way to achieve their own ends. Russell effectively summarized this revisionist view:

> England's conversion to Protestantism was superficial and incomplete . . . Catholics were not un-English, however hard John Foxe might try to depict them so . . . England was a country divided by the Reformation and that division lasted. The central decision after about 1580 was between those converted to Protestantism and those conforming to it. After 1660 the conformists got the better of the converts. Whiggery was the converts' attempt to get their own back.[4]

There were two other crucially important factors which guided the actual process of events. The monarchy, as the one recognizable source of power, could be effectively challenged only in two ways. One was the availability of an army with which to make the challenge and this did not exist in England until the entry of the Scottish army into the picture in 1640. This accounted for the successful attempt to dethrone Charles I. Secondly, any opposition to a particular king would need a recognized 'Pretender' to the throne as an alternative means of power. This helps to explain the central importance of James, Duke of York, during the Exclusion crisis of 1682 and the long-term success of William of Orange and Mary in 1689. Oliver Cromwell's interregnum was the exception which proved the rule. He failed ultimately because he had no real claim to be a 'Pretender' to the throne. His rule was never legitimized in the eyes of the people, according to the contemporary norms of thinking.

The great debate among historians concerning the explanation and interpretation of seventeenth-century conflicts is still continuing,[5] though I believe that the revisionists have made an irreversible breach in the walls of the Whig interpretation of seventeenth-century English history. Recent work has shown that it is particularly difficult to use labels such as 'Puritan' and 'Anglican', 'Whig' or 'Tory', in order to identify neatly the 'great divide' between people at this time. Such categorization was needed by Whig historians to identify the 'heroes' who were on the side of the glorious future and the 'traitors' who were trying to spoil things. The real world was much more fluid and confused, much less clear-cut in its outlook, apart from those essential assumptions of thought which all shared. We can still make some use of these terms, for convenience, as long as we see them in the context of this real world of the seventeenth century, with its own commonplaces and assumptions of thought.

There is no doubt whatsoever that it was an age of conflict and that this conflict both influenced, and was influenced by, contemporary historical writing. This influence has been charted already with regard to the constitutional and political struggles,[6] but we shall be concerned here with its operation in the area of religious life and thought. From the complex and often confusing conflicts,[7] with their various shades and sometimes changes of opinion, we may attempt to draw out certain broad lines of religious thought which produced different views of the English past.

The main body of opinion in England throughout the seventeenth century was characterized by the view that the national (Anglican) Church was a support to monarchy, which represented the unity of the nation-state, and an aid to personal salvation. The one historiographical concept shared by all of Protestant England was that nationalist view of the past which had been embedded in the statutes of the Reformation Parliament. Anglicans and Puritans shared the thinking that the religion of England had come directly from apostolic origins, not via any other foreign church or country. It had been part of the unique and independent way of life and thought of the English nation. Like all the other national institutions, the Church was of native origin. It had been retained in spite of interference from abroad by the Papacy during the medieval period. The Reformation had simply restored it to its pristine native state. It was England's destiny now to defend it against Popish attack and to work for its extension to the newly discovered parts of the world. This was to be part of England's imperialistic mission.

The main divide within the Protestant nation developed around the second part of the dualism of thought, which contained the official view of the English past. This was the emphasis on the erastian nature of the Anglican Church as a religious institution governed by the State. Certain groups now developed different views about the proper relationship between the Church and the temporal authority. All sides appealed to history to prove their case.

It was while William Laud was Archbishop of Canterbury (1633–45) that Charles I allowed the emergence of a 'High Anglican' view of the Church to come to the centre of the stage. This stressed the high authority of bishops, derived from episcopal and historic succession from the first apostles, and also the duty of conformity on the part of the nation in general to orthodox religion as outlined by the episcopate. The Court of High Commission and the self-accusatory *ex officio* oath were the unpopular instruments used by the Laudian regime to enforce religious conformity on the secular State. All this was possible only because of the support of the king. Laud was working as chief minister. This emphasis on ecclesiastical power became a source of conflict in the political situation. Laud was executed after Cromwell's victory in the Civil War in 1645 and Charles himself suffered the same fate four years later.

The period 1649–1660, dominated by the powerful figure of Oliver Cromwell as Lord Protector (from 1653), witnessed the complete effacement of kingly and clerical authority. These years had an important influence on the religious and intellectual history of England. They saw the flowering of ideas from seeds sown at the Reformation – anti-clericalism, rationalism, latitudinarianism and secularism. Such ideas, together with the religious scepticism which followed the breakdown of a united church structure, greatly strengthened the view that the State authority should control the Church.[8] During the interregnum the episcopacy was abolished, only to be replaced by a form of State theocracy under Cromwell, which proved to be even more unpopular and out-of-line with any traditional form of Church–State relationship in England. It became evident that the only workable constitution must involve a return to monarchy and the Church.

The Church which returned with the restoration of monarchy in 1660 was not the same in character as the Laudian Church. Indeed the new Cavalier Parliament was determined to restore it to its proper role as the buttress of monarchy. The bishops were admitted again to the House of Lords. The Licensing Act of 1662 made sure that the Universities and the printing presses were controlled by Anglicans. The Act of Uniformity (1662) ensured a monopoly of power in the State to those who conformed exactly to the religious requirements of the Anglican Church. All this was part of the Clarendon Code (1661–5), those parliamentary measures which aimed at re-establishing the Anglican Church. Yet there was an important difference.

If the Church was to resume its work as a support of monarchy against fanatical extremes and civil disorder, it was itself prevented from exercising the same type of power in the State which it had wielded under Laud. The new Parliament was very careful to ensure that the Church was kept in its 'proper' place, given it at the Reformation, of subservience to the State authority. The Court of High Commission and the *ex officio* oath were not restored in 1660. The royal licence was required before a synod could be called. Church laws depended on the approval of the king as Supreme Governor and its preaching was controlled by his instructions. The offices of the Church, including all bishoprics and deaneries, were in the gift of the king.

So it was that between 1660 and 1688 the Anglican Church held much the same position in English society as it had during the reign of Elizabeth I. Meanwhile, however, important developments were taking place within it. On the one hand there were the successors of the Laudian divines who extolled the spiritual authority of the Church validated by its apostolic foundation and succession. For them the historical and traditional processes, by which that authority had been handed down from generation to generation, loomed large.

It was from this group, with their high-principled beliefs in the sanctity of hereditary monarchy as well as the apostolic Church, that the churchmen and scholars known as the 'Non-Jurors' emerged after 1688. These were men who, having sworn an oath of allegiance to James II, refused to take the new oath to William and Mary which was required after they had replaced James II by the

'Glorious Revolution' of 1688–9. The Archbishop of Canterbury was one who lost his position as a result of this. Among these Non-Jurors were some outstandingly good scholars who, by their patient researches and publication of original documents, were pioneers of true scholarship on the medieval period. After losing office at the Revolution and being driven 'underground', these men were less encumbered by considerations of duty to monarchy and began to take their exalted view of the Church to lengths which were unprecedented in Anglican thought. They began, in fact, to assert the complete independence of the Church authority in spiritual matters. This line of thought was drawn out particularly in opposition to the extreme erastianism adopted by the new Whig bishops such as Gilbert Burnet. In this way the Non-Jurors presented the first challenge to the idea of royal supremacy over the Church within English Protestantism since the Henrician Reformation. They were adopting the same view about the division between Church and State authority as that of pre-Reformation Catholics – 'Give unto Caesar the things that are Caesar's, and to God the things that are God's.' This motivation, together with their exceptional ability as historical scholars, enabled them to make the first important breach in the official version of the English past established in the 1530s, but for the most part their work was done 'underground' and has remained there until now.

The Revolution of 1688 was, however, a triumph for the 'Low Church' party and a consolidation of the main principles of English Protestantism which were now tied closely to the newly emerged and politically triumphant Whig party. From the time of the Restoration in 1660 a new line of thought appeared within Anglicanism which connected with the new scientific and rationalistic spirit of the age of Newton, Boyle and Harvey, together with the philosophy of Bacon and Locke. Its adherents opposed not only the idea of the divine right of monarchy, but also the concept of a spiritual authority in the Church derived from uninterrupted apostolic succession through the ages. As latitudinarians, they were intent on abandoning the dogmatic view of Church authority, doctrine and practice. They believed in a 'rational' approach to Christianity, rather than the spiritual authority of the historical Church. The divisions which had fragmented Protestantism as a result of doctrinal arguments could best be healed, they thought, by an appeal to 'right reason' acting as a platform for Protestant unity based on a comprehensive approach. Similarly, they were not interested in history, as such, except insofar as it could be used to frighten Protestants into uniting against perceived Catholic threats at home or abroad.[9]

At the Revolution of 1688 the 'Low Church' party was not hampered by a belief in the divine right of kings and so was psychologically better prepared for decisive action. Just as the Puritans tended, generally speaking, to be connected with parliamentary opposition to James I and Charles I, so these low churchmen tended to ally, on the whole, with the Whig party in the reign of Charles II and James II. The successful Revolution was going to provide political advantages to the Whigs whose emergence as a distinct political group accompanied their attempt to exclude the Catholic James from the throne in 1679. They were soon to play a dominant part in British politics, powerful under William III and Anne and ensuring the Hanoverian succession in 1714. They remained in power until 1780, returned again in 1830 and evolved into the Liberal Party *c.* 1867.

The Church which emerged after 1689 was more Protestant, in the erastian sense of the word, than it had ever been before.[10] One of the newly appointed bishops was Gilbert Burnet who had been responsible for the original invitation to William III to invade England and who was the chief agent of propaganda for the new regime.[11] Burnet's classic statement of the official version of the English past, his *History of the Reformation* (1679–1715), formed an important link in English historiography between the old official version, established by the Reformation statutes, and the new Whig interpretation of history which was to dominate English historical writing in England up to the second half of the twentieth century. The latter was built upon the former, and its message was easily assimilated into the structure of the official version. But the old version gained from its new association with the 'idea of progress', born as we know it in the seventeenth century[12] and with the ethos of 'rationalism' which Burnet also added, suiting it ideally for the world of the 'enlightenment' and 'the age of reason' in the eighteenth century. Let us note at this point that Thomas Cromwell and Gilbert Burnet, two of the greatest propagandists in English history, were fundamentally involved with the building and the extension of the official version of the past. Both were agents of governments which were reshaping English life and thought, and both also felt it necessary to reshape the nation's memory, to coincide with the revolutions which were taking place.[13]

WILLIAM PRYNNE AND THE PURITAN OUTLOOK ON THE PAST

Puritanism is a convenient but sometimes misleading label, covering a wide range of Protestant views.[14] Basically Calvinist in theology, Puritans were united only in their wish to distance themselves further from Catholicism and in their opposition to the dogma, ritual, and episcopal organization of the Anglican Church. They believed that the Reformation had not gone far enough in discarding the 'Trappings of Popery'. They were completely opposed to the idea of a spiritual authority, handed down by apostolic succession and expressed through the episcopal order and ecclesiastical hierarchy. One of the central ideas through which many of them could express their clear opposition to Catholicism was erastianism – the secular control of the Church. They were usually to be found supporting parliamentary opposition to monarchy and reached their height of influence during the Cromwellian Protectorate when Puritan forms of worship and structure replaced the Anglican liturgy and episcopacy. After the Restoration, Puritanism was subsumed into the wide range of nonconformity which refused to accept the stipulations of the Clarendon Code.

Many Puritans maintained a completely erastian view of the place of religion in the English past and they accepted also the nationalist interpretation of that past. Their contribution to English historiography was completely in line, therefore, with the official view and has nothing of substance to add to Foxe in this respect. We should nevertheless pay regard to the outstanding representative of Puritan historiography in the seventeenth century.

William Prynne (1602–69) was a remarkable exponent of Puritan thought. His biographer writes that, 'This glorification of the state animated his attacks on the enemies of the state church. . . . Prynne was essentially secular. The state was the highest expression of man'.[15] He was imprisoned and had part of his ears removed in 1634 for insulting Charles I and his queen Henrietta Maria, who was a known enthusiast for the stage, in his *Histrio Mastix: The Players Scourge, or, Actors Tragedie* (1633). This was a huge work attacking stage plays. He continued producing pamphlets while in prison, now attacking Archbishop Laud and other Anglican churchmen. The rest of his ears was removed in 1637. While in prison he was branded on both cheeks with the letters 'SL' (seditious libeller). In 1640 he was released by the Long Parliament. He now began to write pamphlets attacking first the Independents, then the Army, then the

Parliamentarians, and finally Cromwell himself and his Protectorate government. He was imprisoned again (1650–3). Finally he supported the Restoration of Charles II, became MP for Bath, and most interestingly for us, Keeper of the Records in the Tower.[16]

Despite his erratic personal career, Prynne was no mean scholar and managed to publish about two hundred books and pamphlets. During the Protectorate he had come to support the cause of tradition and the need for a balanced constitution as opposed to the ideas of the extremists. He produced massive documentary evidence to show that the House of Commons was not immemorial, but went back only to the reign of Henry III. His *Brevia Parliamentaria Reviva* (1662) was his most important work and a notable achievement in the field of constitutional history. However, he had no such insights in the field of ecclesiastical history, nor could he emulate Sir Henry Spelman in understanding the place of the Feudal Law in English and European history.

Prynne's life illustrates very well the danger of categorizing people under labels of any sort, which is always a temptation for the historian. Always in real life there is the possibility of people changing their minds, developing, or acting 'out of character'. It also illustrates the way in which, when carefully used, a person's life can exemplify a certain contemporary assumption of thought which lies deeper than the conventional labels or categories and covers a very wide range of society.

Prynne's publications over a long period show that, although he might change his mind and his position about many other things, he maintained a complete consistency in his conventional view of the English past within the framework of the old official interpretation. He emphasized throughout his life the themes of erastianism, nationalism and anti-Popery. The titles of his publications are more than usually self-explanatory and illuminating as to their contents. In 1640 he published *Lord Bishops, none of the Lords Bishops, or a short discourse, wherein is proved that Prelaticall Jurisdiction is not of Divine Institution*, a typically Puritan tract. Then in 1643 came *The Treachery and disloyalty of Papists, to their soveraignes, in doctrine and practice . . . Or Second part of the Treachery and disloialty of Papists*. Also in 1643 came *Romes MasterPeece, Or the Grand Conspiracy of the Pope and his Jesuited Instruments, to extirpate the Protestant Religion, and to re-establish Popery*. In 1655–8 he produced his *Exact Chronological Vindication and Historical Demonstration of our British, Roman, Saxon, Norman, English Kings Supreme Ecclesiastical Jurisdiction*. At the time of the Restoration of the Monarchy in 1660 Prynne wrote *A Seasonable Vindication of the Supreme Authority and Jurisdiction of Christian Kings, Lords, Parliaments, as well over the Possessions, as Persons of Delinquent . . . Churchmen.* Finally, a year after his death, in 1670, *The History of King John, King Henry II . . . King Edward, wherein the ancient sovereign dominion of the kings of England . . . over all persons and causes, is asserted and vindicated* was published, with its sub-title, *An exact history of the Pope's intolerable usurpations on the liberties of the Kings subjects of England and Ireland.*

All these works, particularly those of the later period when he was Keeper of Records, were rich in documentation but completely conventional in interpretation with regard to the official version of the English past. They supply a perfect example of the way in which materials and documentation do not of themselves further the cause of historical understanding. When the conventional framework is strong enough, it can assimilate the results of such detailed research into its own system. So this man, whose work in calendaring records has earned him a praiseworthy niche in the history of historiography, produced an account of the past which was no whit less insular than its counterparts of the sixteenth century. Secondly, we see in this Puritan historiography an example of the way in which a closed circle of logical argument, based on a theoretical basis which is taken for granted, can remain detached from historical reality and can remain immune from any attempt to break it from the inside. It needs someone with a wider sense of perspective to look at evidence in a new way, to make a breakthrough in such circumstances. We have seen the same phenomenon among Marxist historians in the twentieth century, who have assimilated their detailed research into a preconceived circle of logical argument. This happens particularly when a historian's personal beliefs are based on a philosophy of history and he or she is not ready to be surprised by any evidence.

Significantly, Prynne's training had been in the Common Law tradition and his main theme, as the titles of his work suggest, was that the kings of England had been recognized always as the independent and supreme authority in legal, ecclesiastical, civil and spiritual matters. The story of England's past, up to the time of the Reformation, was seen as a struggle between the forces of light and the powers of darkness. The former was represented by the English kings who tried to defend the true English religion and England's national independence against 'papal and prelatical Usurpations, Innovations'[17] which threatened from the outside.

GILBERT BURNET: OFFICIAL HISTORIAN OF THE ENGLISH PAST

Gilbert Burnet (1643–1715) was the outstanding exponent of Low Church views in the second half of the seventeenth century. These views became increasingly influential in the Anglican Church after 1660, and finally triumphed in the aftermath of the 1688 Revolution in which Burnet played a central role.

Burnet's *History of the Reformation* (1679–1715) was the most officially approved work in the whole historiography of the Reformation in England. Indeed it may be described as a piece of institutionalized historiography. He was given the task of writing it by leaders of the Established Church, who were worried by the recent French edition of Nicholas Sander's *De Origine ac Progressu Schismatis Anglicani* in 1678,[18] and by the leaders of the incipient Whig party who wanted to wield any available weapon against the prospect of a future Catholic king in the shape of James, Duke of York. It was the time of the 'Exclusion Crisis'.[19]

The work was produced under official auspices. Burnet enjoyed the protection and support of the Lord Chancellor, the Attorney General and the Master of the Rolls. The Bishops of Winchester, Coventry and Lichfield were leading patrons of the enterprise, while 'almost all the Eminent Clergy of that time promoted the design'.[20] When the work reached its last stages, it went to the official authorities for approval – to the Lord Chancellor and to Bishops Lloyd and Tillotson. The official stamp of approval was given it 'as a Work very fit to be made publick' by Mr Secretary Coventry who 'doth therefore allow it to be Printed and Published'. In January 1680 the House of Lords ordered that 'the Thanks of this House be given to Dr Burnet, for the great Service done by him to this Kingdom, and the Protestant Religion'. The Commons passed a similar vote of thanks.[21]

The great popularity of Burnet's work was owing to the fact that it appeared during a time when the fictitious 'Popish Plot'[22] and the Exclusion Bill crisis had raised public opinion against 'Popery' to fever pitch. This was a time when the new Whig group was enjoying a forerun of its later long dominance in English life and Parliament. In these circumstances, Burnet's work 'took quiet Possession of the Belief of the Nation'.[23] The first classic statement of the Whig view of the past was written before the Whig 'reign' proper began with the 'Glorious Revolution' of 1688–9, by which William of Holland and Mary (daughter of James II) became king and queen of England.

The work itself is a striking statement of the official version of the Reformation and of the English past. At its core is the defence of the erastian proceedings of the Henrician Reformation – the working out of regal supremacy in ecclesiastical affairs. Burnet wrote in an *Epistle Dedicatory* to Charles II:

> The first step that was made in the Reformation of this Church, was the restoring to Your Royal Ancestors the Rights of the Crown, and an entire Dominion over all their Subjects: of which they had been disseised by the craft and violence of an unjust Pretender.[24]

He was concerned to show how English kings 'did at first erect Bishoprics, grant Investitures in them, call Synods, make Lawes about Sacred as Civil Concerns; and in a word they governed their whole Kingdom'.[25] Indeed, Burnet saw the assertion of the erastian position as one of the main marks of the genuine Anglican as opposed to those who, by their 'popish tendencies' were endangering the Established Church of his day. He was determined to show that the authentic religion of England had always been erastian in character.

Together with this defence of erastianism, Burnet asserted the primitive freedom and independence of the English nation from control by any foreign authority, spiritual or temporal. He denounced violently the papal 'encroachments' upon this independence during the medieval period.[26] His attitude towards the medieval period was that it was so backward that it was not worth studying anything so useless and decadent, and he boasted of his ignorance of it:

> Indeed I am not out of countenance to own that I have not much studied those Authors of the medieval period. . . . If any one has more Patience than I, can think it worth while to search into that *Rubbish*. . . . To dig in Mines were not to me a more ingrateful imployment. I am content to take these things from, second hand.[27]

Here we see emerging the adaptation of the old official view of the past to the philosophy of progress and the Whig interpretation of history. History was a ladder of progress. The historian literally looked down upon the past and its peoples with an attitude of superiority and condescension, which is a foolproof recipe for not understanding anyone, either of the past or of the present. This was an attitude towards the past which was endemic in the Whig interpretation, and it was taught later to generations of undergraduates at Oxford and Cambridge in the nineteenth century. From these history graduates were to come people, like Lord Macaulay, who were to take up important positions in the English colonies. They transferred their sense of superiority to the 'strange' peoples of the past to 'strange' colonial peoples of the present. In both cases the salient fact was that these peoples were different in mentality from the contemporary English people, the former separated from them by time in history, the latter by space in geography. The attitude ensured that neither group was understood by most English historians and civil servants. Macaulay famously and typically wrote that 'one shelf of English books is worth more than all the libraries of India'.

Burnet was one of the outstanding latitudinarians[28] and rationalists of the Anglican Church in the second half of the seventeenth century. He was a member of the Royal Society with a keen interest in science, a typical figure of the post-Restoration period with its belief in the supremacy of reason and its exciting applications in various fields of natural science. It was a time when the idea of progress made its first great impression on English society – a suitable environment for the birth of the Whig interpretation of history as a ladder of progress. Along with this went an impatience with the past which seemed of little use except where it could serve practical purposes in the present.

Indeed, Burnet was not really a historian at all in the accepted sense of today. The evidence is precisely that he was not interested in the past, except where it could be used as a weapon in the present.[29] He had fled abroad on the accession of James II in 1685, when he joined William of Orange at The Hague where he was 'the most prominent refugee'[30] and was 'admitted into all his councils'.[31] He prepared the document which purported to represent the Protestants of England's invitation to William to come to save them from 'Popery and Arbitrary Power'. William prepared 80,000 copies of this document to bring with him to use as propaganda in England.[32] In 1688 William invaded England with a Dutch army and Burnet as his chaplain. The extent of his usefulness to the new regime as the central figure in the propaganda of the new government was soon made evident in a series of sermons given before the new king and Commons, the theme of which was 'the Deliverance of this Kingdom from Popery and Arbitrary Power, by His Highness the Prince of Orange's Means'.[33] These sermons were printed 'by his highness's Special Command' and Burnet received the official thanks of the Commons for them.[34]

The theme of these sermons introduces another very important link between the old official version and the new Whig historiography. From now on, specifically in the last volume of Burnet's *History* (1715) and in English historiography afterwards over the next two centuries, 'Popery' is identified with 'Arbitrary Power' and 'Tyranny' in Whig historiography and in the minds of English people. In the great march of progress, the Reformation freed the English people from 'Popery', and the 'Glorious Revolution' of 1688 freed them from 'Arbitrary Government', which was closely associated with James II and 'Popery'.

The reward for Burnet's usefulness and his Whig principles came in the shape of the first vacant bishopric after William's accession, that of Salisbury. His important work for the new regime gave him a position of weight and status in society. He was a redoubtable figure in the world of politics and religion. People were afraid to oppose anything he had written or said, as is evident from a perusal of the private correspondence of the Non-Jurors and of 'neutral' people who had some connection with them.[35] He was an important advisor to the new government which appointed, chiefly upon his advice, fifteen new bishops in three years, all of them latitudinarians and supporters of the new regime.

The link between the old official view of the past and the new Whig interpretation is neatly demonstrated in a sermon preached by Burnet in 1688, which depicts William of Orange as saving England from falling again under 'Popery' and 'slavery':

As this is a yoke, so it is foreign to us; we owe no dependence to the See that pretends to be Mother-Church; we received not the Gospel from any sent by them. The Christian Religion was in this Island for Several Ages before we had any Commerce with that See; nor were we ever subject to it any other way, than as a Prisoner in the Power of him that took him; we have all the just Titles to an entire Exemption from any acknowledgement of them; for even at the time when we were a Province to the *Roman* Empire, tho' the See of *Rome* had all its Authority from the Dignity of the City, and that this could go no further than the Empire; yet even then we were not put under them, much less can it be pretended that the Empire now being dissolved, and at an end, we owe any Homage there any more: And tho' we did run the common Fate of the rest of *Europe* of falling under the prevailing Superstition of some dark Ages; yet this Nation did even during the Darkness, maintain its Liberty the best it could: It had not force enough for a great while to get the better in the Dispute; but it felt the rigour of that Bondage so heavily, that it broke thro it at last, and being once made free, it was a strange Presumption to imagine, that a Nation which has ever retained such a generous sense of Liberty, could return to so severe and so ignominious a Servitude; and yet our Enemies hope even to have gained this Point . . . we ought still to guard against them. They hate us, because we dare to be Freemen and Protestants. They have Skill and Cunning enough to wait for every Opportunity, and to improve it: This is a *breaking in* that is to be dreaded, as we do the Inundations of the Sea, or the Eruptions of a devouring Fire.[36]

Burnet's *History of the Reformation* is written within the ideological framework of this passage and is the first in the long line of Protestant–Whig histories which portray the freedom and continuous success story of the English nation in terms of the Reformation and the 'Glorious Revolution' of 1688.[37]

The three volumes which constitute the work appeared in 1679, 1681 and 1715, each of them motiviated by considerations of contemporary political expediency. Nevertheless the author's influence and prestige made it a 'Canonical Book' and 'one of our ancestorial traditionary "Standard ecclesiastical authorities"'[38] during the following two centuries. It is also important because it provoked a number of much more interesting and original treatments of the Reformation and the medieval period from certain non-juring scholars[39] whose work has remained in comparative obscurity.

Burnet was actually commissioned to write his *History* because of the qualities he had shown already in his Whiggish *Memoirs of the Duke of Hamilton* (1676) and in his various anti-Popish tracts.[40] On his own admission, and on the observation of others, he knew little about the subject of the Reformation when he undertook the task.[41] He was given a list of dates and observations by Bishop Lloyd and told to proceed from that.[42] To Burnet, the need to provide a basis for Protestant unity in the present was far more important than giving a correct account of something that was dead and gone, and he was quite prepared, for example, to falsify a document in this cause.[43] In this sense the *History* is fundamentally unhistorical in character. It was written simply to meet the contemporary need of finding some basis for unity within English Protestantism which was becoming increasingly fragmented. Burnet's task was to achieve this by exploiting the contemporary and irrational fear of 'rising Popery'. This was a much more important reason than the published one: to contradict the statements in Nicholas Sander's book, published in France, accusing the English Church of schism. The second half of the seventeenth century, during the interregnum and afterwards, had seen the growth of various religious sects and free-thinking bodies, as well as the main split between the views of 'high' and 'low' churchmen. All this represented a serious threat to religious and political stability in an age when religion was of such public as well as private significance.[44]

The attempt by broad churchmen or latitudinarians to solve this problem by 'comprehension' – that is, to regard everything doctrinal as non-essential apart from a hard core of religious belief which was based upon 'right reason' – had run into difficulties. As one conscientious, but perplexed, contemporary wrote in a private letter to a friend, 'ye difficulty still remains, for tho my following right reason may satisfy myself, yet it cannot satisfy another, who says right reason tells him ye contrary. Now who shall be judge in this matter'.[45]

There was, however, another method of attempting to mend the increasing disunity within English Protestantism. For all Protestants shared one belief: that the Church of Rome was their common enemy. A common front could be set up by inventing, emphasizing and exaggerating the threat of 'rising Popery' in England. Moreover, anti-Catholic propaganda could also serve an important political interest. The Whig party used it intensely in their campaign to try to push through the Exclusion Bill in 1678, designed to keep the Catholic James, Duke of York, from succeeding to the throne on the death of his brother, Charles II. The fictitious Popish Plot (1678), invented by two of the most improbable people to have influenced English history, was supposed to contain a plan to massacre Protestants and place James II on the throne. One of the most judicious of our modern historians observes that 'the nation had gone mad' after 'two of the vilest liars in the world concocted the story of the Popish

Plot'.[46] Thirty-five completely innocent Catholics were hounded down and indiscrimately executed in a frenzy of public panic. Another modern historian finds it difficult to comprehend the irrational credulity of the English public at this time, in accepting the lies of such men as Titus Oates and Israel Tonge.[47]

The fear was irrational in terms of the small number of committed Catholics then in England. Even the often exploited danger of invasion by a foreign Catholic power never happened. In fact, it was the commercial rival, the Protestant Dutch, who raided the Thames in 1667, and their leader who conquered England and took the throne in 1688.

The same method was to be used to concentrate political and religious opposition against James II during his reign and to justify the new Whig regime after the Revolution. The main theme of Burnet's sermon in 1689 was 'remember we are Brethren, fellow Christians and fellow Protestants that must have been destroyed together, and therefore must now support and bear with one another'.[48] The design in his *History of the Reformation* is precisely the same: 'to unite us more firmly among ourselves, to bury and for ever Extinguish the Fears of our Relapsing again into Popery'.[49] In 1689 he was placed on a commission for achieving 'comprehension', but this proved to be a far less effective method of closing Protestant ranks and uniting the nation.

The third volume of Burnet's *History* appeared thirty-four years later, in 1715. The only reason which Burnet gives for its appearance is that the earlier volumes of 1679–81 had awakened the nation to the dangers of rising 'Popery' to such good effect, 'that if the like Dangers seem to revert, it may not be an improper Attempt to try once more to awaken a Nation that has perhaps forgotten past Dangers, and yet be nearer them than ever'.(The first unsuccessful Jacobite rebellion on behalf of James Edward Stuart took place in 1715 in Scotland and northern England.) He warned that 'Popery' may well come in because 'Our old Breaches are not healed, and new ones, not known in former Times, are raised'.[50] He recited again the horrors ready to overtake English Protestants and the danger to their lives and property, unless they sank their differences in opposition to 'Popery'. He tells us that the reason for writing the *History* was to warn the English people about all this.[51]

The vested interest of the property-holding class in the official version of Reformation historiography had been apparent in the hostile reception given to Sir William Dugdale's *Monasticon* (1655) by the

Protestants, who feared a plot to restore Catholicism, and the gentry in Parliament, who feared that their title deeds to monastic lands would be called into question by the publication of so many monastic charters,[52] although the book was of a purely scholastic and academic nature. It is significant therefore that Burnet, in the introduction to his third volume of the *History*, held the threat of the papal resumption of Church lands over the English gentry, as his final attack on the favourers of 'Popery'.[53] Similarly, the very first document in the famous 'Collection of Records', added to the third volume, is a Bull of Pope Paul III concerning the recovery of Church lands which had been alienated to the Farnese family in Italy. It has no relevance to English history at all, but is given first place in Burnet's collection 'as no small Piece of Instruction, to all who are possessed of any Estate so alienated from Churches, Monasteries, or Hospitals'.[54]

This 'Collection of Records' was added to the third volume to give an air of authority to the main work, 'so that the Reader will perceive full evidence of the truth of this History'.[55] It achieved this aim, and even today Burnet is accredited with 'being conscious of the need for accuracy' and 'having a nineteenth-century reverence for archive or record material'.[56] In fact Burnet had the utmost disrespect for records. He questioned their value and spoke 'so much in derogation of *History* . . . as a Thing which is in itself so uncertain and not to be depended upon'.[57] His approach to records was flippant.[58] He admitted to having no practice in the use of them,[59] nor had he the scholastic ability or temperament to pursue such research.[60] The idea of including records, to provide an air of authority, had been given him by a friend[61] and he relied on others to copy them.[62] Consequently Burnet's most careful editor concludes,

the numerous and important blunders made by the author and his amanuensis in the process of transcribing . . . The present editor is not obliged to adjust the different causes to which the error may be distributed. . . . It is sufficient for him to say that, after making allowances for all the alterations in the spelling both of common words and proper names, there remained about ten thousand downright mistakes made in the original folios, and which have appeared in every subsequent edition down to the present day.[63]

All this was well known to the non-juring scholars who, in their private papers, pulled the *History* to pieces.

Much has been made, too, of the lists of 'corrections' offered by certain critics, published in the *History*, to reveal that Burnet 'was disarmingly ready to admit his mistakes'.[64] This was done to achieve just that effect on his readers. We know, in fact, from the private papers of scholars such as Strype and Thomas Baker and Nicholas Battely that they knew they could send him only lists of comparatively trivial errors which made no difference to the message of the book, but they kept to themselves their knowledge of Burnet's real distortion of evidence which took place in order to assist his propaganda.[65] When such a distinguished scholar as Henry Wharton published, anonymously, a list of the important mistakes and actual misrepresentations, the reaction was very different. It is clear from the private papers of the Non-Jurors that the political climate and Burnet's prestigious position as defender of Protestantism and the nation, would not allow open contradiction, unless they were prepared to face some sort of ostracism and persecution.[66]

One of the most interesting examples of a complete distortion of the evidence, of which the Non-Jurors knew, is the case of a manuscript of Luther, kept in Corpus Christi College Library, Cambridge. One of Burnet's main interests, as we have seen, was pursuing the cause of unity among Protestants. One method – the most effective as it turned out – was to instil panic about the threat of 'Popery'. The other was the idea of 'comprehension', by which Protestants should drop 'unimportant' matters of dogma and find unity on the essential truths which were amenable to 'right reason'. A very able non-juring scholar, Dr George Hickes, showed in 1695 that Burnet had deliberately perverted the sense of a manuscript of Luther, giving it exactly the opposite sense to its true meaning, to make it seem that Luther was in favour of such 'comprehension'.[67] Hickes went to great lengths to conceal his authorship of this criticism, but there is no doubt of his authorship. Both the 'Collections of Records' and the 'Lists of Errors' were literally façades, to facilitate the success of the book which continued to be regarded as a basic authority on the English past until well into the nineteenth century. It was reprinted in 1820, 1825 and 1829, significantly at the time when Catholic emancipation was in the air and many people wanted ammunition against it. Foxe's 'Book of Martyrs' became especially popular at the same time and for the same reason.

What can we say about all this? Burnet represented a particular ideology, spawned by the idea of progress and the excitement of scientific discoveries in the second half of the seventeenth century.

He had his counterpart in the contemporary French sceptic, Pierre Bayle, who led the 'Pyrronistic' thinkers in their attack on historians who believed in any possibility of achieving historical truth. Mabillon and his fellow monk-scholars defended the validity of history as an independent discipline on the Continent. The non-juring scholars, partly inspired by Mabillon, adopted the same role in England. This debate is resurrected from time to time in European history. Today we have the post-modernist sceptics claiming that there is no such thing as historical truth, while practising historians mount the defence of traditional disciplines and the veridical basis of their subject.

Burnet was a 'théoricien', in Paul Hazard's phrase.[68] The Whig interpretation was to be characterized by its theoretical working out of concepts, like 'Progress', in history, rather than a concentration on the narration of 'facts'. Like Foxe before him, Burnet fused 'causes', 'changes', 'great issues' and 'ideas' coherently together into an epic unity. It is this feature of his work which has attracted the admiration of several modern observers, from Charles Firth to John Kenyon.[69] However, it was achieved by subordinating factual truth to the ideas he wanted to propagate. Burnet, like Thomas Cromwell, was a natural propagandist who knew the power of history – be it true or false – over the minds of people. He was an intelligent man who believed in the Protestant cause, which he could see breaking up. Unity was needed to save that cause and the nation. It could be achieved by 'comprehension' and instilling the fear of 'Popery' as an outside threat to them all. He used historical propaganda, without worrying over its historical truth, in order to achieve his ends, and he could certainly tell an epic story.

The whole affair raises interesting issues of historiography which is the subject of another study.[70] The Non-Jurors viewed historical study in an entirely different way, and set high standards of technical scholarship, so it cannot be said that Burnet's deficiencies were *simply* a product of his own time. However, he may well have been the victim as well as the master perpetrator of an ideology which dominated English life at that period.

What was really needed for the next great advance in historical writing was the fusion of technical scholarship with continuous narrative and analytical discussion. This great fusion was only to come a century later, in the work of John Lingard who set out the classic case against 'philosophic' history and also set standards of source criticism which have not been surpassed.

THE CONTRIBUTION OF THE NON-JURING SCHOLARS, 1680–1730

The supremacy of the State in ecclesiastical affairs was one of the main pillars of the official version of the English past. The whole cause of English Protestantism in the seventeenth century, in the broadest sense, was bound up with this concept. It was something which united most Anglicans and Puritans, or Nonconformists. Historical writing since the Reformation had been built upon the assumption that this concept had been an abiding part of Christianity in England from the very beginning.

Already, however, Charles II's 'uncompromising churchmanship'[71] and his 'assumed role of "unusual bishop"'[72] had allowed the undergraduate Peter Heylin to express an opinion in Oxford in 1627 in opposition to his Regius Professor of Divinity, that the Established Church owed more to the Church of Rome than to the Waldenses, Wycliffites and Hussites.[73] Heylin became a chaplain to Archbishop Laud and much later in life produced his *History of the Reformation* (1661), which displayed his opposition to the more extreme Protestant activities in matters of belief and discipline and to their attack on Church lands and authority. As indicated by its title, 'Ecclesia Restaurata', Heylin's work stressed a continuity in which the Reformation was an essentially clerical movement for self-reform of the Church, assisted by the king. The reign of Henry VIII was simply a prologue, useful because it freed the Anglican Church from Rome, but allowing too great a restraint on the rights of the Church. Heylin's book was, however, lacking in both scholarship and popular appeal.

Other Anglican divines had pursued the theme of the apostolic foundation of the Church of England, independently from Rome. James Ussher, Archbishop of Armagh, in his *Discourse of the Religion anciently practised by the Irish* (1623), had sought to demonstrate the independence of the Celtic Church from papal authority and he was concerned in his *Treatise on the Originall of Bishops* (1641) to show the apostolic origins of the episcopal system in England. Edward Stillingfleet, who was to become Bishop of Worcester in 1689, wrote his *Origines Britannicae* (1685) in another attempt to show an early British Protestant Church, independent of Rome, but with an episcopal form. Establishment figures such as Archbishop Wake and John Inett, in his *Origines Anglicanae* (1704–10), were going to reiterate it. Thomas Fuller, in his *Church History* (1655), expressed the view that, whereas the episcopal form was most like the primitive Church, it was not necessarily a characteristic of the reformed Church. John Strype (1643–1737) formed a fine collection of original documents, including the Lambeth State Papers and the Parker and Wharton manuscript collections. He also published *Lives* of Archbishops Cranmer (1694), Cheke (1705), Grindal (1710), Parker (1711) and Whitgift (1718). He saw the Reformation very much through the eyes of the Establishment and his scholarship was poor and inaccurate.[74] None of these made any significant attempt to challenge the official version of the English past. The Non-Jurors, however, were in a different category with regard to scholarship, and they were provoked into making a significant breakthrough in the conventional story of the past in opposition to the extremely erastian position taken up by English historians after 1689.

The Non-Jurors believed that monarchs possessed their authority by Divine Right, which meant that it could never be removed by man. They had resigned or been dismissed from their positions in Church and State in 1689 because of their reverence for legitimate monarchy. They had already taken the oath of allegiance to James III, and they could not break that by giving another oath to William III. So they were men of conscience who cared about the truth in general. In spite of this belief in the monarch's divine right to rule, they bitterly opposed the concept of absolute and independent supremacy in the king or the State over the Church. They did not see the regal authority as absolute and above all other authority. Rather, there was a hierarchy of divine authority, they held, in which the regal authority was only a part, and not the supreme part. In spiritual affairs the authority of the Church, which had come down in apostolic succession from the first apostles, must be superior to the temporal.[75] This was explosive stuff indeed.

It was this anti-erastian standpoint of the Non-Jurors which separated them from all other Protestants and affected their whole outlook on the English past. They believed in a 'catholic' or universal Christianity which, perfect in the apostolic period, had formed the basis of both the Roman and British Churches. Both these Churches had fallen away from the original doctrines and discipline of the original catholic Truth. They were interconnected insofar as either, or both, had retained that Truth, and were separate insofar as either, or both, had deviated from it.

This belief about the nature of the early Church, together with an increasing insistence on the doctrine of apostolic succession[76] –

and therefore on the idea of historical continuity – made the Non-Jurors more sympathetic with the medieval Church and world, which to all other Protestants represented the backward 'Dark Ages', not even worth studying. It was this sympathetic attitude which made it possible for them to see the medieval world, and the Reformation, in clearer perspective, for no historian can understand what he 'looks down on'. On the other hand, their insistence on the idea of the independence of the various national Churches,[77] and their opinion that neither the British nor the Roman Churches had any authority over the other, obscured their historical vision. They projected a contemporary idea of nationalism into the English past and were unable to achieve a proper understanding of the international or universal nature of the Church before the Reformation. Nor did they understand the relationship between England and the centre of Church government in Rome.

The Non-Jurors believed that there was a spiritual authority on earth, and this had been handed down from Christ Himself. He had given His authority to the first apostles and this had come down from them, by apostolic succession, to the Church bishops of their own day. Just as the Church was independent of the State, so was the spiritual authority supreme in spiritual and ecclesiastical matters. This spiritual authority in England was contained, for the Non-Jurors, in the autonomous English episcopate, independent of both the Pope and the English State.

In fact the ecclesiastical authority of the English bishops in the medieval period was merely a reflection of the authority of the Catholic Church, centred on the Papacy in Rome.[77] Sometimes it was necessary for the Non-Jurors, in answering the historical arguments put forward by Burnet and the other erastians, to turn to this supreme authority of the Papacy, to show the independence of the spiritual order. When, for example, an erastian argument was put forward to show that the English king at a particular time was exercising an ecclesiastical authority independently of the English bishops, it was only by showing that the king had a special grant or dispensation from the Pope for doing so, that they could show that it was no basis for an erastian argument.

This sort of appeal to the outside authority of the Papacy, could not be taken to its logical conclusion by the Non-Jurors. They had their own belief in the independent and autonomous nature of the English national Church to defend against the 'Papists'. In the works of the Non-Jurors, therefore, the appeal to papal authority is used only in isolated and specific cases when their 'backs were against the wall' in opposition to some argument or other put forward by the erastian opposition, and always in a polemical context. It is never allowed to run into a generalization about the nature of the medieval Church in England as essentially part of the Universal Church; neither is it used in works which are non-polemical.

The historiographical significance of this manoeuvre on the part of the Non-Jurors in their anti-erastian warfare is that it enabled them, occasionally and undesignedly, to split the unity of that dualism of thought contained within the national-erastian view of the past for the first time in English historical writing since the statutes of the Reformation Parliament under Henry VIII. Their opposition to the second (erastian) factor was sometimes sufficiently strong and persuasive to make them displace the first (nationalist) factor along with it. On those occasions, when the authority of the Papacy was needed to demonstrate the futility of the alleged historical precedents put forward by the exponents of erastianism, such as Burnet, then for the first time in English historiography that authority was not attacked as a usurpation or encroachment upon the rights of the English people.

This provided the first important breach in the conventional framework of thought, and it needed great intensity of anti-erastian feeling to achieve it. Nor were the Non-Jurors themselves ready to go through the breach which they had made. The importance of their contribution does not arise merely from their recognition of the existence of papal authority in England during the medieval period. It lies, rather, in the fact that, because of the demands of their arguments against erastianism, they were sometimes forced into admitting the validity, historically speaking, of this papal authority. It was no great jump, objectively, from the recognition of the validity of papal authority in some particular medieval episode to the full recognition of the nature of that authority in medieval England. It was lack of sympathy rather than of knowledge which obscured the insight of the non-juring historians at this point and prevented them from going any further than they did in contributing towards our understanding of the English past.[78]

To place their contribution in perspective, however, we should pay some more attention to the climate in which the Non-Jurors were living. It will be sufficient here to illustrate this by looking at the position of one of these scholars. Thomas Hearne (1678–1735) led a lonely and persecuted life in early eighteenth-century Oxford.[79] Because of his refusal to take the oath to the new Hanoverian dynasty in 1715, he had to resign his official posts in the University, including that of librarian in his beloved Bodleian where he had worked since 1700. Of humble origins, and a poor man for a great part of his life, he had family problems, though he himself never married.[80] When asked, on one occasion, why he had not written a History of England, Hearne replied that 'I had already writ and published too many things of Secret History since I have so often [been] troubled on that score'.[81] Indeed Hearne had learned from bitter experience. When publishing his edition of Roper's *Life of Thomas More*, Hearne had been warned that he must not attach the name of Oxford or the Theatre, where his scholarly editions were printed, to this work. The University authorities told him: 'We have nothing to do . . . with what you print. Roper was a Papist. There are Letters in the Book that may do us harm, you will be called before the Parliament. We will not meddle. You must not bring us to trouble by putting either Oxford or the Theatre'.[82]

The severest blow came after Hearne had published, in his edition of *Camden's Elizabeth* (1717), a preface in which he had commented adversely on Henry VIII and Elizabeth. Hearne was brought before the Vice-Chancellor of the University who said that he would 'give me leave to print nothing, that I should be put in the Court, that two Justices would tender the Oaths to me, that in my Preface to Camden's Elizabeth . . . I was a Papist'. The Vice-Chancellor had added that 'I had abused K. Hen VIII and Q. Eliz. and slurr'd the Reformation, and he insinuated that I ought to retract what I had said'.[83] The outcome was that Hearne had been forbidden to print or publish anything, and it was only after a year that he was able to get the sentence rescinded. He wrote, 'They have been very severe here. Those I formerly looked upon as friends have proved Enemies.'[84]

Another interesting feature of the preface to *Camden's Elizabeth* was the questioning by Hearne of the authority of Foxe's *Acts and Monuments*. In May 1718 John Strype wrote to Dr Charlett, Master of University College, Oxford, concerning this:

I have not read his long Preface. Yo give me one passage in it, and I heartily go along with yo and yr Friends at Oxford therein, viz. yr Dislike of yt rude character he gives of Mr. Foxe's Martyrology. The very charge ye Jesuite Parsons laid upon it. It ws in Q. Elizabs Reign from ye Time it came forth in such esteem yt it was appointed (as ye know) to be fixed in al Parish Churches [sic] with ye Great Bible . . . Sr . . . I understand Mr. Hearne hath given ye University great Offence.[85]

In June, Charlett wrote back:

I am much concerned for the credit of Mr. Fox and his History and therefore not a little offended at the vain and bold malice of T.H. who is grown Incorrigible & Intolerable, and Incurable possessed with legion of Pride, Arrogance & Conceit, and . . . turns his pen agst the Honor and Methods and Persons & Laws introducing and supporting the Reformation . . . T.H. has abused so many of all Ranks, always in favor of Popery and agst ye Reformation, that you need not ask the Reasons of the University's displeasure.[86]

Hearne's boldness was often a source of anxiety to his non-juring friends. Browne Willis wrote to him in 1715 after the publication of Burnet's third volume: 'I wish you may not give great offence by setting upon Burnet, tho: he deserves it. I speak this out of caution; for you know how the times stand.'[87] On the same day he wrote to a mutual friend concerning Hearne whose name he does not dare to write: 'all I can say is that if − sd. nothing of the Bp. or the less the better for his circumstances.'[88]

Indeed, even the stubborn Hearne was subdued to some extent, for, having considered publishing something written by Catholics in Elizabeth's reign, he adds that this is 'a matter that must be considered and well weigh'd before I could resolve it this time'.[89] So we see how a man, who had given up all chances of career and preferment, being ready to 'cheerfully undergo all Barbarities that I meet with, being resolved to do nothing agst my Conscience',[90] was yet prevented from publishing Catholic views on the subject of the Reformation, and this nearly two hundred years after the time of the events in question.

It is very illustrative of the change in climate of society as the eighteenth century advanced into the age of the 'enlightenment' that by the time of his death in 1734, Hearne had become a figure of ridicule rather than persecution. The exponents of the new rationalistic and 'philosophical' culture looked down on the labours of learning and erudition, especially where these had been employed in the study of the medieval period. In 1736 there appeared the *Impartial Memorials of the Life and Writings of Thomas Hearne, by several Hands* which had the following lines around the frontispiece:

> *Hearnius* behold in Closet close y-pent
> Of sober Face with learned Dust besprent;
> To *future* ages will his Dulness last
> Who hath preserv'd the Dulness of the Past.[91]

Similarly, when Hearne's beloved books were being sold,[92] a sheet was attached to the inside cover of his own manuscript catalogue, with the scornful words: 'Pox on't quoth Time to Thomas Hearne. Whatever I forgot You learn'.[93]

In the *Impartial Memorials* Hearne was ridiculed for the very virtues which we now regard as his greatest editorial virtue, namely his refusal to change the original in any way. He painstakingly included in his editions, as critics scornfully noticed, words that were 'plainly redundant', as well as those which are 'manifestly wrong',[94] though he added notes to show that he knew of the mistakes while still copying them faithfully. The *Memorials* are summarized in their concluding remark that 'after *wasting* not *employing*, a Life of Fifty odd Years, on the Tenth Day of *June, 1735*, this *Studier* and *Preserver* of *Monkish-Trumpery* gave up the Ghost'.[95]

As a great historian once remarked, when attacked by his critics, 'Time and experience must decide between us',[96] and history often does set people and events in proper perspective, given due time. Foxe, Burnet and Hume are no longer read as serious historians of value, and we do not know even the names of the authors of the *Impartial Memorials*. Thomas Hearne's name, however, stands high now as an editor of medieval texts. A distinguished medievalist of the twentieth century writes: 'Hearne had a respect for the sanctity of an original authority which had been shared by none of his predecessors and he worked with an extraordinary accuracy, even when judged by the most rigid standards.' As a result, Hearne's editions 'set up new standards in the editorship of such texts' and constitute 'a work of national importance'.[97] The first historian to recognize immediately the value of Hearne's work, while dismissing that of most other English historians, was John Lingard.[98]

Hearne's most interesting and innovative work on the Reformation itself, like that of other Non-Jurors, was confined to his own manuscript papers which have never seen the light of day until now.[99] This must be the subject of another study, for we are here concerned only to show the kind of environment which the Non-Jurors had to combat in making their important, if limited, contribution to the shape of the English past and to the general nature of the Reformation in England.

The outstanding Non-Juror publication of narrative history was the *Ecclesiastical History* (1708–14) of Jeremy Collier (1650–1726), a clergyman who refused to swear the oath to William and Mary and was outlawed in 1696 for his public support of non-juring principles. He became the leading Non-Juror after the death of Dr George Hickes in 1715. Collier was able to get away with his *History* because his written narrative is not out of line with the official version. Intriguingly, his most interesting and important contributions are made, not in the body of the work, but in the long preface where he is concerned to deny the extremely erastian claims of other historians. Here he chooses, significantly, not Foxe or Burnet as his target, but the very non-Establishment figure of William Prynne who had offended so many that, by now, and long after his death, there seems to have been no one to stand up for him.

In the preface, Collier begins by considering Prynne's 'two volumes of Records, where he treats of the Saxon and English kings' supreme ecclesiastical jurisdiction'.[100] He is careful to add that, 'In examining this point, I desire the reader would take notice of the dispute is only with Mr Prinn, and not understand me as if I had any design to state the extent of the regale or pronounce upon the supremacy, Having premised this, I shall proceed to a brief essay.'[101]

This kind of qualification was necessary if a book was to be accepted for publication at this time, when approval of the royal supremacy over the Church was taken as a sure sign of the true Protestantism of any writer.[102] Similarly Prynne could be attacked openly as a Puritan, whereas Burnet was too much of an establishment figure to be dealt with in the same way. Precautions against likely accusations of 'Popish tendencies' are to be found scattered here and there in the published works of the Non-Jurors and are eloquent of the suspicion under which they worked.[103] It is very interesting, and sometimes amusing, to compare the published statements of Non-Jurors on the Reformation with their private comments in their own letters, manuscript papers and diaries – particularly where Burnet's *History* was concerned.

So Collier proceeds to deal with Prynne's arguments for the royal supremacy of the English kings in the medieval period. Prynne had referred to King John's sending a prohibition to the Chapter of Lisieux against their electing a bishop without his consent. He had also mentioned John's appeal to the Pope in defence of his rights. Collier responds: 'Now an appeal in the common notion of it, as everybody knows, imparts an application to a superior authority; and yet Mr Prinn is so unlucky as to cite these two instances among his records for the king's ecclesiastical supremacy.'[104]

Collier replies to another of Prynne's historical arguments: 'It is true that the see of Carlisle was endowed and partly founded by king Henry I, but then this was not done without authority from the pope procured for this purpose'.[105]

> Mr Prinn, in pursuit of his design to establish precedents for the royal supremacy asserts that the king as supreme ordinary, has a right to exempt chapels and churches from episcopal jurisdiction; and yet the three records which he cites in proof of this point plainly declare these privileges of exemption were all granted by the see of Rome.[106]

Again, Collier comments in his preface:

> It is somewhat surprising Mr. Prinn should overlook these matters, considering he has printed three letters of king Edward I, in which he writes to the pope, to request him to confirm the exemption of the chapel at Boscham, to give him leave to choose a confessor for himself, and to grant one of his clerks a dispensation for pluralities. Now all these one would think, are very slender signs of an ecclesiastical supremacy.[107]

In his preface, therefore, we find that Collier appeals to the ecclesiastical authority of the Papacy in order to reject the historical arguments of his erastian opponent who had died some forty years before. Yet, in the main narrative of his *History*, where his main concern is not to disprove erastian claims, Collier is bound by the conventional insularity of thought on the subject of the medieval Church in England. So he writes in his main narrative: 'the English Church stood upon their ancient right, and would not submit to every imposition of the court of Rome.'[108] Furthermore, he completely misrepresents the context in which the papal legateship was conferred on Archbishop William of Canterbury in Stephen's reign:

> This archbishop was the first of his see who took the title of Pope's legate. This new distinction gave occasion for further encroachments of the supremacy, and brought the English Church into a state of servitude; for now the Archbishop's authority looked dependent and precarious, and seemed derived from the court of Rome. In his legatine commission Pope Honorius III empowers him to convene the clergy, to exercise discipline and make constitutions for the government of the Church. All which favours carried dishonour and subjection along with them, and suppose the archbishops of Canterbury unqualified for the functions of a primate without a licence from the Pope.[109]

In his treatment of the Reformation itself, Collier describes the rejection of papal supremacy under Henry VIII as a step which 'carried a new face and was something of an Ecclesiastical Revolution', but 'many of the Bishops who had consulted the *Records*, and examined the Practise of the *earliest Ages*, were not disinclin'd to this Change'.[110] No attempt is made to identify these 'Records'. When, previously, the English bishops had refused their consent to an act which forbade the seeking of dispensations from Rome, this refusal was 'because of the unlimited sway of the Popes over the English Church for several ages'.[111] Collier supports Burnet's arguments, 'approved by Antiquity', for the rejection of the papal supremacy, though he is courageous enough to say that he does not agree with Burnet's erastian comments on the royal supremacy over the Church.[112]

Collier, then, views the break with Rome as something which might have seemed revolutionary on the face of it, but which was really a return to the state of things described by the 'records' of 'antiquity'. It was extraordinary that a scholar writing an *Ecclesiastical History* should not have bothered to attempt to trace these records. He was content to accept the vague references to historical precedents made in the Henrician statutes. On the other hand, his aversion to the royal supremacy in the ecclesiastical sphere brings him to a momentary recognition of the 'novelty' of the Act of Supremacy. He describes how Henry VIII consulted the

Universities, the clergy in convocation and several religious houses before this Act was passed and adds that, 'These were thought proper expedients to make way for the regale, to take off the charge of novelty, and reconcile the subject to the act'.[113] The point is not emphasized, but slips out, so to speak, as an anti-erastian aside.

All this would seem to indicate that he was psychologically unprepared to take certain matters further because this would threaten his own position, despite his scholarly mind and a strong inclination to oppose erastian statements where this could be done prudently. If we compare Collier's unpublished statements on the episodes of the Reformation itself with the unpublished comments by several Non-Juror scholars on subjects such as the Divorce Question, the Dissolution of the Monasteries, or the treatment of the Marian and Elizabethan periods,[114] it becomes very clear what could and what could not be stated openly in published works at this time.

There is an important passage in which Collier clearly indicates the dilemma with which the Non-Juror scholars were faced when the two lines of thought, the anti-papal and the anti-erastian, came together. Generally speaking the two parts of the original official version are kept safely apart, as when Collier separates one line of argument in his preface from the other line of argument in the main narrative of his work. In the following passage, however, in which Collier is opposing the typically erastian arguments of the common lawyer, Sir John Davis, he seems suddenly to stop short in his anti-erastian argument and to stand aside, for a moment, to consider the real implications of what he is saying. Then he is immediately forced onto the defensive against the dreaded charge of being 'popishly inclined'. He writes:

> The case of praemunire, reported by Sir John Davis, argues learnedly against the pope's encroachments, but then the case mistakes, in affirming the pope's jurisdiction in England began with the Norman Conquest; for it is plain, this prelate pretended to a superintendency over the English Church before that period. To give an instance or two: the pope granted an exemption from episcopal visitation to the Abbey of Malmesbury in the reign of King Ine, in the eighth century. Pope Leo III removed the metropolitical see from Lichfield, and restored it to Canterbury in the ninth century. And in the eleventh century King Edward the Confessor, in his letter to Nicholas II salutes him as supreme governor of the Church,

sends to him for a dispensation, and received his legates; but after all there is no good consequence from fact to right; neither have I any intention to argue for the excessive pretences of the see of Rome. However, the disproof of the pope's spiritual authority in this island, does not infer that it must necessarily be lodged in the crown. There is a third seat for this privilege, and this is, the bishops of the country. To proceed . . .[115]

Realizing that he has gone too far in the 'Popish' direction while pursuing his anti-erastian argument, he quickly returns to a hasty and unsubstantiated assertion of the autonomous authority of the English Church as expressed in its bishops.

Collier had to stop his anti-erastian argument short of recognizing the validity of papal jurisdiction. Yet, in those parts of his work where he is able to break through the national-erastian framework imposed on the English past, he is able to do so precisely by recognizing the validity of this jurisdiction and arguing from it.

The same intriguing process can be seen at work in the controversy between Gilbert Burnet and the great medievalist, Henry Wharton. Wharton, educated at Cambridge, became chaplain to the Archbishop of Canterbury and had worked on the medieval records in Cambridge and Lambeth. He took the oath to the new regime in 1688 and so was not technically a Non-Juror. His career, opinions and writings, however, place him obviously among them.[116] From 1689 onwards he was faced with the hostility of the Whig bishops as well as the suspicion of his non-juring friends.[117] He never gained preferment and died, a disappointed and perhaps embittered man, at the age of thirty, worn out, it was said, by over-exertion at his studies. Yet his *Anglia Sacra* (1691) is a work of 'permanent importance'[118] which entitles him to the title of founder-member of English medieval studies.

In 1695 Wharton dared to publish, though anonymously, a slim volume entitled *A Specimen of Some Errors and Defects in the History of the Reformation of the Church of England, Wrote by G. Burnet, D.D., now Lord Bishop of Sarum*. It was published under the pseudonym of Anthony Harmer. This is a highly significant work, though largely unnoticed, in the history of historical writing in England. Wharton, an outstanding scholar, feeling that he could express himself more liberally under a pseudonym, makes some extraordinarily important statements in this book, which are examined more closely in another study.[119] Here I will refer to it only as an example of my main argument in this chapter.

Burnet had written, for example, that the Pall sent from Rome to Cardinal Pole in Mary Tudor's reign was a novel device, instituted by Pope Paschal in the twelfth century 'for the engaging of all Archbishops to a more immediate dependance on that See'.[120] Wharton comments:

> I cannot sufficiently admire, that any learned Man should commit so great a Mistake. None, conversant in the History of the Church can be ignorant that the Custom of sending Palls from *Rome* to Archbishops owning any Dependence upon that See, or Relation to it, began many hundred years before Pope *Paschal*, the Second. Pope *Gregory* the First had sent a Pall to *Augustine*, the first Archbishop of Canterbury, and all the Archbishops from him to the Reformation did singly receive Palls from *Rome*, if sudden Death did not prevent them before the Reception.[121]

In the *Specimen* Wharton takes many other instances of Burnet's ignorance, misunderstandings and misrepresentation of the Church in medieval England. Yet, like Collier, this fine scholar could not build a true picture of the ecclesiastical system in England at that time, because the main spur to his work was 'the desire to discover in the past a justification of the ecclesiastical system he served'.[122]

So, in the above passage, he is able to score heavily off Burnet's profound ignorance on the question of the Papal Pall, but he is also careful to safeguard his own High Anglican position by referring to the Pall being sent to archbishops owning dependence 'or Relation' to the Papacy. Similarly, in the *Anglia Sacra*, which he published openly and which is not concerned with opposing erastianism, Wharton, in spite of the excellence of his documentary work, leaves the nationalist aspect of the official version of the English past completely intact. For example, he attacks Archbishop William, in the reign of Henry I, for undermining the independence of the English Church by accepting the legatine office from the Pope. According to Wharton, the Papacy had previously possessed no jurisdiction in England.[123]

The process can be illustrated again from the hitherto unknown and 'underground' manuscripts of Thomas Baker (1656–1740). He resigned a living in 1690 and a fellowship at St John's College, Cambridge, in 1717, rather than take the necessary oaths to the new line of kings. He had been allowed, however, to retain his rooms in that college, and there he lived most of his life in a 'confined, Monastic way of living'.[124] He was a man of sensitive but equable temperament who managed, unlike Thomas Hearne, to live on terms of friendship with an extraordinary range of people, including Burnet himself – much to the astonishment of Hearne. Indeed it is amusing to compare the shattering criticisms of Burnet's *History* in Baker's private manuscripts, with the very mild and unimportant comments sent by him to Burnet, at the latter's request.[125] Even then, he begs Burnet not to use any of his corrections 'that might give Offence to the Church or Religion'.[126] Thus, where Burnet had used a source on Henry's side on the Divorce Question, Baker proves that it is incorrect by comparing it with original documents, but still writes to Burnet, 'But I suppose your Lordship may follow your Authority; and then all is well'.[127] Again, pointing out apologetically that there are good sources to prove that Henry used threats and corruption to get favourable opinions from the Universities on the Divorce Question, Baker quickly adds, 'but I am not concerned to make them good'.[128]

The grateful Burnet wrote back that, 'It is some satisfaction to me yt: so exact a searcher into ye transactions of those times has not discover'd more capital mistakes.'[129] The servile notes which Baker sent to him were just what Burnet wanted. They did not affect his theme and at the same time he could claim that he was intent on making his *History* as correct as possible by publishing these harmless corrections as part of his book.[130] All this showed a certain natural timidity in Baker, but also a fear of betraying the Protestant cause. It throws some more light on the crisis of conscience which must have afflicted so many among the non-juring scholars living in the political and social climate of those times.

Baker was in fact an excellent scholar who published very little, but left a great collection of manuscript notes and collections to the British Museum and Cambridge University Library. In the Cambridge library I discovered a copy of Burnet's *History*, owned by Baker, in the margins of which Baker has left a stream of his handwritten scholarly notes and observations, the quality of which showed that he could have written an extremely important history of the Reformation. His reason for not doing this is made clear in a letter to Hearne, who had asked him to write a life of the Catholic martyr, Bishop Fisher, a Chancellor of Cambridge University and a particular benefactor of Baker's own college, St John's. Baker had become very interested in Fisher and developed a great admiration for him. He had collected a number of original documents in preparation for a Life of Fisher, and Hearne knew that Baker was the best person in England to do so, but Baker replied: 'what you say of undertaking Bp:Fisher's Life, I have often thought of, but to tell you the truth, I dare not venture, since right cannot be done him without giving great offence, & I would either do him right, or nothing at all.'[131]

The previous year, Baker had received a letter from Bishop White Kennett in which the latter had attacked Fiddes' *Life of Wolsey*, because 'in ye opinion of us Whiggs as they calls [sic] us yre sems to have been a wrong cast of his eyes in favour of Popery and some prejudice to ye Reformation'.[132] This seems to have been a warning shot across the bow. So, although Baker had written years previously that, 'We have several things concerning Bishop Fisher amongst the archives of the College. . . . I hope to do him some right before I die',[133] he never did in fact ever publish a life of Fisher.

It is from the hand-written notes in Baker's copy of Burnet's *History* that we can take the final illustration of the process by which the Non-Jurors could break through the barrier of the official version of the past, as a result of their determination to disprove an erastian argument. Burnet, having described the founding of some new bishoprics by Henry VIII, was concerned to give a precedent for such action on the part of the secular ruler in England. In a very good example of the conventional treatment of the papal authority in medieval England, Burnet had written,

And in *England*, when the Bishoprick of *Lincoln*, being judged of too great an Extent, the Bishoprick of *Ely* was taken out of it, it was done only by the King with the consent of his Clergy and his Nobles, Pope *Nicholas* indeed officiously intruded himself into that matter, by sending afterwards a Confirmation of that which was done. But that was one of the great arts of the Papacy to offer Confirmation of things that were done without the Popes. For these being easily received by them, that thought of nothing more than to give the better countenance to their own Acts, the Popes afterwards founded a Right on these Confirmations. The very receiving of them was pretended to be an acknowledgement of a Title in the Pope. And the matter was so artificially managed that Princes were noozed into some approbation of such a pretence, before they were aware of it. And then the Authority of the Canon law prevailing, Maxims were laid down in it by which the most tacite and inconsiderate Acts of Princes, were construed so much senses, as still advanced the greatness of the Papal pretensions.[134]

Baker wrote in the margin, alongside this piece:

That this was not done only by the King is very plain from Eadmer, an Author beyond exception, who liv'd in the same time. . . . It was done with the consent (not of Pope Nicholas, for that is a mistake) but of Pope Paschal . . . Pope Paschal's Letter or Bull to Anselm ArchBp: of Cant: is printed in Selden without Date: In a very antient Chartulary of the Priory of Ely, It is dated thus, Dat Per Manum Eonis Roman: an:Dom:Incarn: 1108: Pontificatus autem D:Paschal 2:Papae anno 10 mo: The King's Charter is likewise there put down, dat:as in Seldon, only It is sayd, Indication:anno 20: & ad ye conclusion 16:Kal:Novembr: as in the monast:p. 95, where the subscribers names are added ex ipso autographo.[135]

Baker disliked the idea of the temporal ruler being deemed to have the right to interfere in the government of medieval bishoprics. He shows here that the spiritual jurisdiction of the Papacy was needed for the king's action in a passage which shows, even in abbreviated form, the scholarship which was typical of the Non-Jurors.

The Non-Jurors' contribution towards the modern state of scholarship on the nature of the Church in medieval England was a by-product of their concern to oppose the arguments of erastian writers among their fellow Protestants. They were unable either to draw the proper general conclusion from it, or to work out the implications of this general conclusion concerning the revolutionary nature of the Reformation. In their published work on the Reformation they could not follow the same process which enabled them occasionally to break through the national-erastian framework of the official version of the medieval period. There was no longer the possibility of their appealing to the Papacy to refute the erastian arguments of Henry VIII, since as Anglicans they could not but approve the rejection of Papal authority in the Henrician Reformation. Yet their opposition to erastianism in all its shapes and forms still informed their historical insight so that they were able to make some very important contributions towards the understanding of certain episodes of the Reformation itself, but only in their own unpublished manuscript papers. Here we find well-researched accounts of subjects such as the Divorce Question, the Dissolution of the Monasteries and the reigns of Mary and Elizabeth, which were not to be repeated, apart from by John Lingard, until the revisionist movement in English historiography in the latter half of the twentieth century.[136]

Their significant, if incomplete, challenge to the official view of the English past was important because it was the first scholarly attempt in England to break the closely bound dualism of thought which dominated English historical writing on pre-Reformation England for four centuries. This in fact was more important than the detailed attack which they were able to mount, from their 'underground' position in society, against the erastian statements of Foxe, Prynne and Burnet on the internal episodes of the Reformation itself. The whole nature of the Reformation as a revolution in English society could only be understood by means of a better understanding of medieval history, and to this they contributed greatly. This line of scholarly interest in the medieval period came to an end in England in about 1730, with the decline of the non-juring movement.

Another important feature of their work was that it represented the only appearance in England of the type of group scholarship which characterized the great development of historical writing in France during the same period, associated with the Bollandist and Maurist monks. And, finally, the Non-Jurors are important because they made contact with continental developments and were inspired and influenced by the work of Jean Mabillon and his fellow monk-scholars, at a time when England as a whole remained comparatively isolated. It was this contact which stimulated the extraordinary standard of scholarship which appeared in the work of the Non-Jurors during the period 1680–1730.[137] This will be another story.

It was to be another century before the appearance of a figure who could challenge and undermine both aspects of the dualism of thought created by Henry VIII and Thomas Cromwell. John Lingard was the first to appreciate the basic work done by the Non-Jurors and made good use of their preparatory work in the publication of accurate texts of original documents.[138]

THREE

Common Law and the Isolationist View of the English Past

In English history during the medieval period there had been three important spheres of law which affected the lives of all English people. Two of them were international in character and one national. Native English law could be traced back to the arrival of the Anglo-Saxons in England. The great F.W. Maitland reminded us, 'in order to avoid any glib talk about primitive institutions', that:

> Teutonic law (for what is true of England is also true of the continent) when it is first set in writing has already ceased to be primitive; it is already Christian, and so close is the connection between law and religion, that we may well believe that it has already undergone a great change.[1]

Maitland felt it necessary to avoid such 'glib talk' because there had been a minor 'Gothic' theme in English historiography in the late sixteenth and seventeenth centuries, which stated that the Common Law of England, together with its concomitant institutions of freedom (including Parliament), all developed continuously from their earliest origins in the primitive forest life of Germany,[2] from where the Anglo-Saxons had come. This theme was taken up again in the second half of the nineteenth century.[3]

I refer to it as a 'minor' theme because it never achieved the status of a major myth, capturing the mind of the whole English people, as did the official version of the English past. It never had behind it the great propagandist machinery of the nation-state and its institutions, as did the official version. The major figures in the common-law camp were firmly committed to this more orthodox, official view. Sir Edward Coke (1552–1634), for example, was Speaker of the House of Commons and then Attorney-General in

Elizabeth's reign, and went on to become the first to hold the official title of Lord Chief Justice of the King's Bench in the reign of James I. A modern authority has described Coke's outlook:

> Coke's mind, it is clear, was as nearly insular as a human being's could be. He saw the law he idolized as the immemorial custom of England, and he imagined it as being immemorial purely within the island. . . . The purely insular character of his ideas could hardly appear more clearly; the law is immemorial in Britain and ancient Continental law merely happens to agree with it.[4]

Coke's view of the past, contained in his *Institutes of the Laws of England* (1644), combined perfectly with the official view put forward in the Reformation statutes, and this view was dominant in England from the sixteenth to the twentieth century.

Both Coke and William Rastell, who was perhaps the first to put forward the 'Gothic' view, were wrong. But it was Coke, whose mind brooked no comparison of English law with that of any other country, who demonstrated more characteristically the nature of the small circle of logical argument which enclosed so tightly the English people's view of their past. The reason why Rastell and Coke were wrong is that neither of them was able to accept, from the national-erastian viewpoint which they shared, that some of the more important roots of English law were to be found in the Catholic Church, which christianized it, and in the Roman law.

It was immediately after the coming of Augustine in 597, sent by Pope Gregory the Great, that we get the first utterance of English law in the dooms (laws) of Æthelberht of Kent (601–4). They were written in the English or Anglo-Saxon language, but expressed in the Latin alphabet of the clerical writers. It was this marriage with Roman and Christian civilization which not only inspired the recording of these laws, but decided to a significant extent their content.[5] So the earliest laws of the English were inspired by and reflected the interests of the Universal Church alongside that of the secular kingdom. It was the presence of the same Church which led to the later improvement of Anglo-Saxon law and culture.[6] This was the fact which could not be assimilated into the thinking of the national-erastian mentality of common lawyers in the sixteenth and seventeenth centuries. Once admitted, it would have been sufficiently explosive to have broken for ever the small circle of logical argument which bound their view of the English past. For this meant that their law, legal institutions and culture, were neither national nor erastian in origin. The first non-Catholic scholar to detonate this explosion was F.W. Maitland in his 1887 lectures at Cambridge on *The Constitutional History of England* which were published posthumously in 1908. It was to be a long time into the twentieth century, however, before the work of this now acknowledgedly great scholar[7] became fully accepted in the academic world, and its impact had not even yet destroyed the great myth and the folklore associated with the official version of their past in the minds of many English people.

The Anglo-Saxon law, then, combined the particular needs of the English people with those of the Universal Church of which they formed part. This law survived the Norman Conquest and was confirmed by William the Conqueror. Indeed the Normans were some way behind the English in the making of written law.[8] This native law had always been administered, though, in different localities through local courts. It was in the reign of Henry II that English law was brought under central control and administered through the king's justices. It now became the same law *common* to all English people. This was the birth of the Common Law proper.[9] At the same time, it became separated from the Canon Law of the Church which also underwent a great development at this time. The Common Law was based on custom and precedent and, unlike the Canon Law, had no unified basis of theoretical philosophical or theological principles which could make it into a coherent whole. It was not studied as an academic subject until the fifteenth century[10] and did not have the same status as the universal Canon Law.

Maitland traced the Roman influence on English law from the early seventh century through to the thirteenth century, when he showed, for example, the influence of Azo, the famous Doctor of Canon Law at Bologna University, on Henry Bracton, the English judge and ecclesiastic who wrote the important *De Legibus et Consuetudinibus Angliae* (1235–59), the first treatise on the laws and customs of England. The Romanization of English law went on until the reign of Edward I whose legislation stopped it, the consequence being that from then on 'English law becomes always more insular, and English lawyers become more and more utterly ignorant of any law but their own'.[11] From this time, too, we see the emergence of lawyers as a large and powerful class in English

society: 'if our lawyers had known more of Roman law, our law –
in particular our land law – would never have become the
unprincipled labyrinth that it became.'[12] This was the class from
which the king's judges were chosen, and which was to emerge
triumphant in the English scene at the Reformation, when the
study of Canon Law was forbidden. It was the common-law attitude
of mind which played a central part in shaping the insular and
isolationist view of the English past. This, in turn, played a leading
part in creating the English attitude towards the outside world. We
can see its influence still at the end of the second millennium. Only
at the very end of the twentieth century did the New Labour
government bring the European Law of Human Rights (equivalent
in some ways to the medieval Canon Law) back into the centre of
the English legal system.

The Feudal Law was associated with an international system of
land tenure common to the various countries of medieval Europe.
In this system, land was held by a vassal from his lord in return for
a pledge of homage and certain services and obligations. In times of
danger or war, the main service was military in character when the
king could demand help of his chief tenants who, in turn, could
expect the same from their sub-tenants. There was much law
associated with this system, to ensure its proper functioning. It
existed in Anglo-Saxon England in embryonic form, but did not
achieve its fullest expression until the coming of the Normans,
when military demands became paramount and the castle and
'knightly quota' were firmly established in English society.
Feudalism was already in decline, however, by the thirteenth
century, when the needs of society had changed, paid soldiers were
taking the place of feudal conscripts and the king's courts had
already taken over the work of the old local land feudal courts.[13]
Similarly, the role of the knight gradually became ceremonial or
picturesque rather than of military importance.

The other system of international law in medieval England was
the Canon Law of the Catholic or Universal Church. In an
important sense this went back, as we have seen, to the coming of
Augustine. The earliest written law in England was concerned with
the protection of the Church in Kent during the time of
Æthelberht (601–4) who had been converted by Augustine.[14]
Likewise, Ine of Wessex (688–95) called a meeting of bishops and
secular advisers, with 'a great assembly of God's servants', to
establish 'just laws and just royal dooms' for 'the welfare of souls

and the state of our realm'.[15] This concern for the protection of the Church continued to accompany the development of English law up to and beyond the Norman Conquest. The influence of Roman law on English law during this period also came through the Church,[16] but it was in the late twelfth century that the distinctive Canon Law as we have come to know it came into being.

It was then that the law of the Universal Church was 'elaborated into a great system of jurisprudence',[17] based on the moral and spiritual principles of Christian teaching and covering the whole of England and beyond, to wherever the Church spread. This unifying legal system was centred on Rome, to which appeals could be sent from all the nations of Christendom for final decision at the papal court. It was the practical means by which the great unification of Christian Europe, based on the principles of Christian scholastic humanism, was created in the twelfth and thirteenth centuries.[18] The Canon Law became one of the great subjects of study in the European universities – particularly Paris and Bologna – alongside Theology, Philosophy and Medicine. Indeed R.W. Southern has recently reminded us that 'the combination of Roman and canon law formed the central core of all European legal studies'.[19]

England was very much part of this European unity. Lanfranc had been a teacher and theologian of European status, both at Bec and Canterbury, and before 1200 Canon Law was being taught at Oxford.[20] Maitland emphasizes the importance of Canon Law in the ordinary life of the English people: 'Canon law administered by the ecclesiastical courts regulated for all Englishmen some of the most important affairs of life . . . all matters relating to marriages and testaments. . . . A great deal of the ordinary private law even of our day can only be understood if we remember this.'[21]

The great struggle between Henry II and Archbishop Thomas Becket reflected the existence of the Canon Law alongside the Common Law of the king's courts. Canon Law was the more coherent, principled, structured and universally respected. It was a normal and very important part of the life of all English people up to the time of the Reformation. Later nationalist historians always regarded the rejection by the papal court of some appeal or other from England as an example of prejudiced 'foreign' interference with England's national independence and liberties, but in fact the papal court was dealing daily with hundreds of appeals from all over Europe, according to the universal principles of the Canon Law. Henry VIII was acting in a perfectly normal way when he appealed in the first place to the papal court on the divorce issue. The abnormality occurred in his reactions when that particular appeal was not granted. The Reformation Statutes of Appeals and Supremacy were the direct result of that decision. They changed things suddenly. Henry VIII forbade the study of Canon Law in England which was then isolated from Europe, from international law, for the first time in a millennium.

These statutes introduced for the first time what we may call the 'common-law attitude of mind' towards the English past, which was part of the official version, backed by all those powers of propaganda and persuasion (including terror tactics) which proved to be so effective. This attitude of mind and outlook was based on the Reformation statutes and the vested interests of the legal profession in England. It stressed the part played immemorially in England by the Common Law which was claimed to be of purely native origin. It denied the validity of the roles played by the Feudal Law and, even more importantly, the Canon Law, which had in fact both been essential parts of the life of England as of the rest of Europe. It omitted some facts altogether, such as the leading part which Archbishop Stephen Langton of Canterbury had played in the introduction of *Magna Carta* (1215). Langton's appointment by the Pope to the Archbishopric of Canterbury, according to the rules of Canon Law (but opposed by certain vested interests in England), had been the reason for the conflict between King John and the Papacy.[22] This common-law outlook took for granted the independent and self-sufficient character of legal life in England before the Reformation and regarded the Feudal and Canon laws as interference by foreign powers. Thomas Cromwell had seen the advantages of this legal outlook in helping him build the new nation-state of England. He had written that view of the past into the preambles of the Reformation statutes. It was another legacy which Cromwell handed onto the future generations of Protestant historians and it is another channel through which he influenced the history of historical writing in England.

The law was a particularly important influence in shaping English historiography, as well as all other aspects of English life. In the seventeenth century it played a central role in the constitutional conflicts of the age. The common lawyer identified the English Constitution and Parliament itself with the 'ancient custom' or Common Law of England, a concept which the Commons used from time to time in their arguments with the king.[23] An important advance in English historiography took place when Sir Henry Spelman and Robert Brady were able to examine the Feudal Law of western Europe and, in so doing, rediscovered the same Feudal Law in medieval England. This was a by-product of their attempt to show that the Common Law, on which Parliament based its rights, was not the only important sphere of law in the English past. The Feudal Law, emphasizing the king's authority, had played an important part, too, in creating English institutions and an understanding of it was needed to explain not only English law, but also the English Parliament itself.

There was no similar rediscovery, however, of the role of Canon Law in the English past, because none of the antagonists in the internal conflicts, political or religious, in seventeenth-century England were inclined to pursue this matter. It is another striking illustration of the way in which government-inspired action in the sixteenth century to erase completely the Catholic past from the minds of the English people was so successful. Spelman, in particular, had one of the most perceptive and inquiring minds among English historians, but even he did absolutely nothing to rediscover the much more important sphere of Canon Law in the life of medieval England. It is also an example of the way in which historians sometimes need a sufficiently good reason to pursue their researches, leading to important discoveries. Certainly it is a rather chilling reminder of the extent to which a closed-mind mentality was involved in that small circle of logical argument which characterized the official version, and of the isolation and insularity of English thought at this period. Anything connected with 'Popery' was a taboo subject. Anyone delving into any aspect of the Catholic past was likely to be accused of 'Popish tendencies', which could have serious repercussions.[24]

The proper appreciation of the role of Canon Law in the English past was more important than the discovery of the Feudal Law as a key to an understanding of that past. The law of the Church had had a much longer and greater influence on the lives of all English people. It had been the inspiration behind the very birth of written English law at the dawn of English history. A great achievement of twentieth-century medieval scholarship in England has been the recognition of the part played by the papal jurisdiction and the Canon Law in the life and development of England itself and in uniting it with Europe. Nor did the Canon Law, unlike the Feudal

Law, decline in influence and importance in the later medieval period. It remained a vital part of English life up to 1533.[25]

Feudal Law in England was certainly analogous and contemporary with its counterpart on the Continent. Advances in scholarship on the English feudal system came about as a result of the study by Spelman and Brady of similar feudal institutions in Lombardy and Normandy.[26] The Canon Law system, however, was not simply analogous and contemporary with its European counterpart over a much longer time, but was actually and essentially a working part of that wider system. We cannot separate them even for the purpose of making comparisons. The Canon Law system in England, like the English Church itself, functioned only as part of the greater whole of Christendom, centred on the Papacy in Rome, wherein lay the only authority capable of appointing the bishops and archbishops in England. We might find an English feudal lord operating in a purely English context. The whole position and function of an English bishop at the same period depended on his place in that wider ecclesiastical system, having its centre in Rome.

In his specialized work on 'the relations of the English Church with the centre of Church government in Rome', Professor C.R. Cheney observed, concerning the English clergy: 'Their conception of the Church required a Church of which the pope was doctrinal head and in which government involved constant intervention by Rome in the affairs of the provinces. There must be a pope – he held the plenitude of power.'[27] The same scholar also noticed that, 'a study of the decretal collections shows that England provided a great deal of the judicial business which gave rise to decretals and that Englishmen played a large part of their collection.'[28]

Z.N. Brooke showed in his important work, *The English Church and the Papacy*, that in the eleventh and twelfth centuries 'the law of the Church, the whole law and not a selected part of it, was the law of the English Church', and 'as I now see it, the English Church was in mind at one with the Church as a whole throughout this period'.[29] W.A. Pantin gave evidence of the same state of affairs in the fourteenth century.[30] W.T. Waugh showed that the 'dealings of Englishmen with Rome', as evidenced from 'the number of entries concerning England in the papal registers', suffered no 'appreciable diminution' by the Statute of Praemunire in 1393.[31] F.W. Maitland, who started all the scholarship on the subject in the twentieth century, had turned to the leading English canonist of the fifteenth century to reveal his 'conservative curialism' and his complete recognition of the papal ecclesiastical jurisdiction over the Church in England.[32]

The Canon Law, then, reflected the unity of the Catholic Church, centred on the Papacy. The proper study of this legal system would have been the quickest route for post-Reformation historians towards a proper understanding of the nature of the medieval Church as essentially part of the Universal Church and of England as essentially part of the wider world of Christendom. This route was blocked effectively, however, by Henry VIII's attack on the Canon Law and his refusal to allow it to be studied henceforth in England. It was a necessary action by the Henrician revolutionary regime to 'cover its tracks', and again it was extremely effective. Its tracks were covered for four centuries, as far as the academic world was concerned, and are still covered as far as most English 'lay' people are concerned.

The statutes of the Reformation Parliament transferred complete control over the Church from the Papacy to the king in England. At the same time, the 'King's Ecclesiastical Law' was substituted for the Canon Law of the Universal Church. Overnight, so to speak, the English Church became a self-contained body, isolated from the wider Church and ruled over by the head of the new nation-state. F.W. Maitland considered that no step that Henry took was more 'momentous' for England.[33] From now on, the Common Law was to be supreme and the secular sphere dominant at the expense of the religious. It started the process of secularization of life in modern England. The common lawyers, with their vested interest in the revolution, were going to play an important part in maintaining the official view of the English past.

Paradoxically, the common lawyers, who had gained so much from the Henrician Reformation and its introduction of the idea of royal supremacy, found themselves in the seventeenth century on the side of Parliament in the arguments between it and the Stuart kings. For, in those arguments, some of the Commons laid great stress on the idea that the law – the Common Law of England – was older than the monarchy itself, and therefore superior to it in authority. One by-product of these arguments, as the Commons became more confident in their status, was that the prestige of the Common Law became even greater. It became connected in the minds of English people with their nation's 'freedom' from 'arbitrary government' as well as from 'foreign interference' and

'Popery'. This meant that the common lawyers' view of the past was impressed still more on the 'English mind'. This was the age in which the law had its most important influence in shaping people's thoughts about the past.[34] It was preparing the soil for the seed of the Whig interpretation of history which was contained in Burnet's *History of the Reformation* (1679–81). While looking for precedents to show that their law had always been above the king, the common lawyers were intent also to prove that it had been superior to any other type of law which may have intruded itself, unwantedly, into English life. This strengthened again the closed-mind mentality, isolationism and insularity of the English outlook on its own past and on the outside world. It prohibited any attempt to recognize the wider framework of life and thought in which their ancestors had lived.

The refusal of the common lawyers to see the Feudal Law in England against the continental background is best interpreted as an implication of their general view of English history in terms of a closed system in which the Common Law reigned supreme. Their opposition to the Canon Law, however, contained much more than this. The Canon Law had remained a living part of English life up to 1533 and was still very much alive in the rest of Europe. Moreover, the rejection of this law had formed a central part of the Reformation statutes. The whole process of the Reformation in England began over the Divorce Question and the king's failure to get his own way in this matter of Canon Law. The common lawyers owed their predominant position in England to these statutes which had ousted the Canon Law and left the legal field in England clear for them.

Consequently, the refusal to recognize the position of Canon Law in medieval England, and to see it in its European setting, was much more definite and conscious, and therefore more rigid and unyielding, than their attitude to the Feudal Law, which was, in any case, of only academic interest in the seventeenth century. Similarly, the vested interests of the established Church and of those landed gentry who had profited from the Dissolution of the Monasteries (and who dispensed law in the localities) were thrown against any attempt to shake the official view of the past. To have attempted to interfere with this would have seemed like treason and treachery in a society which was geared and committed to the Protestant cause and which was shaken by emotionally charged rumours of 'Popish Plots'. This explains why great progress was made in the seventeenth century towards a better understanding of the feudal system in medieval

England, whereas no progress was made in historical writing on the place of the Canon Law in that same age – with one obscure exception which I shall consider below.

The two leading and most powerful common lawyers expressed their attitude to the question in a work significantly entitled, *England's Independency upon the Papal Power Historically & Judicially Stated. By Sir John Davis, Attorney General in Ireland. And by Sir Edward Coke, Lord Chief Justice in England . . . For the Convincing of our English Romanists & Confirming of those who are yet unperverted to the Court or Church of Rome* (1674). Sir John Davis's description of the Common Law in another work is very illuminating and significant:

Briefly, it is so framed and fitted to the nature and disposition of this people, as we may probably say it is connatural to the Nation, so as it cannot possibly be ruled by any other Law. This Law therefore doth demonstrate the strength of wit and reason and self-sufficiency which hath been always in the People of this Land, which have made their own Laws out of their wisdome and experience, (like a Silkworm that formeth all her web out of her self onely) not begging or borrowing a form of a Commonweal either from *Rome* or from *Greece* as all other Nations of *Europe* have done; but having sufficient provision of law and justice within the Land, have no need *Justitiam, & Judicium ab alienigenis emendicare*, as King John wrote most nobly to Pope Innocent the Third. Matth. Paris. Mag. p. 215. En populus sapiens & intelligens, gens magna: as it is said of God's chosen people. 4. Deut.[35]

This passage brings together, as in a jigsaw, the component pieces which made up the picture of the intelligent Englishman's outlook on his past and on the world around him in the second half of the seventeenth century: the Common Law, purely of native origin, showing forth the superiority of the English in wisdom and self-sufficiency; isolationism, English civilisation being a product only of native intelligence, not based, as the rest of European civilization was, on the imported values of Greece and Rome; the English, a truly 'great' people, in fact, God's 'chosen people'.

It is not difficult to see how such appeals to national pride enlisted the enormous power of English nationalism onto the side of the official view of the English past, for nationalism and Protestantism were mutually supportive in the sixteenth century.[36]

The compelling power of this view over the English people was that it told them what they wanted to hear. Conversely, the great problem facing historians who, much later, challenged this view was to get people to see what they did not want to see.[37]

Another leading common lawyer, Sir Matthew Hale, who wrote *The History of the Common Law of England. Written by a Learned Hand* (1713), stated that,

> all the Strength that either the Papal or Imperial Laws have obtained in this Kingdom, is only because they have been received and admitted either by Consent of Parliament, and so are part of the Statute Laws of the Kingdom, or else by immemorial Usage and Custom in some particular Cases and Courts and no otherwise.[38]

This was asserting that no other system of law had ever existed in England by its own authority.

Ecclesiastical historians also had a vested interest in disowning the Canon Law of the past. Nowhere, perhaps, is the general insularity of English historical thought from the Reformation up to the twentieth century more apparent than in the series of *Concilia*, the scholarly collections of ecclesiastical councils and synods of the medieval period, made by ecclesiastical historians in England. These also provide us with a perfect example of the way in which the availability of original documents does not in itself guarantee a proper understanding of historical truth. The original documents can be misread and misunderstood if there is no proper understanding of the context in which they were written and of the assumptions of thought which lie behind them. The failure of interpretation is even more significant when weighed, as in this case, against the remarkable erudition and the high standard of detailed scholarship achieved in these collections.

The distinguished names associated with them are Sir Henry Spelman (the *Concilia*, 1639), Bishop White Kennett (*Ecclesiastical Synods*, 1701), Bishop Edmund Gibson (*Synodus Anglicana*, 1702; *Codex Juris Ecclesiastici Anglicani*, 1713), David Wilkins (the *Concilia*, 1737) and Haddan and Stubbs (*Councils and Ecclesiastical Documents*, 1869–73), all of whom added greatly to the source materials available for the study of the medieval Church in England. Yet the advances in historical technique and knowledge manifested in these works failed altogether to affect the old framework of insular thought about the nature of the Church in medieval England. The mass of documentation was fitted neatly into the old official view which remained completely undisturbed in its main aspects – and this over a period of more than two centuries.

Each of these great collections was based on the ones that went before. On the question of the origins of the 'independent' British Church, for example, Wilkins reprinted the mistaken speculations made by Spelman a century earlier[39] and also included some apocryphal documents at the beginning of his first volume to support these contentions.[40] White Kennett's historical scholarship was marred by his insistence upon the 'ancient independence of the British Church before it succumbed to Papal tyranny'.[41] William Wake, concerned to demonstrate the 'King's Ecclesiastical Supremacy', and 'the authority of Christian Princes over their Ecclesiastical Synods',[42] saw the presence of papal authority in medieval England as an unjustified usurpation upon the regal control which had been exercised over the old British Protestant Church.[43] In the *Concilia* of 1737, David Wilkins was 'not concerned with the part taken by the English delegations at the General Councils', for the 'European point of view . . . was entirely foreign to him'.[44]

Most significant of all is the case of William Stubbs (1825–1901),[45] a cleric who became Regius Professor of Modern History at Oxford (1866) and was later appointed to the bishopric of Chester (1884) and then Oxford (1888). There is no doubting the scholarly distinction of Stubbs who 'may be said to have created the discipline of English medieval history single-handed'.[46] He has been accredited quite recently – and wrongly in my view[47] – with being the first to place the study of history in England on a professional basis by introducing the critical methodology of the German, Ranke.[48] Stubbs edited eighteen volumes of medieval texts for the Rolls Series. His two main works, *Select Charter and other illustrations of English Constitutional History to 1307* (1870) and the *Constitutional History of England* (3 vols, 1874–8), provided the pattern and methodology for English medieval studies in the Universities for the first half of the twentieth century. The latter work has been described as 'one of the most astonishing achievements of the Victorian mind'.[49] The reputation of this scholar played no small part in maintaining the official view of the past in academic circles. Undergraduates trained in his ideas were to provide the nucleus of the teaching profession in the public and grammar schools for the next half-century. It was in the face of such weighty opposition that F.W. Maitland made his great breakthrough in historical understanding of the nature and place of the Canon Law in medieval England in 1898.[50]

Yet Stubbs was quite monumentally wrong about the nature of medieval England and the English Church at that period. He failed to see the wood for the trees in his great and detailed knowledge. He still thought that medieval England was an independent nation, buttressed by an autonomous national Church. One later writer attributes this error to Stubbs' 'uncritical attitude towards legal tradition',[51] while another suggests that he was 'always first and foremost a cleric, and bound by his profession to receive the clerical tradition'.[52] Another reason may be that he was much influenced by Ranke and the latter 'believed that the nation was the divinely created unit at work within universal history, with each nation having its own appointed moment of destiny'.[53] The myth of the 'elect people', which was so much a part of the official view of the English past, could have had a special effect on Stubbs, who was intent on showing the progressive development of English institutions from their 'origins' in the German forests. Whatever the reason, we are forcibly reminded that sometimes the attitude of mind of the historian can be more important than his detailed scholarship in improving our understanding of the past.

The two great contributions to feudal studies in the seventeenth century were made by Sir Henry Spelman[54] and Robert Brady. Spelman was the leading light in the Society of Antiquaries which, at the beginning of the seventeenth century, included men of the calibre of John Selden and Sir Robert Cotton, and which first introduced the analysis of institutions and laws, as opposed to simple narration, into English historical writing. Spelman had more historical insight than most other historians of the century.[55] It was he who inaugurated a proper understanding of the Feudal Law in medieval England by seeing it as part of a wider European phenomenon and making comparisons between the system in England and that on the Continent[56] – a remarkable achievement in the light of English insularity of mind at this period. It is again eloquent of the religious climate of the age that this remarkable scholar, who 'avoided many of the mistakes of other historians',[57] failed to make any breakthrough in the insular framework surrounding ecclesiastical studies. In his famous *Concilia* we find the man who had illumined the social and economic aspects of medieval England fully accepting the idea of an early Protestant

Church, together with a self-contained autonomous system of ecclesiastical law in medieval England.[58]

Robert Brady,[59] physician turned historian at Cambridge, was a strong supporter of the monarchy and his contribution to feudal studies was guided by his interest in the constitutional conflict between king and Parliament in the later Stuart period.[60] It was in opposition to the Whig argument that the Common Law was above the royal authority and had always been paramount in England that Brady turned to the field of Feudal Law to demonstrate the character of this international system and its importance in the life of medieval England and to the central authority of the monarchy. But whereas the Feudal Law might be invoked to buttress the rights of monarchy against the claims of Common Law, the universal Canon Law of the Church could be invoked only to set limits to those rights, as it had done effectively in English history up to 1534. Therefore it was not invoked.

Brady, who had become Master of Caius College, Cambridge, attacked the Canon Law in conventional manner, as the intrusion of a foreign influence upon the powers of monarchy and upon the original purity of the Feudal Law. This intrusion had been caused, he argued, by the confusion and weak monarchy during Stephen's reign in the twelfth century.[61] So far was Brady from recognizing the Canon Law in its proper role as a normal, accepted and important feature of English life up to the time of the Reformation, and so far was he from understanding the nature of England before the Reformation and the true character of that event as a revolution in the history of England.[62]

The whole weight of the ruling influences in seventeenth-century England was against the proper understanding of the position of the Canon Law in England in the medieval period. Apart from the ecclesiastical historians and the common lawyers themselves, the common-law approach to the past was shared by all Protestant England. It was a national assumption of thought which seemed impregnable.

One gleam of historical insight into this area came indirectly and unintentionally. For out of the clash between Whigs and Non-Jurors at the end of the century, there flew a spark of understanding of the vital role of Canon Law in the English past. The Non-Jurors resented the extent to which Church law of any kind had been pushed out of the picture by the common lawyers, to their own advantage and to the diminution of all

Church authority. This led Jeremy Collier to an interesting discussion of the common lawyers' capacity for writing history. When confronted by the 'precedents' put forward by the common lawyer and Lord Chief Justice, Edmund Coke, for State control of the Church, Collier replied that, 'the learned of this profession are generally unqualified to determine in the question of the king's spiritual supremacy' because 'they lay the whole stress of the argument upon the opinions of men of their profession; upon precents in temporal courts, and provisions in parliament'. They were 'unskilled in divinity', 'unacquainted with the history of the Church', and 'unacquainted with the sentiments and practice of the primitive Church'.[63] This was, indeed, the first and very significant criticism of the common-law outlook on the English past made by an English Protestant.

Collier himself, when dealing with a topic which had overtones of a 'State versus Church' issue, could sometimes offer slight, though penetrating comments on the working of the ecclesiastical law in medieval England. For instance, when dealing with the controversy between Thomas Becket and Henry II, he turned to the Canon Law in order to explain and defend Becket's position at one point:

> the trial of clerks in the king's courts was expressly condemned by pope Alexander. Now considering the maxim then current, such a censure must needs have had great force in misleading the archbishop's judgment: for by the canon law, it is expressly determined that the orders of the see of Rome are to be observed in all parts of Christendom.[64]

This statement contains, by implication at least, a recognition of the international character of the Canon Law, its assertion of the headship of the Papacy and of the fact that this was the system as it was understood by Becket. It would have been difficult, if the question had been pressed, to reconcile this historical explanation of Becket's attitude as Archbishop of Canterbury with the conventional concept of a national, independent ecclesiastical jurisdiction in medieval England. The question was not pressed because neither Collier nor his erastian opponents were interested in drawing the general conclusion which it implied. They did not *want to see* the logical conclusion. Apart from such isolated anti-erastian asides, Collier's main narrative was written completely within the conventional framework of the autonomous English Church.

It seemed that there was nobody in seventeenth-century England with the will, as well as the knowledge, to break the conventional insularity of thought on this subject which was an important key to the proper understanding of the English past. The commonly held assumption of thought in this area seemed impenetrable.

Here we come to an interesting phenomenon in the history of historical writing in England – a historical work which has been completely unnoticed. It illustrates the way in which an individual, isolated scholar can sometimes make a contribution which is so far ahead of its own time, so much against the prevailing assumptions of his society, that it can remain hidden in obscurity until centuries later.

In 1687 a particular contribution was made towards Reformation studies, which in fact went further than any other work written in England (apart from John Lingard's *History*) during the intervening centuries to anticipate the findings of twentieth-century academic scholarship. This extraordinary achievement was made possible because someone actually used the key of the Canon Law to interpret the English past. The work was published at the one time during these centuries when it was possible for such a view of the past to have appeared at all in England. This was during the short, three-year interval (1655–8) when James II was on the throne and encouraging a very short-lived period of Catholic scholarship at Oxford and Cambridge.[65] Within two years this attempt foundered and its supporters suffered renewed persecution or exile. Yet the work in question anticipated the celebrated work of F.W. Maitland in English legal history by two centuries. The writer himself has been all but unknown to English historians, warranting the merest mention in general histories of the period, only as an example of 'Roman Catholic encroachments during James II's reign'.[66] The work itself has never been mentioned at all. Neither Maitland nor Lingard, the founder of modern historiography in England, knew anything about it.

Obadiah Walker (1616–99) is in fact one of the very interesting personalities in English history of the seventeenth century. He was a very versatile man, making incursions into many different fields of study and inquiry, which were marked with a startling degree of fresh insight. He wrote the purely historical notes to the *Life of Alfred* (1678), the scientific *Consideration on Optics* (1679) and part of the first volume, dealing with Greenland and Russia, of Pitt's *English Atlas* (1680). He also wrote a work on rhetoric and *Education, Especially of a Young Gentleman* (1673), which went to six editions and made him a 'writer of some note on liberal education'.[66] There has never been an English study of him, but the French author of the only modern treatment of him describes him as an economist, a humanist, a philosopher and a notable theologian.[67] Burnet made it his business to know of him,[68] but no modern writer has noticed his work on the Reformation.

Walker, a Yorkshireman from Darfield, near Barnsley, had been a disciple at Oxford of Abraham Woodhead, a theologian and mathematician who was also interested in history and had been converted to Catholicism in about 1650. As an ardent royalist in the Civil War, Walker had been expelled from Oxford under the Cromwellian regime and had travelled widely on the Continent. He was reinstated at the Restoration to his fellowship at University College, becoming a close friend of Anthony Wood and being largely responsible for getting the latter's *Historia et Antiquitates Univ. Oxon*, published in 1674. Walker's prestige as a writer, educator and administrator earned him the unanimous support of the fellows of University College and he was elected Master in 1676.

Several fellows of the Oxford colleges had been expelled for becoming Catholics at this time[69] and after Walker's election to the Mastership, rumours began to grow around him. He had in fact become a Catholic in 1673. An example of the sensitivity of public feeling had occurred already when Richard Reeves, 'a suspected Papist', was expelled from Magdalen College in 1673. The exponents of the theory of an early British Protestant Church were natural antagonists of the Papal representative, St Augustine, and had accused the latter of procuring the murder of Celtic monks at Bangor.[70] One of the chief charges levelled against Reeves was that he had written a letter in which he had 'defended . . . St. Austen the monk his not consenting or knowing of the death of the monks of Bangor . . . but that St. Austen was dead before that time'.[71]

In 1678 Walker edited a work entitled *Alfredi Magni Anglorum regis*, to which he contributed a preface and notes. Immediately he was violently attacked for supporting, in these notes, that an *entente* had existed between the Pope and King Alfred, and for wanting in this manner to justify the authority of the Papacy in England at this period. In fact the only 'crime' committed in these notes is an indication that King Alfred the Great was on friendly terms with the Pope and respected him greatly. The sequel to this episode is related by Anthony Wood who tells us:

In the latter end of this month Octob. 1678 Mr. Walker, head of Universitie College, accused openlie in the parliament house for a papist . . . that he expressed himselfe popishly affected in many things in his notes on King Alfred's life written by Sir John Spelman – as, thus, Sir John Spelman saith that 'King Alfred fell out with the pope', and that 'they could not agree together'. Mr. Walker saith in his notes and proves it that they did agree and that King Alfred had a great respect for him. . . . So that had not Mr. Walker a friend in the house who stood up for him, he would have had a messinger sent for him.[72]

Another attack was made upon Walker's historical notes and on Wood's *History of Oxford* in Parliament in the spring of 1679 by Sir Harbottle Grimston, for 'many unseemly things of the reformation said'. Gilbert Burnet seems to have been the motivating force behind this attack.[73]

Walker's most productive period of historical writing was between 1681 and 1688. This obviously coincided with a more favourable political climate. During these years the dangers of the Popish Plot scare and the Exclusion Bill crisis had passed. Charles II, riding on a short-term wave of popularity after the failure of the Rye House Plot,[74] was able to dissolve Parliament in 1681. When James II came to the throne in 1685 the way was open, for the first time since the Reformation, for the publication of books which ran counter to the official view. In 1686 Walker openly declared that he was a Catholic, and others followed suit at Oxford. They received the protection of James II, who in October of that year licensed Walker to print 'Romanist' books at Oxford. In 1685 Walker's *Life of Christ* was censured by defenders of the Establishment and the Vice-Chancellor's order of prohibition was obtained against it, but James himself arrived in Oxford a few days later and publicly approved of the work. Walker's series of tracts entitled the *Theses on Church Government* appeared in 1687 and it is with one of these in particular that we shall be concerned.

Walker's peculiar position as Catholic head of an Anglican college came to an end with the Revolution of 1688. In Wood's diary, under 14 December 1688, we find 'F. news that Mr. Obadiah Walker was seized and committed . . . to Maidstone gaole'.[75] In 1689 a mandate was sent out against Walker as suspected of high treason[76] because he had changed his religion and led others to do the same. He was sent to the Tower where he remained until 1690.

After this Walker fades completely from the public scene. The next we hear of him is in the following extract in the diary of Thomas Hearne in 1695:

> After Mr. Walker was turned out of University coll. for being a papist, he lived obscurely in London, his chief maintenance being from the contributions of some of his old friends and acquaintances; amongst whom was Dr. Radcliff who (out of a grateful remembrance of favours received from him in the College) sent him once a year a new suit of clothes with ten broad pieces, and a dozen bottles of the richest Canary to support his drooping spirits. The Dr. Hudson (from whom I received this story) was informed by Dr. Radcliff himself.[77]

The last trace I can find of Walker is a cheerful letter from him to Ralph Thoresby, the noted antiquarian, in 1695 in which he sent the latter some coins of historical interest, promised his best services and congratulated him on 'the augmentation of your plentiful collection, and wishing you still more'.[78] Walker died in London in 1699.

Between 1686 and 1687 there appeared a series of tracts on Church government, written by Walker, among which is one of special interest to our theme. It is entitled *Church Government, part V, a Relation of the English Reformation and the lawfulness thereof, examined by the Theses deliver'd in the four former Parts*, and was published at Oxford in 1687.

The significance of this work, hidden away among the dusty shelves of an old library, derives from the fact that it treats the Reformation in purely legalistic and institutional terms, which allows of a much greater degree of detachment from its detailed 'internal' events than that afforded by the usual approach. This was the sort of book which Henry VIII and Cromwell had attempted to block from ever appearing in England, by their banning of the study of Canon Law in this country. Walker concentrated on certain institutional features of the movement which had been lost sight of amid the polemical controversies of such issues as the Divorce Question or the Dissolution of the Monasteries. He was not concerned with personalities in the movement. Walker approached the matter in the same way as did F.W. Maitland, the legal historian, two centuries later. Like Maitland, he showed in a perfectly calm and logical manner that the Revolution in England constituted a fundamental revolution and complete break with the past and with the ecclesiastical structure and the legal system which had always existed in England before.

In the seventeenth century narrative history was the crude product of a 'scissors and paste' type of approach. It was a kind of stringing together of passages almost directly transcribed from previous writers of one's own side and almost completely devoid of any serious attempt to produce either independent narrative or some kind of historical analysis of laws and institutions. There had emerged, however, from the activities of the Society of Antiquaries at the beginning of the century – when scholars such as Spelman, Selden and Sir Robert Cotton provided the main impetus – a new kind of historical work: 'It was a kind of history that went behind the chroniclers, and surpassed the old narrations by the analysis of institutions and laws.'[79] It took historical scholarship aside from the usual cut and thrust of polemical history. An important moment for the history of historiography was to be when these two forms of historical writing – the narrative and the critical analysis – came together to form the modern vehicle of historical scholarship.[80] This did not happen in the seventeenth century, when the two forms of historical writing were kept apart and were used by different types of people – the scholars on one side and the propagandists on the other. Burnet was outstanding among the latter because he had brought materials from other chroniclers together into a cohesive and dramatic form through which he expressed his propagandist epic in a heightened form. Walker's tract was in the scholarly tradition.

Walker was not concerned to write narrative history in his work on the Reformation; neither did he borrow from the chroniclers. His was the first work produced in England on the Reformation which was an objective analysis of ecclesiastical laws and institutions, and the manner in which they changed at this turning-point in English history. It was the first time in England since Henry VIII had forbidden the study of Canon Law that a writer actually used this law as a key to explain what had happened in the Reformation. In this way Walker was able to by-pass the conventional framework of thought within which the old chronicles had been hidden behind the isolationist, erastian and nationalist viewpoint of ecclesiastical historians and common lawyers. Walker supplied a new type of viewing mechanism, so to speak, which was needed to place the previously distorted picture into perspective.

We may notice, in the first place, that Walker was not interested in arguing polemically in the usual way about the internal events of the Reformation itself. This was quite new. We learn, for instance, that Henry sought the divorce 'whether because scrupulous in Conscience . . . or whether because much enamoured of another Lady, *Ann Bullen*'[81] and Walker was not a bit concerned to prove the point, one way or the other. On the very controversial question of the consummation of Prince Arthur's marriage with Catherine of Aragon, Walker commented, 'you may see, if you have the curiosity, what is said *for* the consummation of that marriage in *Fox* . . . p. 958. Edit. 610, *against* it in *Sanders de Schism* Angl. I. p. 40'.[82] Again the matter is left to the reader. For Walker, this matter, which had been made into a *cause célèbre* by all previous historians, was merely a digression from his main theme: 'I have made this Digression to shew you the diversity of opinions, which was in this difficult matter that you may see the Pope stood not alone in his judgement: and how the several interests of several times justified and condemned the same thing.'[83] The whole tone of detached interest here is completely different from that of all previous writing on these controversial issues of the Reformation.

Walker's main task was to analyse the nature of ecclesiastical institutions in pre-Reformation England. He showed that the Church in England had been part of the Universal Church and that it depended on and accepted the spiritual and ecclesiastical authority of the Papacy. Commenting on the precedents for anti-papal legislation put forward by Protestant historians, Walker showed that there certainly had been conflicts between several of the English kings and the Papacy in medieval England. These conflicts, however, had not been about the rights of papal authority to exist in England, but about the precise limits of the Papacy's spiritual authority and the king's secular authority, which each recognized in the other. There had been no question of the English monarchy denying papal authority. It was accepted as part of the normal life of English people.

So Walker described the Reformation, with the Act of Supremacy and the Act against Appeals, as a complete revolution in English history, changing the nature of ecclesiastical institutions and forcing a complete break with the past. He noted that the official view was that '*Henry* the Eighth made no new Law . . . that these Statutes of Henry the Eighth were only declarative of old Law, not enactive of new Law'[84] and that this was backed by all the leading common lawyers of the day from the Lord Chief Justice of England down to the most ordinary person. Walker claimed that they were all wrong, all making a huge mistake in their understanding of the English past. The interesting fact is that he was right and everybody else was wrong.

The most famous of the medieval statutes which had been used from the time of the Henrician government itself, to demonstrate that the papal authority had not been acknowledged as valid by medieval English people, were the various Statutes of Provisors and Praemunire, especially the 'great' statute of 1393. The official version of that statute had been used to frighten the clergy into submission in 1529–30. All Protestant historians had used it since then as clear and incontrovertible evidence of the strong feelings of national independence and autonomy being expressed against the usurping claims of the Papacy to authority in England. Walker went to the heart of the matter immediately, by making a detailed and full-scale analysis of the issues involved in these particular statutes.

Certainly the statute of 1393 had prohibited the bringing of Bulls or Sentences of Excommunication from Rome, but this had been with reference only to certain cases where the proper temporal rights of the king, which the Papacy recognized to be in the monarchy, were thought to have been infringed. Walker pointed out that neither the king nor Parliament questioned for a moment the papal authority in spiritual matters in England. He wrote:

Again you may find perhaps Appeals, Bulls &c. prohibited in general, without the King's consent first obtained therto: But this is not out of an intention of suppressing all such Appeals of Ecclesiastical Law or Censures whatsoever coming from the Pope or other Spiritual Authority abroad, or out of an intention of denying these in several cases to be rightfully belonging unto them; but only out of an intention to examine them first, whether any thing were contained in them prejudicial to the Temporal or Civil Rights, and Emoluments, and Priviledges of the Prince and of his Subjects, that the Mitre not encroach upon the Crown; both which have their certain limits of Jurisdiction, and may do wrong one to the other. Such authority as this (then) in Church matters you may find exercised by former Princes of England; or perhaps some other power used by them against the Church, and defended by the common lawyers of those days, more than is justifiable. But, on the other hand, I think you will not find either assumed by the Prince or allowed to him by any Statutes before the time of *Henry* the Eighth, such Powers in Ecclesiastical matters, as some of these following. Namely a *Power* to correct and reform all Errors and Heresies in Religion. . . . A *Power* to restrain all Forreign Appeals and Censures from thence, not only in all Cases mixt with the Interests of the Temporal Government, but also in all matters meerly Spiritual and of Ecclesiastical Cognizance.[85]

Such passages as this held the key to the proper interpretation of the ecclesiastical institutions of the medieval period and no modern historian has stated the case better. The question of the Statutes of Provisors and Praemunire was seen correctly for the first time in England since the Reformation, in terms of a legal issue between the two mutually recognized authorities – the universally accepted spiritual authority of the Papacy and the nationally accepted temporal authority of the king – as to where exactly the dividing line between their spheres of jurisdiction lay. This should be compared with the conventional terms of interpretation, still popular in the twentieth century, of a Protestant-nationalist attempt to reject the Pope's spiritual authority in England.

The real problem of understanding involved in this matter was a question of different assumptions of thought. The medieval English people simply assumed that the two authorities, spiritual and temporal, existed side by side, and there was no problem normally in having a dual allegiance, to Pope and king, in different areas of life. Post-Reformation English people gradually forgot the concept of dual allegiance. Within the very different context in which they now lived their lives – that of the all-powerful nation-state in which only one authority covered every aspect of life – they learned a totally different set of assumptions of thought. This new set regarded anything other than complete and total obedience to the king in all things as treason and treachery. Soon it became impossible for people living in post-Reformation England to understand the thinking of their ancestors. The problem was solved for them by government propaganda and a long series of historians who simply read their new way of thinking back into the minds and writings of people of the past. It always needs a creative jump of the imagination to understand the assumptions of thought endemic in people who are different from ourselves, whether the difference is in historical or geographical terms. Such imaginative creativity is at the centre of historical work.

Walker's tract was, of course, intended to serve a religious interest. Its whole point was to show that, according to the premises of Church government he had described in the preceding tracts, the whole concept of the royal supremacy over the Church was invalid and unlawful, judged against the universal code of law which had governed Church life. Walker's aim was religious, but his analysis was correct and was repeated two centuries later by F.W. Maitland, who felt obliged to disarm opposition by stating that he had no religious interest to declare.[86] This also indicates that a religious interest in itself is not the same as prejudice, as long as there is self-knowledge and a primary concern for the truth in the historian's mind. Indeed, in these circumstances, such interest can be a positive spur to uncovering the truth, as it was in Walker's case.

Walker rightly saw the assertion of the royal supremacy as the centre-piece[87] of the Reformation in England, the lynch-pin of the whole movement. He was able to show that it was carried out by government as an act of State.[88] The significance of this tract lies in the fact that Walker adopted a method of approach to the Reformation – along legal and institutional lines – which enabled him to produce a work of real historiographical significance. His approach lifted his work from the battlefield of polemics to the level of genuine historical understanding of the past.

Walker's general approach to his subject and the arguments he used were to be repeated two centuries later by the great English legal historian, F.W. Maitland, in his *Roman Canon Law in the Church of England* (1898), which immediately involved him in a dispute with the learned Bishop William Stubbs and indeed with the ecclesiastical and legal professions.[89] Maitland had expected this and had already asserted his complete disinterest in the religous aspects of the question. During the intervening two hundred years, and indeed until now, Walker's tracts have remained completely unnoticed. They exemplify the way in which historical discoveries or understandings sometimes have to be repeated much later, because the climate of the age – the social, religious and political pressures – may be too inhospitable to allow the first revelation. Seventeenth-century society was not able to look frankly and realistically at its medieval past. There were too many vested interests involved in maintaining the official view, which confined that past within an isolated, nationalistic and insular framework. That view was now an assumption of thought in English society. As such, it was not to be challenged. Obadiah Walker's work, like the man himself, was buried in obscure silence. There is some satisfaction in being able to break the silence on his behalf. As Kierkegaard said, 'A living man is certain to stop talking. But once a dead man begins calling out (instead of keeping quiet as is usually the case) then who is to silence him?'

FOUR

The Medieval Background to Reformation Historiography

THE ROLE OF PERSPECTIVE IN HISTORICAL UNDERSTANDING

It was impossible for English historians to understand the true nature of the English Reformation as a revolution in English history until they had first known and understood the character of medieval England. The national-erastian and isolationist view of the English past emerged originally from the Reformation statutes themselves. It had then been applied retrospectively to the Anglo-Saxon and medieval periods in an *a priori* manner by the Reformers themselves. This had given a theoretical and logical unity to their interpretation of the whole of English history. The circle of argument was logical, but always too small to take into account the real life and the real history of the English people. It was lacking in historical perspective and therein lay its falsity. The isolation of the English after the Reformation, however, contributed greatly to the impenetrability of this view of their past.

The logical circle of argument contained in this theory became increasingly rigid and impenetrable when it was repeated by English historians, ecclesiastics, common lawyers and the Establishment itself over the next three centuries, until it became an assumption of thought, something taken for granted, something which seemed so obviously true and good for the English nation that no one was allowed to contract out of it and speak or write in opposition to it. It was buttressed by social and political persecution against anyone who deviated from it. Certain attitudes of mind resulted – superiority, insularity, a feeling of separation from others, unwillingness to learn from outsiders. These attitudes were cemented by national success in a series of wars against European neighbours and in acquiring a vast empire overseas over the next three centuries.

This view of their past was able to retain its force partly because English historians lacked an interest in and understanding of the period preceding the Reformation. It was not likely that the official version of the past would be overthrown by people who were historians of the Reformation itself. That movement certainly was nationalistic and erastian in character and there was nothing in its subject matter to show that the extension of the theory to the whole of the English past was unwarranted. Moreover, the theory itself was accompanied by the opinion that the study of the 'Dark Ages' was itself useless and retrogressive. This attitude developed particularly during the seventeenth century when the idea of progress, teaching that each generation was an improvement on the last, began to grip the imagination of the English people. It was associated with the glittering successes of scientific discoveries in this century. All this made historians and others look down, in a literal as well as metaphorical sense, on the people of the past, from their higher rung on the ladder of progress.

Such a view would inevitably be an obstacle to the English understanding of their ancestors in England, as well as their colonial subjects in the new world overseas. Just as Burnet asserted in the seventeenth century that he would rather work in coal mines than study the medieval period, Lord Macaulay, in the nineteenth century, was able to boast of the infinite superiority of English culture over that of India. The attitude which guided the English people's view of their past also influenced their outlook on the contemporary world.

There was, then, a complete failure among English historians to place the Reformation in its proper historical perspective and to see it in relation to the ideas and institutions which had characterized the earlier history of England. They wrote as if English history had started with the Reformation and nothing worthwhile had existed before. Even today, the idea that the Reformation emerged from an age of darkness and corruption is alive in the non-academic world, because the great rediscovery of the medieval world in the work of twentieth-century medievalist scholars has not penetrated to the popular level in school textbooks and other forms of popular education.

Two outstanding medievalists of the twentieth century have written very perceptively of this phenomenon. W.A. Pantin writes:

The study of the fourteenth century, as of the later Middle Ages generally, has suffered much in the past from a habit of reading history backwards, of trying to trace signs and causes of the great changes to come, and of thinking of the period as the 'eve of the Renaissance' and 'the eve of the Reformation'. I think that the proper and really fruitful method is to tackle the problem from the other end, and to ask ourselves, how does the fourteenth century grow out of the thirteenth century? In what respects is it a logical continuation or a mishandling of opportunity? A climax or an anticlimax?[1]

Sir Maurice Powicke, an all-too-rare example of the distinguished medievalist who has written on the Reformation, comments:

Our difficulty in comprehending the course of events is doubtless partly due to the fact that to the modern mind English history does seem to begin with the Reformation. . . . Our categories are more closely defined, and as we find it hard to think of England as other than a Protestant country, so we are disposed to feel, if not to think, that the Reformation was, as it were, a rebound to the normal, and the more self-conscious because it appears to have been so easy. This attitude is nothing more than a form of our insular self-satisfaction, and the ease with which King Henry made himself supreme was due to a situation precisely the opposite to that which we imagine. Ecclesiastical opinion had become distracted by a long indulgence in compromise.[2]

The conventional view of the English Reformation could be shaken only by a better understanding of the medieval world which preceded it. Only then could it be placed in true historical perspective. The general context of English life before the Reformation had to be rectified before the particular events of the Reformation, and indeed its whole nature, could be properly understood. When all this has been done, it becomes quite clear that the very word 'Reformation' is a historical misnomer which itself helps to support the official version of the past, especially at the popular level where there is very little, if any, awareness of revisionist work on the subject at an academic level.[3]

The Non-Juror scholars are important primarily because they were able to make the first significant advance toward a better understanding of the medieval period. It is a paradox that, while their own religious outlook and prejudices prevented them from really understanding either the medieval period or the Reformation itself, their work still represents the first real breakthrough in that national-erastian circle of argument which had dominated English historical thought since the events of the 1530s.

From 1660 to 1730 there was an extraordinary revival of scholarly interest in the medieval world.[4] Important collections of medieval Church councils and synods in England were published by some of the Whig bishops in the early eighteenth century. These were inspired by the need to defend the authority of bishops against those who advocated the independent rights of the lower house of the Convocation of Canterbury, in what became known as the 'Convocation Controversy'. These works, concerning points of ecclesiastical precedence and procedure, certainly added much detailed knowledge, but were so insular in character as to make no real impact on a better understanding of the medieval past.

The contribution of the Non-Jurors was different in two respects. Firstly there was their 'distinction . . . in all fields of medieval investigation' which was 'one of the most striking phenomena of the time'.[5] Secondly, their belief in the apostolic succession made them claim a continuous and legitimate descent from the medieval Church in England. They claimed that this was 'their' Church and they denied that any fundamental break had occurred at the Reformation. They were alone among English Protestants, therefore, in having a sympathetic outlook on this Church and an interest in uncovering its past glories. From among several significant figures such as Dr George Hickes, Thomas Baker and Thomas Hearne, whose most penetrating historical contributions were left mostly in their manuscript papers, we shall concentrate here on one representative of the group, who was courageous enough to put forward his views in print, albeit anonymously, to illustrate the original work of which this group was capable in the field of medieval history and the way in which their scholarship anticipated the findings of twentieth-century research.

Henry Wharton, the son of a Norfolk vicar, was educated at Cambridge where he graduated in the year 1683–4, after studying Classics, Philosophy, French, Italian and Mathematics. For some time afterwards he worked as assistant to William Cave, the ecclesiastical historian who produced the *Historia Litteraria* in 1668, and had the opportunity of working on the medieval manuscripts at Cambridge and in the Royal Library at St James. In 1668 Wharton, an able and industrious student, won the friendship and the patronage of Sancroft, Archbishop of Canterbury, who made him one of his chaplains. Wharton took the opportunity of doing a

140

great amount of work on the Lambeth manuscripts. He was the only one of Sancroft's chaplains to remain with him at Lambeth at the time of the Revolution when Sancroft refused to take the oath of allegiance to William and Mary and consequently lost his office. We have seen already how Wharton's own views incurred the hostility of the new Whig episcopate. He lost all chance of advancing his career and eventually returned to his benefice at Chartham in 1694 where he died at the young age of thirty.

Ill health and an early death cut short Wharton's life as a scholar. We catch a glimpse of his mood in the letters written towards the end of his life. They show a frustrated and lonely figure, prevented by sickness from pursuing his beloved historical studies.[6] A contemporary described an incident during his last days:

> Some daies before Mr. Wharton left Canterbury, I was frequently with him at Mr. Archdeacon's house; & one day He opened his trunk & drawers & shewed me his great Collections concerning ye state of our Church, & with a deep sigh, told me, yt all his labours were at an end; & yt his strength would not permit him to finish any more of that subject . . . he sd. His strength failed him & when he came to London He should never be able to do anything about it.[7]

In fact he had already achieved enough in his great work, the *Anglia Sacra* (1691), to carve a permanent niche for himself in the history of historical writing in England.

Wharton indeed may be called one of the founders of English medieval studies in which his work occupies a prominent place. A modern authority describes his *Anglia Sacra* as a work of 'permanent importance . . . a book which has remained indispensable to the study of English monastic chronicles'. Again, it is 'a pioneer work of the first importance' with which 'the comparative study of English monastic chronicles for the first time became possible'. It provided 'a collection of materials that might subserve a scientific history of the medieval Church in England'.[8]

In a letter of 1689 Wharton tells us something of his motive for beginning his collection of medieval chronicles:

> Considering that the history of our church before the Reformation was little known . . . I resolved to make a collection of histories purely ecclesiastical and publish them together;

believing that otherwise they might be for ever lost, and that this might contribute much to an exact ecclesiastical history of our church, if ever it should be undertaken.[9]

He explained that he had carried on his researches up to the time of the Reformation because so few of the chronicles reached that point: 'I found it necessary to continue all of them to that period', to do which 'I have turned over innumerable registers, histories etc and procured much from other persons'.[10] Shortly before he died, he wrote that 'I believe I have got together about almost all which England can afford relating to a History of the Ecclesiastical Affairs & Bps of it before the Reformation'.[11]

It was precisely on the basis of this detailed research into ecclesiastical history between the period covered by the chroniclers and the Reformation itself that Wharton was able to speak with authority on the medieval background to the Reformation. He was certainly the greatest authority on this period in English historiography up to the modern period and his private papers show a knowledge of the later medieval period which conflicts altogether with the official version of decline and decay and anticipates the findings of the most modern scholarship on this period. It is exciting to discover that the work of today's 'revisionists' at the end of the twentieth century was anticipated by Wharton two centuries ago.

The extraordinary fact is that, in spite of his unrivalled knowledge and scholarship, Wharton's greatest work, the *Anglia Sacra*, did not break the mould established by the official version of the nature of the medieval Church in England. It is on the basis of this book that Wharton has been acclaimed as a founder of medieval studies because he supplied the materials on which modern scholars could work. No one has really brought to light his own observations, published anonymously in a rather obscure book which contains the most significant part of his work from our viewpoint.

The *Anglia Sacra* was not written to contest the prevailing erastian views of the period and consequently Wharton did not reveal his own personal views and historical interpretations in this work, which is simply an invaluable collection of documentary material. It was quite a different matter, however, when he decided to confront and oppose the most official expression of the erastian viewpoint on the past, Gilbert Burnet's *History of the Reformation*. Again we find that only the stimulus of anti-erastianism could make the scholarly Wharton reveal his own findings and observations about the Church in medieval England. For those interested simply in the progress of scholarly knowledge, the most important effect of Burnet's propagandist work was that it provoked Wharton into writing a response in which he revealed his own historical insights.

In 1693 there appeared in London *A Specimen of Some Errors and Defects in the History of the Reformation of the Church of England by Gilbert Burnet, D.D., now Lord Bishop of Sarum*. It was published anonymously under the pseudonym of Anthony Harmer, but Burnet himself soon guessed the truth. For there was only one man in England capable of writing this particular book. Indeed it is probably true to say that no other man in England could have written it before the blossoming of medieval scholarship around the middle of the twentieth century. It is also a rather sobering thought that a scholar in 1693 was able to present a picture of the later medieval period as an age of promise and vigour, which has only just been rediscovered by our modern academics, and which the 'lay' people of today have still not had the chance to discover. Such is still the dominant effect of the official version, with its story of medieval decline and decay which was only checked and turned round by the Reformation.

In this slim volume of 200 pages, taking the form of a critical commentary and analytical discussion rather than a continuous narrative, we have the considered views of an outstanding scholar who was able to take his stance from the medieval viewpoint, looking forward, so to speak, to the events of the sixteenth century and the Reformation. This approach provided the complete antidote to the universal disease among historians at that time, of reading history backwards, of looking back at the medieval period to justify the events of the Reformation. It is of enormous historiographical importance. Nothing approaching its penetrative power in terms of exact detailed scholarship, supporting a completely fresh view of the past, was seen again until the late twentieth century.

The central criticism of Burnet's work was made obvious at the start of the *Specimen*. It is simply that Burnet was ignorant of the medieval period. Wharton makes the comment that we can now see as apt, not simply in relation to Burnet's work, but to English historiography in general up to the twentieth century.[12] It is 'necessary . . . for anyone who undertaketh to write the History of our Reformation to be well acquainted with the State of things before the Reformation'.[13] This seems a trite enough comment now, but when Wharton made this point, it was a valid criticism of all Protestant historians and would remain valid until our own century. Wharton showed that Burnet was ignorant not only of the manuscripts, Rolls, Records and Charters of the medieval period, but also of the sources which had been printed in the seventeenth century, such as Dugdale's *Monasticon* and Spelman's *Councils*. It was in answer to this rather devastating point that Burnet boasted of his ignorance of things medieval.[14]

Wharton acknowledged that his book would be unpopular:

These are the Errors and Defects, which I have observ'd. . . . For my performance herein, I expect not either praise or thanks from the present Age; much less from the Historian; yet I thought it a Duty to Posterity not to permit it to be led into mistakes in any thing relating to the Reformation of this Church by Errors contained in an History published in our times, with Pomp and seeming Authority.[15]

It is no wonder that Wharton was not able afterwards to gain preferment in his career. It is interesting also that the hostility which he obviously expected acted as a spur to good scholarship in Wharton. Nicholas Battely, another antiquarian, made this point when he wrote, with reference to the *Specimen*: 'I have little thought of being able to find any Error in it; because it so much concern'd ye bold animadvertor to be exact, punctual & on good grounds.'[16]

A main theme in the official view of the English past was the idea that papal usurpations and interferences in medieval England had increased towards the end of that period until Englishmen, led by their Patriot-King, were provoked sufficiently at last to throw off the insufferable burden by taking the actions involved in the Reformation. This was then seen as a popular movement to reassert national freedom and independence against the increasing stranglehold of a foreign aggressor who was also 'anti-Christ'. So, for example, Burnet emphasized that papal encroachments had increased in the fourteenth and fifteenth centuries, in spite of the Statutes of Provisors and Praemunire which were attempts by the English people to stop them.[17] Cardinals had illegitimately procured and executed a legatine power in England during this time. Wharton replied that this was not true:

A competent knowledge of the History of the *English* Church would have prevented so large a mistake. No Cardinals before

Wolsey, had procured and executed such Legatine Power in *England* since those Laws were made. Cardinal *Beaufort* of *Winchester* indeed had procured it, but could never execute it, being inhibited by King Henry VI, by the advice of Archbishop *Chichley*, and forced to renounce his pretended Power: As for the Legatine Power of the Archbishop of *Canterbury*, which was claimed and exercised by them in Quality of *Legati nati*; that was not in the least contrary to these Laws, nor ever was so accounted; being annexed perpetually to the See of *Canterbury* ever since the Year 1200, and always belonging to them, without any new or distinct Bull.[18]

Again, Burnet was expounding a fiction that was used effectively by Protestant historians to rouse the nationalist spirit of Englishmen, when he stated that the Popes, 'not satisfied with their other Oppressions, did by Provisions, Bulls and other Arts of that See, dispose of Bishopricks, Abbeys and lesser Benefices, to Foreigners, Cardinals and others that did not live in England'.[19]

Wharton tells us that this is 'a very wide mistake', since the Popes never did such a thing in the case of bishoprics until about thirty years before the Reformation 'when it was not done without the Kings good liking and in Vertue of some secret compact between them'. In the case of the abbeys, Wharton says that 'from the first Foundation to their Dissolution, the Popes never gave any one to a Foreigner, not residing', and on the question of Cardinal Abbots, he commented that 'there never was any besides Cardinal *Wolsey* and of him it is well known that he had his Abbey from the gift of the King, and lived in England'.[20] Burnet's views continued to be offered as causes of the Reformation in England, however, until well into the twentieth century.[21]

On the whole problem of the disposition of bishoprics in late medieval England, Wharton has an illuminating statement to make. The official version stressed that the Popes had been able to increase their interference in English affairs because of the weaknesses of certain English kings who had allowed them to dispose of bishoprics in England. This had increased until Henry VIII had restored the national and secular control of the Church in England which had been a feature of the pristine days of old.

Wharton was the first English scholar to point out that the Reformation was the result of an exactly opposite process from that which was popularly supposed. He was able to show:

Indeed for about sixty years before the Reformation our Kings had got the better of the Popes in this matter, and drawn the disposition of Bishopricks to themselves, yet not altogether (for the Popes by their authority and pleasure disposed of *Worcester* at least three times within that term).[22]

This awareness of the increasing spirit of compromise affecting the papal authority in England in the fifteenth century was a significant contribution towards a proper understanding of the background to the Reformation. The fact that so many leaders of the Church were appointed on the kings' advice, sometimes in return for services rendered, meant that the Church had been weakened in the face of secular attack when the crisis arose in England. The case of Cardinal Wolsley's career is the most significant example of a weakness which meant that in the end only Bishop Fisher stood firm among the bishops against Henry's revolution. It was this kind of weakness at the top, rather than popular support from below, which explains the quick demise of the Church in the face of political terrorism. This has not been fully understood in English historiography until very recently.[23]

Wharton in fact was able to show that there were signs of vitality and vigour in the life of the Church in the pre-Reformation era. For example, where Burnet had written that, whereas there were suffragan bishops in the early life of the Church, these had been put down everywhere by degrees until the Reformation revived their appointment in England,[24] Wharton replies: 'If the Historian had pleased to acquaint himself with the State of the Church in *England* before the Reformation, he could not have been Ignorant, that for about 200 years before the Reformation, Suffragan Bishops had been frequent in *England*.'[25] Burnet claimed that there were few sermons given 'in the time of Popery',[26] but Wharton comments that, though this may have been true of the 'ancient times of Popery', it cannot be applied to the later period: 'for some time before the Reformation Preaching seems to have been more frequent in England.'[27]

With regard to the importance of ecclesiastical convocations in English life, Burnet said that nothing could be found in the records concerning the constitution of convocations in pre-Reformation times, but Wharton replies that, 'It might be undeniably demonstrated from the Acts of many Convocations, for above 200 years before the Reformation, until that very time, that the

Constitution of Convocations was all along in this respect the same.' He goes on to give proof, 'So that the matter of Fact is put beyond all doubt'.[28]

As another example, we may take the case of monks and monasteries. These had been given a very bad press in English historiography ever since Cromwell had used the 'Visitors' Reports' (1535) as the excuse for dissolving them in 1536. Not until the magisterial volumes of David Knowles' *Monastic Order in England* (1949) was a properly authoritative consideration given to this subject, but Wharton was able already to make some comments which were truly remarkable for his time. Again, in answer to Burnet's typical attacks on the monks, Wharton showed the importance of the tenth-century monastic reform led by Dunstan, and then indicated that there could have been scope for another such reform, instead of the Dissolution:

immediately before the Reformation, many of the great Monasteries were so many Nurseries of Learning and the Superiors of them very Learned themselves and Promoters of Learning in others. Such were *Kidderminster*, Abbot of *Winchelcombe, Goldwell, Prior of Canterbury, Voche Abbot of St. Austins, Wells Prior of Ely, Holybeach Prior of Worcester, Webbe Prior of Coventry, and many others.* I do not hereby Apologize for the Laziness of the Monks in the middle Ages; but maintain that both in the time of Edgar, and some time after, and immediately before the Reformation, they deserved a contrary Character to what the Historian giveth of them; and that even in the worst times they were far from being Enemies, and Opposers of Learning; as he would have it believed.[29]

These contributions by Wharton to the picture of pre-Reformation England are important because they question, at strategic points, the conventional framework of Reformation historiography, which was built around the idea of the age of 'light' emerging from the age of 'darkness'. Burnet's view on this was almost universally accepted in his own day[30] and for two centuries afterwards. Even in 1984 we were told that this view 'is still a potent influence in our thinking'.[31]

As a final example, it is interesting to find Wharton again anticipating recent scholarship,[32] in opposition to Burnet's statement, replying that in economic terms, 'The case of Vicars was not so bad before the Reformation, as after'.[33] He goes on, in a long passage based upon 'abundant testimony' from 'our ancient Registers and Records', to show that the triumph of the Common Law over the Canon Law at the Reformation and the control of benefices passing to lay hands, meant that vicars were worse off than before. In some cases laymen 'hired poor curates to serve them, at the cheapest rate they could, and still continue to do so'.[34]

Wharton's views, as expressed in the *Specimen*, were radically different from the official account of the Reformation as a popular reaction of English patriotism and freedom against foreign domination. Wharton himself was not able to make the obvious generalization which a modern medievalist would make from the facts at his disposal. As a High Anglican of non-juring principles, he was committed to a belief in the continuity of the later Anglican Church from its medieval counterpart. It was only in these passages of analytical discussion of isolated episodes, written in conscious opposition to the erastian arguments of Burnet, that Wharton was able to break through the conventional assumptions of thought. His commitment to the concept of ecclesiastical continuity in England made him unwilling and therefore unable to recognize the revolutionary nature of the Reformation and the very real break with the past which it represented. In his own main work, the *Anglia Sacra*, where he was not concentrating on opposing erastianism, he was unable, in spite of his great knowledge and scholarship, to transcend the conventional view of the English past. Here, he leaves the *nationalistic* version perfectly intact and even attacks Archbishop William, in the reign of Henry I, for undermining the 'independence' of the English Church by accepting the legatine office from the Pope.[35]

So far in this chapter I have examined the way in which greater perspective could be given to the historiography of the Reformation in England when that subject was looked at from the viewpoint of an Anglican medievalist in the late seventeenth century. Yet this perspective was still only partial. To illustrate the way in which historiography can be of real use in placing history in proper perspective, I will now proceed to a fuller historiographical treatment of three issues of the medieval period which were of strategic importance during the Reformation itself. They were used as crucial evidence in favour of the official version during the 1530s and thenceforward became an accepted part of the English people's view of their past. One of them played a direct part in the 'war of nerves'[36] conducted by the Henrician government against the clergy in 1530. This approach will also serve to indicate the pervasive and extraordinarily insidious effect of the official version of the English past, even on the minds of some of our better modern historians.

THE HISTORIOGRAPHY OF THE CONFLICT BETWEEN ARCHBISHOP THOMAS BECKET AND KING HENRY II

The conflict between Archbishop Thomas Becket and King Henry II has caught the imagination of English people throughout the centuries. The strength of the characters involved and the great issues at stake provide a very dramatic context for the story. It inspired one of the great works of English medieval literature, Chaucer's *Canterbury Tales* (begun *c.* 1387), and a play by one of the major figures in English literature in the twentieth century – T.S. Eliot's *Murder in the Cathedral* (1935).

The conflict was indeed a matter of the highest drama. It symbolized one of the great lessons of Christian teaching: 'Give unto Caesar the things that are Caesar's; and to God the things that are God's.' The view taken about these events by later generations, looking back at them, tells us a great deal about the values of these later peoples as well as those of medieval times.

In the medieval world, both the spiritual and the temporal areas of life were accepted as essential parts of the normal human condition; each had its proper structure of authority for human guidance and for service of the community's needs. At the Reformation, the State took control of the Church in England and now there was only one authority in charge – the State. This prepared the way for other great changes. Assumptions of thought changed over a long period of secularization in English life.[37] The problem arose in historiography when one group of people, with certain assumptions of thought, tried to read these same assumptions back into the minds of their medieval ancestors who in fact had very different ways of thinking. Consequently, these later generations failed to know or understand the thinking of their own ancestors over a period of four centuries.

The epic struggle between the strong Archbishop of Canterbury and the strong king of England in the twelfth century has now been properly placed within the context of an English Church which considered itself essentially part of the spiritual unity of the Universal Church, centred on the Papacy, while owing political allegiance to the king of England. The legal nature of the conflict has, of course, long been evident, but the real issues involved have not been properly understood until well into the twentieth century. Past misconceptions on the subject mean that it is now insufficient to state that Becket was fighting for the freedom of the Church. It is necessary to define what this phrase means. In the words of a modern authority, describing Becket's stance, 'the freedom of the English Church, he repeats again and again, means the freedom to obey the Pope, to be under papal government as the rest of the Church was; he is fighting not only the battle of the English Church, but of the whole Church and the Pope.'[38] The Canon Law was essentially the expression of papal ecclesiastical government on a universal level. It was against encroachments made by the temporal power upon Canon Law that Becket was fighting. The principle of papal government was not in question, and both sides assumed the spiritual and ecclesiastical headship of the Papacy. In practice, however, Henry II's desire to extend the power of his own courts over the Church and its personnel would have impeded papal government of the Church as administered through the Canon Law. Professor M.D. Knowles has summarized the struggle as follows:

As the struggle wore on, the precise object for which the archbishop fought had changed its appearance to his eyes. At the beginning it had been the forensic rights of the Church, and the clerical order; then it had become at Clarendon the freedom of the English Church as part of the universal Church in its relation with Rome; finally it had broadened into a defence of the rights of God against Caesar.[39]

Becket's victory, achieved through his martyrdom, meant that Henry II's attempt, by the Constitutions of Clarendon (1164), to encroach on Church rights[40] had failed.

Essentially then, the struggle was between the spiritual and temporal jurisdictions in England, between the legal rights of the Universal Church as expressed through that part of it which was in England, and the legal claims of the King's Courts in England. These courts had already gained in prestige and authority, becoming the 'common' law over all England under Henry II. The king was now tempted to extend their power at the expense of the

Church in ways which would have impeded the normal working of the Canon Law, but without in any way trying to 'take over' the Church or denying its independent authority in spiritual matters. The quarrel was about where the boundaries between the rights of the two authorities should lie, in order to allow the proper functioning of both. Neither side denied for a moment that the other had its own independent rights, but it was the king, in this case, who was encroaching on what had been accepted previously as the Church's preserve in certain important matters.[41] Bearing in mind this context of the controversy, as modern scholarship has come to regard it, we may now turn to the history of historical writing on this subject to see why the real issues were so long obscured, and why, at various stages, important contributions were made towards a better understanding of it.

At the time of the Reformation, Thomas Becket had been for more than three centuries one of the most popular of English saints and thousands of pilgrims from home and abroad had visited his shrine at Canterbury. Chaucer's *Canterbury Tales* is a description of the personalities on one of these pilgrimages to Becket's shrine. It is not difficult to understand Henry VIII's embarrassment by this living refutation of all that he was doing in taking over control of the Church in England and forbidding all appeals to Rome. In 1538 a proclamation appeared, stating that Thomas Becket was no saint, but a rebel and a traitor. He had been canonized only because he upheld the usurped authority of the Pope against the legitimate rights of the king. From now on all traces of respect for him must be obliterated. Any disagreement with this official verdict on Becket would incur the penalty of imprisonment.[42]

All the essentials of the future historiography of the subject are laid down firmly in this proclamation. The main line is clear. Becket was a traitorous rebel who supported the usurped claims of a foreign power against the proper supremacy of his own sovereign. In this way the medieval episode was assimilated into that concept of national sovereignty which was born in the statutes of the Reformation Parliament. It was enforced with all the enthusiasm and rigour of any revolutionary government wishing to wipe away the past from the memory of its people. All the passages in Fabyan's *Chronicle* which had originally glorified Becket, in the pre-Reformation editions of this work, were hastily omitted in the later editions.[43] It was the kind of procedure with which were to become very familiar in the history of twentieth-century totalitarian regimes.

John Foxe, writing after the Reformation, eagerly took up the theme in his highly influential 'Book of Martyrs': 'If the cause makes a martyr, as is said, I see not why we should esteem Thomas Becket to die a martyr, more than others whom the prince's sword doth here temporarily punish for their temporal deserts.' Becket's cause was clearly 'a rebellion against those to whom we owe a subjection'. Neither can he be excused from the charge of being 'a plain rebel against his prince'. Becket was 'a stubborn trespasser; ergo no martyr'. Foxe referred to his 'plain rebellion', his 'stubborn wilfulness', his 'seditious' complaint to the Pope against the king. Becket had acted 'contrary to all honesty, good order, natural subjection, and true Christianity, whereupon followed no little disquietness after to the king, and damage to the realm'. Beckett's end was useful in teaching an erastian lesson to others: 'to teach all Roman prelates not to be so stubborn, in such matters not pertaining to them, against their prince, unto whom God hath subjected them.' Indeed the whole affair of Becket's enterprise 'against the king's laws' was placed by Foxe within a wider erastian argument; for if only the emperors had used their proper powers against the Popes, they could have prevented much future trouble:

> if they had used the law of the sword against them, and chopped off the heads of one or two, according to their traitorous rebellion, they had broken the neck of much disturbance . . . and all because the superior powers either would not, or durst not, practise the authority given unto them of the Lord, upon those inferiors.[44]

This official version of the subject remained dominant in England until the advent of modern scholarship. In the seventeenth century, the Anglican, Thomas Fuller, saw Becket as 'a stubborn defender of the vivacious clergy against the secular power'. While in exile Becket had allied with Pope Alexander and just as that Pope was exiled by the Emperor 'for pride and insolency', so, too, 'our Becket smarted for the same fault from king Henry'. When Becket returned from exile, he 'increased his insolence against the king and all his subjects'.[45]

The Puritans thought the same, and in 1666 William Prynne described the 'papal and prelatical Usurpations, Innovations, in the Reigns of Stephen, Henry II, Richard II', and the 'schisms, rebellions and treasons of Archbishops and Bishops during their reigns'.[46]

Gilbert Burnet attacked Becket for his disloyalty to his king and master; he had supported a foreign power and his actions served 'to embroil the kingdom'. Referring to Henry VIII's attack on Becket's shrine, Burnet reflected on Becket's 'disloyal practises' which 'made the king resolve to unshrine and unsaint him'.[47] The common-lawyers' attitude to Becket was, of course, unfriendly. Sir Matthew Hale was speaking for them all when he attacked the 'insolence' of Becket who had deigned to oppose the native Common Law of England in favour of a foreign code which had been designed as the vehicle of a foreign power, to interfere in English affairs.[48]

The first important advance towards a better historical understanding of this medieval episode came with the *Ecclesiastical History* of Jeremy Collier, the Non-Juror, published between 1708 and 1714. Collier pointed out that Henry VIII wanted

> to strike at the reputation of this prelate, and bring disgrace upon his memory; for Becket's character, it is plain, must be somewhat unserviceable to the regal supremacy; and though this claim was not set up by the crown at that time of day, yet the archbishop contested very warmly for the privilege of the Church with Henry II.

As to Becket's conduct during the dispute, Collier said that though it 'was not altogether defensible, he was far however from being guilty of that gross mismanagement with which he is charged'.[49]

Collier, as a Non-Juror, was very sympathetic with Becket's stand for the independent rights of the Church against the State. He noted that Becket declined judgment by the King's Court because 'he had appealed to a higher court; that this was enough to bar their proceedings, supposing he had been otherwise within their jurisdiction'. When Becket returned to England in 1170 and was commanded in the king's name to absolve the suspended and excommunicated bishops, 'He told them that it was not within the authority of an inferior jurisdiction to set aside the sentence of a superior court; and that the pope's censure could not be reversed by any mortal'.

Since Becket stood for the rights and freedom of the spiritual authority, Collier was able to disapprove of the servility of the English bishops who supported Henry II against him. Moreover, when Becket based his assertion of these rights on the obedience due to the Papacy, Collier was still willing to support him. In the face of opposition from his own English bishops, Becket 'appeals to the Pope and carries his cross erected into the court'. Again, when Henry II sent ambassadors, including the Bishop of London, to the Pope, requesting that legates should be sent to England to make a final decision against Becket, Collier records the occasion:

> 'But', says the bishop of London, 'we desire they may be empowered to decide the matter without any further appeal.' 'No,' says the pope, 'that privilege is my glory, which I will not give to another: whenever that archbishop is brought upon his trial, it shall be before me; for it would be strangely unreasonable to command him back to England, for his enemies to sit upon him.'

As a Non-Juror, committed to a belief in the autonomy of the Anglican Church, Collier did not openly proclaim papal rights over the Church in England when he dealt with this episode. However, his enthusiasm for the cause of Becket against his secular opponents made him sympathize for the moment with Becket's only means of defence, which was the spiritual authority of the Pope. Indeed, while discussing the papal reaction to the situation, Collier came to the very edge of modern understanding of the ecclesiastical system in medieval England. The following passage is looking at the episode from the viewpoint of the centre of Church government in Rome, which no other Protestant had been able to do. Becket had gone to the Pope and offered to surrender his post. The Pope's advisers, however, argued against this, and said:

> that the archbishop had ventured his life and fortune, and run the utmost hazard in defence of the spiritual authority; that this decision would be a leading case, that if the archbishop sunk in the contest, the rest of the bishops of the Catholic Church would sink with him, the regale carry all before it, and the pope's power dwindle and be lost. It was therefore highly expedient to restore the prelate to his post, though against his inclination, and to stand by him who had entered the lists in behalf of the whole Church. This opinion prevailing, the archbishop of Canterbury was called in, restored to his charge by the pope, who promised to abet his interest and to take care of him.

Collier, while acknowledging the right of the civil power to hear civil cases in the King's Court, showed that the precedents in England were on Becket's side, in his opposition to the trial of clerics in the King's Court. For example, when Odo, Bishop of Bayeux, was seized by William the Conqueror,

> He insisted upon his being a clerk, claimed privilege of his character, and alleged that none could try a bishop but the Pope. The king in his answer, owned the privilege: 'For', says he, 'I do not seize you either as a bishop or a clerk, but as earl of Kent, and under lay distinction.'

Again Collier showed that 'In the contest between Archbishop Anselm and the kings, William Rufus and Henry I, it was taken for granted that none but the pope had any right to try the archbishop'. He cited the great medieval lawyer, Henry de Bracton, as another support for this view and showed that Becket was acting properly within the accepted Canon Law.

Collier's portrayal of the dispute and of the personality of Becket was as accurate, informed and balanced as anything which has been produced by modern scholarship. He praised his courage as one who was 'prepared to die for the cause of God and in defence of the rights of the Church'. He could be blamed for leaving the kingdom without the king's leave, for his vacillation in the first place over the articles of the Clarendon Code and for certain 'indefensible lengths of noncompliance'. He is acquitted, however, of being a traitor to the king and nation, the main charge made against him in the official version, and he did not procure from the Pope the excommunication of the king,[50] as the other writers had said. Writing of the medieval writers who had praised him, and the post-Reformation historians who had vilified him, Collier commented:

> from these, I conceive the truth will be found betwixt the two extremes, and that he was neither so great a saint as the first, nor so great a sinner as the latter would make him. And that as one strained the privileges of the Church too high; so the others seem prepossessed in favour of the crown, and laid too much weight in the secular scale.[51]

Such expressions of moderation and balance did not, however, save Collier from attack in his own day. He was, after all, opposing the conventional view which had gained double strength from the sixteenth-century glorification of monarchy and the increasingly erastian influence of English Protestantism in the seventeenth century. Moreover, High Anglicans, and even Non-Jurors such as Henry Wharton in his *Anglia Sacra*,[52] saw Becket as one who had betrayed the independence of the English Church. The antiquarian, Nicholas Battely[53] expressed this opinion very well when he wrote to a friend:

> Now I pray, May it not be considered, yt Tho: Becket, tho he dyed in vindication of ye privileges of ye Church, yet he was ye first betrayer of ye Rights of his See. He made ye greatest breach upon ye Authority of ye Primacy of Canterbury by resigning ye Archbishoprick back in ye pope's hands, and receiving it again from him, as ye donacon of ye Pope. And indeed, it is ye honour of the Blessed Martyr Tho. Cranmer yt he was ye first who began to claim ye primacy & retrieve ye Rights of his See from being slavishly subjected to ye Roman Power.[54]

The Whig bishops were, of course, much more extreme in their condemnation of Becket and of Collier. White Kennett,[55] for example, accused Collier of 'advancing . . . Churchmen . . . against the Powers of Sovereign Princes . . . not only in the case of Anselm, but of that greater Incendiary Thomas Becket'.[56]

In the last analysis Collier was supporting Becket simply as the champion of the independent rights of the spiritual order in England against the encroachments of the temporal ruler. In order to defend Becket's stand, it was necessary for Collier to adopt the viewpoint of Becket himself, and of the Papacy. Almost without thinking on these occasions, he was regarding the Church in England as part of a much greater whole. This happened, however, only when, in pursuit of some anti-erastian argument, he became oblivious to the general implications of the point which he was making. Nor did he ever allow these episodes to affect his main framework of conventional thought. He believed mistakenly in the autonomy and the independence of the medieval Church in England. Nevertheless, with the exception of John Lingard,[57] no later historian in England produced such a true account of the nature of the conflict between Becket and Henry II until well into the twentieth century.

THE HISTORIOGRAPHY OF THE RELATIONS BETWEEN KING JOHN
AND THE PAPACY

This subject contains two key episodes. In 1205 the monks of
Canterbury, as was their right under Canon Law, elected Stephen
Langton to be Archbishop of Canterbury, but their choice was
opposed by King John, supported by the English bishops. The Pope
decided in favour of Stephen Langon, a man 'of moral and
intellectual greatness'[58] who was to play an important part in the
events leading to Magna Carta. John would not accept this
appointment, until 1213 when he finally submitted to the Pope's
decision on the matter. The second key point in the story was the
context in which John made this final submission. The matter was
a very 'live' issue in the minds and writings of the post-Reformation
chroniclers and historians who strictly followed the government
line. It was used continually as a classic example of one of their
main themes – papal 'foreign' aggression interfering with the native
rights of the English king and his people. It played no small part in
shaping the outlook of English people towards their past and
towards the Papacy.

The conflict between John and the Papacy, however, lacked one of
the ingredients of the previous controversy between Becket and
Henry II. It did not involve a struggle between the spiritual power of
the Church and the temporal power of the king in England. The
historians who dealt with this question emphasized the intrusion of
the foreign power of the Papacy on the dignity and rights of the
English nation as reflected in its bishops and its king. It did not
concern directly the spiritual independence of the English Church
in the face of regal claims to supremacy in ecclesiastical affairs. It
was not a subject, therefore, which was likely to draw forth the
anti-erastian sentiments of the Non-Jurors. Consequently no
progress was made in the historiography of this subject in England,
apart from John Lingard's work,[59] until the twentieth century. Even
then the minds of detached, professional historians were blinkered
in some respects by the hypnotic power of the old official version.

Herbert Butterfield has described the 'glorification of King John'
in the Tudor chroniclers of the post-Reformation era, reminding us
that we should see this in the light of 'the Protestant fervour of
Tudor historians, the reaction against monastic chroniclers, the
adoration of monarchy, the hatred of rebellion even though it
might be against a wicked tyrant'.[60] We have seen that the reign of

King John was used as government propaganda in a play by John Bale, instructed by Thomas Cromwell,[61] after the Act of Supremacy was passed in 1534. It was to remain a source of anti-Catholic propaganda throughout the sixteenth century. This is well illustrated in John Foxe's *Acts and Monuments* (1563). He writes:

> After the popish prelates, monks, canons, priests, &c saw thus their crafty juggling by their feigned prophet who foreshadowed King John's doom would not speed, notwithstanding they had done no little harm thereby, to help the matter more forward, they began to travail and practise with Pope Innocent on the one side, and also with the French king on the other; besides subtle treasons which they wrought within the realm, and by their confusions in the ear, whereby they both blinded the nobility and commons. The King thus compassed about on every side with enemies, and fearing the sequel thereof, knowing the conspiracies that were working against him, as well by the pope, in all that ever he might, as also by Philip, the French king, by his procurement; and moreover his own people, especially the lords and barons, being rebelliously incited against him; as by the pope's curses and interdictions and dispensations with all those that would rebel against him, commanding them, to detain from him such homage, service, duties, debts, and all other allegiance, as godly subjects owe and are bound to yield and give to their liege lord and prince: all which things considered, the king, in the thirteenth year of his reign, because the French king began to make sharp invasion upon him within his own realm, sent speedy ambassadors to the pope as to the fountain of all this mischief, pretended to work and entreat his peace and reconcilation with him, promising to do what ever the Pope should command of him in the reformation of himself, and restitution of all wrongs done to holy church and make due satisfaction there – for unto all men that could complain.[62]

The English prelates at this time were described by Foxe as 'that mischievous progeny of antichrist' who had raised an 'outrageous cruel noise' against 'their natural King'. He added a reference to 'the tyrannical inderdiction under which he had continued six years and three months. But before the repleasement thereof, he was miserably compelled, as hath been declared, to give over both his crown and sceptre to that antichrist at Rome.'[63]

The whole emphasis here is upon affronted national dignity and rebellious treason against the king. We have a picture of the Pope, stirring up rebellion in England and procuring the invasion, if possible, of England by other foreign Catholic powers in order to extend his own power. There are, too, 'the traitorous vassals' in England who assisted the Pope in his designs.

All this was powerful propaganda and highly emotive material in Elizabethan England, with its developing cult of nationalism and sovereignty and its warfare against Catholic Spain.[64] It was material well suited to the propagandist purposes of the Elizabethan government, which was attempting in all ways possible to strengthen national unity against the outside threat of Spain and the incipient opposition from the Puritans in the Commons. It certainly contributed to the continuing rise of English xenophobia which had been born in the 1530s.[65]

In the seventeenth century there was no deviation from this conventional interpretation. Thomas Fuller, usually a more moderate exponent of the official version, wrote in his *Church History* (1655) that King John was indeed 'suffering unjustly because he would not willingly part with his undoubted right' in the affair of the Canterbury election. His main attention is directed to the later events of 1212–13:

> behold the miserable condition of king John, perplexed with the daily preparation of the French king's invasion of England, assisted by many English malcontents and all the banished barons. Good patriots, who, rather than the fire of their courage should want fuel, would burn their own country which first bred them. Hereupon king John having his soul battered with foreign fears, and foundered within by the falseness of his subjects, sunk on a sudden beneath himself to an act of unworthy submission and subjection to the pope.

To complete the picture he writes: 'king John on his knees surrenders the crown of England into the hands of Pandulphus the papal legate, and also presented him with some money as the earnest of his subjection, which the proud prelate tramples under his feet.'[66]

The Puritan and anti-clerical William Prynne saw in the incident of the election of 1205 an attempted defence by King John of the 'English Kings supreme ecclesiastical jurisdiction' against 'Popish and Prelatical Usurpations'. He noted the final 'unworthy prostitution' of 'undoubted Rights and Privileges' to 'Tyrannical Usurpations' in the forced submission of John to the Papacy in 1213.[67] This emphasis by Prynne on the erastian aspect of the affair rather than the purely nationalist interpretation is due to the particular design he was pursuing in this work and may be regarded as something exceptional in the historiography of this subject.

Gilbert Burnet justified Henry VIII's severities against 'Papists' during the Reformation by referring to historical precedent: 'two of his own ancestors, Henry II and king John, had been driven to great extremities, and forced to unusual and most indecent submission, by the means of the popes and their clergy.'[68]

It is significant that the Non-Jurors had nothing to contribute to the historiography of this subject. They did not feel the need to defend their own Church against erastianism in this case and so were not provoked or stimulated into producing anything new. Committed to their belief in the autonomy of their national Church, they were as ready as any other Protestant Englishmen to condemn the interference of the Papacy in English affairs. Jeremy Collier, for example, saw the question of the Canterbury election of 1205 as an issue between the Pope and the monks of Canterbury on the one hand, and the English bishops on the other; on such an issue there was no doubt where Collier stood: 'it has been the practice of the court of Rome to depress the rights and authority of the bishops; so that when there happened any debate between them and the monks, the conclave generally declared for the latter.'[69] Concerning the conference between John and the papal legate in 1211, he was as anti-papal as any other Protestant writer of the time, referring 'to what flaming excess they carried their encroachments upon the civil power'. Here was Collier giving full play now to his belief in a national Church which was independent of any outside control during the medieval period. Whereas he had introduced the Canon Law to defend Becket's stand against the King's Courts, he did not invoke the same law to justify the rights of the Canterbury monks against the English bishops in 1205, though the same Canon Law was involved.

Again, Collier wrote in the conventional style, appealing to English national feeling, when he repeated the old story that Pandulph, the papal envoy, told John in 1213, 'that the King of France lay at the mouth of the Seine with a formidable fleet and army, that he had an authority from the pope to seize his dominions, and that his holiness had conveyed the sovereignty of the English crown to that prince and his successors'. John was 'driven to this compliance' with the legate's terms by the 'hard language' of the Pope and the 'terror of the interdict'. Meanwhile Pandulph 'managed himself with great haughtiness upon this occasion, and trampled the money under his feet which the king gave to him as an earnest of his vassalage'.[70]

In the second half of the seventeenth century the idea that England was likely to be invaded by Louis XIV of France and have Catholicism thrust upon its people was a centrepiece of anti-Catholic propaganda. It was certainly an important part of the Whig interpretation of past and present history. The mistaken idea that the Secret Treaty of Dover (1670) between Charles II and Lousis XIV contained clauses promising that a French army would be used to force Catholicism on England was much in vogue up to the second half of the twentieth century,[71] although Lingard had actually published that Treaty for the first time in 1830 and proved that the story was untrue.[72] After the events of 1688–9, the exile of James II and the Whig ascendancy in the reign of William and Mary, this interpretation of King John's subjection to the Papacy during the medieval period would have had an immediate impact on English readers. The subject itself was by now part of English folklore.

The later historiography of King John and the Papacy is very illustrative of the durability over centuries of the official version. It stressed the attempts by the Pope to extend his power and influence in England by fair means or foul, to subvert the rights of the English bishops in the Canterbury election of 1205, and to gain John's ignominious submission in 1213 by deposing him and inviting Philip Augustus of France to invade England and seize the English throne. This version remained current in English historiography, with only one exception, until the middle of our own century.

W.S. McKechnie, in his study of *Magna Carta* (1905), referred to the 'triumph of papal arrogance' in the election of Stephen Langton as Archbishop of Canterbury in 1205, and noted that the astute Pope Innocent III was quick to see an opportunity for papal aggrandizement in England.[73] Even in the 1957 edition of W.E. Lunt's *History of England*, the old approach is still going strong:[74]

The pope who was thus confronted with two candidates for the archbishopric was Innocent III. He did more perhaps than any other pope of the Middle Ages to exalt the power of the vicars of Christ on earth. He was not the pope to let slip the opportunity presented by the disputed election to advance the papal authority. . . . The excommunication failed, as had the Interdict, to bring about the triumph which Innocent III desired.[75]

In fact, however, two specialist studies of this episode by two of the most distinguished of modern medievalists changed its interpretation completely. Sir Maurice Powicke, in his *Stephen Langton* (1928) wrote:

A busy pope like Innocent III was advising the Church on such points very frequently; his quarrel with King John would appear to him a very serious case among hundreds of cases relating to elections in all parts of Europe. I doubt if the insularity of English historical inquiry from the days of William Prynne onwards has had as misleading consequences in any matter as in its treatment of this quarrel. We must, to start with, rid our minds of any idea that the pope was only concerned to exert his authority. He was concerned to see that the law of the Church was carried out.[76]

Then, in 1938, M.D. Knowles, in an essay on 'The Canterbury Election of 1205–6' commented:

The disputed Canterbury election of 1205, which led to the final election in Rome of Stephen Langton, and that in turn to the Interdict and submission of John to Innocent III, form one of the most familiar episodes in English mediaeval history, and have been recounted times beyond number. Almost all, whether scholars and specialists or compilers of text books, who have written since the chief sources for the narrative appeared in the Roll Series some fifty years ago, have followed very closely the account given by Bishop Stubbs in his introduction to the Historical Collections of Walter of Coventry. It is the purpose of this note to point out that a number of incidents in the narrative as given by Stubbs cannot be accepted as historical facts.[77]

Stubbs, for instance, said that Innocent dismissed the claim of the bishops to take part in the election, without trial; in fact their claim was dismissed only after due trial. Again, 'on this point the claim of the monks was canonically irrefragable: they were the sole capitular body and had been repeatedly recognised as such by Rome'. So, also, the celebrated 'secret election', held by the monks, only took place in fact when they heard that John, 'acting in collusion probably with the bishops', had already sent to Rome, 'hoping to get Innocent's acceptance of a specific candidate'. Finally, as against Stubbs' statement,[78] the decision in favour of Langton was a unanimous one. Knowles used the papal register of Innocent III to show exactly where Stubbs had been mistaken.

> In conclusion, it may be suggested that it is unhistorical to attribute to Innocent III a deep and far-sighted design throughout all these negotiations. Rather, he proceeded in this case as in the contemporary cases of Glastonbury and Evesham, to allow the machinery of litigation to have full play according to the canons, regarding himself as the supreme administrator of legal justice. Only when the business of the courts had run its course did he act as the supreme ruler of Christendom.[79]

An even more dramatic change in interpretation of the other episode in the story – the 'humiliating' submission of King John to the Papacy – which had featured to great effect in anti-Catholic historiography over four centuries, was made even later. A long line of distinguished historians in the twentieth century, including Stubbs, K. Norgate, G.B. Adams, S. Painter, W.S. McKechnie, W.E. Lunt and Sir Maurice Powicke himself, all followed the chronicler Wendover in relating the conventional story of the deposition of John by Innocent III and of that Pope's invitation to Philip Augustus to seize the English throne.[80]

In 1948 C.R. Cheney at Cambridge produced the first full-scale scholarly treatment of the episode. He expressed surprise 'that historians have not been more concerned about the difficulty of accepting this testimony', namely that of the medieval chronicler, Wendover. In fact Lingard had made this same point in 1819.[81] Cheney showed, by collating the various chroniclers with the records, that 'the details of Wendover's narrative cannot be other than the products of imagination', so that 'in the history of this episode, fiction has successfully masqueraded as fact for more than seven hundred years'. Cheney proved that John was in fact 'never formally deposed by the pope' and there is no reason whatever to believe that Innocent invited Philip Augustus to invade England.[82]

The best modern account strips the story of those colourful elements which had been used from the time of the Reformation itself to inflame the nationalist feelings of English people against Catholicism. The episode is placed within a different historical context of diplomacy and strategy on a wider scale than that evisaged by Anglocentric post-Reformation historians who read their own narrow categories of nationalism, insularity and Protestantism back into the world of medieval England, where these concepts did not exist as they were known later. Cheney concludes:

It confirms the impression gained from other sources that the royal interdict and excommunication did not seriously trouble royal government and that John's difficulties were of a different origin, though they were aggravated by the displeasure of the Church. As the events of these years now appear, the Pope was more of a statesman than he seemed when we believed in the various unheeded sentences of 1211, 1212 and 1213. He measured his words according to his means and did not declare deposition when he could not enforce it. On the other hand, this episode suggests that John was still strong enough in 1212 and 1213 to choose the time and manner of his reconciliation with the Church. The pope was more anxious to pardon a prodigal than the king to solicit the forgiveness of his spiritual father. John's final acts of submission and homage were not the fruit of sudden desperation: they were the consequences of an embassy sent to Rome six months earlier. If it is true, and it may well be, that John acted on his own initiative when he made England and Ireland vassal states of the papacy, he made his intention known in Rome before Pandulph left for England; the formula of surrender shows that the act was premeditated. The terror-stricken tyrant and the domineering priest disappear from a story of well-calculated diplomacy by two men, each of whom had qualities of greatness.[83]

THE HISTORIOGRAPHY OF THE STATUTES OF PROVISORS AND PRAEMUNIRE

In 1922 W.T. Waugh showed by internal and external evidence that the 'Great Statute of Praemunire' of 1393 was merely something of a diplomatic pawn in the legal contest over patronage rights between the King's Court and the Papal Curia. It had not been taken very seriously by anyone at the time of its enactment. Waugh commented that 'for examples of how the meaning of an act can be distorted and its range extended, there is no need to look further than the notorious achievements in later times of the very statute we have been considering'. He was at pains to point out that 'Neither the statute of 1393 nor any other measure passed in England during the middle ages sought to prevent all exercise of the pope's authority in the country.[84] In 1949 G.R. Elton noted that the statute of 1393 was 'an attack on Rome's invasion of patronage rights, not an attack on Rome';[85] and in 1955 W.A. Pantin, a specialist on the fourteenth century, wrote:

> It is therefore a mistake to imagine that the Statute of Praemunire (or for that matter the Statute of Provisors) was a general or direct attack on papal authority or papal supremacy as such; it was not the first blast of the Reformation. Its only purpose was to prevent the pope from meddling with those cases (such as patronage) which the king had always claimed as temporal not spiritual matters.[86]

This is the accepted position of modern scholarship on the subject.

Nowhere, perhaps, is the false use of history to serve present expedience better illustrated than in the use made by Henry VIII of the old Statutes of Provisors and Praemunire in the period 1529–34. This episode also conveys the atmosphere created by a king intent on political terrorism as a means of getting his own way. By 1529 it was becoming clear that Wolsey was not able to procure papal permission for the divorce which Henry was seeking. Wolsey had become useless to the king and, moreover, he represented, as legate, the Pope's authority in England. In 1529 Wolsey was convicted under the old Statute of Praemunire (1393) of having accepted and misused the position of papal legate back in 1523. He died on his way to meet his end.

Encouraged by the success of this ploy, Henry began his campaign against the Church in England. In 1530 writs were made against eight bishops and seven other churchmen, again for offending against the old medieval statute which was being cynically misinterpreted so as to be exploited as a dangerous weapon. The charge was 'absurd', but in this 'legal fairyland'[87] anyone and everyone was in danger. Henry immediately extended the charge to cover all churchmen, who suddenly became liable to life imprisonment, the forfeiture of all their possessions and very possibly a worse fate still. The real terror lay in the vagueness and unpredictability of Henry's sudden moves and in the ruthless manner in which English law was being misused to achieve the king's ends. To avoid a worse fate, the clergy were forced to admit their own guilt and pay a sum of £118,840 to appease the king. He proceeded immediately to make them acknowledge him as 'Protector and Supreme Head of the English Church and Clergy'. They insisted on adding the clause, 'as far as the law of Christ allows', but he made them abandon this two years later. In this way the old medieval acts 'furnished Henry VIII with perhaps the most formidable weapons used by him to destroy Wolsey and to intimidate the clergy',[88] so preparing the way for him to become complete master in his own domain. Then in 1533 the same technique was used to make that domain independent of any outside authority.

The Act in Restraint of Appeals to Rome (1533) was epoch-making in separating England from the rest of Europe, both Catholic and Protestant.[89] By now Thomas Cromwell, the 'virtuoso of statecraft',[90] had been called in by Henry as his first minister. G.R. Elton has shown, by collating the various manuscript drafts of this act,[91] how the initial intention – gaining a divorce – was finally translated, through Cromwell's interventions, into a broader and more political statement about the nationally autonomous character of the English Church under the king. One factor which remained present throughout the evolution of this Act was the dependence of this new political statement on the supposed precedent set by the fourteenth-century Statutes of Provisors and Praemunire. These were used to justify the Act against Appeals.

The Act against Appeals announced the freeing of the English nation and people from the intolerable usurpations of a foreign power. It was the duty of all English people to withstand 'the Ambition and usurpacion of all foreign powers'. The new stand is taken on existing laws and on the 'somewhat mystical sovereignty of the crown',[82] as stated in 'dyvers sundrie olde autentike histories and Cronicles'. The Act claimed that the Statutes of Provisors and Praemunire had asserted the Crown's supremacy over the spiritual and temporal jurisdictions, to the exclusion of the Papacy, but this had been thwarted by further and persistent papal encroachments. All this would now be put right. The king's rights would be preserved 'from the Annoyance as well of the see of Rome as frome the usurped auctorities of other foreyne Potentates attempting the dymynysion or violacion thereof'.[93]

From 1533 onwards English historians followed the Henrician government's line and built their picture of the historic Act against Appeals on the earlier Statutes of Provisors and Praemunire. John Foxe, in 1563, stated that these statutes brought both spiritual and temporal cases within the king's jurisdiction, so that 'the pope is restrained of his usurped power, authority and jurisdiction within this realm of England'.[94] Thomas Fuller, in 1655, referred to the Statute of Praemunire 'which mauled the papal power in England', and went to add that 'Some former laws had pared the pope's nails to the quick, but this cut off his fingers'. This statute 'gave such a blow to the church of Rome that it never recovered itself in this land, but daily decayed till its final destruction'.[95]

Gilbert Burnet made great play of the old statute as proving the superiority of the temporal over the spiritual power in England: 'In this Dispute then between the Spiritual and Temporal Power we see the Parliament judged the matter'. This, he asserted, was a valid precedent for the further assertion of State power over the Church at the Reformation: 'by the same right that they judged one point, they may judge other Points' and 'their Judgment was as valid under *Henry* the Eighth, as under *Richard* the Second'.[96] This was bound to produce an interesting reaction from the Non-Jurors in defence of the spiritual authority against erastianism.

In fact Burnet's description of the Reformation as an erastian movement was, of course, correct – the State undoubtedly took control over the Church – but his justification for it was based upon a false appeal to historical precedent. The Non-Jurors mistook the essential character of the Reformation and as a result they had no need to justify it by a false appeal to history. They denied the revolutionary and the erastian nature of the Reformation itself, stressing the continuity of their own Church with the medieval Church; therefore, they did not have to find erastian precedents for it in the medieval past. Jeremy Collier, in his *Ecclesiastical History* (1708–14), was able, therefore, to provide the best exposition of the Statutes of Provisors and Praemunire to be found in English Protestant historiography up to the twentieth century.

Nothing is clearer than that his treatment of these statutes is the product of a conscious attempt to refute the erastian arguments which writers such as the common lawyer, Sir Edward Coke, and Burnet were drawing from the official view of them. His concern to make this refutation was strong enough at that moment to override the other view to which the Non-Jurors were committed, namely that which saw the medieval Church in England as an autonomous and independent body.

Collier struck at the heart of the erastian argument when he indicated that Sir Edward Coke had extended the whole purpose and meaning of the Statute of Praemunire: 'all application to a foreign jurisdiction, either in the court of Rome or elsewhere, to the prejudice of the king's crown and regality fall within the penalty of the statute. And here he stretches the word 'elsewhere' to a very large sense, and points it against the ecclesiastical courts in the realm.'[97] It was because Coke had extended it to the English ecclesiastical courts that Collier felt obliged to defend the position of the English Church, but his own defence extended to the rights of the Papacy as well. This comes out clearly when Collier is dealing later with Henry VIII's unjustified extension of the remit of praemunire in order to bring the English Church to its knees in 1529–30. Attacking the validity of Henry's proceedings against the English clergy, he wrote:

The purview of these acts of provisors and praemunire seems plainly set forth in the preamble. And what is that? It is to secure patronages from papal provisions; it is to prevent the impeachments of judgments given in the king's courts, it is to guard the prerogative from the encroachment of the conclave. Now what way does it appear that a moderate exercise of the legatine commission was inconsistent with the rights of the subject, or the jurisdiction of the crown above-mentioned? Might not Wolsey make use of his own legatine authority in convening national synods, voting for the passing or nulling of canons, and doing other things of a spiritual nature, without encroaching upon any branch of property or prerogative? One would think there were many powers within the verge of this authority, inoffensively practicable. Further it is observed that several English archbishops, since the making of these statutes, have acted as pope's legates without any prosecution from the state; and, which is more, it appears pretty plainly that those lords and other persons of figure who exhibited the articles above-mentioned against cardinal Wolsey, were not of opinion that the legatine authority was necessarily subversive of the king's prerogative, or inconsistent with the laws of the land.[98]

Collier here put the proper limitations upon the scope and meaning of these fourteenth-century statutes. He saw that they involved the protection of the king's law against encroachment, without denying for a moment the validity of the Canon Law administered by the Papacy.

It is very significant, too, that Collier turned to the preamble of the Statute of Praemunire for the definition of the terms of reference involved. This preamble, ignored by Henry VIII, Thomas Cromwell and all later Protestant historians who followed their lead, was essential to an understanding of the proper purpose and meaning of the statute of 1393. It had been given careful attention by the makers of this statute themselves: 'The truth probably is that the enacting part of the statute was not regarded very seriously. It was badly drafted. . . . In sharp contrast is the long preamble, obviously drawn up with care.'[99]

All this provides a very good example of the way in which a document can be misread and misinterpreted by historians unless they know the essential assumptions of thought which lay behind it – especially the normal relationships between the two authorities mentioned in this particular statute. The mistakes of later historians might well be attributed to this factor, but the first 'mistake', by the Henrician regime, was a deliberate and cynical exploitation of this medieval statute, which set the precedent for later historians.

It is highly significant also that, whereas Collier invoked the proper meaning of the fourteenth-century statute to disprove the historical basis of Henry VIII's attack on the English clergy in 1529–30, he did not repeat the operation to reveal the fallacies in the historical claims made by the preamble to the Act against Appeals to Rome in 1533. Precisely the same error was involved, but the Appeals Act, from Collier's viewpoint, was more directly concerned with enacting the national rather than the erastian part of the Reformation in England.

The preamble to the Act against Appeals provided the lynch-pin for a historiographical framework which was to include the concept of an early British Church of apostolic foundation completely independent of Rome[100] and an interpretation of medieval English history which stamped every sign of papal authority as a foreign encroachment or usurpation. The need to confirm and illustrate this view, and to buttress it with every kind of argument, became the main preoccupation of Protestant–Whig historians.

The desire to show the early independence of the British Church was the plainly stated motive behind the revival of Anglo-Saxon studies in Elizabeth's reign, with the publication of Matthew Parker's *De Antiquitate Britanniae Ecclesiae* (1566) and the foundation of the Society of Antiquaries (1566). The Church histories of the Laudian school, such as Peter Heylin's *Ecclesia Restaurata* (1655), the works of the Non-Jurors at the turn of the seventeenth and eighteenth centuries and the works of some English Church historians of the nineteenth century[101] all indicate the same. They all wanted to show, by appealing to early history, that the modern Church of England was independently founded in early days and then restored to its primitive purity at the time of the Reformation, after a period of papal encroachment and abuse in the medieval period.

Even when more elaborate accretions to the framework, such as the legend of an early apostolic foundation by St Paul or Joseph of Arimathea, had been dismissed by advancing scholarship[102] the enduring quality of the framework itself is evident in the treatment given to the Statutes of Provisors and Praemunire in the late nineteenth and early twentieth centuries.

So the scholarly Bishop Stubbs failed to see these statutes in their proper context and therefore did not understand their true meaning. Indeed the comprehensive meaning which Stubbs gave to the Statute of Praemunire of 1393 was the very meaning which had been attached to it by Henry VIII for the first time in 1529. This meaning was based not merely on a failure to see the statute in its proper context, but also on the actual omission of important words of restrictive effect which had been included in the original text of the statute.[103] In this respect, Stubbs, at the end of the nineteenth century, was far behind Jeremy Collier, who had achieved a proper understanding of the statute two centuries before. Indeed Stubbs' understanding of it – the old official version – was still dominant well into the twentieth century.

W.W. Capes in 1900 described the statute of 1393, with those of 1353 and 1365, as 'the great bulwark of the independence of the National Church'.[104] Sir James Ramsey wrote in 1913 of 'the great statute of Praemunire, the most anti-papal Act of Parliament passed prior to the reign of Henry VIII; the Act from which the rapid decline of Papal authority in England is commonly dated'.[105] And E.W. Gwatkin in 1917 saw in this statute 'the will of the nation expressed by Parliament' by which 'papal interference was shut out of England as far as law could shut it out'.[106]

It was not until the whole context had been set right, until medieval England was seen, at last, as a self-conscious part of a greater whole – the Christian community of Europe – that these episodes could be interpreted within their proper historical context. Obadiah Walker had achieved this understanding in the later seventeenth century. Jeremy Collier had made an important contribution at the beginning of the eighteenth century. John Lingard made his exceptional contribution to English historiography as a whole in the first half of the nineteenth century. But all these were isolated, if prophetic, voices in the history of historical writing. F.W. Maitland began the 'academic' movement towards a proper understanding of medieval England in 1898.[107] Z.N. Brooke re-affirmed the 'revisionist' view of the period from the Norman Conquest to the reign of King John.[108] W.A. Pantin authoritatively expressed it for the fourteenth century, during which the Statutes of Provisors and Praemunire were passed:

> This English ecclesiastical unit was called by the convenient name of the English Church (*ecclesia Anglicana*). Such a name did not of course imply any of that claim to ecclesiastical autonomy which was afterwards made in the sixteenth century. Nothing could be more clear than that the fourteenth-century English Church was very consciously part of the universal Church, in ecclesiastical government and in its intellectual and spiritual life.[109]

And later works in the twentieth century showed that this situation pertained in England right up to the time of the Henrician Reformation.

EPILOGUE

Together with the emergence of the true picture of the ecclesiastical system in medieval England, there came the refutation of the concomitant features of the official view of the English past which had accompanied the distorted view of the medieval period: the concept of an early Protestant British Church which had been established by one of the Apostles and contained the purity of the true Christian faith.[110]

As early as 1912, the Welsh historian Sir John Lloyd, in his *History of Wales*, wrote: 'no theological differences parted the

Roman from the Celtic Church, for the notion that the latter was the home of a kind of primitive Protestantism, of apostolic purity and simplicity, is without any historical basis.'[111] J.C. McNaught, a Scottish scholar, commented in 1927: 'As a result of our investigations we have come to the conclusion that the early Celtic Church, so far from being independent of Rome, in the sense of repudiating the papal supremacy, was simply a part of the Catholic Church, and with the whole of the Church acknowledged the Pope as its head.'[112]

It is clear that there was a certain interdependence between the various concepts contained within the official view. These formed a circle of logical argument. The idea of the Reformation as a return to the past was the initial idea, the centrifugal feature. The whole of English history was brought into agreement with the initial view of the break with Rome, as described in the Henrician statutes. Then the other parts were used to confirm the character of the Reformation itself. Previous English history was interpreted as an original 'golden' age, spoilt during the medieval period by the encroachments and interferences of the Papacy, but revived again by the Reformation which restored its national freedom to the English people. Later English history was to be interpreted as the great success story of the 'elect nation', leading to a position of imperial superiority in the world, with the Reformation and the 1688 Revolution as the two greatest stepping-stones in the story. There was a strong vein of political theology holding it all together and giving it a pleasing coherence. Thomas Cromwell, John Foxe and Gilbert Burnet had all contributed to this political theology. By this, I mean a certain theological view of politics and history which could be brought to buttress the idea of the English nation-state and empire. Cromwell's input was to introduce the theology of 'obedience' to the State; Foxe introduced the apocalyptic interpretation of English history; and Gilbert Burnet connected up these ideas with the Whig interpretation and the 'idea of progress' which carried the myth on into the age of 'enlightenment and reason', and indeed into the modern world of the twenty-first century.

Modern academic research has gradually undermined and destroyed the circle of logical argument, but has had little immediate effect on the nation's thinking in the way, for example, that Foxe's book did. The old view, which as a great myth became part of English folklore, still grips the imagination and feelings of many English people. The new research has not yet reached the public. Too much of it has been confined to academic monographs and articles, meant only for trained historians. There is in fact quite a strong tradition in England that professional historians should write for an audience of their colleagues, rather than for the public at large. There has been too little done in the way of writing up the results of historical research and scholarship in a way which is user-friendly for the more popular market. Too little of it has been made available for school textbooks. Yet we are now at a stage of history when it is very important that people at large should know more about their past, in the perspective established by the medievalists and revisionist historians of the twentieth century. It is this wider perspective which is needed for the teaching of new and important truths. The great myth concerning their past is now much more of a hindrance than a help to the English people in finding a new role for themselves in the new millennium. The truth lies not in small logical circles of argument, but in the widest and deepest perspective. The new historical perspective could help them to plan for the future in a much more realistic and helpful way, for example, by emphasizing the importance of community values and cooperative action, rather than a selfish kind of individualism and nationalism, devoted to 'cut-throat' competition as its highest value.

There is a common factor informing all three of the above historiographical case studies. It is to do with something which is again at the heart of being a historian. Before reading documents, one should have some knowledge of the general context in which they were written, including the relationship between the parties involved. Otherwise, words can take on meanings which are quite different from those intended by the writers, even, on some occasions, producing interpretations which are exactly opposite to the meanings intended. In all three of the above cases, for example, there were certain assumptions of thought present. Nobody in England was questioning the right of papal authority to be there. They all took this for granted and did not even bother to write down this obvious point. Therefore, some parties could express their grievances, real or imagined, in quite uninhibited terms because both sides knew that there was no question of challenging papal authority in spiritual matters. Without this knowledge, however, historians could – and in post-Reformation times did – read into these documents all sorts of challenges to papal authority itself which did not in fact exist. Then there is the evidence of people, like the chronicler Matthew Paris, who are always grumbling against all authority, simply because they do not like authority. This too can be completely misleading concerning the real nature of the case. In this sort of situation, the vital clues as to the nature of fundamental relationships which held society together are not always to be found in the documents themselves. Only the historian who has 'steeped' himself in the atmosphere of the period and is sensitive to the necessary 'vibes' behind the documents will be able to interpret them properly. One senses a sureness of touch in Sir Maurice Powicke, for example, when he is dealing with medieval evidence. I feel far less happy on the occasions when historians of more modern history are 'looking back' and making judgments on the same evidence.

One clear example of this process of misreading documents is shown in the way in which historians misunderstood and misinterpreted the documents of the medieval period because they did not understand the underlying and often unstated relationship between the Church in England and the rest of the Universal Church, centred on the Papacy. This particular misunderstanding and misinterpretation took place consistently over a period of centuries, as shown in the three historical case studies examined above.

Another example of the same process has been revealed recently in a study of medieval economic history, entitled *Property and Power in the Early Middle Ages*.[113] In the past, economic historians have tended to approach evidence such as gifts, bequests, sales and grants of immunity in medieval history with the crude working concept of 'Land equals power'. This working tool is derived from an understanding of society in modern times and is inadequate and often inappropriate when dealing with medieval society where other underlying assumptions existed.

In the medieval period, 'community', concepts and categories such as 'transaction', 'reciprocity' and other aspects of the Christian moral law which formed the basis of all relationships, were the norms. If these concepts and categories are applied as working tools, the same medieval evidence is made to reveal much deeper truths about the relationship between property and power in that period. This is equally true, whether the case studies are taken from eleventh-century Wales, England, Saxony, Byzantium, twelfth-century Tuscany or Merovingian and Carolingian France. One very interesting case study, for example, is that of Erkanfrida, a French lady of the Carolingian period, who endeavoured, after the death of her husband and against other powerful male claimants, to keep control of certain property near Trier. Alone it would have been impossible, but the power she was able to use arose from 'an impressive number of saintly supporters, and . . . a friendship network spanning heaven and earth'.[114]

We are reminded of the powerful nature of those great concepts of spiritual and secular community, transcending death, which held society together during the medieval period; without understanding them, it is impossible for modern historians to gain a full understanding of that period and its people. This new study, edited by Wendy Davies and Paul Fouracre, is therefore a highly significant and important contribution to the historiography of economic history. It changes the 'viewing mechanism' through which historians will in future look at the documents and other evidence available for the medieval period.

Another example of what I mean is the treatment of the Crusaders by historians since the sixteenth century. Protestant historians, their assumptions based on their own categories of thought, invariably describe the Crusades as displays of Catholic bigotry. Marxist historians, likewise, have inevitably discovered that their main motivating force was economic. However, in the second half of the twentieth century historians have started to re-examine the subject of the Crusades from the viewpoint of the medieval people who were involved in them. These people, like any other cross-section, were a mixed bunch, but there now seems little doubt that, among all the other mixed motives, there was a real and primary urge, driven by their religious faith, to respond to the call of the Church in defence of the Holy Places of Jerusalem: 'Fresh attention has been given to the religious and cultural climate which gave birth to the movement, to the ties of kinship and patronage which sustained it and the outlet which it provided for the chivalric values of society.'[115]

The historian, then, has to immerse him- or herself in the atmosphere of his or her period, if he or she is to become aware of the 'essential commonplaces' and assumptions of thought which underlie and inform the documentary evidence. He or she has to have respect, sympathy and a liking for the people who lived in it and will need to have great sensitivity to those 'vibes' which will make it possible to 'read between the lines' of a document. Above all, one must be aware of the great danger of 'hindsight', the temptation to read the present back into the past. The historian must allow the documents to speak for themselves, with the help of sensitive insight, without allowing preconceived notions to distort them. The danger is particularly great when the historian believes in a theory of progress, allied to the idea that there is an inevitability about events which means that the victors must always be right because they are 'on the side of the future'. Having achieved all this, then, the historian will have achieved that elusive but all-important sense of perspective.

The Protestant–Whig historians fell at all these hurdles, and consequently failed to understand the world of medieval England and the true nature of the Reformation which changed things so radically. Herbert Butterfield described 'the recovery and exposition of the medieval world' as something which 'still remains as the greatest creative achievement of historical understanding',[116] against which judgment we must measure the worth of the historians who contributed to it.

One of the great medievalists of the twentieth century helps us to see the Henrician Reformation through the eyes of someone who understood better than most the values of the world which it was replacing. Sir Maurice Powicke looks at surrounding events as seen through the eyes of Sir Thomas More. More 'stands out as the one person who saw quite clearly what Henry VIII's revolution meant'. He 'was the witness . . . who had brooded over the state of Christendom. He was wise, witty, urbane, observant, critical, caustic, yet full of pity'. He believed passionately in the unity and peace of Christendom, and in the truths behind them. Although he had 'no illusions about the state of Europe', he 'could not stand the denial of the unity of Christendom, and that men should take advantage of the troubles of the time to decry this unity for the sake of power or money'. He 'could see no rhyme or reason in the incessant wars, no justice in movements which spoiled the poor, no wisdom in the destruction of great institutions and ancient loyalties because they were not all they should be'. More knew the importance of all the issues involved. This 'leader in the new learning', who was 'interested in the discovery and exploitation of the empty spaces of the earth' and whose ideas in the field of social reform were so modern, was quite prepared to die the death of a martyr 'in and for the faith of the Holy Catholic Church'.[117]

FIVE

Enlightenment and Romanticism in English Historiography

THE SECULARIZATION OF THOUGHT

One of the most important aspects of the intellectual history of England and other European countries after the sixteenth century was the emergence of a phenomenon which can be summarized most conveniently as the secularization of thought. In the medieval world the authority of revealed Christianity, as expressed through the Catholic Church and the Scriptures, was accepted throughout Christian Europe. The Church provided the religious and moral framework within which the social, political, cultural and economic life of Europe took place. The different countries also worked within the self-conscious unity of Christendom. The secular rulers and their governments had important and acknowledged roles in the Christian scheme of things, but they were important parts of a greater whole and they could not claim absolute power or authority. In the spiritual sphere, the authority of the Church was higher than them and all people were ultimately of equal importance in the sight of God. The architecture of the period, finding its finest expression in the great cathedrals and churches, is eloquent of the Christian faith which was at the centre of European civilization and culture. The whole of Europe was called to the defence of the Holy Places of Jerusalem in the Crusades. The peace and unity of Christendom was more important than political divisions within Europe. It is difficult now to appreciate the central part which religion played in public as well as private life in medieval Europe.

This is not to say, of course, that there were not all the failures, abuses and compromises which usually accompany the attempt of any human community which is trying to live according to a

177

religious and social ideal, but these existed alongside saints, philosophers, statesmen and scholars whose example portrayed the value of their basic beliefs. Outstanding men of the Renaissance in the sixteenth century, such as Erasmus and Thomas More, had the insight and foresight to see clearly the consequences which would follow the breakup of Christendom. This was their great objection to the 'Reformation', though they were reformers themselves. The correspondence between Erasmus and Martin Luther shows a certain degree of collaboration in their concern to remove abuses in the Church, until Erasmus realized that Luther was intent not on reform, but on revolution; then there was a great break between them, which symbolized the great divide between the medieval world and the modern era as it was going to emerge.

The Reformation and the concomitant rise of the the new nation-states broke the unity of Europe. In England, as in Germany, Protestantism was exploited by the rulers to help them to achieve their political ambitions. In post-Reformation England State authority was in control of all aspects of life, including the religious. The divisions within Protestantism which emerged, and the Civil War and Interregnum of the seventeenth century, left religious life in England in a very fragmented condition. There began to develop in post-Restoration England new ways of looking at the life of society as a whole and of the place of man in the universe. There was a gradual rejection by certain thinkers of the concepts of revealed religion as expressed through the doctrines of the Church. This began to be replaced by a purely human interpretation of life and its meaning. 'Rationalism' came to mean a reliance on the powers of human reason above the authority of religious doctrine. Francis Bacon's advocacy of the utilitarian end of human reason and John Lock's 'sensation-psychology' provided the seventeenth-century seedbed of the new intellectual ethos and prepared the way for the 'age of reason' and 'enlightenment' in the eighteenth century when, for the first time, the place and significance of God in the cosmos was questioned. This had fundamental effects on society.[2]

The glittering successes achieved by the application of science in the second half of the seventeenth century, associated with such names as Harvey, Boyle and Newton,[3] provided a suitable background for the development of these ideas.[4] It is not surprising, in these circumstances, that the 'idea of Progress', with its emphasis on purely secular ends and its visionary prophecies of an earthly Utopia, has been traced to the latter half of the seventeenth century.[5] The vision of man's *unaided* march to perfection in an earthly paradise first appeared at this time and continued to drive the thought of Europeans up to modern times. But the unprecedented human tragedies associated with the two world wars of the twentieth century introduced doubts about man's capacity to rule unaided over himself and the universe.

It has been demonstrated[6] that interest in and study of the medieval period in England ended with quite remarkable abruptness in about 1730. At about the same time the age of erudition and technical scholarship, associated with the Non-Jurors in particular, also ended. The whole tenor of historiography in the eighteenth century was to be quite different from that which preceded it.

Already, towards the close of the seventeenth century, the influence of the secularization of thought on historical writing had become apparent. Burnet was in many ways a herald of the eighteenth century, for example, in his concentration on ideas, illustrated or worked out in history, rather than on the veracity of the facts themselves. History was to be regarded as a source of teaching concerning the nature of man and his place in the universe. Facts became less important than historical 'laws' which could be 'deduced' from the past. The important end was to discover the fundamental laws of human nature and of the natural world, which were unchangeable. Then history was simply the application of these laws to the facts of any particular period. History became 'philosophy, teaching by example'.

Sceptical thinkers of the eighteenth century sought to discover eternal truths and laws in the natural world and in history.[7] They were not interested in the humdrum occupations of fact-finding and source criticism. They were more concerned with the 'truths' which lurked beneath the surface of historical events than in the events themselves. It may perhaps be said that those people who rejected the revealed truths of Christian doctrine were now looking for the great truths of life in history or in nature. With the new fashion of thought came an attitude of scorn towards the erudite scholars of the preceding age and, indeed, for the whole of medieval history up to the 'Renaissance'. 'Philosophical' thought, expressed in elegant style and language, became the main criterion for excellence in the work of the historian.

A benefit resulting from this was the development of narrative history. The concentration on general ideas led to attempts to describe the way in which society changes and develops, the way in which the structure of society in one age changes into that of the next. The lack of technical scholarship and source criticism, however, meant that historical writing was not properly 'earthed', so to speak, and was too far separated from the real world of factual events. The next great step forward in historiography in general was when the two skills – narrative writing and technical scholarship – came together to make the modern vehicle of historical writing as we now know it. From this point of view, it is arguable that historical writing in England, up to this point, had actually 'fallen back' from the standard set up in the *fusion* of both skills seen in the Venerable Bede's *Ecclesiastical History of the English People* (731). Bede was a superb storyteller and he was extraordinarily reliable as a source for facts.

The danger of 'ideas' becoming divorced from facts was to be seen in the development in later history – particularly in Germany – of *historicism* (a belief that historical events are determined by 'Laws'). The philosophies of Hegel and Nietzsche were applied to history in such a way as to provide the background for the emergence of Marxist Communism and Fascism respectively. Both these historical ideologies had their own small circles of logical argument which were applied to history. Both sets of ideologists then claimed that history was the basis and justification for their actions – with disastrous effects for humanity in the twentieth century. Historical writing in England had already been affected considerably by the ideology of the 'elect nation' and was going to be affected, to some extent, at the end of the nineteenth century by the ideology of the 'nation's spirit', which expressed itself in history during its 'moments of destiny'.[8]

All this, in a peculiar way, was an expression of the secularization of thought, the imposition of a 'man-made' and 'man-centred' form of 'revealed religion', replacing the God-given revelation mediated through the Church and the Scriptures. It seems that the religious instinct is set deep in all human beings and will seek expression in a variety of other ways, if not fulfilled in an authentically religious form.[9]

THE AGE OF 'ENLIGHTENMENT' AND 'REASON'

David Hume wrote his *History of England* between 1754 and 1762. The outstanding representative of the English 'enlightenment', he was first and foremost a philosopher, who believed that history was a useful field for the illustration of his main philosophical tenets. In his *Enquiry Concerning Human Understanding* (1748), he wrote, concerning the study of history: 'Its chief use is only to discover the constant and universal principles of human nature, by showing men in all varieties of circumstances and situations, and furnishing us with materials from which we may form our observations and become acquainted with the regular springs of human action and behaviour.'[10] During the century after the publication of his *History* Hume was probably the most influential and prestigious of the historians of English history (nearly 200 editions of his *History* have appeared). His account of the Reformation was the most representative expression of Reformation historiography in the eighteenth century.

Hume's interpretation of the English past was certainly new. It was English history seen from the completely secularist viewpoint, which would be equated today with that of secular humanism. For the first time in English historiography of the Reformation we find a writer who has no religious interest or sympathy to declare. Hume was not a believer in Christianity and therefore it was quite unnecessary for him to try to support the truth of any particular belief. He was not, however, unprejudiced. His attachment to the secular beliefs of the 'enlightenment' made him particularly prejudiced against any expression in history of 'revealed' religion or of the Church as custodian of this revelation.

Significantly, Hume's version of the Reformation was not fundamentally different from Burnet's. Both fell easily into the framework of the Whig interpretation and the theory of progress, and into that of the old official version itself. The conventional interpretation of Catholicism, as seen in Foxe and Burnet, was that of a system of superstition and imposture, by which, during the 'dark ages' of the medieval period, a wicked priesthood had exploited a credulous populace. Like Burnet, Hume was much more interested in general truths than in the veracity of the historical facts. Neither of them had any real interest in the techniques of historical research and source criticism. Both thought it entirely legitimate to fill in gaps in historical knowledge with conjectures and generalizations out of their own heads.

Hume, like Burnet, knew nothing and cared less about the medieval period, towards which they both shared an attitude of contempt. He wrote of the 'dark ages', dominated by superstition and obscurantism. For him, any form of religious belief was anathema. He referred often to the tricks and impostures used by a malevolent clergy over the people. The latter were enslaved, in his view, by superstitious beliefs which had been designed to maintain clerical power. Speaking of the Council of Trent in the sixteenth century, he wrote, in typical vein:

> It is the only general council which has been held in an age truly learned and inquisitive, and as the history of it has been written with great penetration and judgment, it tended very much to expose clerical usurpations and intrigues, and may serve as a specimen of more ancient councils. No one expects to see another general council, till the decay of learning and the progress of ignorance shall again fit mankind for those great impostures.[11]

The Reformation, for Hume, was a great step forward towards the age of 'enlightenment and reason'. Although religion was not ousted altogether from England, the supremacy of the State over the Church was a definite step in the right direction. The gigantic fraud of clerical power and control had been unmasked and overthrown. So far he was at one with Foxe and Burnet. Hume regarded the royal supremacy and the erastian aspect of the Reformation in England as its greatest glory, though for quite different reasons than those held by previous English supporters of the official view. For Hume, these achievements meant that from then on real progress could be made towards the complete secularization of thought, placing man instead of God at the centre of everything.

The most famous English historian of the eighteenth century was Edward Gibbon (1737–94), best remembered for his famous *The Rise and Fall of the Roman Empire* (1776–88) in which he blamed the early Christian Church for the fall of that empire. Gibbon, like Hume, saw history in terms of rational laws and processes and had no sympathy with 'revealed religion' which claimed to have derived its doctrine from a source above, but not opposed to, reason. He also regarded the Reformation as an erastian movement which shook off the shackles of clerical control and enabled human reason to assert itself independently. It represented, therefore, a great step forward towards the 'enlightenment' of the eighteenth century. A kind of complacent nationalism is wedded to the general theme of human progress in Gibbon's thought:

We contemplate the gradual progress of society from the lowest ebb of primitive barbarism, to the full tide of modern civilization. We contrast the naked Briton who might have mistaken the sphere of Archimedes for a rational creature, and the contemporary of Newton, in whose school Archimedes himself would have been a humble disciple. And we compare the boats of osier and hides that floated along our coasts with the formidable navies which visit and command the remotest shores of the ocean. Without indulging the fond prejudices of patriotic vanity, we may assume a conspicuous place among the inhabitants of the earth.[12]

The Reformation was a very important stage in this story of national progress in England:

Till the period of the Reformation, the ignorance and sensuality of the clergy were continually increasing; the ambitious prelate aspired to pomp and power; the jolly monk was satisfied with idleness and pleasure; and the few students of the ecclesiastical order perplexed rather than enlightened their understanding with occult science and scholastic divinity.[13]

Gibbon concluded therefore that 'the protestant and the patriot must applaud our deliverance' from the mental bondage of the medieval period.[14]

It is evident, then, that one of the two main interpretative ideas of the old official version of the English past – the assertion of State control over the Church – remained completely intact during the eighteenth century. But what of the other interpretative idea, enshrined in the nationalist and isolationist approach to the English past?

It would seem at first glance that the eighteenth century, with its concentration on generalizations, 'enlightenment' and 'rational' approaches to history, would find little room for the narrowly national or isolationist interpretation of the past. Outside England itself, this observation would be true. Vico in Italy, Voltaire and Montesquieu in France, Schlözer and Gatterer in Germany, and even the Edinburgh school, represented by Adam Ferguson and John Miller, were concerned with various aspects of universal history. It would have been strange indeed if, against this background, there had been no signs at all of wider interests in English historiography, and, in fact, a gigantic 'universal' history was produced in England as a cooperative work by several minor authors. This work, however, was simply a compilation from other writers, a compendium of the different national histories, and, apart from criticisms of it from the artistic and scholarly viewpoints, the whole plan behind it was rejected by continental historians such as Schlözer, who said that this 'aggregate of national histories' was not what was meant by 'universal' history.[15]

The truth seems to be that English historians in the eighteenth century were unable to shake off that general insularity of thought created by historical, historiographical and geographical forces which remained an essential part of their environment. Hume, as we shall see, in spite of his Scottish partiality against England, was particularly insular in outlook. Even so representative a figure of the 'enlightenment' as Bolingbroke, the Tory political philosopher who wrote *The Idea of a Patriot King* (1749), was affected by it.[16] Gibbon was another typical product of the 'enlightenment', anti-clerical and 'rational'. His early decision 'not to learn German – it was far too barbarous a language – insulated him from some of the bracing scholarly breezes blowing on the Continent'.[17]

Not surprisingly, then, Hume falls completely within the old nationalistic category of Reformation historians since the sixteenth century. His scholarship is notoriously suspect and inadequate,[18] as one might expect from a man who believed that most knowledge is not perfectly certain, and who was not really very interested in facts: 'I have inserted no original papers, and entered into no detail of minute uninteresting facts. The philosophical spirit which I have so much indulged in all my writings, finds here ample materials to work upon.'[19] He knew little European history and was only really conversant with seventeenth-century history. His *History* was simply the application of general theories concerning the nature of man to a set of data which he was content to take, as it suited him, from the old chroniclers or from previous historians such as Foxe, Burnet and Strype.

Certainly Hume was more detached than his predecessors in his discussion of the religious conflicts and personalities of the sixteenth century. Events, for him, were decided according to 'the operation of those principles which are inherent in human nature'.[20] Queen Elizabeth, for example, is described as 'an excellent hypocrite', a person who 'was herself attached to the protestants chiefly by her interests and the circumstances of her birth'. She was an admirable ruler whose foreign and domestic policies were determined completely by motives of self-preservation.[21] This was a far cry indeed from Foxe's view of Elizabeth and of the religious mission which she had been appointed to perform. A refreshingly unprejudiced treatment is afforded to religious conflicts of the age, but this is because Hume was not really interested in these conflicts, nor could he understand them. He applied the secular motives and standards of his own day to the people of the sixteenth century and he was much further from understanding them than either Foxe or Burnet – despite their violent prejudices.

Hume left the official framework of Reformation historiography, as established in the Henrician statutes, entirely intact. In his account of the Anglo-Saxon Church, he wrote that the Papacy 'advanced every day on the independence of the English Church'.[22] Introducing his treatment of the celebrated Statutes of Provisors and Praemunire, he remarked that 'It is easy to imagine that a prince of so much sense and spirit as Edward would be no slave to the court of Rome'. These statutes 'speak in plain terms, of expelling by force the papal authority, and thereby providing a remedy against oppressions which they neither could nor would any longer endure. Men who talked in this strain were not far from the reformation.'[23] Hume's account of the Reformation itself is fundamentally the same as that of Foxe and Burnet, except that he is less interested and less passionate in his description. He saw the movement in terms of a successful bid for freedom by the English people, led by their king, against 'the yoke of papal authority'.[24] He described how 'The parliament was again assembled and Henry in conjunction with the great council of the nation, proceeded still in those gradual and secure steps by which they loosened their connections with the See of Rome and repressed the usurpations of the Roman pontiff'.[25]

Both Foxe and Hume were insular in their outlook on the past, but their insularity was expressed in quite different ways. Foxe, deeply affected by the religious issue, thought that England had a role in the Protestant apocalyptic plan, to lead, to defend and to spread the Reformation in Europe. Hume expressed his appreciation of the unique quality of the English nation's role in terms more suitable to the eighteenth-century outlook. He was pleased to state that 'of all the European churches which shook off the yoke of papal authority, no one proceeded with so much reason and moderation as the church of England' which 'had preserved itself in that happy medium which wise men have always sought, and which the people have so seldom been able to maintain'.[26]

It is significant that, while Hume was a Tory, his *History* did not mark a break in the supremacy of the Whig interpretation of the past. He was prejudiced against the Puritans because of the trouble and civil strife caused by their 'religious fanaticism', but he was sympathetic with the erastian-minded Anglican Church because it had made itself subservient to the State and had a useful stabilizing influence in English society. He was very much on the same wavelength as Burnet in this respect. The popularity of his work[27] meant that for a whole century – until it was superseded by the even more popular Whig masterpiece of Macaulay in the mid-nineteenth century – English historiography was dominated by Tory writers. The fact that this change took place without affecting the official version of the past indicates that the ideology contained within this piece of folklore was more fundamental to the English people's view of their past, more closely connected with their deepest prejudices and assumptions of thought, more part of their cultural outlook in the eighteenth century, than any difference of mere party politics. It was part of their *national* folklore. As a very recent observer has commented,

> the cultural hegemony of 'Whig' history in eighteenth-century England was essentially independent of any literary or scholarly movement, because it was as much a working political tradition as a view of history, and this was also true of Victorian England.[28]

As we have seen, this myth of the English past could be displaced only by a proper understanding of the medieval period. The historical writers of the eighteenth century completely failed to understand the medieval period because their own viewpoint was fundamentally unhistorical. They could look on the past only through the eyes of the present, and they judged it only by their own standards. They were not interested in the medieval period because they were 'so sure of being right on the subject of life and the universe' that they felt that the different values of the past were beneath their consideration.[29] A very recent commentator on the eighteenth century remarks that 'We can now appreciate the arrogance behind polite society's confident assertion of "Reason", which in fact only reflected the prejudices of the semi-educated of a certain place and time'.[30] Yet Gibbon in particular strove to show one stage of the history of Rome, with its particular institutions,

changing into another. The very attempt to describe this process –
though we may or may not agree with his historical analysis –
was an important contribution to the art of historical writing as
we have come to know it.[31]

REACTION: THE ROMANTIC MOVEMENT 1780–1830

It is significant that no history of the Reformation as such was
written in the eighteenth century. The religious passions of the
seventeenth century had cooled so much that comparatively little
interest was shown in the subject, apart from its consideration in
the general histories noted above. However, between 1780 and
1830 there were various currents of change operating within
English society and historiography.[32] The self-conscious
nationalism of the English had continued and increased during the
war with France in the American colonies and, especially, with the
coming of the French Revolution and the Napoleonic Wars. We
know that Protestantism, wars against Catholic Spain and France
and the conquest of an overseas empire were the three driving
forces in defining this self-conscious nationalism at this time.[33]

The English people looked askance at the terrible happenings in
France during the Revolution – the violent attack on monarchy, the
bloodshed and internecine conflicts, the denunciation of religion
and tradition – all in the name of the 'Goddess Reason'. It seemed
that the 'enlightenment' had succeeded only in driving people crazy.
Then there came the attack on other nations, driving Napoleon to
full-scale war against England. William Wordsworth had been
thrilled initially at the tone of the French Revolution's aims:
'Liberty, Fraternity and Equality'.

> Bliss was it in that dawn to be alive,
> But to be young was very heaven.[34]

However, having visited France during the troubles, England's
foremost poet experienced the 'still, sad music of humanity' and
returned with different views. He and his friends were to be the
harbinger of a new epoch in English culture and historiography,
which we know as the 'Romantic Movement'.

Before the turn of the century, this new movement was making
itself felt in England. A reaction against 'rationalism' expressed
itself in a variety of ways, including a greater interest in the past,

in tradition and in the roots of their nationality. The importance of religion in the life of individuals and of nations began to be reasserted.[34]

Edmund Burke was the greatest political thinker of the new era, and possibly of all eras, in English history. Originally on the Whig side of English politics and an opponent of the government's treatment of the American colonists, his criticism of the French Revolution in the famous *Reflections on the French Revolution* (1790) marked his final break with the Whigs. His insistence that freedom could only exist within the limits of tradition and constitutional continuity provided the centrepiece for future Tory politics. He opposed the rationalistic and pragmatic approach to history and to politics, stressing the importance of tradition and religion in the making of people's character.[35] He was equally opposed to radical extremism and government oppression.

Sir Walter Scott was the main link between English Romanticism, with its interest in the remote, mysterious past, and historical writing. His historical novels, culminating in *Waverley* (1814), exercised an important influence on English writing and helped to direct popular interest back to historical awareness. This revived interest in the past is vividly expressed in the *Rural Rides* (1830) of William Cobbett, who remained a Tory democrat at heart in spite of his extremely radical and anti-establishment views.[36] Cobbett was not a historian, but he used Lingard's work as the basis of his own *History of the Reformation in England and Ireland* (1824–7) in which he argued that the Reformation was a conspiracy of the rich against the poor. Cobbett's work was the first to emphasize this view,[37] which had in fact been put forward by the 'rebels' in risings associated with Robert Aske in Yorkshire (1536) and Robert Kett in Norfolk (1549). Cobbett's claims were exaggerated in some respects, though later work supported his central thesis, just as his attack on the Reformation for destroying 'Merry England' has recently received scholarly support.[38]

One interesting aspect of Cobbett in the history of historiography is the exemplification in him of a peculiar way in which historical understanding can sometimes be developed by the ordinary 'layman'. Cobbett was a bluff, honest, courageous and plain-speaking Englishman,[39] with a strong sense of justice and fair play. During his life he was imprisoned and had to flee to America for challenging certain conventions and commonplaces which others took for granted. For example, he said that flogging in the army was wrong. He was no great scholar. On the other hand, his mind had not been blinkered by the official version of things. He was freer than most to *see* what he *looked at*. The *Rural Rides* is a description of his travelling around England on horseback and making personal observations on all and sundry as he is passing through different neighbourhoods. The book is full of amusing incidents, some of which are historiographically speaking highly significant.

For example he visited Malmesbury in September 1826 and looked at the ruins of the old abbey and the ancient market cross. This leads him to some interesting aesthetic and historical reflections:

> the abbey is used as the Church, though the church-tower is a considerable distance from it. It was once a most magnificent building; and there is now a *doorway* which is the most beautiful thing I ever saw, and which was, nevertheless, built in Saxon times, in 'the *dark* ages'.
>
> There is a *market-cross* in this town, the sight of which is worth a journey of hundreds of miles. Time, with his scythe, and 'enlightened Protestant piety', with its pick-axes and crow-bars; these united have done much to efface the beauties of this monument of ancient skill and tastes . . . ; but in spite of all their destructive efforts, this cross still remains a most beautiful thing, though possibly, and even probably, nearly, or quite, a thousand years old. There is a *market-cross* lately erected at Devizes, and intended to imitate the ancient ones. Compare that with this, and then you have, pretty fairly, a view of the difference between us and our forefathers of the 'dark ages'.

In October of the same year he passed through Fairford:

> which is quite on the border of Gloucestershire, [and] is a very pretty little market-town, and has one of the prettiest churches in the kingdom. It was, they say, built in the reign of Henry VII; and one is naturally surprised to see that its windows of beautiful stained glass had the luck to escape, not only the fangs of the ferocious 'good' Queen Bess . . . but even the devastating ruffians of Cromwell.

This beautiful church is in fact the only one in England to have retained a complete set of medieval stained glass windows and is very well worth a visit.

Visiting Bury St Edmunds in December 1821, he reflected, 'Bury, formerly the seat of an abbot, the last of whom was, I think, hanged, or somehow put to death, by that matchless tyrant, Henry VIII.' In Reigate, in October 1825, he recalls the old priory and all the benefits derived by the community from it. Then coming to Beaulieu Abbey in the New Forest in October of the following year, he again muses on the scene:

> The little church or chapel, of which I have been speaking, appears to have been a very beautiful building, by what remains of the arches . . . the interior is partly a pig-stye and partly a goose-pen. Under that arch which had once seen so many rich men bow their heads, we entered in to the goose pen.

Cobbett goes away and finds out all he can about the history of Beaulieu Abbey, concluding that it did a great deal for the public good, for the monks were not as greedy as later landlords. Visiting Tenterden in Kent (August 1823), he admired the old medieval church on the hill, observing the 'very fine sight' of people leaving the church, 'the dress and beauty of the town', but remarks that now 'shabbily-dressed people do not go to church'. He deplored the practice of having 'pews' where the finely dressed people sat: 'Those who built these churches had no idea that worshipping God meant going to sit to hear a man talk out what he called preaching. By worship they meant very different things.' Worshippers were expected to stand or kneel: 'all were upon a level before God at any rate.' Cobbett tells us that he is a Protestant of the Church of England, but has to make observations according to his sense of truth and justice.[40]

All this is a useful example of how people can learn history by using their eyes in an unblinkered way. Similarly all history teachers will have learned much from those pupils who ask the unexpected question, or who give the unexpected answer to what seem a conventional question. Cobbett represents a quite exceptional phenomenon. He and Sydney Smith[41] were in a category of their own at this time, seen, in a way, as two 'outsiders' and two fine examples of 'Englishry' at its best.

The two representative English historians of this 'Romantic' phase were Sharon Turner (1768–1847) and Robert Southey (1774–1843). Turner's work illustrates all the new trends. He was motivated by religious, nationalistic and romantic ideals to probe into the early history of England. He thought that, 'the period of Anglo-Saxon history which preceded the invasion of England was worthy of greater attention because to contemplate the infancy of celebrated nations is among the most pleasing occupations of human curiosity'.[42] His *History of the Anglo-Saxons* (1799) was a noteworthy achievement, for which he made use of Celtic poetry, the Cotton manuscripts in the British Museum, and other original sources. The work, however, had many defects of scholarship, among which were faulty translations, uncritical use of sources and the 'common failing of ignorance of Continental research'.[43]

Then, between 1814 and 1823, Turner produced his *History of England*, which was inferior in many respects to his previous work on the Anglo-Saxon period. Here he used no new materials and showed the same lack of sympathy with and knowledge of the medieval period which was such a marked feature of previous English historiography. His Protestant and nationalist prejudices were much more pronounced in this work which is dominated by the idea of English progress from barbarism to the highest form of civilization.[44] The introductory chapter of thirty-five pages is concerned with 'The Corruptions of the Antient Catholic Church' and is sufficiently lurid in character. Typical of the whole is this extract from his description of medieval churchmen: 'Avarice was their character, from the highest to the lowest, and they were never satisfied. Luxury, profligacy . . . and every species of flagitiousness and abomination were in practice among them, and the fountain of all this depravity was the Roman court. Their ignorance equalled their vices.'[45] All this is nothing but a completely unsubstantiated repetition of conventional accusations made by previous purveyors of the official version of the past. It was obviously meant to heighten and justify the events of the sixteenth century, as the 'Dark Ages' gave way to the new age of 'light', when

> that intellectual principle, which animates and guides the human frame, displayed in all things an excited and investigating curiosity, awakening from the sleep of its former contentedness, and never to be deadened or satiated again. . . . The change was the more striking to the imagination, from the comparative darkness and destitution of the middle ages which had preceded. . . . The sanguinary dominion of Rome over the English nation; the tyranny of the papal hierarchy.

The darkness had gone and the way was open for religious and intellectual advance.[46]

The interesting aspect of Turner's *History* is that, while having nothing new or original to contribute to Reformation historiography, it constituted a link between the views of John Foxe and David Hume and the imperialistic jingoism of nineteenth-century England. From Hume and the 'enlightenment' Turner inherited the view of the Reformation as a movement which cast off the obscurantist and superstitious beliefs of medieval religion and set the stage for the advancement of the modern intellect, culture and civilization.[47] His religious concept of England's unique and providential agency in all this was distinctly reminiscent of Foxe. He was writing just after England had been the life saviour of Europe against the Napoleonic threat of domination and tyranny, when this view of England's special role in the destiny of Europe was particularly popular. The following extracts illustrate these historiographical strands coming together in his work. He was anxious to point out that

It was the resolution and perseverance of the English government and people, which encouraged and enabled the Northern hemisphere of Europe to throw off the yoke of Rome, and to complete its religious independence; and . . . If England's efforts had failed to maintain the liberation which it had commenced within itself and promoted elsewhere, the European world would have been subjected, with unpitying rigour, to that reign and inquisitorial tyranny of a jealous papacy and its vindictive hierarchy; and to that compulsory retention and veneration of puerile legends, and of many mercenary rites and doctrines, which by confounding religion with popular absurdity had deteriorated Christianity and the human intellect; and were continually tempting the enlightened understanding to that general incredulity, which it is one of the sins of the papal system, in its vulgar and practical form, to be ever tending to produce in a cultivated age.[48]

So Turner depicted 'a new era in the mind and history of mankind', started by the Reformation in 'the age and reign of Henry VIII'. England had been chosen by Providence to act as leader of the world and was demonstrating this by its imperial power in the new age. The following passage constitutes a kind of manifesto for English historical writing – tied to the chariot wheels of imperialism – in the nineteenth century:

For of what sovereign, before our present Monarch, George IV, and his still revered Father, can it be said, that he has reigned over AN HUNDRED MILLIONS of subjects, united under one sceptre? And though widely disparted in their territorial localities, yet how, in this opening year of 1829, forming altogether one peaceful, prosperous and happy kingdom; with every appearance of subsisting for the increasing benefit of mankind, and in the continued enjoyment of their individual felicities. Fortunate are the young, who are born to witness the meridian splendour of such national phenomenon. Happy are the aged, who cannot depart without the exhilarating view of this interesting aspect; and who had the satisfaction of witnessing its progressive growth, and of knowing that it has not been the scheme or the usurpation of any turbulent ambition. It has been the grand evolution of the providential destiny of our Country, produced by no human contrivance or vicious rapacity. England has been impelled by causes, not originating from herself, to become what she is; and as long as she exercises her sovereignty to promote the peace, the improvements, the morality, the religion, and the happiness of mankind, so long will her aggrandizement be continued, until some other nations arise, if ever any shall, whose superior predominance will still more signally advance the future progress of our emulous, excited, and never-resting order of intellectual being. Nations and cabinets may plan and battle; but that country alone will now become paramount in their political competitions, from whose elevation, the human race will, most universally, derive the largest proportion of general prosperity and of individual comfort. At present, the BRITISH dominion appears to be transcended by no other, in the diffusion of these blessings.[49]

Discernible in such passages is a connecting link between the Protestant 'elect nation', the ideas of progress and enlightenment, and the jingoistic nationalism and imperialism which played such a great part in the psychology of English people throughout the nineteenth century, terminating in the Golden Jubilee of 1887 when Queen Victoria ruled over a quarter of the world's population, when her military and naval forces still ruled the world in terms of power politics, and when British commerce and industry were still expanding on the ruling heights of the world's economy.[50] All these elements came together to define what the English people meant by their national self-consciousness and identity.

Turner was not interested in the history of institutions and, apart from the Providential power in history,[51] he read the past in terms of racial or national character and environment. Despite his romantic interest in the dawn of English history, he was firmly convinced of the intellectual and moral superiority of his own age. He looked down on the past from his elevated rung on the ladder of progress and his view of that past was representative of that of most nineteenth-century English people.

He never understood that England had once been part of Europe. His account of the Reformation is, after all, the old official version, decked up in the language acquired from later ages. The English nation, led by its temporal ruler, broke free from papal control. England's future greatness was based on this movement for national independence and freedom. Queen Elizabeth was the 'greatest founder of the progressive amplitude of our national greatness' and 'the healthful fountain of all our national vigour was that Reformation, of which she became the efficacious supporter, and the most successful champion.'[52] The Reformation put an end to the 'doctrines of the superiority of the papal and sacerdotal power above all temporal authority'[53] and the reign of Elizabeth saw 'the consolidated power of the state' come into its own.

Robert Southey's *Book of the Church* (1724) clearly illustrates the way in which the official view of the Reformation was considered an essential prop to the maintenance of the English Church and State Establishment which guaranteed the safety, security and success of the English people. This work was written at a time when social and political discontent was widespread in England after the Napoleonic wars. Outbursts of internal violence, such as the 'Peterloo Massacre' (1819) and later the Chartist risings, were expressions of political, social and economic unrest, as the more negative features of England's Industrial Revolution were beginning to shake English society. Moreover, there was a movement for Catholic Emancipation in England, after three centuries of deprivation and persecution, and there was increasing agitation in favour of political reform.

Southey's aim was to bring the nation to its senses, to remind his contemporaries of the temporal and spiritual blessings which had been bestowed on them by the Establishment and to indicate that loyalty and allegiance to the Established Church went along inextricably with proper security and order in the State. He wrote explicitly in praise of the role of the Anglican Church in English society:

> We owe to it our moral and intellectual character as a nation; much of our private happiness, much of our private strength. Whatever should weaken it, would in the same degree injure the common weal; whatever should overthrow it, would in sure and immediate consequence bring down the goodly fabric of the Constitution, whereof it is a constituent and necessary part. If the friends of the Constitution understand this as clearly as its enemies, and act upon it as consistently and as actively, then will the Church and State be safe, and with them the liberty and the prosperity of our country.[54]

Southey regarded the Anglican Church as an essentially national institution and the protector of the English constitution. He was therefore opposed to both Catholicism and Nonconformity, which, to him, represented threats to the English Establishment.[55] He found a sense of security in the established institutions of his country. He regarded the social and economic discontent, the new democratic ideas which were to lead to the great Reform Act of 1832 and the Catholic movement for emancipation, which was conceded by the Duke of Wellington (fearing severe disturbances and the strong Irish support for Daniel O'Connell) in 1829, as disrupting influences which threatened these institutions and therefore the security of the country.

Southey also saw the Reformation as the historical basis on which these national institutions stood: 'The result of our Reformation is of such transcendant good', having produced 'an ecclesiastical establishment . . . eminently good and essentially conducive to the general good'.[56] Here he was reflecting a strongly held view which was another vital element in the English people's view of their past. The pursuit of a sense of *security* is deeply felt in the human condition and it was strongly connected in the nineteenth century with the official way of looking at the past. By the nineteenth century this instinct had become a central plank in the Tory, as well as the Whig interpretation of English history.

Sharon Turner and Robert Southey[57] were true representatives of the new historiography – romanticist, nationalistic and pietistic in character – which was part of the reaction in the first part of the nineteenth century against the values of the 'age of reason' which seemed to have proved their bankruptcy in the excesses of the French Revolution. But, of course, history does not fit completely into such convenient categories. There will always be exceptions or 'overlaps' in real life. There was another, and more important, historian at this time, who belonged more to the previous age of the 'enlightenment' in spirit. Henry Hallam (1777–1859) was educated at Eton and Oxford and was a barrister by profession. He wrote as a cultured and educated Englishman, bringing from his profession a calm and detached prose style. His philosophical approach to history was essentially that of the 'enlightenment'. He considered 'the annals of barbarians so unworthy of remembrance',[58] while 'the ecclesiastical history of the Middle Ages presents one long contention of fraud against robbery'.[59] His main charge against the medieval period was that it allowed clerical superstition and fraud to gain too much influence over the State. The Reformation was a movement of 'emancipation', primarily because it succeeded in overthrowing clerical control.[60] Hallam's anti-clericalism is evident in such passages as the following:

It ought always to be remembered that *ecclesiastical*, and not merely *papal* encroachments are what civil governments and the laity in general have to resist, a point which some very zealous opposers of Rome have been willing to keep out of sight. The latter arose from the former, and perhaps were in some respects less objectionable. But the true enemy is what are called High-Church principles, be they maintained by a pope, a bishop, or a presbyter.[61]

His anti-clericalism was motivated by completely different feelings from those of the seventeenth-century Puritans. They were on fire with religious feelings; Hallam looked down on such enthusiasm and emotional involvement. The difference reflects the very real change in atmosphere which took place in English society between the seventeenth and eighteenth centuries. Again this change was not absolute, for John Wesley touched a strong nerve of deep religious feeling among ordinary people in eighteenth-century England, but it pertains to the leading writers and influences in society.

Hallam's *A View of the State of Europe during the Middle Ages* (1818) was simply, in his own words, 'a comprehensive survey of the chief circumstances that can interest a philosophical enquirer',[62] and this intention places his work very much in the same category as that of David Hume. On the other hand, Hallam's work also contains a certain 'mystical' feeling which, though less obvious than in the unrestrained utterances of Turner or Southey, is nevertheless evident in the occasional references to an overruling Providence in history,[63] which remind us that he was also a man who lived in an age which was reacting against the Enlightenment.

His most notable work, the *Constitutional History of England* (1827), though written in a style of judicial impartiality, was another expression of the official national-erastian view of the past. For Hallam, the Reformation was a movement of national liberation from clerical control. The royal supremacy was the high-water mark because it meant that the Church was 'altogether emancipated from the superiority of Rome'[64] while being brought under the control of the State. His complacent and self-conscious nationalism expressed beautifully the sense of pride and superiority which was an inextricable part of the English view of the past in the nineteenth century: 'No unbiassed observer, who derives pleasure from the welfare of his species, can fail to consider the long and uninterruptedly increasing prosperity of England as the most beautiful phenomenon in the history of mankind.'[65] Hallam's work, therefore, had all the qualities needed for it to become 'a work of great and prolonged influence'[66] in the nineteenth century.

In this brief survey of the historiography associated with the official version of the English past between 1730 and 1830 there has been evidence of changes which greatly affected the outlook of English society and English historians, as the age of strongly religious feelings gradually changed into the colder 'rationalism' of the 'enlightenment'. This altered again in the period of the Romantic movement in which there was a fascination with the more poetic, religious and mystical elements in life, in history and in nature.

In this kaleidoscopic scene of a changing society, there is one stable and unchanging feature in the English people's view of their past. All these historians, whether they were Whigs or Tories, rationalist or romantic, had one thing in common. Their view of the English past was contained within that national-erastian dualism of thought which had its origin long before in the statutes of the Reformation Parliament. This was connected with their common view of the medieval period as an age of 'darkness', from which emerged the Reformation, a popular movement led by the king, to free the nation and lay the basis for its future greatness. Along with this went the idea of progress which they applied to the history of post-sixteenth-century England. England's great success in colonial wars with France and Spain in the eighteenth century and in the Napoleonic Wars at the turn of the century, served to confirm the general spirit of confidence and superiority which it had gained from the earlier concept of the 'elect nation'. All these ideas were reflected in the Whig interpretation of history, but in fact the official view of the past was much bigger and deeper than the Whig interpretation. For it affected the thinking of English people across the political, social and cultural boundaries.[67] It was an assumption of thought, the great myth about the English past which had come to define what it meant to be an English person, as opposed to any other kind of human being.

By 1830, however, a new figure had emerged in English historical writing. His work represented something entirely new – a complete breakthrough from the old framework of thought into the modern world of historical scholarship. It completely undermined the premisses of thought on which the great myth was based. His work was to be largely by-passed and his significance largely underestimated in his own century and in ours.[68] The hypnotic effect of the great myth on the popular mind was too strong during these periods to be supplanted by academic research – however powerful and penetrating that might be. His work has never before been subjected to sufficient examination in depth. Various scholars have sometimes 'dipped in' and have recognized his astonishing ability to be right on a whole range of subjects in his *History of England* (1819–30) from the time of the Romans to 1688, where later professional historians, who were specialists in much smaller periods of history, were wrong. We shall be concerned now with John Lingard's extraordinary achievement, how it came about and the reaction to it in English society.

SIX

John Lingard and the Birth of Modern Historiography in England

John Lingard was born in 1771 at Winchester. He came from a family which 'though comparatively in humble circumstances, had been immemorially established at Claxby, a sequestered village at the foot of the North Wolds, in Lincolnshire'.[1] His father was a carpenter, his mother the daughter of a small farmer, both of them Catholics. His mother's family had been impoverished and broken up by fine and imprisonment during the revival of anti-Catholic persecution after the 1745 rebellion of the Stuart cause.[2] At the age of nine, Lingard had personal experience of the Gordon Riots of 1780 which followed the Catholic Relief Act of 1778 and which had spread from the metropolis into several provincial areas.[3] In 1782, having been brought to the notice of Bishop Challoner, he was sent by the latter's successor, Bishop James Talbot, to the English College at Douai where he began his studies for the priesthood. He acquitted himself brilliantly in the course of humanities before entering the school of theology. The educational philosophy at Douai – empirical, classical and critical use of sources – engendered an approach which 'lay at the roots of modern historical consciousness'[4] and of the young Lingard's own training as a historian, a training totally unavailable in England at this time. Now, however, the threat of the French Revolution was making itself felt in Douai and Lingard had experienced its dangers personally.[5] The declaration of war between England and France in 1793 was the signal for flight to the collegians at Douai, the college having been seized and occupied by the revolutionaries.

Lingard returned to England with a small party which included the son of Lord Stourton. Having been invited by the latter to become tutor to his son, he entered the Stourton household.

Meanwhile, another party of students from Douai had found shelter in a small school at Tudhoe, about six miles from Durham. Lingard immediately resigned his appointment and went to join them, becoming the director of this little group in 1794. After one other move, they finally settled at Crook Hall, near Durham, where in October 1794 they resumed their former way of life and education as a college community. Lingard became vice-president and was ordained priest at York by Bishop Gibson in the spring of 1795. He was appointed also as 'prefect of the studies' at Crook Hall and was head for many years of the schools of natural and moral philosophy.

In 1808 the college moved to Ushaw where it still stands, about five miles outside Durham. Lingard remained here until 1811, in the early autumn of which year he left Ushaw to become the parish priest of the secluded mission of Hornby, a small village near Lancaster. He had been offered the presidency of Maynooth College in Ireland, but declined this, as he was later to decline other such offers – including the rectorship of the English College, Rome, and two bishoprics – to adopt a way of life which he preferred. It was also strongly rumoured, after the success of the first volumes of his *History*, that he had been created a cardinal *in petto* (in waiting) by Pope Leo XII in 1826, but Lingard typically made a joke about the whole thing.[6] By this time his uncompleted *History* had been translated into French, Italian and German, and his reputation in Rome and Europe was much higher than it was in England.[7] He was unaffected, however, by any ambition for clerical advancement. From 1811 until his death in 1851, apart from two visits to Rome and occasional excursions to libraries in Manchester, Liverpool and London, Lingard remained at Hornby, confining himself to his work in the little parish there and to his historical researches.

Lingard's interest in history had been apparent during his childhood,[8] but it was during his stay at Crook Hall that his historical talent began to show itself. The extraordinary width and openness of his approach are immediately apparent. In his journal for the year 1800 there are comments such as 'Gibbon read and compared with Fleury, Froissart, Villani, Muratori, Wraxall etc', 'Read Life of Clement XIV in French by Curraciolo', and there are notes on subjects like the wars of the Turks against the Venetians or the character of Philip II of Spain.[9] About this period also, we find letters in which Lingard was already 'commissioning' his scholarly friends – priests who were scattered all over England and abroad – to perform various tasks of historical research in places such as the Chetham library in Manchester and the British Museum in London.[10] It became Lingard's custom at this time to read papers on various aspects of Anglo-Saxon Church history to a small group of friends, and he was persuaded by them to turn these into a book. This was the origin of *The History and Antiquities of the Anglo-Saxon Church* (1806), for which he used many original sources and manuscripts in Anglo-Saxon and Latin. The book was 'an important event in the historical scholarship of the time'.[11]

From the time of the publication of this work, Lingard's friends urged him to extend it into a full History of England, but he hesitated to embark on an undertaking which might be 'injurious to the interests of the college',[12] an early manifestation of the carefulness with which Lingard approached the deep-seated religious and historical prejudices of an English audience. After settling at Hornby, however, he did begin to work on a history, but still thought of it only, as he says, for the use of schools.[13] He soon found, however, that his researches were carrying him far beyond the limits of such an 'abridgement'. The latter was thrown aside and he began to work in earnest on the *History of England* as we know it, filling ten large volumes and covering the time from the first invasion of the Romans up to the accession of William and Mary in 1688. The first three volumes appeared during the period, 1819 to 1824, and the work was completed in 1830. It was revised and updated over the next twenty years as new documentary evidence came to light.

Lingard's situation at Hornby was in many ways ideal for the writing of history. The village parish was very small, and he was able to devote most of his time to his studies, the intensity of which is shown in a letter of 1828: 'I am compelled to devote my whole time to the perusal of works, pamphlets, newspapers, etc, etc. connected with my historical researches, and on that account have for these three or four years found it necessary to abstain from all other reading, however interesting it may be.'[14] He was secluded to an extent which made concentrated study and thought possible. The qualities of calmness and detachment in his work may well have owed something to his situation, for as he wrote himself in another context: 'the same object will often appear in a very dissimilar light to the spectator who views it calmly from a distance, and the man who acts under the influence of public excitement, and with a judgment swayed by the views and prejudices of party.'[15] Nor was he deprived, on the other hand, of the advantages to be gained in experience by contact with the world of public affairs. He enjoyed such company, from time to time, as the judges on the northern circuit – Pollock, Scarlett and Brougham – who made a point of stopping to visit him when they passed that way.[16] It must be a tribute to his common sense and good judgement that he was frequently consulted on the most important questions in the successful struggle for Catholic emancipation (1829), as is seen in the correspondence between him and Bishop Poynter[17] in which his advice was sought and given on certain matters. It was Lingard, for example, who drew up the petition to be presented to the Lords in 1825 concerning emancipation for Catholics. In all these matters he was face to face with the practical issues of the day and is always careful and diplomatic in dealing with them.[18] So we see reflected in his historical narrative that sense of reality which recognizes, for example, the element of the unforeseen.

It is central to the historian's task to be ready to be surprised by the evidence, an approach which stems from a recognition of the element of human free will. It also comes from the preparedness to see things from the viewpoint of the people actually dealing with events, rather than looking back and making interpretations based on hindsight. This ability was a marked feature of Lingard's work, which equipped him to break through the conventional framework of thought on the English past. This approach singles Lingard out from any other contemporary or previous English historian. So he could write, 'we often attribute to policy events which no deliberation has prepared, and which no foresight could have divined';[19] 'it is not often that the adventurer discerns at the outset the goal at which he ultimately arrives. The tide of events bears him forward; and past successes urge him to still higher attempts';[20] 'for many of the improvements in the English constitution we are indebted more to views of personal interest than to enlightened policy'.[21]

He refers ironically to those 'philosophic' historians who 'are apt to attribute to the foresight of politicians those counsels which are in reality suggested by the passing events of the day'.[22] With regard to the Civil War, he comments, 'the controversy between the king and his opponents no longer regarded the real liberties of the nation'.[23] This approach was to be repeated nearly 150 years later when, in the 1970s, the 'revisionist' historians, led by Conrad Russell, made their 'attempt to evade the influence of hindsight' which had 'grossly distorted the story we have been told', in their attack on the Whig interpretation. Russell also adds that the work of the International Commission for the History of Representative Institutions has made it difficult to sustain 'the potentially offensive assumption that the survival of Parliament in England is due to any special virtue in the English'.[24]

Lingard took a very firm stand against the 'philosophical' approach to history, which had characterized the eighteenth century:

> It is long since I disclaimed any pretensions to that which has been called the philosophy of history, but might with more propriety be called the philosophy of romance. . . . If they indulge in fanciful conjectures, if they profess to detect the hidden springs of every event, they may display acuteness of investigation, profound knowledge of the human heart, and great ingenuity of invention; but no reliance can be placed on the fidelity of their statements. . . . They come before us as philosophers who undertake to teach from the records of history; they are in reality literary empirics who disfigure history to make it accord with their philosophy. Nor do I hesitate to proclaim my belief that no writers have proved more successful in the perversion of historic truth than speculative and philosophic historians.[25]

This was a clarion call against Hume and his followers in eighteenth-century historiography, and against any historian who fails to make the proper distinction between history as a professional subject, an independent discipline, with its own methods and limitations, and the other disciplines of philosophy and theology. Lingard was in fact the first figure in English historical writing whom we can identify as asserting the *separateness* of history as a discipline in its own right, with its own methodology. He was in my view the first professional English historian and quite remarkably he set himself standards which have not been surpassed – or even perhaps equalled – in modern historiography. It is revealing, too, that Lingard was trained in both philosophy and theology and was well capable, therefore, of identifying the particular characteristics of historical writing as a separate discipline.

For this reason, Lingard was unaffected by the romantic, mystical, pietistic, or nationalist elements which characterized the Romantic movement and its exponents, such as Southey and Turner. There is no attempt in Lingard, for example, to attribute particular events to a providential agency. He writes quite sceptically, *qua* historian, about the heavenly 'voices' of Joan of Arc, suggesting another explanation without being dogmatic on the subject.[26] The high level of impartiality and objectivity which he achieved in his treatment of religious issues has been recognized[27] and will be confirmed by the most cursory reading of those parts of the *History* where such issues are at stake. The *Oxford and Cambridge Review* had to concede in 1846 that Lingard was 'as free from the perils of metaphysical flights . . . as he is uninfluenced by a religious or political bias';[28] and a modern historian wrote of his *History*, that 'It gave no indication that the author was a Catholic priest, and few of his readers would have guessed it'.[29]

In politics Lingard has been described by one modern writer as 'mildly Whig'[30] and by another as a Tory 'at heart'.[31] It would be impossible to build a case of bias against him. His treatment of the constitutional struggles of the seventeenth century does not reveal any particular partiality and some of his comments are masterpieces of objective judgment.[32] It is significant that the *Edinburgh Review*, the main Whig review of the day, criticized Lingard in 1825 for his lack of 'generous sympathy' with 'the cause of freedom',[33] but by 1831 it had to acknowledge the 'rigorous impartiality, which he uniformly displays on political questions', although he was still not 'Whig' enough for its liking.[34] Lingard's own word on the subject is given in a letter to his publisher: 'Whether my history will be, as you call it, the history of the people, I know not; but I persuade myself that no writer has hitherto set down to the task more free from political prepossession than myself.'[35] Lingard was a patriotic Englishman whose Catholicism was of the English type, akin to that of Thomas More and John Henry Newman. He insisted that English Catholics should be careful to identity and proclaim the essentials of their faith and not confuse these with the 'accidentals', which came with the national cultures of other countries. He disliked any exaggerated forms of ceremony, which he associated with certain continental forms of Catholicism,[36] and was concerned to set proper limits to the extent of papal authority.[37]

He consciously set out to write as an 'unconcerned spectator'[38] and as a 'citizen of the world'.[39] Indeed he expects this as the stance which the professional historian must always adopt. Moreover, he actually achieved this in his work, so that there is no hint of national bias, which constituted one of the major reasons for the originality of his achievement. He was at once, for example, proud of the traditional 'skill and intrepidity' of the British seaman[40] and able to see the lower side of the activities of the Elizabethan heroes – Drake, Hawkins and the rest.[41] He recognized the value of the English Constitution,[42] but realized that it was not simply the product of English wisdom as his predecessors and contemporaries took it to be.[43] There is an extraordinarily balanced tone to his treatment of international issues, whether it be in describing Anglo-French relations of the fourteenth century,[44] Anglo-Spanish relations of the sixteenth century,[45] or Anglo-Dutch relations of the seventeenth century.[46]

Lingard's temperament, as it emerges from his correspondence, was one of simplicity and good humour. His intense dislike of exaggerated or affected language and behaviour was the source of the dry but unmalicious humour which appears from time to time in his narrative.[47] There is no instance of his being provoked into a quarrel with anyone. The villagers at Hornby had a great affection for him[48] and his sense of humour must have been a great help. When he became well known by his writings, the stagecoach used to stop outside his house, where the driver would point out his residence and the travellers would look through his window to catch a glimpse of him at work. When Lingard saw what was happening, he used to place his dog – an obliging animal – to sit on his chair, complete with spectacles and coat. The travellers would then gape in astonishment at the 'celebrated', but rather grizzled, Dr Lingard at work.

Lingard's style is classical in its simplicity and lucidity. It was consciously chosen as the instrument which would best achieve his purpose – a clear narrative conveying simply stated factual information which in fact contained an originally based and explosively new interpretation of English history. Significantly, the revisionists of the late twentieth century also emphasize the importance of narrative as opposed to 'theoretical' history.[49] He was criticized for a lack of 'feeling and pathos' which most contemporary writers exhibited, and for his 'lifeless coldness', together with the lack of 'moralising' or 'philosophic' passages to which English readers had become accustomed.[50] He disliked bigotry, intolerance or fanatical display of any kind[51] and from whatever quarter. Also there is nothing dogmatic about his work, in the sense that Macaulay's History is dogmatic.[52] There is a continual awareness in Lingard of the inadequacy of source material to be able to explain *everything*.[53]

LINGARD AND THE ROLE OF AUDIENCE REACTION[54]

There is abundant evidence that Lingard's historical work was met with great suspicion and hostility by Protestant England. The *Edinburgh Review* commented frankly in 1825: 'as the author approaches indeed to the critical period of the Reformation . . . he will require to be watched as closely in his account of our free constitution as of our Protestant Church.'[55]

The *Westminster Review* of 1827 looked back and observed:

> A history of England by a Roman Catholic priest was assuredly destined to be met with coldness and suspicion. It required merit of a very high order to contend successfully against the prejudice of a nation of protestants, glorying in the reformation of their ancient creed, and eyeing with jealousy and apprehension the adherents of the once predominant faith.[56]

English people in the first decades of the nineteenth century had all that hostility to and fear of Catholicism which had been bred into them by three centuries of unmitigated literary and oral tradition on the subject. The saving of the nation from Popery was celebrated annually on 5 Novenber and the tradition sometimes manifested itself more dangerously in phenomena such as the Titus Oates Plot (1678) or the Gordon Riots (1780). The suspicion and hostility were always there. Popular literature of the decade 1820–9 reflects the ferment in the years preceding Catholic emancipation (1829), when anti-Catholic hostility expressed itself in 'No-Popery' campaigns, meetings and petitions.[57] This was the decade during which Lingard's *History* appeared.

The recourse to history took a primary place in the various tracts written against Catholic emancipation. The Massacre of St Bartholomew (1572) and the Irish Massacre (1641)[58] figure very largely in popular tracts such as *Christian Martyrdom: Being Authentic Accounts of the Persecutions Inflicted by the Church of Rome on the Protestants* (1826) and *The Accusations of History against the Church of Rome* (1825). That extraordinary *enfant terrible* among Anglican clergy, Sydney Smith,[59] pointed out that one of the main reasons for anti-Catholic clamour was the belief 'that the Catholics alone have been persecutors' which was propagated by 'men who love party better than truth'.[60]

Another reason for the preconceived hostility to Lingard's work was fear for the safety of the national Church, which was synonymous with that of the nation. Dr Kipling, Dean of Peterborough, had already attacked an earlier work of Lingard in which the latter had used the phrases 'the new Church of England' and the 'modern Church of England'. These were, said Dr Kipling, 'seditious words in derogation of the established religion' for which Lingard was 'amenable to a court of justice', since 'the church by law established in this country is so inseparably interwoven with the British Constitution, that whatever is calumny on the former must be calumny on the latter'.[61]

Paradoxically, this kind of expected public reaction was of positive advantage in Lingard's case. It was a positive spur to good scholarship and impartial presentation. Psychologically, it became almost an obsession with Lingard that he should be able to prove demonstrably whatever he wrote, so that no one could accuse him of partiality. As a Catholic priest he certainly wanted to serve his Church, but he saw that the best way to do this was to tell the historical truth and to prove it. This was a personal force which led him to his highly original and important activity in the areas of source extension and source criticism. It was in this field that he was to become a figure of the first importance in English historical writing.[62]

Even more interestingly from the viewpoint of the student of historiography, this concern of Lingard to establish his credentials with his readers made him reveal, to an unprecedented extent, the ways in which he reached his conclusions. His readers are invited, so to speak, into his historical workshop where they can share with him the techniques which he developed to test the authority of his sources. This has made it possible for the researcher to follow him every step of the way in the process of comparing and collating sources, according to a systematic use of certain auxiliary techniques,[63] in a way that has not been possible with any other historian of which I know. It was a result of Lingard's need to bring the reader alongside him, in order to gain his trust, and this was the result of the peculiar historical circumstances in which he was writing his *History*.

Lingard saw clearly that his first task was to remove prejudice from the minds of his readers, 'for prejudice in general indisposes Protestants not only yielding to argument, but even from listening to it'.[64] He wrote to a friend just after the publication of his first volume in 1819:

> Through the work, I made it a rule to tell the truth whether it made for us or against us, to avoid all the appearance of controversy, that I might not repel Protestant readers, & yet to furnish every proof in our favour in the notes. . . . In my account of the Reformation I must say much to shock Protestant prejudices & my only chance of being generally read by them depends on my having the reputation of a temperate writer. The good to be done is by writing a book which protestants will read.[65]

His concern to avoid any imputation of partiality or controversy is evident throughout Lingard's correspondence. For example, he had written a controversial pamphlet in his younger days and now wrote anxiously to his publisher to ask whether he thought that a reprint of it might affect his good name as a historian.[66]

Indeed, Lingard's caution in the face of a hostile audience accounts for a few instances in which his work falls short of the very high standard of professional detachment which he usually achieved as a historian. He mentioned certain things, not because they should be included on historical grounds, but merely because to omit them might provoke a charge of prejudice.[67] In one such instance, he is criticized by a modern writer for being too harsh on the Catholic concerned.[68] In another important instance, when he is in fact breaking completely new ground and giving modern shape to the account of a famous episode in medieval history, which had been used mistakenly and continuously for propaganda purposes in the official version since the sixteenth century, Lingard actually omits to mention where he found his source for a certain charter in case it might provoke prejudice:

> It is true . . . that I might originally have made the matter more clear by stating where I had found the charter: but I did not do so then. Why? Because it was an experiment. I was beginning my career as a historian of England: I knew the prejudices marshalled against me: and I was afraid that if I had said that I found it in the Vatican, it would immediately have been proclaimed a fraud &c &c.[69]

This, too, was concerning an episode which was not fully or correctly recorded by other English historians until the middle of the twentieth century.[70]

To be fair to Lingard, we should not attribute his impartiality simply to the factor of audience reaction. As with Mabillon, Lingard was inherently a man of great integrity for whom the truth mattered greatly: 'Piety and truth must never be considered as separable, for honest and genuine piety will never come into conflict with the truth.'[71] This is one of his fundamental attributes as a historian and it is clearly revealed in his private papers.

Lingard's scholarly, unprejudiced and uncontroversial approach was something entirely new to English historical writing. Previous historians of all sides had regarded it as their duty to defend their own side and attack the other.[72] The originality of Lingard's approach in this respect provoked the criticism of several of his fellow Catholics who felt that he was letting his own side down in parts of his work. Bishop Milner, who tried to get the Irish bishops to join him, and Mgr Talbot, for example, denounced Lingard's *History* as a betrayal.[73] It was in reply to such attacks that the values at the heart of Lingard's activity as a historian are revealed. He wrote to a friend in 1820, just after his first volume had appeared:

Your friend thinks I should have occasionally assumed a tone of piety & betrayed something more of a bias towards the Catholic cause. I think that if I wished to do good, I ought to have written as an indifferent spectator. Time and experience must decide between us. Should their verdict be against me, no one will deplore my misjudgment more than myself.[74]

Even more directly, he wrote to another friend in the same year, defending himself against another complaint that he had been prejudiced against the monks in his account of the Dissolution of the Monasteries: 'Perhaps he would have me deny the whole charge. . . . To have met the charge by denying it would have been to have acted contrary to my conscience since I believed it in many respects true.'[75] We shall see[76] that Lingard in fact had dealt with this subject in his usual manner of carefully weighing and balancing the evidence before reaching his conclusions, much along the same lines as a modern specialist has done.[77] Lingard adds to the above letter the observation that not only would it be morally wrong but also 'contrary to sound policy' to prevaricate with the truth.[78]

The anticipated audience reaction also affected greatly the style in which Lingard presented his work. He deliberately chose an unadorned style as the best vehicle for the original scholarship which he was putting before a highly suspicious and hostile English audience whose basic historical presuppositions he was going to contest. Facts rather than eloquence were needed to overcome deeply rooted prejudices, when he was telling people what they did not want to hear. These facts had to be as incontrovertible as possible. This was in complete contrast to Lord Macaulay who was to become celebrated for his literary eloquence when telling the public what they wanted to hear[79] in the nineteenth century. Lingard wrote in 1819, the year in which his first volume appeared: 'But style is become with me a secondary object. The task I have imposed on myself of taking nothing on credit but of going to the original authorities, is so laborious that I have no time to throw away on the graces of style.'[80]

It is noticeable, however, that once having gained his first hearing, and with this a degree of confidence,[81] Lingard became more eloquent in the later volumes of his first edition and in the later editions themselves.[82] Again, when dealing with a completely non-controversial subject such as the Great Plague of London (1665–6),[83] he revealed a real ability for vivid description and powerful suggestion in creating the atmosphere of the time. The *Edinburgh Review* commented that the Plague 'has never been noticed by any historian in more than a few lines. Dr. Lingard has made good use of his materials, and may fairly challenge comparison with the well-known account of the plague at Athens by Thucydides.'[84] It is interesting that the major characteristic of Lingard's narrative style – his concentration on putting the facts in the right order – is another feature of the work of the modern revisionist historians. Conrad Russell has mentioned this as a characteristic feature of their own work as opposed to the theorizing and generalizations which the Whig historians imposed on the facts.[85]

THE METHODOLOGY OF LINGARD'S ATTACK ON THE OFFICIAL VERSION
OF THE ENGLISH PAST

The abiding insularity of thought, which had bound English historiography since the sixteenth century, strongly affected all aspects of the English people's outlook. It was buttressed by three main defects. One was the ingrained habit among English historians of regarding previous writers of their own side as authorities, rather than going to original sources. Secondly, English historians did not look outside England for their sources. They can hardly be blamed for this, since most continental archives were not open to scholars until the second half of the nineteenth century, but they did not even recognize the need to look at events from another nation's point of view. Thirdly, the science of source criticism as an essential tool of the historian had not begun to be developed in England.

The writer who wished to break through this insularity of thought was faced with a much greater challenge than we can now possibly imagine. The obstacles ranged from deeply rooted and intensely held prejudices, to the lack of proper techniques of source criticism and to the physical unavailability of original sources. All this represented a challenge to Lingard which was arguably the greatest faced by any English historian. So far, we have looked at the factors which came together around the 1820s to provide a conducive environment for the challenge to take place. Tolerance of Catholics had reached a stage when, for the first time, the challenge was just possible. Indeed, the hostility and suspicion of the audience could now become a spur to good scholarship in the challenger. Nothing could have happened, however, if a writer with exceptional personal qualities and extraordinary ability as a historian had not been there at the right time to take up the challenge. One of the fascinating features of historical development lies in such interaction between personal and impersonal factors.

Up until Lingard English historians had been pleased to accept the official version of their country's past which had come down to them. They had no reason to change anything. Lingard, however, was interested in changing the story. His Catholicism was undoubtedly the main driving force behind his enthusiasm and determination to seek new sources, but there was no division between his Catholicism and his seeking of the truth, which was another of his passions. To Lingard, they went together. One of the major reasons for Lingard's importance in historiography is found in his stated intention of taking nothing on credit from previous writers, but of going back to the original sources from which he would rewrite the history of the country's past. He wrote in 1806 in the preface to his *Anglo-Saxon Church*: 'My object is truth; and in the pursuit of truth I have made it a religious duty to consult the original historians. Who would draw from the troubled stream, when he may drink at the fountain head.'[86]

He dedicated himself to this task, which was something completely new in English historical writing. His success in this matter was conceded by a contemporary reviewer of the first edition. The *Edinburgh Review* of 1825 admitted:

> He possesses what he claims. . . . He has not copied at second hand from other compilers . . . to borrow his own metaphor, he has not drawn from the troubled stream, but drank from the fountain head. His narrative has accordingly a freshness of character, a stamp of originality, not to be found in any general history of England in common use.[87]

He was the first English historian actually to state that he was going to write only from original sources. It is much more impressive that he actually did so. This has been shown by a detailed study of the way in which he used his sources.[88]

Generally speaking, Lingard had little respect for previous English historians. We find in his letters remarks such as 'The authority of Strype and Burnet I laugh at',[89] or 'who would pin his faith on Burnet?'[90] and again: 'Why do you want the hallucinations of Hume? From me it is impossible that you can get them. I have never looked into Hume since I left Ushaw, unless on three occasions for passages to which my attention was directed by others. I have not time to take and read for that purpose.'[91] He confided to his publisher in 1826, that Sharon Turner had an over-romantic approach to history: 'Between you and me . . . he sometimes makes very silly and visionary discoveries'.[92] Writing near the end of his life, he wrote of Macaulay's celebrated *History of England*: 'It will not do. Macaulay does not write history. One half of the quotations from him are of no authority. . . . You might as well believe all the skits and witticisms & falsehoods which are prevalent during a contested election.'[93] This judgment on Macaulay's lack of source criticism was to be confirmed a century later.[94]

It was Lingard's intention to avoid the mistakes which had been repeated by his predecessors, by basing his narrative as far as possible on original materials. For example, while preparing his volume on Elizabeth's reign, he wrote that 'it is my wish to compose it entirely (or at least as far as may be) from the original letters and papers',[95] and 'I trust that by collating so many original letters and papers, I shall be able to make a history of Elizabeth etc. something different from those we now have'.[96] It was not surprising that Sir Cuthbert

Sharp, who produced his own *Memorials of the Rebellion of 1569* in 1840, wrote to Lingard in 1837, saying that, 'Yours is the only history I can rely upon – the herd of historians follow in the same track.'[97]

It is significant, however, that Lingard did share the same admiration that modern scholars have learned to have for the splendidly accurate editions of original documents published by the 'antiquarian' scholars of the seventeenth century – especially those of the Non-Jurors. He made good use of such publications by Sir Henry Spelman, Henry Wharton, Browne Willis and Thomas Hearne. Lingard wrote, for example, to a helpful friend in 1818, while preparing his *History*:

> Now of the books I most want, it may chance that you have some, or that some of your catholic friends, who would be so good as to lend me them, may have them. They are principally Hearne's publications. I have a few of his publications; and lately wrote to London to buy a few others. I had persuaded myself that an octave of two volumes would not cost above 30/-. What was my surprise, when I found from Booker that he could get none under five guineas. This was what my finances would not bear; and unless I borrow them, I must continue my journeys to Manchester to consult them.[98]

For his account of the medieval period, Lingard used the works of these scholars, such as Hearne's editions of the chroniclers and Wharton's *Anglia Sacra*, and for the Anglo-Saxon period he made use of the documents published by Henry Gale and Sir George Hickes.[99]

Lingard was particularly keen on discovering and using any documents in England which had not been used before. He asked the Jesuits at Stonyhurst for any 'information or documents which you may possess respecting Mary or Elizabeth of England, or Mary of Scotland (I mean such as are not easily accessible)'.[100] He received from them several documents,[101] including a 'manuscript account of the Gunpowder Plot by Fr. Gerard', a missionary priest who had been accused of complicity in it.[102] This helped Lingard to 'disclose many important particulars which must have been otherwise unknown'[103] in an account which has been acknowledged as the first important statement on this subject: 'Until Lingard . . . historians made few attempts to increase our understanding . . . he used two sources hitherto untapped.'[104] Again, the Duke of Norfolk's library contained valuable materials, including a manuscript life of Philip Howard, which the editor of *State Trials* had failed to secure.[105]

From Sir Thomas Clifford Lingard gained a document from the family archives, an extremely important original document which would have left an important gap in English history if it had not been retrieved and published. It enabled him to become the first English historian to see the original of the Secret Treaty of Dover (1670) between Charles II and Louis XIV. This document had come down from the Lord Clifford who had been a member of Charles II's 'Cabal'[106] and it had never been published. This had enabled Whig historians, from the time of the event itself, to write that Charles II had arranged, in this secret treaty, for a French army to come over to force Catholicism onto the English people. This was, of course, a potent piece of anti-Catholic propaganda in England, from 1670 onwards, warning all English people of what would happen if ever a Catholic came to the English throne. Lingard disproved this story by publishing the text of the Secret Treaty for the first time in 1830.[107] The treaty says that when Charles II openly declared that he had become a Catholic, if there was an uprising among his enemies to depose him, Louis XIV would supply him with soldiers to put down that attempt and enable him to keep his throne. The old version still appeared in reputable academic works through the twentieth century, and as late as 1995,[108] which is a signal instance of the extent to which Lingard's work had been ignored. In a modern edition of English documents, published in 1967, this secret treaty still had to be printed from the only source available: Lingard's *Appendix* to his ninth volume, headed 'This important treaty was kept secret till the year 1830, when the late Lord Clifford permitted me to publish it from the original in his possession.'[109]

This was an age when many important manuscripts and original documents were still in private hands. Some eventually went to public repositories, some were to be lost for ever. Lingard understood the importance of all this, which explains his frantic pursuit of them before they were lost. Manuscript sources in the shape of despatches or private letters were provided for inspection by Lord Hardwick, the Duke of Hamilton, the Earl of Shrewsbury, the Duke of Northumberland, Sir Bourchier Wray, Lady Stafford, Philip Howard of Corby Castle and Mr Butler at Burton Constable. We find Lingard writing to a Scottish library to ask if there were any manuscripts there and 'chasing' anybody who had possession of original materials. A Mr Leigh, in Devonshire, had 'several original letters between Walsingham & his underlings' and Lingard's reaction was, 'as I cannot prevail on him to let me have them I have urged him to publish them himself'. Mr Kyle, a Scottish bishop, had 'about 60 letters of Mary of Scotland, originals from her to the Archb. of Glasgow' in cipher, and Lingard was looking for someone who would be able to decipher them. Such examples illustrate the task confronting Lingard when the concept of public repositories for original materials was still in its infancy and when many important papers were lying around in various parts of the country.[110]

Apart from his pursuit of original sources in private hands, Lingard naturally used the repositories and archives which did exist, and also many lesser libraries. From the Lingard correspondence there emerges a picture of a nationwide network of 'agents' who peformed 'commissions' for him in various places. At the British Museum Library, a number of helpers were used, including one 'Peter', a Mr Kaye, Thomas Wright and Tierney. Henry Gillow was given work to do at the Chetham Library, Manchester, and the Durham Library; he was also sent to examine manuscripts in the Dean & Chapter Library at Durham. Mr Whedall worked for Lingard at the Oscot Library, and Mr Kirk at Lichfield. Searches were undertaken for him in the library at Lancaster and in the library at Norfolk House. Mr Upcot at the 'London Institution' and Mr Palgrave, 'sub-commissioner of records', were also helpful to him.[111]

Lingard's personal impact on the State Paper Office is worth recording. He writes in a letter of 1827:

You perhaps know that I had copies of some of the papers in the state paper office respecting the [Gunpowder] plot. Office copies of everything were made and sent to Mr. Peel by his order. . . . Well, Sir, my researches have given birth to more; and now nearly a hundred papers on plot [sic] have been discovered.[112]

Lingard gained permission from Lord Lansdowne to visit the State Paper Office, and, armed with an order to examine papers concerned with the Commonwealth period, he went. However, he was not allowed on this occasion to see papers connected with the Gunpowder Plot which 'were not comprised [sic] in Lord Lansdowne's Order', for 'of Catholics they appear very jealous'. But

'It is my intention on my next visit to have these papers included in my order and to ascertain the truth'.[113] These original papers feature in Lingard's account of the plot in his *History*.[114]

The remarkable fact is that Lingard was the first historian to use such manuscript sources in writing the history of England. It was nearly two decades later that Ranke, the German pioneer of 'scientific' history, came to understand that sixteenth-century history could not be written from printed materials alone. When Ranke produced the first volume of his *History of England Principally in the Seventeenth Century* in 1858, he used Foxe, Strype, Hallam, Froude and Sharon Turner as authorities for the sixteenth century, and did not use the Harleian or Lansdowne manuscripts as Lingard had done. Nor did Ranke recognize, as Lingard did, the major role of Thomas Cromwell in the Reformation movement in England.[115] Ranke was too much influenced by the 'mystical' idea of the spirit of the 'nation' working out its 'moment of destiny' in history,[116] in spite of his later and extensive work on public records.

All the available collections of printed documents were used extensively by Lingard and he made it a life-long task to keep his *History* up to date by taking cognisance of any new publications of documents and using them in his new editions. In the 'Preliminary Notice' to his sixth edition, published in 1848, two years before his death at the age of eighty, he lists the new published information which had become available since his previous editions, and which he has woven into the text of his new edition. By now, the aged scholar was fighting valiantly, and still with good humour, against loss of memory, loss of eyesight and painful illness;[117] yet his work-rate and enthusiasm seemed to be unflagging.

The new sources used for this last edition of his work included Benjamin Thorpe's *Ancient Laws and Institutes of England* and John Kemble's *Codex Diplomaticus Aevi Saxonici* and the *Homilies of Ælfric* on the Anglo-Saxon period. For medieval England, there was Dr Giles' twelve volumes of *Patres Ecclesiae Anglicanae* which contained the valuable accounts of eye-witnesses and letters 'from the most celebrated characters in the western church at that period'; also Thomas Duffus Hardy's *Close and Patent Rolls* for the reigns of John and Henry III, published for the Record Commission. These had given much new information on subjects like the quarrel between Henry II and Becket, and John's relationship with the Papacy. Sir Francis Palgrave's *Parliamentary Writs* had been printed, also for the Record Commission and 1830 had seen the start of the publication

St Augustine was Pope Gregory the Great's 'Apostle to the English'. He landed at Ebbsfleet, Kent, in 597 and became the first archbishop of the new ecclesiastical centre of Canterbury. In bringing the Angles and Saxons together under the See of Canterbury, he took the fist step towards English unity. Bede used evidence from Canterbury for his *Ecclesiastical History of the English People* which created the concept of a single English people. (Photograph: Tony Horsey. Reproduced with kind permission of the Dean and Chapter of Canterbury Cathedral.)

Tomb of the Venerable Bede, Durham Cathedral. Bede (673–735) was a monk at Monkwearmouth and Jarrow. The father of English history and 'the most learned man in Europe', he was the only English 'Doctor of the Universal Church'. His *Historia Ecclesiastica gentis Anglorum* first visualized the English as a single people and is a landmark in their development. (Photograph: by kind permission of The Dean and Chapter of Durham.)

King Alfred the Great (848–99) adopted Bede's idea of a single and united English people. The founder of England on the basis of Christian values which would ensure its survival, he 'worked to bring England increasingly into continental civilization'. (Photograph: Paul Newman.)

St Boniface baptising converts (above) and suffering martyrdon in AD 754 (below). He had 'the greatest influence on Europe of any Englishman'. (Staatsbibliothek Bamberg: Msc. Lit. 1, f. 126v.)

St Thomas Becket (1118–70) was martyred in defence of the Catholic Church. (Photograph: Sebastian Strobl. Reproduced with kind permission of the Dean and Chapter of Canterbury Cathedral.)

Geoffrey Chaucer (*c.* 1340–1400) was an outstanding combination of English genius and European culture. His *Canterbury Tales* depicts a cross-section of 'Englishry' on pilgrimage to St Thomas Becket's shrine:

'to Canterbury they wende.
    The holy blissful martyr for to seke.'
(By courtesy of the National Portrait Gallery, London.)

Window in Lady Julian's cell, St Julian's Church, Norwich. Julian of Norwich (*c.* 1342–1424) was an English mystic, whose *Revelation of Divine Love* speaks with a distinctively English voice to her fellow members of the Universal Catholic Church. She became very popular again in the twentieth century. (By courtesy of The Julian Centre, Norwich.)

Henry VIII (1491–1547). (By courtesy of the National Portrait Gallery, London.)

EARL OF ESSEX.

Thomas Cromwell, 1st Earl of Essex (1485–1540). The first 'Minister for Propaganda' in English history, he propagated the 'Great Myth' of the English past, in order to disguise the unprecedented revolution in English life caused by the Henrician Reformation (see ch. 1). (Artist: Hans Holbein. By courtesy of the National Portrait Gallery, London.)

Thomas More (1478–1535) was a great Englishman, European and Christian humanist. This prophetic and central figure in English history combined a patriotic sense of 'Englishry' with other allegiances to the Universal Church and European civilization. He died for his Catholic beliefs and the common good, in the face of the absolutist claims of the new nation-state. (Photograph: the author.)

Erasmus (c. 1466–1536), the great Dutch Christian humanist, was a friend of More. Representative of the northern Renaissance, he stood, like More, for peace and European unity in the face of rising and warring nationalisms, combined with the divisive effects of the Reformation. (© Hulton Getty.)

John Milton (1608–74) – the idea of the 'Elect Nation'. John Foxe and others had established the Protestant interpretation of an apocalyptic view of English history. Milton, in his pamphlets *Of Reformation* (1641) and *Animadversis* (1642), brought this thinking to the conclusion that England was 'the one nation chosen by God to fulfil His purposes in the world'. This was to have a great effect on the way the English thought about themselves and the outside world up to the twentieth century.
(By courtesy of the National Portrait Gallery, London.)

Thomas Hearne (1678–1735) represents the fine but inhibited scholarship of the non-juring school of historians, much of whose work was 'underground'. Persecuted by the Establishment and ridiculed by the Enlightenment, he is now recognized for his accurate editing of original texts, 'a work of national importance'. (By kind permission of St Edmund Hall, Oxford.)

David Hume (1711–76), philosopher and historian of the age of 'Enlightenment' and 'Reason', saw history as 'philosophy teaching by example'. His atheistic and sceptical outlook provided a secular interpretation of the 'Great Myth'. His *History of England* was dominant in England 1754–1850. (Artist: James Tassie. By courtesy of the National Portrait Gallery, London.)

Robert Southey (1774–1843), 'Lake Poet' and historian, was part of the Romantic Movement in reaction against the Enlightenment. His work continued the 'Great Myth': his *Book of the Church* (1824) saw the Reformation and the Anglican Church as the main props to the security of the Establishment. (Artist: Robert Hancock. By courtesy of the National Portrait Gallery, London.)

John Lingard (1771–1851) was the founder of modern historical writing in England. His work undermined the 'official version' and the 'Great Myth'. A patriotic Englishman, he wrote consciously as a 'citizen of the world' and broke the mould of Anglo-centricity (ch. 6). (By kind permission of Ushaw College, Durham.)

Cardinal John Henry Newman (1801–90), Englishman, Christian humanist and universalist. (Artist: Emmeline Deane. By courtesy of the National Portrait Gallery, London.)

Lord Macaulay (1800–59), the celebrated representative of the Whig interpretation of English history. The main 'burden of his song was English superiority, and his *History of England* (1849–61) was extremely popular and influential in the 'great age of Empire'. (By kind permission of the Master and Fellows, Trinity College, Cambridge.)

Sir G.M. Trevelyan (1876–1962), last in the line of immensely popular Whig historians. (By kind permission of the Master and Fellows, Trinity College, Cambridge.)

Sir Herbert Butterfield. His *The Whig Interpretation of History* (1931) was the first conscious ideological attack on the official version of the English past. It was 'one of the most powerful and influential essays in the history of English historiography' and was eventually to lead some historians in new directions and to new insights. (Reproduced with kind permission of the Master and Fellows of Peterhouse, Cambridge.)

of the volumes from the State Paper Office on the reign of Henry VIII. For Elizabeth's reign, Sir Cuthbert Sharp had published the *Memorials of the Rebellion of 1569* (1840) and Labanoff the *Recueil des Lettres de Marie Stuart* (1844), while some original documents had also been printed in Thomas Wright's *Queen Elizabeth and Her Times* (1838).

Between 1838 and 1840 there had appeared the important compilations of documents by C.P. Cooper, secretary to the Record Commission, entitled *Recueil des dépêches, rapports, instructions et memories des ambassadeurs de France en Angleterre et en Ecosse pendant la XVI siècle*. Lingard made good use of these, together with the newly printed *Bowes Correspondence* and *Leicester Correspondence*. For the seventeenth century Thomas Carlyle had published a 'large collection of documents' in his *Letters and Speeches of Oliver Cromwell* (1845), and Lingard warns his readers that, while he has made use of the printed documents, he did not regard Carlyle's own commentary in this work as usable. Lingard also describes the way in which important despatches of the French ambassadors in the reigns of Charles II and James II had come into his possession since his first edition, from the original materials collected from the French archives by Mazure who 'possessed unrestricted access to the archives of the Ministère des Affaires étrangeres de France'. Other collections of important original documents used and their authors are acknowledged in the footnotes of the various volumes of the sixth edition.

Lingard's determination to use only originals, and to pursue them assiduously, becomes even more extraordinary when we compare his work with the type of sources commonly used by contemporary English historians. Henry Soames said that he based his *History of the Reformation of the Church of England* (1826) largely on Foxe, Burnet and Strype and obviously saw nothing wrong in this. His conclusion, not suprisingly, was that there 'can be no doubt that an attentive perusal of the evidence published in illustration of England's defection from papal Rome will generally lead to the conclusion that her ecclesiastical Reformers attained important, and even also necessary ends, through wise and unexceptionable means'.[118] Sharon Turner, in his *History of the Reigns of Edward VI, Mary and Elizabeth* (1829), makes the same uncritical use of these old propagandist writers. His pages are filled with lengthy references and quotations from the unreliable writings of Foxe and Burnet. Significantly, Turner and Soames felt no concern about showing their uncritical and complete reliance on these 'authorities'. They were following the accepted norms of their time, which shows just how far Lingard was ahead of his time.

Similarly, no one in England had ever approached the Anglo-Saxon or medieval periods with the appropriate critical apparatus before Lingard, or in his own day. Henry Hallam expected no criticism when he repeated the old view that there could not have been any real learning during the 'Dark Ages'. Like Burnet, more than a century earlier, he is proud to admit that 'I pretend hardly any direct acquaintance with these writers',[119] by which he is referring directly to the Venerable Bede, Alcuin and others. Lingard regarded Bede as sufficiently trustworthy to be a primary source and modern historians have come to the same conclusion about Bede, who is 'the master of a living art', and his *Ecclesiastical History* belongs to 'the small class of books which transcend all but the most fundamental conditions of time and place'.[120] On the other hand, both Soames and Hallam gave great weight to the medieval chronicler, Matthew Paris: 'the most spirited, copious and interesting of that class.'[121] Paris had been used since the sixteenth century as a convenient weapon with which to attack the medieval Church. Lingard showed for the first time that he was very unreliable, unless his evidence could be confirmed by other and more authoritative documents. No modern medievalist since the mid-twentieth century would now regard Paris on his own as safe evidence for anything.[122]

LINGARD'S PLACING OF ENGLISH HISTORY WITHIN A EUROPEAN CONTEXT

An even greater significance becomes apparent when Lingard began to extend his search for original documents to continental archives. For the first time in English historiography an English historian was intent on looking at English history from a wider point of view. The Anglocentric approach had completely dominated English historical writing. Lingard was motivated to produce a history which was 'something different from those we now have' and it was also his firm belief that it was the historian's duty 'to contrast foreign with native authorities, to hold the balance between them with an equal hand, and, forgetting that he is an Englishman, to judge impartially as a citizen of the world'.[123] This was an astonishing breakthrough in thinking, contrary to the age-old insularity of English historical writing, and we cannot over-emphasize its significance. Even today historians are struggling with its implications, and new insights and perspectives are being achieved, which Lingard anticipated more than 150 years ago – such as those gained by looking at the 1688 Revolution from a European rather than an Anglocentric viewpoint.[124]

Lingard was the first English historian to use the Vatican and other Roman archives. He had contacts in Rome[125] who were invaluable before the European archives were officially opened in the last quarter of the nineteenth century. G.A. Bergenroth, who published the first Calendar of Spanish State Papers relating to England in 1862, wrote in 1860 that 'Rome may be richer. I have tried hard to get access to the papal records. . . . The fact is that the Roman Archives are inaccessible to any independent authority'.[126] Yet Lingard was getting information from them some forty years before this.

In 1817 Lingard visited Rome 'in great measure', as he wrote later, 'for the purpose of consulting authorities'.[127] He armed himself with a letter from Bishop Poynter to the people 'who might be useful in getting me admission to the MSS. of the Vatican'.[128] Having reached Rome, Lingard still found it very difficult to get at the archives. Cardinal Litta kept on putting him off from day to day, until at last Cardinal Consalvi 'took me under his protection' and 'I was compelled to appeal to his authority to compel Monsigr. Nebbia to let me have what I wanted, who at first would do nothing, because forsooth Monsr: Marini (I think that was the name) was absent'.[129] Lingard wrote:

> Nothing could exceed the kindness of his Eminence [Cardinal Consalvi]. He sent for Monsignor Baldi, and in my presence told him to order, in his name, all the officers to give me every facility, and to procure for me such MSS as I should then mark down in writing. But although they obeyed, everything had been thrown into so much confusion by the French [Napoleon's incursions into Italy and the Vatican, 1809] that I did not procure all the codices I wanted.[130]

We learn from Lingard's journal on this visit to Italy of his keen interest in manuscript material wherever he found it. He wrote, for instance: 'Verulli is a large town with 16,000 inhabitants. Its library is one of the best in Italy: it has two very ancient MSS.'[131]

The homeward journey was also made instructive, for he found manuscripts in the Ambrosian Library, Milan, which he wanted to consult.[132]

The next chapter in the Roman story came with the establishment of an old pupil of Lingard at Ushaw College, Robert Gradwell, as rector of the English College, Rome, in 1818. From now on Gradwell was Lingard's 'agent' in Rome and there are many letters and sheets of extracts from manuscripts extant which bear witness to his services in this capacity. Lingard wrote to Gradwell in 1818, that 'I shall not hesitate to employ you in Rome; know [sic] your goodness'.[133] From 1818 to 1831 Gradwell was receiving instructions from Lingard on a variety of subjects, including 'the opinion of foreign courts respecting Perkin Warbeck in [sic] reign of Henry VII',[134] the letters between Henry VIII and Anne Boleyn which had a bearing on the Divorce Question,[135] Cardinal Pole's letters on the English situation in the reign of Henry VIII,[136] the career of Mary Queen of Scots,[137] Cardinal Allen,[138] the Massacre of St Bartholomew,[139] Fr. Garnet and the Gunpowder Plot[140] and Cromwell and James II.[141] Manuscript material was also sent from the archives of the Franciscan Convent of St Isidore.[142] Lingard's use of a charter discovered in the Vatican archives threw new light on the subject of King John's homage to the Pope in 1213;[143] and on most of these subjects, Lingard provided the first modern account.

Another foreign source which Lingard had originally found in Rome at the Barberini archives were the famous reports of the Venetian ambassadors 'respecting the state of every realm to which they were sent'.[144] The report which Lingard had found in 1817 contained a 'most ample and interesting account of England during the three first [sic] years of the reign of Queen Mary', and this material was included in his fifth volume[145] on the reigns of Mary and Elizabeth.[146] By 1827 Robert Gradwell had found more of these despatches and sent extracts from them to Lingard[147] who used them as an outside and valuable source on such subjects as the policy of Oliver Cromwell and the technical differences between English and Dutch ships during the sea war of 1653–4.[148]

Lingard recognized the value of these ambassadors' reports long before Ranke saw their importance, and he searched everywhere for them. He discovered some in the Lansdowne manuscripts[149] and others in the manuscript collections owned by Henry Howard at Greystoke Castle, which provided important information on such matters as the financial state and expedients of the government under Edward VI, a description of the boy king, and the military state of England on the eve of the Spanish Armada.[150] Finally, Lingard used for his later editions the *Ragguali*, published in 1837–8 by Rawdon Brown at Venice, which included reports on Henry VIII, Queen Catherine and Anne Boleyn.[151]

Lingard was not averse to imposing upon the most distinguished ecclesiastics. Gradwell himself became a bishop in 1828 and another agent used by Lingard was the future Cardinal Wiseman. Writing in his usual forthright manner to Wiseman in 1834, he said, 'If in any researches that you make for me, you can derive any assistance from Card. (I believe he is Card.) Capacini, you have to right to demand it, in consequence of his promise to Dr. Gradwell, which he cannot forget.'[152]

Lingard also wanted to use the despatches of other ambassadors in England. He knew that the despatches of the imperial ambassador, Renard, who was in England during Mary Tudor's reign, were deposited in the library at Besançon. He was determined to use them. A chain of helpers was enrolled, including a Mr Tuite, Dr Poynter, the Archbishop of Besançon and a 'gentleman at Besançon' who actually consulted the despatches. Lingard made lists of the information he required and of the questions which he thought might be answered by the materials at Besançon. The librarian there made extracts from the documents which were sent to Lingard. He was able to make good use of them in his treatment of the reign of Mary Tudor. Lingard wrote to his publisher in 1823, enclosing a note to include in the *History*:

> By comparing the printed despatches of Noailles the French ambassador at the accession of Mary, with the manuscript despatches of Renard the imperial ambassador at the same period Lingard has been enabled to lay before his readers a correct account of the intrigues which led to the marriage of the queen with Philip of Spain, and of the origin, the objects, and the progress of the insurrection under Wyatt. . . . The whole of this part of the volume may be pronounced new to English readers, and an important addition to our history.[153]

Similarly, for the period of Charles II and James II, Lingard was able to use the despatches of the French ambassadors, Barillon and Bonrepaus. M. Mazure, the keeper of the archives at the Depot des Affaires Étrangeres in Paris, had 'copied with his own hand the whole series' and 'at his death I purchased for £5 all his papers, and by that means became possessed of exact copies'.[154]

It was on the subject of the authenticity of a manuscript in the King's Library in Paris that Lingard first incurred the oppositon of John Allen of the *Edinburgh Review*. Allen had denied the authenticity of this manuscript, but Lingard enrolled the services of an expert, M. Buchond, to prove its authenticity and used it in his account of the captivity of Richard II.[155] A Mr T. Langan transcribed materials for Lingard in Paris, as did Mr Charles Browne Mostyn, who sent some valuable information on the Massacre of St Bartholomew, based on the despatches of the papal nuncio, Salviati.[156] Lingard was the first English historian to give the now accepted version of the Massacre[157] – that it was not a long and carefully premeditated act, but a panic measure on the part of a desperate Catherine de Medici. By contrast Lord Acton, Regius Professor of Modern History at Cambridge (1895) and one of the most learned men of his day, got it wrong for most of his life.[158]

In the Lingard correspondence we also find his attempts to gain materials on English history from the archives in Portugal and Malta;[159] and he tried to establish contact with those in Germany.[160] Perhaps the most interesting and revealing story, however, of his connection with foreign archives is that which tells of his researches, by remote control as it were, in the great Spanish State Archives at Simancas.[161]

The Spanish State Archives were not opened until 1844 and the first publication of Spanish sources relating to English history appeared eleven years after Lingard's death, in the 1862 work of a German scholar, G.A. Bergenroth.[162] Bergenroth wrote in 1860 about his visit to the State Archives at Simancas that, 'I am the first who has come to this remote village in the interests of English history';[163] but in this he was mistaken.

The ancient castle of Simancas was the place chosen by Philip II of Spain in 1566 as the great repository for the mass of letters and documents which had been accumulating at the royal court throughout the sixteenth century. The cautious and suspicious nature of the Spanish monarch is reflected in the strict regulations, formulated by Philip, which governed entry to these archives and which remained substantially unchanged until 1844. Nobody was allowed access to the originals; a special note, signed by the king's own hand, was necessary to obtain a copy of any document; this permission was given very rarely, and never to foreigners; no fire was allowed in the archives, even in the depths of winter – and this is one of the colder places in Spain.[164]

Lingard was using information which had been gained for him from these archives as early as 1820, before any other English historian had even thought of looking in that direction for material on English history. Such information helped him to give the modern shape to many important aspects of Anglo-Spanish relations in the sixteenth century. Here again, it was a matter of Lingard's replacing the conventional Anglocentric viewpoint with a Eurocentric approach.

The Spanish monarchy was the pivotal point of European politics and diplomacy in the sixteenth century, for here was the famous Hapsburg European Royal Family, ruling the Holy Roman Empire. The correspondence of the various Spanish envoys with Ferdinand and Isabella, Charles V and Philip II contained the keys to many problems not only of Spanish history, but also of the history of Germany, France, Italy and England. It was impossible to understand certain aspects of English history without knowing the Spanish side of the story. Lingard understood this. He had two friends who lived at the English College or Seminary in Valladolid, just eight miles east of Simancas. They were given instructions by Lingard to obtain information on certain matters from the archives at Simancas. They managed to do this with a remarkable degree of accuracy, as we now know, in spite of great difficulties.

One of the subjects which formed the first episode of the Spanish 'story' was the background to the marriage of Prince Henry and Catherine of Aragon which had been delayed from 1505 to 1509. The young Henry had 'protested' in 1505 against the pre-contract made for his marriage with Catherine, who was the widow of his elder brother, Arthur. The official version of English history looked retrospectively and Anglocentrically at this event, reading into the delay and protest real doubts concerning the validity of the marriage. This version would obviously strengthen Henry's case twenty years later, when he wanted to divorce Catherine to marry Anne Boleyn.

Lingard knew that the key to the matter would probably lie in the correspondence between Henry VII and Ferdinand of Spain during those early years before the first marriage, for European diplomacy and politics were often closely connected with royal marriages. The key to the problem was probably lying among the dusty archival shelves at Simancas. Lingard wrote to his friends in Spain, who first of all sent him an account of the events by the Spanish historians,

Mariana and Zurita.[165] This in itself was interesting and new to English historiography, but Lingard, of course, wanted more. He needed to base his account on original documents, and to check secondary sources in the light of these documents – this was one of his rules of source criticism. There was only one thing to do and Lingard wrote again, instructing his friends to get into the State archives and look at the original documents for these years.

Alexander Cameron, following Lingard's instructions, was able, somehow or other, eventually to gain the required information from the archives. He wrote to Lingard, giving a detailed account of the financial negotiations which preceded the marriage in 1509, complete with dates, sums of money involved, methods of payment and the various strategies adopted by both sides to gain the upper hand in the diplomatic manoeuvring. On the subject of the 'protest' of 1505 Cameron wrote:

> A correspondence was carried on between Ferdinand and Henry till the death of the latter; the correspondence turns principally on the payment of Catherine's portion. Henry complained that the payments were not made at the stipulated times; Ferdinand in reply offered different excuses. . . . Henry the seventh in a letter . . . 1507, tells him that he could get a far better match for his son than Catherine, twice as much money, but that he preferred her on account of her beauty and her virtue, and that he was resolved to stand to his engagement (*guardor los pactos*) as evident proof that he had no doubts of the validity of Pope Julius' dispensation. . . . The Protestation was evidently a political device intended to work on Ferdinand's fear. Henry pretended that he was at full liberty to conclude the marriage or not, just as he pleased . . . Ferdinand was obliged to accede to all his demands. This is the sum of what I have been able to find.[166]

It was evident from the Spanish papers that the delay in the marriage of Henry and Catherine, including the episode of Henry's protestation, was part of a prolonged piece of wrangling between Ferdinand and Henry VII, designed to gain a tactical advantage for the cleverer party – an interpretation which was perfectly consistent with the shrewd character of Henry VII and the diplomatic ability of Ferdinand. In 1489, when the marriage of Catherine and Arthur had been arranged, Ferdinand had held the diplomatic advantage and made good use of it. When Arthur died in 1502, the European scene had changed. Henry VII was now far more secure on the English throne and Ferdinand was now more the suppliant. Henry liked his new position and tried to avail himself of it to advantage during the period 1502–9. Whether there was a real or merely a feigned possibility of Henry VII's abandoning the idea of a Spanish marriage for his son in 1505, the essential fact remained that, as Lingard described it,[167] the protestation of 1505 was a diplomatic tactic on the part of Henry VII, not a personal expression of conscience by the future Henry VIII. This, too, is how modern historians have come to understand the episode.[168]

Thinking within the ideological framework of the official version of the English past, English historians had seen the historical questions of the sixteenth century in terms of an Anglocentric religious controversy. They had also read later events back into the minds of people of an earlier period. So the episode of 1505 had become connected with the later Divorce Question, the centrepiece of the Henrician Reformation. It was used mistakenly as a convenient piece of propaganda for the official version of the past, which commenced in 1533–4. Lingard's introduction of foreign source material placed the whole business within a wider framework of European diplomacy which was much more closely related to the political realities of the situation in 1505. It is a detailed point which serves to illustrate well the nature of Lingard's role in English historiography, of widening the perspective and placing events within a European perspective. He wrote to a friend of the 'new information which I have supplied & which he will not find in any other English writer, respecting the delay of Catherine's marriage',[169] and, in a footnote to the text in his *History*, he noted:

The English historians seem entirely ignorant of the causes which for so many years delayed the marriage of Henry and Catherine. For the preceding narrative I have recourse to the Spanish historians Zurita and Mariana, and have compared their statements with the records at Simancas, which have been copied for me by a friend in Spain.[170]

Lingard was also sent extracts from the Spanish ambassadors' reports of Elizabeth's reign. These threw new light on the character and policy of Philip II. For example, one letter from the Spanish king to his ambassador in London revealed that Philip had not known of Pius V's intention to excommunicate Elizabeth in 1570 until his ambassador had informed him of it. It also revealed that Philip considered the excommunication 'as of very doubtful policy, & only to be justified by his ardent zeal'.[171] Philip showed himself in these letters to have been 'particularly slow in entering any promises of assistance to English malcontents'. The Duke of Alva showed the same attitude and 'most vehemently opposed every project of that invasion that was proposed to Philip'.[172]

Facts such as these from the Simancas documents made a great difference to Lingard's treatment of the subject. English national feeling had been invoked against the twin threats of Spanish invasion allied to Popery in the sixteenth century, and this had left its stamp on English historical writing. English Protestants and nineteenth-century English liberals gladly accepted the 'Black Legend', depicting Philip as a 'monster of iniquity', which had been created by William the Silent's *Apologia* (1572). This hostile presentation of Philip can be traced in all the Protestant historians of the sixteenth and seventeenth centuries, and then in Robert Watson's *History of the Reign of Philip II* (1777) and through the influential works of the nineteenth century such as those of J.A. Froude, J.L. Motley and W.H. Prescott.[173] Lingard's contemporary, Sharon Turner, described Philip as 'the vindictive arm of the Papacy',[174] himself subject to the terrors of the Inquisition, while he planned the Catholic invasion of Protestant England. Philip was indeed 'the relentless enemy of every patriotic Englishman'.[175] Thus was exemplified and confirmed the xenophobic English attitude towards the 'Papacy' and the 'foreigner', which had been initiated in the 1530s.

Lingard, by using Spanish materials, was able to show that factors of politics and national interest influenced Philip's actions just as they guided Elizabeth's. Philip was certainly not a servile instrument in the hands of the Papacy, with which his own relations were sometimes acrimonious. We have been told that Ranke was the first historian to produce this new view of Philip, after his researches into the reports of foreign ambassadors found in various archives on the Continent[176], but this is a mistake. The modern portrayal of the Spanish king had emerged before Ranke in the work of Lingard, whose treatment of Philip, based partly on the materials from Simancas, anticipated the findings of modern scholarship and provided the first balanced account of Philip and his relations with England. From Lingard we learn that Philip, a man of fortitude, was naturally slow and cautious. He had not supported his wife Mary Tudor's persecution of Protestants in England, and his confessor had preached strongly against them.[177] On the subject of the papal excommunication of Elizabeth, Lingard noted: 'It has been supposed that this bull was solicited by Philip; but in a letter to his ambassador in England (June 30), he says that he never heard of its existence before it had been announced to him by that minister, and attributes it to the zeal rather than the prudence of the pontiff.'[178]

Lingard tells us that the rebellion in the Netherlands was caused by the 'arbitrary notions' of Philip by which he managed to antagonize every section of the community; and the Spanish Inquisition was certainly an 'odious Institution'.[179] Yet Lingard was also the first English historian to disprove the old legend that Philip had arranged a meeting with the French monarch at Bayonne to plan the Massacre of St Bartholomew and the total extirpation of Protestants in Europe.[180]

Again, in his treatment of the Spanish Armada, Lingard broke new ground in English historiography, with a balanced interpretation of events. Elizabeth had provoked Philip into sending the Armada which might well be seen as an act of self-defence. She had 'intercepted his treasure [from the colonies], had given aid to his rebels [in the Netherlands] and hired foreign mercenaries to fight against his armies, and had suffered her mariners to plunder and massacre his defenceless subjects on the high seas and in his American dominions'. By 1583, the political situation in Portugal, France and the Netherlands was favourable enough for him to begin making plans against England, but he was still cautious and slow to act. Finally, Elizabeth's sending of an English army to the Netherlands in 1585 was 'equivalent to a declaration of war' and the execution of Mary, Queen of Scots, in 1587 hastened it. Philip was forced into action, exchanging his usual caution and procrastination for sudden temerity.[181]

With regard to the immediate preparations for the Armada, we are told that 'of all men, the Spanish king should have been the last to acknowledge in the pontiff the right of disposing of the crowns of princes'. He had declared war without hesitation against Pope Paul IV on a previous occasion and his general, the Duke of Alva, had 'dictated the terms of peace in the Vatican', but now 'revenge and ambition taught him a different lesson'. A document from Simancas gave Lingard the details of Philip's preparation for the Armada, including his demand for money from the Pope, 'the renewal of the censures promulgated against Elizabeth by former pontiffs' and his plans to have the investiture of the English throne conferred on himself.[182]

Lingard is proud of 'that contempt of danger and that spirit of enterprise which had long been characteristic of the British sailor' and in the final outcome 'the Spaniards had learned to respect the courage and power of their enemy'.[183] He noted the 'spirit of commercial enterprise' which 'seemed to pervade and animate every description of men during the reign of Elizabeth', but also observed correctly that this had 'awakened under Mary'[184] – a remark which was very novel in his day.[185]

Lingard praised the good qualities in Elizabeth who showed, under crisis, 'the characteristic courage of the Tudors'[186] and gave evidence of her 'humanity' by 'refusing to dip her hands in innocent blood' when advised by some to execute the 'leading men in the Catholic body' in England.[187] He praised, too, the majority of English Catholics who 'displayed no less patriotism than their more favoured countrymen' and produces original materials to show that 'The Catholic peers armed their tenants and dependants in the service of the queen; some of the gentlemen equipped vessels, and gave the command to Protestants; and many solicited permission to fight in the ranks as privates against the common enemy'.[188]

When publishing his volume on Elizabeth in 1823, Lingard could claim that he had 'joined much important information from the archives of Simancas in Spain, where Philip II deposited all the dispatches which he received from his ambassadors in the different courts of Christendom' and that from this and other sources, he had 'derived much information . . . which in a great measure has hitherto been withheld from the knowledge of the English reader of history'.[189] Certainly his account of the whole episode of the Armada is a masterly display of detached and professional writing, quite unknown in Lingard's day and indeed for a very long time afterwards. It provides a good example of an approach which, for Lingard, must always be that of the true historian:

I have strictly adhered to the same rules to which I subjected myself in the former editions . . . to watch with jealousy the secret workings of my own personal feelings and prepossessions. Such vigilance is a matter of necessity to every writer of history, if he aspires to the praise of truthfulness and impartiality. He must withdraw aloof from the scenes which he describes, and view with the coolness of an unconcerned spectator the events which pass before his eyes, holding with a steady hand the balance between contending parties. . . . Otherwise, he will be tempted to make an unfair use of the privilege of the historian; he will sacrifice the interests of truth to the interest of party, national, or religious, or political.[190]

There is evidence among the Lingard papers of extracts copied for him from the Simancas archives on other matters. One letter of 1825 from a Mr Sherburne, has extracts in Spanish amounting to about 1,650 words, with the enclosed note: 'These different extracts were taken in the archives of Simancas after a careful reading of the original documents.'[191] Another letter of 1825, sent from Cameron (at Valladolid) to Sherburne (now back in England) for forwarding to Lingard, contains extracts comprising about 1,380 words. Cameron wrote:

You will have seen by my last scrawl that I was desirous to serve Dr. Lingard to the utmost of my power. . . . But, as Dn. Tomas no longer presides over the department [at Simancas] I was obliged to request a friend to introduce me to his successor. After a long delay he disappointed me, and would only give me a line of recommendation. I gave the comission [sic] to Dn. John, who went to S. [Simancas] on the caballo of San Francisco. . . . He met . . . with a paper of which he took some notes, and which I shall subjoin.[192]

Throughout the Simancas correspondence there is reference to a shadowy figure in the background who maintained a studied obscurity. This was the friendly official at the archives, the one who supplied materials for 'oral', then 'ocular' inspection. It was Don Tomas Gonzalez, canon of Plasencia, who, in 1815, had been chosen by Ferdinand VII of Spain, to restore order in the Simancas archives after the confusion cuased by 'the depredations of the French invader [Napoleon 1809], subsequent neglect, and the partial return of the papers which followed the peace'.[193] He succeeded in his mission, making, for example, a set of indexes which were later used by Bergenroth,[194] and also finding time to make extracts from the sixteenth-century documents which he published in the *Memorias de la real academia de la historia* (1832). Volume VII of this work was devoted to Anglo-Spanish relations in the reign of Elizabeth: *Apuntamientos para la historia de Felipe II . . . y la reina d'Inglaterra*. Lingard made use of this publication in his later editions. Don Tomas left the archives in 1832 which was a blow to the chances of research by Lingard's helpers in Spain; his absence through ill-health in 1825 had previously obstructed their research. He died at Madrid in 1833.

Throughout this description of Lingard's contact with foreign archives, we have been aware of the unsatisfactory nature of the means by which he gained his information. His helpers were educated amateurs and the information they sent was in the form of extracts from the documents. Lingard was well aware of the dangers and took his own precautions.[195] He used these materials very carefully. Sherburne seems to have been a more able and critical researcher than Cameron. Both of them worked under Lingard's supervision; they searched for material under each 'head of enquiry' which was sent to them. This type of supervision, though restrictive, had its advantages. Neither of them was entirely dispassionate in his search for evidence, and Cameron in particular was so anxious 'to discover the practices of Elizabeth'[196] that there was a danger of his sending opinions instead of facts. Lingard exercised a restraining influence, demanding facts and names to substantiate any opinion that they sent to him and they were willing to admit when an opinion could not be verified by the documents. Moreover they both made it quite clear in their letters when they were merely expressing opinions and when they were actually stating facts derived from the documents: it was in these facts alone that Lingard was interested. Sherburne was particularly good at basing his statements on the documents; he also copied out extracts for Lingard and was much more ready than Cameron to break free from the restrictions of his special commission and introduce 'unconnected gleanings' of his own from the documents. Sherburne was also definitely copying his information by the end, not merely having an 'ocular' inspection of it.[197]

Yet that the agents managed to convey the meaning of the documents accurately may be seen by comparing their extracts with the archival materials when these were finally published.[198] We would now say, of course, that the historian should see the documents for him or her self, but it was impossible for Lingard to travel abroad. Moreover the continental archives had not been opened for use. The fact remains that he was the first English historian to see the need and to have attempted – with considerable determination, ingenuity and success – to use documentary information from foreign archives, in order to see events in English history within a European perspective. He was able to break through the insularity of English thought on the subject of the English past, to see events from a Eurocentric rather than an Anglocentric viewpoint. This was a major achievement at this time, and no one has yet been able to repeat it, in terms of a complete history of England, using all the information from foreign archives which has since become available to all scholars.

LINGARD'S NEW DESCRIPTION OF THE ENGLISH PAST

We have seen how the old historiographical framework of thought, established in the sixteenth century and dominant in England until the twentieth century, was built around certain key concepts which supported one another in a small circle of logical argument to produce the official view of the English past. One of these concepts was that of an early British Church, founded by one of the original Apostles, which was national and erastian in character and completely separate from the Universal Catholic Church. The second concept was that the papal role in the medieval period was encroaching and trespassing on English liberties and independence in Church and State. The third concept was that of the Reformation as a movement of national liberation and freedom in the sixteenth century, which restored the English Church and State to their original national and erastian forms and, in so doing, laid the foundations for England's divinely appointed role as the 'elect nation', destined to lead Protestantism in the old world of Europe and in the new world of the widespread colonies abroad.

Lingard's monumental work, in ten volumes, based on original sources gathered from foreign archives as well as those of England, together with a sophisticated system of source criticism and technical scholarship, undermined each of these concepts and constructed a new framework for historical writing on English history as a whole, as well as the nature of the Reformation in particular. This was the achievement of one man, with an exceptional range of languages at his disposal, facing the official view of the past which had been built up over centuries to become part of English folklore and was integral to that system of assumptions which made up the national way of looking at things, conscious and subconscious.

The idea of a primitive British Church, nationalist and Protestant in character, founded in England directly by one of the early Apostles, had in fact slightly predated the Henrician statutes. It had existed in the works of certain English Protestants who were exiles in Antwerp during the period 1525–35. Some of these exiles, like Frith, Barlow, Roye and especially William Tyndale, had pointed back to a primitive Church of Protestant purity in England. Their version was evangelistic in character and needs to be distinguished from the official version, inspired by the political thinking of Thomas Cromwell in particular.[199] However, Cromwell quickly borrowed Tyndale's theological ideas to bolster the ideology of the new nation-state;[200] and the evangelistic theory of an early Protestant Church was also to be assimilated later into the politically motivated official version of the past. John Bale, an 'agent' for Cromwell, developed the idea of this early Church and handed it on later to John Foxe, who combined the official version with an apocalyptic, Protestant view of English history. The concept of an early English Protestant Church satisfied the need to provide the proper pedigree for the 'elect' nation, as it came to be seen in the seventeenth century, which had never had to borrow any important idea from anyone else. The English people had retained the purity of faith, specially brought to them by one of the Apostles, until papal power had encroached and interfered with it during the medieval period, after the Norman Conquest. This ideology was still dominant in Lingard's day.

In 1819, the Bishop of St David's wrote concerning the Church of England:

> Its origin was purely apostolical. To the labours and preaching of the great Apostle of the Gentiles St. Paul, we are indebted for the first introduction of the Gospel. . . . The rejection of the Pope's authority in the *seventh century* stamps the first feature of its Protestant character . . . its independence on the Church of Rome during the Saxon Government, down to the Norman Conquest. From the accession of the Norman Princes to the beginning of the sixteenth century, subject to the Pope . . . It was then . . . that the *ancient faith* and worship of the primitive Church was restored.[201]

He saw the English Church as the true vehicle of Christianity. The Catholic Church was in a state of schism, having isolated itself by breaking away from the English Church.[202] In 1835 Henry Soames, in his *Anglo-Saxon Church*, wrote of the 'high antiquity of Britain's conversion' and considered St Paul, 'the great Apostle of the Gentiles as not improbably the founder of our national Church'. This early Church had not been connected with Rome, but with Asia, 'the cradle of our hold faith'.[203]

Lingard commented on this concept in the first volume of his *History*, published in 1819, saying that the writers who claimed St Paul or St Peter as the founder of Christianity in Britain had based their conclusions 'improbable as they are in themselves . . . on the most slender evidence; on testimonies which are many of them irrelevant, all ambiguous and unsatisfactory'.[204] He went on:

> Nothing can be less probable in itself, nor supported by ancient testimony than the opinion that Britain was converted by oriental missionaries. The only foundation on which it rests is, that in the seventh century, the Britons did not keep Easter on the same day as the church of Rome. That, however, they did so in the beginning of the fourth century is plain from Eusebius (Vit. Con. iii. 19), Socrates (Hist. v. 22) and the Council of Arles (Spelman, pp. 40, 42). . . .
>
> It is surprising that so many modern historians should have represented the Britons as holding different doctrines from those professed by the Roman missionaries, though these writers have never produced a single instance of such difference. Would Augustine have required the British Clergy to join in the conversion of the Saxons, if they had taught doctrines which he condemned? Bede has related with great minuteness all the controversies between the two parties. They all regard points of discipline. Nowhere does the remotest hint occur of any difference respecting the doctrine.[205]

Lingard then described how Christianity had come to Britain as part of its gradual extension throughout the Roman Empire, of which Britain formed a part.[206] This is now the accepted shape of the historiography of the early Church in Britain, but the old view survived in England until well after Lingard's time.[207] He wrote to a friend, with some sense of frustration, towards the end of his life, of the state of knowledge at Oxford University on this subject: 'I find it quite an admitted fact among them that St. Paul preached here, and that the Britons were supplied with mssionaries from the East, and had nothing to do with Rome, till the conversion of the Saxons.

Even as late as yesterday, I had here the senior fellow of a college in Oxford who believed that to be the case.'[208] The myth lingered on, in the popular mind, until well into the twentieth century. One still comes across examples of it today.

The second great pillar of the official view was the complete misreading of the nature of medieval England. It saw English people during this period as continually snarling their defiance of the papal authority which had taken from them their original freedom as a nation. This was the 'dark age' of the nation's history. Lingard was not an uncritical enthusiast as far as the medieval period was concerned. He had no romantic illusions about faults and failings of people in that age, as of any other. He wrote to a friend, complaining of certain Catholics who were 'outrageous praisers of the middle ages' and who 'ought to be stopped'.[209] He recognized, however, that during that whole period, England was self-consciously part of the Catholic Church and that medieval English people had not looked at life in a defiantly nationalist way, although they were patriotic and concerned to maintain their own rightful privileges.

This new outlook was highly significant because it completely changed the viewing mechanism through which historians examined the world of medieval England. To get this right was suddenly to get everything into proper perspective and to give a very different meaning to the statutes and other documentary evidence of the period. It was to see life in medieval England as it actually was and to experience how it actually felt to be an English person and also a loyal member of the Universal Church. The original documents, which had long been available to English historians through the scholarly editions published by the Non-Jurors and others, were now to be seen through different eyes and interpreted properly, because they were seen in the perspective of the real thoughts and assumptions of thought of the people who wrote them. This was after three centuries of misunderstanding arising from the failure by English historians to recognize the assumptions of thought of their medieval ancestors.

So Lingard recognized that the Canon Law of the Universal Church was something which medieval English people regarded as a normal part of their lives, rather than as a foreign code of law which had been thrust upon them by an alien power for its own tyrannical purposes. Similarly, he appreciated that they regarded the Papacy as an essential part of their religion, not as an enemy intent on usurping and extending its power in England. Starting from such new premises of thought, Lingard was able to place the religious and political conflicts of the period within a new context, and to give a new meaning to the attitudes behind, and the words used in, the documentary evidence from the medieval period. It was not that Lingard had any sentimental or romantic attachment to the past, which characterized various writers of the Romantic movement. It was simply that he understood the way in which the institutions of the medieval period worked. He understood something which had been completely forgotten by English people, such was the power of the official view of the past over their finds and preoccupations in the centuries after the enactment of the Henrician statutes and the creation of the new nationalism which came in with these statutes. They had forgotten that it was perfectly possible for English people to be very patriotic and obedient to their kings, while belonging to the Universal Church and giving it their allegiance in spiritual matters. This had been the situation in fact for nearly 2,000 years before the statutes of 1533–4, but within a few generations it became extremely difficult for English people to understand that such a situation could exist. Indeed they believed that it had never existed. Such was the power of the great myth created by the official view of their past.

If the 'greatest achievement of historical understanding' was the 'recovery and exposition of the medieval world',[210] then Lingard made a most significant contribution towards this achievement in English historical writing. The Non-Jurors had taken important steps towards it by their sympathetic interest and publication of scholarly editions of medieval documents, but they had fitted all this into a context which was out of perspective and so they had never really understood the world of medieval England. Their contribution had been stimulated by their anti-erastian sentiments, rather than by a proper understanding of the nature of the medieval Church in England. Lingard established the proper context and assumptions of thought of that world, so that all the details suddenly fell into place and took on a new meaning. For example, people in the medieval period certainly grumbled and complained from time to time about authority, as all of us do, but this did not mean that such grumbling, sometimes conveyed in the documents, meant that they were actually questioning the right of that authority to exist. The documents would not usually convey the basic assumptions because everyone took these for granted. Documents are written for the use of those in the present, not for future historians as we sometimes assume.

To illustrate the precise nature of the gap between Lingard and the greatest medievalist among the Non-Jurors, we may compare their treatments of the episode of 1125 when Archbishop William of Canterbury had obtained a grant of legatine authority from Pope Innocent. Since there was no erastian element involved in this episode, Henry Wharton was not able to interpret the facts properly. Both he and Jeremy Collier attacked the archbishop for submitting disgracefully to a foreign authority and jeopardizing the independence of the English Church by his action in this matter.[211] Lingard sees it in a different light altogether:

> Wharton . . . is very severe on the memory of this prelate, whom he accuses of having, by the acceptance of the legatine authority, subverted the independence of his church, and enslaved it to that of Rome. Had William, indeed, believed, with Wharton, that the pope previously possessed no jurisdiction in England, he would have deserved this censure; but he acknowledged, like his predecessors, the papal authority (See Malm. 112–116), and, if he objected to the admission of foreign legates in England, it was not because the church of Canterbury was independent, but because the authority of legate had been previously granted by the popes to the archbishop of Canterbury. Inaduitum scilicet in Britannia cuncti scientis, quemlibet hominem supra se *vices apostolicas* gerere nisi solum archiepiscopum Cantuariae. Ead. 58. See the grants to the archbishops Tatwine, Plegmund, and Dunstan in Malmesbury de Pont. ii. 116.[212]

The contributions of the Non-Jurors to a proper understanding of the English past was made in spite of their general ideas about the medieval period and the nature of the Reformation itself. Lingard's contribution to the subject was a direct result of his having set the whole historical context in proper perspective.

Lingard understood that medieval England belonged within an essentially European context, not only in the religious sphere, which was the core of society's life, but also in the political, economic and social areas, since these were influenced considerably by the religious beliefs and values which informed life as a whole.

His lengthy treatment of the feudal system as it existed in England before the Norman Conquest (forty-eight pages) and after the Conquest (twenty-four pages), all based on original sources, makes it obvious that feudal institutions were common to European countries and were brought to England from other parts of Europe, both before and after the Conquest.[213] F.W. Maitland was later to complain that 'From the end of the seventeenth century onwards our English law grew up in wonderful isolation; it became very purely English and insular'.[214] Lingard, like Spelman before him (in the sphere of feudal law), already knew that during the medieval period, 'English law . . . was a member of a great European family, a family between all the members of which there are strong family likenesses'.[215] England, in fact, had never existed before the sixteenth century as an independent nation-state, isolated from Europe. Later specialists in medieval history would go further in filling in additional details, but it was Lingard who had established the proper context. To illustrate his achievement we can now look at his own treatment of those three strategic episodes of medieval history – historiographically speaking – which were examined earlier.[216]

Lingard prefaced his account of the conflict between Henry II and Thomas Becket with a long description of the development of the system of Church law which had grown up 'from the commencement of Christianity'[217] in England. For the first time in English historiography, with the exception of Obadiah Walker's 'lost' tract, the Canon Law was placed within the context which is given it by modern scholarship, starting with F.W. Maitland in 1898.[218] It was revealed by Lingard as an international system of law, centred on the Papacy in Rome. Becket was described as defending the rights of the Universal Church, which included the people of England, in England. Lingard also deals with the relationship between this structured system of international law, studied in the universities of Europe and based upon fundamental Christian principles, and the less sophisticated system of Common Law which had grown up in England:

> confused and uncertain, partly Anglo-Saxon, partly of Norman origin and depending on precedents, of which some were furnished by memory, others had been transmitted by tradition. The clerical judges were men of talents and education: the uniformity and equity of their decisions were preferred to the caprice and violence which seemed to sway the royal and baronial justiciaries.[219]

This long description – fifteen pages – of the two legal systems is a key section in establishing the new viewpoint and in reinstating the Canon Law as an integral part of English life in the medieval period. It crystallizes the idea of English history as being essentially part of European civilization, while containing its own particular culture and institutions as well. This section, written in very simple and undramatic terms, contains the ideas which were finally – in the following century – to change the nature of the way in which academic English historians viewed their past. It is interesting to reflect that we are now, at the end of the second millennium, about to see another international system of European law, that of Human Rights, being reinstated as an integral part of the legal system in England.

Having established this new context, Lingard treated the whole affair in a detached and objective manner. Becket was 'this extraordinary man, a martyr to what he deemed to be his duty', and one 'who, since his death has been alternately portrayed as a saint and hero, or as a hypocrite and traitor, according to the religious bias of the historian'.[220] Extreme statements on both sides of the contest were qualified 'by recollecting the warmth of the two parties, and the exaggeration to which contests naturally give birth'.[221] The reader is given an accurate and clear-cut account of the standpoints maintained by the two sides in the dispute as well as a balanced narrative of the development and final outcome of the contest.

Turning to the episode of the relationship between King John and the Papacy and the Canterbury election of 1205,[222] Lingard described Pope Innocent III as deciding the case impartially according to the universal law of the Church, rather than as the power-bent foreigner – a familiar figure in all Protestant historiography – seeking to extend his unwanted and improper influence in England.[223] In his treatment of the events of 1213 and the submission of King John to the Papacy, Lingard used an unpublished document from the Vatican archives and other 'authentic documents still extant' to show that the accounts of the chroniclers Wendover and Matthew Paris, hitherto accepted as the two main authorities, were full of errors and could not be accepted as good evidence. In an important and scholarly appendix Lingard anticipates some of the findings of modern medievalists in the mid-twentieth century.[224] He begins: 'In most narratives of this transaction so many errors are found, that I may be allowed to state the naked facts, as they exist in authentic documents still extant':

The foregoing statement, drawn from authentic sources, shows how little credit is due to Matthew Paris, and also to Wendover, whose work Paris copies and occasionally interpolates. The narratives of both these writers abound with errors. They tell us that the 15th May, on which the proceedings with Pandulph (the papal envoy) occurred, was the vigil of the Ascension, whereas the Ascension fell that year on the 23rd. of May. They are full of the transactions between the king and Pandulph, but know nothing, at least say nothing, of the more important proceedings between the king and the legate. They pretend to give us copies of the charters granted to John, but imperfect and falsified copies, which had led them and their readers into error. They affirm that John did homage to Pandulph; yet give as the form of homage the oath of fealty. Paris, moreover (but for this he has not the authority of Wendover) describes Pandulph after the homage, receiving the money, and trampling it in this pride underfoot, though, as the reader has seen, the money was not paid till several months afterwards.

I may add that the titles of several instruments in Rymer seem to have been copied out of Paris, and are equally calculated to mislead the reader. They are evidently contradicted by the contents of the documents to which they are prefixed. Even the certificate of the King's absolution (Rym. 112) is no certificate; he was not absolved till several months afterwards, and the instrument itself contains not a word on the subject. There occurs in it a clerical error. By the omission of a word, John is said to have done homage by oath and charter, whereas he only promised by his charter to do it.[225]

All this is very significant. From the time of Archbishop Parker's editions of Paris' chronicles in Elizabeth's reign, they had been regarded as unassailable and powerful evidence for the official view of English attitudes towards the Papacy in the medieval period. In 1948 Professor Cheney, in his scholarly account of this episode, expressed surprise at the way in which historians had accepted so easily the authority of chroniclers such as Wendover – and these had included even Sir Maurice Powicke. In 1958 another modern scholar in a specialist work on Matthew Paris, wrote:

It is high time that the ghost of Matthew Paris' anti-papalism was laid. He did not understand politics, though he was keenly interested in them, and his anti-papalism is by no means ideological. He never thought about the theory of papal power: he merely had a grudge against authority. He resented all attempts at interference with his own material interests, and the king suffers just as much from his tirades as does the pope.[226]

However, Lingard was already, in 1820, using one of his techniques of source criticism to devaluate the authority of Paris as a reliable source. This particular rule was that a chronicler or contemporary writer must not be taken as first-class evidence, unless his reliability has been confirmed by comparison with contemporary documentary evidence. Lingard writes: 'Paris tells us . . . but I have learned to doubt the assertions of that writer, when he is not supported by other documents. . . . He has already told us . . . Unfortunately for the credit of the historian, these letters are still extant, and prove to be exactly of an opposite nature. . . . See them in . . .'.[227] This was an example of Lingard's distinction between an 'authentic' and an 'original' source.[228]

So here we have Lingard anticipating M.D. Knowles' specialist account of the 1205 election[229] and C.R. Cheney's expert demolition of the authority of the chronicler, Matthew Paris – well over a century before them both. Not one of Lingard's contemporaries was capable of the level of scholarship he achieved, and indeed this judgement could be extended to cover English historians over the next hundred years as well, including Bishop Stubbs. Lingard must be placed in the company of the very best medievalists of the second part of the twentieth century and not one of them was engaged in writing a complete *History of England* in which at least the same standard of scholarship is sustained throughout.

Apart from his use of techniques of source criticism, Lingard also makes a point of general historiographical interest here, which struck at the very heart of the Protestant–Whig approach to historical writing:

Though the principles of morality are unchangeable, our ideas of honour and infamy perpetually vary with the ever-varying state of society. To judge impartially of our ancestors, we are not to measure their actions by the standards of the present manners and notions; we should transport ourselves back to the age in which they lived, and take into account their political institutions, their principles of legislation and government.[230]

He went on to show that in the thirteenth century the state of vassalage was not necessarily degrading, that many princes of Christendom had been in that state at one time or another, and that John's father, Henry II and his brother Richard, had both entered into that state. Again John had acted with the advice and consent of the great council of barons 'whence it may be fairly presumed that there was something in the existing circumstances which formed in their opinion a justification both of the king and of themselves'. Again, it meant that the influence of the Papacy could be used to buttress the position of John and his posterity on the English throne against internal rebellion and outside attack by France.[231] Such comments were only possible from one who understood the unity of Christendom, with the Papacy at its head and the common background of the feudal institutions in Europe in the medieval period. They could not have been understood by all those English historians who, looking through the eyes of English nationalism and Protestantism, saw the Papacy as a foreign and alien power, intent on encroaching on the powers of the independent nation-state of England.

Lingard knew that he was facing deeply rooted and long-established prejudice on this subject. He was placing it within the context of a European society which was very different from the post-sixteenth-century world. He had to proceed very carefully and here is Lingard 'stooping down', so to speak, to get alongside his readers, understand their difficulties and help them out of the prejudices from the position in which they *were* rather than from where they *ought* to be:

> This transaction has heaped everlasting infamy on the memory of John. Every epithet of reproach has been expended by writers and readers against the pusallinimity of a prince who could lay his dominions at the feet of a foreign priest and receive them back again as a feudatory. It was certainly a disgraceful act; but there are some considerations, which if they do not remove, will at least extenuate his offence.[231]

Indeed, he was afraid, in the first instance, to say that he had discovered an important document on the subject in the Vatican archives, because of the suspicions which that would arouse.[232] Lingard was not surprised, therefore, when the expected reaction came, and the contemporary critics declared themselves 'a little astonished to find' that he 'has put in an elaborate plea to extenuate the infamy of John in this abject submission to the church of Rome'.[233] Lingard's version of the context is the one now accepted by modern scholars, in which 'the terror-stricken tyrant and the domineering priest disappear from the story of well-calculated diplomacy',[234] and in which the Pope's decision to ratify the election of Stephen Langton, who was to play a very important role in the making of Magna Carta in 1215, as Archbishop of Canterbury is extremely important for later English history.[235]

Before discussing the famous Statutes of Provisors and Praemunire of the fourteenth century, the misinterpretation of which had played such an important role in the Reformation itself,[236] as well as in later historical writing, Lingard thought it necessary again to describe the context in which these statutes were passed. This is another of those key sections of his *History* where Lingard turns aside from the main narrative to adjust the viewing mechanism, so to speak, so as to change completely the way in which the English public had been used to looking at the medieval period for three centuries. His own understanding of the essential commonplaces of medieval society enabled him to achieve a proper understanding of these statutes while, as we have seen,[237] English scholars were going to get it wrong for another century after Lingard. He describes the context as any modern medievalist would do:

> In this I may direct the attention of the reader to the state of the English Church during the fourteenth century. The rivalry which has already been mentioned still existed between the civil and ecclesiastical judicatures, and each continued to accuse the encroachments of the other. That their mutual complaints and recriminations were not unfounded, will appear probable if we reflect that the limits of their authority had not been accurately defined, and that many causes had different bearings, under one of which it might belong to the cognizance of the spiritual, and under another to that of the civil judge.[238]

He then goes on to describe the real reason behind these statutes, which previous and later English historians saw as a national expression of the wish to be free from the yoke of subjection to a foreign power. His description is again centrally important in changing the conventional view of the past:

From the preceding detail the reader will have collected an accurate notion of the controversy. Of the primacy of the pontiff or of his spiritual jurisdiction there was no question; both these were repeatedly acknowledged by the commons in their petitions and by the king in his letters. But it was contended that the pope was surrounded by subtle and rapacious counsellors who abused, for their own emolument the confidence of their master; that by their advice, he had 'accroached' to himself a temporary authority to which, as it invaded the rights of others, he could have no claim; and that when repeated remonstrances had failed, it was lawful to employ the resources of the civil power in the just defence of civil rights. It was in vain that the pontiff, on account of his pre-eminent dignity in the church, claimed a right to dispose of its revenues for its advantage; the new statutes were put into execution, and the same legislators who received with deference the doctrinal decisions and disciplinary regulations of their chief pastor, visited with the severest penalties of the law the clergymen who procured from him the provision to a benefice in opposition to the rights of the patron.[239]

This approach was completely new to Engish historiography. It placed the subject within a new context. The conflict was between two mutually accepted authorities as to where the boundary between them lay, not a struggle between a nation of patriots fighting valiantly against a foreign intruder, as later historians had read it. Lingard's work was providing a new and penetrating light on the medieval scene, in which events were being considered from the viewpoint of the people actually taking part in them, not from that of a later generation reading their own thoughts back into the minds and words of their predecessors.

It was precisely because he had a proper understanding of the medieval background that Lingard was able to place the Reformation itself into a proper perspective. His treatment of it was the first scholarly, rather than polemical, account in English historical writing.[240] Having got the medieval background right, he needed only a soberly written and factual narrative of events in the Reformation to show its revolutionary nature, without having to stress the point. He was well able and willing to describe faults and abuses in the Church, which provided the opportunity for the attack on it,[241] just as he had revealed any abuses of papal authority in medieval England.[242] Like Thomas More, Lingard recognized faults in the Church, but did not see them as the real reason for the Reformation in England, which was the king's determination to get the divorce. He was able in fact to prove many of the Catholic contentions in the detailed story of events as they unfolded,[243] and he recognized the very important role of Thomas Cromwell's 'boldness and ingenuity' in realizing the king's design.[244] His treatment, however, is always even-handed and objective. Describing the execution of Anne Boleyn, for example, he makes his own comment on the historiography of the subject:

> To have expressed a doubt of her guilt during the reign of Henry, or of her innocence during the reign of Elizabeth, would have been deemed proof of disaffection. The question soon became one of religious feeling, rather than historical disquisition. Though she had departed no further than her husband from the ancient doctrine, yet, as her marriage with Henry led to the separation from the communion with Rome, the Catholic writers were eager to condemn, the Protestant to exculpate her memory. In the absence of those documents which alone could enable us to decide with truth, I will only observe that the king must have been impelled by some most powerful motive to exercise against her such extraordinary, and in one supposition, such superfluous rigour.[245]

To take another example of this insistence by Lingard on approaching his materials in the spirit of 'historical disquisition' rather than 'religious feelings', we can look at his treatment of the contentious subject of the Dissolution of the Monasteries by Henry VIII and Thomas Cromwell:

> The monks of different descriptions amounted to many thousands; and in such a multitude there must have existed individuals whose conduct was a disgrace to their profession. But when this has been conceded on the one hand, it ought to be admitted on the other, that the charges against them are entitled to very little credit. They are ex parte statements, to which the accused had no opportunity of replying, and were made to silence inquiry and sanctify injustice.

The commissioners themselves were not trustworthy witnesses: 'all were stimulated to invent and exaggerate, both by the known rapacity of the king, and by their own prospect of personal interest'. They were men 'of very equivocal character, who had solicited the appointment and had pledged themselves to effect, as far as it might be possible, the extinction of the establishments which they should visit'.[246] Lingard's statements are verified by reference to the original documents. The episode illustrates Lingard's normal practice of weighting the value of a source and of 'getting behind it' to assess its reliability. He used a wide range of official primary sources for this subject, including original documents from the British Museum, Parliamentary Journals and state papers, as well as documents already printed in collections by Rymer, Strype, Stevens, Hearne, Browne Willis and Henry Wharton.[247]

It is significant that one Catholic critic accused Lingard of being prejudiced against the monks in his treatment of this question, but in fact his account is simply the first balanced treatment of the subject in English historiography. Lingard also points to the familiar tactics of terror employed by the Henrician government in these proceedings; non-compliant monks were imprisoned or executed to 'terrify their brethren'.[248] Lingard's description of the strength and character of the 'Pilgrimage of Grace' as a popular movement in defence of the monasteries[249] has been repeated in the most recent statement on the subject in 1997, as opposed to earlier twentieth-century statements.[250]

Similarly, Lingard was the first English historian to recognize the central importance of Thomas Cromwell in the Reformation. Lingard gives a very full account of Cromwell's role, including his political ideas, his plans for their implementation and his position of influence in seeing through, for example, the submission of the clergy, the royal supremacy and the Dissolution of the Monasteries. He was the man 'whose counsels had first suggested the attempt and whose industry had brought it to a successful termination'.[251] Again, state papers and other original materials are used as the basis of the account.

Lingard's treatment of Mary Tudor's reign was the first balanced account in English historiography and it should be borne in mind that Pollard was still making a 'grotesque caricature'[252] of her, nearly a century afterwards. Lingard made quite clear his own views of the Marian persecution: 'the infamy of the measure . . . these horrors . . . barbarous executions . . . The foulest blot on the character of this queen'.[253] Yet he places it in historical perspective:

> It was the lot of Mary to live in an age of religious intolerance, when to punish the professors of erroneous doctrine was inculcated as a duty . . . by the leaders of every religious party. Mary only practised what *they* taught. It was her misfortune rather than her fault, that she was not more enlightened than the wisest of her contemporaries.[254]

While 'the mind is struck with horror', it 'learns to bless the legislation of a more tolerant age, in which dissent from established forms, though in some countries still punished with civil disabilities, is nowhere liable to the penalties of death'.[255] Lingard then proceeded to describe Mary's integrity, the decency of her court, her real concern for the people of England, her sound moral character and compassion for the poor. We are also informed of her support of the Universities and of important steps taken by Parliament in her reign to advance the cause of justice in England by legal reforms. Mary supported the commercial interests of England, and it was during her reign that the great history of England's commercial development began. Despite the loss of Calais, we are reminded that 'she had the honour of concluding the first commercial treaty with Russia'.[256] Lingard even notices, albeit in a footnote,[257] an observation of the Venetian ambassador in Mary's reign concerning the reformed system of taxation in England. We can certainly claim that Lingard provided the first modern and balanced treatment of the reign of Mary Tudor, as opposed to the long line of Protestant–Whig historians who saw it as 'sterile' because in their eyes it did not lead to the future. It is interesting to compare Lingard's account with a very recent statement in 1996: 'Far from "sterility" being the keynote of this decade . . . many fertile and enduring reforms were discussed or initiated in the 1550s. Among the most significant was the switch in the theory of taxation.'[258]

Finally, we may look at Lingard's treatment of Elizabeth I. From the time of Camden's *Annales Rerum Anglicarum et Hibernicorum Regnante Elizabethae* (1615), the English people were taught to see Elizabeth as a paragon of all the virtues of sovereignty, the queen whose work, together with that of her father, Henry VIII, laid the foundations of England's greatness in the modern world. Coming to the modern era, Mandell Creighton's *Elizabeth*, published at the end of the nineteenth century, concluded with the 'uncritical and adulatory picture' which was 'to remain the twentieth-century norm'.[259] Sir John

Neale's *Queen Elizabeth* (1934), republished to great acclaim in 1952 with the new title, *The First Elizabethan Age*, was even less well balanced than Creighton's account. For Neale, 'Elizabeth could do no wrong, her indecisiveness was masterly temporization, her aversion to novelty a laudable desire for stability, her vanity self confidence, her mistakes compromises forced on her by others; in any difference of opinion between her and her ministers she was invariably right.' Her 'outrageous bad manners, her aggressive bullying, her sexist behaviour, her ruthless authoritarianism' were all ignored or attributed to strain. Neale described foreign affairs and foreign monarchs, such as Philip II of Spain, as Elizabeth saw them, for Neale's knowledge of European history was limited. But his description of Elizabeth remained pre-eminent and was reflected in the later accounts of A.L. Rowse and Conyers Reade.[260] In 1993 John Kenyon remarks that 'it is surprising that there has not already been a bluntly revisionist biography'.[261]

A 'bluntly revisionist' account of Elizabeth I had already been given a hundred years before Neale published his first biography. In 1823 Lingard provided an account which gave all the corrections required in a well-researched and balanced revisionist work. Lingard had stated his intention of doing this by using only original sources[262] and he succeeded in doing so. We have already seen that he used the Spanish sources to give a new account of Philip II, one that is far superior to Neale's because it was Eurocentric rather than Anglocentric in perspective.[263]

Lingard ascribed the ascent of England to a nation of first rank under Elizabeth to the 'spirit of commercial enterprise' which had revived in the reign of Mary, and was carefully fostered in that of Elizabeth. This

> gave a new tone to the public mind, and diffused a new energy through all ranks of men. Their views became expanded; their powers were called into action; and the example of successful adventure furnished a powerful stimulus to the talent and industry of the nation. Men in every profession looked forward to wealth and independence; all were eager to start in the race of improvement.

The foreign policy adopted by her ministers was also effective in increasing England's power, though 'it may be difficult to reconcile with honesty and good faith'. They were 'perpetually on the watch to sow the seeds of dissention, to foment the spirit of resistance, and to aid the efforts of rebellion in the neighbouring nations', a policy which was applied to France, Spain, the Low Countries and Scotland.

Government policy was usually a matter of practical compromise between the queen and her ministers. They had great problems with her 'habitual irresolution'. 'To deliberate appears to have been her delight, to resolve a torment.' She was mean-minded and this, too, was a hindrance to her ministers and their policies. Her treatment of Mary, Queen of Scots, exemplified her weaknesses, but we must also remember her position:

> Elizabeth may perhaps have dissembled; she may have been actuated by jealousy or hatred; but if we condemn, we should also remember the arts and frauds of the men by whom she was surrounded, the false information which they supplied, the imaginary dangers which they created, and the despatches which they dictated in England to be forwarded to the queen through the ambassadors in foreign courts, as the result of their own judgment and observation.

Her natural ability and accomplishments were great. She had the bravery of the Tudors, but she was also vain, irritable, authoritarian, bullying and coarse. She wanted to be remembered as the 'virgin queen', but 'the woman who despises the safeguards must be content to forfeit the reputation of chastity'. Her behaviour, particularly towards Dudley, showed that 'she was become regardless of her character and callous to every sense of shame'. But, though 'haughty and overbearing' at Court, she 'condescended to court the good-will of the common people' in the country.

Under Elizabeth the administration of justice was corrupt partly because of her own predecessors, partly because of her own acceptance of bribes and her interference in private cases. The Court of Star Chamber 'inflicted the severest punishments for that comprehensive and undefinable transgression, contempt of the royal authority'. Courts of commissioners were occasionally appointed 'for the public or private trial of offences' and the queen, 'from her hasty and imperious temper, manifested a strong predilection' for the courts martial which dealt with 'whatever could be supposed to have the remotest tendency to sedition'. She assumed the discretionary power of 'gratifying her caprice or resentment by the restraint or imprisonment of those who had given her offence'. Many new felonies and treasons were created and 'the ingenuity of the judges gave these enactments the most extensive application'. All this, together with the acts 'inflicting death for religious opinion', meant that Elizabeth was 'not sparing of the blood of her subjects'.

Perhaps the most significant statement of Lingard, placing him firmly in the ranks of the most recent revisionists at the end of the twentieth century, concerns the nature and role of the Elizabethan Parliament. Here it is important to quote at some length from Lingard's account:

> Elizabeth firmly believed, and zealously upheld the principles of government established by her father – the exercise of absolute authority by the sovereign, and the duty of passive obedience in the subject. The doctrine with which the lord keeper Bacon opened her first parliament, was indefatigably inculcated by all his successors during her reign, that, if the queen consulted the two houses, it was through choice, not through necessity, to the end that her laws might be more satisfactory to her people, not that they might derive any force from their assent. She possessed by her prerogative whatever was requisite for the government of the realm. She could, at her pleasure, suspend the operation of existing statutes, or issue proclamations which should have the force of law. In her opinion, the chief use of parliaments was to vote money, to regulate the minutiae of trade, and to legislate for individual and local interests. To the lower house, she granted, indeed, freedom of debate; but it was to be a decent freedom, the liberty of 'saying ay or no'; and those that transgressed that decency were liable, as we have repeatedly seen, to feel the weight of the royal displeasure.

Lingard quotes the earlier remark of Michele, the Venetian ambassador, that 'in point of fact the kings of England were become absolute lords and masters; and that, like the grand Turk, they had established a council similar to that of the Bashaw'.[264]

Lingard was in fact anticipating modern researchers such as Conrad Russell, concerning the *ad hoc* nature of Parliament in the sixteenth century, in contrast with the Whig view, sustained in the twentieth century by scholars such as Wallace Notestein (*The Winning of the Initiative by the House of Commons*, 1924) and Sir John Neale (*The Elizabethan House of Commons*, 1949; *Elizabeth I and her Parliaments*, 1955–7), that the Elizabethan House of Commons demonstrated a progressive development towards its modern place of constitutional importance under the benign eye of a queen who could foresee its future importance to the nation. John Neale was knighted for his services to his country as a historian. John Lingard has received little or no recognition.

We shall see later[265] that Lingard provided a view of the 'Glorious Revolution' of 1688–9, based on continental sources as well as domestic, which challenged one of the most cherished assumptions of thought in Whig historiography – that England had invited its saviour from abroad, in the shape of William of Orange, to carry on the torch of liberty and freedom from popery and arbitrary government. He provided the first interpretation of these events which was not narrowly Anglocentric in character, using continental sources to place them within a wider European framework, from which they could take on a new meaning. Lingard's interpretation was not to be repeated until a 'great breakthrough in scholarship' in 1996, published in the United States by two historians of non-English descent (*The World of William and Mary: Anglo-Dutch Perspectives On the Revolution of 1688–89*, ed. Dale Hoak and Mordechai Feingold). As one reviewer of this work states very succinctly:

In 1688–9 William conquered England and took the crown for himself. This simple fact, obscured by generations of Anglocentric interpretation, is glaringly obvious once the 'Glorious Revolution' is seen from a European perspective. And it has been one of the lasting achievements of the academic reassessment, prompted by the Revolution's tercentenary, to restore that European viewpoint.[266]

Lingard, however, had already done this, writing in isolation, more than 160 years before, and no one had since noticed. Time and again, Lingard achieved extraordinary understandings of history, simply by adopting a simple narrative form, based on original research and a highly developed system of source criticism, but without any dramatic utterances which might have brought more attention to his work. But, then, he was deliberately careful to avoid dramatic utterances, not to frighten off his readers.

Lingard's greater significance in the historiography of the Reformation is not connected so much, however, with his original scholarship and balanced treatment of the 'internal' issues of that movement, important though these breakthroughs were. It is related, rather, to the fact that he was able to place the whole movement within its proper perspective as a great and radical change in English history, a great break in continuity and in tradition. This is explained fully, if again undramatically, in Lingard's usual sober style and with his usual economy of phrase. Henry, in the Reformation Parliament, set out 'to exclude the authority hitherto exercised by the pontiffs' and the 'resolution was taken to erect a separate and independent church within the realm'. Henry's 'supremacy in religious matters had been established by act of parliament' and 'its known opponents had atoned for their obstinacy by suffering the penalties of treason'. However, 'Penal statutes might enforce nonformity; they could not produce convictions. The spirital supremacy of a lay prince was so repugnant to the notions to which men had been habituated, that it was everywhere received with doubt and astonishment.' Thus a 'religious revolution' was wrought in England, which 'provided the most important innovations'.[267]

Here we have reiterated that view of the English past expressed by Thomas More in 1535, which had been silenced afterwards in England for three centuries. It was a view which was capable of changing, not only the historiography of the Reformation itself, but the whole picture of the English people's view of their past. For it was a change in perspective, looking at everything in a new way, and when one changes the viewing perspective, the whole picture is changed. It is in such moments as these that the greatest advances in historical writing take place. Centuries of accumulated facts can suddenly take on a completely new shape and design, whereas previously they had simply been pushed, however awkwardly, into the old framework of historical thought.

Lingard's simple statement was in direct opposition to the official view which was dominant in England from the sixteenth to the later part of the twentieth century. That view stated that the Reformation was a popular and patriotic movement, led by the king, to throw out the hated and usurped authority of the Papacy in England.[268] Recent work in local history from different regions of England has confirmed the view that the Reformation was not popularly supported.[269] It has confirmed Lingard's view that it was imposed from above, by an Act of State. Where necessary, political terror, bribery, persuasion and propaganda were used to gain the acceptance (passive at least) of an 'unenthusiastic and conservative' people.[270] For we know that Tudor governments had a great range and variety of methods at their disposal when they wanted to force something through, and Cromwell, in particular, was extraordinarily adept at finding ways of achieving the king's objective. Penry Williams summarized this research in 1995 by stating that, 'The one thing that can be said with certainty about England in 1558 is that it was not yet Protestant' and that most people were not yet committed to the Reformation.[271]

Lingard also noticed that the Statute of Succession (1534) 'provided safeguards and created offences hitherto unknown; and thus stamped a new character on the criminal jurisprudence of the country', and this 'served as a precedent to subsequent legislatures'.[272] This has been confirmed again by Penry Williams who notices that the Treasons Act of 1534 was considerably extended in 1571 and that 'By 1585 it was now treason to belong to a particular category of person, a remarkable extension of the law'.[273]

Lingard was able to place the Henrician Reformation within its proper perspective, as the greatest revolution in English history. With Lingard, the three-centuries-old official view of the English past was undermined and the whole story reconstructed within a different framework. He effectively destroyed the Great Myth. The new picture was that of an England which, for more than a thousand years, had been part of European life, culture and religion. For a great deal of that time it has belonged also to a social, economic and legal structure which covered most of Europe. As a result of the unprecedented action of the Henrician government, a real break occurred in the continuity of English history. At that time the Church was the greatest centrifugal factor in forming community. England had belonged to the Catholic Church, so it was part of an international or European community. From 1533–4 onward, England had its own national Church and it became increasingly a nationalistic community, learning completely different ways of looking at the outside world and its peoples. This was to give a new orientation to England's development for the next three centuries, and it also created a new psychology in the English people. During this time the English people were given a completely distorted view of their past and their historical identity. This greatly affected their view about themselves and everyone else.

In Lingard's day, however, an academic undermining of the great myth was not sufficient. The Establishment in England, the great institutions of State, were obviously opposed to the destruction of the myth. Most people could not read. Those who could read were content to accept what they wanted to hear, in an age when England was on 'top of the world'. Various factors had to change before the old myth could be undermined at a popular level. The conditions at the end of the twentieth century are now right for it to happen, but the work of the revisionist school of historians is still the preserve of only a minority of English people. It may well be that in the new conditions of Europe and the world at the beginning of the next millennium, English people may be very glad to learn that they are really Europeans, by historical identity, after all.

LINGARD'S IMPORTANCE IN ENGLISH HISTORIOGRAPHY

In terms of the development of historical writing as a craft, Lingard holds a place of primary importance in English historiography. His work represented a fusion of the technical scholarship, which had started in the seventeenth century but was greatly developed by Lingard, with the art of continuous narrative and analysis of institutions, together with the description of the historical development of a community, which had been the main positive feature of eighteenth-century historiography.

Lingard's technical scholarship represented a major step forward in historical writing in England. His exceptional ability at being right in his historical judgments and interpretations has long been recognized. Lord Acton, Regius Professor of Modern History at Cambridge, and 'the most widely read, surely, of modern historians, could declare that "Lingard has never been found wrong"',[274] and that 'Lingard's *History* . . . was so far superior to the books that preceded it. . . . The impartiality of scientific research is our surest ally if we adopt it'.[275] Another Cambridge scholar, A.W. Ward declared that 'there has never been a more vigilant recorder of facts than Lingard, or one whom criticism was less successful in convicting of unfounded statements'.[276] G.P. Gooch wrote that Lingard produced 'the first modern narrative of the two critical centuries of English history',[277] a prophetic remark which he did not substantiate or elaborate on in any way. Philip Hughes, a modern Tudor historian, describes Lingard as 'a master historian', adding that, on one matter, 'Another 130 years of scholarship have not added substantially to what he wrote in 1823', and on another, 'Lingard's judgment of a hundred years ago and more, still stands'.[278] The most recent commentator describes him as 'The English Ranke'.[279] But only an in-depth study of Lingard's work can reveal the techniques of source criticism which he imposed on himself and which lay behind his extraordinary achievements as a historian.

In 1960 Herbert Butterfield wrote that 'now that we are beginning to study the ways in which critical techniques actually developed . . . some historians, like the Catholic Lingard, are acquiring an unexpected significance'.[280] This remark was based on his knowledge of research work, involving an in-depth study of Lingard's use of sources, which had just been completed,[281] and has not yet been published. The great development of technical scholarship in seventeenth-century England had been seen in the erudite and accurate publications of the texts of original documents. This work was the first stage in the history of modern scholarship, dominated in Europe by the towering figure of Jean Mabillon, the Bollandist monk, whose great work, *De Re Diplomatica* (1681) remains the foundation of the modern study of the *authentiticy* of historical documents. Mabillon had a great influence on non-juring scholarship in England, for these English scholars regarded Mabillon's work as setting the standard towards which they were striving, which has again been shown in unpublished research.[282]

The second great stage in the development of technical scholarship was when historians began to look behind the original source, to identify and *assess its credibility* as a witness to the truth. Lingard was the first English historian to make this distinction between an 'original' and an 'authentic' (by which he meant 'credible') source. He states it in explanation to a critic who had accused him of prejudice in his use of sources in discussing the infamous Massacre of St Bartholomew (1572) in France. Lingard's extreme sensitivity to any charge of prejudice made him publish a booklet of some hundred pages in order to explain his thinking on the matter:

I said, that I had compared 'the most authentic documents'; he [the critic] makes me say that I compared the 'original documents'. The charge is unintentional, but it is not immaterial. By 'the most authentic documents', I mean documents of sufficient authority to deserve credit, as coming from men, who either were the original devisers of the massacre, or received their information from the original devisers, of the massacre. Such persons may be admitted as authentic witnesses. But the 'original documents' of the reviewer are not confined to such evidence: he extends the denomination to the numerous writings on the subject, published within a few years after the event; of which the far greater part proceeded from those who possessed not the means of ascertaining the real origin of the tragedy, and who wrote only from hearsay, conjecture, and passion. Such writing cannot be classed among 'the most authentic documents on the subject'.[283]

Lingard is here using 'authentic' to mean 'credible' or 'reliable', as opposed to 'original'. The critic, John Allen of the *Edinburgh Review*, had not seen the difference. It was Lingard's application of this method of testing the credibility of a source which enabled him to interpret the evidence properly, so as to give the now accepted view of this subject, as against the popular view in nineteenth-century England.[284]

Interestingly, too, just as Lingard made this important statement concerning source criticism in his booklet, *A Vindication of Certain Passages in the Fourth and Fifth Volumes of the History of England* (1826), in answer to John Allen's mistaken criticism, so, too, had Jean Mabillon written his *De Re Diplomatica* (1681), in answer to a senior scholar-monk who had questioned the authenticity of a certain document which Mabillon had pronounced genuine. The two books represent the two important stages in the development of modern historiography, setting out the rules by which, in Mabillon's case, one set about proving the *authenticity* of a document and, in Lingard's case, the *credibility* or *reliability* of the source as a witness to historical truth. The most important contribution of Daniel Papebroche,[285] in the seventeenth century, and John Allen, in the nineteenth, to historiography was to provoke Mabillon and Lingard into publishing the rules of evidence behind their historical judgements.

In getting behind the source and testing its credibility by applying various techniques, Lingard can be shown to have been the first English historian to have created and worked systematically with rules of source criticism and evaluation.[286] Indeed, as far as I know, he was the first to do this in the history of historiography. It was this factor, above all, which accounts for the great accuracy and reliability of his work in spite of the fact that it covered the whole of English history up to 1689. Time and again he was to be proved right about a certain episode when later and more specialist writers – even in the twentieth century – were still getting it wrong. His *History* was built upon the foundations of rules of source criticism and evaluation which he developed for himself, without necessarily thinking of the universal importance of what he was doing. It was something which simply seemed necessary for him to achieve his aims as a historian, and he did not look further than this. Mabillon had reacted in just the same way in the seventeenth century. Lingard wanted to show that the official version of the English past was faulty and he invented the technical scholarship which had not existed hitherto and which was required to enable him to do this. Mabillon had wanted to defend his own personal judgment about the authenticity of a certain document. Both cases illustrate the way in which very important developments in historiography can take place, starting from a personal initiative, but attaining universal importance as their general significance becomes understood.

To appreciate Lingard's craftsmanship, one has to get behind his narrative to examine the way in which he actually used and evaluated his sources, to look closely at the process by which the sources are translated into the narrative form. Fortunately Lingard's method of work enables the researcher to do this, because he wanted to share with his readers the process by which he came to such different conclusions from the official version of the English past. It is a fascinating story which must be told in a separate and more specialized study of Lingard as a historical craftsman,[286] but it is the most important factor accounting for his success in dismantling the official view of the past. He used the authorized editions of original documents produced by the best seventeenth-century scholars as a platform for the next stage of examining the 'source of the source'. He looked behind the original documents, using a wide range of rules, to evaluate and elucidate the level of authority of the source being used. Indeed, not only was Lingard the first English historian to work consistently with these techniques, but it is not clear that any modern historian has equalled him in this respect. This is because I know of no other historian who has gone to such lengths to reveal his sources and the processes by which he has evaluated them.[287] This is particularly impressive when we consider the vast sweep of English history which he examined assiduously in this way.

Why then, is Lingard still largely unknown? In the nineteenth century, the usual reaction of the most influential historians such as Macaulay and Hallam was simply to say that what Lingard was saying could not possibly be true, because it was going against what everyone knew to be true and 'we must abandon all faith in public fame if it were really unfounded'.[288] As we have seen, there were still too many vested interests in maintaining the official version, which also seemed to fit in completely with England's status in the world. We should notice, though, that in more academic circles there seems to have been some grudging respect for him in practice. For example, we find, rather unexpectedly, that his *History* was on the list of set or recommended books at Cambridge and Oxford towards the end of the century, and, even more surprisingly, when Longmans started the publication of its twelve-volume *Political History of England* in 1905, the editors mentioned in the prospectus that 'Lingard was still the standard complete history of England'.[289]

In the twentieth century I believe that another reason for lack of interest in Lingard among academic historians is that he was categorized as someone who had not been trained in the English Universities, which meant that he did not have the professional pedigree to be taken very seriously, and his image has come down, if at all, as that of 'an enlightened Roman Catholic' and no more. If that is the case, then we must be reminded that history teaching only became an independent discipline in terms of an Honours Graduate Course, at Oxford in 1872 and at Cambridge in 1875.[290] Lingard had received probably the best academic preparation for a future historian available for an Englishman, at Douai College in France, where there was an important emphasis on source criticism.[291] He was arguably, too, the most well equipped of all English historians in his knowledge of languages, ancient and modern.[292] Of course, he had never been attached in any way to Oxford or Cambridge and ignorance of his work and lack of interest in him may well have been part of a general insularity of outlook which has existed as much among academics in England, as in anyone else. Moreover, Lingard was a humble Catholic parish priest throughout his life. Could he then really have been a giant in the history of English historiography as well? Again we must be reminded that, having received the best possible training, he then had, as a celibate parish priest of a small village parish, the time he needed to achieve the great task which he had set himself. That is why he never wanted to move. Even among Catholics in England, Lingard is virtually unknown except to a few academics. To the lay

Catholic, his name is most likely to be familiar as a name in the parish hymn books, as the writer of one of the most well known of traditional hymns 'Hail, Queen of Heaven'.

The claim that Lingard is the father of modern historial writing in England is based on his insistence on the importance of using original sources, his extension of these sources to archives outside England itself, his creation of the techniques of source criticism and his ability to combine this technical scholarship with the art of continuous narrative, covering a great theme of historical development over nearly two thousand years. He also fulfilled – perhaps uniquely in English historiography – the requirements laid down a century later by the great French historian, Marc Bloch:

> In historical works of a serious nature, the author generally lists the files of the archives he has examined and the printed collections he has used. That is all very well, but it is not enough. Every historical book worthy of the name ought to include a chapter, or if one prefers, a series of paragraphs inserted at turning points in the development, which might be entitled: How can I know what I am about to say.[293]

Lingard is a suberb master-craftsman to whom young historians could well apprentice themselves.

I can think of no other English historian who has achieved so much. The significance and extent of his achievements have not been recognized hitherto by his own country or by English historians of historiography. On a professional level we may recall his words that 'time and experience must decide between us';[294] his time of recognition may yet come. In pastoral and personal terms, I suspect that it would matter more to him to know that, after his death, the non-Catholic villagers of Hornby set up their own memorial to him in their local parish Church, 'erected by his friends'.

SEVEN

The Official Version in the Victorian Period and in the Twentieth Century

Lingard's achievement in dismantling the official version of the English past was disregarded by the mainstream of English historical writing in the nineteenth and, to a great extent, the twentieth centuries. Histories of England continued to be isolationist, nationalistic, Anglocentric, 'whiggish' and Protestant in their interpretations.[1] For much of this time there seemed every reason for the English to applaud the official view of their past which had produced such a glorious present. The Golden Jubilee of Queen Victoria, 'Queen of England and Empress of India', in 1887 signalled that England was the most prosperous country in the world. Her power was dominant in the political, military and naval spheres. A quarter of the world's population lived in the British Empire. England had led the Industrial Revolution and its manufacturing capacity was still expanding. These conditions were to linger on for another half a century. The English people could hardly have been blamed for feeling that, somehow or other, they must be a superior nation, which partly explains the 'insatiable progress of Victorian imperialism'.[2] One could hardly have expected them to accept, under these conditions, another view of the past which would have made them seem less special as a nation or people.

Popular historians and university professors of history in the nineteenth and first half of the twentieth century did not waver from the official view, apart from a few medievalists who followed a lonely track, established by F.W. Maitland at the turn of the century. Writers of popular histories continued to support it throughout the twentieth century, and academic historians of the modern period began to challenge it only in the latter half of this century, when the 'revisionists' started to probe and question certain aspects of it.

During most of this time the English reading public were getting what they wanted to hear from their historians. Lord Macaulay has been described by a modern historian as, 'unquestionably the greatest of the Whig historians' and his interpretation of English history was 'the established version for nearly a century'.[3] His *History of England* (1849–61) was 'compulsively readable . . . . one of the best sellers of the century . . . and it had never since gone out of print'.[4] The 'burden of his song' was English superiority and this 'appealed to national patriotism'.[5] His work expressed ideas which were 'universally popular' and 'expressed them in such a way that it flattered the self-esteem of the English people'.[6] The *History* brought Macaulay great wealth and a peerage – as Lord Macaulay of Rothley Temple (1857). He was undoubtedly the supreme Establishment figure of his age in the world of historical writing. It is significant that the first reductive estimate of Macaulay's *History* – apart from Lingard's judgment – has been made only very recently in 1997 by P.R. Ghosh. He concludes that any enduring status for Macaulay could rest only on his work as an essayist, not on his *History*.[7] His *Essays Critical and Historical* (1834), though brilliantly written, have been described in our own day as 'dogmatic, overbearing and irredeemably shallow',[8] while Lord Acton – who admired his great talent – called them 'the key to half the prejudices of our age'.[9] We have long known, of course, that his work completely lacked the type of source criticism and wider outlook which characterized Lingard's *History*. Lingard himself made it a rule not to mention Macaulay, though we know from his private letters his opinion that, 'Macaulay does not write history'.[10] Macaulay, I think, was an extremely gifted writer who was lifted up by public opinion to the status of a great historian – which he was not.

Two examples, one of which is an attack by Macaulay on Lingard, will illustrate very well the way in which, in the circumstances described, Lingard's work was sidetracked by contemporary and later historians. These will also reveal much of the contemporary attitudes of mind on the subject of the official version of the English past. One is concerning a straight piece of political history, an area in which Macaulay has regularly been regarded as particularly astute.[11]

Macaulay, relying on the reports of Sir William Temple, the English diplomat involved, accepted the popular view that the Triple Alliance of England, Sweden and Holland, negotiated against Louis XIV of France in 1667, was a masterpiece of English diplomacy by which yet another European tyrant had been stopped in his tracks by English intervention – a particularly popular idea in the post-Napoleonic age. Lingard, however, had simply applied to the evidence two of his normal rules of source criticism: to compare foreign with domestic sources in dealing with international questions, if one was to avoid an Anglocentric interpretation; and to consider carefully reasons why a particular source may be 'interested' and therefore possibly prejudiced. On comparing Temple's account with the French diplomatic documents, and with the papers of Louis XIV himself,[12] Lingard concluded: 'Much praise has been lavished on this negotiation, as if it had arrested Louis in his career of victory, and preserved the independence of Europe; but in fact, it accomplished nothing more than the French king had offered, and was desirous to effect.'[13] He showed that Louis in fact was the master of the international situation at this time and had willingly accepted the conditions of the ensuing treaty, only because they were pawns in the game of long-term advantage which he was playing. This of course was a completely new and 'shocking' statement on the subject, giving Macaulay the opportunity to make his famously dismissive remark, that Lingard was one whose 'great fundamental rule of judging seems to be that the popular opinion cannot possibly be correct'.[14] A century after Lingard had written, G.M. Trevelyan, OM – as famous in the twentieth century as an Establishment figure as Macaulay, his grand-uncle, was in the nineteenth – repeated the official line:

In 1668 an English diplomat in the Low countries, Sir William Temple negotiated with great skill the Triple Alliance of England, Holland and Sweden to check the French advance on the Rhine and in the Spanish Netherlands. The effect was instantaneous. Louis was compelled to accept the terms of the Treaty of Aix-La-Chapelle.[15]

It was ten years later, in 1949, that an outstanding specialist on the Stuart period, Sir George Clarke, wrote that this Triple Alliance had long been regarded by historians as 'a master stroke of diplomacy', partly because 'Temple, one of the best living writers of English prose, took many opportunities of writing in his own praise'.[16] In 1952 another Stuart specialist, Maurice Ashley added:

But meanwhile the French king had arranged a secret treaty with the Emperor, head of the Hapsburg family. Louis XIV had good reason for being willing to make peace with Spain in the spring of 1668 (for why bother over a small part of the Spanish Empire if the bulk of it might be coming his way?) – and the Triple Alliance contributed little to his decision.[17]

Thomas Munck, writing in 1993 on the European scene at the time of the Triple Alliance, observes that 'France had both the resources and the contacts to exercise a paramount influence on international relations'.[18] One has to bear in mind, of course, that Lingard claimed no particular specialism in the Stuart period. He was writing a history of England from the time of the Romans up to 1668. Macaulay's *History* dealt with the period 1668–97.

The second illustration concerns the celebrated 'Irish Massacre' of 1641 in which English historians had always alleged that the Irish Catholics had committed the most terrible premeditated massacre of Protestants in Ireland, by means of the most devilish cruelty. This story had achieved high status in anti-Catholic mythology and propaganda in England and was still being used extensively in the 1820s as an argument against giving emancipation to English Catholics.[19]

The old version described the unprovoked murder of some 200,000 men, women and children, with sub-human cruelty. One pamphlet on the subject was entitled, 'The Rebels' Turkish Tyranny', with accusations of terrible cruelty. It was no wonder that 'news of the Irish massacre raised public excitement to fever height'[20] in England. Lingard's balanced account of this is as follows:

> The reader will be surprised that I have not alluded to the immense multitude of English Protestants said to have been massacred . . . 200,000 men, women and children . . . murdered, many of them with exquisite and unheard-of tortures . . . and that the same has been repeated by writers without number. But such assertions appear to me rhetorical flourishes, rather than historical statements. They lead the reader to suppose that the rebels had formed a plan to surprise and murder all the Protestant inhabitants; whereas the fact is, that they sought to recover the lands which, in the last and in the present reign, had been taken from them and given to the English planters. . . . That in the prosecution of this object

many lives would be lost on both sides is evident. . . . But that no such premeditated design of a general massacre existed and no such massacre was made, is evident from the official despatches of the lords justices during the months of October, November and December.[21]

Lingard went on to quote the official despatches to prove his point. Here, again, we see two of his rules of source criticism at work: never to use 'popular' accounts which were not substantiated by official records; to weigh carefully the value of any evidence used. To assess the number of Protestants killed, he went to the findings of the commissioners who investigated the rising, and who, in their examinations, 'collected those which had been made upon oath, and consigned them to another book, attesting with their signatures that the copies were correct'.[22] This attested evidence led him to the conclusion that, in total, just over 4,000 people were killed by the rebels, while 8,000 others died as a result of the rebellion. Lingard commented:

That they [the Irish] suffered as much as they inflicted, cannot be doubted. But the blame of such barbarities should not rest solely with the perpetrators on either side; it ought to be shared by those who originally sowed the seeds of these calamities by civil oppression and religious persecution'.[23]

Lingard expected an incredulous response to his statement, for, writing to a friend, while engaged in the preparation of this volume, he said, 'Several small pamphlets etc have been published against my account of the Massacre of St Bartholemew. Perhaps as much may be said against the account in my next vol of the Irish massacre. . . . I find the Irish less guilty than I suspected and their adversaries at least equal to them in cruelty.'[24] The response was indeed as expected. Thomas Keightley in his own *History of England* (1839) joined forces with the more celebrated Henry Hallam: 'We share Mr. Hallam's opinion of Dr. Lingard's attempt to disprove by mere scraps of quotation, an event of such notoriety that we must abandon all faith in public fame if it were really unfounded.'[25] This time, a century later and to his credit, G.M. Trevelyan got it right. He observed:

Land spoliation, social inequality . . . goaded to frenzy by religious persecution, could not but result in terrible atrocities.

Some four or five thousand Protestants perished by massacre, and a still greater number from cold, hunger and ill-treatment. Rumour, crossing the channel, told tales yet more ghastly than the truth. While England was celebrating the memory of Guy Fawkes, she learnt that the Catholics of Ireland had massacred the Protestants. All Englishmen, equally ignorant of Ireland, were agreed that the task which Cromwell long afterwards accomplished must be set about at once.[26]

Godfrey Davies wrote in 1937: 'They [the Irish] were necessitated to take up arms, they say, for the preservation of religion . . . and the natural and just defence of their country. It is safest to leave it at that.'[27] John Morrill, comments succinctly in 1996, that 'the rebellion was a pre-emptive strike by Irish Catholics, desperate to disarm the Protestant community before it launched a pogrom against them.[28] The most recent specialist book on the subject broadens the issues. M.P. Maxwell, writing in 1994, summarized the main conflict as 'England's nationalist expansion' against 'the Catholic religion's supra-nationalism'.[29]

In the second half of the nineteenth century, when England's commercial and imperial power was soaring to its apogee, the main preoccupation of English historians, following Macaulay's example, was to celebrate the great national success story; this started an era which was to last until well into the second half of the twentieth century, when the Whig interpretation of English history flourished unopposed. The English past was regarded universally as a continuous story of the development of liberty, self-government and imperialist expansion, still stressing the Reformation and the Glorious Revolution of 1668 as the great stepping-stones. The editor of J.R. Green's immensely popular *Short History of the English People* (1874) comments: 'The role of historians now, was to act as bards, not as regards the royal praise singers, bit as the collective men of the people, to recall the glories of the past and trace the unbroken thread of liberty and self-government.'[30]

The popular historian, Green (the first to attempt to write *social* history for a wide audience), and the Oxford academics, A.E. Freeman, W. Stubbs, J.E. Froude, A.F. Pollard and S.R. Gardiner, were all intent on praising the long and continuous development of progress and freedom from Anglo-Saxon times. Stubbs in the medieval period, Froude and Pollard in the Tudor age and S.R. Gardiner's work on the Stuart period all revealed great powers of scholarship and research. They did much towards laying the foundation for twentieth-century scholarship in these fields of history, but they were all insular and Anglocentric in their approach and all of them managed to contain their work within the Protestant–Whig interpretation of English history. As a result this interpretation continued to dominate historical writing in England until well into the second half of the twentieth century. More importantly, these men and their students were the teachers of the graduates who became teachers of history in schools and training colleges, and their books decided the content of countless textbooks used lower down the educational ladder. With the introduction of compulsory education for an ever-increasing number of people from the time of W.E. Forster's Education Act of 1870, the official view of the English past became more firmly fixed and more all-pervading than ever as it became taught to *everybody* in school. There was less chance than ever now of a new William Cobbett appearing, who would look with such simplicity at what he saw around him that he could derive new meanings about the past from the environment of the present.

In the latter part of the nineteenth century expressions of another, Teutonic myth appeared: that all these great qualities of the English, driving the engine of continual progress in English history, were derived from the ancient origins in the forests of Germany; that they had inherited, for example, the 'moral earnestness' of the Teutonic spirit which had predestined them to accept Luther's call from the Fatherland in the sixteenth century.[31] This was a theme which had arisen in muted form during the seventeenth century when there had been attempts to drive the remote ancestry of the English Common Law back to the German forest communities,[32] but this has been pushed aside by the insularity of the chief common lawyers who were not willing to look outside England itself for its origins.[33]

J.R. Green, at the commencement of his *History*, asserted that 'For the fatherland of the English race we must look far away from England itself'. The political and social organization of the early English 'must have been that of the German race to which they belonged' and 'the religion of the English was the same as that of the whole German family'. Indeed,

It is with reverence such as is stirred by the sight of the head-waters of some mighty river that one looks back to these tiny

> moots . . . where the men of the village met to order the village
> life and the village industry, as their descendants, the men of a
> later England, meet in Parliament at Westminster, to frame
> laws and do justice for the great empire which has sprung
> from this little body of farmer commonwealths in Sleswick.

Describing the land of Hengest at Ebbsfleet, Green remarks that 'no
spot in Britain can be so sacred to English men as that which first
felt the tread of English feet'.[34]

So, too, was William Stubbs, the most prestigious medievalist of
his day, affected with the idea of England's belonging to the
Teutonic race. This is a primary theme in his mind and it is
interesting to recall that he was a great admirer of the German
historian, Leopold von Ranke, who believed intensely in the divinely
created role of the *nation* within world history, and in the idea that
each nation had its appointed moment of destiny. Stubbs wrote that
'The English Nation is of distinctly Teutonic or German origin' . . .
sharing the German primaeval pride in purity of extraction' and
aware that they belonged to the 'stock of our forefathers'.[35]

It is significant that Stubbs, a Tory and Anglican bishop, had no
qualms at all about accepting the Whig interpretation of English
history. For him England was a Teutonic nation, unaffected by any
significant influence from Rome or Latin Europe. It was their German
blood which had endowed the English with the qualities of self-
reliance, self-government, leading to national liberty and self-
fulfilment. His 'blatant nationalist and organic terminology'[36] and his
nationalist interpretation of the English past were to be a powerful
influence on later English historians and students. Stubbs' deserved
reputation as a brilliant scholar and the quality of his scholarship
meant that 'his shadow still lies across the Oxford school of Modern
History in 1980' and his three-volume *Constitutional History of
England* (1874–78) has 'held its own for nearly a hundred years as
the *Ur*-text on English medieval history'.[37]

However, this also meant that his faults and prejudices were to
have an undue influence on twentieth-century historians, for 'some
of his most dubious assumptions are still at the root of our
historical thinking'.[38] His was certainly a major force during the
twentieth century in maintaining some of the main elements which
underlay the official view of the English past: a certain conscious
distancing from Latin Europe, 'rejecting the notion of any
significant Roman or Frankish influence on the developing

constitution';[39] the retrospective reading of a modern-type nationalism into the institutions of Church and State of medieval Europe; the discerning of a continuous organic progress towards modern institutions; and the attribution of all this to certain superior qualities of self-reliance and independence, racially inherited from their Teutonic ancestors, which made English history a 'special case'. Some of this was to be repeated a century later in Elton's *The English* (1992).[40]

Yet this distinctive line of the Teutonic inheritance never became a core part of the *Great Myth* itself – as it affected the mass of English readers – conveyed by the old official version. It did not fit easily into the much stronger, older and more popular view enshrined in the official version: that everything of value had been born and bred within England itself, independently of Germanic or any other influence. Nor did this 'teutonic' view ever have the machinery of the State behind it – as it was later to have in Hitler's Germany – to drive it on and make it dominant by propaganda and terror. In England these tactics had been used in the sixteenth century to support the official view, and it is clear that, without such state machinery behind it, determinedly pushing it along, it would not have been possible to have created the Great Myth in English historiography. A certain trend or coterie of historians at any particular time – such as this Germanic theme among English historians at the turn of the nineteenth and twentieth centuries – would not of itself be sufficient to do this. Nevertheless, there were still rumours, during and after the Second World War, that Hitler had not really wanted to crush the English because they were part of the Teutonic race.

Another powerful and contemporary ideology, related in some ways to the Teutonic myth, which 'hardened' nationalist ideas in English politics and historiography at this time, stemmed from the publication of Charles Darwin's *Origin of Species* in 1859.[41] The idea of evolutionary progress was soon applied, mistakenly, to other aspects of life and it seemed particularly pertinent to the Whig interpretation of history. Just as proponents of the official version had gladly assimilated the idea of progress in the seventeenth century and the concepts of the Enlightenment in the eighteenth, so now in the second half of the nineteenth century, it incorporated evolutionary theory (including 'the survival of the fittest'). The English past was now expressed in terms of several stages of natural and evolutionary progress by a superior people. The

Reformation and the Glorious Revolution of 1688 represented the two main stages. There was also the added offshoot of the concept of the survival of the fittest, which again could be used to demonstrate how the English nation had progressed or evolved because of its superior qualities of character, derived from 'German stock'. J.R. Green, whose general *History of the English People* was extremely popular at this time, was certainly influenced by Darwin's evolutionary ideas. Their influence was to appear again in the work of Stubbs, A.F. Pollard, and later still, to some extent, in that of J.E. Neale in the middle of the twentieth century.[42]

Meanwhile the influential Sir John Seeley,[43] Professor of Modern History at Cambridge (1869–95), in *The Expansion of England* (1883), described the growth of the British Empire as an inevitable development of the great imperial mission destined for Britain. J.A. Froude, in his *History of England from the Death of Cardinal Wolsey to the defeat of the Spanish Armada* (12 volumes, 1856–70) and *English Seamen in the Sixteenth Century* (1895), also concentrated on the expansionist glories of England. His glorification of the nation, though based on extensive research and archival material, was entirely within the old, national, insular and erastian perspectives. He saw the Reformation as the triumph of the English people as they overthrew the foreign yoke of the Papacy to regain their national independence and freedom, to establish the base for their glorious expansion overseas. It was a more detailed and scholarly account of the old version, though still delivered in a partisan manner and with an obviously anti-Catholic prejudice. Froude's description of Mary Tudor, for example, later repeated by Pollard, was a 'grotesque caricature',[44] as it always was in the Whig interpretation. From that viewpoint, Mary represented the failed past, while the Protestant Henry VIII and Elizabeth I stood for the glorious future. His main theme, in dealing with the Reformation, was similar to that of Burnet in the seventeenth century, though Froude's scholarship was infinitely superior. E.A. Freeman, appointed Regius Professor of History at Oxford in 1884, wrote a monumental work on *The History of the Norman Conquest* in five volumes (1867–9) which presented his belief in the superiority of the British Constitution. A close friend of J.R. Green and Stubbs, he was defective in his own scholarship and 'all his work is infected with anti-Semitism and a violent though selective xenophobia'.[45]

Mandell Creighton, who became Professor of Ecclesiastical History at Cambridge in 1884, was the first editor of *The English*

Historical Review in 1886 and became Bishop of London in 1897. He specialized in the Tudor period and his last work, *Queen Elizabeth* (1896), 'held the field for more than thirty years'. It portrayed a 'profoundly Whiggish' view that around Elizabeth 'the England which we know grew into the consciousness of its destiny' and his conclusion gives us 'that critical and adulatory picture which . . . was to remain the twentieth-century norm'.[46]

Tudor studies in the early twentieth century were dominated by the great output of A.F. Pollard, at University College, London. He created and occupied the Directorship of the Institute of Historical Research. His work was based mainly on printed material from the published calendars, especially the *Letters and Papers of Henry VIII*. His books include *England under Protector Somerset* (1900), *Henry VIII* (1902), which 'held its own for the next sixty years as the standard life', the very popular and influential *Factors in Modern History* (1907), which 'certainly in its time . . . had a powerful influence on our fathers' and grandfathers' thinking about the sixteenth century',[47] the *Political History of England 1547–1603* (1910) which 'held its own into the 1930s as a teaching aid', the brief *History of England* (1912) for the 'Home University Library', *The Evolution of Parliament* (1920) and finally *Wolsey* (1929).

Pollard concentrated more on the political character of the Reformation, rather than the religious. It marks the beginning of the twentieth-century preoccupation with the secular rather than the religious element in history. In this way his work provided a new picture, but the picture was still very much in the old frame of the official version. The most recent survey stresses Pollard's 'insularity' as the most striking aspect of his work. He rarely went outside England and was not well read in European history. He was extremely nationalistic and his Anglocentric view of the English past fell into both the Whig tradition and 'the "historical Darwinism" of J.R. Green, who influenced him profoundly'.[48] For Pollard, the Reformation represented a natural stage in the evolution of England towards national greatness. His *History of England* was subtitled 'A study in Political Evolution', to accompany his *Evolution of Parliament*. His view of Henry VIII as leading one of the great stages of evolution and anticipating the future development of the nation to its ultimate destiny was a perfect example of the old version, adapting itself to the ideological climate of the new age:

As England's world status came increasingly under threat in that uneasy lull between the Boer War and the Great War the intensely nationalist picture presented by Pollard's books had increasing attractions. His portrayal of Elizabeth as a national symbol is a curious reversion to sixteenth century iconography.[49]

Pollard died in 1947. The 'torch' was passed on to his pupil, J.E. Neale, whose work on the 'evolution' of the House of Commons in Elizabeth's reign revealed the influence of Pollard and J.R. Green. Neale's famous *Queen Elizabeth* (1934) was widely acclaimed by academics and the public. Its long-lived success was based partly on its scholarship and style, but also on its:

> glorification of England's past greatness, its mood of nationalist euphoria, which the public found comforting in a decade of disillusion, depression and fear. They continued to draw comfort from it during the Second World War and on into the austerity-ridden era of the Welfare State; at the dawn of a much trumpeted 'Second Elizabethan Age' in 1952 the book's title was changed accordingly.[50]

Neale's unbalanced and adulatory description of Elizabeth I as an embodiment of England's national glory was repeated by other English national historians, such as A.L. Rowse. It still awaits proper reassessment and revision. No historian since Lingard has been able to produce a balanced view of Elizabeth I, seen from the perspective of a 'citizen of the world'.

Sir John Neale's outstanding contribution to our detailed knowledge of the Tudor period is contained in his three volumes on *The Elizabethan House of Commons* (1949), followed by the two volumes of *Elizabeth I and her Parliament* (1955 and 1957). His Whiggish thesis that there was a continuous development or evolution in Parliament's authority during Elizabeth's reign 'owed something to the Darwinian theories of Pollard'.[51] It has now been severely questioned by the work of revisionists such as Conrad Russell, whose researches have shown the reign as 'a period of consensus, punctuated by minority demonstrations which ended in futility'.[52] Moreover, Neale's viewpoint was as insular as Pollard's, and, like the latter, he had an inadequate knowledge of European history.[53] He described continental people, such as the Dutch or

Philip II of Spain, as Elizabeth saw them. This was Anglocentricism at its extreme; here again we must make the glaring contrast between Neale and what Lingard was able to achieve, using the Spanish sources as well as the English, in 1820.[54]

The historiography of seventeenth-century England has much the same story to tell in the nineteenth and twentieth centuries. The classic Whig statement showed a continuous development of Parliamentary authority in the seventeenth century, resulting in the final triumph of freedom at the Glorious Revolution in 1688 when arbitrary government was banished for ever. Samuel Rawson Gardiner, who became Professor of History at King's College, London in 1877, spent his life pursuing the most detailed research into seventeenth-century English history, almost on a year-to-year chronological basis. From 1863 he published a series of books which took his account up to 1656 by the time he died in 1901. His *Constitutional Documents of the Puritan Revolution* (1889) was 'a set book for the Oxford History School and continuously in print to this day' and his work as a whole was regarded for the first two decades of the twentieth century as completely objective and authoritative. In fact all this extremely detailed research was placed into a framework which told the old Whiggish story of the Stuart period:

> he wrote his history backwards, like any common-or-garden Whig: the king was always wrong, even if he was legally and morally right; his opponents were always right, even if they were legally and morally wrong. Moreover, every incident in the struggle between them . . . pointed in the same direction; it was part of an inevitable and irresistible process.[55]

Gardiner's account of the seventeenth century was totally in line with the Whig interpretation. His great reputation for scholarly learning and the mass of detail he accumulated gave great authority to his work.[56] His general interpretation was not really challenged until the work of the revisionists, starting in the 1960s when Conrad Russell and others, studying each Parliament in individual detail, found no evidence for a continuous line of development in terms of independent authority; on the contrary they were able to reveal several 'retreats' from one Parliament to another. The assault on the old Whig, Anglocentric view of the 'Glorious Revolution' of 1688 had to wait until the publication of a book in 1996, written by two non-English scholars, who used continental sources to achieve a new 'European' viewpoint. This was the result of an academic reappraisal which had been going on since the tercentenary of the Revolution in 1988–9. Lingard was the only English historian to have been there before, in 1830.

The last in the long line of popular and avowedly Whig historians who exercised a great influence over the English people's view of the past was G.M. Trevelyan, grand-nephew of Macaulay. He became Regius Professor of History at Cambridge in 1927 and was appointed by Sir Winston Churchill as Master of Trinity College in 1940. He was also admitted to the Order of Merit by George V in 1930 and, like Churchill, was one of the very few non-scientists to be elected to the Royal Society in the twentieth century. Such were the honours bestowed by a grateful country on the most popular historian of his day, whose best-known works on English history were his *History of England* (1926) and the *English Social History* (1940). The first was 'Whiggish' in character, depicting 'Britain . . . the mother of parliaments' achieving 'what other nations have found incompatible', while 'At the Reformation the English, grown to manhood, dismissed their Latin tutors . . . Britain had become a world by itself'.[57] *English Social History* was published first in America, then in England in 1944:

> He regarded it as a contribution to the war effort, which in its way it was . . . its flag-waving patriotism, its intense nostalgia for the English past, its chauvinistic assumption that England had always been great and England had always been right, catered for an obvious public need in the weary closing stages of the war, and the disillusioning postwar years of continued austerity and imperial decline.[58]

The influence of this book on the minds of the English reading public was enormous: 'the public adored it, and it is still one of the best-selling books of all time'.[59] Trevelyan was indeed an 'authentic phenomenon', who had a greater cultural influence on his own time than any other historian of the twentieth century. But 'outsiders' were less impressed. An American writer described his work as 'ardently national' with a 'militant assertiveness of the superiority of English institutions'; and a French reviewer of the *Social History* dismissed it as 'un pamphlet de propagande nationaliste et xénophobe', written with 'complaisance et d'auto-satisfaction'.[60] Meanwhile the young Herbert Butterfield had written his important *The Whig Interpretation of History* (1931).

Trevelyan was the last Whig historian to exercise such a great influence on the English public at large, but this was not the end of the Whig interpretation itself. Its influence on the minds of practising historians has been perhaps the most durable phenomenon in the history of English historical writing, expressing itself in a variety of forms and guises, even after its chief dangers and weaknesses had been made clear by Butterfield. One of the most tempting of its attractions was that it seemed to do so much for the English national spirit and morale, especially in times of national crisis. Butterfield himself wrote of confidence-boosting qualities produced in the English by this view of their past during the particular stresses and strains of the Second World War.

In *The Englishman and his History* (1944), Butterfield described the help to English morale provided by the Whig view of the uninterrupted progress of England and its institutions. He later attacked L.B. Namier's methods of writing history because they tended to undermine English morale and idealism without replacing them with any thing else; for 'I happen to believe that history is a school of wisdom and statesmanship' for the benefits of future 'public servants and statesmen' who need ideals to work towards.[61] Butterfield was right in emphasizing the need for idealism and principles in public life. It is important, however, that they are based on *true* views and perspectives of the past, which form a realistic basis for guidance in our public life. This will be particularly important as we look to the past for guidance to our future in the new millennium which is facing us with its many problems and opportunities.

Even when modern historians could not be called 'Whiggish' in the most blatant sense, there can still be evidence of the warping effect of the old way of looking at particular aspects of the past. Geoffrey Dickens, for example, wrote his *The English Reformation* in 1964 and this understandably became a very popular and influential textbook, at undergraduate and sixth-form level. Dickens looks back at the pre-Reformation period and over-emphasizes the importance of Lollardy in its own day as 'the abortive Reformation',[62] because he is reading it too closely in the light of what happened later in the sixteenth century. A very recent scholar observed in 1996: 'Lollardy might be considered retrospectively as a kind of 'pro-Protestant' movement within the late fourteenth and early fifteenth centuries. Within the context of their own time, they may be seen as they saw themselves, as one of many currents of reformation and dissent within the Church.'[63]

We have been reminded again recently, in Greg Walker's *Persuasive Fictions: Faction, Faith and Political Culture in the Reign of Henry VIII* (1995),[64] of the tendency among historians to consolidate dissenting individuals or groups into united sects and so exaggerate their importance. Before the Reformation the Church was the main centrifugal force in creating community and society. This was a commonplace, an assumption of thought which was taken for granted in this period, even by those who would wish to introduce reforms and changes. To regard Lollardy as the 'abortive Reformation' of its day is to misread the documents of Lollardy by interpreting them outside the normal assumptions of thought of that day. A specialist in the later medieval period reminds us that 'there is a temptation to regard the Henrician Reformation as a natural evolution from medieval developments' which it was not.[65] One of the new breed of revisionist historians now tells us that Geoffrey Dickens' perspective and method 'have been undermined by the impact of revisionism'.[66] If the Reformation had not happened in the sixteenth century, as it might not have, Lollardy could not have been regarded as 'the abortive Reformation'. This view is essentially a reading of later history back into the past.

Coming into the last decade of the twentieth century, it is intriguing to find that the most influential of the Tudor academic historians in the second half of this century seems to fall victim to the temptation to read history backwards when he set out, at the end of his career, to write a history of *The English* (1992). After a lifetime of productive achievement as a scholar of the Tudor period, Sir Geoffrey Elton was appointed to the Regius Chair of History in Cambridge in 1983 and was knighted in 1986. He had arrived in England as a refugee from Prague in 1939 and had risen to the top of both his own profession and the English social establishment. He wrote *The English* out of a sense of gratitude to the English.[67]

This book, written at the end of the millennium by one of the best known of England's professional historians, is of more than usual relevance to the main theme of our study. For, as soon as Elton leaves his detailed documentary knowledge of the Tudor period to look at England's history as a whole, in his first book intended specifically for a wider and more popular audience, he begins to write like a Whig historian, within the main framework of the old official view of English history. He becomes concerned to discern and praise the admirable continuity of England's development and growth from its earliest days, towards its unique greatness. The whole exercise is so significant and illustrative as a historiographical phenomenon that it deserves some detailed attention.

No one can doubt Elton's mastery of the documentary sources for the Tudor period, though one might not follow him in his interpretation of the facts or in his view of the personalities and issues involved. His intense, documentary research has been described as 'teutonic' in that 'his attitude is most akin to that of the great German nineteenth-century masters'.[68] He was exceptionally perceptive when dealing with Thomas Cromwell's 'Revolution in Government' because he thought in very much the same way as Cromwell, sympathizing strongly with his objectives and admiring his achievements. He conducted his own historical researches with the same qualities of efficient and methodical thoroughness which characterized Cromwell's political work. He believed strongly, as had Stubbs, Freeman and Ranke, in the merits of a strong and centralized nation-state, governed by a strongly centralized government. For Elton, Cromwell had created the machinery for such a state and used the Common Law as the instrument to carry out his revolution in English life and to impose it on the people.

There are some indications, too, that Elton shared with previous historians, such as Stubbs, Green and Freeman, a certain 'pan-Germanic' view of the English past.[69] He certainly saw England as a 'fundamentally Germanic people',[70] 'that identifiable branch of the Germanic nations',[71] and drew the line clearly between them and their Celtic neighbours.[72] He is keen to show that, from the first, the English people could 'lay claim to a high degree of self-sufficiency'.[73] With regard to the early Anglo-Saxon laws, he is pleased to announce that 'Latin did not enter the game'.[74] So it was that this people 'managed to organise itself from within its own conventions and resources.'[75] Elton fails to recognize adequately the bi-lingual nature of Anglo-Saxon culture, in which Latin played the major part in the written aspect. He stresses rather the role of English as the 'main Germanic vernacular that had achieved the status of a literary medium: it was a written language used by administrators, chroniclers, thinkers and poets'.[76] This is a matter of perspective. It is not so much a matter of what he says, but of whether he is putting things together in the proper relationship with one another. Since language is a main centrifugal force in creating community and culture, this *emphasis* on the vernacular as opposed to Latin conveys a false impression: that Anglo-Saxon England was more independent and self-sufficient, as opposed to being part of the common culture of Europe before the Norman Conquest.

Elton remarks on the continental influence resulting from the Norman Conquest. He comments again, 'certainly a first impression must be that 1066 marked a major, indeed an enormous break in continuity'. It was after the 'subterranean years' of the temporary ascendancy languages following the Conquest that the English language was to 're-emerge' during the thirteenth century as 'easily the most adaptable and most varied means of communication ever put together by man'.[77]

Elton seems inclined, too, to read later history back into the medieval world, to emphasize the early stage at which English people became recognizable in their modern garb, so to speak. He asserts that, from 1272 onwards, 'the English nation had unquestionably arrived' with its 'characteristic mixture of tolerant superiority and grim xenophobia'; 'this nationalism rested on a powerful streak of chauvinism – of hatred for foreigners'.[78] It is towards France in particular that Elton identifies this xenophobic attitude in the later medieval period. Again, he follows in the path of earlier 'Germanists' such as Stubbs, Green and Freeman, who sought German origins and influences on English institutional developments, but sought to underplay the significance of French influence on England. But the truth lies in perspective.

Stubbs' pupil, T.F. Tout, who became Professor of History at Manchester, recognized this fault and made some perceptive comments in his *France and England: Their Relationship in the Middle Ages* (1922). He showed that France and England had enjoyed a mutually enriching relationship within the wider Latin civilization which they shared, Even when the Hundred Years War took place, it did not cause the mutual animosity between two peoples which one would expect under modern conditions of war; for 'The "foreigner" still was not so much the national enemy as the neighbour from a rival borough or the next county'.[79]

> Medieval battles, then engendered less ill-feeling than modern ones, partly because they were looked upon as part of the rule of nature, partly because they were, as between France and England, waged between peoples who had almost everything in common and, besides, had a very imperfect conception of national solidarity.[80]

Tout saw the Reformation as isolating England, for the first time, from French influence. Speaking of the renunciation of Latin – the 'common tongue of the west' – as the language of the liturgy at the Reformation, Tout adds, 'In this and in more important ways the Reformation built up further walls of separation between the two peoples. After the Reformation, religion was no longer an integrating but a separating force. Side by side with the national state arose the national church.'[81] Stubbs' influence on medieval studies at Oxford, and on twentieth-century historiography has been great, but Tout, as early as 1906, warned us, concerning his *Constitutional History of England*, that 'much evil has, I am convinced, accrued in Stubbs's own university from the excessive cult of this great book'.[82] F.W. Maitland and T.F. Tout shared the view that Latin and Catholic culture was of prime importance in the life of the English people up to the sixteenth century. Both of them saw the Reformation as an isolating movement, causing a great break in the continuity of English history.

More recently, Matthew Vale has reaffirmed Tout's view of the 'close and fruitful contact' between England and France during the period 1216–1340. They 'shared a common civilisation and culture' and it would be 'extremely misleading' to see a consistent and continuous hostility between them. If the 'relative harmony' was affected by 1340, it was certainly not the result of 'national sentiment':

> It is sometimes forgotten that Anglo-French relations in the thirteenth and fourteenth centuries, possessed many of the qualities of a family history. Sir Maurice Powicke was quite right to emphasize the domestic quality of high politics, when so much depended upon dynastic marriages, connections and alliances within an enlarged family circle.[83]

Vale emphasizes, too, the 'local' character of the combat in Aquitaine, where the English extensively used French soldiers whose allegiances were shaped by local rather than national considerations.[84]

War, of course, is always brutal, but there were certain elements in medieval warfare between European states which distinguished it from that in other periods. The enemy could not be completely depersonalized when both sides shared a common religious and cultural value system, and when the modern weapons of mass killing by remote control were not available.[85] In the medieval period 'many conflicts only affected society significantly in its upper ranks' and the social effects of war were less disruptive than in ancient times when whole peoples were reduced to slavery, or in the modern age when entire populations were dispossessed or transferred and when the whole community has directly suffered the effects of war.[86]

During the medieval period, too, the universal Canon Law of the Church was more concerned with the good of the whole community at all levels than with any particular sectional interests involved in the war. It was intent on showing how people should behave towards one another in times of conflict. It set out not only the moral conditions for a 'just' war, but also rules to safeguard the non-combatants in the wider community. During the Hundred Years War, for example, the French canon lawyer, Honore Bouvet, wrote the *Tree of Battles*[87] in 1389, in which he defended the interests of the community by indicating the various immunities, rights and protections which non-combatants should enjoy, and the limitations of the power of the soldier under Canon Law. So, too, in England, another canon lawyer, Nicholas Upton, produced his *De Studio Militari* (1440) which again reminded the combatants on both sides of the rights of the public.

There must have been a natural heightening of feeling among combatants and others during the conflict, but it would be mistaken to see this in terms of mutual national hatred between the peoples. It is significant that some people 'questioned whether any war could be worthwhile or just when fought between Christian and Christian' for 'the doctrine of Christian love, such as Langland voiced in *Piers Plowman*, seemed incompatible with war'.[88] Indeed, as the authority on medieval warfare remarks, 'Christian and courtly values . . . were foreign to martial values even when they in some cases integrated them'.[89] Even seven years after the outbreak of the conflict between England and France, Richard de Bury, Bishop of Durham, was able to travel extensively in France (1344–5). He showed no anti-French prejudice, described Paris as '*paradisium mundi*' and revealed 'no nationalistic ill-will or chauvinistic animus' in his writings.[90]

The xenophobia associated with modern nationalism could not arise under these conditions. The English did not become xenophobic as a *nation*, against other *nations*, until their country had become a sovereign, independent nation-state, isolated from the Continent and western Christendom, and taught by the unprecedentedly powerful propaganda of the centralized Tudor state to distrust and hate 'foreigners' who had now become simply the inhabitants of other European *nations*. The old Canon Law, which had concerned itself with universal moral concepts appropriate for *all people*, was now cast out of England and replaced by the English Common Law, from which there was no appeal outside the nation. There was now no commonly accepted code of conduct by which international relations could be judged. The door was open for the new world of power politics.

Moreover, the majority of 'outsiders' or 'foreigners' in western Europe were associated with the Papacy, which had now become the main source of evil, hatred and fear, the very symbol of anti-Christ, according to the new theological and political propaganda in England. This made it possible for the first time for the people of other countries to be depersonalized or dehumanized as the 'enemy'. The isolation of England bred more fear and distrust. In these circumstances xenophobia could breed and become an unbridled passion. This accounts also for the extraordinarily durable history of anti-Catholic persecution in England itself; Catholics, according to this way of thinking, were *ipso facto* aliens, who pretended to be English but were really intent on the destruction of the nation. This helps to explain, too, the gullibility of the English public in succumbing to bouts of frenzy, fear and distrust. The last of these, the 'Gordon Riots' in 1780, led to the killing of about 300 innocent people, in reaction to the Catholic Relief Act of 1778.

Elton is misreading the past, therefore when he tries to trace English nationalism and its accompanying xenophobia, back to 1272. He read the assumptions of thought of the later, post-Henrican age back into the previous period, a process which the medievalists are continually warning us against. Vale writes in 1996:

A renewed tendency to seek for signs of emergent national identity – if not of nationalism – during the later Middle Ages has also been discernible in some recent works . . . we must be wary of transporting modern doctrines and concepts of the State into thirteenth and fourteenth century conditions.[91]

It is very easy to misread the actual documentation of the later medieval period, unless certain assumptions of thought belonging to the people who wrote them are constantly kept in mind.

Similarly, Elton refers to the concept of the 'elect nation' in medieval England, which he derives from the 'theology' of the Plantagenet kings, anxious to pursue their ambitions in France.[92] These ambitions in fact were largely *dynastic* rather than *national*. This again is an example of reading later concepts into the minds of an earlier people whose assumptions of thought were quite different. The Plantagenet kings, who ruled England from 1133 to 1486, belonged to one of the most notable families in European history, and they were certainly *European* as well as *English*. They were very closely tied to the Continent by religion, family, marriage, land and trading links. Such sentiments as Elton found in their writings, while they pursued their dynastic ambitions in France, were simply medieval pieties with which they coloured their personal ambitions – such as a general feeling of being endowed with God's special favour. These utterances should not be identified with the post-Reformation view of England as the 'elect nation', for there was to be a completely different set of assumptions of thought behind this phrase as used by John Milton in the seventeenth century. J.W. McKenna points out that it was only after the Tudor revolution in the 1530s that England's claim as the 'elect nation' could 'be received as a plausible political ideology': 'The influence of that mighty idea can be read in the works of John Foxe, the words of John Aylmer, the Golden Speech of Elizabeth I and the chauvinistic rhetoric of John Milton.'[93] In the England of Milton's day, Calvin's theology had given this phrase a much more narrowly selective interpretation than it could ever have had in the Catholic teaching of medieval Europe.[94]

Finally, Elton claims that, in the fourteenth century, England turned hostile to the Papacy: 'King and Parliament joined hands in attacks on papal rights, and in defence of national independence', and 'the new relationship was adverse to the notion of a Church standing above national boundaries'.[95] Medievalists have shown quite clearly, however, that the popularity and authority of the Papacy, as Head, on earth, of the Universal Church, was as strong as ever on the very eve of the Reformation, and that papal authority, as opposed to its particular applications, had never been denied by king or Parliament. As Peter Heath puts it, 'The progress from Praemunire to Protestantism was not one of evolution, but revolution'.[96]

Unfortunately the work of the great medievalists in the twentieth century, 'brilliant though it was, was for the most part too technical for the man in the street, even the educated man in the street'.[97] The highly significant fact here is that even a historian of Elton's status and specialist knowledge of the Tudor period could still, in 1992, misinterpret the English past in the same way as did the old followers of the official version, from the time of the Henrican statutes onwards. Such is the force of the official version on the minds of historians as well as the 'man in the street'.

Nor is it simply a matter of Elton's failure to understand the religious mentality of the medieval world. This arises partly from his lack of sympathy with that mentality – in short, he prefers Thomas Cromwell to Thomas More.[98] But he also concedes that

> Inevitably, given my foundation and preferences, I am bound to concentrate on political and ideological events. Family relationships or habits of procreation seem to me historically less fascinating; they tell us about this or that human being but not about a collection of them, and they do not really change through time. After all, so many attempts to define the commonplaces of human behaviour in historical categories have proved mistaken.[99]

Some of us would say, however, that the changes in the 'commonplaces of human behaviour', according to their historical context, constitute both the most difficult challenge to the historian – because they are rarely written down – and, at the same time, provide the most important keys to the proper interpretation of the documents of the past. Certainly, it is impossible to understand the inter-state relationships of medieval Europe without a complete appreciation of the importance of 'family relationships' (like those of the Plantagenets) and their effects on human thinking and behaviour.

Elton believed that English history as such came to an end in the early nineteenth century when it was replaced by the concept of 'British' history, which included its Celtic neighbours. This phase, in turn, came to an end with the collapse of the British Empire. Looking at the gloomy picture which he saw around him as he wrote *The English*, at the end of his career, he hoped that the English will 're-emerge from their British phase' to show the one characteristic which once 'marked them out among the nations', that is 'the ability to tolerate variety'. He also wishes that they will 'come again to respect the rights of the individual: the rights not of Man but of English men and women'.[100]

The beginning of a new approach to Reformation historiography started at the beginning of the twentieth century in the works of the great medievalist and Cambridge scholar, F.W. Maitland. He was a legal historian who was able to show that the English Church, law and institutions were once part of the much wider community of western Europe. He revealed the great influence of Roman law and of the Catholic Church on English life up to the Reformation, which he demonstrated to have been a drastic break in the continuity and direction of English life. Among his most important works were *The History of English Law before the time of Edward I* (with Sir F. Pollock, 1895), *Roman Canon Law in the Church of England* (1898), *English Law and the Renaissance* (1901) and *The Constitutional History of England* (published posthumously in 1908). His seminal thinking and depth of scholarship were allied to exceptional intellectual clarity and an extraordinary detachedness from contemporary prejudices and vested interests. He remains one of the greatest of English scholars. His work was too original to be popular and his influence never extended to the level of popular reading. Stubbs differed from Maitland on the subject of the nature of the medieval Church in England. Stubbs' influence on the academic world of their time was much wider, but we know now that Maitland was right in seeing the pre-Reformation Church and its legal system as essentially part of the universal Catholic Church, not as an independent national Church. There is no doubt that Maitland's work was the inspiration for later medieval scholars such as T.F. Tout, Stubbs' greatest pupil, and Z.N. Brooke, who took the matter further in his book *The English Church and the Papacy* (1930).[101]

Since the 1930s a series of outstanding medievalists – F.M. Powicke, M.D. Knowles, C.P. Cheney, W.A. Pantin, R.W. Southern, Sir Frank Stenton (on Anglo-Saxon England) and others – have thrown great beams of scholarly light on a period of which Thomas Arnold, Regius Professor of History at Oxford in 1841, had written: 'I could not bear to plunge myself into the very depths of that noisome cavern, and to toil through centuries of dirt and darkness.'[102] Perhaps the great mark of the final achievement of these medievalists was when Dom M.D. Knowles, a Benedictine monk, was appointed to the Regius Chair of *Modern* History at Cambridge in 1954 – and he was the authority on medieval monasticism. Their work made it possible for us to see that other historians, specialists in later periods, have often read history backwards, attributing to medieval people the assumptions of thought which belonged to the post-Reformation world. They also brought to fruition that greatest of historical discoveries, which was the re-creation of the medieval world and its achievements.

These medievalists, however, rarely ventured into the later period of the Reformation. When they did, as in the case of F.M. Powicke in his short essay on *The Reformation in England* (1941),[103] or in David Knowles's last section of his magisterial *The Monastic Order in England* (1949), they were able to give glimpses of a very different view of the Reformation from the one the official version had allowed. This was the viewpoint of the people who lived through these events, who were just coming out of the medieval world and were looking contemporaneously rather than with hindsight at what was happening around them. Both were written by master historians who were rejecting the Whig interpretation of history, not in any self-conscious way, but simply because it did not make sense to them as medievalists.

The first conscious, ideological attack on the official version of the English past had been made already by the youthful Herbert Butterfield in his *The Whig Interpretation of History* (1931), which described 'The tendency in many historians to write on the side of Protestants and Whigs . . . to emphasize certain principles of progress in the past and to produce a story which is a ratification if not the glorification of the present.'[104] This short book was one of the most powerful and influential essays in the history of English historiography, and was eventually to set many historians working in new directions. However, its effects were delayed until after the Second World War, and it was in the second half of the twentieth century that it bore fruit in a new generation of historians. Even Butterfield himself was so affected during the Great War by the need to strengthen English morale in the face of the enemy, that he developed a certain sympathy with the confidence-boosting effects on the country of the Whig interpretation in English historical writing, though I would not agree with those who think that he had actually been converted to the Whiggish view or that he thought this was the proper way to write history.[105]

The first ground-breaking work from the university world, by a Tudor historian, to divert from the old official view of sixteenth-century history, was Professor J. Scarisbrick's authoritative *Henry VIII* (1968), which at last replaced Pollard's account of 1902 as the definitive biography of the king whose actions caused the greatest break in continuity in English history. While taking full account of Elton's portrayal of Thomas Cromwell's instrumental importance, Scarisbrick restored Henry VIII to his place as the chief policy maker in the revolutionary proceedings of the 1530s and the one who was ultimately responsible for them.[106] He also emphasized the importance of the divorce as the occasion without which the Reformation might not have happened. There is no hint of writing from hindsight in Scarisbrick's work and he makes us see that the Reformation was not part of any unavoidable pattern of continuous 'progress' in English history. He restored the essential character of the popular risings of 1536 in the north – the 'Pilgrimage of Grace' – as chiefly a protest against the Reformation. They were strong enough to have overthrown the regime, had not Robert Aske and other leaders trusted the king's word to negotiate with them. This raises a question which, to the Whig historians, would be 'thinking the unthinkable'. What would have happened to the rest of English history had Robert Aske been successful in overthrowing the regime? To the Whig historians, the Reformation was successful and it had to be inevitable because it led to the future in which they lived. If it could be shown that the Pilgrimage of Grace could have succeeded, then it had to be chiefly about something other than opposing the Reformation, because English history would make no sense at all to them without the Reformation.

Scarisbrick's book on Henry VIII was followed, later, by his *Reformation and the English People* (1984), in which he wrote:

> the basically Whiggish and ultimately Protestant view of things is still a potent influence on our thinking. Diluted, residual, secularised, that influence may now be. But we still find it difficult to do without this model of late medieval decline and alienation – followed by disintegration and then rebirth and renewal. . . . We have been content with the image of the Tudor regime unleashing and then riding on the back of the tiger of popular anti-clericalism, anti-papalism and so on.[107]

In 1985 Professor John Bossy produced his *Christianity in the West*, which effectively challenged the very use of the word 'Reformation', as a Whiggish term which tends to prejudge historical issues, with its implication that a superior form of religion was replacing the old. He also highlighted the fact that Christianity, before the

Reformation, meant primarily the body or *community of Christ's people*, whereas afterwards it often came to mean a body of different *isms*.[108] This was a key insight into pre-Reformation assumption of thought. It was the Church which had been the main force in creating community at every level of life, from local parish to the whole of Europe. To attack the Church was to attack society. After the Reformation, with open divisions in Christianity, there was no centrifugal force strong enough to create community at an international level, and there was no international law yet to replace the Canon Law.

The Stripping of the Altars. Traditional Religion in England c. 1400–c. 1580 (1992), by the Cambridge historian, Dr Eamon Duffy, gives a very detailed and well-researched account of the revolutionary impact of a radical break and discontinuity with the English past; here again there is no element of 'progress' or inevitability about the account. Much of this change has resulted from the findings of research workers at local level, describing the impact of the Reformation in various English counties.[109] Other historians have looked at certain changes which happened across the face of England. R. Hutton's *The Rise and Fall of Merry England. The Ritual Year, 1400–1700* (1994)[110] shows the way in which many popular social customs associated with the ritual year, in the lives of ordinary English people, were undermined and rejected by the newly imposed theology. P. Marshall's *The Catholic Priesthood and the English Reformation* (1994)[111] emphasizes the drastic changes in the life of the clergy. Several changes of mind and doctrine, forced on the clergy after 1529, affected morale and status in the relationship between them and their flocks. Anti-clericalism was a result rather than a cause of the Reformation. In 1996 B.A. Kümin's *The Shaping of a Community. The Rise and Reformation of the English Parish c. 1400–1560* revealed a flourishing parish life in the late medieval period and the negative effects the Reformation had on this life. The parish was taken over by the State for its own purposes, which caused great change and discontinuity in parish life.[112] Other works have appeared, presenting revisionist views of the Reformation. Christopher Haig edited the thought-provoking *The English Reformation Revised* (1987)[113] and produced his own *English Reformations: Religion, Politics and Society under the Tudors* (1993),[114] showing the diverse strands of thought and action which existed under the term 'Reformation', of which religion was represented only in one evangelistic element.

In 1995 there appeared the first volume of Professor R.W. Southern's *Scholastic Humanism and the Unification of Europe*,[115] which, perhaps more than any other single work, is likely to change the ways in which historians look at the medieval past and its achievements. Far from a picture of the modern world emerging from the 'dark ages' we are now shown that the real achievements of the modern world are based on the thinking of our medieval ancestors. This work reveals Christian humanism as the great achievement of the High Middle Ages, inculcating the whole of society in western Europe with a system of ordered thought and behaviour, based on a universal system of moral law in its widest sense. This affected life at every level, including the social, political and economic aspects. The belief in an ordered meaningful universe provided a great stimulus for creative and investigative inquiry. It established the seed-bed of ideas which led to the Renaissance and also to the later scientific achievements of more modern times. By the twentieth century, however, the massive secularization of society had pushed out the spiritual core which had given ultimate meaning, order, coherence and purpose to that all-embracing Christian humanism. Europeans are now left, at the end of the second millennium, with the residual effects of this achievement, but without the values and beliefs which inspired it and gave it meaning. We have problems of disorder and confusion at all levels of life, similar to those which had featured at the end of the first millennium. There is a great need again for values which can sustain order, meaning and coherence in the contemporary world. Southern's reconstruction of the past is almost the opposite to that of the old official version and its Whig concomitant of continual progress. It also presents us with much food for thought as we enter the new millennium.

In the 1970s the revisionist movement in seventeenth-century English historiography started, associated particularly with Conrad Russell, a young London University historian. This constituted a frontal attack on the old Whig interpretation of the age of the Stuarts. It attacked particularly the idea that there had been a continuous and conscious movement, in opposition to the arbitrary rule of the Stuart kings, towards parliamentary government, moving inevitably through the first great stage of the Great Rebellion of 1642 and reaching its apogee with the Glorious Revolution of 1688. The revisionists challenged this view and, with it, the authority of Burnet, Macaulay and S.R. Gardiner, on whose general interpretation seventeenth-century historiography had been established. Russell's detailed study of successive parliaments revealed no conscious or continuous development towards parliamentary government. Indeed, he was able to show that this was not the framework of ideas within which seventeenth-century members of parliament thought. It was a later attitude of mind transferred back to an earlier age. Russell published his *Parliaments and English Politics, 1621–29* in 1979. In 1990 there appeared *The Causes of the English Civil War*, followed in 1991 by his major study, *The Fall of British Monarchies*.

Other historians took up the cause of 'revisionism'. Kevin Sharpe, for example, in his 1983 study, pointed to the real attempts to reform and reinvigorate central and local government during Charles I's period of 'Personal Rule', and showed that, given more time, they might well have succeeded.[116] Esther Cope could find no evidence of widespread opposition to Charles I's policy during this period in her *Politics without Parliaments* (1987). In the Whig version, this period of 'Personal Rule' had featured as an attempt at arbitrary government which had upset the nation and caused the king's downfall. The revisionists argue that the real reasons for the Civil War and its outcome have more to do with factors like the financial crisis experienced by the monarchy and the appearance of the Scottish army on the scene in 1642. Russell, however, has also had his critics[117] and it may be some time before the history of this period falls into a more balanced perspective. But the Whig interpretation, as such, will never have the same force again among academic historians.

Russell describes the main features which characterize the revisionists' approach:

> revisionism has always been directed against the historiographical assumptions Whigs and Marxists have held in common . . . the notion of progress . . . a tendency to use history as a way of explaining why events led to their ultimate conclusion . . . the attempt to evade the influence of hindsight on the story has happened in other fields of historical investigation, including the origins of the English Reformation, and in all of them, historians writing in the 1970s have been attempting to argue that hindsight has grossly distorted the story we have hitherto been told . . . an attempt to avoid the pressure to assume, *a priori*, that the result we are investigating was inevitable. . . . Revisionism has also been an attempt to

restore the study of political narrative history. To let the search for causes or explanations take priority over the establishment of the correct story is to put the cart before the horse . . . we must establish the course of events by treating it as a subject worthy of study in its own right, and then and only then attempt to analyse its causes.[118]

The political narrative – establishing the correct sequence of events – may itself need revision because of the mistakes of previous historians and also taking into consideration new documentary evidence which has come to light. Also, and very importantly, the revisionists were 'reluctant to assume as the Victorians did that England is always a special case'.[119] It is interesting to reflect that on all these counts of the revisionists' general approach to historical writing John Lingard could very appropriately be called the 'father' of this group of historians writing in the late twentieth century, 150 years after him – and they probably know nothing about their predecessor.

From its very beginning in the sixteenth century, the official view of the English past had been narrowly nationalistic and Anglocentric, assuming that England was a special case and treating it largely in isolation from its neighbouring countries in the British Isles and from continental Europe. Events in these other countries were treated from the English viewpoint and their importance was judged according to their impact on English history. This, from the historiographical viewpoint, was a problem of perspective. For example, the vital part played by William of Orange in the 'Glorious Revolution' of 1688 was treated solely from the English 'internal' perspective in the Whig interpretation. William was seen as the 'saviour' who answered the call from the English to save their freedom and Protestantism, the one, therefore, who played an important role in their inevitable progress towards democracy, success and power. A very recent scholar has observed that 'the Glorious Revolution is crucial to the Whig interpretation of British history, central to the notion of British uniqueness'.[120]

However, recent academic work, inspired initially by the tercentenary of the 'Glorious Revolution' has placed it within a European rather than an Anglocentric perspective. This change of perspective puts the whole subject in a different light. It immediately becomes clear that this really was a conquest of England by the opportunist William of Orange who, seeking his own and

Holland's advantage, took the English crown for himself, with the considerable military support of his Dutch army and assisted by the provocations of Louis XIV. The 'call' from the English Protestants was in reality a document put together by that arch-propagandist, Gilbert Burnet, which a few other of his political cronies in England signed on behalf of all 'English Protestants'. Burnet was already with William at The Hague, planning the move. The Whigs in England were not sufficiently cohesive to have engineered it. The Tories, who were much the more significant group, quickly acquiesced when they saw which way things were going, and went along with the tide. The people of England were in confusion, ready to follow any definite lead. James II panicked and fled the country, leaving the vacuum to be filled by a foreign prince who had married his daughter. It was an extremely successful 'coup d'état', in which a small group of determined and capable individuals played a primary part – and none more so than Burnet who became propagandist-in-chief to the new regime.

The new Establishment had a vested interest in obscuring the nature of what had happened and very quickly – almost contemporaneously with the events themselves – the whole takeover was being interpreted as a Whig-inspired English movement to save the country from 'Popery' and 'arbitrary government'. William had brought his own press with him for propaganda purposes, and the leaflets and pamphlets were quickly and widely distributed. Thus was born the idea of the 'Glorious Revolution', representing the next great step after the Reformation along the road to England's freedom. No notice or credence was taken of the fact that it was James II, and his brother Charles II before him, who were the first English kings to try to establish religious toleration for all in their Declarations of Indulgence (1662, 1672, 1687, 1688), and that it was the Establishment which had wanted, in measures such as the Clarendon Code, to prosecute minority religious groups. Every English Establishment coming afterwards has been committed to the Whig interpretation of the events of 1688.

Academic research stimulated by the tercentenary of 1688 resulted in a new account which was published in the United States in 1996: *The World of William and Mary: Anglo-Dutch Perspectives On The Revolution of 1688–89*, edited by Dale Hoak and Mordechai Feingold. This is a Eurocentric account the like of which has not been seen before in Britain, except in John Lingard's *History*. In 1830 Lingard had used foreign sources (especially the papers and letters of the French ambassadors and agents, D'Avraux and Barillon, who were at the centre of European politics at this time) to place the 'Glorious Revolution' in the context of continental politics and the opportunistic ambitions and initiatives of William of Orange.[121] Lingard had also pointed out for the first time that the supposed 'memorial' sent to William by the Protestants of England, inviting him to invade, was in fact the work of Gilbert Burnet, in exile at The Hague, which he had learned from d'Avraux.[122] It is also clear from Lingard's account that William's success was by no means inevitable. It had depended on several mistakes made by James II, including certain panic measures, which had alienated his supporters, and the decision to flee the country. James II's panic measures, caused by the fear of what might happen, brought upon himself the very dangers of which he was afraid. Lingard's account was so 'new' and so 'up-to-date' with our present knowledge, simply because he portrayed the sequence of events, based on original foreign as well as domestic sources, without attempting any particular interpretation himself. His concentration on getting the political narrative right, rather than expressing causes, interpretations or generalizations, gave his work a certain timeless quality. His account of the 'Glorious Revolution' is quite consistent, therefore, with the account in this recent work by Hoak and Feingold.

The propaganda campaign behind the Whig interpretation is of great interest. We know that William brought with him Burnet, printers and printing presses. We also know that Burnet immediately began to preach a series of propagandist sermons in London, almost contemporaneously with the passing events.[123] It was only with the publication recently, however, of Dr Tony Claydon's *William III and the Godly Revolution* (1996),[124] that sufficiently detailed attention has been given to the expert use of propaganda by the new regime. Claydon reveals the central part played by Bishop Gilbert Burnet who had become a prime agent of William at The Hague and returned with him at the 'Revolution'. Burnet was the man in charge of the propaganda campaign. Indeed Claydon terms it the 'Burnetine ideology'. Conveyed through official sermons and pamphlet publications, it was designed to 'sell' the legitimacy of the new Establishment, to gain the support of Parliament and to further the alliance between Holland and England as leaders of Protestantism against 'Popery' in Europe. The propaganda included 'fast days' and pronouncements of official 'Thanksgivings' for the 'Glorious

Revolution and an emphasis on the 'Courtly Reformation' (another idea of Burnet) established by the new king and queen, as the central theme. William's right to the throne was vested in his role as the divinely appointed leader of moral and religious reform. The recourse to a suitable interpretation of history to justify current proceedings became a principal tool of propaganda, as it had been in the 1530s under Cromwell. In this way the Whig interpretation of the 'Glorious Revolution', and of previous English history leading up to it, came into being. Its creator was Gilbert Burnet.

The last decade of the twentieth century has witnessed the first real attempt to view English history as part of the wider British and European scene. In 1991 Jondorf and Dumville edited *France and the British Isles in the Middle Ages and Renaissance*,[125] which describes the cultural links and exchanges between these two neighbouring parts of Europe in the seventh and eighth centuries. He also discusses how Franco-British culture was created from the twelfth century onwards by the cross-fertilization of languages – Latin, French, English and Celtic – which produced the media for literary and intellectual life in Europe. In 1994 *England in Europe 1066–1453*, edited by Nigel Saul,[126] again emphasized the strength of the religious, cultural and political bonds which held England and continental Europe together during the medieval period, while in the same year *England and Normandy in the Middle Ages*, edited by D. Bates and A. Curry,[127] showed the same multiplicity of connection in all areas of life, including art, architecture and other areas of cultural interchange. Again in 1994, Jeremy Black, Professor of History at Exeter, published his *Convergence or Divergence? Britain and the Continent*, which demonstrates the ecclesiastical, cultural, political and economic links between Britain and continental Europe since Roman times. Indeed, Black argues that there continued to be a certain degree of mutual influence and involvement until 1918. The experience of the two world wars was, in his view, mainly responsible for Britain's insularity and hostility towards Europe in the twentieth century. In this respect, I believe that he has underestimated the longer-term influence of the Reformation, the rise of the nation-state and British imperialism in separating England and British life from that of continental Europe since the sixteenth century. Nor can he envisage the possibility of a future for Britain's relationship with the rest of Europe on any other basis than that of the nation-state: 'the notion of a European community is of value if its institutional pretensions and prerogatives do not range too widely and are restricted by the preservation of a major role for the nation-state.'[128] There is, however, no reason, apart from its dominance in the last four centuries of European history, to assume that the nation-state will last for ever in its present form.[129] It was not always so in the past, and the likelihood is that it will not always be so in the future. This may be one of the areas of life in which we may have to learn to outgrow the past in order to make proper preparations for the conditions of the future.

In 1996 B. Bradshaw and J. Morrill edited *The British Problem: 1534–1707*. We learn that during this period 'Britain' was used by English people mainly as a 'synonym for England',[130] and that 'the central drive of English kings was to expand to the north and west'[131] at the expense of Ireland, Scotland and Wales. John Morrill emphasizes in his introduction to this work the radical and revolutionary importance of the two main acts of the Henrican Parliament, in changing the life of England and of Britain. He writes that there are a 'few defining moments, wherein changes take place which produce a fundamental new climate in the environment'. Certain changes produced by the Henrican Reformation Parliament represented such a break in the history of the English and the British people: 'It can be said that the passage of the Act in Restraint of Appeals (1533) and of the Act of Supremacy (1534) was just such a defining moment in constituting a rite of passage . . . from one stage to another.'[132] In 1996 Professor Black also wrote *A History of the British Isles*, in which he makes his own observations on previous historiography in Britain: 'The Whiggish approach to British history emphasized a Protestant identity for the nation . . . a nationalistic self-confidence that combined a patriotic sense of national uniqueness with a xenophobic contempt for foreigners, especially Catholics.'[133] He also makes the important distinction between the results of recent academic research and the continued march of the old interpretation of the English past in more popular historical literature:

In most academic circles Whig history is apparently dead, displaced by the scholarly developments of the last sixty years. At the popular level, however, trusted historical images are still popular, generally reflect Whiggish notions and often have little to do with academic developments. In addition the academic works that sell best and are most accessible to the general reading public are generally those written in a traditional fashion.[134]

This helps to explain why the hold of the Great Myth, based on the official version, on the minds of English people is still very apparent and very influential. It provides the basis for a set of 'politically correct' assumptions of thought, such as the 'thousand years of our independent national sovereignty', to which politicians feel able to appeal for popular support when all else fails, in campaigns for 'Britain against Europe'. That myth asserts that the English were never really Europeans, that they ought to keep to themselves and rely on their own resources, as they have always done, and they should be ready once again to reject defiantly the attempts by foreigners to destroy their historical freedoms and independence.[135]

Yet common sense, the influence of television, together with increasing experience of life, culture and sport in continental Europe, are also beginning to exercise an influence. The building of the Channel Tunnel between England and France stands as a signpost to the new millennium. Many English people are beginning to see advantages for themselves, in terms of human rights and justice, ensuing from the judgements of the European Courts in these matters. English workers are seeing that the Social Chapter has much to offer them in terms of their human dignity and standard of life. The final outcomes of the BSE crisis concerning British cattle is showing that, after all, it was not our European neighbours who made the mistakes, acted unreasonably and were in the wrong – in spite of the great tirade in much of the British tabloid press against the 'outrageous behaviour of the foreigners'.

In the contemporary debate as to whether or not Britain should be part of the process for European unification, a clarification of Britain's real historical identity and deepest cultural and religious roots could play a very important part in the decision. For when people have to make a critically important decision concerning their future, it is often such considerations of historical identity and root values which play the most influential role in their thinking.

EIGHT
Epilogue

Historical myths are often very revealing. The first myth concerning Europe was grounded in its classical past and is contained in a Greek legend. It tells how 'Europe' came from Europa, daughter of the King of Tyre, and Jupiter. They settled in Crete and their children became the first 'Europeans'. Europe certainly finds its identity essentially as a community or family of people, rather than a physical entity. Its people share a religious, moral, cultural and historical identity. They have been shaped initially by the heritage of Greece and Rome, and then, over the last two millennia, by the beliefs and values of the Christian faith.

The great majority of the present constituents of the European Union are Christian, mostly Catholic, but also Orthodox and Protestant. Their ethical and social values find their origin and still largely find their meaning in the Judaeo-Christian tradition, in spite of the secularization of life which has taken place in the twentieth century. Of the additional six states mentioned in Jacques Santer's 'Agenda 2000' (July 1997) as qualifying for consideration for entry into the Union, four – Poland, Hungary, the Czech Republic and Slovenia – are Catholic. The other two – Estonia and Cyprus – are Protestant or Orthodox. With their entry, the European Union would extend from Ireland in the west to Poland in the east, both nations very Christian in character.

With the great secularization of life in modern Europe came the rise of secular beliefs in such economic or political systems as Communism, Fascism and Capitalism. Looking back, at the end of the twentieth century, all these are increasingly seen as having failed to produce the necessary answers to people's needs. There is a recognition among more and more observers of the contemporary scene that an exclusive concentration on economic and political considerations – important though they are in themselves – is inadequate because they are comparatively short-term in character. These considerations find their proper meaning and perspective only within the context of spiritual, religious, moral and cultural values, where the deepest needs and true identity of people are to be found. Food is essential: people must eat in order to live, but they do not live in order to eat.

Similarly, the interdependence of the various elements in human life and the universe is becoming increasingly obvious. We cannot really separate out elements like economics, politics and defence from questions of religion, culture and morality. Indeed, the attempt to separate these elements has been one of the chief mistakes of modern European history. They all belong, in perspective, to the essential unity of life.

The greatest challenge facing Europe in the new millennium is to restore this perspective and to place its political and economic strategies within those traditional values which are the true basis of its identity. These values meet the basic needs of people within the changing political and economic contexts of the modern world. The Christian ethic and social teaching are expressed today in concepts such as respect for the individual person, human rights and dignity, democracy, justice, welfare provision, freedom and environmental care, all of which make an *ethic* which enjoys very high status throughout the world. It is probably true to say that all *peoples* in the world are now aspiring to achieve objectives in terms of this ethic.[1]

If policies were constructed to apply the values of this ethic sensitively and imaginatively, with proper respect for the cultural variety of individual local regions of Europe, there would be powerful forces working in support. These policies would have the enormous advantage of working with history, with the beliefs, values, experience and cultural traditions which constitute the heritage of the European past. They would be working in continuity with the past. Such values would also be capable of meeting the needs of the present and the future. The process of including the new entrants from Eastern Europe might be helpful in shifting emphasis from shorter-term economic considerations to the longer-term considerations of spiritual, moral and cultural identity in the minds of the European Parliament and Commission. The truth, as always, lies in getting the various elements of European unity in the right perspective.[2]

The process by which it became academically acceptable to regard medieval England as very much a part of Europe was started by the epoch-making work of a great legal historian, F.W. Maitland.[3] He was followed during the twentieth century by a number of distinguished medieval historians. Recently, Sir Richard Southern, most eminent of contemporary medievalists, has made another breakthrough. He has shown that the Christian scholastic teaching not only was the basis of European unification in the medieval period, but also had a much greater influence on European life and thought up to the twentieth century than has been appreciated previously.[4] Yet the influence of the great isolationist myth, that England has always lived an essentially independent existence, has continued to dominate popular thinking in England.[5]

In January 1973 certain economic and political pressures forced England into joining the European Economic Community. However, the mental outlook of many of its people, to which their view of the past contributed so greatly, was very slow to adjust to the new realities of the situation. H.G. Koenigsberger asked a question in 1964 which is probably still pertinent: 'Must ever our most up-to-date text books stick to the indefensible separation of "English" from "European" i.e. Continental history?'[6] Recently, a distinguished European, George Steiner, a scholar long resident in England, remarked that he had been regarded for a long time as an 'outsider' and 'too continental' for certain English tastes. He observed that '"continental" is a complicated word in certain English mouths' because it conflicts with English feelings of 'inwardness'.[7]

From the time of the inception of ideas concerning a united Europe in the second half of this century, there have been particular problems for English people. Very few initially wanted to have anything to do with the idea. In 1967 a distinguished journalist in England wrote that 'Britain is not genuinely European . . . whenever a major international issue arises . . . her *instinctive* reaction is a markedly non-European or even anti-European'.[8] Progress was made, guided by grudging acceptance of the realities of the new situation in which England found itself in the world. The English government accepted the jurisdiction of the European Courts of Justice and Human Rights. This acceptance means that for the first time since the Act in Restraint of Appeals (1533) it is possible for appeals to be made to a higher court outside England against legal decisions made in England. It is only very recently that the 'New Labour' government incorporated the European Law of Justice and Human Rights into English law, so that for the first time since the medieval period England will belong to a European-wide system of law which is concerned with the universal application of human rights and justice.

Already there are signs of the civilizing effects of this new system of appeals outside England. One example is the question of equal rights for men and women. Yet one of the most popular English newspapers reacted as follows to the early manifestations of this concept:

> from the European Court of Justice, came a devastating and expensive ruling that all British men are entitled to free NHS prescriptions from the age of 60 . . . an outside body is ruthlessly instructing [us] . . . how to behave. . . . What were our M.P.'s doing while foreign judges tore up British laws and British practices? Raging against this alien intrusion? . . . it is a sad truth in this ancient democracy . . . [our] M.P.'s have surrendered to Brussels.[9]

Similarly there is significant opposition to the Social Chapter of the Human Rights legislation, by which, for example, there should be a minimum wage for all workers and a maximum working week of forty-eight hours, with four weeks' paid holiday a year. English people were told that this would be unworkable in England, without disastrous effects on its 'competitive edge'. There are obvious comparisons between many of these modern-day concerns of the European Courts of Justice and Human Rights and the international Canon Law, centred in Rome, which was concerned in the medieval period with questions such as the 'just wage' and other forms of protecting the weak against exploitation by the strong. Both are rooted in the Christian philosophy of the essential and equal dignity of all human beings. Another interesting example is the decision in the European Court of Human Rights (17 December 1996) that English law had breached the human right of silence in the Guinness Fraud Trial in England.[10] This right was inherent in the teaching of medieval scholastic philosophy.

Three elements have been present in the way in which English people have defined their own nationalism since the sixteenth century. One was Protestantism, which, in its broadest sense, has meant a shared anti-Catholic mentality. Secondly, there was the empire and a shared sense of pride in the acquisition of vast colonies overseas. Thirdly, there was the series of wars against Spain, France, Holland and Germany, which stimulated a sense of shared danger and pride in victory and consolidated a sense of national unity against outside threat.[11] These factors have lost their potency at the end of the twentieth century and there have been signs of a lack of direction in England's attitudes and policies up to 1997, with obvious confusion about the best way forward for the future. The General Election of 1997 encapsulated much of the internal debate on these issues, with the 'attitude to Europe' proving the central focus at issue between the main parties.

I have suggested in this study that there was another deeper, and even more durable force behind the rise and maintenance of a nationalist and insular mentality in England. This force has been associated with the other factors, yet is essentially different from them and can continue to exist when the other factors have lost their effect. The psychological force of a very strongly held historiographical myth developed all the power of a folk memory in the minds of most English people. It has been all the stronger because it has existed and still exists in certain assumptions of thought and attitudes which are so deeply embedded that they are not stated or questioned at a rational level. It is the great myth that England has always been separate and independent from mainland Europe and has always had its own national institutions, born unaided out of the national wisdom and strength of character of the English. It asserted that England owed nothing and borrowed nothing of importance from the mainland peoples[12] and was separate from them and superior in its splendid isolation.

This myth is based on a false understanding of the past. England, for the first millennium of its history, was increasingly part of the life and culture of Europe. In particular, it belonged to the Universal Catholic Church, which was the main centrifugal force behind European unity and community. For much of that time, it also shared with Europe that feudal system which informed so much of its political, economic and social life.

There was, indeed, a natural sense of 'Englishry' which expressed itself in its own cultural genius and, in steps like Magna Carta, towards its own freedoms at a national level. As Sir Maurice Powicke has written in his aptly titled *Ways of Medieval Life and Thought*, there are historical questions which 'cannot be answered by reference to the later categories of history':

They ought not, in my view, to be answered by those who see nothing in the thirteenth century but the fight for a new nationalism. There was, I feel, a sense of Englishry, going back to pre-Conquest days, penetrating and influencing from top to bottom the English which we can dimly see, but it was a responsive, not essentially an anti-clerical, anti-foreign thing. It was to find its full expression later, in Chaucer and Langland and the great English mystics, in More and Colet and Shakespeare – not in the growlings of churlish defiance.[13]

Professor David Knowles also tried to put into words 'a certain blend of qualities that is peculiarly English, and that throughout the ages . . . has been embodied again and again in great Englishmen',[14] among whom he cites the Venerable Bede, Alfred the Great, Chaucer, Thomas More, Shakespeare and Samuel Johnson. These qualities include seriousness, simplicity, sanity, loyalty, trust, warm-heartedness and a keen sense of pathos.[15] Such qualities, together with a great 'bull-dog' tenacity and courage in the face of adversity, describe well the particular strengths of the English people at their best. These strengths were partly undermined by that official view of their past which produced, for example, the vein of xenophobia and extreme, irrational anti-Catholic prejudice which lasted for so long. They were also affected by ideas of themselves as 'the elect nation', and by the glittering successes which came with victories in war, colonial conquests on an unprecedented scale and great national wealth from prosperous trade and industry. Beneath it all, however, these are still essentially the strengths of character which can reassert themselves, given new challenges and opportunities of a different sort.

The history of Europe over two thousand years has been essentially that of a great society of peoples, sharing fundamentally the same religious, cultural and moral values. Men like Erasmus and Thomas More had dual citizenship, so to speak. More was a typical Englishman of the best sort, but he was also a European, very conscious of those shared values which informed European history and culture. Within this greater unity, there was room for a great diversity and variety of local cultures.[16] Unity in essentials works in harmony with diversity of cultural expression. We know that an isolated culture tends to atrophy, whereas cultures thrive from fruitful contact and cooperation within a greater unity of values. Daffyd ap Gwilym's poetry, for example, revealed the fruitful marriage between the Welsh bardic tradition and European influences in Welsh literature of the fourteenth century, both existing within the unity of European culture. He is regarded as the most eminent Welsh poet of the medieval period.

The sixteenth century saw the break up of the old European unity of culture and religion, with the emergence of the new nation-states which spent a great deal of the next 400 years engaged in internecine warfare in Europe and in the fight for supremacy in trade and colonial expansion. One suspects that Erasmus and More could foresee something of this prospect. Both were severe critics of faults in the Catholic Church, but Erasmus broke with Luther and More broke with Henry VIII on this great issue. They wanted reform, not a revolution which would throw out certain universal values – including European peace and unity – enshrined in the unity of Christendom. England rose to the top of these fighting nationalisms, reaching the summit of its success as a nation and imperial power during the late nineteenth century. Since then there has been 'the story of Britain's slide down the slippery slope from palmy greatness to anxious mediocrity'.[17] But this has happened – perhaps to a lesser degree – to other European nations as well over the last four centuries.

Europe now seems to be moving towards the older vision of unity and partnership among all its peoples. The catastrophic wars between France and Germany in particular have persuaded the leaders of both these countries to seek a means of avoiding such wars again, and of establishing a permanent peace in Europe. This is the main political aim behind the movement towards European unity, and it is nobler than most of those which have guided European 'power politics' over the last four centuries. It will be an appropriate objective with which to face the new millennium, especially when extended to a worldwide dimension.

After a long period of isolation, in the shadow of its mighty neighbour, a small country like Wales, for example, has already produced in the twentieth century a literary figure who combines the Welsh cultural heritage with a deep knowledge, understanding and appreciation of the culture of Europe. Saunders Lewis, playwright and poet, saw in the medieval literature of Wales 'a unique expression of the "philosophica perennis" of Catholic Christendom'[18] and he astonished most of his fellow countrymen by becoming a Catholic. He is regarded as the greatest Welsh literary figure of the twentieth century. His themes are universal. Nominated for the Nobel literature prize in 1970, he was a cultural figure well ahead of his own time and may not have been properly understood by many of his contemporaries. He wrote in Welsh and remains a towering and prophetic figure in Welsh culture today, pointing the way forward to a

Wales which can once again take its place among the other European cultures. Scotland and Ireland have shown the same signs of awakening.[19]

But what of England's future in the new millennium? It could be, from a new viewpoint, that its greatest years were not after all those of its glittering but transient triumphs in war and imperial expansion, just as the greatest days of France may not have been the period of *la gloire* under Napoleon. Certainly nobody would claim that Germany's greatest days were under Hitler. Looking back, does aggressive competition and war ever lead, even for the victorious nation, to real glory in terms of the happiness of its people? Is our vision for the new millennium to be one of seeking peace, unity and partnership between peoples, or is it still to be one of seeking the national advantage in some sort of cut-throat competition with others bent on the same end?

The debate concerning Europe continues in contemporary Britain during these opening years of the twenty-first century. Britain has seemed to be the least enthusiastic of the major countries about the process for European unification. The idea of dual citizenship is extraordinarily difficult for many English people to accept. The main problem, I submit, is at the subconscious level of the 'folk memory', incorporating the Great Myth. It has been the main factor in making English people look at things in a different way and adopt different attitudes from those of most other European countries.

Brave decisions have to be made. History does not repeat itself, but a true knowledge of one's past can provide an important reservoir of experience which can assist in the making of such decisions. Great opportunities and challenges are facing the countries of Europe in the new millennium. Perhaps the greatest of these will be the chance to put into practice a new vision of Europe, united again by a system of common values, one of the most important of which will be toleration and respect for people of all races, countries, religions. Within such a Europe there will be opportunities for freedom of expression by various and diverse local cultures. Such a framework might be a federal structure or a commonwealth of countries on the model of the British Commonwealth. Whatever form is agreed upon, England would not lose its own Parliament, as opponents sometimes seem to imagine. Each state would retain its own parliament to ensure democratic control of its own government. There would be no great shift of power to Brussels, only better and more democratic means of controlling the powers which already exist in Brussels. The federal structure has built-in machinery to ensure the protection of regional differences.[20]

Such a vision of the future will depend, however, on European countries feeling a sense of common identity and certain common values as well as common interests.[21] This is the essential prerequisite for greater European integration towards unity. What identity and what values? It is difficult to think of a value system which could replace the Judaeo-Christian tradition, which historically has been at the root of European culture and civilization. In Britain, we know, from various polls taken on this matter, that even when parents do not attend a place of worship, the majority of them believe in God and want their children to be educated within a Christian value system; this is as good a test as any in discerning people's most deeply held feelings and convictions. While Christian influence may have declined in the twentieth century, its values still give us the best understanding of what Europeans hold in common – of what it means to be European.

Christian values would have the power and tradition to attract sufficient support throughout Europe to form a consensus among the majority. They underpin so much of our existing life and thinking, though we sometimes forget the connection. The Christian belief in the spiritual nature of men and women, the sacrosanct worth, uniqueness and dignity of each individual, for example, lies at the root of the great respect for individual persons reflected in our legal system: 'a person is innocent unless he or she is proved to be guilty', or 'even the guilty must be treated with respect and humaneness', 'the State is for the individual, not vice-versa'. Similarly the equal worth of all human beings in the sight of God lies at the heart of European thinking about issues such as human rights, peace, justice, democracy, subsidiarity and solidarity. This holds true in spite of the fact that so many Christians have themselves misinterpreted or transgressed their own fundamental laws of love of God and their neighbour.

Christianity itself had developed[22] to become more ecumenical in the widest sense, showing respect and tolerance for people of all faiths and none, working with 'all people of good will' in partnership to serve the needs of all mankind. Religious leaders could have an important part to play alongside statesmen in working for a united Europe.

EPILOGUE

A great Englishman of the nineteenth century, Cardinal Newman (1801–90) lived out in his own life and seminal writings his universal view of Christianity and its relationships with human society.[23] Newman is now increasingly recognized as a truly prophetic figure in English, European and even world history. His thinking has come to fruition in its great impact on the modern Christian outlook, in particular on the Second Vatican Council. He will become one of the most influential English thinkers in shaping Christian history in the new millennium.

Another Englishman, Cardinal Basil Hume, Archbishop of Westminster and President of the Council of European Bishops' Conference, spoke to the fifth symposium of European bishops in 1982 of the contemporary situation in Europe:

> The situation which confronts the Christian Church in our continent is complex and difficult. There are political divisions between East and West. There are profound social and cultural differences between the North and South of the continent. There remain in Europe religious divisions caused by often bitter religious history which has separated Catholics and Protestants. Despite these difficulties, the continent retains a spiritual unity which arises from a shared history and from common Christian values.[24]

This was a very realistic statement of the problems facing any movement towards unity, but at the same time there was a clear insistence on the firm basis on which such a movement could be founded. Significantly, too, the sudden and dramatic collapse of Communism in Eastern Europe, since these words were spoken, reinforces their message concerning the true spiritual identity of Europe. The human spirit of these peoples in Eastern Europe survived and then rose to express its essential need for freedom. What looked like an insuperable barrier of political and military power collapsed before it in a sudden, unexpected and most extraordinary manner.

Also the ecumenical movement has brought Christians more closely together, while the Second Vatican Council (1962–5) made highly significant and important statements concerning freedom of conscience, religious freedom and respect for other religions and all people. All this has prepared the way for the rebuilding of a Christian value system as the core of that common identity which

Europeans will need to recognize in the next millennium as a true basis for their unity.

The English people in particular will need to develop a sense of historical and cultural identity with their European neighbours. Their comparatively recent experience as a world power and their present status as centre of a commonwealth of countries of different cultures could help them to make a very special contribution towards the movement for unity in the new Europe.

To meet the needs of the new millennium, the English people need to recover the flexibility of mind which belonged to their pre-Reformation ancestors. Thomas More, Chaucer and other writers were able to express their country's natural genius within a wider context of European culture. English Christians paid temporal allegiance to their English sovereign and spiritual allegiance to the Universal Church. People were English *and* European. The narrowing effect of the national-erastian view of their past (together with the new theology of absolute obedience to the state ruler), introduced by the Henrican government, was to fix with great rigidity the idea that English identity was defined by absolute and sole allegiance to the national ruler who controlled everything. In England it became impossible after the Reformation for 'true Englishmen' to belong to a wider concept than England itself, whether it be the Universal Church or Europe. The English people now need to recover this flexibility by overcoming the rigidly narrow, nationalistic sense of identity taught relentlessly to so many generations by the official view of their past.

Sir Richard Southern's publication of the first volume of his planned three-volume work on *Scholastic Humanism and the Unification of Europe: Foundations* (1995) could well prove to be of great historical significance. The culmination of a lifetime's fruitful activity by one of the most distinguished of English historians,[25] this work offers a fine example of the way in which history and historiography can sometimes interrelate. Southern's work was made possible only because of his daily contact from 1969 to 1981 with the library at St John's College, Oxford, which contained the shelves of medieval books which had been thrown out at the Reformation, only to be restored by Archbishop Laud between 1595 and 1640. This had been part of Laud's attempt, as Fellow and later President of the college and Archbishop of Canterbury, 'to bring Oxford and the Church of England back into contact with the earlier tradition of European learning'; it reflected 'his inspiring vision of the re-integration of the learning of the Middle Ages with that of his own time'.[26] His imprisonment and execution (1645) under the Long Parliament brought an end to that attempt, but Southern's work on these materials in St John's Library during the latter part of the twentieth century may well contribute to a reintegration of the principles of Christian humanism with the culture of our time at the beginning of the new millennium.

Southern's work posits that Christian humanism formed an important base for European unification in the medieval period, for the Renaissance and for the world of modern science. This has not been properly understood before. He shows that the great schools of Christian scholastic studies at Paris and Bologna in the eleventh and twelfth centuries produced principles and values which were to permeate the life of Europe at every level and in every area. These underpinned the intellectual life, the culture, the government and the social and legal structures of western Christendom.[27] They coloured the thinking and behaviour of ordinary people throughout Europe. Gratian's *Decretum* (1139) was the 'first masterpiece of Scholastic Humanism', attracting artists as well as jurists, basing its fine intellectual foundations in 'the events of ordinary life and full of human situations'.[28]

All this provided a sense of common identity among the peoples of Europe, the basis for European unification. Moreover, this Christian humanism provided the root for the flowering of the Renaissance in the fifteenth and sixteenth centuries – of which Thomas More and John Colet were the greatest exponents in England – and also for the later developments in mathematics and the natural sciences from the seventeenth century to the twentieth. This Christian humanism declared that the universe and all its parts were filled with meaning, and it was the business of the theologian, the philosopher, the scientist, artist, poet and all other students to research, discover and celebrate this meaning from their different viewpoints. The aim was to push the boundaries of human inquiry and discovery as far as they would go in all directions. Theirs was 'an attempt to make the created universe, and its relationship to the eternal being of God, as fully intelligible as the limitations of fallen nature allow' and the methods used were the same in investigating order in all created things and in all human relationships. The nineteenth-century English poet, Robert Browning, understood this when he made his *Fra Lippo Lippi*, the late fifteenth-century Italian painter, say:

This world's no blot for us
Nor blank; it means intensely, and means good:
To find its meaning is my meat and drink.[29]

The relationship between Christian humanism, the Renaissance and modern science is exemplified by the life and work of Leonardo da Vinci (1452–1519), the great Italian painter, sculptor, architect, engineer and scientist. He is acclaimed by the world at large as one of its great geniuses. His notebooks contain many examples of the way in which he anticipated the findings of modern science by working on his own mathematical and scientific premisses. The inspiration for all this was his Christian humanism: 'If this outer carcass of man seems marvellously created, consider that it is nothing compared to the soul which has informed it', 'I let stand without touching the crowned letters' [the Scriptures] . . . for they are the Supreme Truth', 'Oh God, you sell all things to men at the cost of their effort', 'If you do not know God, you cannot love Him. . . . What is the undefinable thing which would cease to be if it were to be formulated – the infinite which would be finite if it could be defined'. There is a limit to man's abilities: 'Even more the spirit in the universe. But the finite cannot be extended into the infinite.'[30]

Twentieth-century secular humanism retained from its medieval origin the motivating 'desire to extend human powers to the utmost', but abandoned the spiritual and religious dimensions at its heart, which had informed and underpinned all human activities and behaviour with a meaningful, deep,[31] and interrelated structure of religious and moral values. It was the dominance of secularization in twentieth-century humanism which pushed out the spiritual and religious from that vast scheme of things and left man isolated in his pursuit of false gods to worship. Perspective and meaning were lost, and man himself degraded. Gone, too, was the framework of values, order and meaning within which people had thought, worked and behaved. The world of the twentieth century was lived to some extent on the residue of the past, but witnessed order breaking down at many levels of life. Ultimately, as Herbert Butterfield pointed out, there are only two basic stances from which we can consider the world and human life. Either it is all accidental, or it has meaning. If it has meaning, then we are predicating the existence of God.[32] Rampant secularization of thought in the twentieth century produced its own philosophy of meaninglessness, and from this is spawned disorder. Carl Gustav Jung, 'one of the great thinkers of this century',[33] wrote that 'man cannot live without meaning'. Perhaps we need look no further for the present lack of order in the world around us.

George Steiner, considering the sterility of European culture at the end of the millennium, pointed out that the wonderful achievement of landing men on the moon – the apogee of scientific and technical endeavour – could not produce 'one great poem, picture or metaphor' to celebrate it in cultural or spiritual terms. He observes:

> The only manifest energies are those of money. Money has never smelt more sharply, it has never cried more loudly in our public and private concerns . . . there are at present fewer and fewer voices which articulate a philosophy, a political or social theory, an aesthetic which would be both in the European inheritance and of world relevance.[34]

Mikulás Teich writes that a very new type of society is needed if the scientific and technical revolution of the twentieth century is 'to come into its full human and humane heritage'.[35] Another contemporary observer of the changing scene at the end of the millennium, Lord Asa Briggs, makes an interesting comment on the 'march of time'. He points to the end of the idea of continual material progress towards a secular Utopia, which has been a main driving force behind western civilization over the last three centuries.[36]

There is evidence that many people, anxious about the increasing disorder in society, are looking again for certain 'core values'. In Britain the former Tory Prime Minister, John Major, urged the return to 'basics', by which he apparently meant a return to traditional Christian values. The present Prime Minister, Tony Blair, wrote, in a piece entitled 'Why I am a Christian', 'there is a desire in the modern world to retrieve and re-establish a sense of values, of common norms of conduct . . . there is an increasing rejection, interestingly among young people, of an amoral society'.[37] Blair, a committed Christian before he became a politician, has been described as a Christian Democrat.

It has been a perennial part of the historical process in all civilizations that a core set of values is passed on from one generation to the next as the basis of any cohesive society. At the end of the present century, it seems that our society has not succeeded very well in this respect. Our young people are certainly moral and spiritual beings, but many have not inherited the beliefs and values which have been at the core of European and British civilization: 'the hungry sheep look up and are not fed.'

In Germany Chancellor Helmut Kohl stressed his Christian Democratic principles in leading the movement towards a united Europe. His main aim was to establish peace and order in Europe on a permanent basis. He wanted to ensure that there is no return to the strident type of nationalism anywhere, but particularly in his own country. The French President, Jacques Chirac, was in alliance with Chancellor Kohl in this pursuit of peace.

Chancellor Kohl was following in the footsteps of Dr Konrad Adenauer, founder of the Christian Democratic Union in 1945 and Chancellor of the West German Federal Republic in 1949. Adenauer was far-sighted enough after the Second World War to foresee the danger that his own country, in pursuit of German reunification, might have been tempted to make a deal with the Soviet Union, thus threatening the security of Western Europe. His strategy for peace in Europe was to bind West Germany into the European Union. In this he was supported by the founding father of the new Europe, Jean Monnet, who was equally determined to avoid any repetition of internecine warfare in Europe. The primary aim of Adenauer, Monnet, de Gasperi and Robert Schuman was to create permanent peace by establishing European unity. Economic strategies, important though they were, remained essentially tools and instruments by which the primary political aim could be achieved.

The nation-state is a human artefact which has been in existence for only some three or four centuries. History is continually changing and it would be unwise to suppose that this particular form of political unit will not undergo change or replacement sooner or later. There is no reason to suppose, as many people seem to do, that there is anything perennial or immortal about the nation-state.[38]

The founding fathers of the new movement for the European Union were very conscious that one could not achieve European unity by a full-frontal attack on the entrenched position of the sovereign nation-state. They understood the subtler forces behind historical change and how these usually work. Monnet himself made the very perceptive and illuminating remark that 'We are uniting the people, not forming a coalition of states'.[39] Similarly, the European Commission seems to be:

handling the British . . . simply by not using words like 'federalism' and 'constitution' in the hope that otherwise very reasonable objectives can be accomplished without ruffling British feathers . . . [caused by] tabloid prejudice and political manipulation. . . . Yet the debate on certain clear issues must take place if truly democratic values are to be upheld.[40]

In Britain, until the General Election of May 1997, there has been a situation which has been termed 'Democracy in crisis'.[41] Unlike in France and other parts of Europe, the Tory government was following a policy of centralization, so that decision making was taken further away from the people at local level. The same government conceded more power to Europe, in military, economic and financial matters, than the British public seemed to understand, but at the same time drew back from political involvement in Europe and kept to a politically correct use of language concerning the 'independence of our sovereign nation-state'. In fact, both Britain and Europe have been in great need of more democratic control of their decision-making powers. Europe is well aware of this, so that 'subsidiarity' – a principle of Catholic social teaching first enunciated in these terms in a papal encyclical of 1930 and confirmed strongly in Pope John XXIII's encyclical, *Pacem in Terris* (1963) – has now become 'a pillar of European policy' under the Maastricht Treaty.[42] It means that the decision-making process in all human organizations should be made at the lowest appropriate level consistent with good government. It derives ultimately from the concept of the dignity of all human beings born in the image of God. It equates with the more commonly known democratic aim that decisions should be taken as closely as possible to the citizen.[43] This will be needed to safeguard democratic control of European institutions, as well as the variety of regional differences and cultural identities.

In Britain, too, there have been all too many signs in the press of negative attitudes and 'snarling defiances' against the attempt to build a united Europe. The Tory government up to 1997 felt constrained for the most part to speak in terms of assumptions of thought deriving from the Great Myth of the English past, as the Tory Opposition under William Hague continues to do. It is extremely important now that the English people can free themselves from the imprisonment of a false view of their historical identity.[44] They can do this by gaining a true understanding of their past in the perspective of the last two thousand years of their history. If they can achieve this understanding, then they will have a role of central importance to play in the next millennium in the creation of a new European unity, by bringing their own unique experience and understanding of democracy and its application to a united commonwealth of peoples.[45]

Anthony Sampson, commentating on the British scene before the General Election of 1997, observed that the British were rightly proud of their past tradition of democracy which could be immensely valuable to Europe, but instead they were in danger of losing it at home under a succession of Tory governments. Their influence abroad had been diminished by their misplaced fear of European unity. Their own valued institutions, such as the law, the Church of England, the monarchy, the universities and local government, had all lost influence in the face of a remarkable and dangerous centralization of power within their own state. While 'British politicians relish their unique history of freedom, voters have to look to Strasbourg [the Court of Human Rights] as their ultimate protection'. Sampson continued:

> Looking back over thirty years at Britain's institutions – whether schools, law courts, engineering institutions or banks – I see them still trapped in closed circles: they frustrate any attempts at reform as they turn in on themselves. The schools still do not equip Britons with the languages and knowledge to move confidently in the contemporary world, particularly on the continent. The media are still preoccupied with the English-speaking world and remain caught up with a mutual love affair with parliament which prefers to ignore Europe. The Law still cannot connect up with a European convention which provides stronger human rights for the citizens. Yet in the meantime many adventurous young Britons are finding fulfilment on the continent beyond: academics escaping from back-biting high tables, engineers looking for a more respected profession, or businessmen looking for more enterprising customers. Even ordinary tourists discover that the French, Germans or Italians can help to teach the British how to run railways, education or cities.[46]

S. Weir and K. Boyle observed, in May 1997, that 'Nothing perhaps expresses the island mentality of the United Kingdom more succinctly than the length of time the idea of human rights has taken to make any impact on British politics, the courts and domestic culture'.[47] The English will have to choose between becoming whole-hearted Europeans, learning from their neighbours and teaching them as well, or becoming involved in a 'retreat back into a more dangerously insular mentality'.[48]

What are we to say finally to the sceptics – sometimes incorrectly termed realists – who claim that any seeking of peaceful order and unity in Europe in the new millennium is far too Utopian, even if if were desirable? Barbara Ward, Lady Jackson, an economist of distinction, said that the idea that people could not extend their normal behaviour in establishing methods of peace and order in their own nations to wider political units was nonsense. It was simply a challenge to the human will and intelligence to look at the world around them with a wider and more open perspective. It is a growing-up process in the development of humanity:

> If freedom for us is no more than the right to pursue our own self-interest, personal or national, then we have no claim to the greatest vision of our society. . . . There has to be a new start, new policies, a new approach. Otherwise we prepare for our own defeat, simply by default.[49]

She argues that we are now in a period when scientists, having discovered the essential interdependence and delicate balance of the natural systems, are learning greater humility and sensitivity in handling their discoveries. Their work is inextricably linked with other great laws and values which govern the world and the human family. The underlying unity of scientific law was known to the Greeks and the medieval scholastics. The 'underlying law of human brotherhood and obligation' was 'most passionately proclaimed by the Hebrew Prophets' and again confirmed by the Christian humanism of the medieval Christian legal system. This is now proclaimed in the Catholic social teaching on *solidarity* which points to the simple but dynamic truth that we are all responsible for one another in the human family. The dynamic power of this concept has been seen in its use by the workers of Poland (1981–9), leading to the drastic demise of the Communist regime there and, consequently, to its collapse in the whole of Eastern Europe. This is also a central tenet of the Maastricht Treaty and is a sufficiently powerful and dynamic force to act as the basis for European and world unity.

Lady Jackson's conclusion, in 1976, regarding these fundamental laws underlying science and human brotherhood, was:

Today they came together in a new fusion of vision and energy to remind us of our inescapable unity even as we stand on the very edge of annihilation. The scientist and the sage, the man of learning and the poet, the mathematician and the saint repeat the same warning: 'We must love each other or we must die'.

It could be that the time is becoming ripe for a great step forward: 'it is just possible that this fusion of new knowledge and ancient wisdom could release a more potent explosion of moral energy than any earlier attempt to convert humanity from the false gods of greed and power.'[50]

Christopher Dawson, one of the few English historians of this century who completely broke free from insularity of mind and who contemplated deeply on the historical identity and culture of Europe, wrote just after the mid-century concerning the state of Europe after two world wars:

the catastrophes of the last thirty years are not only a sign of the bankruptcy of secular humanism, they also go to show that a completely secularized civilization is inhuman in the absolute sense – hostile to human life and irreconcilable with human nature itself . . . the forces of violence and aggressiveness that threaten to destroy our world are the direct result of the starvation and frustration of man's spiritual nature. . . . The recovery of a Christian culture is therefore . . . essential . . . this social ideal which has become so pale and remote to the individualism and secularism of . . . the modern world.[51]

In 1996 an important ecumenical statement emerged from the Oxford historian Felipe Fernández-Armesto (Catholic), and Derek Wilson (Anglican). They conclude their important study, *Reformation: Christianity and the World 1500–2000* thus:

today secularism is on the defensive, while religions are back – active powers in the reshaping of a spiritually changed world. Christianity, in particular – until recently divided and beleaguered – has made an unpredictable comeback. In Eastern Europe the churches have emerged in strength from the ruins of

Communism. In the West they are challenging the new paganism of consumer societies. In Latin America they have made and contained political revolutions. They have launched the most dynamic movement ever to have convulsed Africa. They have helped to wrench political policy into new directions in the USA. Their evangelising power has broken out in patches in Eastern Asia. . . . A generation ago, the history of Christianity could be indulged as an antiquarian pursuit, now it is an urgent part of the agenda for anyone who wants to be ready for the future.[52]

The authors look backwards and forwards at the end of the millennium in this survey of the relationship between Christianity and the secular world between 1500 and 2000. They believe that creative and dynamic developments have occurred in ecumenical Christianity, which will play an important part in shaping the post-secularist history of the new millennium.[53] Fernández-Armesto is also the author of the recent work, *Millennium*, which appeared in 1996.[54]

Grace Davie's findings in *Religion in Britain since 1945: Believe without Belonging* (1994) again radically challenge the convention that secularism is an irresistible and inextricable part of being 'modern' in contemporary Britain. She points to the enduring and revivifying qualities and manifestations of religious belief in diverse contexts in modern Britain. This book is also a timely reminder of the failure of modern British culture to deal with the essential human need to 'belong'.[55] There is a great vacuum in the essential area of community building at the end of this millennium. There is something very important here to be learnt from the medieval world.

In 1963 Pope John XXIII summoned the Second Vatican Council (1962–5). He had been elected Pope in 1958 at the advanced stage of seventy-seven. He was very wise and very simple, exuding an extraordinary and quite unconscious air of sheer goodness to everyone who met him. He wanted to confront the prevailing culture of the twentieth century with the pertinence of Christian belief and values. This Council was to produce several documents which are important, not only for Catholics but for all people. Bishops from all over the world attended and contributed. The Council set out the guidelines for the Church's contemporary role, *The Church in the Modern World* (1965). The purpose and practical effect of the Council documents was to establish an *aggiornamento* or dialogue with the modern world in terms which it could understand. Pope John wanted 'to open the windows' of the Church and to let in 'fresh air' from outside. This Council provided the basis for the policies on which the Catholic Church throughout the world will organize its life and mission of service to all people in the new millennium. They are still being gradually absorbed.

The policies themselves are all derived from the Gospels and the first principles of Christian teaching, but developed and 'translated' to meet the understanding and needs of men and women living in the modern world. The dignity of the human person and the freedom and sacrosanct nature of the individual's properly informed conscience are restated and are translated into the responsibility of affording and ensuring religious freedom and respect to everyone. Again, the belief that all men and women are of equal dignity and importance, because they are all created by God, in His image and likeness, and are brothers and sisters in God's human family, is translated into the Catholic social teachings on human rights, justice, racial equality and concepts such as subsidiarity and solidarity.

This Council's effect on Catholic attitudes, its new openness to the Protestant world, to other religions and to the secular world, and its willingness to learn from many of the insights that come from all of these, were main factors in helping to bring Christians together in the second half of the twentieth century and in establishing positive relationships with other peoples of different religions and of none. One of the sixteen documents of the Council is the decree on *Ecumenism* (1964). In *The Church in the Modern World* (1965), the first two sections are concerned with 'The Dignity of the Human Person' and 'The Community of Mankind'. Other sections deal with 'The Proper Development of Culture', 'Economic and Social Life', 'The Life of the Political Community' and 'The Fostering of Peace and the Promotion of a Community of Nations'.[56] Christianity is essentially *personal* and *universal* in character.

In 1963, before calling the Council, Pope John had produced for the world his encyclical letter, *Pacem in Terris*. Again, he wrote it not simply for Catholics and other Christians, but specifically and significantly 'to all men of good will', just as the Second Vatican Council (1964–5) was to address itself to the role of the Universal Church in serving the needs of all men and women of every nation, colour and creed.

Pacem in Terris is concerned with the great moral principles of 'Order in the Universe' and 'Order in human beings', which are familiar to those unacquainted with the tradition of scholastic humanism and which stem from the incalculable value of the human person. It applies the same (but much-developed) Christian principles which were used in the twelfth and thirteenth centuries to create the unification of Europe to the question of peace and order in today's world. The word 'Order' is used in the scholastic sense of 'good', 'reasonable', 'just' and 'appropriate', when weighed against the deepest needs of human beings. Its detailed sections are concerned with 'Order' in the relations between individuals, between individuals and the State, between individual states, and between individual states and the world community. Drawing from first principles of Christian thought, it encapsulates all the wisdom of the Judaeo-Christian tradition, which, more than with anything else, has created European culture over a period of two thousand years. This wisdom is then applied to the modern world, incorporating all the new knowledge which has become available from all fields of study up to the present, and placing it all within a coherent system of values which gives meaning, direction and purpose to the people of today.

For example, one of the explicit statements in *Pacem in Terris* which is of great relevance for us today concerns the rights of minority groups in the face of political moves towards 'political autonomy and national integration'. Based again on the innate dignity of all human beings, the principles are set and applied: 'One thing is clear and beyond dispute: any attempt to check the vitality and growth of these racial minorities is a flagrant violation of justice; the more so if exertions are aimed at their very extinction.' But to achieve balance and perspective, such minority groups should not 'magnify unduly their own racial characteristics' or 'rate them above those human values which are common to all mankind, as though the good of the entire human family should subserve the interests of their own particular race'.[57] Ways of achieving positive and fruitful association, without losing their own identity, are discussed: 'They should realise that their constant association with a people steeped in a different civilization from their own has no small part to play in the development of their own particular genius and spirit.'[58] Again, 'Truth calls for the elimination of every trace of racial prejudice'; people have the right 'to the means necessary for maintaining a decent standard of living', and to wages which allow a 'standard of living consistent with human dignity'. Workers have 'the right to meet together and to form associations with their fellows'; 'the common good is something which affects the needs of the whole man'.

Such rights are balanced with personal responsibilities and duties, due to other members of society and incumbent upon everyone. Other sections deal with 'the proper balance between population, land and capital', the rights of political refugees and disarmament. The main thrust of the document is towards the strategy of peace, based upon justice, at all levels of human relationships. This encyclical also asserts the principle of human 'solidarity' – we are all responsible for one another – and the principle of 'subsidiarity',[59] both of which are now at the very centre of the political strategy for European unification. Similarly, its section on 'The Essentials of the Common Good' has been echoed in the important and well-received document of the same name, issued as guidance to voters in Britain by the Catholic bishops before the 1997 General Election.[60]

Already the machinery has been set up in Europe to extend normal human behaviour in settling disputes peacefully, to areas wider than the nation-state. The European Courts of Justice and Human Rights have been established and have already begun to exercise a civilizing influence on English life, in spite of the press accusations of their 'demeaning of a sovereign Parliament'. These courts have extended human rights to everyone, including refugees or other people who may be at odds with individual states. There is an international court to deal with violation of human rights during warfare, after the Bosnian atrocities; the Social Chapter has been introduced to establish the basic conditions for human dignity in Europe, including the concept of the minimum wage and reasonable working hours for a decent standard and quality of life.

The values displayed in such enterprises are derived ultimately from the old principles of Christian humanism which recognized that economic and political structures are meant to serve the interests of people, enabling them to become more fully human. People do not exist simply to serve these structures. The Church itself is for the individual, and not vice-versa, Therefore, these principles are meant to be superior to matters of economic or political expediency, which should not be allowed to supersede them if we are to achieve the quality of life associated with a truly human community. These age-old values of Christian humanism are also those with which the society of the peoples which we call Europe can most identify, since they lie at the root of our civilization. They are capable, in their developed form, of meeting the needs and demands of the new millennium. They represent the best opportunity of holding these peoples together in the peace and order of community.

We can take heart, too, from the considered statement of the scientists gathered under the auspices of the United Nations Educational, Scientific and Cultural Organization in 1986, who declared that, 'We are not condemned to war and violence because of our biology. Instead it is possible for us to end war and the suffering it causes'. Professor Rotblat, Nobel Prize winner, set the challenge in 1996: 'War must cease to be an admissible social institution. The abolition of war must be our ultimate goal', in which he was echoing the earlier comment of Pope John Paul II, that war must not any longer be on the human agenda.

Sir Richard Southern says that the rediscovery of Christian humanism at work in the medieval scholastic schools was stimulated by Pope Leo XIII's encyclical, *Aeternis Patris* (1879) which 'created a scholarly activity of unparalleled force in the history of medieval studies'.[61] Indeed, without the help of the scholarship produced 'under its impulse', Southern says that hardly any of the chapters in his *Scholastic Humanism and the Unification of Europe* could have been written. It was the encyclical of 1879, therefore, which revealed, indirectly, this great framework of principles and rational thought which underpinned the comparative peace and order of Europe during the twelfth and thirteenth centuries.

It may not be too imaginative, perhaps, to think that a document like *Pacem in Terris*, written nearly a century later, could have a similar effect, if its principles were to be applied not simply to the *study* of comparative peace and order in a past era of European history, but to the actual establishment of these conditions in the new millennium. We have already witnessed the power of two of these principles of social justice (solidarity and subsidiarity) working to produce great, sudden, and completely unexpected changes in the political and economic realities of eastern Europe after 1980 when the Polish *Solidarnhosc* was founded in Poland under Lech Walesa. Then the two principles became central tenets of the Maastricht Treaty (1991) as a basis for European unity. 'Subsidiarity' is there to ensure the protection and care of the individual cultural identities of smaller regions; 'solidarity', to ensure that poorer regions can be helped by the stronger, for their mutual benefit. 'Solidarity' can also obviate the danger of a 'Euro-Fortress' mentality, because its ultimate dynamic is universal, being grounded in the values of Christian humanism.

Certainly Pope John XXIII exuded brotherly love to everyone, which made him one of the most universally loved and respected figures of the twentieth century. He embodied the very spirit of peace and unity, based on love and justice, in the human family. This was founded on his belief in the brotherhood of man under the Fatherhood of God, upon Whom we are all completely dependent. This guarantees the dignity of each individual person and the equal worth of all people and constitutes the greatest and most hopeful vision for the society of the human family in the future.

Already the quest for unlimited material progress is under critical scrutiny, for 'the paradox of progress has shattered progressivist fallacies. We have advanced so much and improved so little'; and the 'old understanding' of secularization as the essential mark of modernity is now being seriously questioned in the face of evident signs of the 'persistence and resurgence' of religion as the most enduring feature of the human condition.[62] Paul Johnson has described the faults which have led to 'catastrophic failures and tragedies': 'the rise of moral relativism, the decline of personal responsibility, the repudiation of Judaeo-Christian values and not least the arrogant belief that men and women could solve all the mysteries of the universe by their own unaided intellects.' The big question for the future, he claims, is whether or not these faults can be eradicated: 'On that would depend the chances of the twenty-first century becoming, by contrast, an age of hope for the future of mankind.'[63] Similarly, a contemporary social scientist, N. Dennis, has pointed to the weakening of the family and its associated culture of life-long monogamy as the major cause for rising crime and general disorder in our society at the end of the twentieth century.[64]

The greatest challenge for people in this new millennium will be to rejuvenate and revitalize those spiritual and moral values relating to the fundamental needs of human beings. These values provided the basis for European (including English) order, culture and civilization in the past and now need to be developed and applied to the world of today. Norman Davies, historian of Europe over the last two thousand years, remarks, 'Europe, like nature itself, cannot abide a vacuum. Sooner or later the European Community in the West and the successor state in the East must redefine their identities . . . and their allegiances.'[65] Another contemporary historian, D. Urwin, depicts the 'Community of Europe' as an 'extraordinarily resilient idea endowed with great regenerative power'.[66]

In England, Will Hutton, commenting on the contemporary

scene, sees the need to combine the values of individualism and choice, which have dominated life in modern Britain under the Tory governments, with other values such as 'commitment, stakeholding, citizenship, the public good and cooperation' which are 'even more deep rooted in British culture'. We must learn that 'wealth, for example, should be seen as more than a single increment to GNP, its object is to promote human well-being'. If these values are accepted again, then 'Britain does have a remarkable chance to transform itself and its institutions' and to emerge as more socially cohesive and effective.[67]

Christian humanism represents an organic system of values capable of responding to universal and perennial human needs. It is capable of developing to meet the needs of people in the next millennium. It also provides the most successful balance between the sacrosanct dignity and freedom of each individual person and the rights inherent in the building of community. The modern world has overemphasized individualism and only succeeded in depreciating the value of human life, because it has excluded the spiritual element. Christian humanism proved itself successful in building community in the medieval period because it did not posit a contrast or contradiction between the individual and society. The rights and responsibilities of both were safeguarded in relation to God and the moral and natural law. It was the spiritual concept which held the balance and guaranteed the dignity of man and the rights of society. Society was not an isolated abstract, but a description of people living in a community which existed to satisfy the social side of their nature. Law existed to make people free by regulating the weaker sides of human behaviour.[68]

Without such a framework of values for the society of the future, rapidly increasing advances in science and technology could again become the tools for further acts of war, provoked by human pride, selfishness and greed. With such unbridled and unprecedented power at their disposal the people could indeed perish.

The great issue facing Europe and the world in the new millennium can be summarized in very simplistic terms. Human history has demonstrated the struggle between good and evil, between the great aspirations of the human spirit and those forces of self-destruction and disunity stemming from the selfishness and pride which lurk in human nature. The Old Testament holds the mirror up to these forces of destruction in such vivid word-pictures as the stories of Cain and Abel or the Tower of Babel – names which have become part of the world's general vocabulary. Modern psychiatry has discovered the same forces working in human nature. The New Testament provides the answer for mankind: love is the only key which unlocks the cell of our dark selfishness and gives us true freedom, freedom from fear. Love of God is necessary to overcome our human pride and to see ourselves in true perspective in all our frailty and dependence on Him, as well as in that eternal importance which we derive from Him. Love of neighbour is necessary to overcome our selfishness and to enable us to live together as one family on this planet.

The situation has changed. The Kyoto Summit on Global Warming (December 1997) represented the first demonstration of the *practical reality* and urgency now of human interdependence, shared expectations and combined resources – the essential 'togetherness' of the human family. Global markets and economics and new communication technologies emphasize the 'global village'. A new way of thinking is being forced upon us. The startingly new, relevant and creative question for statesmen and women in the new millennium will be increasingly recognized as 'What will be most beneficial generally and in the long run, for the people of the world, of Europe and ourselves, since we must all live together properly, or perish together?'

The great enemies at this stage in our response to the challenge are fear, pessimism, cynicism, hopelessness and unprepared idealism. But we are in a new situation. Humility and forgiveness and unexpected wisdom can sometimes be learned most effectively when we are on the brink of recognizable disaster. As Felipe Fernández-Armesto has written, in the conclusion to his *Millennium*, 'No earlier age had means to such awareness of such comprehensive menace, or such an awesome chance'.[69]

This 'awesome chance' was, I think, expressed by Nelson Mandela, when he spoke to the British Parliament and proposed 'a new universal order in which we shall all be our brother's keeper'.[70] Christian Democratic leaders should not fail to respond to this challenge. Britain itself could truly become 'a beacon to the world',[71] by openly pursuing a *vision* of politics based on Christian values and principles and thus giving a dynamic coherence, criteria, meaningfulness and purpose to its policies in the third millennium of the Christian era. In this way England would be truly keeping faith with its real historical identity, as created by Augustine, Bede, Boniface and Alfred the Great in the first millennium, and as celebrated by Chaucer, Julian of Norwich, William Langland and Shakespeare in the second. So too would their Celtic neighbours in Britain, with their own strong Christian traditions. I suspect, too, that there would be popular and increasing support in Britain, Europe and elsewhere.

As a historian, I am aware of the surprising and unpredictable nature of historical development, stemming ultimately from human free will. As a Christian, I can be no other than hopeful and ultimately expectant for the future. Alfred the Great founded the English nation on Christian values, stating that they would provide the only sure basis for its survival against all nihilistic enemies in the present and the future. I share his beliefs, finding no better words to conclude this study than his own:

I hold, as do all Christian men [and women], that it is Divine Providence that rules and not fate.[72]

Afterword

'There will come a time when you, France, you Italy, you, England, you, Germany, all you nations of the continent, without losing your distinct qualities, your glorious individuality, will merge into a higher unity and form the European brotherhood'

Victor Hugo (1849), quoted by H. Young, *This Blessed Plot* (1998).

In the Spring of 2002 my wife and I spent a few weeks in an area of northern Italy which could well be described as the centre of Europe. The mountain ranges of the Alps and the Dolomites bring together the borders of Italy, France, Germany, Switzerland and Austria. Across Austria to the north-east and the Adriatic to the south-east beckon the slavonic lands of Eastern Europe, recently liberated from nearly half a century of Communist domination. They are now bidding for entry to the European Union, from which they have much to gain and to which they have much to contribute.

This mountainous central region is marked by the tracks of the past, revealing the age-old routes which our ancestors created for movement between different parts of ancient Europe. We followed one such old mountain road in the Dolomites between Italy and Austria. The remains of the past were fascinating. The road itself was one of those old Roman roads to be found all over Europe, including Britain. Alongside it there were some shaped boulders to be seen from time to time, with circular indentations around them. Official notices indicated that these had been found on the original road. The indentations had been made by the iron-clad wheels of Roman chariots, two thousand years ago. Also, from time to time, there were 'Stations of the Cross', such as can be seen in all other parts of Christian Europe, fixed to rocks at the roadside, reminding us of the religion which created our modern European civilization.

It was in this south Tyrolean mountainous and borderland area, in 1991, that the amazing find was made of 'The Iceman'. Erika and Helmut Simon, a couple from Nuremberg, had wandered from the marked mountain trail in 1991 and discovered a corpse sticking out of the glacier ice and meltwater in a rocky gulley. They thought it must be that of a recent mountain climber. It turned out to be from the fourth millennium B.C. and its discovery captured world-wide attention as that of the oldest, 'preserved', European.

We visited the South Tyrol Museum of Archaeology at Bolzano where the mummy and an extensive range of his belongings, found on or near him, are exhibited, including his axe with a copper blade (the only complete prehistoric one ever found), bow and arrows, long flint dagger with a wooden handle, a retoucheur (tool for more intricate work on flint) - the only known example of its kind, a roughly meshed net (probably for catching birds); and a back-pack. The find led to intense scientific inquiry into the area of comparative cultural findings in the region. It particularly interested me that 'stones with pictures on them were probably related to the cult of the ancestors' – evidence of some kind of religious worship, which seems to be a constant feature of human life, through the ages.

The other interesting feature is something which has been discovered by intensive scientific research on the remains, including examination by X-ray and various procedures of the most advanced forms of forensic science. The man, aged in his forties, was murdered. There is an arrow head still in the back of his shoulder. He was shot in the back, some distance lower down the mountain, probably by a rival hunter, perhaps from a rival tribe. He escaped to higher ground, lay down to rest; and bled to death.[1] In this earliest finding of human life in Europe, we find the age-old problem of man's inhumanity to man, probably arising from 'economic' or 'political' competition. European history has been littered with internecine wars, increasing in magnitude as science and technology have advanced, reaching a climax in the twentieth century.

* * *

Roman law and civilization played a great part in providing a political framework for European life in the first half of the first millennium A.D. The beliefs and value system of the Christian religion became the greatest influence in shaping European life and culture in the medieval period. Christianity played the major part in bringing about the unity of Europe, culminating in the period of the twelfth and thirteenth centuries described so admirably by the late Sir Richard Southern in his seminal work on *Scholastic Humanism and the Unification of Europe* (1995–2001).[2]

This scholastic humanism, based on the Christian scriptures, but integrating into its philosophy the ideas of the Greek thinkers, Plato and Aristotle, provided the ethical values and principles underlying a great framework throughout Christendom. Its prime exponent was St. Thomas Aquinas whose writings became text-books of Christian teaching. Human nature, good in itself, but with inherent flaws – pride and selfishness – was guided within a balance between individual and communal rights and responsibilities. This system did not mean, of course, that there were no transgressions by individuals or nations. Pride, selfishness and perverted religious thinking, still expressed themselves in bouts of intolerance and strife, especially in relations between the Christian and non-Christian world. But it did provide a framework of universally accepted ethical criteria within which a remarkable degree of European unity was established and expressed in European law. These criteria were derived from the Christian belief in the supreme dignity and importance of each individual human being created uniquely by God and possessed of an eternal soul. These individuals were designed to live in community with one another; and so the community, too, had its own rights. These beliefs constituted the ultimate foundation of all expressions of Christian humanism in western philosophy. Indeed it is not clear that there has ever been a stronger ethical basis for any form of humanist thinking, in spite of the many instances of the human failure to live up to the principles and ideals involved.

This unity within Europe was shattered by the break-up of Christendom at the Reformation and the rise of warring nation states, driven by the concepts of raison d'état, power-politics and economic mercantilism; and increasingly unfettered by the ethical and moral principles of Christian humanism. It was what great European Christians like Thomas More (1478–1535) and Desiderius Erasmus (1466–1536) had foreseen and feared. The process began in earnest in the sixteenth century and reached its climax in the two great World Wars of the twentieth century. It saw finally the rise of the monstrous totalitarian power systems - Fascist and Communist - which denied any form of humanism. They became a law unto themselves, treading brutally underfoot every concept of human dignity and rights and inflicting unprecedented human misery and suffering in Europe and the wider world.[3]

After the end of the Second World War in 1945 there was a general feeling that humanity had gone 'off the rails'. The old values of European civilization had been discarded and humanity brutalised. In 1948 it was thought necessary for the newly constituted United Nations to issue its Declaration of Universal Human Rights. At the same time there started a movement which will be regarded, I think, by future historians, as one of the most extraordinary and significant developments in European and world History.

It happened because of the quiet determination of a small group of Christian Democrat statesmen in Europe to ensure that all this would never happen again. Their work had none of the trappings of glory, pomp and power, associated with the triumphal proceedings of previous European leaders, intent on national glory and power. One might almost say that its true significance has been unnoticed as yet by many people, especially the British. It was a movement designed to establish the Union of Europe, in such a way as to make future internecine wars impossible.

Already, the ideology for the re-establishment of a Christian ethic in Europe had been set out in the work of the French philosopher, Jacques Maritain (1882–1973), especially in his *Introduction à la Philosophie* (1920) and *True Humanism* (1941). He had spent most of his long life restoring and applying the philosophical methods of the great medieval philosopher, Thomas Aquinas, to modern problems across the whole range of areas in society, including politics, law, economics, culture and education. He was the foremost among a number of modern 'Neo-Thomist' thinkers whose philosophical methodology started with concrete facts before moving to theory, moved from the known to the unknown and insisted that 'supernature' (ideals) must be built upon 'nature' and the natural law. They emphasized again the importance of establishing a proper balance between the rights and responsibilities of individuals and those of the community in which they lived and worked. Their work was meant precisely to find in the Thomistic philosophy, solutions to the problems facing post-1945 Europe. Their ideas were to bear fruit after 1945 in the work of several continental statesmen and economists of the newly established 'Christian-Democratic' parties in Germany, France and Italy. Their work is little known, except peripherally, in Britain.

The first European statesman to lay the foundation of the new thinking was, significantly, the German, Dr Konrad Adenauer (1876–1967). Mayor of his native city of Cologne continuously since 1917, he had been imprisoned by Hitler in 1933 for opposing the Nazi regime and he had witnessed the horrors inflicted by it on Germany and the wider world. In 1945 he founded the Christian Democratic Union and worked with General de Gaulle for post-war reconciliation between France and Germany. In 1919 he became Chancellor of the West German Federal Republic and was determined that the 'German experience' under Hitler would never happen again, especially when the future advent of German re-unification would once again restore Germany to full strength.

He appears to have been the first European statesman to determine that his own country would never again be tempted to use its strength for warlike purposes. His method was devastatingly simple, but unprecedented. He would start with the concrete facts of economics and politics; and so arrange them that the more intangible end of lasting peace in Europe would be achieved. He would bind West Germany so tightly into the European community by economic and political interdependency, that it would be practically impossible for France and Germany to go to war with one another again. Unlike de Gaulle, who doubted Britain's readiness for the venture, Adenauer would later support Britain's application for entry to the Common Market. His successor, Chancellor Helmut Kohl, whose brother had been killed in the Great War, pursued the same policy with the same end in mind. He became leader of the Christian Democratic Union in 1976 and Chancellor in 1982.

Another of these thinkers and statesmen was Jean Monnet (1888–1979), the French economist who had originated Churchill's offer of union with France in 1940. He created and applied the plan for the modernisation of France under de Gaulle in 1945. He put forward the 'Schuman Plan' to co-ordinate European coal and steel production in the European Coal and Steel Community which was to become the Common Market. Robert Schuman (1886–1963) was the French Prime Minister (1947–48) and Foreign Minister (1948–53) who proposed the 'Schuman Plan' in 1950, with the same ideology as that of Konrad Adenauer in mind. It was implemented in 1952 and was the foundation of the European Community. Another member of the group was Alcide de Gasperi (1881–1954), the Italian statesman who founded the Christian Democratic Party in Italy. As Prime minister of Italy (1945–53) he worked persistently, in conjunction with his French and German colleagues, for European peace through unity achieved by economic and political bonding.

This group of Catholic elder statesmen shared an ideology. They were of a similar age range. They had seen in person the final cataclysmic stages of the internecine warfare which had ravaged

Europe for four centuries. They had seen what had happened when political and economic dominance had been the main aims of European nations. They determined that politics and economics should now become the servants of the people rather than the masters in European affairs. These would become the means and not the end. The end – the 'supernatural' or 'ideal' – was to be a lasting peace in Europe, built upon the proper management of the 'natural' and concrete propensities for economic and political security and prosperity.

So European states would now be bound together, firstly economically and then politically, by such ties of interdependence – consolidated by appropriate and mutually agreed legislation – that war between them could never be possible again. Economics and Politics were no longer to be causes of war, but the very instruments of peace. this unprecedented plan, simple in its audacity, required great good will, great resolution, great patience, perseverance and determination, to overcome the inevitable difficulties, snags, disappointments and set-backs. Human nature had not changed, but was being managed in a different way. Inducements were used instead of threats; endless negotiation instead of the turning of backs to one another. There was nothing brilliant or dramatic about it. The prosaic character of the whole process has hidden the tremendous nature of its achievements. There was no glorious triumphalism about it; no victors; no losers. It was a process by which European countries were learning to swim together or to sink together; and in such circumstances everybody seemed willing to swim.

Many observers, particularly in England and at the start of the enterprise, scoffed at the 'unrealistic', 'unworkable', 'naive', 'simplistic' and 'idealistic' idea of bringing different nations, with their own selfish interests, national pride and long history of internecine warfare, into such a partnership. Many just waited for it to collapse, with a sense of sceptical detachment; and were too ready to say that it had failed whenever it met an obstacle. Looking back after half a century, we can only marvel at the success of these early thinkers and planners. Seemingly impossible steps forward have been taken and a series of important treaties signed, committing them all to closer inter-dependence. Like a spider's web, a mass of mutually-accepted threads of very detailed legislation has been spun, within which the nations of Europe have become increasingly interconnected, economically and politically.[4] Almost unnoticed, peace crept in and stayed in Europe. Moreover, there has been a general level of increasing prosperity enjoyed by Europeans at large, especially of course in countries like Luxembourg, Spain, Portugal and Eire, where the standard of living has been greatly improved. There are still problems and differences to be overcome. There always will be in human society. But the original vision has materialised into something so successful that the other countries in eastern Europe are now very anxious to participate themselves.

This extraordinary movement was guided by a value-system which informed it and worked in perfect harmony with its main aims. The original impulse behind it all was the need felt to restore certain religious and moral values which were at the root of European civilization and needed to be restored. These were Christian values. Two of the main principles guiding the development of the European Union are derived directly from the social teaching of the Catholic Church – *solidarity* and *subsidiarity*. The former enshrines the teaching that all people belong to one human family, in which we must express our 'solidarity', our care and concern for all the others. The latter crystallizes the teaching that each person and each nation's identity should be given equal value, irrespective of its political and economic strength. Two other principles, the language of which has developed in secular society, have come to be recognized as inherent and implicit within the Church's own original beliefs; indeed a necessary corollary of them. These are the concepts of *democracy* and *human rights*. It is a signal instance of the Christian Church itself learning from the secular world, from discerning the 'signs of the times' which might in certain instances bring to light ideas which are in fact logical developments of its own basic teachings. It is this organic ability to 'develop'[5] its thinking which enables Christianity to serve the needs of the modern world.

The first significant appearance and extension of 'human rights', as such, in Christian teaching, was in the enclical, *Pacem in Terris*, addressed to the whole world by Pope John XXIII in 1963. They were confirmed in the teachings of the Second Vatican Council (1962–65) which he himself had called into being. Now was firmly established the Christian stance that *all* people of whatever religious belief or none, have inalienable rights as human beings, which have to be respected by everyone, including the Church and State. In particular, human life is sacred and must not be taken in the pursuit of any political or religious cause. Any other stance by Christians on this issue can now be regarded as perverse. When the highest authorities of all authentic world religions – Muslim, Buddhist, Hindu, Jewish – can express their authentic teachings so clearly in this way, then religion can begin to perform its proper role as peace-maker in the world; and perversions of religious teaching, from whatever quarter, can be recognized as such. Indeed, capital punishment, though still used in the USA, is now regarded as degrading and demeaning in Europe.

In 1950 the newly-emerging European Union (the Council of Europe) established the European Commission of Human Rights, with its headquarters in Strasbourg, under the European Convention of Human Rights. The European Court of Human Rights was then established in 1959, to examine and adjudicate on complaints brought by states or individuals. This Court has become increasingly important in the last fifty years, in establishing a value system and a code of conduct for individuals and states throughout Europe. Unlike the UN Convention and Court of Human Rights, the European model has extended the concept from the rights of states to the rights of individuals. Most of its work in fact has been in this capacity as a Court of Appeal to which individuals throughout Europe can bring their appeals against their own governments.

* * *

In the meantime Britain's (or England's) role in all this has been of quite a different and rather a peculiar nature. I say 'or England' in recognition of the fact that England's dominant role in the British political scene has been so dominant in the past that the two terms have been in practice interchangeable. This situation is now changing since Tony Blair's comparatively recent devolution of power to Scotland, Wales and Northern Ireland.

The publication in September, 2000, of the documentation concerning the negotiations for Britain's entry into the European Community (1970–72)[6] presents a very enlightening and intriguing story of the real intentions of the British Government at the time, compared with the British public's perception of what was going on. It becomes apparent that, although the British Government, had a realistic understanding of the need to integrate with Europe, the British public was still hypnotised by the 'Great Myth' of England's immemorial national and sovereign independence. Indeed such feeling was so intense and so closely connected in the popular mind with 'patriotism' and what it means to be English, that no British Government in the twentieth century felt able – for electoral reasons – to reveal the truth of what was happening. They all feared that the messenger conveying such a truth would be shot – metaphorically speaking.

British prime ministers during the second half of the twentieth century seem to have understood the need to integrate with Europe. Even Sir Winston Churchill himself, the very embodiment of patriotism, now appears in the light of Roy Jenkins' recent book, *Churchill* (2001),[7] to have been very far-sighted in his 'Europeanism' in the 1950's. He naturally tried to retain as much as possible of Britain's fading position as one of the world's great powers and it was this aspect which the public was made more aware of at the time. In fact, however, he 'had a full sense of Britain's participatory vocation' in Europe'; and to further this was 'one of his dominant political purposes'.[8] This is true in spite of the fact that, during his second term of office, when the elderly Churchill allowed the euro-sceptic Anthony Eden to run this aspect of Government, Churchill seemed to spend most of his time, extoling the American connection.[9]

Edward Heath's election victory in 1970 and his own enthusiasm for Europe succeeded in removing the sceptical doubts about Britain's intentions, which M. Pompidou shared with de Gaulle. Britain was admitted to membership in 1972, albeit on terms which really meant complete surrender to the requirements of the Community. The papers of Sir Con O'Neill, the senior diplomat handling the negotiations, reveal to us now that:

'We had to get in. What mattered was to get into the Community, and thereby restore our position at the centre of European affairs. It would be in the interest of this country to join the EEC whatever the terms'.[10]

This reveals what his political masters wanted. This, however, was not the way in which the British public perceived it. They believed that Britain was retaining its independence, while benefiting from the economic advantages of the Community.

Edward Heath knew that Britain must, in its own political and economic interests, enter Europe – whatever the cost in terms of its loss of independence. If he had presented the matter in this way to the public, he would not have been elected in 1970. The English people might just have accepted that the British Empire had to be broken up; but they certainly would not have accepted a British

Prime Minister's agreeing to the loss of any of Britain's cherished 'sovereign independence'.

Similarly, when Lady Thatcher signed the Single European Act in 1986, she saw it as means of extending her policy on free enterprise across the single market. In reality it meant, however, that Britain was taking another step into closer integration with Europe. It was bound to result in important concessions to majority voting in the European Community, which would significantly limit Britain's independence. But to the public, Lady Thatcher was the greatest of patriots in her defence of Britain's national and sovereign independence.

In fact, the last fifty years of the twentieth century witnessed the last chapter in the story of the part played by the 'Great Myth' in the history of the English nation. This was the period in which it became a major card in the game of party politics. It was used by leaders of both the Tory and Labour parties at different times, as a vote-catching appeal to 'patriotism' and 'what it means to be English'. Hugh Gaitskell used it in 1962, in opposing Britain's bid to enter the Common Market, saying it would be 'the end of Britain as an independent nation . . . the end of a thousand years of history'.[11] In 1996 the Tory Prime Minister, John Major, used it during his pre-election campaign, warning the British public that the Labour Party would 'in a thousand days, vandalize a thousand years of British history',[12] by pursuing further integration with Europe. The ex-Tory Cabinet Minister, Michael Heseltine was able to write later, however, in 2000, that Britain could be likened to Wessex and other Anglo-Saxon kingdoms. It would one day be 'no more than a quaint and increasingly faint memory'. The process of Britain becoming part of a European federation: 'is as irreversible and unstoppable a process as anything in politics ever is'.[13]

But at the beginning of the twenty-first century the 'Great Myth' that Britain had always been an independent and sovereign nation state – superior, isolated and self-reliant – is still playing a great part in providing the psychological background of subliminal prejudice against Britain's joining the single monetary system in Europe, by adopting the 'Euro'. For what is the 'Euro' to 'eurosceptics' but a threat to the peculiar English coinage which in turn is a concrete symbol of these perceived qualities of being English and not European.

No prime minister of Britain during the twentieth century attempted the leadership task of educating the British public about the need to enter whole-heartedly into a full partnership with other European countries, working for the unity of Europe. Nobody dared, during this time, to take on the electoral challenge of dispelling the 'Great Myth', which has reigned supreme in England for four centuries, up to the present moment. Nobody has inspired the British people with that vision of a lasting peace in Europe which has been one of the most important achievements in world history during the last half of the twentieth century. It seems to have been a phenomenon which has completely missed the attention of the British people; and has certainly not been brought to their attention.

The victory of Tony Blair and 'New Labour' in 1997 constituted a watershed in British politics – perhaps the greatest change in direction in British politics since that of the Henrician Government in the 1530's. The country felt that the need for a change in Government after a very long period of Tory rule, especially in the wake of a number of demoralising examples of 'sleaze' in government. Tony Blair had made the bold, but clever decision, to inform the public openly before the General Election in 1997 that he would be prepared to consider entering fully into the movement for European unity by accepting the next essential step forward – monetary union – but only on certain conditions. He would do so only if the famous five economic criteria, established by his Chancellor, Gordon Brown, were met, thereby completely safeguarding Britain's economic position. Secondly, he would do so only if the British public then voted in favour in a national Referendum. The caution and safeguards here reveal Blair's own appreciation of the power of the 'Great Myth' over the public mind. They did in fact provide the necessary reassurance for the biggest step forward so far in electoral terms. Blair duly and famously won the election in 1997, indicating that the British public was prepared at least to listen to the argument under these conditions - a huge step forward in preparing the ground for the task of leadership in this momentous matter.

*   *   *

Meanwhile, there have been very significant developments in Europe and the World during the last half century. One of the most important is the relationship between the European Union and the United States of America, a matter which bears very critically on Britain's choice of a way forward in the twenty-first century.

The USA emerged from the Second World War in 1945 as the greatest super-power in the world. It has remained so. It had led the world in the defence of Europe and the defeat of Hitler during that War. It went on to make a highly significant contribution (12 million dollars) to the European Recovery Programme (1948–52), known as the 'Marshall Plan'. It was the massive power of the USA, too, which held in check the threat to Europe and the world, from the totalitarian system of Soviet Communism during the 'Cold War' which went on into the last decade of the century. It might well be argued that it was the great protective power of the USA which allowed Europe to get on with its amazing experiment, during this fifty years, of establishing a lasting peace in Europe.

But this position of unparalleled power has also given the USA too great a propensity to use it unilaterally; and worse still, it has tempted the USA into an increasingly confident belief in its moral legitimacy. The USA is now spending nearly 500 billion dollars a year on its military 'security'. The European Union has no intention of competing with this; though it does spend a great deal of money on foreign aid (more per capita than the USA). This is where power becomes extremely dangerous. This is what Lord Acton meant when he said in the nineteenth century that 'Power corrupts and absolute power corrupts absolutely'. It requires a deep understanding that such power is dangerous, to save it from becoming a corrupting influence. It is safe only when used for the service of others, under proper international authority.

The greatest danger will arise for the USA and for the world, if it is perceived as misusing its enormous power for 'protectionist' and selfish reasons rather than serving the common good. In that case the USA would be part of the problem, rather than part of the solution in the process of establishing world peace. This is why such power can only be used at the behest of the United Nations Security Council and never unilaterally by the USA on its own. There is a sense in which the USA has nothing to fear but fear itself. The recent 'Home Security' Bill pushed through by Bush (23 Nov. 2002) to discover terrorists, is perceived by many as a real threat to essential freedoms in the USA. The horrific events of September 11th, 2001, were a sobering reminder that no human power, however great, is invulnerable. One result of an abuse of power today could be that 'clash of civilizations' which Samuel Hartington a former security adviser in the USA has predicted.[14] But this need not happen. There is another path to follow.

The fifty years of peace in Western Europe, in which the strength of the USA played a major part, allowed the movement for European Unity to grow apace. The fifteen nations of Western Europe are all now well settled in the Community. In October, 2002, however, the European Union made the epoch-making announcement that eight post-Communist countries from Eastern Europe (together with Cyprus and Malta), are all likely to be admitted to full membership in 2004. The significance of this in European history can hardly be exaggerated. The Eastern European countries, repressed and economically stagnated under Communism, are now going to be helped by the prosperous West. It will mean a great input of economic energy to bring their standard of life abreast of the others; but this has been done already for countries like Eire and Spain. In turn there will be a greater and richer mixture of diversity and multi-cultural experience, deepening the strength of the European Union. What is developing is a prosperous Europe, of 500 million people, economically and politically united, living according to the values of democracy and human rights and the principles of solidarity and subsidiarity. Europe will be a Continent of 25 nations living in durable peace and prosperity, after four centuries of perhaps the worst internecine warfare in world history. There will be difficulties, as, for example when the much needed reforms of the Common Agricultural Policy begin to operate fully;[16] but this should not disguise the merits of the achievement. It will be an unprecedented example of diversity within unity, in its scale, methodology and nobility of purpose. It will constitute a brotherhood of 25 nations, working together in peace for the common good. The celebrated victories of previous European 'giants' such as Charlemagne or Napoleon, are left in the shade in comparison with this extraordinary achievement.

Yet this achievement has hardly been recognized in Britain or the USA. The perception in America, especially, is that Europe is a 'weakling' (in terms of defence budgets and willingness to deploy military force) which is not up to the challenges of the modern world. In fact, however, the European Union, while shunning military might, is arguably the world's most dynamic political bloc today. Twelve of its states have abolished their own ancient currencies – some as old as themselves – to introduce an ambitious single monetary system (the 'Euro') from which there is no way back. The EU is about to bring in to itself ten Eastern European nations in 2004; with Romania and Bulgaria following in 2007. It is continually introducing new instruments such as cross border police raids or EU arrest warrants, while the first constitutional convention since 1787 (Philadelphia) is now taking place in the EU Parliament. There are some signs, too, indicating that the slower-moving EU economy might in the long run prove steadier and bigger (in terms of numbers) that of the USA.[17]

The European Union does not have war on its agenda. It is not much interested in power or military force, except for occasional peace-keeping commitments in areas such as Kosovo, where joint action is needed by the UN to stop crimes against humanity such as 'ethnic cleansing'. Its main motivating force in foreign policy is to pursue a 'civilising mission', whereby its principles of democracy, human rights and 'good governance' can be accepted in other areas such as Africa, the Middle East and the Far East. Moreover it believes it has found the formula for perpetual peace between nations based on economic and political ties of inter-dependence; and wishes to export this invaluable gift to other peoples. It believes in a world where strength is not so important and unilateral action by the strongest power is ruled out of order. Rather, it has discovered a system whereby all nations are governed by mutually accepted rules of behaviour, under-pinned by a moral consciousness which has replaced the concept of power-politics. In short, Europe, has achieved an advanced post-modern form of civilization, ahead of the rest of the world. Its attitude to the rest of the world is: 'Taste and see that what we have discovered is good'.

The USA, on the other hand, believes in achieving 'good' ends by force; by unilateral action if necessary against the perceived evil which is identified in a certain person or country. The aim is to eliminate that evil by superior military strength. So the USA is continually increasing its expenditure on defence, already greater than any other nation – to something which is now nearing 500 billion dollars a year. Yet, it is beginning to learn that military might on its own cannot destroy the present evil of terrorism. It is apparently obliterated in one place and then reconstructs itself, to appear somewhere else. This is especially the case when the terrorist is someone – the suicide bomber – who is quite ready to die for his cause; and is quickly replaced by someone else. In the face of such transnational terrorism, power politics is no longer a relevant or appropriate defence. The answer must be ultimately in terms of removing those conditions – injustice, inequality, poverty, failure, despair, hopelessness – in which the seeds of terrorism thrive. In the shorter term, the answer, for the USA, lies in working in co-operation with allies through the one universally-recognized and representative world authority – the United Nations, which enshrines the values of democracy and human rights.[18] The best possible strategy for the USA, in its own interests as well as those of the world at large, is to put its great military strength at the disposal of the United Nations Security Council. It would form the core of a strong and effective 'international police force', well able to deal with any breaches of international law. On the other hand, any arrogantly unilateral action by the USA could lead to a 'clash of civilizations' – the template for which is already tragically displayed in the continual cycle of violence characterising the conflict between Israel and Palestine.

*   *   *

Tony Blair has discerned the four major roles which he should pursue in the new Millennium. He has stated quite clearly that there should be no isolation for Britain. The swift advance of globalisation means that this is just not possible in any case. The good of each country now is inextricably connected with the good of the world. In this sense there is no longer any valid distinction between domestic and foreign policy.[19]

In the first place, he intends that Britain should be a force for good in the world, opposing terrorism, putting its own house in order in terms of human rights and helping to extend these to other countries. We are all inter-dependent and the actions of each country rebound for good or evil on itself and on the rest of the world. This is the sense in which he says that Britain, while no longer a super-power, must be a 'beacon to the World'.[20]

Secondly, Blair is intent that Britain should occupy a leading and influential role as an integral part of the developing European Union. Thirdly, he wants to maintain, as far as possible, Britain's special relationship with the USA. Fourthly, he can then occupy a 'pivotal role', acting as a bridge between the newly-united Europe and the USA. Fifthly, because of its own experience as a former world power and leader of the Commonwealth, Britain is well placed for bringing as much influence as possible to bear on world development, in terms of helping the developing countries, such as in Africa, out of their poverty and by extending the principles of democracy, human rights and global ethics throughout the world. This is his great vision of Britain's role in the new millennium, made evident in all his speeches in Britain and around the world.

After his election in 1997, Blair immediately began to speak with a completely new voice in British politics. Instead of socialist ideology, he began to speak passionately of the importance of values. He had become a practising Christian before he had been a politician and his Christian convictions run very deeply.[21] He has been described as a Christian democrat and the description is apt.

On being elected, with a massive majority in 1997, he immediately presented the new paradigm of a Government existing to serve the people; and required his MPs and Ministers to go out as 'ambassadors' to show this in their work. [Sir Hartley Shawcross had welcomed Labour's previous landslide win in 1945 quite differently: 'We are the masters now'.] If inspired by his own Christian beliefs, Blair is 'inclusive' in his appeal, so that British Muslims and Hindus, for example, also greeted his statement. In foreign policy, Blair sets out his objectives in terms of 'doing good in the world', contrasting with the traditional British view that 'we have only interests, not friends'. There is much truth in the remark made after his first speech to all the new MPs at Church House in London, that he has 'christianised politics' in Britain. The only British Prime Minister who remotely bears comparison with him in this respect is William Gladstone (1809–98).[22] He invests greatly in getting *everyone* to belong and contribute to 'the common good' and wishes to include all who have been marginalised. He injects something which is badly needed in a sceptical, weary and sometimes cynical world, become indifferent to politics - inspired and eloquent leadership in pursuit of a vision of a better world for all.

In his first key-note speech to the New Labour Party Conference, in 1997, he portrayed a new vision for Britain's future, returning it to its older historical role as 'one of the great innovative peoples' who once brought the world 'the Magna Carta' and should now play a leading role in the new Europe. Indeed Europe represents 'a great opportunity' for Britain rather than the 'threat' which the Tories perceive it as being. It provides an opportunity for a great extension of democracy and human rights:

'The chains of mediocrity have been broken, the tired days are behind us. We are free to build that model 21st nation, to become that beacon to the world'.[23]

He went on to speak of the values underlying his policies:

'compassion . . . social justice . . . the struggle against poverty and inequality . . . liberty . . . basic human solidarity. Ours is a simple enough vision. But it will require a supreme national effort'.[24]

Such was the immediate rhetoric following his electoral victory. Soon, some very interesting changes in Government policy began to take place. Robin Cook, the new Foreign Minister, produced a mission statement for Britain's new foreign policy shortly after the creation of the new Government. In this, for the very first time we find an explicit and central reference to an 'ethical dimension'. This was important because it set a new target against which the Government itself could be answerable in future, if it fell short. Until then, Britain's foreign policy had been guided explicitly only by 'national interests' – nothing more had been expected.

Globalisation has been a central feature of change in the world. In the last half century, the world has become a much smaller place in terms of trans-national and trans-continental developments in communication, high technology, big business and expanding business markets. An increasing understanding of environmental forces, such as global warming, has also led to the need for global action. No individual nation is equipped to deal with these new conditions in isolation. The old English idea of itself as an independent and sovereign nation state is now not only undesirable but impossible.

So, almost without the British people realising it, the old 'Great Myth' about the English past is redundant as well as mythical. New and much wider political institutions are needed to manage such forces. More importantly, in order to control and humanise the great forces of global economics and the new technology now available, a global ethical system of moral values, under-written by legal sanctions, is essential. Otherwise the new world situation will become infinitely more dangerous in its effects on mankind, than anything which has gone before.

Tony Blair has been quick to comprehend all this. He has embraced the idea of Human Rights as the basis for such a moral code; and introduced it into British Law in 2000. The Human Rights Act rests on the value of the equal dignity and worth of every human being - a basic Christian teaching. This has been a momentous step in breaking through British isolationism and making it part of Europe again. Even more importantly, it forms a central pillar in the new architecture of political, economic and social life of Europe in the new Millennium.

Human Rights can also form the basis of a new concept of the 'Common Good' in Britain, Europe and the World. It stipulates the right of every human being to freedom of religious worship. Secularist thinkers have often pointed to the part played by religion in wars and persecutions of the past. They have prophesied the decline and death of religion in the new Millennium and seen this as an advantage for world peace. But the horrors caused by atheistic totalitarianism in the twentieth century denies this argument. It is impossible to dispense with religion because it responds to the basic human need to be loved, to see meaning in life, to belong to something bigger than oneself, to pursue what is good, beautiful and true. Religion responds to man's spiritual needs and is an essential part of the human condition. Like the need for water, food and love, it is part of our humanity and cannot be 'outgrown' or dispensed with. Religion, too, is one of the main motivators of community building, which is essential to human beings. This is an aspect of life which has been underestimated in the modern world at the cost of much human suffering and frustration.

The real enemy here is the one within. All religions have experienced in their histories, the danger of perversions, of warped, unbalanced or fanatical extremism or exclusionism, incorrectly described as 'fundamentalism'. This is a kind of religious fascism which teaches hatred and exclusion of others. It has distorted beyond recognition the central teaching of all the authentic religions in the world, from time to time and has led to views and actions which are the very antithesis of their own central beliefs and teachings. An abuse of religion in this way is similar to an abuse of political power or the abuse of science; but much worse because it turns the very remedy for evil into another cause for evil. Such perversions have indeed been one of the causes of war and violence in the past in Europe and in other parts of the world.

One of the most important and significant developments, therefore, in the second half of the twentieth century in the Christian world of the west, has been the recognition by the main Christian bodies, that the principle of human rights, with all its implications, is in fact an implicit and essential part of their own faith system, even though it has been dormant, misinterpreted, or overlooked, in the past. Christians who have attacked the human rights of others have always been betraying their own central and fundamental belief in 'loving your neighbour as yourself'.

Pope John Paul II, for example, has emphasized continuously the doctrine of Human Rights, as a fundamental part of the Christian global ethic; and asked, on the part of the Catholic Church, for forgiveness for its past transgressions in this area. This has been a main theme of many of his statements on his innumerable visits to all parts of the world. Concerned about the perilous state of humanity, he voiced his alarm in his Christmas message for World Peace in 2001. The cataclysmic events in the USA on 11th September, 2001, demonstrated the frightful power of warped religion in the modern world. He called a meeting of leaders of all world religions to be convened in Assisi in January 2002, to affirm humam solidarity which crosses all boundaries, national, racial or religious. All religions should be able to agree on a God of peace and compassion; and on respect for one's neighbour. The modern world is a pluralistic society which depends for its health and survival on a proper understanding among all religious groups of what true religious means. It also demands the duty and preparedness of religious leaders to disown and condemn any signs of perversion or fanaticism among their own groups. This is an essentially important part of the movement for world peace. We are beginning to learn again that, whether we like it or not, religion is one of the most powerful influences on the vast majority of people in the world. It can be the major contributor towards world peace; but religious perversion can be a contributor to war. Religious leaders, then, have a major and indispensable responsibility to speak out for the authentic values of their religion. They themselves are the only ones really capable of delegitimising any perversion of their own religion, seeking to justify the taking of human life.

Important developments have taken place in this area. British Muslim leaders were forthright in their condemnation of the atrocity of 11 September, 2001, in the USA. The calm voices of these moderate Muslim leaders were speaking for the vast majority of peace-loving and orthodox Muslims. Similarly with regard to the Israeli-Palestinian conflict in the Middle East, the Chief Rabbi of Great Britain and the Commonwealth, Jonathan Sacks, has expressed his great sadness: 'I regard the current situation as nothing less than tragic. It is forcing Israel into postures that are incompatible in the long run with our deepest ideals'.[25] Kofi Annan, Secretary-General of the United Nations, spoke during the Bosnian crisis, of the great need: 'to restore religion to its rightful role as peacemaker and pacifier'.[26]

Dr Hans Küng, the Swiss Catholic theologian, has asserted: 'No peace between the nations without peace between the religions; no peace between the religions without dialogue between the religions; no dialogue between the religions without research into their theological foundations'. He is founder and president of the Global Ethic Foundation in Tubingen, Germany. His *A Global Ethic for Global Politics* advocates a semi-official body called the Council for a Parliament of the World's Religions to bring together a consensus of all those moral teachings which every faith has in common. Kung, at the age of 31, was one of the most influential theologians (a council *peritus* or expert) in the epoch-making Second Vatican Council, called by Pope John XXIII.[27]

Tony Blair, significantly, has become a close friend and admirer of Kung's work. Kung believes that politicians need to understand the importance of religions in the world and have a vital role to play in advancing a global ethic. Blair insists continuously that global politics needs to be underpinned by such an ethic. Küng has been invited to Downing Street. Blair was invited to speak at Tübingen in 2000. Of all the world's political leaders, Blair speaks with the greatest conviction from the moralist viewpoint. He speaks of the need for all 'the children of Abraham' to come together and make a new world.[28]

Behind Blair's frequent demand for reforms in world governance is the Gladstonian principle that in the long run 'What is morally right cannot be politically wrong; and what is morally wrong cannot be politically right'. Blair has said:

'Nations act out of self-interest. Anything else is delusion. But recognising we are part of an international community is our self-interest'.[29]

He insists that globalisation has presented challenges that can be met only if nations accept a doctrine of 'international community' and cooperate together. In his Tübingen address, he said:

'None of the big issues facing us all – trade, finance, the environment, nuclear proliferation, organised crime and drugs – can be tackled today by nations acting alone. The history of the last 100 years and more shows the vital importance of renewing the institutions of international cooperation and of building alliances between the main players . . . Increasingly our problems are shared . . . our societies and economies are threatened where no understanding to solve these problems exists; and benefit where it does'.[30]

The European Union, for Blair, is the prime example to the world of how nations with shared interests can work together: 'The EU is the most obvious manifestation around us of the need for all nations to cooperate'.[31]

Blair has important and respected admirers. Hans Küng sees him as a man of extraordinary vision, surer of what he wants to do for the common good of Europe and the world, than either Helmut Kohl or Gerhard Schroeder when they became chancellors of Germany. Küng says that people in Britain expect Blair to change everything overnight; but it is essential that he should move gradually and with conviction – 'not try to do everything at once'.[32] Klaus Schwäb, the German economics professor who founded the World Economic Forum has expressed his amazement at what Blair has been able to do in his comparatively short term of office;[33] and praised his qualities as a political moralist.[34]

Tony Blair is one of those rare people who is a visionary and a man of action at the same time. He believes that it is Britain's role to do good in and for the world; and in doing so, it will serve Britain's own interests as well. There was a real moral compulsion about his determination to stop the 'ethnic cleansing' and crimes against humanity which took place in Kosovo (1999–2001) when 200,000 of the surviving Albanians fled the province in the face of the oppressive and persecuting Serb regime of Slobadan Milosevic. Britain took a leading part in the joint Nato force which intervened under the terms of the UN Security Council Resolution, mandating the entry of an international force to stop crimes against humanity and to restore stability to the region.

Britain's role was particularly important in this and in the peace-keeping afterwards because of the nature of its own small (in comparison with American) but extremely well-trained and well-armed specialist force. As a result the Milosevic regime was forced out and he himself was voted out of power by his own people. In July 2002 the presidents of Yugoslavia, Bosnia and Croatia met to work out plans for mutual cooperation - an extremely important step in establishing peace and stability in the Balkans which has been a trouble-spot in Europe throughout modern history. Meanwhile Milosevic is standing trial at the Hague for his crimes against humanity. Similarly Blair has tried to act the role of an international peace-maker, in his frequent visits to other trouble spots in the world, meeting, for example, the leaders of India and Pakistan as well as those of Israel and Palestine; while Britain's peace-keeping force has been prominent in helping to establish peace in such places as Sierra Leone and Angola.

Blair has a similar and deeply-held moral commitment to helping the under-developed countries of the world. Here, again, he argues convincingly that this policy is morally right; but also makes good sense politically and economically. He describes the condition of Africa – its sufferings from poverty, disease, war and sometimes bad governance – as a 'scar on the conscience of the world'. Britain has played a leading part in all the meetings and conferences designed to solve the problems of world poverty, sanitation and global warming; from the Kyoto summit in Japan (1997) to the recent huge gathering at the world summit in Johannesburg (2002). Here there are many frustrating problems and obstacles, caused ultimately by lack of a concerted political will; but like all great movements, small steps forward are being taken on a path from which humanity cannot afford to deviate.

Britain took the lead in pressing for debt relief in the G8 meetings of the world's leading industrial nations and in other global forums such as the World Bank. The idea became part of 'Britain and Jubilee, 2000'. It was originally put forward by CAFOD, a London based Catholic charity; and was powerfully supported by Pope John Paul II in 1994. The Alliance of British Churches then founded 'Jubilee' in 1996, making it first a national, then an international 'idea whose time has come'. Tony Blair's Government ended the campaign by announcing the most far-reaching package of debt relief ever. Gordon Brown praised the Churches' contribution to the campaign at a Jubilee rally in December, 2000:

'Were someone to ask Stalin's famous question – "How many divisions has the Pope?" in terms such as "How much international clout has Christianity?" the answer, in the light of global debt relief agreed so far, would have to come back as "100 billion dollars and counting"'.

But some of the wealthiest governments of the northern hemisphere have not yet proved willing to give up making a net profit out of their relationship with the poor countries of the southern hemisphere. The repayment of debt, especially to the USA, along with the exploitation of unfair terms of trading (including protectionism of their own industries) by the strong against the weak, are main causes of poverty in developing countries. Economic mismanagement, civil wars and political corruption by the rulers of some Third World countries, are also contributary causes. Blair has spoken out vigorously in various speeches on these matters in various parts of the world.

The lead given by Britain's strategy could be an example for the western world. It agreed to cancel the debt of twelve countries immediately, including some of the poorest. Eight more will need to introduce reforms indicating that the money provided by debt relief will be used to help the poor. The debt owed by twelve others – too unstable politically and militarily to undertake such conditions – has been 'frozen' awaiting developments. Such agreements are designed to target real benefits to the people concerned and to encourage good governance.

It is with regard to Africa that Blair has stated his position on globalisation and on Britain's new role in the world most clearly. Since 11th September, 2001, he has targeted his strategy particularly on the problem of terrorism in the world. All these issues are collected into a coherent and integrated vision of the way forward in his speeches in Africa.

Addressing the Nigerian parliament in February, 2002, he rejected criticism at home that he was concentrating too much on world affairs at the expense of domestic policies. British interests were bound up with those of Africa. Terrorist attacks emerged from the seething sense of injustice and bitterness experienced by 'failed states'. This could happen in Africa:

'You need our support . . . but we need you to succeed. If Africa gains, we gain. The world will be safer and more just. When an African child dies every three seconds the developed world had a clear duty to act. No responsible world leader can turn his back on Africa.'[35]

In the same speech, he called on rich countries to open their markets to trade and urged them to provide logistical and financial support for peace-keeping in African countries. The western world has become rich through economic progress. Africa remains dogged by poverty, disease, war and corruption:

'The vision of globalisation driven by a global ethic, by global values, is not utopian. It is modern realism.'[36]

He continued with a telling passage:

'The events of September 11 illustrated dramatically that the security of each of us depends on the prosperity of us all. In today's inter-dependent world there can be no secure future for any of us unless we manage globalisation with greater justice. There has never been a time when self-interest and mutual interest were so dependent on each other. Which are the nations that export drugs and terror, extremism, weapons of mass destruction that threaten the world's stability? The prosperous? The democratic? No, it's the failed states, the dictatorships, the economically and politically bankrupt that do so. What we know today – what we saw was horrifyingly brutal in New York on September 11 – is that globalisation no longer applies just in technology, trade, capital, culture and communications. Politics is global. The threat of weapons of mass destruction, religious fanaticism and terror cannot be escaped.'[37]

Defending the New Partnership for Africa's Development Initiative being drawn up by the G8 countries, Blair commented: 'It is not impossible idealism, it's a down payment on a decent future.'[36]

He called on G8 counries to 'practise what we preach' on free trade by offering poorer countries in Africa duty-free and quota-free access to western markets. Africa was a potential market of 750 million people, for investors. We should commit:

'not only to a reduction of overall tariff levels in the World Trade Organisation next round, but the abolition of some which hit African countries the hardest.'[38]

From Nigeria, Blair flew on to Ghana and visited British peace-keeping forces in Sierra Leone, before attending a seminar on development in Senegal.

Blair was the main ally of the USA, after September 11th (2001), in their legally sanctioned pursuit of Osama Bin Laden and his Al-Qaida terrorist network, hosted and sponsered by the oppressive Taliban regime in Afghanistan. This involved the military action of the British special force. Afghanistan, dominated by its Taliban regime, had long been one of the most notoriously dangerous centres of terrorism and one of the most difficult to subdue, as the Russian army had discovered earlier. This decisive action proved to be successful. The Taliban regime was removed and the Al-Qaida network disrupted, though Bin Laden himself had disappeared.

The aftermath was particularly important to Tony Blair. He had determined from the start to bring about proper development for the repressed people of Afghanistan. In June, 2002, Michael Alridge reported for the BBC[40] on the newly elected President and Government of the country. Comparative stability, security and freedom had been established for the people, under the UN security force led by Britain. Kabul had been transformed; there were educational programmes established. It will take more time, of course, before Afghanistan develops. Such things cannot be achieved overnight. The recent murder of the newly-elected Vice President indicates that conditions are nowhere near perfect yet. But an important start has been made in aided human development for the people there.

By now Blair's reputation as an international statesman in the eyes of Europe, America and the Third World, is extraordinarily high. British people, with all their inbred ironical scepticism, have begun to realise this only at a very late stage. There has been much criticism of Blair's concentration on foreign affairs, at the expense of home affairs – a charge which would be very difficult to sustain. The notion of the inter-dependence of nations in the new world of globalisation, means that there is very little gap between foreign and domestic policy. This is a concept that British people have not yet properly understood. It struck a new chord, therefore, when Blair commented that his policy with regard to Afghanistan related directly to domestic affairs in Britain. Afghanistan was the main centre for the harvesting of opium crops. These produced the largest supply of drugs which ended up in Britain, causing one of the biggest problems in British society and affecting the lives of thousands of ordinary British people. Money from the drug trade went to finance the terrorist network centred in Afghanistan, but extending to all parts of the world. Britain, therefore, had an important stake in what was happening in Afghanistan. This problem still exists. Only a successful political, economic and social reconstruction of Afghanistan will solve it; but Blair's words ring very true: that in the modern, inter-dependent world, there is little distinction between domestic and foreign policy.

AFTERWORD

Blair has shown considerable consistency in his support for international law. He sees the need to strengthen this and the role of the United Nations as essential contributions towards the building of world peace. From the same viewpoint, it is essential to provide the means by which war criminals and those who have committed crimes against humanity can be brought to justice. In 2001, the former Bosnian Serb general, Radislav Krystic was sentenced at the Hague to 46 years in jail for the genocide of 7000 Bosnian Muslim men and boys in Srebrenica in July, 1995. Then, most importantly, the Serbian Head of State, Slobadan Milosevic, was brought to trial in 2001. He is an atheist who had exploited perverted religious and nationalist prejudice in Serbia to start a wave of 'ethnic cleansing' against the Muslim population. The action was important because it showed that heads of state are no longer immune from punishment under international law, for crimes against humanity. It showed, too, that the human rights of Muslims or members of any other religion, would be protected by the UN against 'ethnic cleansing'. Tony Blair felt a strong moral compulsion to act and British forces played a major part in the success of this enterprise and the later peace-keeping operations.

Coming closer to home, there was the equally important case of the Chilean dictator, General Pinochet, who had seized power from a democratically-elected Government in Chile, by military force. Under his rule (1973–78) more than 3000 people were killed or disappeared. Britain had acceded to the International Convention Against Torture. Pinochet had stated in 1974 that 'torture is the tool with which we will exterminate our enemies'.[41] Pinochet visited Britain for medical treatment in 2000. The British Government decided that he had no immunity from prosecution as a former head of state. He was brought to trial before a British court for crimes against humanity in spite of the considerable opposition of some, such as Lady Thatcher, who declared indignantly that he had been a 'good friend' of Britain's during the Falklands war against Argentina. The final decision was waived on health grounds, and he was sent back to Chile where he was finally brought before a Chilean court. The case was important again because it established before the world that heads of state who commit crimes against humanity can no longer get away with it – an extremely important step forward in the movement for human rights throughout the world. Meanwhile Milosevic had been voted out of power by his own people after his defeat by the UN force.

Another interesting example of the world-wide spread of human rights was the arrest (12 July, 2002) of General Galtieri who had led Argentina into the attack on the Falklands. He and his fellow military junta members were brought to trial for crimes against humanity. Both Chile and Argentina needed to show, for their own self-assurance, that they now live in the world of human rights.

In Britain itself, four important achievements stand out in Blair's premiership so far. Three of them were integral parts of the Government's programme of constitutional reform, aimed at modernising Britain and making it into a strong and confident democracy in the twenty-first century. Firstly there was the great reduction of the number of hereditary peers in a reconstituted House of Lords – a logical move for a modern democratic state. Secondly the devolution of authority to Scotland, Wales and Northern Ireland has given new life – culturally, economically and politically - to these countries. Just as the external Empire overseas was broken up after 1945; so now, the internal 'colonisation' of neighbouring countries, which started with the 'Act of Union' with Wales (1536), was rescinded. This action was important because it reflected the spirit of the principle of subsidiarity in the European Union - the respect for and recognition of the rights of smaller countries. It shows the coherent way in which Blair tends to apply in practise, the principles in which he believes. It was a way of righting, where possible, wrongs which had taken place in the past. Both these reforms will, I believe, become more important in the wider perspective taken by future historians.

Nothing perhaps has been more indicative of Britain's insularity of thought than its slowness in the second half of the twentieth century to appreciate the importance of the human rights movement which was developing on the Continent. Nothing perhaps will change British society so much in the new Millennium as Blair's third reform - the epoch-making Bill of Human Rights in 2000.

The fiftieth anniversary in 1998 of the promulgation of the Universal Declaration of Human Rights by the United Nations, was celebrated throughout the world; but it had not always been so. The 'Cold War' between Russia and the West continued through most of the second half of the twentieth century. During this time appalling abuses were inflicted by anti-democratic regimes in the West, especially in Latin America. The West turned a blind eye to these events because these regimes were 'useful' to it. In Russia, community rights were asserted at the expense of individual human freedoms, such as those of speech and religious worship which were also denied to its peoples in Communist-dominated Eastern Europe. The United Nations itself was more concerned at this period with the rights of states rather than individual human beings.

During this time human rights, in their fullest sense, found a friend in high places in the person of Popes John XXIII and John Paul II. The Church had come late into the field of human rights, but when it did arrive; it came in a big way. It started with John XXIII's great encylical: *Peace on Earth* (1963), in which he made the first detailed Christian statement on human rights. He also called the 2nd Vatican Council (1962–5) which gave a central place in Christian teaching to human rights. This was followed by John Paul II's personal commitment and promotion of human rights expressed continuously on his many visits to various countries throughout the world. It proved to be a marked feature of his papacy. His moral support for the Polish workers in their bid for freedom through 'solidarity', proved to be conclusive in 1989; and this was to lead in the most dramatic manner to the unexpected collapse of Communism throughout Eastern Europe.

In 1998 the Catholic Bishops' Conference of England and Wales published their own British version and extension of Christian teaching on human rights.[42] This integrated the pragmatic Anglo-Saxon Common Law tradition (from Magna Carta to Thomas Paine and John Locke) with the more philosophical approach of continental thinkers. It emphasized the indivisibility and universality of human rights. People could not pick and choose which ones they wanted. It applied to all individuals and to all nations and races in the world. These were inalienable rights; they belonged to all human beings, worthy or unworthy. They were based ultimately on scriptorial revelation concerning the dignity and eternal value of each human being; and also on the natural law discourse concerning people's fundamental needs.

The bishops conceded readily that the language of human rights had started outside the Church; and indeed these rights had been sometimes violated in the past in the name of the Church which had regarded them as a secular weapons to be used against it. They have now come to understand that these principles are implicit in their own fundamental beliefs. It is a remarkable example of what is meant by the 'development' of religious thinking; and by this same process its Christian message becomes more obviously relevant to the needs of the modern world (a process described by

John XXIII in 1962 as the 'aggiornamento'). It is vitally important now that other major religions undergo the same 'development', to ensure that religion becomes a major influence for world peace. Human rights have now become criteria by which the Christian Church will evaluate and judge its own actions. It is important that other religions – Jewish, Muslim, Buddhist, Hindu - do the same. This would contribute fundamentally to the cause of peace in India, Pakistan, the Middle East and Asia.

All religions will need to adopt another development, also, to make them relevant to the needs of the pluralistic society of the modern world. They need to accept the fact that there should be a separation of Church from State. A theocracy, in which religious law is supreme and applied to all citizens, is not consistent with a pluralist society. In the case of Christianity, its Founder stated clearly that this was not the nature of His religion. He specifically resisted the offer of worldly power, when tempted by the Devil in the desert. Again He said: 'My kingdom is not of this world'; 'Give unto Caesar the things that are Caesar's and to God the things that are God's'. Christians therefore cannot accept the idea of a theocracy. Sharia law (Islamic) or Canon Law (Christian), for example, by their very nature, cannot apply to all citizens in a pluralistic society. State law, on the other hand, does apply to all citizens of that particular state, though it must observe the needs of religious Freedom. The separation of Church and State is essential when we are striving to achieve the conditions for peace in a multi-ethnic, multi-cultural society which is pluralistic in character. Blair and Küng are trying to achieve a global ethic containing the main moral teachings of all the major religions, which could sustain such a society in the modern world.

The actual Bill of Human Rights enacted by the Blair Government in October, 2000, brought the European Convention of Human Rights into the law of Britain.[43] This is enormously significant — one of the events of which the true importance will be recognized only at a later stage, when historians, looking back, will be able to place it in its true perspective. Nothing will be more important in changing the direction of British life and history from its four-centuries-old divergence into insularity, back into the mainstream of European life and history. The law covers and colours such a great part of our lives; and the European – indeed universal – character of the law of Human Rights, will inevitably make citizens of Europe and the wider world, of us all. In the opinion of that great legal historian, F.W. Maitland, nothing was more momentous in separating England from Europe than Henry VIII's dismantling of the international Canon Law of the Catholic Church which had existed alongside the national Common Law in medieval England.[44] In the same sense, nothing will be more momentous in changing us into Europeans again (as well as Britons) than this new Act of 2000. The new law will, in the long run significantly change British culture and way of life as our own 'distinct qualities and glorious individuality' will remain, but be enhanced and developed by closer contact with other cultures. The very nature of the law of human rights will contribute to a much greater appreciation, by each country involved, of the great bonds which hold together the family of human kind; and of the very real sense in which we are all inter-dependent.

In more detailed form, the Act will mean that British people are now able to enforce their human rights directly, without having to go to the European Court of Human Rights in Strasbourg. The Act's aim is to establish a new *culture* in which citizens will recognize the human rights of others, balanced against their mutual responsibilities. All public authorities without exception will need to be mindful of human rights in all that they do. Ministers of State have to ensure that any new legislation introduced into Parliament has to be compatible with them. This British Bill also emphasizes the roles of good education and good citizenship which must accompany the new legislation, in creating this new culture. All this gives a unique quality to the British model of a Bill of Human Rights, enshrined in the Act.

The Act demonstrates, too, the importance of democratic principles which, together with these human rights and responsibilities, reflect the inherent dignity and equality of all human beings, irrespective of age, sex, religion, race, nationality or anything else. The political philosophy involved is a true reflection of the Christian heritage as 'developed' in the last fifty years. It is an extremely important and exciting cultural development in Britain, combining as it does continuity with the past, together with constructive adaptation to the needs of the modern world in the new Millennium.

The Act will change eventually many of our assumptions of thought and ways in which people think and behave. It will affect institutions in Church and State as all begin to look critically at themselves in the light of human rights and at themselves in the light of it. Its implications are immense for us all. They still have to be discerned, drawn out and developed in fundamentally important aspects of legal, political, social, economic, medical, cultural and religious life in Britain[45] That is why the Human Rights Act is a turning point in British history.

The establishment of a political settlement in Northern Ireland based on the 'Good Friday' agreement, was a major achievement of Blair's Government, in spite of the recent set-backs during the Summer of 2002. The process contained the same elements of tireless patience, negotiation, creative embiguity and determination to achieve peace, which characterised the movement for European Union on the Continent. Here again, Blair's personal contribution has been of great significance. He personified the qualities mentioned above. Interestingly, too, he adopted the same stance as John Paul II in his belief in the 'purification of memory', by unprecedently expressing his sorrow, on behalf of the British Government, for past injustices committed in Ireland in its name. Against the advice and opinion of many others, he saw this as the only way forward from the Christian as well as the political viewpoint. Then he demonstrated his willingness to go to extraordinary lengths to achieve the basis of a just and peaceful settlement in a situation which was recognized throughout the world as one of the most intractable. Much more than going the legendary 'extra mile' for peace, Blair proved himself to be a marathon runner in this respect. His approach was different from that of any other British Prime Minister since Gladstone; and he achieved something - so far - which no previous British statesman (including Gladstone) has managed to do. There is a sense, too, in which Blair has used his experience in Ireland as a template for his approach to and management of other intractable problems. The 'Home-rule' arrangement has been temporarily suspended in Ireland at the moment, but I believe that the peace process there is now ultimately unstoppable.

Blair, like all human beings, has made mistakes and experienced failures in his dealings with several issues during his Premiership. One thinks, for example of the Bernie Ecclestone issue and the ill-fated attempt to interfere in the appointment of his favourite candidate for the office of first minister in the Welsh Assembly. The costly and futile building of the Millennium Dome, was peculiarly inappropriate for the purpose. It seemed to many to be doomed from the start. It was an expensive failure in itself and more importantly in its symbolism it was a real error of judgement. It served only to obscure the infinitely greater importance and appropriateness of an event which truly celebrated the meaning of the new Millennium – the passing by the British Parliament of the Act of Human Rights. This was in reality the ideal celebration of the great Christian event in 2000AD, marking a completely new phase in British history.

Another error of judgement, in my view and now in his own, was Blair's failure to start the radical restructuring in the Education and Health services much earlier than he has done. He recognised this in his speech to the Labour Conference in Blackpool (October, 2002) in his statement that 'We have not been bold enough'; and has now commenced the restructuring in a big way. Looking at his first term of office, the expectations he raised for improvement in these services were impossible to meet without urgent action which should have started immediately after his election in 1997. Blair asked the nation to judge him on his success in meeting his stated targets of improvement in these areas; and it will be a formidable task to fulfil these during his second term of office.

I believe, too, that he was not sufficiently 'bold' after his election in 1997, when on a great wave of popularity and national support, together with his unprecedented New Labour majority in the Commons, he could have both educated and led the country into greater integration with Europe, by joining the preparations for monetary union – by 'striking when the iron was hot'.[46] This failed opportunity has meant an unnecessary delay in proceedings. Britain could by now be playing a leading role in Europe and be in a better position to play the other 'pivotal' role between Europe and the USA if he had played the card of a national referendum on the matter in 1998. But, of course, he had pre-empted this by his promise of its depending on the 'Five Economic Tests'. He is now at a greater risk of not being successful. My own instinct, however, is that Britain will inevitably join the 'euro' – because in Blair's own words, it is its 'destiny'. Blair's lack of confidence in 1997 was understandable and resulted only in a slightly damaging postponement of the matter. Europe however urgently needs reassurance that Britain has left behind its old insularity and become sufficiently 'European-minded' to adopt a leadership role. At the moment I believe that Europe sees Blair as a future leader, but has doubts about his country's position.

These real or perceived failings should not be allowed, however, to obscure the very real and important ways in which Blair has changed the direction of British politics at home and abroad. He has done enough to suggest that he has the qualities needed to be an outstanding statesman in Britain, Europe and the World. Whether he will become so regarded will depend, I believe, on how he now deals with three great challenges which face him. One is domestic. He has nailed his flag to the complete and successful restructuring of the main public services – Health and Education – and his domestic policy will be judged on the results of this.

The other two challenges pertain to his standing in Europe and in the wider world. The first of these two is of course whether or not he can be the first British Prime Minister to lead his people into the position which they held quite naturally until the sixteenth century. This is the position of recognising that they hold several important identities at the same time. They are Welsh, Northern Irish, Scottish or English; they are all British; they are also all Europeans; and they are also citizens of the world. Blair has already moved, by devolution of powers, towards getting them to recognize their first two identities. The next major step is the recognition that they really are Europeans and have been for much the greater part of their history. If he can achieve this, then he will be able to lead them into acceptance of monetary unity with the rest of Europe, which is a vital stage forward in the planned development of a newly united Europe. Britain has been the only major player in European politics to contract out of this so far. Now a decision has to be made which will be vital to Britain's becoming a 'leading and central player' in Europe, which Blair has already identified as one of his main aims.

Blair has been quite clear about his own positive attitude to Europe, especially in his speeches outside England. Significantly it was in Scotland (May, 2001) that he became the first British Prime Minister in four centuries to openly attack the 'Great Myth' about the English past in a speech which rather neatly summarised the theme of *The English Nation: The Great Myth*. He gave a new interpretation of what 'patriotism' means for the British. He said that Britain was a nation which had:

'ancient European roots stamped through and through, dating as far back as St. Augustine's mission to Kent and the Roman invasion . . . London was a great European city in Roman times . . . Edinburgh was a jewel of European civilization in the Middle Ages'.[47]

and he added, a little defiantly, perhaps with an English audience in mind:

> 'We are all products of that history, whether we like it or not'.[48]

He stressed that it was a mythical patriotism which sought to isolate Britain from Europe. Patriotism in the twenty first century 'centred on Britain's key alliance with Europe'. The Tories saw Europe as 'the source of all our problems', but:

> 'such isolation is not standing up for Britain. It is relegating Britain to the sidelines of a Europe in which British jobs and influence are intimately engaged'.[49]

Then, in his speech to the New Labour Party Conference at Blackpool, in October, 2002, he spoke briefly but strikingly and very revealingly on the matter of accepting the 'Euro' and entering the single European currency:

> 'It is our destiny to do so'.[50]

There is no doubt now that Blair himself understands the true nature of the English past and sees re-entering Europe as a return to our deepest roots.

Yet Blair has not really started to involve the great British public in a serious debate on the matter. They are, at the moment, subject to the whimsical changes of the economic climate for their views on the matter. As I write the latest gallop polls indicate a majority of the public against the 'Euro'. One of the main reasons seems to be the fact that British tourists have perceived that prices have increased in continental hotels and restaurants as these have exploited the coming of the 'Euro' to 'round-up' their figures and so benefit from this 'one-off' situation. This happened also when the metric system was introduced. It is the sort of ephemeral factor which ought not to be a serious consideration in a debate of such epoch-making importance. There is also the natural opposition engendered, at a subliminal level, by four centuries of exposure to the 'Great Myth' of the English past, acting as a psychological barrier against any notion of 'giving away' part of our 'immemorial national and independent sovereignty'.

The debate concerning the 'Euro' really does represent a turning point of profound importance in British history. The quality of that debate up until now has been very poor – with no mention at all of the real nature and purpose of the movement for European unity. Even from Tony Blair, we have only heard in detail the structure of the famous five economic 'tests', designed by Gordon Brown, to ensure that Britain will not lose out economically by joining the 'Euro'. The only mention of a more transcendent factor has been Blair's somewhat mysterious phrase uttered very recently – 'It is our destiny'.[51] What did he mean? No one seems to have inquired. Could it have been only a throw-away, 'off the cuff' remark? – or something which he feels about most deeply.

In my view the European vision of life without war, which is at the heart of the Union, has a somewhat better chance of being accepted by most human beings, than most visions have - if it can be shown to be possible. I have no doubt that the Welsh, Scottish and Irish people would support it very readily. 'Subsidiarity' means great gains for them, in terms of their own culture and prosperity in any case, as has been demonstrated by what has happened in Eire, Luxembourg, Portugal and Spain, since they joined the Union. I believe that the English people, too, could be equally inspired by and attracted to the vision of a lasting peace in Europe (with England part of it), if they were given a chance to understand what was really behind the European Union.

This would be especially the case if it were demonstrated that the European Union has proved to be the most successful attempt in history, to establish a lasting peace in Europe; and perhaps, potentially - by example and by the extension of the principles involved - in the world. The English, I believe, could forgo their renowned scepticism and ironic detachment if the facts were put before them; if they understood the real nature of their own history; and if they could perceive a truly inspiring role for their own country in the world of the new millennium.

England 'lost an Empire and failed to find a role', in the second half of the twentieth century. The 'glory' days of empire and world supremacy proved to have been transitory and to have cost the loss of millions of lives of ordinary people, together with the misery and disruption inflicted on many more. But now a scene is opening out at the beginning of the new Millennium, when there is the opportunity for Britain (including the English) to assume a role which is infinitely more noble and inspiring than any before.

Europe has been the main 'shaper' of World history in the last few centuries[52] and, with the help hopefully of the USA, it has the vision, ideas and influence to continue exercising such an influence. Britain, with its experience of Commonwealth, the influence of the English language, its world-wide prestige, its special relationship with the world's greatest super-power, its Christian heritage and the values now stemming from it, has the opportunity of taking a leadership role in Europe. Britain also happens to have a leader now with the necessary global vision, the eloquence to proclaim it and the will to implement it in practice.

Not since the days of Bede, Boniface and King Alfred, has Britain had the chance to play such an inspiring role in Europe. The British, being a pragmatic nation, will need some solid pieces of evidence to support any visionary proposal. This is there for them in the evidence of a 'miracle' which has happened in a previously war-torn and weary Europe – the coming of a lasting peace and prosperity, built on human rights and democratic principles. The English, I believe, could be enthused in the face of a really worth-while project which already has a good track record for success. All this is dependent, however, on their being able to show that they have, at last, really understood what is happening in Europe and genuinely want to become part of it. This can only happen if Britain decides in the coming referendum that they want to participate in the essential next step of a single monetary currency in Europe – which, in many ways will help to bring European countries even closer together as well as leading to greater prosperity. If the answer is 'yes', then the British will begin to understand more of the realities of Europe, to feel part of it, and to experience a sense of ownership of the vision. They have a great deal to offer. It is time for Tony Blair to use his inspiring qualities to revivify the British people with a new sense of enthusiasm. He has to show them the real reasons why Britain should accept the single monetary system in Europe. The British people will respond, I think, under the right leadership, and have a chance to show their mettle.

It is a part of a process of human development which all peoples will experience. The world of the third millennium will need its citizens to have multiple identities, to respond to the needs of the new 'global village', while retaining all those 'distinct qualities' and 'glorious individuality' which are important parts of their humanity. The days of narrowly confined and constricted nationalism are over. The British people were once Europeans as well for the greatest part of their history. They will now need to show themselves capable of becoming people with several identities. The Human Rights Act will help, culturally as well as legislatively to establish a new global climate for all citizens of the world. The willingness to adopt a multi-identity approach, is going to be an essential part of world citizenship in the third Millennium.

Only after Tony Blair has led his country into becoming fully part of Europe can he achieve his second aim of seeing Britain become the 'pivotal bridge' between Europe and the USA – another of his stated aims. This is enormously important for various reasons. The great difficulty and the great opportunity in the situation lie together in the unquestionable fact of reality – the position of the USA as easily the most powerful nation on earth. The USA suffers from the 'English disease'. From the time the Pilgrim Fathers first settled in America in the seventeenth century, they and their successors have thought of their new country as 'superior', 'indifferent', 'special' – with a divine mission of leadership in the world.[53] English people were taught to think in the same way from the sixteenth century onwards,[54] but have now had to face the truth, in the second half of the twentieth century – that, basically they are of the same value as everyone else. Historical and geographical factors were ultimately responsible for making first England and then the USA the most powerful nations on earth; and the USA is still in this position.

This feeling still exists in the Bush Administration which tends to think that there is some sort of moral legitimacy inherent in this supreme power. It is always difficult in any case for the possessor of supreme power to refrain from using it. There is also the temptation to think and sometimes act as if the normal rules which apply to everyone else do not apply to Americans, for what the latter perceive to be good reasons. This is especially the perception of the European Union, since the Bush Administration has proved itself to be extraordinarily 'protectionist' and 'self-interested' from its inception. This Administration, for example, has insisted on maintaining tariffs to protect its steel industry against the 'open market' approach adopted by the European Union. It has contracted out of the anti-ballistic missile agreement, against European wishes; refused to sanction the targets set at Kyoto and ratified by all countries of the European Union, to protect the world's climate against the over-production of carbon gases; refused to ratify targets to reduce unfair trading methods which exploit the poor and developing countries of the world (as recently at Johannesburg,

2002); and has threatened the disruption of the new International Criminal Court, set up in 1998 by the Treaty of Rome (for the apprehension of criminals against humanity) and long desired by the European Union, by insisting that USA citizens uniquely be exempted from its jurisdiction.

Terrorism has been the most recent threat to humanity and since the terrible events of 11th Sept. 2001, Bush has declared war against the 'axis of evil' – countries which harbour or assist terrorists. His threat of taking unilateral action has been set aside by the persuasion of Blair – much appreciated by the European Union – and others; and by the UN's supportive resolution to insist on Saddam Hussein's acceptance of the weapons inspectors who will search Iraq for evidence of biological, chemical weapons or nuclear potential. These inspectors have just started their work there (26th Nov. 2002).

The European Union is also completely opposed to terrorism, but has less faith in crude military strength, unilaterally employed by the strongest power against weaker regimes, as the successful key to the situation. The pursuit of justice is always right, but the use of reprisal, in the form of unmitigated force used against the innocent and guilty, is politically inept. It does not help to rid the world of terrorism which has its breeding ground in the bitterness and resentment already felt by weaker, backward and often exploited countries, against the rich and powerful people. The European Union and Blair wish to solve all problems, according to the template which the former has used in Europe and the latter in N. Ireland – endless and patient negotiation. If force is necessary, according to the criteria of a 'just war', then it should be used only with the sanction of the United Nations Security Council, the only body representing the whole world as opposed to any particular vested interests; and therefore able to use legitimised force for the common good. One hopes now that Iraq will comply with all the demands set out in the UN Resolution.

All this has been a severe test for Tony Blair's political abilities. So far he has used his pivotal role to very good purpose. He has proved himself to be Bush's 'best friend' on the international scene, acting strongly and supportively in defence of America after the unprecedented attack of 11th September, 2001. He bolstered the USA's action against the Al-Qaida and the Taliban regime in Afghanistan. He has convinced the rest of the world of the great danger to everyone imposed by the international terrorist network. He has repeatedly warned the world of the danger represented by the stock of illegal weapons which Saddam Hussein is suspected of having and indeed has used in the past against his own people.

Yet few can doubt now that it is Blair's strong and persistent influence which has played an important part in dissuading Bush from using his great power to destroy Saddam Hussein and his regime in Iraq, by unilateral action. Blair knows that it is essential that Bush should act through the UN, in order to avoid a possible 'war of civilizations' in the Middle East. Yet he knows that Hussein wants to split the western alliance and that only the knowledge of impending disaster in the form of an American attack, has held him back from defying the West. Blair has been walking a tight rope with great skill, holding the alliance together and keeping both the European Union and the USA on side, though their natural methods of approach differ greatly.

The events of Friday, 8th November, 2002 were a considerable tribute to Blair's prestige, patience and skill. The fifteen members of the Security Council of the United Nations, representing the whole world, including Syria who stood for the Arab countries, voted unanimously to accept the Resolution that Iraq must either disarm or be disarmed.

If this strategy succeeds, it may well come to be regarded again as epoch-making. Blair's faith in the United Nations and his important influence in Washington, were vindicated. It was certainly a diplomatic triumph for the Bush-Blair approach; but also much more than that. Blair's role as a pivotal force for good in the world - in this case between Europe and America – was exercised at the highest level and achieved a result of great importance for the world. His method of patient negotiation and determination, was proved to be very effective at the highest level. The strength, credence and status of the United Nations reached an unprecedented peak of importance, which will be of great significance in world history. The USA acted, almost in spite of itself and after 'chafing at the bit' for quite a time, in a way which increased its world prestige greatly. It held back its massive strength, and put it at the disposal of the proper, representative and legal authority, in terms of international law.

All this could augur well for the future. The USA had got used to the methodology of unilateral action, which seemed to get them what they wanted. But now we are in a different world, and the USA has experienced circumstances getting out of hand in the face of global terrorism. Sharon is discovering the same in his futile attempts to crush terrorism in Palestine by mighty force. One hopes that

President Bush will have gained from the experience of seeing how effective in the present world scene, is the tactic of working through the UN. The UN itself will benefit from being able to have a substantial core to its 'international police force', willing to act at its behest to establish peace in troubled areas. Bush may, hopefully, taste and see that this is the best way of dealing with terrorism. The next use of this methodology could be to establish the mutual recognition of Israel and the Palestinians' right to exist separately as independent states, with borders returning to the 1969 arrangement according to the Oslo Agreement. This is certainly high on Blair's agenda as a priority issue. He wants a grand settlement of this issue which is probably the singly most important part of the Middle East problem. Up to date, Bush has simply concentrated primarily on getting rid of Saddam Hussein. It may well be that he will come to see these two issues in different perspective.

One of the main factors in the world situation at the moment is the attitude of the USA, given the supreme military power which it holds. The USA, at the deepest level, has a Christian heritage of its own. It is a democratic and pluralist society which believes in toleration and the separation of Church and State. There are fundamental values which Europe, Blair and the USA hold together. The one great difference lies in their attitude to power and military might. At this moment (27 Nov. 2002), the USA has slipped into a role – putting its power at the service of the UN – which is incomparably more reputable, noble and beneficial to its own security as well as that of the world at large, than its unilateral interventions abroad in the second half of the twentieth century. Many of these latter actions – in Latin America and the Middle East and Asia – have been perceived by some as 'throwing its weight around' and have built up resentments and enmities against the USA. Its perceived unilateral support of Israel against the Palestinians may be seen by future historians as one of the root causes of the terrorism instigated in various parts of the world by the 'enemies of America' and culminating in the horrors of II September, 2001.

If the USA could change its attitude and policy, recognize the merits of the European strategy for peace, listen carefully to its good friend, Tony Blair, and regard its own mighty power as something which needs to be safely confined to multilateral action, at the behest of the UN, then the USA could find its own proper role in the new world of the third Millennium. Combining its great strength, with the philosophy of the European Union and with

Tony Blair occupying a pivotal role between them, the trio could represent a great influence for disseminating democracy, justice, freedom and human rights in the world at large.

This becomes more of a possibility when we realise that there is a great deal of opposition in the USA itself against the old attitudes. General Wesley Clarke, former Supreme Commander of Allied Forces in Western Europe, Richard Holbrook the USA ambassador to the UN under Clinton, are just two notable examples of those who opposed the idea of unilateral war with Iraq. Christian groups in the USA, such as the Catholic bishops and the leader of Bush's own Baptist denomination, spoke against it; and Al Gore, the presidential rival made a very blunt speech in opposition to it (Sept. 2002):

'After September 11, we had enormous sympathy, goodwill and support around the world. We've squandered that and in one year we've replaced that with fear, anxiety and uncertainty, not at what the terrorists are going to do, but at what we are going to do'.[55]

Many Americans have been affected by the old 'English disease' – thinking of themselves as 'chosen', different and superior people[52] but this myth cannot survive long into the inter-dependent 'global' age in which we are now living. Perhaps we are at the point when it will be left behind both in England and in America. Perhaps this is another area in which Tony Blair can offer some good advice to President Bush.

Tony Blair, is a political moralist with strong views about making the world a better place to live in for everyone. He believes that ultimately we are all inter-dependent in the global system of the modern world. What is harming one country cannot fail eventually to have harmful effects in all others. Beneficial action taken in one country cannot fail to improve the lot of others as well. This is an extension into secular politics of the Christian economy of the effects of good and bad actions in the world. Blair would have been very receptive, therefore, to a message sent to him by Cardinal Hume, on behalf of all the English and Welsh Catholic bishops, just before he took up his one year's term as President of the European Union in January, 1998. Cardinal Hume hoped that Europe would continue its progress with the cardinal principles of *solidarity* and *subsidiarity*, as set out in the Maastricht Treaty (1992) firmly in mind. He went on to warn against the development of a 'Fortress

Europe' mentality of protecting and securing itself agains the 'outside' world:

> 'We share and respect creation with all the peoples of the world; we recognise the image of God in peoples of differing cultures; and we are brothers and sisters who care for those who belong to us.'[56]

This is a clear example of where political thinking and Christian values were exactly on the same wave-length.

The vision presented by the European Union, in spite of many obstacles still to be overcome, represents an inspiring way forward for Europe and the World at large. It is expanding rapidly. In 2004 the ten eastern European countries (together with Malta and Cyprus) will be accepted into the Union, greatly increasing its population to about 500 million. This will mean the unification of eastern and western Europe, according to the principles of *solidarity* and *subsidiarity*. The material standard of life in the east will be brought up to western standards. In turn, western Europe, itself blighted spiritually by intensely materialistic standards, should gain from the spiritual heritage and experience of countries, like Poland. They have suffered much and know the importance of human values, to which science, technology and political power, should always be subservient. Such experience will be invaluable to a 'people's Europe' in Tony Blair's phrase. He is a foremost supporter of the extension of the European Union in this way.

The next great extension of these principles could well be into areas where other cultures and other religious heritages prevail. The vision is not restricted by geography. It is becoming increasingly clear that the future of these cultures could depend greatly on their ability to develop in ways which makes them compatible with the needs of the modern world. Most of these societies would, of course, be outside the European geographical hegemony; but there is one notable exception.

Turkey is very anxious to join the Union and represents a very interesting case. Its application has not been considered to have much chance of success because of its poor human rights record, and its political and economic conditions. The recent elections in Turkey (31 Oct. 2002) swept aside the old parties and brought the new 'Justice and Development Party' into power. Its leader, Tayyip Erdogan is a devout Muslim who has been Mayor of Instabul. He claims to have thrown off the old Euro-scepticism in his own politics. He wishes to join with the secularist parties in trying to persuade the European Union to accept Turkey's application to join. If the Union follows its original intention in debarring Turkey, it could well strengthen the anti-western groups there; and might cause social and political violence. Perhaps the Union could reconsider Turkey's application.

Turkey is a considerable Sunni Muslim country of 67 million people. Its position, between the Black Sea and the Mediterranean, bounded to the east by the USSR and Iran and to the south by Iraq and Syria, makes it an important link between Europe and the Muslim world. Very recently (16 Nov. 2002), Abdullah Gul, a proxy prime minister for Mr Erdogan[57] was installed, as his Islamic-rooted Justice and Development Party announced sweeping plans for economic and social reforms to meet European standards. This could become the first Muslim society organised on this basis.

If this were to be successful, it would be a model of immense importance to the whole Muslim world. The *Arab Human Development Report* (UNDP, New York, 2002), written by Arabs, recommended the need of just such changes if the Arab countries were to succeed in the modern world.[58] Since 2000 Turkey has abolished the death penalty, reformed its civil code, restored civil rights in the Kurdish provinces and lifted the ban of Kurdish broadcasting – all in an attempt to comply with EU demands. Very recently (9th Nov. 2002), the EU enlargement commissioner, Guenter Verheugen said 'the new Turkish Government must put an immediate end to torture, prosecute those accused of human rights abuses and free political dissidents.'[59]

Valéry Giscard d'Estaing of France, writing in *Le Monde*, objects to Turkey joining the EU, because it is an 'asiatic state' which would be a threat to the EU. It would 'press for Morocco and other Middle East states to be admitted until the whole concept of Europe would become meaningless'.[60] EU officials, however, have reassured the new Muslim-based Turkish Government that it could still be admitted eventually, as long as it met the entry requirements required of all candidate states, whether Christian or not.[61] The situation demonstrates how attractive the European Union is becoming to other cultures. If Turkey continues to act favourably towards EU requirements, it would be a real opportunity for 'development' in Turkey and perhaps more widely in the Middle East.

The influence of a statesman with Tony Blair's wide and deep, global vision is sorely needed by Europe in this sort of situation; but his influence in Europe is limited because Britain, so far, has still not acted in a way which convinces Europeans that it is now committedly European in its approach. On the important matter of a unitary monetary system, Britain is still perceived, on this issue, to be judging things *solely* in its own interests, without regard to other and wider considerations.

Similarly on another important matter for the European Union, Blair's influence is much needed. Most of the European countries recognize that there has to be drastic reform of the Common Agricultural Policy by which subsidies are used to protect farming interests, particularly in France. They all realize that something has to be done about this to meet the legitimate demands of the ten eastern European countries expected to enter in 2004. Blair is probably the foremost statesman, thinking also of the effects of this 'protectionist' policy on developing countries such as Africa, which are prevented by these subsidies from exporting their main – sometimes their only – saleable produce to Europe.

This explains the 'blazing row' which took place at the end of October (2002) between Blair and Jacques Chirac when the latter went back on deals made with the World Trade Organisation at Doha, to liberalise European trade to help the world's poor. Blair has a passionate commitment to help developing countries and this showed in a real display of emotion. Here is a situation where Europe needs Blair's influence to guide it in a direction which it must take sooner or later in any case. But here again, Blair can hardly exercise proper influence when he himself is leading a country which has not as yet committed itself to the 'euro'. Acceptance of the 'Euro' has become an important 'litmus test' as to the truly European commitment of the British people.

Blair's influence as a 'pivotal bridge' between Europe and the USA will again be very much needed when the problem of Iraq is resolved and the much more centrally important question of a settlement between Israel and the Palestinians has to be decided. There is no doubt from his many statements on the subject, that Blair (and Europe) sees the solution in terms of re-establishing the Oslo Agreement by which Israel would have to withdraw from its 'occupied' Palestinian territories and allow the establishment of two mutually recognized and independent states of Palestine and Israel, living alongside one another in peace. This is the only settlement which could restore lasting peace to the area. The USA has held the greatest lever of power in the area, especially over Israel. The obvious and sensible step forward, now, is for the United Nations to step in, supported by the USA, Europe and all other interested parties, to solve the problem. Israel has already failed to meet past UN resolutions. The USA is perceived by Europe as favouring Israel and thus dangerously antagonising the Arabs.

Tony Blair could play an extremely important part again in his 'pivotal' role between Europe and the USA. He would be regarded by all reasonable people as a neutral observer. He condemns terrorism, but he also condemns the causes of terrorism. He has visited the area himself to speak both to the Israeli leaders and to Yasser Arafat, leader of the Palestinians; in fact he has met the latter on more occasions than any other western leader. The peaceful settlement of this problem in the middle east could do more than any other single action, to eliminate the causes of terrorism and to avoid the 'clash of civilizations' mentality.

* * *

Blair's task now must be that of educating his own people, to enable them to come to a proper understanding of the vision which the European Union has for its own role in the world of the new millennium. A comcomitant of this is that Britain would need to shed once and for all the last vestiges of insularity and isolation which the 'Great Myth' of the English past has cultivated and sustained so successfully for the last four centuries. Only then can Britain grasp the opportunity of taking a leading role in helping Europe to achieve its own vision of a United European 'brotherhood of peoples', living in lasting peace and prosperity together. Only then, too, could Britain play its full part in helping to extend the vision of peace, toleration, justice, human rights, democracy and freedom under international law, to other parts of the 'global village' which the multi-ethical, multi-cultural and pluralist society of the world of the third Millennium is becoming.

It seems that the various aspects of this vision are going to be encapsulated in the bid to gain the support of the British for a 'yes' vote in the national referendum which may possibly take place in 2003 on whether or not the nation accepts the single European monetary system – 'Euro' – as its own. It will be of great practical significance, bringing together even more closely, more simply and transparently, the economic system of Europe, for everyone's benefit. If there is a positive result, it will symbolise that the British will have at last recovered their self-conscious identity – for the first time since the sixteenth century – as a great European, as well as a distinctively British, and then English, Welsh, Irish or Scottish people. It will constitute a watershed in British history, appropriately enough at the beginning of this new Millennium.

Tony Blair is the youngest, most visionary and most moralistic statesman among world leaders at this time. He has more 'standing', in the sense of personal prestige, than any other political leader; and has developed into an outstanding orator. He has the ability as a global thinker and man of action, to contribute largely and importantly to the development of Britain and the outside world in the path of peaceful living. There is about him, too, mixed in with human weaknesses, a certain passionate sincerity and inspirational quality which is badly needed in a world grown indifferent to politics. This, I believe, accounts for his extraordinary success in Britain and outside it, in terms of public acceptance.

As is always the case with political moralists, he can be accused of inconsistency and imperfections. He knows, for example, that he can do little at the moment about Russia's treatment of Chechnya or China's offences against human rights, though both these nations are making some progress[62] through greater contact with the West. Sometimes, too, it has been difficult to disentangle Britain – in the transitional state of arms dealing – from previous agreements to supply, for example, Hawk jets to Zimbabwe or the USA with special parts for planes which have been sent later by the USA to Israel. It is good that political opponents bring up these charges against the Government, to keep it on the defensive in such matters. It was Robin Cook, however, who, when he was Foreign Minister, who tried to give some perspective. He listed the guiding principles of Government foreign policy in 2000 as: building more bridges and fewer barriers; confirming that the global interest now becomes the national interest; extending global values such as democracy and human rights; confirming the belief that the greater Britain's standing is in Europe, the greater it will be in the world; and making it clear that the most immediate challenges to all countries were now transnational forces which needed to be dealt with at an international level. Then he added:

'I flatly reject the cynical view that, because we cannot make the world perfect, we should give up on trying to make it better . . . The obligation on us is not to put everything right, but to do what we can to make a difference. We will therefore take every realistic step to pursue diplomacy for democracy'.[63]

The political moralist must insist that the end does not justify the means. He knows, however, that practical politics is often limited by the art of the possible and prudence has to be exercised in considering the practical effects of certain actions. In my view Blair is a sincere Christian Democrat who is trying to take his country with him in the noble task of making Britain and the outside world a better place in which people can improve their quality of life. He has brought moral qualities and a global vision into British politics, which, if he can gain the support of the British people in the coming referendum, will change its direction and establish a new and more important role for Britain in the twenty-first century.

This new role will have a vital continuity with the Christian values which lie at the root of our civilization; but these will be developed and expressed in a way which makes them increasingly relevant to the needs of the modern world in the new Millennium. Tony Blair, then, is following the sage words of Alfred the Great who founded the English nation on Christian values and stated that they would 'provide the only sure basis for its survival against all nihilistic enemies in the present and the future'.[64]

* * *

When Victor Hugo expressed so confidently the vision of the future contained in the heading to this Afterword in 1849, it must have appeared realistically impossible for it to ever be realized. Similarly, it would have been impossible for a British person to imagine in 1849 that a new system would be established in Britain by which the wealth of the country would be brought in (by income tax) and redistributed to ensure a minimum standard of living and health service for everyone – there would have been too many difficulties barring the way for it ever to happen.

Now, in 2002, we are in the privileged position of seeing Hugo's vision and those of others, taking shape before our eyes. The world is in many ways a much smaller place now than Europe was in Hugo's time. A Continent now is a much smaller place than a nation was then. Enormous developments in transport, communication and information technology have made the world into what we now call a 'global village'. I believe that great things are possible if world leaders follow certain paths which are becoming increasingly clear as alternatives to any catastrophic 'clash of civilizations'.[65] It will be possible to achieve remarkable goals if modern technology is used as a means of improving the world's quality of life. Imagine, for example, global values such as *solidarity, subsidiarity, democracy* and *human rights*, guiding and using modern technology, to establish a cosmopolitan redistribution of the world's adequate wealth to ensure a minimum standard of life and health service for everyone. There will be many difficulties to overcome; but I do not see it as impossible.

'Without a vision, the people perish'. It may be fitting, then, to conclude this postscript with a new and even greater vision for the third millennium, and with only a slight alteration of Hugo's words:

'There will come a time when you Europe, you Asia, you Africa and you, America, all you Continents of the world, without losing your distinct qualities, your glorious individuality, will merge into a higher unity and form the world-wide human family'.

Edwin Jones,
Swansea,
April 2003

Notes

1. Cf. below, pp. 159–60. It was the purpose of stained glass windows in medieval England to praise God and teach the Christian faith as part of the community's way of handing on their values from one generation to another, in the church which was the centre of community life: 'they proclaim the central truths of the Christian religion in a direct and public manner', S. Brown and D. O'Connor, *Medieval Craftsmen, Glass Painters* (British Museum Press, 1991), p. 11.

2. Cf. 'Protestantism became destructive, and, from the viewpoint of those who love what they see, was an unmitigated disaster', K. Clarke, *Civilization* (BBC and John Murray, 1969–70), p. 159. The same sentiments are in A. Graham-Dixon, *A History of British Art* (BBC Books, 1996).

3. S.A. Kierkegaard, *Enter-Eller/Either-or* (1843). He was a Danish philosopher (1813–55), considered to be the founder of modern Existentialism, which exaggerated the isolation of the individual in order to stress his/her importance in the modern world of mass industrialization. The great 'heresy' of the second half of the twentieth century in England has been the imbalance created by an emphasis on extreme individualism at the expense of community values, which are in fact essential for the well-being of the individual as well as society. Cf. 'Other people are my enemy' (Jean-Paul Sartre); 'There is no such thing as society' (Margaret Thatcher). Cf. 'Before the upsurge of economic individualism in the 1980s came the even more widespread "me-firstism" in the 1960s. All classes were affected. The civic spirit thing was replaced by the free-spirit thing', Peregrine Worsthorne's Essay, *Daily Telegraph*, 19 April 1997.

4. Cf. 'if we want a new start we must look to the past', Melvyn Bragg, *Speak for England* (Book Club Associates, 1976), introduction, p. 1. Bragg describes how, in a moment of personal crisis, he returns to his roots in order to make his vital decision.

5. T.S. Eliot stated in his *Notes Towards the Definition of Culture* (Faber, 1948) that all meaningful cultures had a core of religious beliefs at their centre. Cf. 'To deny the necessity of a united Church was in effect to deny that there was such a thing as society. . . . In 1500 it was the Church, rather than anything else which turned individuals into a society', C. Russell, *The Oxford Illustrated History of Tudor and Stuart Britain*, ed. J. Morrill (Oxford University Press, 1996), p. 258.

PREFACE

1. For the power of 'artificial' or 'collective' memory, see S. Rose, *The Making of Memory* (Bantam Press, 1992), pp. 326–7. Cf. '"invented traditions" seek to establish continuity with a suitable past', Eric Hobsbawm, *The Invention of Tradition*, ed. E. Hobsbawm and T. Ranger, (Cambridge University Press, 1983), p. 2. Cf. D. Marquand believes that it would be difficult to invent an English identity from traditions preceding the Acts of Union with Wales, Ireland and Scotland, and preceding the Empire. See *Uniting the Kingdom? The Making of British History*, ed. A. Grant and K.J. Stringer (Routledge, 1995).
2. See R. Rex, 'The crisis of obedience: God's word and Henry's Reformation', *The Historical Journal*, 39 (41), 1996. Cromwell borrowed the idea from William Tyndale, *The Obedience of a Christian Man* (1527), to justify the Act of Supremacy (1534), see ibid., p. 881. Rex says that 'the new prominence henceforth accorded to obedience by the Henrician regime is for the first time thoroughly explored in this paper', ibid., p. 863.
3. Cf. 'England once lay in the mainstream of European development and after the sixteenth century it became an eccentric tributary', V. Bogdanor, 'Remembering and Forgetting', *Twentieth Century British History*, vol. 7, No. 2 (Oxford University Press, 1996), p. 256.
4. Cf. 'The English do not need nationalism and do not like it; they are so sure of themselves that they need hardly discuss the matter', *Englishness, Politics and Culture, 1880–1920*, ed. R. Colls and P. Dodd (Beckenham, Crown Helm, 1986), Preface.
5. *Nationalisms in Europe 1915 to the Present*, ed. S. Woolf, (Routledge, 1996), p. 1.
6. Ibid., p. 2. 'the most consistent thread of [Enoch] Powellite philosophy has been the advocacy of the nation state as the fundamental and the truest expression of collective identity', Editorial, *Daily Telegraph*, 19 April 1997.
7. Cf. pp. 235, 252.
8. E.J. Hobsbawm, *Nations and Nationalism since 1780* (Cambridge University Press, 1990, 2nd edn 1997). A. Hastings, *The Construction of Nationhood* (Cambridge University Press, 1997), pp. 1–66. For the complexity of this subject, see the different approaches taken in *Concepts of National Identity in the Middle Ages*, ed. S. Forde, L. Johnson and A.V. Murray (Leeds Studies in English, 1995). I believe it is simplest and safest to see it as the medieval people did. Cf. p. 252.
9. J. Bossy convincingly renounces the very term 'Reformation', with its implications of an improved form of Christianity replacing an inferior sort, *Christianity and the West, 400–1700* (Oxford University Press, 1985). A.G. Dickens stresses the importance of the Lollards as precursors of the Reformation, 'The Abortive Reformation', *The English Reformation* (Batsford, 1964), ch. 2. C. Haigh argues that there were

several reformations, all of which were political except for one evangelical strand, *English Reformations* (Oxford, 1993). P. Collinson says that Protestant England was not born until well into Elizabeth's reign, *The Birthpangs of Protestant England* (Macmillan, 1992). G.R. Elton, in his various works, J. Scarisbricke, *Henry VIII* (Eyre and Spottiswoode, 1968), and E. Duffy, *The Stripping of the Altars* (Yale University Press, 1992), all maintain the view of the Reformation as a revolution imposed by government and enacted by parliamentary statue under Henry VIII. D. Loades has recently confirmed its revolutionary nature in his *Revolution in Religion. The Reformation in England, 1530–1570* (University of Wales Press, 1994). Certainly the revolution, by state enactment (1532–6), created the conditions from which Protestantism and other features such as sectarianism, individualism and secularization were to emerge.

10. Modern nationalism, stressing the supremacy of the individual state, is a very different phenomenon from the medieval sense of Englishry or patriotism which sat easily alongside belonging to the Universal Church and the Christian culture of Europe. Erastianism, or the supremacy of the State over the Church in ecclesiastical matters as in all else, is named after the Swiss Protestant advocate of this position, Thomas Erastus (1524–83).

11. This idea was actually born among certain English Protestant refugees who had fled to Antwerp in 1525 to escape Henry's wrath against heretics. It was different in origin, therefore, from the official view of the past, but soon became part of it with the intervention of John Bale, see below, pp. 50–1.

12. Cf. 'The use of the term "English" as a synonym for "British" is more than just a slovenly application of the word, but represents a series of assumptions about the central right of England to speak for Britain, and by the imposed silence, the inability of the Welsh, Irish and Scottish races to challenge effectively those assumptions . . . it reproduces the imperial philosophy in which the mother country represents the greater whole', K. Lunn, 'Reconsidering Britishness', *National Identity in Contemporary Europe*, ed. B. Jenkins and Spyrus A. Sofos, (Routledge, 1991), p. 87. Cf. 'When the *Oxford History of England* was launched a generation ago, "England" was still an all-embracing word. It meant indiscriminately England and Wales, Great Britain, the United Kingdom and even the British Empire', A.J.P. Taylor, *English History, 1914–1945* (Oxford University Press, 1965, repr. 1992), p. v. Cf. 'The English use Britain as a synonym for England', J. Morrill, *The British Problem, 1534–1707*, ed. B. Bradshaw and J. Morrill (Macmillan, 1996), p. 10. For further reading on this matter, see C. Harvey, *Cultural Weapons. Scotland's Survival in the New Europe* (Abacus, 1992); H. Kearney, *The British Isles. A History of Four Nations* (Cambridge University Press, 2nd edn 1994), p. 320; M. Hughes, *Divided Ireland. The Roots of the*

Modern Irish Problem (University of Wales Press, 1994). M. Hechter's *Internal Colonialism. The Celtic Fringe in British National Development, 1536–1966* (Berkeley and Los Angeles, 1975) is the fullest account of the assimilation of the Celtic countries into the English hegemony. See also K. Robbins, *Nineteenth Century Britain. Integration and Diversity* (Oxford University Press, 1988). For a rather different account, which suggests more cohesive factors behind the creation of the 'British nation', see L. Colley, *Britons. The Forging of the Nation, 1707–1837* (Yale University Press, 1992). The complexity of the issue and the different views about it are portrayed by the various contributors to *The British Problem: 1534–1707*, ed. B. Bradshaw and J. Morrill.

13. F.W. Maitland has been described recently as 'the greatest of Cambridge scholars', C.N.L. Brooke, in his foreword to Z.N. Brooke, *The English Church and the Papacy* (Cambridge University Press, new edition 1989), p. xiii; and even more recently as 'arguably the greatest of all historians of medieval England', *The Companion to British History*, ed. J. Gardiner and M. Wenfeld (Collins and Brown, 1995), p. 493; and 'By common consent . . . one of the great British historians', *The Oxford Companion to British History*, ed. J. Cannon (Oxford University Press, 1997), p. 609.

14. John 10:10.

15. For a convenient summary of the documents of the Second Vatican Council, see *Outlines of the 16 Documents: Vatican II*, prepared by V.M. Heffernan (Fowler Wright Books, 1968). For an authoritative analysis of Christian humanism, see *The Mind of Pius XII*, ed. R.C. Pollock (W. Foulsham & Co. Ltd, 1955), especially 'The Complete Man', pp. 13–30. For a perceptive description of the integration of tradition and theology with human experience and contemporary perspectives, see P. Sheldrake *Images of Holiness. Explorations in Contemporary Spirituality* (Darton, Longman and Todd, 1987). For Newman's Christian humanism, see C.S. Dessain, *John Henry Newman* (Nelson, 1966), p. 61.

16. See, for example, *What is History Today?*, ed. J. Gardiner (Macmillan, 1988). Gardiner refers to 'the retreat from faith in impartial truth' and other strands of thought, which have produced a 'new pluralism' in the theory of historiography. For a very capable and convincing response by practising historians, in defence of objective truth, the integrity of history as an independent discipline and the foundations of traditional scholarship, see J. Appleby, L. Hunt and M. Jacob, *Telling the Truth About History* (W.W. Norton Press, USA, 1996): 'A democratic practice of history . . . encourages skepticism about dominant views, but at the same time trusts in the reality of the past and its ultimate knowability.' It is necessary to have 'faith in the ultimate goal of education: the rigorous search for truth usable by all peoples'. The challenges of 'relativism, post-modernism, nihilism and various forms of solipsistic thinking' are dealt with ibid., pp. 11–12, 308. It is noticeable that the 'postmodernist' sceptics such as Rorty, White and, more recently, K.

Jenkins are not themselves practising historians. For another comment on scepticism in general, see J. Horgan: 'What explains this skepticism? For these scientists, as for any other intellectuals, truth-seeking, not truth itself, is what makes life meaningful. . . . Post-modernism stresses that all future revelations will eventually be ephemeral as well. They sacrifice the notion of absolute truth so that they can seek the truth forever', *The End of Science. Facing the limits of Knowledge and the Twilight of the Scientific Age* (Brown and Co., 1997), pp. 271–2. For a neuro-scientist's 'utter rejection' of post-modernist scepticism, see S. Rose, *Making of Memory*, p. 311. Cf. C. Behan McCulloch, *The Truth of History* (Routledge, 1998), pp. 308–9.

17. See *Science*, 15 August 1997.
18. It was in opposition to Bayle and other 'Pyrronistic' sceptics who were challenging the validity of any sort of historical evidence – and thereby the use of history as an independent discipline – that the great Jean Mabillon wrote his *De Re Diplomatica* (1681), which was to be the foundation work for development of the ancillary sciences by which the authenticity of documents could be established. See P. Hazard, *La Crise De La Conscience Européenne 1680–1730* (Paris, 1935), i, chs 1 and 2: Cf. A. Momigliano, 'Ancient History and the Antiquarian', *Warburg Institute Journal*, iii (1950), pp. 286–313. In England, F.W. Maitland pursued his historical research so 'that mankind should believe what is true, and reject what is false' (quoted in D. Andrew Penny, *The Historical Journal*, 40(1), March 1997, p. 123). For John Lingard's attitude on the question, see below, pp. 175–6.
19. Cf. 'There still remains an unresolved, although possibly fruitful dilemma in historical scholarship: whether to continue to address the community of trained historians, or to break out decisively into the popular market which can, arguably, be captured without any loss of critical standards. . . . the French historical profession of the present day has made the decisive breakthrough, whereas its English counterpart has been disinclined to do so', S. Bann, *The Inventions of History. Essays on the Representation of the Past* (Manchester University Press, 1990), p. 13.
20. Sir H. Butterfield to E. Jones, 28 September 1967 (in the author's possession).

INTRODUCTION

1. See, for example, H. Thomas, *Christianity in Roman Britain* (Batsford, 2nd imp., 1993), pp. 355, 362. For influences from Aquitaine, Italy and Byzantium, see C.R. Dodwell, *Anglo-Saxon Art: A New Perspective* (Manchester, 1982). Cf. P. Wormald, 'Aethelwold and his Continental Counterparts', in *Bishop Aethelwell. His Career and Influence*, (Woodbridge, 1988), pp. 13–42; W. Levison, *England and the Continent in the Eighth Century* (Oxford, 1946). From the eighth century: 'within the whole of the settled western world, for all the divergencies

and contrasts in traditions, a social and religious uniformity that looked to Rome . . . was coming into being', H. Loyne in *Welsh Society and Nationhood. Historical Essays presented to Glanmor Williams*, ed. R. Davies, R. Griffiths, I.G. Jones and K.O. Morgan (University of Wales Press, 1984), p. 18. Cf. The need 'to place the English Church of the tenth and the eleventh centuries where it certainly saw itself but is too rarely seen by its later historians: in the mainstream of Western Christendom', V. Ortenberg, *The English Church and the Continent in the Tenth and Eleventh Centuries* (Clarendon Press, 1992), p. 4. For Franco-British cross-fertilization, linguistic and cultural exchange from the seventh century onwards, see *France and the British Isles in the Middle Ages and Renaissance*, ed. G. Jondorf and D.N. Dumville (Boydell Press, 1991). We have become increasingly aware of the strength of the religious, cultural, economic and political links between England and the Continent during the medieval period: see *England in Europe*, ed. N. Saul (Collins and Brown, 1994); and J. Black, *Convergence or Divergence? Britain and the Continent* (Macmillan, 1994).

2. Historians have tended to underestimate the importance of religion in the history and development of societies. Recently there has been a greater recognition of the centrality of religion to a nation's identity, culture, life and history. See, for example, J. Wolffe's *God and Greater Britain, 1843–1945* (Routledge, 1994). C.J. Sommerville, *The Secularization of Early Modern England. From Religious Culture to Religious Faith* (New York, Oxford University Press, 1992), argues that the secularization of English society began with the Reformation. See P. Heath, *The Church and the Shaping of English Society, 1215–1535* (Arnold, 1996), and *Religion and Society in Early Modern Britain*, ed. D. Cressy (Routledge, 1996), both of which show the great influence of the Church on English people. Cf. K. Robbins, *History, Religion and Identity in Modern Britain* (Hambledon Press, 1996), for the role of religion in the development of British identity and 'Britishness' during the modern period of British insularity. Cf. *Religion in Victorian Britain*, ed. J. Wolffe (Manchester University Press, 1997).

3. During the Middle Ages, the Universal Church saw to it that everything had an international dimension. Cf. 'Medieval Christianity coloured men's views at every level', J.M. Roberts, *The Triumph of the West* (BBC, 1985), p. 104. R. Fletcher, *The Conversion of Europe from Paganism to Christianity 371–1386 AD* (HarperCollins, 1997), p. 2.

4. For these details see Bede, *Ecclesiastical History of the English People* (Penguin, 1991), pp. 65, 70. Pelagius (*c.* 360–*c.* 420) was a monk from Wales or Ireland who taught the heresy that man could attain salvation by the exercise of his own will, without the aid of Divine Grace.

5. Cardinal Hume reminded this ecumenical gathering in Canterbury Cathedral that Gregory the Great's successor, John Paul II, in his encyclical *Ut Unum Sint*, asked the help of other church leaders and

theologians to make the Papal role recognized universally as essentially a service of love. Cf. Gregory the Great described himself as 'The servant of the servants of God'.

6. See *Bede, Ecclesiastical History of the English People* pp. 72, 98. Bede writes of Pope Gregory that he had shown so much zeal for the conversion of England, that 'we may rightly call him our own apostle', ibid., p. 98.

7. A letter from Pope John Paul II to 'My Venerable Brother, Cardinal George Basil Hume, 27th May, 1997'. Published in *Catholic Herald*, 23 May 1997.

8. Ibid.

9. C. Dawson, *The Making of Europe* (Sheed and Ward, 1932), p. 211.

10. H.A.L. Fisher, *A History of Modern Europe* (Eyre & Spottiswoode, 3rd imp., 1949), i, p. 151.

11. G.M. Trevelyan, *History of England* (Longman, 1947), p. 78.

12. See N. Saul, 'Medieval England: Identity, Politics and Society', *The Oxford Illustrated History of Medieval England*, ed. N. Saul (Oxford University Press, 1997), pp. 3–4.

13. See J. Bowle, *England. A Portrait* (Readers' Union, Ernest Benn, 1968), p. 17. Cf. *Alfred the Great. Asser's Life* (Penguin, 1983), p. 29. For the most recent edition of the *Chronicle*, see *The Anglo-Saxon Chronicle*, trans. and ed. M. Swanton (J.M. Dent, 1997).

14. J. Bowle, *England*, p. 21.

15. See *The Oxford Companion to English Literature*, ed. M. Drabble (Oxford University Press, 1994), p. 17.

16. Faro was the last Moorish stronghold to be recaptured in 1249. Contrast the situation later, in 1596, when the Earl of Essex burned Faro to the ground and sent the books of the bishop's library there back to the newly founded Bodleian Library in Oxford.

17. His great epic poem, *Lusiads*, described the age of Portuguese exploration 'por mares d'antes navegados' (through seas none had sailed before).

18. D. McCulloch, *Thomas Cranmer* (Yale University Press, 1996), p. 632. Cranmer's *Book of Common Prayer* was to have a great influence in England 'in the realms of language and cultural identity', ibid., p. 630.

19. See Ann Williams, *The English and the Norman Conquest* (Boydell Press, 1995), pp. 218–19. Cf. M. Watkin, 'The French Linguistic Influence in Medieval Wales', *Transactions of the Hon. Society of Cymmrodorion* (1918), pp. 146–222; and a more updated account in Marie Surridge, 'Romance Linguistic Influence in Middle Welsh', *Studia Celtica* (1966). Alongside the Latin and French media for the expression of intellectual and cultural 'Welshry' there was also their own vernacular: 'At the end of the eleventh century, Wales already had a long and distinguished history, unsurpassed as far as vernacular literature was concerned, by any of the emerging states of Western Europe', F.G. Cowley, *The Monastic Order in S. Wales 1066–1349* (University of Wales Press,

1986), p. 139. All these influences were to come together to provide the richness and quality in the work of Dafydd ap Gwilym in the fourteenth century.

20. A. Williams, *English and the Norman Conquest*, pp. 214–15.

21. See below, p. 232.

22. In the 'clas' (monastic group) system in Wales, Welsh scholarship in Latin was of a high calibre. The famous Welsh scholar, Asser (d. 909), was enlisted from St David's to become tutor to King Alfred. He wrote a *Life of Alfred* in Latin (893) and a *Chronicle of English History*. Another example was Gerald of Wales (Giraldus Cambrensis, 1146–1212) who studied at St David's, Paris and Oxford and wrote the *Itinerarium Cambrensis*. Welshmen studied at the Universities of Bologna, Perugia, Rome and Paris, as well as at Cambridge and Oxford (where 400 Welsh names were listed) during the medieval period. The period 1435–1535 was a 'great century' of 'remarkable poetic creativity'. 'Faint echoes' of Continental humanism were heard in the work of Tudor Aled. Richard Whitford of Flintshire was a friend of Thomas More and Erasmus and helped to bring the great Dutch scholar to England in 1499. See C. Davies, *Welsh Literature and the Classical Tradition* (University of Wales Press, 1995), pp. 3–4, 34–5, 52. Cf. Sir Glanmor Williams, *The Reformation and Wales* (Oxford University Press, 1997), p. 30, note 31.

23. See N. Saul, 'Medieval England: Identity, Politics and Society' (Oxford University Press, 1997), pp. 1–5.

24. M.D. Knowles, *Saints and Scholars* (Cambridge University Press, 1962), p. 15.

25. Ibid., pp. 17–18.

26. See *The Complete Works of Geoffrey Chaucer*, ed. W.W. Skeat, (Oxford University Press, 1951), introduction, p. xv.

27. 'The Tale of the Wyf of Bathe', ibid., ed. W.W. Skeat, p. 579.

28. Cf. 'He depicts with tolerance and relish most of the characters since thought typical of England as they jog along the chalk downs to Canterbury in the restless spring', J. Bowle, *England. A Portrait*, p. 57. This was the time of year: 'Than longen folk to goon pilgrimages . . . To Caunterbury they wende, The holy blisful martyr for to seke', *Works of Chaucer*, ed. Skeat, p. 419.

29. M. McKisack, *The Fourteenth Century 1317–1399* (Oxford University Press, 1959), p. 527. The most recent text of this poem is *Piers Plowman. Parallel Text Edition of William Langland*, ed. A.V.C. Schmidt (Longman, 1995).

30. *The Vision of William Concerning Piers The Plowman*, ed. W.W. Skeat, (Oxford University Press, 1886, repr. 1979, 2 vols), i, p. 3.

31. Cf. J. Bossy, *Christianity in the West 1400–1700* (Oxford, 1985), p. 171.

32. Cf. J. Angus, *The Handbook of English Literature* (The Religious Tract Society, n.d.), p. 53.

33. See M. McKisack, *The Fourteenth Century*, p. 527.

34. *Piers Plowman*, ed. Skeat, i, pp. 446–7.
35. Cf. T. Merton, 'The English Mystics' in *Mystics and Zen Masters* (Farrar, Straus & Giroux, New York, 1967), p. 140. Cf. T. Merton, *Conjectures of a Guilty Bystander* (Doubleday, New York, 1966), pp. 191–2. For Julian's work as 'art' (with the Gospels, St Augustine and Plato), see Iris Murdoch, *Existentialism and Mystics. Writings on Philosophy and Literature* (Chatto and Windus, 1997), p. 459.
36. S. Upjohn, *All Shall Be Well. Revelations of Divine Love of Julian of Norwich* (Darton, Longman and Todd, 1992), pp. 1, 192, 185, 52. Cf. *In Love Enclosed*, ed. R. Llewelyn (Darton, Longman and Todd, reprint, 1992), p. 54. Cf. Julian of Norwich, *Revelation of Divine Love*, ed. Marian Glasscoe (Exeter Medieval Texts, University of Exeter Press, 1985), chs 27, 30. Cf. Plaque in Julian Cell, Norwich.
37. S. Upjohn, *All Shall be Well*, p. 11. Cf. S. Upjohn, *Why Julian Now* (Darton, Longman & Todd, 1997).
38. Cf. S. Upjohn, *All Shall be Well*, pp. 52, 54, 62, 131. Cf. 'Julian of Norwich, an anchoress of the fourteenth century, has captured the imagination of our time in a remarkable way', G. Jantzen, *Julian of Norwich, Mystic and Theologian* (Society for Promoting Christian Knowledge, 1987), p. 3. Cf. M. McLean, *Julian, Woman of our Day*, ed. R.L. Llewelyn (Darton, Longman & Todd, 1985), introduction.
39. T. Turville-Petre, *England the Nation: Language, Literature and National Identity, 1290–1340* (Clarendon Press, 1996).
40. See below, pp. 16, 234–5.
41. See R.R. Davies, *Domination and Conquest: The Experience of Ireland, Scotland and Wales, 1100–1300* (Cambridge University Press, 1990). It did not extend to the actual incorporation of Wales until 1536.
42. P. Heath, *Church and Realm 1272–1461* (Fontana Press, 1988), p. 356. Cf. 'The Act in restraint of appeals (1533) reminds us that the Pope stood at the apex of ecclesiastical jurisdiction in England and was, despite all the writs and statutes of medieval times, resorted to by English litigants in all manner of cases – matrimony, divorce, tithes, testaments, and so on'. Ibid.
43. R.W. Chambers, *Thomas More*, p. 391.
44. G. Marsden, *History Today*, 47(4), April 1997, p. 20.
45. See R.W. Chambers, *The Place of St Thomas More in English Literature and History* (Longman, 1937), pp. 77, 83–4. Cf. Lord Campbell, Lord Chancellor: 'After three centuries . . . we must still regard his murder as the blackest crime that ever has been perpetrated in England under the forms of law', quoted R.W. Chambers, *The Place of Thomas More*, p. 114. Cf. Sir James Mackintosh: 'No such culprits as More had stood at any European Bar for a thousand years: the condemnation of Socrates is the only parallel in History', quoted ibid. England's most deadly satirist of human follies, Dean Swift, described More as the person 'of the greatest virtue this kingdom every produced', quoted ibid., p. 35.

46.   *William Roper and Nicholas Harpesfield, Lives of St Thomas More*, ed. E.E. Reynolds, p. 178.

47.   Ibid., p. 178.

48.   Ibid.

49.   See R.W. Chambers, *The Place of Thomas More*, p. 118. Also P. Hughes, *The Reformation in England* (Hollis and Carter, 3rd edn, 1954), i, p. 281.

50.   Cf. above, pp. 8–9.

51.   T. More, *The Utopia*, ed. H.B. Cotterill (Macmillan, 1952), p. 117.

52.   Ibid., p. 121. For further discussion of the relationship between More's Christian humanism and his political views, see J. Hexter, *The Vision of Politics on the Eve of the Reformation: More, Machiavelli and Seyssel* (Allen Lane, 1973), and R.P. Adams, *The Better Part of Valour: More, Erasmus, Colet and Vives on Humanism, War and Peace* (University of Washington Press, Seattle, 1962).

53.   It is not in G.M. Trevelyan's *History of England*.

54.   T. More, *The Utopia*, pp. 53, 94, 130. cf. interestingly 'it should be lawful for every man to favour and follow what religion he would.' People could proselytise peacefully, but use 'no violence . . . displeasant and seditious words . . . [on pain of] banishment or bondage', Ibid., p. 131.

55.   Nelson Mandela's speech at Westminster Hall, 11 July 1996.

56   The Reformation was 'a relentless torrent, carrying away the landmarks of a thousand years', E. Duffy, *The Stripping of the Altars. Traditional Religion in England c. 1400–c. 1580* (Yale University Press, 1992), p. 593. Cf. D. Loades, *Revolution in Religion. The Reformation in England, 1530–1570* (University of Wales Press, 2nd edn, 1995). C. Hill sees the break with Rome as 'momentous'. It led to 'England being cut off from the Continent', *Reformation to Industrial Revolution* (Penguin, 1992), pp. 3, 25. Cf. The Acts in Restraint of Appeals (1533) and of Supremacy (1534) constituted one of those 'few defining moments when changes take place which produce a fundamental new climate and environment', J. Morrill, *The British Problem 1534–1707*, p. 19. In Wales, the Reformation and Act of Union produced 'drastic and long-lasting changes. For good or ill, in politics, law, administration, religion and culture, Wales would never be the same again'. Henry's actions resulted in 'cutting England and Wales off from western Christendom', G. Williams, *Renewal and Reformation, Wales 1415–1642* (Oxford University Press, 1993), preface, p. vii. The Reformation also undermined the social customs of England: see R. Hutton, *The Rise and Fall of Merry England. The Ritual Year, 1400–1700* (Oxford University Press, 1994). Cf. 'There were profound and far-reaching consequences for the country when Henry made himself supreme head of the Church of England', D. Loades, *Chronicles of the Tudor Kings*, ed. D. Loades, (Bramley Books, 1996), p. 163. For the changes affecting the life-cycle of ordinary people, see D. Cressy, *Birth, Marriage and Death: Ritual, Religion and the Life-cycle in Tudor and Stuart England* (Oxford University Press, 1997). In

contrast, modern work has stressed the continuity and survival of Anglo-Saxon law, customs and institutions after the Norman Conquest.

57. See C.J. Sommerville, *Secularisation of Early Modern England*. Cf. 'The Reformation not only subordinated the national church to the King, it also subordinated parishes to squires', C. Hill, *Reformation to Industrial Revolution*, p. 35. For later developments in fragmentation of religion and secularization, see J. Morrill, *The Tudors and Stuarts* (Oxford University Press, 1992), pp. 135–7.

58. J. Lingard, *History of England*, (J.C. Nimmo and Bain, 6th edn, 1883 rep.) v, pp. 35–6. This was the first instance of centralized control of education in England and Wales. The Welsh proto-martyr was a teacher, Richard Gwyn – hanged, drawn and quartered in Wrexham, 1584.

59. D. Loades, *The Reign of Mary Tudor* (Longman, 2nd edn, 1995), p. 402.

60. R. Rex, 'The crisis of obedience', p. 863.

61. Ibid., p. 883.

62. Ibid., p. 871.

63. 'In one sense the Tudors were perceived and perceived themselves as agents of God', D. Loades, *Power in Tudor England*, (St Martin's Press, New York, 1997), p. 8.

64. Cf. D. Loades concerning Henry VIII: 'He had emancipated himself from the Canon law. . . . By 1540 he had redesigned the law of God to suit himself, and established the principles that it was subjected to the same legislative process as the Common Law of England. This made him, in one sense, the most absolute monarch in Christendom. . . . The kings of France and Spain, however great, recognised limits which the King of England had transcended', *Chronicles of the Tudor Kings*, introduction, p. 9. Thomas More, following medieval scholastic theology, said at this trial that human law could bind only a person's words and actions. A person's thoughts were between him and God, a matter of Divine Law. Therefore he had the right to silence, without any appropriation of guilt. See R.W. Chambers, *The Place of Thomas More*, p. 116. The European Court of Human Rights decided (17 December 1996) that Ernest Saunders' human right of silence had been breached in the Guinness Fraud Trial in England. The right to silence was overthrown in 1996 in England, against the wishes of most senior legal opinion. This decision at Strasbourg could lead to its restoration in British law.

65. Cf. 'England of the sixteenth century had her state trials and incomprehensible confessions . . . those accused of treason were exposed to any forms of persuasion the government cared to use', L. Baldwin Smith, 'English Treason Trials and Confessions in the Sixteenth Century', *Journal of the History of Ideas*, (1954), xv, No. 4, pp. 471–2. Cf. L. Baldwin Smith, *Treason in Tudor England. Politics and Paranoia* (Jonathan Cape, 1986).

66. See below, p. 280 note 84.

67. A. Toynbee, *A Study of History* (Oxford University Press, 2nd edn,

1931), i, pp. 17–18. Cf. 'Britain is an island and this fact is more important than any other in understanding its history', R. Strong, *History of Britain* (Hutchinson, 1996), foreword, p. ix.

68.   See *England in Europe*, ed. N. Saul; and J. Black, *Convergence and Divergence*

69.   See D. Hay, *Polydore Vergil: Renaissance Historian and Man of Letters* (Oxford, 1952), pp. 174–5.

70.   Caused by British failure to take earlier preventative action.

71.   See below, pp. 260, 281 notes 97 and 98.

72.   W. Holdsworth, *A History of English Law* (6th edn, 1938), i, p. 591.

73.   D.M. Loades, *Politics and the Nation, 1450–1660*, p. 181: section on 'Propaganda and Control', pp. 180–9.

74.   For the importance of the Feudal Law, see J.G.A. Pocock, *The Ancient Constitution and the Feudal Law* (Cambridge University Press, 1957). For the Canon Law, see E. Jones, 'English Historical Writing on the Reformation in England, 1680–1730' (Ph.D. thesis, University of Cambridge, 1958), ch. 1, pp. 43–73.

75.   The selling of monastic lands to the gentry created a 'major vested interest' and a 'near insuperable carrier against the restoration of the old order, which stood firm for generations', J. Scarisbrick, *Henry VIII* (Yale University Press, 1997), foreword, p. xviii. Ibid., p. 338.

76.   See J. Scarisbrick, *Henry VIII*, pp. ix, 1–2. Cf. 'The notion that Protestantism swept to power in England on a wave of revulsion against the Church, does not stand up to scrutiny', D. Newcombe, *Henry VIII and the English Reformation* (Routledge, 1995), p. 2. Similarly in Wales: 'there was virtually no sign of deep-seated opposition to the faith as taught by the Church, nor any serious criticism of it', G. Williams, *Renewal and Reformation*, p. 137. Anti-clericalism was a result rather than a cause of the Reformation: see P. Marshall, *The Catholic Priesthood and the English Reformation* (Clarendon Press, 1994). The humiliating series of changes forced on the clergy after 1529 greatly affected the relationship between them and their flocks. Cf. C. Cross: 'A spate of recent books and articles has stressed the essential satisfaction of the English people with the Church in the early sixteenth century and the unpreparedness of the laity for radical change', *The English Historical Review*, cxi, No. 444 (November 1996), p. 1266. Cf. G. Marsden: 'The old idea promoted by nineteenth-century Protestant historians, that vitality had entirely ebbed from the devotional practices of the Church at ground level, has been more and more contradicted over the past twenty years', *History Today*, 47(4), April 1997, p. 18. For the 'vigorous, adaptable and widely understood' character of late-medieval Catholicism, see E. Duffy, *Stripping of the Altars*, p. 6. Cf. 'Revisionist historians now question the long-held view of the Roman Catholic Church in England and Wales as riddled with abuses and in terminal decline on the eve of the Reformation. It is now argued that without

Henry VIII's marital engagements, there could have been that spiritual
and moral renewal which would have revitalized the old faith', and any
account of the Welsh Church on the eve of the Reformation 'must take
account of the increasing vitality in the second half of the fifteenth
century', G. Elwyn Jones, 'The Historical Background', *A Guide to Welsh
Literature c. 1530–1700*, ed. R. Geraint Gruffydd (University of Wales
Press, 1997), p. 77. Cf. concerning the pre-Reformation Church: 'there
was no sense of crisis . . . there can be little doubt that it was giving its
members what they wanted to receive. . . . There is little evidence of
spiritual doubt, but much of undemonstrative acceptance', R. Horrox,
*Fifteenth Century Attitudes and Perceptions of Society in late medieval
England* (Cambridge University Press, 1994, repr. 1996), p. 12.

77. J. Scarisbrick, *Henry VIII*, pp. xvii, 329, 338–9.
78. *The Utopia of Sir Thomas More*, ed. H.B. Cotterill (Macmillan, 1952)
     pp. 50–1. Cf. 'In parishes all over England, decent, timid, men and
     women set themselves to do just that. It was not for them to rule the
     winds . . . the conscience of the prince was in the hands of God, and the
     people must make shift to do as best they could under the prince', E.
     Duffy, *Stripping of the Altars*, p. 542.
79. See above, pp. 33ff.
80. H. Butterfield, *The Whig Interpretation of History* (Bell, 1931).
81. Cf. 'Tudor security required an extension of English hegemony within
     the British Isles – Wales, Ireland and Scotland. Accordingly Henry
     undertook or continued the wider task of English colonization that was
     completed by the Act of Union with Scotland in 1707', J. Guy, *The
     Tudors and Stuarts* (Oxford University Press, 1992), p. 33. Cf. C. Hill: 'A
     natural concomitant of the suppression of local liberties is an ideology
     of nationalism', *Reformation to Industrial Revolution*, p. 36. Cf. 'the
     imperialistic design' and 'the burgeoning imperialism' of Henry VIII,
     leading to the Act of Union with Wales, B. Bradshaw, 'The Tudor
     Revolution and Reformation in Wales and Ireland: The origins of the
     British Problem', *The British Problem: 1534–1707*, p. 53.
82. L. Colley, *Britons*, p. 374.
83. For example, see Bobi Jones, 'The Roots of Welsh Inferiority', *Planet*
     (Lewis & Sons, Llandyssul), March 1974, pp. 53–72. He notes: '1536,
     the date of the Act of Union with England, is usually noted as a
     turning-point in the history of our country' and that 'legal or objective
     inferiority conferred on the Welsh language in the 16th century
     produced a subjective sense of inferiority in the Welshman regarding his
     own identity and character: feelings of shame and even of guilt evolved
     soon after the Middle Ages . . . and gradually settled down into a
     chronic inferiority complex regarding this one thing, his Welshness',
     ibid., p. 35.
84. See P. Collinson on the institutional, xenophobic and often irrational
     nature of anti-Catholic prejudice in England, 'No Popery: the

mythology of a Protestant nation', *The Tablet* (25 March 1995), pp. 384–6. Cf. 'We have established that anti-Catholicism had to do with the affirming of a nation', ibid. This published lecture by Patrick Collinson, Regius Professor of History at Cambridge, has been reprinted in *Prejudice in Religion: Can we move beyond it?* ed. P. Cornwall (Geoffrey Chapman, 1997). The part played by English xenophobia in this phenomenon is noticed by D. Loades, *The Reign of Mary Tudor* (Longman, 2nd edn, 1995), p. 396. Cf. 'a deep and anti-Catholic prejudice, as much xenophobic phenomenon as a theological one, had taken deep root within important strata of the English political nation. It was a latent force but easily aroused and immensely powerful', W.T. MacCaffray, *Queen Elizabeth and The Making of Policy, 1572–1588* (Princetown University Press, 1981), p. 266. B. Coward comments that 'the emotional, irrational fear of Popery was diffused throughout seventeenth-century society', *The Stuart Age* (Longman, 2nd edn, 1994), p. 199. K. Sharpe writes of 'Anti-Popish hysteria and popular politics' in *The Personal Rule of Charles I* (Yale University Press, 1995), p. 209. P. Lake analyses this 'irrational passion and prejudice' in 'Anti-Popery: The Structure of a prejudice', *The English Civil War*, ed. R. Cust and Anne Hughes (Arnold, 1997), pp. 181–210. C. Hydon confirms the importance of anti-Catholicism in shaping British attitudes and mentality in the eighteenth century. He shows that it was still a vibrant force and the Gordon Riots (1780) were mainly an expression of religious hatred, fanned by virulent government propaganda; see his *Anti-Catholicism in Eighteenth Century England c. 1714–80* (Manchester University Press, 1994). Frank H. Wallis has shown the same for the nineteenth century, indicating the Reformation as being an important part of the vituperative Protestant tradition, in his *Popular Anti-Catholicism in Mid-Victorian Britain* (Lewiston, New York, 1993). P. Ghosh has very recently observed that one of the 'key characteristics of the English middle class was anti-Catholicism' in 'Macaulay: the Heritage of the Englightenment', *The English Historical Review*, cxii, No. 446 (April 1997), p. 363. L. Colley sees this prejudice as the main cementing element in the establishment of British nationalism from the eighteenth century and on into the nineteenth and twentieth centuries, *Britons.*, pp. 18–54.

85. Catholics were given the vote in the Catholic Emancipation Act of 1829.
86. See E. Jones, Ph.D. thesis, pp. 188–280.
87. See D. Douglas, *English Scholars* (1939), pp. 223, 240, 243.
88. See E. Jones, Ph.D. thesis, pp. 115–30.
89. Cf. 'As a result of the Reformation England was denied the direct benefit of such schools of learned discipline as the reform of the Religious Orders on the Continent provided. We had no Bollandists to inculcate

sound principles of hagiology, no Maurist community to construct gradually a science of diplomatic'. C.R. Cheney, 'Introduction', *English Historical Scholarship in the 16th and 17th Centuries*, ed. L. Fox (Oxford University Press, 1956), p. 5.

90. See below, pp. 81, 83, 87, 88, 90.

91. See below, p. 174.

92. See E. Jones, 'A Study of John Lingard's Historical Work, with special reference to his treatment of the reign of Elizabeth I', M.A. thesis (University College of Swansea, 1956).

93. See below, p. 184.

94. G.P. Gooch, *History and Historians in the Nineteenth Century* (2nd edn, 1952), p. 273.

95. P.R. Ghosh, 'Macaulay: the Heritage of the Englightenment', p. 395.

96. Mr Hugh Gaitskell's speech at the Labour Party Conference, 1962, strongly opposing Britain's entry into the European Economic Community.

97. Mr John Major's speech to Tory Party Conference, October 1996. Edward Pearce describes the negative attitude towards Europe taken by some Tories: 'We have Europe and the single currency – Chancellor Kohl doing by economic means what Hitler failed to do in the 1940s', 'Times and Tides', *History Today*, 47(6), June 1997, p. 5.

98. Cf. 'The English do not need nationalism and do not like it. They are so sure of themselves that they need hardly discuss the matter', *Englishness: Politics and Culture, 1880–1920*, ed. R. Culls and P. Dodd (Beckenham Croom Helm, 1986), preface. Cf. 'There is a terrible danger that the British people, drugged by the seductive mantra "It's time for a change", are stumbling, eyes glazed into an election that could undo 1,000 years of our nation's history', in huge lettering, framed by the Union Jack on the front page of the *Daily Mail* (30 April 1997), together with a double-page inside editorial comment on 'The Battle for Britain – Our very survival as an independent nation is at stake in this election. All other issues pale into insignificance'.

99. Cf. 'no modern Western states can withstand the forces of interdependence', J. Young, *Britain and European Unity, 1945–1992* (Macmillan, 1993), p. 173. Cf. 'History ties the two countries together and will not be denied', H. Bell, *France and Britain, 1940–94: The Long Separation* (Longman, 1997), p. 297.

100. Cf. Charles Handy, *Beyond Certainty, The Changing World of Organisations* (Arrow Books, 1996).

101. R.W. Southern, *Scholastic Humanism and the Unification of Europe vol. I* (Blackwell, 1995), pp. 17–21. Cf. 'At the deepest level, it is in its Christian nature that the explanation of the success of medieval society in shaping the future must lie', J. Roberts, *The Triumph of the West* (BBC 1985), p. 108.

102. Cf. 'To Trevelyan and his generation, the Second World War spelt the

end of civilisation and the "death knell" of spiritual values', D. Cannadine, *The Next Hundred Years*, ed. H. Newby (National Trust Publications, 1995), p. 18.

103. For the great escalation in the size and number of war implements since the seventeenth century, see *The Oxford Illustrated History of Modern War*, ed. C. Townshend (Oxford University Press, 1997).

104. R. Bartlett, *The Making of Europe 950–1350* (Penguin, 1994), introduction, p. 1.

105. A. Toynbee, *A Study of History* (Oxford University Press and Thames & Hudson Ltd, 1972), foreword, p. 10.

106. R.F. Foster, *Mr. Paddy and Mr. Punch: Connections in Irish and English History* (Allen Lane, Penguin, 1993), pp. 93–4.

107. See *The Reformation in National Context*, ed. B. Schribner, R. Porter and M. Teich (Cambridge University Press, 1994), in which P. Collinson has written the chapter on England. Cf. 'The early Protestant reformers were staunch supporters of the English monarchy', C. Hill, *Reformation to Industrial Revolution*, p. 36.

108. *Macaulay. History of England*, ed. H. Trevor-Roper (Penguin, 1979), editor's introduction, where he is describing the Whig interpretation.

109. J.W. Young, *Britain and European Unity, 1945–1992* (Macmillan, 1993), pp. 182–3.

110. R.W. Southern, *Scholastic Humanism*, pp. 1, 13.

111. Ibid., pp. 21–2, 23.

112. Ibid., p. 13.

113. Southern refers to the long-lasting 'misconception', from the sixteenth century 'almost to the present day' that 'the Bible was diminished by the schools'. It was in fact their 'sovereign text book', ibid., p. 103.

114. Ibid, p. 22.

115. *Outlines of the 16 Documents: Vatican II*. See 'Declaration on Religious Freedom' (pp. 102–5); 'Declaration on the Relationship of the Church to Non-Christian Religions'; 'Decree on Ecumenism' (pp. 57–64); 'Decree on Eastern Catholic Churches' (pp. 64–6); 'Declaration on Religious Freedom' (pp. 105–9); 'Pastoral Constitution on the Church in the Modern World' (pp. 38–53). Cf. 'Catholics should also cooperate with their separated brethren, and all men seeking true peace' (p. 53). 'The Church rejects every persecution against any man . . . the Church opposes any discrimination or harassment of men because of race, color, condition of life or religion. And urges Christians to live in peace and good fellowship with all men' (p. 105). Cf. 'The Church respects and esteems non-Christian religions because they are the living expression of the soul of vast groups of people. They possess an impressive patrimony of deeply religious texts. They have taught generations of people how to pray. They are all impregnated with innumerable "seeds of the Word" and can constitute a true "preparation for the Gospel"', Pope Paul VI, *Evengelii Nuntiandi*.

116. Cf. C. Longley, *The Tablet* (25 January 1997), p. 98. Dr Zaki Badawi, head of the Muslim College in London, warmly welcomed *The Common Good*, saying that the social teaching contained in it was perfectly acceptable to Muslims.

117. B. Ward, *The Home of Man* (Penguin, 1976), p. 294.

118. K. Lunn, 'Reconsidering Britishness', p. 98. Cf. K.O. Morgan comments on contemporary Britain: 'Most powerfully of all the British expressed a deep sense of history.' He refers also to the 'mystique of national identity' in their thinking', *The Oxford History of Britain* (Oxford University Press, 1992), vol. 5, p. 146.

119. A. Sampson, *The Essential Anatomy of Britain* (Hodder and Stoughton, 1992), p. 160. Sampson adds that, at that time, British voters and politicians refused to take the European parliament seriously, which weakened their own democracy as their government became more centralized and more interlocked with Europe.

120. J. Northcott, *The Future of Britain and Europe* (Policy Studies Institute, 1995), p. 342.

CHAPTER I

1. In his *Assertio Septem Sacramentorum*, a reply to Luther's *The Babylonish Captivity of the Church* (1520).

2. Quoted by J.R. Tanner, *Constitutional Documents* (Cambridge, 1922). p. 48, note 1.

3. See E. Duffy, *Stripping of the Altars*, pp. 4–6.

4. G.R. Elton, 'The Evolution of a Reformation Statute', *The English Historical Journal*, lxiv (1949), p. 182.

5. Cf. 'he learned to think in terms of function and efficiency. . . . On the other hand, he was no agnostic and, in so far as his cool temperament allowed, he appears to have been genuinely attracted by ideas which stemmed from Luther', A.G. Dickens, *The English Reformation* (Fontana, 8th imp., 1976), p. 158.

6. For the debate concerning the exact importance of Cromwell's role in government, see G. Elton, 'A New Age of Reform?', *Historical Journal*, 30 (1987), pp. 709–16. A.G. Dickens, *English Reformation*, and J. Guy, 'Thomas Wolsey, Thomas Cromwell and the Reform of the Henrician Government', *The Reign of Henry VIII, Politics, Policy and Piety*, ed. D. MacCulloch (Macmillan, 1995), pp. 203–27.

7. Writing in 1324, Marsilio was 'the most portentous of medieval rebels' whose book was 'a prophetic forerunner of the Protestant erastianism of the sixteenth century, the democratic theory of the nineteenth and the State worship of the twentieth', A.G. Dickens, *English Reformation*, p. 123.

8. See R. Rex, 'The crisis of obedience', pp. 863, 881.

9. Ibid, p. 894.

10. See G.R. Elton, *England Under the Tudors* (Methuen, 1955), pp. 130–7.

Cf. 'it cannot reasonably be questioned that Cromwell supplied their chief guiding force', A.G. Dickens, *English Reformation*, p. 161. Cf. J. Scarisbrick, whose view I share: 'Cromwell's care of his business was all-embracing and immediate, this does not mean that he had ultimate responsibility for all policy . . . he was the executant of the king's designs. In executing them he doubtless left his own imprint on them. It was for him to convert them into statutory form, to give them precision and draw out their full meaning. He may have determined timing and sequence, shown what was possible and what was not, what was necessary and what was not, and intervened with decisive suggestions. But he neither worked alone, nor was the true initiator of these royal undertakings', *Henry VIII* (Eyre and Spottiswoode, 1968), p. 304. Cf. 'especially after 1529, Henry VIII was in overall control of state affairs', *Henry VIII* (Yale University Press edn, 1997), foreword, p. xi. But Cromwell was allowed to conduct the propaganda campaign in his own way. See R. Rex, 'Crisis of Obedience', p. 881.

11. G.R. Elton, 'The Evolution of a Reformation Statute', p. 178, note 2.
12. *Documents of the English Reformation*, ed. G. Bray (James Clarke & Co. Ltd, 1994), p. 78. Cf. 'it is certainly of considerable interest that under the ascendancy of Thomas Cromwell the preambles to the Acts of Parliament regularly included justificatory references to the chronicles', D. Hay, *Polydore Vergil, Renaissance Historian and Man of Letters* (Oxford, 1952), p. 167.
13. *Sources of English Constitutional History*, ed. C. Stephenson & F.G. Marcham (Harper, 1937), p. 308.
14. J. Scarisbrick, *Henry VIII* (1968 edn), p. 304.
15. *Documents of the English Reformation*, ed. G. Bray, pp. 113–14.
16. F.W. Maitland, *Roman Canon Law in the Church of England* (1898), p. 92.
17. 'The rule of law was fundamental to the thought of the age and to the way men acted and behaved', R. Palliser, *The Age of Elizabeth. England under the later Tudors, 1547–1603* (2nd edn, 1992), p. 349.
18. See J. Scarisbrick, *Henry VIII*, (1968 edn).
19. The most recent description is: 'While the notion that the move to political integration resulted from the necessity to enforce a breach with Rome, which was likely to prompt serious opposition from the Welsh, is now regarded as much too simplistic, there is no denying the concern with which the Privy Council viewed the Welsh reaction to the Reformation changes', G. Elwyn Jones, 'The Historical Background 1530–1700', p. 7. Professor Jones also notes that 'there was little popular support for the religious changes' and 'Protestantism had not taken firm root' in Wales. In Elizabeth's reign, there was 'no great enthusiasm for the new order among the majority' and evidence of the 'prevalence of Roman Catholic practices such as the use of the rosary'. Cf. The Reformation in Wales only 'came of age' in the second half of the eighteenth century, Williams, *Wales and the Reformation*, pp. 30–2,

402. Some prominent Catholics, such as Morris Clynnog, Owen Lewis, and Gruffydd Roberts, went abroad to train for the priesthood. Roberts also produced an important Welsh 'Grammar' (published in Milan in 1567). However, the role of the Welsh gentry, leaders of local society, was decisive: 'Generally, the temptation afforded by the opportunity to acquire church lands was stronger than religious devotion . . . and tied them, irrevocably as it proved, to the Tudor state' and its policy of anglicization in culture and religion. Ibid., pp. 8–9. There were exceptions, gentry who remained Catholic and appear on the rolls of 'recusants', for example, Owen of Hengwrt, Wynns (Gwydir), Stradlings (Glamorgan), Carnes (Ewenny) and the Herberts.

20. Cf. 'In effect the Tudor Reformation marked the extension to the religious sphere of the existing policies of centralisation and cultural imperialism', *Conquest and Union. Fashioning a British State, 1485–1725*, ed. S.G. Ellis and S. Barker (Longman, 1994), p. 58.

21. *Sources*, ed. Stephenson and Marcham, p. 314.

22. 'The "empire" of Henry VIII is the nation state contracting upon its insularity. The object . . . is to deny the subjection of the insular power to any external authority, temporal or spiritual, and it thus embodies the fundamental principle of Henry VIII's Reformation', *Tudor Constitutional Documents*, ed. J.R. Tanner (Cambridge, 1922), p. 40. Henry had wanted to base his claim for spiritual authority on the role of the Holy Roman Emperor, but found that this, like other specific precedents, could not be substantiated.

23. G.R. Elton, 'The Evolution of a Reformation Statute', p. 181.

24. *Tudor Constitutional Documents*, ed. J.R. Tanner (Cambridge University Press, 2nd edn, 1951), p. 48, note 1.

25. Ibid.

26. *Documents of the English Reformation*, ed. G. Bray (1994), p. 79.

27. E. Gibson, *Codex Iuris Ecclesiastici* (1713), p. xxviii.

28. H.W.C. Davis, 'The Canon Law in England', *Zeitschrift der Savigny-Stiftung Fur Rechtsgeschichte*, xxxiv (1913), p. 353.

29. J. Scarisbrick's view is that these 'outrageous' threats, based on 'fabrications', were all part of Henry's scheme to force Pope Clement into submission on the Divorce question. See *Henry VIII* (Yale University Press edn, 1997), foreword, pp. xv–xvi.

30. *Select Documents of English Constitutional History*, ed. G.B. Adams and H. Morse Stephens (Macmillan, 1921), p. 241.

31. Such as Bishop Fisher and Prior Haughton of the Carthusians. The latter had shown 'balanced sanity' and 'sweet rigour' as prior of his community. He now set the example to 'that part of his community', which showed 'gallant faith and selflessness' and followed him to the gibbet or died in chains'. See A.G. Dickens, *English Reformation*, p. 88: 'They died for a conviction as sincerely felt as the love of God which had first led them to the hard and high paths of the Carthusian life.' Dickens

concludes that 'The Tudor age bred no nobler Englishmen than these, and inhumanity of their punishment must remain among the fouler blots upon the record of Henry VIII'. Thomas More had tried his vocation with these Carthusians at the London Charterhouse, from the age of eighteen to twenty-two.

32. See above, p. 283 note 10.
33. G.R. Elton, 'The Evolution of a Reformation Statute', p. 184.
34. J. Kenyon, *The History Men* (Weidenfeld and Nicholson, 1983, 2nd edn, 1993), pp. 2–3.
35. Ibid. Cf. Williams, *Wales and the Reformation*, pp. 1–2.
36. J. Kenyon, *History Men*, p. 3.
37. S. Woolf, *Nationalism in Europe*, ed. S. Woolf, introduction, p. 2.
38. D. Loades, *Power in Tudor England* (St Martin's Press, New York, 1997), p. 1.
39. D. Loades, *Chronicles of the Tudor Kings*, introduction, p. 9.
40. See G.R. Elton, *The Tudor Revolution in Government* (Cambridge, 1953).
41. J. Kenyon, *History Men*, p. 4.
42. Ibid. Cf. A.G. Dickens, *English Reformation*, p. 168. For a fuller consideration of Vergil, see D. Hay, *Polydore Vergil.*
43. J. Kenyon, *History Men*, p. 4.
44. Ibid.
45. A.G. Dickens, *English Reformation*, p. 168.
46. See T. Mayer's essay in *Tudor Political Culture*, ed. D. Hoak (Cambridge University Press, 1995).
47. A.G. Dickens, *English Reformation*, p. 168.
48. R. Horrox, *Fifteenth Century Attitudes and Perceptions of Society in late Medieval England*, ed. R. Horrox (Cambridge University Press, 1996), p. 12.
49. See below, pp. 72, 244.
50. For these details, see H. Butterfield, *The Englishman and his History* (Cambridge University Press, 1944), pp. 17–23.
51. Ibid.
52. For these details, see J. Kenyon, *History Men*, p. 9.
53. See E. Jones, Ph.D. thesis, p. 246.
54. Ibid., pp. 135–83.
55. J. Kenyon, *History Men*, p. 9.
56. Ibid., p. 8.
57. *Oxford Companion to English Literature*, ed. M. Drabble, p. 941.
58. J. Kenyon, *History Men*, p. 10.
59. H.R. Trevor-Roper, *Queen Elizabeth's First Historian* (1971), quoted in J. Kenyon, *History Men.*
60. See below, pp. 208ff. Cf. J. Lingard, *History of England*, vi, pp. 649–65.
61. See below, p. 184.
62. For the history of this myth, see G. Williams, 'Some Protestant Views of Early British Church History', *History*, xxxviii (1953).

NOTES

63. L. van Norden, 'Peiresc and the English Scholars', *Huntingdon Library Quarterly*, xii (1948–9), No. 4, p. 370. Cf. T.D. Kendrick, *British Antiquity* (1950), p. 140. Cf. H. Ellis, Cambridge University Library MS., Add. 4479, ff. 55–6.

64. J.G.A. Pocock, *The Ancient Constitution and the Feudal Law* (Cambridge University Press, 1967).

65. J. Kenyon, *History Men*, p. 6.

66. Quoted in ibid.

67. Ibid.

68. Quoted in ibid.

69. Ibid.

70. See below, ch. 7.

71. J. Ussher, *Discourse of the Religion anciently practised by the irish* (1623) and *Treatise on the Originall of Bishops* (1641). E. Stillingfleet, *Originae Britannicae* (1685). See E. Jones, Ph.D. thesis, pp. 14–15.

72. See below, p. 161.

73. See 'The Faerie Queene', *The Oxford Companion to English Literature* (1992), p. 336.

74. W. Shakespeare, *Richard II* (Act 2, Scene 1).

75. Cf. P. Milward, *The Catholicism of Shakespeare's Plays* (St Austin Press, 1997). H.S. Bowden, *The Religion of Shakespeare* (1899).

76. See E.K. Chambers, *William Shakespeare: A Study of Facts and Problems* (1930). Quoted in B. Hodek, *The Complete Works of William Shakespeare* (Spring Books, London, n.d.), p. xvi.

77. Cf. above, p. 63.

78. B. Hodek, *Works of Shakespeare*, pp. xi–xii.

79. See P. Herman's essay in *Tudor Political Culture*, ed. D. Hoak (Cambridge University Press, 1995).

80. See P. Milward, *Shakespeare's Religious Background* (1989) and Bowden, *Religion of Shakespeare*. The seventeenth-century Anglican, Richard Davies, reported that Shakespeare had 'died a papist'.

81. A. Hastings, *Construction of Nationhood*, pp. 207–8.

82. M. Creighton, 'John Bale', *Dictionary of National Biography*, iii (1885), p. 41.

83. R. Rex, 'Crisis of Obedience', p. 881.

84. Ibid., p. 883.

85. W. Haller, *Foxe's Book of Martyrs and the Elect Nation* (New York, 1963), pp. 58–9.

86. Cf. His use of the 'visitor's reports' before the Dissolution of the Monasteries and his attempted bribery to gain favourable opinions from the Universities in favour of the divorce.

87. See below, p. 53.

88. E. Duffy, *Stripping of the Altars*, p. 6.

89. W. Haller, *Foxe's Book of Martyrs*, p. 62.

90. M. Aston, 'Lollardy and the Reformation', *History*, xlix, No. 166 (June 1964), p. 150.
91. W. Haller, *Foxe's Book of Martyrs*, p. 63.
92. Ibid., p. 76.
93. J. Foxe, *Acts and Monuments*, ed. S.R. Cattley (1852), ii, p. 331.
94. Ibid., p. 14.
95. Cromwell was 'essentially a cold man . . . who killed for a purpose only and as rarely as possible . . . but who showed no weakness . . . once he had decided on a course of action', G.R. Elton, *England under the Tudors*, p. 128.
96. J.F. Mozley, *John Foxe and His Book* (1940), p. 129.
97. See Andrew Penny, 'John Foxe's Victorian Reception', *The Historical Journal*, 40(1) (1 March 1997), p. 127.
98. J.F. Mozley, *John Foxe and his Book*, p. 129.
99. W. Haller, *Foxe's Book of Martyrs*, p. 130.
100. G.A. Williamson, introduction, *Foxe's Book of Martyrs* (1965), ed. G.A. Williamson, p. xxix.
101. C. Haigh, introduction, *The English Reformation Revisited*, ed. C. Haigh, (Cambridge University Press, 1987), p. 2.
102. J. Scarisbrick, *Henry VIII* (Eyre and Spotiswoode, 1968), pp. 386–7.
103. See K.R. Firth, *The Apocalyptic Tradition in Reformation Britain 1530–1645* (Oxford University Press, 1979).
104. Penry Williams, *The Later Tudors. England 1547–1603* (Clarendon Press, 1995), p. 115.
105. M. Aston, 'Lollardy and the Reformation', p. 150.
106. K.R. Firth, *Apocalyptic Tradition*, p. 110.
107. Ibid., pp. 106–8.
108. Quoted in ibid., p. 165.
109. Quoted in ibid., p. 167.
110. Ibid., pp. 236, 256.
111. See N. von Maltzahn, *Milton's History of Britain. Republican Historiography in the English Revolution* (Clarendon Press, 1991).
112. See below, p. 58.
113. K.R. Firth, *Apocalyptic Tradition*, p. 253.
114. D. Morgan and M. Evans, *The Battle for Britain: Citizenship and Ideology in the Second World War* (Routledge, 1993), p. 88.
115. K.R. Firth, *Apocalyptic Tradition*, p. 247.
116. W. Haller, *Foxe's Book of Martyrs*, p. 14.
117. E. Duffy, *Stripping the Altars*, p. 593.
118. See W. Haller, *Foxe's Book of Martyrs*, p. 87.
119. A. Tillotson, *Sermons on Education* (1665), p. 162.
120. L. Colley, *Britons*, pp. 26–7.
121. See below, p. 191.
122. L. Colley, *Britons*, p. 27.

123. Sydney Smith, *The Works of the Rev. Sydney Smith* (3rd edn, 1845), iii, pp. 291–2.

124. For these details, see L. Colley, *Britons*, pp. 24–6.

125. D. Andrew Penny, 'John Foxe's Victorian Reception', p. 113.

126. L. Colley, *Britons*, p. 29.

127. Ibid., p. 31.

128. Ibid., p. 33.

129. See J. Uglow, *Hogarth, A Life, a World* (Faber & Faber, 1997), pp. 463–5. Also L. Colley, *Britons*, pp. 30–4.

130. L. Colley, *Britons*, p. 43.

131. Ibid., p. 53.

132. A.G. Dickens, *English Reformation*, p. 154.

133. Niccolo Machiavelli (1469–1527), an Italian 'politician'. In *The Prince* (*Il Principe*) he describes ways in which rulers can build up their states (and themselves) by the opportunistic manipulation of other people, often by amoral means and by exploitation of their weaknesses. His name is synonymous in modern history with cunning and cynical statecraft.

134. For example, Paul Josef Goebbels, a former journalist, was appointed Minister of Propaganda in Hitler's Nazi Party in 1933. He brought all cultural and educational activities under Nazi control and led a war of nerves against intended victims at home and abroad. He described the invasion of Poland, which started the Second World War, as a purely self-defensive action by Germany.

135. J. Scarisbrick, *Henry VIII* (1997) foreword, p. xiii.

136. Ibid.

CHAPTER II

1. I follow here the thinking of C. Russell. Cf. *Unrevolutionary England, 1603–42* (The Hambledon Press, 1990), p. xxvi.

2. See below, p. 228.

3. For the most recent survey of the religious scene after 1660, see J. Spurr, 'Religion in Restoration England', *The Reigns of Charles II and James VII and II* (Macmillan, 1997).

4. C. Russell, *Unrevolutionary Britain*. Cf. C. Russell, 'Parliamentary History and Perspective, 1604–29', *The English Civil War*, ed. R. Cust and Ann Hughes (Arnold, 1997), pp. 32–62. 'The conflict between "court' and "country" was not fought between members of Parliament and the king; it was fought out within the members "own minds" ', Ibid., p. 56.

5. Cf. J.H. Hexter, 'The Birth of Modern Freedom', *Times Literary Supplement* (21 January 1983), pp. 51–4; *Parliament and Liberty from the reign of Elizabeth to the English Civil War*, ed. J. Hexter (Stanford University Press, 1992); Ann Hughes, *The Causes of the English Civil War* (Macmillan Education, 1991).

6. See J.G.A. Pocock, *The Ancient Constitution and The Feudal Law*.

7. See A. Milton, *Catholic and Reformed. The Roman and Protestant Churches in English Protestant Thought, 1600–1640* (Cambridge University Press, 1995). This is an interesting analysis of religious thought and culture, and their role in the years leading to the Civil War. See also, P. Collinson, *The Religion of Protestants. The Church in English Society 1559–1625* (Clarendon Press, 1982), and *The Birthpangs of Protestant England: Religious and Cultural Change in the Sixteenth and Seventeenth Centuries* (Macmillan, 1988).

8. Cf. 'By 1660 both Erastianism and the lay movement had become dominant in the English ecclesitical tradition, and both tended to articulate concerns which had pre-occupied Interregnum anticlericalism . . . the Erastian triumph at the Restoration was quite complete. Convocation accepted its subordination to parliament, and in the countryside the parson abandoned to the squire whatever ambitions he may have retained from the age of Laud. But although an awareness of the reduced political and economic position of the parish clergy must have made some impression on popular attitudes, it is certain that the greatest effect was felt in the parliamentary classes where Erastian control was ingrained', J.F. Mucleur, 'Popular Anticlericalism in the Puritan Revolution', *Journal of the History of Ideas*, xvii (1956).

9. See 'Burnet and the Whig Historiography', E. Jones, Ph.D. thesis, pp. 73–92.

10. Cf. With reference to the words 'Protestant Reformed Religion established by law' in the new coronation oath of William III, 'Protestantism (as distinct from the old "Reformed doctrines") means erastianism or the complete subordination of church to state', D. Ogg, *England in the Reigns of James II and William III* (Oxford University Press, 1956), p. 283. Henry Compton, Bishop of London, was the only ecclesiastic to sign the invitation to William of Orange (1688) to occupy the English throne. E. Carpenter's study of him is significantly titled, *The Protestant Bishop* (1956).

11. See below, pp. 72, 244. Cf. T. Claydon, *William III and the Godly Revolution* (Cambridge University Press, 1995), which is particularly enlightening on the 'Burnetine' propaganda in England after the Revolution, concerning the nature of the Court.

12. Cf. J. Bury, *The Idea of Progress* (Macmillan, 1928), pp. 92, 94–6.

13. See above, pp. 33, 60. See below, pp. 72, 244.

14. See P. Collinson's works cited above, note 7.

15. W. Williams, *William Prynne: A Study in Puritanism* (Cambridge, Mass., 1931), pp. 181–2.

16. His appointment to this post 'inaugurated a period in which the keepers were sometimes appointed for their work in propagandist historiography on medieval and constitutional themes', J.G.A. Pocock, *Ancient Constitution*, p. 162.

17. W. Prynne, *Exact Chronological Vindication* (1665), ii, p. 227.

NOTES

18. Nicholas Sander was a Catholic refugee who had written this book, describing the new Church of England as schismatic, while in exile in 1582.

19. See M. Knight, *Politics and Opinion in 1678–81* (Cambridge University Press, 1994). Anti-Catholic prejudice was incited and exploited for political reasons, particularly to 'exclude' James, Duke of York, from the throne.

20. G. Burnet, *Reflections on Atterbury's Book* (1700), p. 23.

21. For these details, see E. Jones, Ph.D. thesis, pp. 17–19.

22. See above, p. 21.

23. G. Burnet, *History of the Reformation* (1715), iii, introduction, p. iii.

24. G. Burnet, *Reformation* (2nd edn, 1681), i, Epistle Dedicatory.

25. G. Burnet, *Reformation* (1715 edn), i, p. 102.

26. Ibid., i, p. 103.

27. G. Burnet, *A Letter Writ by The Lord Bishop of Salisbury To The Lord Bishop of Coventry and Litchfield, Concerning A Book lately Published, called, A Specimen of some Errors and Defects in the History of the Reformation of the Church of England, by Anthony Harmer* (1693), pp. 15–16.

28. Seventeenth-century Anglican clerics who adopted a non-dogmatic approach to church authority, doctrine and practice in order to try to achieve unity among the followers of various Protestant beliefs. This was a particular cause of dispute between the Non-Jurors and Burnet. Dr George Hickes argued that latitudinarianism, together with the tendency to discard everything Catholic, traditional and historical, would lead to 'absolute scepticism'. He referred to Christianity as 'a *Society* which Antiquity, so much undervalued by him [Burnet] called the Catholick Church'. The latitudinarian approach endangered 'every Thing that hath been receiv'd for Catholick and Fundamental in Christianity in the purest Ages of the Church'. He emphasized the importance of 'the *uninterrupted Succession* upon which the Priesthood depends' and which the Latitudinarians seemed ready to abandon. He refers to 'the Divine Authority of the holy Scriptures, which depends so much upon Tradition, That they themselves are not alone sufficient to prove it without the Testimony of the Church', *Some Discourses Upon Dr. Burnet and Dr. Tillotson* (1695), preface and p. 22.

29. See E. Jones, Ph.D. thesis, p. 88.

30. D. Ogg, *England in the Reigns of James II and William III* (Oxford University Press, 1955), p. 196.

31. J. le Clerc, *Life of Burnet* (1715), p. 24.

32. J. Lingard, *History of England*, x, pp. 330–1 and notes.

33. G. Burnet, *A Sermon Preached before the House of Commons on the 31st. of Jan. 1688* (1689), pp. 10, 11, 13. Cf. T. Claydon who describes the propaganda campaign as 'the Burnetine ideology'. Burnet was the creator of the idea of 'courtly reformation' which was a main propagandist plank of the new revolutionary government.

34. G. Burnet, *Sermon, 31st Jan. 1688*.

35. See below, pp. 77, 83, 85, 90, 109. For further details, see E. Jones, Ph.D. thesis, pp. 93–115, 316.

36. G. Burnet, *Sermon, 31st Jan. 1688*.

37. See below, pp. 210, 245.

38. F. Palgrave, *The History of Normandy and England* (1851), preface, pp. xlv–xlvi.

39. See E. Jones, Ph.D. thesis, pp. 22–43, 188–280.

40. T.E.S. Clarke and H.C. Foxcroft, *A Life of Gilbert Burnet . . . With an introduction by C.H. Firth* (Cambridge, 1907), p. 150.

41. G. Burnet, *Reformation* (2nd edn, 1681), i, preface. Clarke & Foxcroft, *Life of Burnet*, p. 151. Cf. G. Burnet, *Reformation*, ed. N. Pocock (1865), vii, editor's preface, p. 1.

42. G. Burnet, *Reformation* (1st edn, 1715), iii, introduction, p. 1. Cf. 'The author's acquaintance with books appears to have been limited within narrow bounds at least at the time when the first two parts of the History appeared', G. Burnet, *Reformation*, ed. N. Pocock, editor's preface.

43. See below, p. 77.

44. J. Morrill speaks of the 'disintegration of Anglicanism and Protestantism' after the Civil War and Interregnum, 'The Stuarts', *The Oxford Illustrated History of Britain*, ed. K.O. Morgan (Oxford University Press, 1994), p. 344. Cf. J. Spurr, 'Religion in Restoration England', pp. 90, 118, 120, 122. Cf. G. Burnet, *Reformation* (1st edn, 1715), iii, p. viii.

45. J. Salter to J. Strype, 30 Oct. 1674, Cambridge Univ. Lib. MSS., Baumgartner I, Strype Corresp., pt. i, f. I. Cf. 'who shall be judg of ye unlawfulness or lawfulness of yr condition: we must not: for then by ye same reason the church of Rome shall be judge & so we should be sure to be condemned as schismatical for separating from her: ye nonconformists must not, for they will as certainly excuse themselves, as we do – in our difficulty', Salter to Strype, 10 Aug. 1674. Ibid. f. 16.

46. G.N. Clarke, *The Later Stuarts, 1660–1714* (Clarendon Press, 1949 repr.), pp. 88–90.

47. See lecture by P. Collinson, 'Prejudice Unmasked', printed in *The Tablet* (March 1995).

48. G. Burnet, *Sermon of 23rd. Dec. 1688* (1689), p. 28. Cf. the title of a tract, written anonymously in 1688: *The Ill Effects of Animosities Among Protestants in England Detected. And the Necessity of Love unto, and Confidence in one another, in order to withstand the Designs of the Common Enemies, laid open and enforced.* This tract is attributed to Burnet in the British Museum Catalogue, but this authorship is questioned in T.E.S. Clarke and H.C. Foxcroft, *Life of Burnet* (Cambridge, 1907), p. 555.

49. G. Burnet, *Reformation* (1st edn, 1715), iii, dedication.

50. Ibid, introduction, p. viii.

51. Ibid.

52. Cf. 'No work which involved the history of real property could be of purely academic interest in the seventeenth century, especially when its theme was related to the central religious conflict of the age', P. Styles, 'Politics and Historical Research in the early Seventeenth Century', *English Historical Scholarship in the Sixtenth and Seventeenth Centuries*, ed. L. Fox (Oxford University Press), p. 69.
53. G. Burnet, *Reformation* (1st edn, 1715), introduction, p. xii.
54. Ibid., p. xv.
55. G. Burnet, *Reformation* (2nd edn, 1681), i, preface.
56. J. Kenyon, *The History Men*, p. 38.
57. See G. Hickes, *Discourses on Burnet and Tillotson*, preface. Cf. E. Jones, Ph.D. thesis, pp. 111–12.
58. G. Burnet, *Letter . . . To the Lord Bishop of Coventry* (1693), p. 20.
59. G. Burnet, *Reflections On a Book Entituled The Rights, Powers and Priveleges of an English Convocation, Stated and Vindicated* (1700), p. 25.
60. T.E.S. Clarke and H.C. Foxcroft, *Life of Burnet*, p. 152.
61. Ibid., preface by C. Firth, pp. xii–xiii.
62. G. Burnet, *Reflections . . .* (1700), p. 25.
63. G. Burnet, *Reformation*, ed. N. Pocock, editor's preface, p. 67. Cf. Thomas Smith, who composed the first proper catalogue of the Cotton collection, compared Burnet's copies of records with the originals in that collection, and concluded that there 'is little or no credit to be given to Dr. Burnet's Collections: he and his Scotch Amanuensis having been guilty of shameful omission and perversions in numerous instances', T. Smith to T. Hearne, 31 Dec. 1705. See E. Jones, Ph.D. thesis, p. 102.
64. J. Kenyon, *History Men* (1993), p. 37.
65. Cf. E. Jones, Ph.D. thesis, pp. 104–8. Cf: 'The Critical Notes on ye History of ye Reformation can never do harm to ye Author [Burnet] or to ye cause, for I have imparted them to no body but yor selfe . . . these . . . will be buryed with me in obscure silence', N. Battley to J. Strype, 23 July 1692, Cambridge Univ. Lib. MSS., Baumgarten e, Strype II, f. 36.
66. See below pp. 83, 88–90. When Anthony Wood of Oxford discovered the ill dealings of Henry VIII's agents who came to Oxford in order to get a favourable opinion on the divorce – as opposed to what Burnet had written – Burnet was 'angry'. Wood's *History of Oxford* was cited in parliament in 1679 as being against the Reformation. Burnet wrote that 'This is writ very indecently: Neither like a Divine, nor a Christian' and accused Wood of being 'a Tool of some of the Church of *Rome*'. See E. Jones, Ph.D. thesis, pp. 104–5.
67. Hickes wrote about this anonymously. We know his authorship because of a letter he sent to his friend Thoresby, which he concluded with: 'I must enjoin you to burn this letter, which makes mention of it', Hickes to R. Thoresby, 14 October 1708. See E. Jones, Ph.D. thesis, p. 101. Fortunately Thoresby did not obey this instruction. The manuscript of Luther, 'Cogitationes Lutheri de sacramento, scriptae

manu propris', is in Corpus Christi College Library, Cambridge, MS. 102, f. 271.

68. P. Hazard, *La Crise de la Conscience Européenne 1680–1715* (Paris, 1935, 3 vols), i, pp. 40–2.

69. See J. Kenyon, *History Men*, p. 39.

70. See E. Jones, Ph.D. thesis, pp. 73–130.

71. B.H.G. Wormald, *Clarendon* (Cambridge University Press, 1951), pp. 306–8.

72. K. Sharpe, *The Personal Rule of Charles I*, p. 284.

73. M. Creighton, 'Peter Heylin', *Dictionary of National Biography*, xxvi (1891), p. 319.

74. The scholarly Hearne made a valid criticism of Strype: 'Mr. Strype hath a large Collection of MSS. Papers, & he is an industrious Man. But then as I take it, he wants both Learning and Judgment and does not know how to make a true and right use of his Papers', Hearne to Anstis, 18 July 1714, Bodleian MSS. copied by Hearne into his Diary, vol. 56, ff. 7–8. This judgment is confirmed by R. O'Day, *The Debate on the English Reformation* (Methuen, 1985), pp. 47–52.

75. See T. Lathbury, *A History of the Non-Jurors* (1845), pp. 286–8. Cf. J. Collier, *Ecclesiastical History* (ed. F. Barham, 1840), ii, 48–50 and Barham's preface, pp. v, vi, ix. Cf. G. Every, *The High Church Party* (1956), p. 73.

76. Cf. R.D. Cornwall, *Visible and Apostolic: The Constitution of the Church in High Church Anglican and Non-Juror Thought* (University of Delaware Press, 1993). Cf. K. Feiling, *History of the Tory Party 1640–1714* (Oxford, 1924), p. 410.

77. See Z.N. Brooke, *The English Church and the Papacy* (Cambridge University Press, 1989), with new foreword by C.N.L. Brooke, foreword and introduction, pp. 1–21.

78. See below, pp. 92, 142ff.

79. 'For my own part, I am now here like a Recluse, & converse much more with the Dead than with the living'. Hearne to Browne Willis, 14 Dec. 1715. Copied by Hearne into his Diary, Bodleian MS., No. 58, f. 100.

80. In a letter from Hearne's lame and indigent father, we hear of a guinea which Hearne had sent 'towards the Buriall charge of your poort Brother Jo', a request for 'any spare Linnen as shirts bands or handkerchiefs or a pair of old stockings which will go into a small bundle', a reference to 'Brother Ned' who 'fell sick and lost his Harvest', to William who 'thanks you for sending him the Guinea to help his charge', and to his father's condition: ''tis hard with me being to pay such Rent that I cannot buy anything of apparel . . . I will endeavour to be content if my Creditors will but let me alone', George Hearne to T. Hearne, 8 Oct. 1716, Bodleian MS., Rawlinson Letters, 26, f. 3.

81. 'Sept 15, 1724', Bodleian MS., Hearne's Diary, 104, ff. 155–6.

82. Hearne to –, 20 Jan. 1717, Bodleian MS., Rawlinson Letters, f. 172.
83. 'Account of the Proceedings against me with relation to Camden's Elizabeth . . .', Bodleian MS., Hearne's Diary, 71, f. 4.
84. Ibid., ff. 16, 18.
85. Hearne to –, 20 Jan. 1717, Bodleian MS., Rawlinson Letters, 26, No. 56, f. 172.
86. Strype to Charlett, 24 May, 1718, Bodleian. MS., Ballard 15, f. 72b.
87. Charlett to Strype, 3 June 1718, Cambridge Univ. Lib. Ms., Strype Correspondence, iv, part iii, f. 258.
88. Browne Willis to Hearne, 18 Feb. 1715, Bodleian MS., Rawlinson Letters, 27 A, f. 129.
89. Hearne to –, n.d., Bodleian MS., Rawlinson Letters, 39, f. 119.
90. 'Nov. 1715', Bodleian MS., Hearne's Diaries, ff. 70–1, 78.
91. *Impartial Memorials . . . By several Hands* (1736), frontispiece.
92. A notice of the sale which took place at 'T. Osborne's Shop, Gray's Inn on 16 Feb. 1736 is in *Lists of Catalgues of English Book Sales 1676–1900 in the British Museum*, ed. A.W. Pollard (1915), p. 246.
93. 'Hearne's Catalogue', Bodleian MS., English miscellaneous, e. 49.
94. *Impartial Memorials*, p. 26.
95. Ibid., p. 60.
96. See below, p. 176.
97. D.C. Douglas, *English Scholars* (1939), pp. 243, 240, 234.
98. See below, pp. 179, 216.
99. See E. Jones, Ph.D. thesis, pp. 231–63.
100. J. Collier, *Ecclesiastical History*, ed. F. Barham (1840), preface, p. lxiii.
101. Ibid.
102. Burnet saw the assertion of the erastian position as one of the main marks of the genuine Protestant, as opposed to those who, by their 'Popish' tendencies, were endangering the Established Church. Attacking these latter, Burnet writes: 'the Independence of the Church on the State, is also contended for as if it were on Design to disgrace our Reformation', *Reformation* (1st edn, 1715), iii, introduction, p. xxii.
103. See E. Jones, Ph.D. thesis, pp. 188–241. Cf. T. Lathbury, *History of the Non-Jurors*, pp. 80, 241.
104. J. Collier, *History*, preface, p. lxiv. Again, it is interesting to find Collier, in his preface, in opposition to Prynne, referring to the papal opinion on the regal supremacy: 'In the last page he [Prynne] makes a lamentable misconstruction of Innocent the Third's letter to King John, and has so little judgment as to make the pope acknowledge the king's supreme ecclesiastical power. That the court of Rome has challenged a temporal jurisdiction over princes we have too much proof, but that they ever owned kings for the spiritual heads of the Church, was never heard of till Mr. Prinn's discovery', ibid., p. lxix. Contrast these remarks of Collier, in his preface, with his conventional statement of the relations

between King John and the Papacy in his main narrative. See below, pp. 134–5.

105. Ibid., p. lxvi.

106. Ibid., pp. lxvi–lxvii.

107. Ibid., p. lxix.

108. J. Collier, *History*, ed. T. Lathbury (1852), ii, p. 98.

109. Ibid., ii, p. 179.

110. J. Collier, *History* (1714), ii, p. 82.

111. Ibid., ii, p. 47

112. Ibid., ii, p. 80

113. J. Collier, *History*, ed. T. Lathbury (1852), iv, p. 263

114. See E. Jones, Ph.D. thesis, pp. 188–280

115. J. Collier, *History*, ed. Barham (1840), ii, pp. 47–8

116. Cf. 'Wharton was irrevocably committed to the Non-juring cause that he had betrayed. He was never happy under the new political regime which he did not hesitate to condemn', D.C. Douglas, *English Scholars*, p. 193

117. Cf. Thomas Hearne admired his work but considered that he was lacking in integrity, *The Remains of Thomas Hearne M.A. of Edmund Hall. Being Extracts from MS. Diaries, collected with a few notes*, ed. P. Bliss (2nd edn, 1869, 3 vols), iii, p. 18.

118. D.C. Douglas, *English Scholars*, p. 179

119. See E. Jones, Ph.D. thesis, pp. 135–50

120. G. Burnet, *History of the Reformation* (1st edn, 1681), ii, p. 340.

121. H. Wharton, *Specimen of Some Errors and Defects in the History of the Reformation of the Church of England, Wrote by G. Burnet D.D., now Lord Bishop of Sarum* (1695), p. 147.

122. D.C. Douglas, *English Scholars*, p. 179.

123. See H. Wharton, *Anglia Sacra* (1691), p. 792.

124. Baker to J. Ward, 2 July 1739, British Museum MS. Add. 6029, ff. 59–60. Cf. 'My life is monastic as my studies . . .', Baker to Wanley, 20 July 1714, British Museum MS., Harleian 3777, f. 56. 'I am out of the world & live in the utmost retirement', Baker to Strype, 22 May 1720, Cambridge Univ. Lib. MS., Baumgarten, 10 Strype Corresp., Baker Papers, Part II, f. 120.

125. See E. Jones, Ph.D. thesis, pp. 198–9.

126. Baker's MS. note on his copy of Burnet's *Reformation* (1715), iii, preface, p. x, This copy is in Cambridge University Library.

127. Baker's MS. note on ibid. (appendix in which Burnet prints Baker's corrections), p. 401. (Cambridge Univ. Lib.)

128. Ibid.

129. Burnet to Baker, 5 Feb 1713, Bodleian MS., English history, d.1, f. 84 (transcript).

130. Ibid.

131. Baker to Hearne, Recd. 23 Sept. 1725, Bodleian MS., Rawlinson Letters, 23, f. 26.

NOTES

132. Kennet to Baker, 28 Mar. 1724, Bodleian MS., English history, d. 1, f. 83.
133. Baker to Thoresby, 23 Mar. 1710, *Letters to Eminent Men Addressed to Ralph Thoresby, F.R.S. Now first Published from the Originals* (1832), ii, p. 236.
134. G. Burnet, *Reformation* (2nd edn, 1681), i, pp. 301–2.
135. T. Baker's MS. note in margin of ibid. (Cambridge Univ. Lib.)
136. See E. Jones, Ph.D. thesis, pp. 188–280.
137. Ibid., pp. 115–30.
138. See below, pp. 179, 216.

CHAPTER III

1. F.W. Maitland, *The Constitutional History of England* (Cambridge University Press, 1961, reprint of 1908 edn), p. 2.
2. See S.L. Kliger, *The Goths in England* (Cambridge, Mass., 1952). Kliger discusses its beginnings in 1567 in the work of William Rastell, pp. 24–5. J.G.A. Pocock warns of the danger of exaggerating this theme, *The Ancient Constitution and the Feudal Law* (Cambridge University Press, 1957), p. 57.
3. See below, pp. 223–5.
4. J.G.A. Pocock, *Ancient Constitution*, p. 56.
5. See 'Dooms of Aethelberht (1601–4)', *Sources*, ed. C. Stephenson and G. Marcham, pp. 2–3. Cf. Maitland's comment that 'We do well to remember that the oldest laws we have . . . are . . . Christian laws', *Constitutional History*, p. 2.
6. Cf. 'The main force which made for the improvement of law was the church, and the church if it was Catholic was also Roman', F.W. Maitland, *Constitutional History*, p. 5.
7. See above, p. 273 note 13.
8. Cf. F.W. Maitland, *Constitutional History*, p. 7.
9. See P. Brand, 'Henry II and the Creation of the English Common Law', *The Making of the Common Law* (Hambledon Press, 1992).
10. I do not consider that P. Brand ('The Court Room and the School Room', in ibid.) has shown convincingly that the systematic teaching of the Common Law began in the thirteenth century; though I think he has made the case for some handing on of vocational information from senior to junior practitioners.
11. F.W. Maitland, *Constitutional History*, p. 21.
12. Ibid.
13. Cf. 'The social structure of England changed greatly between 1189 and 1307. It is quite arguable that "the feudal barony came to an end in the fourteenth century"', F.M. Powicke, *King Henry III and the Lord Edward* (Oxford University Press, 1947), ii, p. 703. Cf. S. Painter, *Studies in the History of the English Feudal Barony* (Baltimore, 1943),

p. 197. Cf. P. Cuss, *The Knight in Medieval England* (Sutton Publishing, 1995), p. 170.

14. See above, pp. 95, 293 note 5.
15. See the 'Dooms of Ine', *Sources*, ed. Stephenson and Marcham, pp. 6–7.
16. Cf. 'the church, Catholic and Roman, carried with it wherever it went the tradition of the older civilization, carried with it Roman institutions such as the will . . .', F.W. Maitland, *Constitutional History*, p. 6.
17. Ibid., p. 11.
18. R.W. Southern, *Scholastic Humanism*, i, pp. 158–62, 317.
19. Ibid.
20. Ibid.
21. F.W. Maitland, *Constitutional History*, p. 11. Cf. 'The fundamental distinction that we draw between real and personal property' derives from the 'division of the law into two departments, the secular and the spiritual'. Also 'Why do we still couple "probate" with "divorce"? Merely because both matrimonial and testamentary causes belonged to the church courts'.
22. See below, pp. 131–2.
23. J.G.A. Pocock, *Ancient Constitution*, pp. 91–123.
24. Cf. above, pp. 90, 108–9.
25. The Act in Restraint of Appeals (1533) forbade any legal appeals from England to Rome. Until then the Canon Law was operating normally in England.
26. J.G.A. Pocock, *Ancient Constitution*, pp. 91–123.
27. C.R. Cheney, *From Becket to Langton. English Church Government 1170–1213* (Manchester University Press, 1956), pp. 84–5.
28. Ibid., p. 97.
29. Z.N. Brooke, *The English Church and the Papacy* (Cambridge, 1931), pp. 101, 226.
30. W.A. Pantin, *The English Church in the Fourteenth Century* (Cambridge University Press, 1955), pp. 2–4.
31. W.T. Waugh, 'The Great Statute of Praemunire', *The English Historical Review*, xxxvii (1922), p. 175, note 219.
32. F.W. Maitland, *Roman Canon Law in the Church of England* (1898), p. 92.
33. Ibid. Cf. Sir William Holdsworth: 'In the preambles to Henry's statutes we can see the gradual elaboration of the main characteristics of those changed relations of Church and State – the theory of the Royal Supremacy. The dual control over things temporal and spiritual is to end. The crown is to be supreme over all persons and causes. The canon law of the Western church is to give place to the "King's Ecclesiastical Law of the Church of England". These great results were achieved by the Reformation Parliament which sat from 1529 to 1536. . . . Both the legal and doctrinal theory obscure the very fundamental change which had taken place at the Reformation. The relations between Church and State, and the position of the ecclesiastical courts had been fundamentally

altered. The church had been brought within the state; and subjected to the power of the crown. That has involved in the course of time other consequential changes. . . . The result of the Reformation was the transference to the state of complete control over the church and the substitution for the canon law of the King's Ecclesiastical law', *A History of English Law* (6th edn, 1938), i, pp. 588, 597–8.

34.   J.G.A. Pocock, *Ancient Constitution*, pp. 29–31.

35.   Sir J. Davis, *Les Reports Des Cases & Matters En Ley* (1674), preface.

36.   Cf. 'The English Reformation must be seen . . . as an assertion of English nationalism. . . . For 250 years protestantism and patriotism were closely interwoven', C. Hill, *Reformation to Industrial Revolution* (Penguin, 1992), pp. 25, 36, 42. Cf. 'Between 1530 and 1580 these same pressures of State converted England into a Protestant country and added the Protestant faith to the sense of national identity which was clearly emerging. By the time of the Armada in 1588 it was about as necessary as loyalty to the Crown, and more necessary than English speech', D. Loades, *Power in Tudor England*, p. 157.

37.   See below, p. 175.

38.   Sir M. Hale, *The History of the Common Law of England, Written by a Learned Hand* (1713), pp. 28–9.

39.   *Councils and Ecclesiastical Documents Relating to Great Britain and Ireland, Edited after Spelman and Wilkins*, ed. A.W. Haddan and W. Stubbs (Oxford, 1869), preface, p. x.

40.   Ibid.

41.   G.V. Bennet, *White Kennett, 1660–1728* (1957), p. 167.

42.   W. Wake, *An Appeal to all the True Members of the Church of England in behalf of the King's Ecclesiastical Supremacy* (1698). Cf. W. Wake, *State of the Church and Clergy of England* (1703), p. 1.

43.   Wake 'considered the Old English Period as one in which the rights of the Crown over the Church were essentially similar to those reasserted by the English monarchy after the submission of the Clergy in 1533, while in the intervening period he postulated those same rights as having been usurped by the Papacy', D.C. Douglas, *English Scholars* (2nd edn, 1951), p. 214 Cf. G. Every, *The High Church Party* (1956), p. 86.

44.   E.F. Jacob, 'Wilkins's Concilia And The Fifteenth Century', *Transactions of the Royal Historical Society*, xv (1932), pp. 120–7.

45.   See H. Cam, 'Stubbs Seventy Years After', *Cambridge Historical Journal*, ix (1948); and J.G. Edwards, *William Stubbs* (1952).

46.   *Oxford Companion to English Literature*, ed. M. Drabble, p. 946.

47.   See H. Kearney, *The British Isles. A History of Four Nations* (Cambridge University Press, 1990), p. 1.

48.   John Lingard was the first English historian to do this, using his own critical methodology.

49.   Quoted in *Oxford Companion to English Literature*, ed. M. Drabble, p. 946.

50. Maitland was aware of the probable reaction to his conclusions See his *Roman Canon Law In The Church of England* (1898), pp. 86–7.

51. Cf. 'he too easily endorsed the tradition which he found in vogue among the ecclesiastical judges of his own day', H.W.C. Davis, 'The Canon Law in England', *Zeitschrift Der Savigny-Stiftung Für Rechtsgeschichte*, xxxiv (1913), p. 351.

52. W. Holdsworthy, *History of English Law*, i, p. 591, note 1.

53. See H. Kearney, *The British Isles*, p. 1.

54. See J.G.A. Pocock, *Ancient Constitution*, pp. 91–124.

55. See H. Butterfield, *The Englishman and his History* (Cambridge University Press, 1944), pp. 35–6.

56. See J.G.A. Pocock, *Ancient Constitution*. Cf. F.W. Maitland, *Why the History of English Law is Not Written* (Cambridge, 1888), p. 12.

57. H. Butterfield, *Englishman and his History*, pp. 35–6. Cf. H.A. Cronne, 'The Study and the Use of Charters by English Scholars in the Seventeenth Century', *English Historical Scholarship in the Sixteenth and Seventeenth Centuries*, ed. L. Fox (Oxford University Press, 1956), p. 77.

58. Cf. Spelman to Whelock, 22 Sept. 1637, Cambridge Univ. Lib. MS. Dd. 3, 12, ii. 3. Cf. Spelman to –, 28 Mar. 1639, British Museum MS., Add. 34500, f. 170. Cf. C. Dodd, *Church History*, ed. M.A. Tierney (1839), pp. 25–6, note 1. Cf. F. Wortley, *Characters and Elegies* (1646), pp. 48–9.

59. See J.G.A. Pocock, 'Robert Brady, 1627–1700. A Cambridge Historian of the Restoration', *Cambridge Historical Journal*, x, no. 2 (1951), pp. 186–204.

60. Ibid.

61. R. Brady, *A Compleat History of England from the first entrance of the Romans under the Conduct of Julius Caesar, Unto the End of the Reign of King Henry III* (1685), Preface to the Norman Period, pp. 296–7.

62. Ibid.

63. J. Collier, *History*, ed. T. Lathbury (1872), iv, pp. 259–60.

64. Ibid., ii, p. 307.

65. G.N. Clarke, *The Later Stuarts, 1660–1714* (Oxford University Press, 1949), p. 119.

66. Ibid. I am not convinced by attempts to ascribe the Oxford Theses to A. Woodhead. See *Recusant History* (Oct. 1981), pp. 406–9.

67. See M. Nédoncelle, *Trois Aspects Du Problème Anglo-Catholique En XVIIe Siècle* (1951), p. 53.

68. Cf. G. Burnet, *Reflections On The Oxford Theses. Relating to the English Reformation, Part II* (Amsterdam, 1688); and *Reflections On The Relation of the English Reformation Lately Printed at Oxford* (London, 1689). Cf. note 72, below.

69. For example, one Timothy Nourse had been expelled from his fellowship at University College on becoming a Catholic.

70. G. Williams, 'Some Protestant Views of Early British Church History', *History*, xxxviii (1953), pp. 230, 233.

NOTES

71. *Life and Times of A. Wood*, ed. A. Clarke (1892). Entry for 'Dec. 21 1673', ii, p. 275.
72. Ibid., '30 Octob. 1678', ii, p. 421.
73. For Grimstone's attack, see ibid., '30 Apr. 1679', ii, p. 449. Cf. A. Wood, *Athenae Oxoniensis* (2nd edn, 1721), ii, p. 933. For Burnet's involvement, see A. Wood, *Athenae*, ii, p. 449 and M. Nédoncelle, *Trois Aspects*, p. 51.
74. A conspiracy, involving the Duke of Monmouth and several prominent Whigs, to assassinate Charles II and his brother, James, Duke of York, as they passed by Rye House on their way to the races at Newmarket.
75. *Life and Times of A. Wood*, ed. Llewelyn Poweys (1932), p. 270.
76. *Calendar of State Papers – Domestic, 1668–69* (1895), p. 76.
77. *Remains of Thomas Hearne*, ed. P. Bliss, i, p. 60.
78. Item '15 Aug. 1695', *Letters to Thoresby* (1832), i, pp. 211–16.
79. H. Butterfield, *The Englishman and his History*, p. 32.
80. Ibid.
81. O. Walker, *Relation of the English Reformation* (1687), p. 21.
82. Ibid. If Catherine's marriage with Henry VIII's eldest brother, Arthur, in 1509, had been consummated, then this would have weakened the case in Canon Law for the validity of her marriage to Henry.
83. Ibid., p. 23.
84. Ibid., p. 24.
85. Ibid., p. 40.
86. See above, note 50, and below, note 89.
87. O. Walker, *Relation of the English Reformation*, pp. 41–3. Cf. J. Sacrisbrick who refers to the Act of Supremacy as 'the central event of the 1530s', *Henry VIII* (Eyre & Spottiswoode, 1968), p. 304.
88. O. Walker, *Relation of the English Reformation*. Cf. F.M. Powicke's statement, below, ch. 7, note 103. Cf. 'The English Reformation was enacted by statute', C. Hill, *Reformation to Industrial Revolution*, p. 35.
89. Cf. 'It may be expedient for me to say that I am a dissenter from both the "English" and the "Roman" and from other churches', F.W. Maitland, *Roman Canon Law in the Church of England* (1898), preface, p. vi. Maitland noticed the part played by English nationalism in the official view of the past, ibid, pp. 84, 86, 89. This was 'the only one of his mature books not published by his University Press . . . The immediate reaction [to it] . . . was one of stunned amazement', G.R. Elton, *F.W. Maitland* (Weidenfeld & Nicolson, 1985) pp. 73–4.

CHAPTER IV

1. W.A. Pantin, *The English Church in the Fourteenth Century* (Cambridge, 1955), p. 2.
2. F.M. Powicke, *The Reformation in England* (Oxford University Press, 1949), pp. 7–8.
3. See, for example, E. Duffy, *The Stripping of the Altars*.

4. See D.C. Douglas, *English Scholars* (2nd edn, 1951).

5. 'In a generation of great learning the most profound scholars were among the Non-jurors', K. Feiling, *A History of the Tory Party 1640–1714* (Oxford, 1924), p. 203.

6. Cf. 'I was obliged by my Physician's advice to resolve upon an immediate journey to the Bath . . . the care of my health & direction of Physicians have forbidden to me all thoughts & care of the Res Literaria, till it shall please God to restore me', Wharton to Charlett, 16 June, 1694, Bodleian MS., Ballard 15, f. 5.

7. N. Battley to J. Strype, 15 March 1695, Cambridge Univ. Lib. MS. Baumgarten 3, Strype Correspondence II, f. 52.

8. D.C. Douglas, *English Scholars*, pp. 176, 185, 186.

9. Wharton to Todd, 28 Oct. 1689. *Letters on Various Subjects, Literary, Political and Ecclesiastical to and from William Nicolson*, ed. J. Nichols (1809), i, 13–14.

10. Wharton to Todd, 28 Oct. 1689. Ibid., i, 14.

11. Wharton to Charlett, 16 June 1694. Bodleian MS., Ballard 15, f. 5.

12. F.M. Powicke was the first medievalist to write even a short essay on the Reformation. See his *History of the Reformation* (Oxford University Press, 1941).

13. H. Wharton, *Specimen* (1693), p. 49.

14. See above, p. 116.

15. H. Wharton, *Specimen*, p. 160.

16. N. Battely to J. Stype, Feb. 1692. Cambridge Univ. Lib. MS. Baumgarten 3, Strype II, f. 43.

17. G. Burnet, *Reformation* (2nd edn, 1679), i, p. 107.

18. H. Wharton, *Specimen*, p. 27.

19. G. Burnet, *Reformation*, (1st edn, 1679), i, p. 107.

20. H. Wharton, *Specimen*, p. 20.

21. Cf. 'After 1400 the provision of aliens to English benefices almost ceased, and papal provision, so far as it survived, was simply one of several ways by which Englishmen got English benefices. Thus the papal provision of aliens to English benefices, contrary to the popular notion, cannot be seriously considered as one of the causes of the Reformation', W.A. Pantin, *The English Church in the Fourteenth Century* (Oxford University Press, 1955), p. 96.

22. H. Wharton, *Specimen*, p. 20.

23. Cf. F.M. Powicke, *The Reformation in England* (Oxford University Press, 1941), pp. 6, 8. Cf. J. Scarisbrick, *The Reformation and the English People* (Basil Blackwell, 1984), pp. 1–2.

24. G. Burnet, *Reformation* (1st edn, 1679), i, p. 158.

25. H. Wharton, *Specimen*, pp. 35–6.

26. G. Burnet, *Reformation*, i, p. 316.

27. H. Wharton, *Specimen*, pp. 56–7.

28. Ibid., pp. 31–2.

29. Ibid., pp. 12–14.
30. Cf. 'Read the beginning of Burnet's *History of the Reformation* in his abridgment . . . his thoughts are very good and the series of affairs that made way for the reception of the Reformation with so much ease are set in a full and proper light', *The Diary of Dudley Ryder, 1715–16*, ed. W. Matthews (1939), p. 111.
31. See J. Scarisbrick, *Reformation and English People*, pp. 1–2.
32. Cf. 'The Reformation saw an extension of lay control over the Church in terms of patronage as well as income', D. Palliser, *The Age of Elizabeth. England under the Later Tudors. A Social and Economic History of England* (2nd edn, 1992), p. 354.
33. G. Burnet, *Reformation*, ii (1681), p. 24.
34. H. Wharton, *Specimen*, p. 66.
35. H. Wharton, *Anglia Sacra. Sive Collection Historarium Partim antiquitas, partim recenter scripturam. De Archiepiscupis & Episcupis Angliae. A prima Fidei Christianiae susceptione ad Annum MDXL. Nunc primum in Lucem editorum* (1691, 2 parts), i, p. 792.
36. See P. Hughes, *The Reformation in England* (Hollis & Carter, 1954), i, pp. 207–22.
37. Cf. C. John Sommerville, *The Secularisation of Early Modern England* (Oxford University Press, 1992).
38. Z.N. Brooke, *The English Church and the Papacy* (1989 edn), p. 209.
39. M.D. Knowles, 'Archbishop Thomas Becket. A Character Study', *Proceedings of the British Academy*, xxv (1949), p. 193.
40. Some of the Constitutions were: the custody and revenues of every vacant archbishopric, bishopric, abbey and priory should go to the king; every suit involving a clergyman, should commence before the king's justices who should determine whether the cause ought to be tried in the secular or episcopal court; no senior cleric should go overseas without the king's permission; appeals in clerical cases should not go to the Papacy without the king's consent.
41. Ibid.
42. Cf. *State Papers: Henry VIII*, xiii, Part ii (1893), No. 1087), No. 133 and preface, pp. xv–xvi. Cf. D. Wilkins, *Concili Magna* (1737), iii, p. 835.
43. Cf. H. Butterfield, *The Englishman and his History*, p. 17.
44. J. Foxe, *Acts and Monuments*, ed. S.R. Cattley (1837), ii, pp. 196, 197, 198, 203, 205, 213, 227, 228, 229.
45. T. Fuller, *Church History of Britain*, ed. J.S. Brewer (Oxford, 1845), ii, pp. 98, 101, 102, 103.
46. W. Prynne, *The first . . . tome of an exact chronological vindication* (1666), p. 489.
47. G. Burnet, *Reformation*, ed. N. Pocock (1865), i, pp. 236, 387, 388.
48. M. Hale, *The History of the Common Law of England* (1713), p. 138.
49. J. Collier, *History*, ed. T. Lathbury (1852), iv, p. 421.
50. Ibid., ii, pp. 252, 269.

51. Ibid., ii, p. 302.
52. H. Wharton, *Anglia Sacra*, ii, p. 523 and notes.
53. Nicholas Battely was a research worker for John Strype. See E. Jones, Ph. D. thesis, Appendix II, 'John Strype and Nicholas Battely', pp. 300–17.
54. Battely to Strype, 3 May, 1692. Cambridge Univ. Lib. MS., Baumgarten, 3, Strype Corresp., ii. f. 35.
55. See W. Newton, *The Life of Dr. White Kennett* (1730).
56. Quoted in J. Collier, *Some Observations on Doctor Kennet's Second and Third Letters Wherein His Misrepresentations of Mr. Collier's Ecclesiastical History Are Lay'd Open and his Calumnies Disprov'd* (1717), p. 3.
57. See above, p. 200.
58. G.M. Trevelyan, *History of England* (Longman, 1947), p. 169. Cf. F.M. Powicke, *Stephen Langton* (Oxford, 1928).
59. See below, pp. 200–3.
60. H. Butterfield, *The Englishman and his History*, p. 19.
61. See above, p. 49.
62. J. Foxe, *Acts and Monuments*, ed. S.R. Cattley (1837), ii, p. 333.
63. Ibid.
64. See L. Colley, *Britons*, pp. 11–55.
65. See W.T. MacCaffrey, *Queen Elizabeth and the Making of Policy 1572–1588* (Princeton University Press, 1981), p. 266.
66. T. Fuller, *Church History*, ed. S. Brewer (1845), ii, pp. 144, 148, 150.
67. W. Prynne, *The first (and second) tome of an exact chronological vindication . . .* (1665), ii, p. 227.
68. G. Burnet, *History*, ed. N. Pocock (1865), i, p. 551.
69. J. Collier, *History*, ed. T. Lathbury, ii, p. 393.
70. Ibid., ii, p. 411.
71. Cf. M. Ashley, *England in the Seventeenth Century* (Penguin, 1952), p. 130.
72. *English Historical Documents*, ed. D.C. Douglas, vol. viii, ed. A. Browning (Eyre and Spottiswoode, 1953), pp. 863–7. The editor acknowledges that this Secret Treaty of Dover is printed from J. Lingard's *History of England* (1874), ix, pp. 251–4.
73. W.S. McKechnie, *Magna Carta* (Glasgow, 1905), p. 28.
74. W.E. Lunt, *History of England*, (New York, 1957) 4th edn., pp. 134–5.
75. Ibid.
76. F.M. Powicke, *Stephen Langton* (Oxford, 1928), p. 79.
77. M.D. Knowles, 'The Canterbury Elections of 1205–6', *The English Historical Review*, liii (1938), p. 211.
78. Cf. *Memoriale Fratris Walteri De Coventria*, ed. W. Stubbs, ii, preface, pp. lviii–lix and xlii–xliv.
79. M.D. Knowles, 'Canterbury Elections', p. 220.
80. See *Memoriale*, ed. W. Stubbs, ii, preface, p. lviii and notes, p. 304. K. Norgate, *John Lackland* (1902), pp. 175; G.B. Adams, *History of England, 1066–1216* (1905), p. 422; S. Painter, *William Marshall* (Baltimore,

1933), pp. 175–6; W.S. McKechnie, *Magna Carta*, p. 31; W.E. Lunt, *Financial Relations of the Papacy with England to 1327* (Cambridge, Mass., 1939), p. 134; F.M. Powicke, *Stephen Langton*, p. 78; F.M. Powicke, *Cambridge Mediaeval History* (1929), p. 317.

81.   C.R. Cheney, 'The Alleged Deposition of King John', *Studies in Mediaeval History Presented to F.M. Powicke*, ed. R.W. Hunt, W.A. Pantin and R.W. Southern (Oxford, 1948), pp. 100–16. Lingard had made this same point in 1819. He had shown the untrustworthy nature of Wendover and Matthew Paris as sources, by comparing their accounts with official records – one of his rules of source criticism. Lingard had consequently discounted their accounts of this episode of King John's relationship with the Papacy in 1819. See his *History of England*, ii, p. 626.

82.   C.R. Cheney, 'Alleged Deposition', p. 116.

83.   Ibid.

84.   W.T. Waugh, 'The Great Statute of Praemunire', *The English Historical Review*, xxxvii (1922), pp. 173–4.

85.   G.R. Elton, 'The Evolution of a Reformation Statute', p. 196.

86.   W.A. Pantin, *The English Church*, p. 85.

87.   A.G. Dickens, *The English Reformation* (Fontana, 8th imp., 1976) p. 150.

88.   W.T. Waugh, 'The Great Statute', p. 173.

89.   Cf. C. Hill, *Reformation to Industrial Revolution* (Penguin, 1992 ed.), p. 30. Cf. A.G. Dickens, *English Reformation*, p. 444.

90.   Ibid., p. 154.

91.   See G.R. Elton, 'The Evolution of a Reformation Statute'.

92.   The Act in Restraint of Appeals is printed in *Documents Illustrative of English Church History*, ed. H.J. Gee and W.J. Hardy (1896), pp. 187–92.

93.   Ibid.

94.   J. Foxe, *Acts and Monuments* (1563), ed. S.R. Cattley (1837), ii, p. 777.

95.   T. Fuller, *Church History*, ii, p. 368.

96.   G. Burnet, *Reflections on The Oxford Theses, Relating to the English Reformation* (Amsterdam, 1688), pp. 55–8.

97.   J. Collier, *History*, ed. T. Lathbury, iii, pp. 210–11.

98.   Ibid., iv, p. 172.

99.   W.T. Waugh, 'The Great Statute', p. 196.

100. The appeal to an early British Church of pristine purity had commenced in fact with some early English Protestants who had fled into exile at Antwerp during the period 1525–35. These had included William Tyndale, Frith, Raye and Barlow. See R. O'Day, *The Debate on the English Reformation* (Methuen, 1985), p. 8.

101. See pp. 196–7 below.

102. See p. 144 below.

103. W.T. Waugh, 'The Great Statute', pp. 173, 204.

104. W.W. Capes, *The English Church in the Fourteenth and Fifteenth Centuries* (1900), p. 92.

105. J. Ramsay, *Genesis of Lancaster* (Oxford, 1913), ii, p. 288.

106. E.W. Gwatkin, *Church and State to the Death of Queen Anne* (1917), p. 106.

107. In his *Roman Canon Law in the Church of England* (1898).

108. Z.N. Brooke asserted that the 'Ecclesia Anglicana' always meant that part of the Universal Church was situated in England, until 'the Reformation altered the whole meaning of that phrase', *The English Church and the Papacy* (Cambridge, 1931), pp. 18–20. This work was republished in 1989, with an introduction by C.N. Brooke, bringing it up to date with some recent research, but with no significant change to its original conclusions.

109. W.A. Pantin, *English Church*, pp. 93–4.

110. See G. Williams, 'Some Protestant Views of Early British Church History'.

111. J.E. Lloyd, *A History of Wales*, (1911), p. 173.

112. J.C. McNaught, *The Celtic Church and the See of Peter* (Oxford University Press, 1927), p. 106.

113. *Property and Power in the Early Middle Ages*, ed. W. Davies and P. Fouracre (Cambridge University Press, 1995).

114. Ibid., p. 111. I am indebted in this whole paragraph, and for this quotation, to the review article on this book by R. Bulzaretti, in *The Economic History Review*, l(2), May 1997, p. 393.

115. See N. Saul, *History Today*, 17(3), March 1997, p. 9.

116. See above, p. 198.

117. F.M. Powicke, *The Reformation in England* (Oxford University Press, 1941), pp. 4–7. See above, p. 13.

CHAPTER V

1. Cf. J. Morrill, 'The Stuarts', *The Oxford Illustrated History of Britain*, ed. K.O. Morgan (Oxford University Press, 1994), p. 344.

2. See J. Redwood, *Reason, Ridicule and Religion. The Age of the Enlightenment in England 1660–1750* (Thames and Hudson, 2nd edn, 1996), introduction, p. 17.

3. Sir Isaac Newton (1642–1727), a scientific genius, who pursued a spiritual quest and retained a mystical view of life and the Universe, recognized that he was making only a contribution towards a better understanding. His *Philosophia naturalis principia mathematica* (1687) was an important stage in the history of science.

4. Cf. G.N. Clarke, *The Later Stuarts 1660–1714* (Oxford, 1949), pp. 359–62.

5. Cf. J.P. Bury, *The Idea of Progress* (Macmillan, 1928), p. 64.

6. Cf. D.C. Douglas, *English Scholars 1660–1730* (2nd edn, 1951).

7. Cf. J. Fruchtman, *Thomas Paine and the Religion of Nature* (John Hopkins University Press, 1993).

8. See below, pp. 223–5.

9. Cf. R.C. Zaehner, 'The Religious Instinct', *The New Outline of Modern Knowledge* (1956). Zaehner, the Spalding Professor of Eastern Religions at Oxford, wrote extensively on the religious instinct, as expressed in man's need to worship, to 'belong' to a reality which is greater than himself, to find meaning in life, to search for love, truth and beauty, to distinguish betwen 'right' and 'wrong'. Zaehner explains that this instinct can express itself in warped or distorted ways, if it is not grounded in authentic religion; for people can worship 'false gods'.

10. D. Hume, *Enquiry Concerning the Human Understanding*, ed. L.A. Selby-Biggs (2nd edn, 1902), p. 83, para. 65.

11. D. Hume, *History of England* (1826 edn), p. 437.

12. *The Miscellaneous Works of Edward Gibbon*, ed. Lord Sheffield (1814, 5 vols), iii, pp. 559–60.

13. Ibid., pp. 562–3.

14. Ibid.

15. See H. Butterfield, *Man On His Past*, pp. 47–50.

16. See J.H. Hayes, *The Historical Evolution of Modern Nationalism* (New York, 4th reprint, 1951), pp. 17–22. Bolingbroke believed that England's own national genius expressed itself in its own national Church.

17. R. Porter, *Gibbon. Making History* (Phoenix Giants, 1988), p. 5. Gibbon records on several occasions in his *Memoirs* 'his gratitude for 'having been born "in a free and enlightened country"',*Oxford Companion to English Literature*, ed. M. Drabble, p. 390.

18. Cf. Lingard who wrote to a friend in 1849: 'What do you want with the hallucinations of Hume? I have not time to take and read for that purpose', Lingard to Walker, 7 March, 1849, Ushaw MS., Lingard to Walker 1846–50, a.I, j. 11.

19. D. Hume, *History of England* (1826 edn), preface.

20. Ibid., v, p. 19.

21. Ibid., v, pp. 264, 327, 59.

22. D. Hume, *History*, (1871 reprint of 1786 edn), i, p. 35.

23. Ibid., i, p. 532.

24. Ibid., v, p. 131.

25. Ibid., ii, p. 139.

26. Ibid., v, pp. 131–2.

27. Hume was a 'consummate stylist'. His *History* 'became immensely popular . . . and appeared in nearly 200 lifetime and posthumous editions', *Oxford Companion to English Literature*, ed. M. Drabble, pp. 483, 482. Cf. J. Kenyon, *History Men*, p. 53.

28. P.R. Ghosh, 'Macaulay and the Heritage of the Enlightenment', *The English Historical Review*, cxii, No. 446 (April 1997), p. 391.

29. H. Butterfield, *Man On His Past*, p. 53.

30. C. John Sommerville, 'Surfing the Coffee house', *History Today*, 47(6), (June 1997), p. 10.

31. See D. Womersley's introduction to Edward Gibbons, *History of the*

Decline and Fall of the Roman Empire (Allen Lane, Penguin, 1994, 3 vols); and R. Porter, *Gibbon*, introduction, pp. 6–7.

32. Cf. T.P. Peardon, *The Transition in English Historical Writing, 1760–1830* (New York, 1933).

33. Cf. Linda Colley, *Britons*, introduction, p. 6.

34. W. Wordsworth, 'Hope For Men', *Wordsworth. Selected Poems*, ed. H.M. Margoliouth (1959), p. 114.

35. Cf. England's wonderful progress towards freedom has been enacted 'under the auspices and is confirmed by the sanctions of religion and piety. The whole has emanated from the simplicity of our national character, and from a sort of native plainness and directness of understanding', E. Burke, *Reflections on the French Revolution* (Everyman, 1910), p. 87. Cf. A. Cobban, *Edmund Burke and the Revolt against the Eighteenth Century. A Study of the Political and Social Thinking of Burke, Wordsworth, Coleridge and Southey* (1929).

36. Initially Cobbett was an anti-radical journalist (in his *Political Register* from 1802), but about 1804 his views began to change and he wrote increasingly for the radical interest.

37. B.H.G. Wormald, 'The Historiography of the English Reformation', *Historical Studies* (Papers read before the Second Irish Conference of Historians, 1958), p. 55.

38. See, for example, T. Thorold Rogers, *Six Centuries of Work and Wages* (1884). This 'established that the degradation of labour began after Henry VIII', B.H.G. Wormald, 'Historiography of the English Reformation', p. 55. For a further discussion of this, see D.M. Palliser, *The Age of Elizabeth. A Social and Economic History of England* (2nd edn, 1992), p. 168. Cf. R. Hutton, *Merry England*.

39. Cf. his essential Englishness described in A. Burton, *William Cobbett: Englishman* (Aurum, 1997).

40. William Cobbett, *Rural Rides*, ed. S.E. Buckley (Harrap, 1950), p. 249. Cf. 'By 1570 churches were centres of preaching instead of ritual', R. Hutton, *Merry England*, pp. 109–10. Hutton's work corroborates some of Cobbett's views concerning the decline of social customs related to the old ritual year after the Reformation. Referring to his own very practical education, Cobbett is pleased not to have become 'as inefficient a mortal' as those 'turned out from Winchester and Westminster School, or from any of those dens of dunces called colleges and universities', William Cobbett, *Rural Rides*, ed. S.E. Buckley, p. 76. For the other references, see ibid., pp. 43, 150, 173, 249, 258, 276.

41. See below, p. 174.

42. S. Turner, *The History of the Anglo-Saxons* (1799), preface, p. iv.

43. See T.P. Peardon, *Transition*, pp. 225–6.

44. Cf. 'May not the progress of the human mind from barbarism to knowledge he viewed in epitome in the history of every nation which has undergone this happy process . . . to display the savage primate

slowly ameliorating into the civilized, moral and scientific man', Turner, *History of Anglo-Saxons*, preface, p. viii.

45. S. Turner, *History of England* (1812–23), introduction.
46. Ibid.
47. Ibid.
48. Ibid.
49. Ibid. (1829 edn), iii, preface.
50. See P. Mathias, *The First Industrial Nation. Economic History of Britain 1700–1914* (Routledge, 2nd edn, 1983).
51. S. Turner, *History of England* (1829 edn), iii, preface.
52. Ibid.
53. Ibid.
54. R. Southey, *Book of the Church* (1824), ii, p. 528.
55. Ibid., ii, pp. 33–41.
56. R. Southey, *Sir Thomas More or Colloquies on the Progress and Prospects of Society* (1831), i, p. 247.
57. Robert Southey was also, of course, one of the famous 'Lake Poets' who lived in the Lake District and was a friend of Coleridge. He became Poet Laureate in 1813. See *Robert Southey: The Critical Heritage*, ed. L. Madden (1972).
58. H. Hallam, *View of the State of Europe During the Middle Ages* (1829), ii, p. 2.
59. Ibid., ii, p. 208.
60. Ibid., ii, p. 366 note *.
61. H. Hallam, *Constitutional History of England* (1827), i, p. 61.
62. H. Hallam, *View of the State of Europe*, preface.
63. Ibid., i, p. 357; ii, pp. 216–17.
64. H. Hallam, *Constitutional History*, i, p. 61.
65. H. Hallam, *View of the State of Europe*, ii, p. 374.
66. *Oxford Companion to English Literature*, ed. M. Drabble, p. 428.
67. Cf. In the eighteenth century 'the Englishman of every class is famous for his insular self-satisfaction and his contempt for the foreigner', B. Williams, *The Whig Supremacy 1714–1760* (Oxford University Press, 1939), p. 1.
68. Apart from G.P. Gooch and H. Butterfield. See below, pp. 213–14.

CHAPTER VI

1. M.A. Tierney, 'Memoir of the Rev. Dr. Lingard', prefixed to J. Lingard, *History of England*, i, p. xxvi.
2. See 'Mrs. Lingard's Narrative', printed by F. Fletcher in *Lingard Society Papers* (Oct. 20, 1924).
3. E. Bonney and M. Haile, *The Life and Letters of John Lingard 1771–1851* (1911), p. 17. Cf. C. Haydon, *Anti-Catholicism in Eighteenth Century England* (Manchester University Press, 1994), shows that anti-

Catholicism and religious hatred, fanned by virulent government propaganda, was still a vibrant force in 1780.

4. J.P. Chinnici, *The English Catholic Enlightenment: John Lingard and the Cisalpine Movement 1780–1850* (Patmos Press, Shepherdstown, 1980), pp. 6–11.
5. M.A. Tierney, 'Memoir', pp. xxxiii–xxxiv.
6. Cf. W.J. Hegarty, 'Was Lingard a Cardinal?', *The Irish Ecclesiastical Record* (Feb. 1953), pp. 87–8. Hegarty argues against the rumour, but we know that the Papacy thought very highly of Lingard's work and judged that his Catholic critics in England did not understand the importance of what he was trying to do.
7. See D.F. Shea, *The English Ranke: John Lingard* (Humanities Press, New York, 1969), pp. 71–3. By an Arrête Special, the University of Paris ordered that a copy of Lingard's *History of England* be placed in every college library in France. Lingard was elected a foreign member of the French Academy. Shea's book is a useful short introduction to Lingard, but he does not seem to have known of the unpublished research of E. Jones, M.A. thesis, nor does his comparison with Ranke really bring out the distinctive contribution of Lingard in the area of source criticism.
8. 'Mrs. Lingard's Narrative'.
9. E. Bonney and M. Haile, *Life of Lingard*, pp. 74–5.
10. Ibid., p. 85.
11. T.P. Peardon, *The Transition in English Historical Writing, 1760–1830* (New York, 1933), p. 277. See also P. Phillips, 'John Lingard and the Anglo-Saxon Church', *Recusant History* (Oct. 1996), pp. 181–7.
12. M.A. Tierney, 'Memoirs', p. xxxix.
13. Ibid.
14. Lingard to Husenbeth, 24 July, 1828. Ushaw MS., Lingard Transcripts, File B.11.
15. J. Lingard, *History of England*, ix, p. 495.
16. See Lingard to Mawman, 29 Aug. 1827, Ushaw MS., Lingard to Mawman 1818–27, File B.3, letter M.62. Cf. 'Pollock, the uncompromising Tory, Scarlett, the equally uncompromising Whig – until his opposition to the Reform Bill drove him into the ranks of the Tories – and Brougham, the future chancellor, gathering round the table of the Catholic priest in his village presbytery, afford a picture which makes us sigh with regret that no echoes of their conversation, except the traditon of its excellence, have come down to us', E. Bonney and M. Haile, *Life of Lingard*, p. 242.
17. Cf. 'it will never be known till his life is really written, and his correspondence published, how great a share he had in the direction of our ecclesiastical affairs in England, and how truly he was almost the oracle which our bishops consulted in matters of intricate or delicate

importance', Cardinal Wiseman, *Recollections of the Last Four Popes* (1859), p. 208.

18. See collection of letters 'Lingard to Poynter', Ushaw MSS.
19. J. Lingard, *History of England*, i, p. 437.
20. Ibid., iv, p. 225.
21. Ibid., cf. iii, p. 212; ii, p. 606; i, p. 579.
22. Ibid., vii, p. 153.
23. Ibid., vii, p. 537.
24. C. Russell, *Unrevolutionary England* (Hambledon Press, 1990), introduction, pp. ix–x.
25. J. Lingard, *History of England*, preface, pp. xvii–xviii.
26. Ibid., iv, p. 27.
27. See E.L. Woodward, *The Age of Reform* (1938), p. 532; and T.P. Peradon *The Transition in English Historical Writing*, p. 279.
28. *The Oxford and Cambridge Review* (1846), ii, p. 38.
29. G.P. Gooch, *History and Historians in the Nineteenth Century* (3rd impress., 1920), p. 284.
30. T.P. Peardon, *Transition*, p. 279.
31. D.F. Shea, *Lingard*, p. 35.
32. J. Lingard, *History of England*, vii, pp. 536–7; viii, p. 241.
33. *Edinburgh Review*, lxxxiii (April, 1825), p. 6.
34. Ibid., cv (1931), pp. 21, 39.
35. Lingard to Mawman, 8 July, 1824, Ushaw MS., Lingard to Mawman 1818–27, File B.3, letter M. 21.
36. We find him, for example, stressing the inexpedient nature of certain ceremonials, like 'Dr. Wiseman's soirées', which have nothing to do with essential doctrine and which, though popular in Italy, 'do not appeal to the Englishman who considers them as "strange and foreign"', Lingard to Walker, Letters of 16 and 18 Feb. 1850, Ushaw MS., Lingard to Walker 1850–1, Folder 7.
37. See Lingard, *History of England*, v, p. 455 note.
38. Ibid., i, preliminary notice, p. xiv.
39. Ibid., (4th edn, 1837), preface, p. vi.
40. Ibid., vi, pp. 480–3, 501.
41. Ibid., vi, p. 480.
42. Ibid., v, p. 230.
43. Ibid., ii, pp. 212, 606. Contrast E. Burke, *Reflections on the French Revolution* (Methuen, 1923), p. 79.
44. Lingard, *History of England*, iii, pp. 183, 191.
45. Ibid., vi, p. 483; vii, pp. 209–10.
46. Ibid., viii, p. 375.
47. Ibid., vi, pp. 604, 582, 540 note 2, 547 note 2, 556 note 1, 566, 603 note 1.
48. See p. 252.
49. See p. 285.

50. *Edinburgh Review*, lxxxiii (April 1825), pp. 4, 6, 7, 3.
51. Cf. J. Lingard, *History of England*, ii, pp. 261, 450; iii, pp. 158–9, 467; v, pp. 485–6; vi, pp. 333, 248; viii, pp. 495–6.
52. See C. Firth, *A Commentary on Macaulay's History of England*, (1938), pp. 53–5, 65.
53. Cf. J. Lingard, *History of England*, ii, p. 306; v, pp. 212, 228 note 1, 464; vi, pp. 381, 356, 164 note 1, 310.
54. I owe this idea to P. Hughes, *History Today* (Apr 1951), p. 62.
55. *Edinburgh Review*, xlii (1825), p. 30.
56. *Westminster Review*, vii (1827), p. 187.
57. See a contemporary's critical view of all this in Sydney Smith, *The Works of the Rev. Sydney Smith* (3rd edn, 1845), ii, pp. 232–3; 253; iii, pp. 49–50, 275 note *, 276, 283, 284, 291, 293, 325–6, 336–7, 347, 365–50.
58. See below, pp. 220–2.
59. Sydney Smith (1771–1845), an Anglican clergyman, superb wit and humane Englishman who campaigned vigorously against slavery, transportation, Game laws, prisons, and in favour of Catholic Emancipation. See H. Pearson, *The Smith of Smiths* (1934); *Twelve Miles from a Lemon. Selected Writings and Sayings of Sydney Smith*, compiled by N. Taylor and H. Hankinson (Lutterworth Press, 1996).
60. *The Works of the Rev. Sydney Smith*, iii, p. 296.
61. Dr. Kipling to Lingard, n.d., Ushaw MS., Gillow Transcripts: Correspondence of Rev. John Lingard-Miscellaneous, f. 28.
62. See E. Jones, M.A. thesis, pp. 54–186.
63. Ibid.
64. Lingard to Oliver, 9 Nov. 1840. Ushaw MS., Gillow Transcripts, Corresp. between the Rev. John Lingard and the Rev. G. Oliver, 11, Code 0, letter 32.
65. Lingard to Kirk, 18 Dec. 1819, Ushaw MS., Lingard Transcripts, File B. 11.
66. Lingard to Mawman, 15 July 1823, Ushaw MS., Lingard to Mawman, 1818–27, File B.3, letter M. 16.
67. Lingard to Oliver, 11 Aug. 1827, Ushaw MS., Gillow Transcripts, Corresp. between the Rev. Dr. Lingard and the Rev. G. Oliver, Code 0, f. 3.
68. D. Mathew, *Catholicism in England* (Catholic Book Club, 2nd edn, 1948), p. 66. This is concerning Fr. Garnet, S.J.
69. Lingard to Coulston n.d., Ushaw MS., Lingard to Various Others 1815–51.
70. See below, pp. 137–8, 201–2.
71. Quoted by M.D. Knowles, 'Jean Mabillon', *Journal of Ecclesiastical History*, 10, (1959), p. 169.
72. B.H.G. Wormald, 'The Historiography of the English Reformation', *Historical Studies* (Papers read at conference, London, 1958), p. 47.
73. Cf. D.F. Shea, *Lingard*, pp. 76–7.

74. Lingard to ?, 10 Dec. 1820, Ushaw MS., Lingard Transcripts, File B. 11.
75. Lingard to Kirk, 25 Nov. 1820, Ushaw MS., Lingard Transcripts, File.
76. See below.
77. Cf. M.D. Knowles, *The Monastic Order in England* (Cambridge University Press, 1949), pp. 692–3.
78. Lingard Kirk, 25 Nov. 1820, Ushaw MS., Lingard Transcripts, File B. 11.
79. See below, pp. 218–19.
80. Lingard to Price, 13 Feb. 1847, Ushaw MS., Lingard Transcripts, B. 10, f. 363.
81. See E. Jones, M.A. thesis, pp. 153–4.
82. Ibid., pp. 166–7, 173–4.
83. J. Lingard, *History of England*, ix, pp. 107–13.
84. *Edinburgh Review*, liii (1831), p. 18.
85. Cf. C. Russell, *Unrevolutionary England*, introduction, pp. ix–x.
86. J. Lingard, *The History and Antiquities of the Anglo-Saxon Church* (3rd edn, 1845), preface, p. vii.
87. *Edinburgh Review*, xiii (1825), p. 2.
88. See E. Jones, M.A. thesis, pp. 182–6.
89. Lingard to Walker, 19 May 1836, Ushaw MS., A. 1, a. 3.
90. Lingard to Walker, 7 March, 1849, A. 3, j. 11.
91. Lingard to Walker, 19 May, 1836, Ushaw MS., A. 1, a. 3.
92. Lingard to Mawman, 1826. Quoted in P. Phillips, 'John Lingard and The Anglo-Saxon Church', *Recusant History* (Oct. 1996), p. 186.
93. Lingard to Coulston, 11 Dec. 1848, Ushaw MS., Lingard to others, 1815–21.
94. Cf. 'The development of a more scientific method of treating historical evidence was one of the great achievements of the nineteenth century. Macaulay stands outside this historical movement', C. Firth, *A Commentary on Macaulay's History of England* (1938), p. 65. See also P.R. Ghosh, 'Macaulay: the Heritage of the Enlightenment', pp. 394–5.
95. Lingard to Kirk, June 1821, Ushaw MS., Lingard Transcripts, B. 11.
96. Lingard to Kirk, 21 March 1822, Ushaw MS. Ibid.
97. Sharp to Lingard, 6 May, 1837, Ushaw MS., Lingard Correspondence N–Y, Miscellaneous, 1806–51, B. 2.
98. Lingard to Gradwell, 28 June, 1821 (?), Ushaw MS., Lingard Transcripts, B. 11.
99. Hickes was the greatest figure in Anglo-Saxon studies among the Non-Jurors. He had learned his craft from Mabillon and his *Linguarum Veterum Septentrionalium Thesaurus* (1703) was an epoch-making event in Anglo-Saxon scholarship.
100. Lingard to Sewell, 7 Dec. 1821, Ushaw MS. 'Lingard Correspondence from the archives of the English Province s.J.', ff. 1–2.
101. See E. Jones, M.A. thesis, p. 56.
102. Lingard to Gradwell, 19 Oct. 1822, Ushaw MS., Lingard Transcripts B. 11.

103. J. Lingard, *History of England*, vii, p. 37 note 2.

104. S.M. Toyne, 'Guy Fawkes and the Gunpowder Plot', *History Today* (Nov. 1951), p. 16. Cf. A. Fraser, *The Gunpowder Plot* (Weidenfeld and Nicolson, 1996), in which Lingard is used as a reference book.

105. Cf. *A Complete Collection of State Trials*, ed. T.B. Howell and W. Cobbett (1816), i, p. 259.

106. An inner group of advisers to Charles II; its name derived from the initials of its members: Clifford, Arlington, Buckingham, Ashley and Lauderdale. It has been seen as a precursor to the Cabinet, but it had no official status and was discarded when politically convenient.

107. J. Lingard, *History of England* , ix. Appendix B, pp. 503–10.

108. M. Ashley, *England in the Seventeenth Century* (Pelican, 1952), p. 130. Cf. *The Companion to British History*, ed. J. Gardiner and N. Wenborn (Collins & Brown, 1995), p. 245.

109. J. Lingard, *History of England*. The treaty is in French. See it reprinted from Lingard in *English Historical Documents*, ed. D.C. Douglas, vol. vii: 1660–1714, ed. A. Browning (Eyre and Spottiswoode, 1967), pp. 745–6.

110. For these details see, Ushaw MSS., Robertson to Lingard, 2 Dec. 1826; Lingard Corresp. N–Y Miscellaneous 1806–31, B. 2; and Lingard to Walker, 11 Jan. 1835. File 'Lingard to Walker', 1837–41 A1, a. 23.

111. For these details, see Ushaw MSS., Lingard to Tierney, 10 Apr., 1837, Lingard Transcripts, B. 10, f. 235; Lingard to Walker, 10 July 1844 and 15 Mar. 1844, File 'Lingard to Walker', f. 6; Thomas Wright to Sharp, n.d. in Lingard Corresp. N–Y Miscell. 1805–51, B. 2; Lingard to Tierney 16 July 1846 in Lingard Transcripts, B. 10, f. 293; Lingard to Gillow n.d. in Lingard to Walker 1846–50, A. 3; Lingard to Whedall, 13 Apr. 1820, Lingard Transcripts, B. 11; Lingard to Walker, 16 Apr. 1849, File 'Lingard to Walker 1846–50, A. 3, letter j. 16; Lingard to Kirk, June 1821, Lingard Transcripts, B. 11; Lingard to Mawman May and October 1825, in Letters to Mawman', B. 3, M. 35 and M. 40.

112. Lingard to Oliver, 11 Aug. 1827, Ushaw MS., 'Corresp. between Lingard and Oliver', code 0, 1, Transcript letter No. 3.

113. Ibid.

114. J. Lingard, *History of England*, vii, p. 37 note 2.

115. Cf. D.O'Shea, *The English Ranke: John Lingard*, p .100.

116. See above, pp. x, 224.

117. See E. Jones, 'John Lingard and the Simancas Archives', *The Historical Journal*, x, i (1967), pp. 74–5.

118. H. Soames, *History of the Reformation of the Church of England* (1826), preface, p. ix.

119. H. Hallam, *View of the State of Europe in the Middle Ages* (2nd edn, 1819), iii, 335 note *.

120. F. Stenton, *Anglo-Saxon England* (Oxford University Press, 1947), p. 187.

NOTES

121. H. Soames, *Elizabeth Religious History* (1839), p. 209.
122. See below, p. 202.
123. J. Lingard, *History of England* (4th edn, 1837), preface, p. vi.
124. See below, p. 243.
125. See below, pp. 185, 186.
126. 'G.B. Simancas, 20 Sept. 1860', *Athenaeum*, No. 1721 (20 Oct. 1860).
127. Lingard to Wiseman, 9 April, Ushaw MS., Wiseman Papers, folder 772–833.
128. Lingard to Poynter, 26 March 1817, quoted E. Bonney and M. Haile, *Life of Lingard*, p. 152.
129. Lingard to Wiseman, 9 Apr. 1834, Ushaw MS., as above.
130. Lingard to Poynter, 26 Mar. 1817, E. Bonney and M. Haile, *Life of Lingard*, p. 139.
131. 'The Rev. J. Lingard's Journal on a tour to Rome and Naples in the Summer of 1817', Ushaw MS. (not numbered).
132. 'Lingard's Journal', quoted in E. Bonney and M. Haile, *Life of Lingard*, p. 154.
133. Lingard to Gradwell, n.d. but it precedes the letter of 18 April 1818, Ushaw MS. 'Copies of the letters of Dr. Lingard from the archives of the English College Rome, 1812–14'. Lingard Transcripts, B. 1.
134. Lingard to Gradwell, 18 April, 1818. Ushaw MS. Ibid.
135. Lingard to Gradwell, 3 June 1819, Ushaw MS. Ibid.
136. Gradwell to Lingard, 22 Mar. 1821 and Gradwell to Lingard, 21 Jan. 1822, Ushaw MS., 'Lingard Transcripts-Gradwell Corresp.' A. 4, ff. 39 and 45.
137. Lingard to Gradwell, 21 Jan. 1822, Ushaw MS. Ibid.
138. Lingard to Gradwell, 19 Oct. 1822, Ushaw MS. 'Lingard Transcripts B. 11'.
139. Gradwell Gradwell, Monte Porzio, 23 Sept. 1826, Ushaw MS. 'Lingard Transcripts-Gradwell Corresp.', A. 4, f. 118.
140. Lingard to Gradwell n.d. 'Lingard Transcripts', B. 11.
141. Gradwell to Lingard, Rome, 9 May 1827, Ushaw MS., 'Lingard Transcripts-Gradwell Corresp.', A. 4, ff. 154–6.
142. Lingard to Tierney, 27 May, 1848, Ushaw MS., 'Lingard Transcripts B. 10', ff. 309–10.
143. See below p. 239. Cf. E. Jones, M.A. thesis, pp. 22–54.
144. Lingard to Gradwell, 3 June 1819, Ushaw MS., 'Lingard Transcripts B. 11'.
145. J. Lingard, *History of England* (1st edn, 1823), v, pp. 15 note 20, 68 note 107, 104 note 41, 110 note 53, 116 note 60, 133 note 85, 136 note 94, 139 note 98.
146. Ibid.
147. Gradwell to Lingard, Monte Porzio, 2 Oct. 1827, and Gradwell to Lingard, Rome, 27 Dec. 1827, Ushaw MS., 'Lingard Transcripts and Gradwell Corresp', A. 4, ff. 159 and 164.

148. J. Lingard, *History of England* (1st edn, 1829), vii, pp. 48 note, 67, 196 note, 41, 174.
149. Lingard to Gradwell, 2 Oct 1827, Ushaw MS. 'Lingard Transcripts-Gradwell Corresp.', A. 4, f. 159.
150. J. Lingard, *History of England*, v, pp. 504 note, 363 note, 385 note; vi, 501 note, 649 note.
151. Ibid., iv, p. 591 note 1.
152. Lingard to Wiseman (at Rome), 9 April, 1834, Ushaw MS., 'Wiseman Papers', folder 772–833.
153. Lingard to Mawman, 10 May, 1823, Ushaw MS., 'Lingard to Mawman 1818–27', B. 3, letter m.18. The story of Lingard's contact with the archives at Besançon can be followed in the correspondence between Lingard and Bishop Poynter in the Ushaw MSS., File B. 11, for 1823.
154. Lingard to Coulston, 11 Dec. 1848, Ushaw MS. 'Lingard to Various Others 1815–51'.
155. J. Lingard, *History of England*, iii, p. 387 note 1.
156. Mostyn to Lingard, Versailles, 23 Oct. 1826, Ushaw MS., 'Lingard Correspondence F–M 1850–51'.
157. See E. Jones, M.A. thesis, pp. 42–6.
158. H. Butterfield, 'Lord Acton and the Massacre of St. Bartholomew', *Man on His Past*, pp. 171–203.
159. Lingard to Poynter, 27 Oct. 1833, 12 Dec. 1825, 5 July, 1826, Ushaw MSS., 'Lingard Transcripts', B. 11.
160. 'With Germany I have no correspondence and therefore am very anxious to follow your advice by opening a communication with Professor Dollinger', Ushaw MS., Lingard to Wiseman, 20 Aug. 1826, 'Lingard to Various Others 1815–51'. Dollinger was Professor of Canon Law and Church History at the University of Munich and a leading German scholar.
161. See E. Jones, 'John Lingard and the Simancas Archives', pp. 57–76.
162. G.A. Bergenroth, *Calendar of State Papers from Spanish sources relating to English affairs* (1862).
163. Bergenroth's letter of October 1860 in 'Foreign Correspondence' of *The Athenaem*, no. 1723 (3 Nov. 1860), p. 593.
164. For these details, see *Correspondance de Philippe II sur Les Affaires des Pays-Bas: D'Après les Originaux Conservés dans Les Archives Royales de Simancas*, ed. M. Gachard (1848), I, Notice Historique et Descriptive, pp. 43–8. M. Gachard adds that 'De tous les historiens et chronistes espagnols, Geronimo de Zurita, qui écrivit, sous les règnes de Charles-Quint et de Philippe II, en qualiteé de chroniste d'Aragon, l'historie de ce royaume . . . parait avoir été le seul qui ait eu accèss aux archives de Simancas', p. 50 note 1.
165. Geronimo de Zurita (1512–80) was patiently zealous 'in the search and use of manuscripts' and a founder of 'critical scholarship in Spain', R.B. Merriman, *The Rise of the Spanish Empire* (1925), iv, pp. 482–3. Juan de

Mariana (1532–1624) had 'modern views of contemporary affairs', ibid., p. 483.

166. Cameron to Sherburne, Valladolid, 20 May, 1820 (forwarded to Lingard, Ushaw MS., 'Lingard Correspondence F–M (1805–48).

167. J. Lingard, *History of England*, iv, pp. 328–9 and note 2.

168. See, for example, G. Elton, *England Under The Tudors* (1955), pp. 39–41. Interestingly, too, J. Scarisbrick has changed his view and now accepts that the papal dispensation granted to Henry and Catherine was canonically sound, *Henry VIII* (Yale University Press, 1997), pp. x–xi.

169. Lingard to Kirk, 15 Nov. 1820, Ushaw MS., 'Lingard Transcripts B. 11.

170. J. Lingard, *History of England*, iv, p. 335 note 2. Writing to his publishers in 1820, Lingard had to explain the spelling and meaning of the word 'Simancas', so unfamiliar were these archives to English people, Lingard to Mawman, dated 1820, Ushaw MS., 'Lingard to Mawman, file B. 3.

171. J. Lingard, *History of England*, iv, p. 335 note 2.

172. Sherburne to Lingard, 19 Feb. 1823, Ushaw MS., 'Lingard Corresp. N–Y Miscellaneous, 1806–51', ii.

173. J.A. Froude, *History of England* (1856–70); J.L. Motley, *Rise of the Dutch Republic* (1855); W.H. Prestcott, *History of the Reign of Philip II* (Boston, 1855–8).

174. S. Turner, *History of the Reigns of Edward the Sixth, Mary and Elizabeth* (2nd edn, 1829), iv, p. 141 note 1.

175. A. Dimock, 'The Conspiracy of Dr. Lopez', *The English Historical Review*, ix (1894), p. 471.

176. R. Trevor Davies, *The Golden Century of Spain, 1501–1621* (1937), p. 119.

177. J. Lingard, *History of England*, vi, pp. 469, 497, 513.

178. Ibid., (4th edn, 1838), viii, p. 56 note.

179. Ibid., vi, pp. 226–7.

180. Ibid., vi, p. 228 and note i, p. 282; also vi, appendix, p. 685. Cf. H. Butterfield, *Man on His Past*, pp. 175, 185, 191.

181. J. Lingard, *History of England*, vi, pp. 497–8. Cf. G. Mattingley, *The Defeat of the Spanish Armada*, pp. 82–4.

182. Ibid., vi, p. 502.

183. Ibid., vi, p. 511.

184. Ibid., vi, p. 479.

185. Mary's reign has been treated in a more balanced way, similar to Lingard's, recently. Cf. J. Guy 'The Tudor Age', *Oxford Illustrated History of Britain*, ed. K.O. Morgan, p. 263.

186. J. Lingard, *History of England*, vi, p. 514.

187. Ibid., vi, pp. 504–5. But she could also be revengeful, vi, p. 525.

188. Ibid.

189. J. Lingard to Mawman, 10 May, 1823, Ushaw MS., Lingard to Mawman, 1818–27, letter m. 18.

190. J. Lingard, *History of England*, preliminary notice, pp. xiii–xiv.

191. Sherburne to Lingard, 16 April 1825, Ushaw MS., Lingard Correspondence N–Y Miscellaneous, II.
192. Sherburne to Lingard, 26 Nov. 1832, Ushaw MS., Lingard Corresp. Ibid.
193. Cf. *Retraite et Mort De Charles-Quint au Monastère de Yuste*, ed. M. Gachard (Bruxelles, 1854), I, preface, p. ii; and W. Stirling, *The Cloister Life of the Emperor Charles the Fifth* (2nd edn, 1853), preface, p. xi.
194. *Calendar of . . . State Papers . . . at Simancas*, ed. G.A. Bergenroth, (1862), I, introduction, p. ix.
195. Lingard demanded facts and names to substantiate any opinion that they sent him. Lingard was only interested when they could show that they were actually stating facts derived from the documents.
196. Cameron to Lingard, 26 Nov. 1832 (re. addressed by Sherburne to Lingard), Ushaw MS., Lingard Correspondence N–Y Miscellaneous 1806–51, ii.
197. Sherburne to Lingard, 28 Feb. 1823, Ushaw MS., Ibid.
198. Compare the extracts from the documents in a letter from Sherburne to Lingard (26 Nov. 1832, Ushaw MS. Lingard Corresp. N–Y Miscellaneous 1806–51, ii), with Lingard's published account of the documents in the *History of England* (4th edn, 1837–8), viii, n.x, p. 458, appendix, and both these with the Simancas documents published in *Calendar of State Papers – Simancas IV*, ed. M.A.S. Hume (1899), pp. 101–6.
199. R. O'Day, *The Debate On the English Reformation*, pp. 8–10.
200. See above, pp. 15–16, 32–3.
201. *Bishop Burgess, English Reformation and Papal Schism, or The Grand Schism of the sixteenth century, in this country, shewn to have been the Separation of the Roman Catholics from the Church of England and Ireland* (1819), pp. 2–3.
202. Ibid.
203. H. Soames, *The Anglo-Saxon Church* (1835), introduction, p. 3.
204. J. Lingard, *History of England*, i, p. 52.
205. Ibid., i, p. 92 note.
206. Ibid., i, pp. 52–3.
207. Cf. Sir G. Williams, 'Some Protestant Views of Early British Church History', p. 229. Even now there are echoes of it: 'the myth of a Celtic Church which was something apart from Rome, a myth which dies very hard', A.D. Carr, *Medieval Wales* (St Martin's Press, 1991), p. 8. I came across an echo of it while on holiday in Cornwall this year (1997).
208. Lingard to Walker, 30 Jan. 1846, Ushaw MS., Lingard to Walker 1840–49, Folder 6.
209. Lingard to Walker, 23 Oct. 1846, Ushaw MS. Ibid.
210. H. Butterfield, *Man On His Past*, p. 33.
211. Ibid., p. 108.
212. J. Lingard, *History of England*, ii, pp. 47–8, note 34.
213. Ibid., i, ch. vii; ii, pp. 208–25.

214. F.W. Maitland, *The Constitutional History of England* (Cambridge University Press, 1961), p. 142.
215. Ibid.
216. See above, ch. 4.
217. J. Lingard, *History of England*, ii, pp. 119–34.
218. F.W. Maitland, *Roman Canon Law in the Church of England* (1898).
219. J. Lingard, *History of England*, ii, p. 125.
220. Ibid., ii, pp. 163, 108.
221. Ibid., ii, p. 127.
222. The monks of Canterbury had elected Stephen Langton. Henry II, supported by the English bishops, opposed this. The Pope decided in favour of Stephen Langton.
223. See above, pp. 131–6.
224. J. Lingard, *History of England*, ii, note B, p. 626.
225. Lingard, *History of England*, ii, p. 626.
226. R. Vaughan, *Matthew Paris* (Cambridge University Press, 1958), p. 263.
227. J. Lingard, *History of England*, ii, pp. 393–4, note 4. Cf. Other rejections of Paris, after comparison with the original records: ii, pp. 403 note 1, 405 note 1.
228. See below, pp. 214–15.
229. J. Lingard, *History of England*, ii, pp. 331–2.
230. Ibid., pp. 332–4.
231. Ibid., p. 331.
232. See above, p. 176.
233. Jones to Lingard, 4 Dec. 1833, Ushaw MS., Lingard Transcripts B. 10, f. 199.
234. See above, p. 138.
235. Cf. A.L. Poole, *From Domesday Book to Magna Carta* (Oxford University Press, 1951), pp. 457–8, Cf. F.M. Powicke, *Stephen Langton*.
236. See above, p. 138.
237. See above, p. 143.
238. J. Lingard, *History of England*, iii, p. 250.
239. Ibid., iii, pp. 264–5.
240. B.H.G. Wormald, 'Historiography of the Reformation', p. 54.
241. J. Lingard, *History of England*, iv, pp. 449–50.
242. Ibid., ii, pp. 413–18.
243. Cf. 'as from Lingard it became increasingly clear that scholarship endorsed many of the contentions on the Catholic side of the age-long argument whether or not certain crucial events had occurred: for example (1) the Catholic contention that the marriage between Catherine of Aragon and Prince Arthur had not been consummated, and that the lawfulness of Henry VIII's marriage had been generally endorsed; (2) the early entrance of Anne Boleyn into the situation governing Henry's actions (though not as early as Lingard thought); (3) the fact of the existence of a draft licence sought from Rome by

Henry allowing him to marry Anne despite his illicit relations with her sister Mary (a fact which can hardly fail to bear upon our judgment of the nature of the conscientious scruples from which Henry claimed to suffer over his relationship with Catherine); (4) the use of bribes to gain verdicts from the European Universities favouring the King's view', B.H.G. Wormald, 'Historiography of the Reformation', p. 56.

244. J. Lingard, *History of England*, v, p. 78.

245. Ibid., v, pp. 93 note 2, 98.

246. Ibid. See footnotes in v, ch. 2.

247. Ibid.

248. Ibid., v, p. 95.

249. Ibid., v, pp. 82–7.

250. See J. Scarisbrick, *Henry VIII*, p. xvii. Contrast A.G. Dickens, *English Reformation*, p. 182.

251. J. Lingard, *History of England*, v, p. 51.

252. See below, p. 226.

253. J. Lingard, *History of England*, v, pp. 482, 483, 486, 526.

254. Ibid., v, pp. 526, 486.

255. Ibid., v, p. 486.

256. Ibid., v, p. 531.

257. Ibid., v, p. 530 note 1.

258. J. Guy, *The Oxford Illustrated History of Tudors and Stuarts*, ed. J. Morrill (Oxford University Press, 1996), p. 263.

259. J. Kenyon, *History Men*, p. 211.

260. Ibid., p. 217.

261. Ibid.

262. See above, p. 179.

263. See below, pp. 190–1.

264. For the above details and quotations, see Lingard, *History of England*, vi, pp. 649–5.

265. See below, p. 244.

266. J. Spurr, *History Today*, 17(3), March 1997, p. 53. I am indebted to John Spurr for this review.

267. J. Lingard *History of England*, iv, p. 449, v, p. 35.

268. See below, p. 239.

269. Cf. 'on the whole English men and women did not want the Reformation and most of them were slow to accept it when it came', J. Scarisbrick, *The Reformation and the English People* (Blackwell, 1984), p. 1. For local studies, see below pp. 240, 316 note 109 R. Whiting argues that traditional religion continued to be popularly supported up to the Reformation, but that the impact of the Henrician Reformation was more extensive and destructive than is often supposed: *The Reign of Henry VIII: Politics, Policy and Piety*, ed. D. MacCulloch (Macmillan, 1995), pp. 203–27. The weight of judgment in modern scholarship, however, is that England could not be called 'protestant' until the 1570s

or 1580s, and then with a majority of 'conformists' rather than 'committed', see above, p. 18.

270. J. Scarisbrick, *Henry VIII* (Yale edn, 1997), pp. 329, 338. Cf. J. Scarisbrick, *The Reformation and the English People*; G.R. Elton, *Policy and Police: The Enforcement of The Reformation in the Age of Thomas Cromwell* (Cambridge, 1972); L. Baldwin Smith, *Treason in Tudor England. Politics and Paranoias* (Jonathan Cape, 1986). R. Whiting writes: 'Punishment for overt opposition ranged from whipping or imprisonment to hanging, beheading, drawing, quartering and public display of bodily parts' as a 'terrible example to others', *The Reign of Henry VIII*, p. 226.

271. P. Williams, *The Later Tudors* (Clarendon Press, 1996), p. 465. Cf. 'Protestant England was born some considerable time after the accession of Elizabeth', P. Collinson, *The Birthpangs of Protestant England. Religious and Cultural change in the Sixteenth and Seventeenth Centuries* (Macmillan, 1992), p. ix.

272. J. Lingard, *History of England*, v, p. 23.

273. P. Williams, *Later Tudors*, pp. 467–8, where it is noticed that the Treasons Act of 1534 was considerably extended in 1571.

274. Quoted in P. Hughes, *Dublin Review*, vol. 167 (1920), p. 274. Cf. 'Lingard's *History of England* has been of more use to us than anything that has since been written; it was so far superior to the books that preceded it. . . . The impartiality of scientific research is our surest ally if we adopt it', Lord Acton, *The Rambler* (new series, xi, Feb. 1859), p. 85.

275. Sir A. Ward, *The Cambridge History of English Literature*, xiv (1916), p. 54.

276. P. Hughes, *The Reformation in England* (Hollis and Carter, 1954), iii, p. 240; ii, pp. 265 note 1, 226 note 3.

277. G.P. Gooch, *History and Historians in the Nineteenth Century* (2nd edn, 1952), p. 273.

278. P. Hughes, *The Reformation in England*, iii, p. 240; ii, pp. 265 note 1, 226 note 3.

279. D. O'Shea, *Lingard*.

280. Sir H. Butterfield, *George III and the Historians* (1957), p. 119.

281. See E. Jones, M.A. thesis.

282. See E. Jones, Ph.D. thesis, ff. 115–30.

283. J. Lingard, *Vindication of Certain Passages in the Fourth and Fifth Volumes of the History of England* (2nd edn, J. Mawman, London, 1826), pp. 10–11.

284. See above, pp. 174, 187.

285. Daniel Papebroche was a senior monk-scholar who had stated that a certain document was not authentic. Mabillon, a much younger scholar, wrote the *De Re Diplomatica* (1681), to demonstrate the criteria which he used in coming to the conclusion that it was authentic. Papebroche, replied in an admirable letter, saying that the young scholar was right, and that he, Mabillon, was the 'master'.

286. See E. Jones, M.A. thesis, ff. 98–153.
287. Cf. 'It must be admitted that historians are reticent about the ways in which they go to work, and that we are profoundly ignorant of the nature of historical thinking', Reviewer, *English Historical Review*, lxvi (1951), p. 455. This comment would still hold true in 1998.
288. J. Kenyon, *History Men*, pp. 193, 194.
289. Ibid.
290. Ibid., p. 150.
291. See above, p. 168.
292. See above, p. 169. He knew Latin, Greek, Hebrew, Anglo-Saxon, French, Italian, Spanish and German.
293. *The Historian's Craft* (1954). Cf. p. 317 note 121.
294. See above, p. 176.

CHAPTER VII

1. N. Ferguson argues that the 'modern historical profession', unlike its scientific counterpart, has not been characterized by 'shifts forward'. Rather, there has been 'a sluggish "revisionism"' in which historians 'are mainly concerned to qualify the interpretations of the previous generation, only rarely (and at a risk to their own careers) challenging its assumptions', *Virtual History. Alternatives and Counterfactuals*, ed. N. Ferguson (Picador Press, 1997), p. 40. This chapter may help the reader to decide on the appropriateness, or not, of this remark.
2. Cf. J. Darwin, *English Historical Review*, cxii, No. 447, June 1997, p. 642.
3. H. Trevor-Roper, *Lord Macaulay. The History of England* (Penguin Classics, 1968), with introduction by H. Trevor-Roper, p. 7.
4. J.W. Thompson, *A History of Historical Writing* (New York, 1942), ii, p. 297. Cf. J. Kenyon, *History Men*, p. 76.
5. C. Firth, *Comment on Macaulay's History*, p. 14.
6. Ibid., p. 65. Cf. Lord Acton described Macaulay as 'amateur' and 'insular'; and certainly a 'great gulf separated Macaulay from the new German pioneers of historical method and source criticism', H. Trevor-Roper, *Macaulay's History*, p. 36.
7. P. Ghosh, 'Macaulay and the Heritage of the Enlightenment', *The English Historical Review*, cxii, No. 446, April 1997, p. 395.
8. *Oxford Companion to English Literature*, ed. M. Drabble, p. 599.
9. Ibid. But the brilliant style in which they were written made them immensely popular, much more so than the *History* itself. Cf. P. Ghosh, 'Macaulay and the Enlightenment'.
10. See above, p. 179.
11. See H. Trevor-Roper, *Macaulay's History*, introduction.
12. J. Lingard, *History of England*, ix, pp. 159–60 note 1.
13. Ibid.

14. *Macaulay's Critical and Historical Essays*, ed. G.M. Trevelyan (1903), ii, p. 38.

15. G.M. Trevelyan, *History of England* (Longmans, Green & Co., 3rd edn, 1945), p. 457.

16. G.N. Clarke, *The Later Stuarts* (Clarendon Press, 1949), pp. 69–70.

17. M. Ashley, *England in the Seventeenth Century* (Penguin, 1952), p. 129.

18. T. Munck, *Seventeenth Century Europe* (Macmillan, 1993), p. 374.

19. See above, p. 174.

20. G. Davies, *The Earlier Stuarts* (Clarendon Press, 1937), p. 115.

21. J. Lingard, *History of England*, vii, pp. 554–5.

22. Ibid., p. 558.

23. Ibid.

24. Lingard to Gradwell (n.d.), Ushaw MS., Lingard Transcripts B. 11.

25. T. Keightley, *The History of England* (1839), ii, p. 529.

26. G.M. Trevelyan, *England Under The Stuarts* (Oxford, 1925), p. 218–19.

27. G. Davies, *Earlier Stuarts*, pp. 114–15.

28. J. Morrill, *The Oxford Illustrated History of Tudor and Stuart Britain*, ed. J. Morrill (Oxford University Press, 1996), pp. 339–40.

29. M.P. Maxwell, *The Outbreak of the Irish Rebellion of 1641* (Gill and Macmillan, 1994), p. 259.

30. J.R. Green, *Short History of the English People* (Folio edition, 1992), ed. R. Hudson, introduction, p. xix.

31. R.W. Chambers, *Thomas More*, p. 389.

32. See above, pp. 94–5.

33. 'The common-law writers took their law to represent the immemorial custom of their country and did not derive it from any source outside their own coasts', J.G.A. Pocock, *Ancient Constitution*, p. 56.

34. J.R. Green, *A Short History of the English People* (Macmillan, 2nd edn, 1917), pp. 1, 2, 4, 7. Both Green and Freeman were 'chauvinistic' Cf. J. Kenyon, *History Men*, pp. 212, 218.

35. W. Stubbs, *Select Charters and other Illustrations of English Constitutional History to 1307* (Clarendon Press, 9th edn, 1929, revised by H.W.C. Davis), p. 1. For Stubbs's 'nationalist interpretation of English history' on which later English historians were to build their accounts, see J. Kenyon, *History Men*, p. 158.

36. Ibid., pp. 158–9.

37. Ibid., pp. 154, 157, 175.

38. Ibid., p. 159.

39. Ibid., pp. 157–8.

40. See below, pp. 231–2, 236.

41. Cf. D. Washbrook, 'After the Mutiny', *History Today* (Sept. 1997), p. 14.

42. See below, pp. 224, 227.

43. J. Kenyon, *History Men*, pp. 176–81.

44. D. Loades, *The Reign of Mary Tudor* (Longman, 2nd edn, 1995), p. x.

45. *Oxford Companion to English Literature*, ed. M. Drabble, p. 368.

46. J. Kenyon, *History Men*, p. 211.
47. Ibid., pp. 211–12.
48. Ibid.
49. Ibid., p. 214.
50. Ibid., p. 216.
51. Ibid., p. 218.
52. Ibid., p. 219.
53. Ibid., p. 217.
54. See above, pp. 190–3.
55. J. Kenyon, *History Men*, p. 230.
56. Another reprint of Gardiner's *History of the Great Civil War* was published in 4 volumes (Windrush Press) as late as 1987.
57. G.M. Trevelyan, *History of England* (Longman, Green & Co., 1926, 3rd edn, 1949), pp. xix, xxi, 29.
58. J. Kenyon, *History Men*, p. 245.
59. Ibid., p. 246.
60. See D. Cannadine, *G.M. Trevelyan. A Life in History* (Harper and Collins, 1992), pp. 222, 228–9.
61. See Ved Mehta, *Fly and Flybottle* (Weidenfeld and Nicolson, 1963) p. 196. Quoted in J. Kenyon, *History Men*, p. 218.
62. A.G. Dickens, *English Reformation*, ch. 2, 'The abortive Reformation'.
63. P. Strohm, 'The 1390s', *Fins de Siecle. How Centuries End 1400–2000*, ed. A. Briggs and D. Snowman (Yale University Press, 1996), p. 11.
64. G. Walker, *Persuasive Fictions: Faction, Faith and Literature in the Reign of Henry VIII* (Scolar Press, 1995).
65. P. Heath, *Church and Realm, 1272–1461* (Fontana Press, 1988), p. 353.
66. C. Haigh, *The English Reformation Revisited* (Cambridge University Press, 1987), introduction, p. 2.
67. G. Elton, *The English* (Blackwell, 1992), p. xii.
68. See J. Kenyon, *History Men*, p. 219.
69. See M. Vale, *England and her Neighbours, 1066–1453. Essays in Honour of Pierre Chaplais*, ed. M. Jones and M. Vale (Hambledon Press, 1989), pp. 200–1.
70. G. Elton, *The English*, p. 2.
71. Ibid., pp. 5, 16.
72. Ibid., p. 4.
73. Ibid., p. 14.
74. Ibid., p. 11.
75. Ibid.
76. Ibid., p. 54.
77. Ibid., p. 55.
78. Ibid., pp. 69, 111.
79. T.F. Tout, *France and England. Their Relationship in the Middle Ages* (Longman, 1922), p. 143.
80. Ibid., p. 146.

81. Ibid., p. 154.
82. Quoted in J. Kenyon, *History Men*, p. 190.
83. For this section, see M. Vale, *England and her Neigbours*, pp. 215, 199, 216; and also M. Vale, *The Origins of the Hundred Years War* (Clarendon Press, 1996), introduction, p. 3.
84. See M. Vale's chapter in *Arms, Armies and Fortifications in the Hundred Years War*, ed. A. Curry and M. Hughes (Boydell Press, 1994).
85. Cf. The depersonalization of modern warfare described in D. Pick's *The Rationalisation of Slaughter in the Modern Age* (Yale University Press, 1996).
86. See P. Contamine, *War in the Middle Ages*, trans. Michael Jones (Blackwell, 1996 reprint), pp. 305–6.
87. See N.A.R. Wright, 'The Tree of Battles of Honore Bouvet', *War, Literature and Politics in the Late Middle Ages. Essays in Honour of G.W. Coupland*, ed. C.T. Allmand (Liverpool University Press, 1976), pp. 12–31. Cf. T. Merton, *Henry's Wars and Shakespeare's Laws. Perspectives on the Law of War in the Later Middle Ages* (Clarendon Press, 1993).
88. P. Heath, *Church and Realm, 1272–1461* (Fontana Press, 1988), p. 110.
89. See P. Contamine, *War in the Middle Ages*, p. 305.
90. M. Vale, *England and Her Neighbours*, p. 216.
91. M. Vale, *The Origins of the Hundred Years War*, p. ix.
92. G. Elton, *The English*, p. 70.
93. J.W. McKenna, *Tudor Rule and Revolution*, ed. J. Guth and J.W. McKenna (Cambridge University Press, 1982), p. 43.
94. Catholic theology teaches that all people are 'destined' (intended) to be saved, but each person has the free will to choose his or her own response.
95. G. Elton, *The English*, p. 93.
96. P. Heath, *Church and Realm*, p. 357.
97. Cf. J. Kenyon, *History Men*, p. 222.
98. See G. Elton, 'Thomas More and Thomas Cromwell', *Studies in Tudor and Stuart Politics and Government*, vol. iv, 1982–1990 (Cambridge University Press, 1992), pp. 144–60. Cf. J. Kenyon, *History Men*, p. 287.
99. G. Elton, *The English*, preface, p. xi.
100. Ibid., p. 234. Félipe Fernández-Armesto has written very recently concerning Sir Geoffrey Elton, that 'his version of the English past misled a generation but he became part of the history he set out to study', *History Today*, 46(12), Dec. 1996, introduction. Armesti sees Elton's idealization of the English as an essay in 'self-anglicisation by a man who reached the pinnacle of success in his career after coming to England: " the country in which I ought to have been born"'.
101. 'The history of the English Church in the Middle Ages has especially suffered from being treated thus in isolation. . . . And for this reason, when its relations with the central government of the Church and its Head the Pope, have been discussed, the impression given is that

foreign policy and relations of the English Church are being described, its contacts with a foreign power to whose authority it is naturally not anxious to be subordinate. If this were a true view, and if such an independent position had been possible, the Church would not have been a real unity, but a federation of independent national Churches. We know that it was a real unity, and was so regarded in all its parts; this is an essential truth, to which we must adhere in spite of apparent contradictions. And if we keep it in mind and contemplate the Church from the centre outwards, we get a very different impression of the English Church from that which is normally current', Z.N. Brooke, *The English Church and the Papacy* (Cambridge, 1931), p. 1.

102. Quoted in J. Kenyon, *History Men*, p. 155.

103. F.M. Powicke began this book with a well-known sentence, quite startling in its simplicity and directness at the time: 'The one definite thing which can be said about the Reformation in England is that it was an act of State', *The Reformation in England* (Oxford University Press, 3rd impr., 1949), p. 1.

104. H. Butterfield, *The Whig Interpretation of History* (Bell, 1931).

105. M. Cowling argued that Butterfield had adopted the Whig interpretation in 1944, 'to use it for patriotic reasons in a time of national crisis, *Religion and Public Debate in Modern England* (Cambridge, 1980), p. 227. J. Kenyon writes, similarly, that Butterfield's 'conversion to Whiggism had already been signalled in . . . 1944', *History Men*, p. 289. I agree with G. Elton who says that Butterfield was simply describing the useful effects of the Whig interpretation in 1994, in raising British morale, but that 'it is not true that he had come to approve whiggism as a right way to record history', *Studies in Tudor and Stuart Politics and Government* (Cambridge University Press, 1992), iv, pp. 272–3.

106. J. Scarisbrick, *Henry VIII*, p. 304. I agree with Scarisbrick on the whole, but I think that R. Rex has shown that it was Cromwell who initiated the strategy of adopting Tyndale's Protestant theology of 'obedience' to the king, as representing 'God's word'. See above, p. 32.

107. J. Scarisbrick, *The Reformation and the English People* (Blackwell, 1984), pp. 10–12.

108. J. Bossy, *Christianity in the West 1400–1700* (Oxford University Press, 1985), p. 171.

109. Cf. M. Bowker, *The Henrician Reformation in the Diocese of Lincoln under John Longland, 1521–1547* (Cambridge University Press, 1981); C. Haigh, *Reformation and Resistance in Tudor Lancashire* (Cambridge University Press, 1975); S. Lander 'Church Courts and the Reformation in the Diocese of Chichester, 1500–1558', *Continuity and Change: Personnel and Administration of the Church of England, 1500–1642*, ed. R. O'Day and F. Heal (Leicester University Press, 1976); R. Hutton, 'The Local Impact of the Tudor Reformations', *The English Reformation Revised*, ed. C. Haigh, (Cambridge, 1987).

110. See p. 278 note 56.
111. P. Marshall, *The Catholic Priesthood and the English Reformation* (Clarendon Press, 1994).
112. B.A. Kümin, *The Shaping of a Community. The Rise and Reformation of the English Parish* c. *1400–1560* (Scolar Press, 1996).
113. *The English Reformation Revised*, ed. C. Haigh (Cambridge University Press, 1987).
114. C. Haigh, *English Reformations: Religion, Politics and Society Under The Tudors* (Clarendon Press, 1993).
115. R.W. Southern, *Scholastic Humanism and the Unification of Europe, Vol. I* (Blackwell, 1995).
116. K. Sharpe, 'The Personal Rule of Charles I', *Before the English Civil War*, ed. H. Tomlinson (1983), pp. 53–78.
117. See J. Kenyon, *History Men*, pp. 264–5.
118. C. Russell, *Unrevolutionary England*, pp. ix–x.
119. Ibid.
120. J. Black, *A History of the British Isles* (Macmillan, 1996), p. 157.
121. J. Lingard, *History of England*, x, ch. iv, pp. 319–26. Lingard tell us how he got at these sources: 'During the reign of Charles II and James II, the documents the most interesting to Englishmen are the despatches from the French ambassadors and agents, detailing their own proceedings, and the most important events in England and Holland. They have never yet been published . . . Mazure . . . [who] possessed unrestricted access to the archives of the Ministere des Affaires étrangeres de France, transcribed, for the sake of accuracy, every separate piece with his own hand. . . . It will undoubtedly be noticed that . . . I repeatedly quote passages from documents hitherto inedited: and it may with reason be asked from what source I procured them. I answer, from the very transcripts which were made by Mazure himself. After his death his papers came into my possession. . .', ibid., preliminary notice, pp. xi–xii.
122. Ibid., x, p. 330 note 2.
123. See above, p. 73.
124. T. Claydon, *William III and the Godly Revolution* (Cambridge University Press, 1995).
125. G. Jondorf and D.N. Dumville, *France and the British Isles in the Middle Ages and Renaissance* (Boydell Press, 1991).
126. *England in Europe 1066–1453*, ed. N. Saul (Collins and Brown, 1994). This was followed by his *The Oxford Illustrated History of Medieval England* (Oxford University Press, 1997).
127. *England and Normandy in the Middle Ages*, ed. D. Bates and A. Curry (Hambledon Press, 1994).
128. J. Black, *Convergence or Divergence. Britain and the Continent* (Macmillan, 1994).
129. Cf. Adrian Hastings does not accept the idea that 'the nation state is

the only political form available for the modern world', *The Construction of Nationhood*, p. 6.

130. *The British Problem: 1534–1707*, ed. B. Bradshaw and J. Morrill, (Macmillan, 1996), p. 10.

131. Ibid., p. 15, 19.

132. J. Black, *History of the British Isles*, introduction, p. xiii.

133. Ibid.

134. Ibid.

135. Cf. the reaction of one of the most popular daily newspapers in Britain to the Dublin EU Summit meeting's proposals on Euro banknotes in December 1996. A huge front page display: 'Has 1,100 years of our history come to this?', followed by an inside editorial: 'They think they can subvert 1,000 years of history with their pieces of coloured paper. They are mistaken' (*Daily Mail*, 14 December 1996).

CHAPTER VIII

1. Tom Stacey, former chief foreign correspondent for the *Sunday Times*, describes the 'honour in which the essential Western ethic, at best un-Americanised, is secretly held throughout the world', and 'the secret spiritual muscle and objective authority of the West's stubbornly Christ-informed core – that ethic which would and does defend human rights, feed the poor, protect the weak, spread healing medicine, champion nature, challenge its own shibboleths, question itself with daring', against which no opposition 'can logically prevail, or indeed seek to prevail', *The Tablet*, 19 April 1997, pp. 508–9.

2. I am indebted for some of the above material to John Haldane, Professor of Philosophy and Director of the Centre for Philosophy and Public Affairs in the University of St Andrews.

3. See above, p. 237.

4. See R.W. Southern, *Scholastic Humanism and the Unification of Europe. Vol. I*.

5. Cf. Various British governments have 'failed to produce or appropriate an explicit vision of British relations with Europe. . . . We can expect reasonably that the British "play intelligently in Europe". To do this you have to recognise strengths and weaknesses. The language of national greatness precludes this', J. Bulpitt, 'The European Question', *The Ideas That Shaped Post-War Britain* (Fontana Press, 1996), pp. 255–6.

6. H.G. Koenigsberger, *History*, xlix (June 1964), p. 220.

7. George Steiner, *Desert Island Discs*, BBC broadcast, 23 February 1996.

8. Peregrine Worsthorne, *Sunday Telegraph*, 26 February 1967.

9. Editorial, *Daily Mail*, 21 October 1995. Cf. 'Another Surrender to Europe', editorial, 27 December 1995, referring to another decision of the European Court of Human Rights.

10. See above, p. 278 note 64.

11. See L. Colley, *Britons*, introduction, pp. 1–10.
12. Cf. 'the British people . . . and the Conservative rank and file think ultimate virtue resides in sovereignty, independence and self-reliance', Paul Johnson, *Daily Mail*, 27 November 1996.
13. F.M. Powicke, *Ways of Medieval Life and Thought* (Oxford, 1949), p. 129.
14. M.D. Knowles, *Saints and Scholars* (Cambridge, 1962), p. 17.
15. Ibid.
16. See C. Dawson, *Understanding Europe* (Sheed and Ward, 1952), p. 57.
17. G. Holmes, general editor of *Foundations of Modern Britain*, preface, p. ix, to J.A.F. Thompson, *The Transformation of Medieval England* (Longman, 1992). The titles of later volumes in this series tell the story of England's rise and fall: *The Emergence of a Nation State* (A.G. Smith), *The Making of a Great Power* (G. Holmes), and *The Eclipse of a Great Power 1870–1975* (K. Robbins). G. Holmes also observes in this general preface that Britain 'belatedly recognised that the days of self-sufficiency as regards Europe, too, were past', pp. ix–x.
18. R. Pennar Davies, *Presenting Saunders Lewis*, ed. A.R. Jones and G. Thomas (University of Wales Press, 1983), pp. 94–5. Cf. 'Saunders Lewis is quite simply the foremost dramatist to have written in the Welsh language. . . . He may almost be said to have invented a dramatic literature for Welsh-speaking Wales, drawing eclectically upon chiefly European modes', J.P. Clancy, *The Plays of Saunders Lewis* (Christopher Davies Press, Llandybie, 1985, 2 vols), i, p. 7.
19. Cf. 'developments in the European community have heightened perceptions of the value of minority contributions to the ideal of a greater Europe. Present debates over the nature and institutions of self-determination are indication enough that the Welsh will enter the next millennium as conscious as they have ever been of their nationhood and the contribution which it can make in enriching a wider world', G.E. Jones, *Modern Wales* (Cambridge University Press, 2nd edn, 1995), p. 320. Cf. C. Harvey, *Cultural Weapons. Scotland and Survival in the new Europe* (Abacus, Edinburgh, 1992); and M. Hughes, *Divided Ireland. The Roots of the Modern Irish Problem* (University of Wales Press, 1944).
20. See Damian Howard, '1996 and All That: The writing on the wall', *The Tablet*, 17 June 1995, p. 765.
21. Cf. 'Since the late Middle Ages, . . . there has been enough common ground among the different parts of western and central Europe to make it reasonable to see that region of the world as a whole'. This region possessed 'distinctive characteristics', 'In particular, Latin Europe (that is the part of Europe that was originally Roman Catholic . . .) formed a zone where strong, hard features were as important as geographical and cultural contrasts', leading to 'an increasingly homogeneous society'; 'By the fourteenth century, a huge part of Europe, including England, France, Scandinavia, Northern Italy and Spain had come to possess a relatively high degree of cultural

homogeneity', R. Barlett, *The Making of Europe* (Penguin, 1994), pp. 1, 2, 3, 291, 313.

22. 'Developmental' here is in the sense conveyed by J.H. Newman in *An Essay on the Development of Christian Doctrine* (1845). In the 'organic' life of the Church, deeper meanings, implications and insights can be drawn, in an 'evolutionary' process, from the original doctrines; but these later developments cannot contradict original and essential doctrines.

23. Cf. 'If Christianity be a universal religion, suited not to one locality or period, but to all times and places, it cannot but vary in its relations and dealings towards the world around it, that is it will develop', J.H. Newman, *An Essay on the Development of Christian Doctrine*, pp. 73, 140.

24. Cardinal B. Hume, 'Address to the Fifth Composium of European Bishops', *Briefing*, 12 (1982).

25. His first book, *The Making of the Middle Ages* (1951), immediately placed him among the front ranks of historians. In 1970 he produced two major works on *Western Society and the Church in the Middle Ages* and *The Medieval Church as a Social and Political Phenomenon. Medieval Humanism.*

26. R.W. Southern, *Scholastic Humanism and the Unification of Europe Vol. I*, preface, p. v.

27. Ibid., pp. 21–2.

28. Ibid., pp. 133, 305, 310.

29. R. Browning, 'Fra Lippo Lippi', *Men and Women* (1855).

30. *The Thoughts of Leonardo Da Vinci*, followed by an unpublished lecture on Leonardo da Vinci's intelligence, by A.D. Sertilanges, trans. R. Scott Walker (Brochure, Le Clos-Luce, n.d.), pp. 4–5.

31. 'Depth' is Tillich's term for the religious dimension of life which 'gives substance, ultimate meaning, judgment and creative courage to all functions of the human spirit', Paul Tillich, *Theology of Culture*, ed. R.C. Kimball (Oxford University Press, 1964), pp. 143–4.

32. H. Butterfield, *Writings on Christianity and History*, ed. C.T. McIntire (Oxford University Press, 1979), p. 8.

33. Carl J. Jung, *Man And His Symbols* (Aldus Books, 1964), introduction by John Freeman, p. 15. It was to Freeman, in a BBC interview, that Jung said he did not *believe* in God's existence because he *knew* it. Cf. Carl J. Jung, *Modern Man in Search of a Soul* (1933).

34. George Steiner, Salzburg Festival Lecture, 1994. Quoted by Mikulás Teich, 'The Twentieth Century Scientific and Technological Revolution, *History Today*, 46(11), Nov. 1996, p. 33.

35. Mikulás Teich, ibid.

36. Asa Briggs, 'The March of Time', *History Today*, 46(11), Nov. 1996, p. 5.

37. Tony Blair, *Sunday Telegraph Review*, 7 April 1996, p. 1.

38. See above, pp. x–xi, 245.

39. Quoted by A.E. Campbell, review in *Twentieth-Century British History*, ii (No. 2) (1996), pp. 283–4.

40. See D. Howard, '1996 and All That', p. 765.

41. A. Sampson. *The Essential Anatomy of Britain. Democracy in Crisis* (Hodder and Stoughton, 1992), p. 161.

42. Leon Brittan, *Europe. The Europe We Need* (Hamish Hamilton, 1994), p. 22. Subsidiarity was 'enshrined for the first time in treaty form at Maastricht'. Cf. 'subsidiarity is just what Britain needs to escape from over-centralisation at home', A. Sampson, *The Essential Anatomy of Britain*, p. 161.

43. A. Sampson, *The Essential Anatomy of Britain*, p. 161. Cf. 'There is no contradiction between strengthening Europe and forging stronger regional and local units'.

44. Cf. 'Euro-Fear': 'We appear to be one tick of the clock away from losing our sovereignty, our independence and not just 1,000 years of history, but history from when the first man fought to protect this country from an invader', reader's letter, *Daily Mail*, 3 January 1997.

45. A. Sampson, *Essential Anatomy*, p. 161.

46. Ibid., p. 160.

47. S. Weir and K. Boyle, 'Human Rights in the U.K.', *The Political Quarterly*, 68, No. 2 (April–June 1997), introduction to Special Issue, p. 128.

48. A. Sampson, *Essential Anatomy*, p. 159.

49. B. Ward, *The Rich Nations and the Poor Nations* (Norton and Co., New York, 1962), pp. 159, 136.

50. B. Ward, *The Home of Man* (Penguin, 1976), pp. 291–3. Cf. the *Scientist* (15 August 1997) reports that in this age of 'post-modernism' when sceptics have been denying the existence of objective truth, Religion and Science are united in their common stance that there is real and objective truth to be discovered. Powerful forces are bringing Science and Faith closer together. Both the American Assocation for the Advancement of Science and the US National Academy of Science have set projects to promote greater dialogue between religion and science; while the British Assocation for the Advancement of Science discussed 'Religion in an Age of Science', at its conference in September 1997. *Science* reports a willingness now among scientists, to discuss their own religious beliefs.

51. C. Dawson, *Understanding Europe* (Sheed and Ward, 1952), p. 252.

52. Félipe Fernández-Armesto and Derek Wilson, *Reformation: Christianity and the World, 1500–2000* (Bantam Press, 1996), preface, p. ix.

53. Ibid., p. 300.

54. F. Fernandez-Armesto, *Millennium* (Black Swan Press, 1996).

55. Grace Davie, *Religion in Britain since 1945: Believing without Belonging* (Blackwell, 1994).

56. See *Outlines of the 16 Documents: Vatican II*, V.M. Heffernan.

57. See *Peace on Earth. Encyclical Letter of Pope John XXIII*, 'Pacem in Terris', 1963 (CTS, 1965).
58. Ibid., pp. 36–7.
59. Ibid., pp. 34, 37, 39, 40, 50, 24–6. 'In the words of Pius XII: "The calamity of a world war, with the economic and social ruin and the moral excesses and dissolution that accompany it, must not on any account be permitted to engulf the human race for a third time" ', ibid., p. 42.
60. See above, p. 28.
61. R.W. Southern, *Scholastic Humanism*, p. 2.
62. Cf. F. Fernández-Armesto, *History Today*, 46(12), Dec. 1996.
63. Paul Johnson, *Modern Times* (Phoenix Giant Press, 1996), p. 789.
64. N. Dennis, *The Invention of Permanent Poverty* (Institute of Economic Affairs, 1997).
65. Norman Davies, *Europe* (Oxford University Press, 1996), p. 1136.
66. D.W. Urwin, *The Community of Europe: A History of European Integration since 1945* (Longman, 2nd edn, 1995). This is the general picture presented by the book, in the spite of the author's rather discouraging remarks, in this second edition, about the unlikelihood of more integration, in the light of the happenings in 1991–4.
67. Will Hutton, *The State We're In* (Vantage Press, new edn, 1996), p. 710.
68. See above, p. 263. An interesting modern expression of some of these ideas is in *The Personal World: John Macmurray on Self and Society*, selected by Philip Cornford (Floris Books, 1996). Tony Blair has been much influenced by Macmurray's philosophy of society (individuals can develop properly only within properly developed communities) and has written the introduction to this book. The conflict between 'self' and 'society' has been endemic in the conflicting political systems of the modern world. Christian humanism resolves this conflict in a way which is fundamentally important for the world of the new millennium.
69. F. Fernández-Armesto, *Millennium*, p. 710.
70. See above, p. 14.
71. T. Blair, Speech to Labour Party Conference, as new Prime Minister, 1997.
72. Alfred the Great, from an exegetic attached to his translation of Boethius, *De Consulatione Philosophiae*. Boethius was a Christian martyr (525), who wrote this work in prison. Alfred translated it in the 890s. It was translated again by Chaucer (*Boece*) and was one of the most influential books during the medieval period.

AFTERWORD
1. See Angelika Fleckinger & Hubert Steiner, *The Ice-Man* (Folio Verleg Bolzano, Vienna 1998, & South Tyrol Museum of Archaeology), 3rd. ed. 2000.

2. Sir Richard Southern, *Scholastic Humanism and the Unification of Europe*, vol I (1995), vol. 11 (2001) (Blackwell, Oxford). Sir Richard died before he could publish the intended third volume of this fine work.

3. See a range of studies which have appeared at the end of the twentieth century, depicting the tragedies and atrocities of that era. For example, J. Glover (Director of Medical Law & Ethics at King's College, London) *Humanity: a moral history of the twentieth century* (Pimlico, 2000), featuring the disastrous combination of modern technology with the destructive side of human psychology, leading to the horrors of the Ist World War, Stalin, Hitler, Pol Pot, and the bombings of Hamburg and Dresden. Anthony O'Hare (Professor of Philosophy at Bradford), *After Progress: Finding the Old Way forward?* (Bloomsbury, 1999) sees the evil of science in reducing life to triviality and horror. Martin Gilbert, *Challenge to Civilisation: a History of the Twentieth Century, 1952–99* (1999) which is concerned with civil liberties and the ill treatment of racial groups as in apartheid in S. Africa, the persecution of Russian Jews, and the massacre in Tiananmen Square). Andrew Conquest's, *Reflections on a Ravaged Century* (Murray, 1999), is an authoritative critique of Soviet and Nazi ideologies which led to the deaths of millions in Europe. Philip Bobbitt, *The Shield of Achilles: War, Peace and the Course of History* (Allen Lane, 2002) sees the old nation-state about to be overtaken by the market state, adapted to gloablisation. See also, J. Lawrence, *Warrior Race: the British Experience of War from Roman Times to the Present*, (2001). N. Ferguson, *The Pity of War*, (Penguin, 1999).

4. Cf. Article by Robert Kagan (senior associate at the Carnegie Endowment for International Peace), *Daily Telegraph*, 10 Aug. 2002.

5. The best description of this process of 'development' in Christian teaching is to be found in Cardinal John Henry Newman's *Essay on the Development of Christian Doctrine* (1852). He was one of the greatest thinkers in the Catholic Church of the modern era and a precursor of the Second Vatican Council.

6. Sir Con O'Neill, *Britain's Entry into the European Community: Report on the Negotiations, 1970–72* (Frank Cass, 2000). See also Hugo Young, *This Blessed Plot: Britain and Europe from Churchill to Blair* (Macmillan, 1998) – a story of missed opportunities.

7. Roy Jenkins, *Churchill* (Macmillan, Pan Paperback, 2001), pp. 813–18.

8. Ibid., p. 818.

9. Ibid., p. 857.

10. Sir Con O'Neill, Op. Cit.

11. Mr Hugh Gaitskell's speech at the Labour Party Conference, 1962.

12. Mr John Major's speech at the Tory Party Conference, 1996.

13. Michael Heseltine, *The Spectator* (9 Sept. 2000).

14. S. Hartington, *The Clash of Civilisations and the Remaking of World Order* (Simon Schuster, 1996).

15. These are Poland, Hungary, the Czech Republic, Slovakia, Slovenia, Lithuania, Estonia and Latvia.

16. See below, p. 34.

17. See Ambrose Evans-Pritchard, 'Eurofile', *The Daily Telegraph*, 23 Nov. 2002.

18. See J. Nye, *The Paradox of American Power: Why the World's Only Superpower Can't Go It Alone* (Oxford Univ. Press, 2002). Nye sees three layers to global politics. One is *military* (in which America is all-powerful); the second is *economic* (with America, Europe, Japan and China more evenly matched). The third and increasingly important is *transnational* issues such as global warming and international terrorism. It is the third in which America cannot act alone.

19. See Blair's speech to the Confederation of Industry in Bangalore, reported in *The Daily Telegraph*, 5 Jan. 2000.

20. See Blair's speech to the New Labour Party Conference just after his election victory, 30 Sept. 1997; and his speech to the Nigerian Parliament, 7 Feb. 2002.

21. Cf. 'His [Blair's] contemplative Christianity ran deeper and was established earlier than I realized. His adoption of Christian Socialism at Oxford was therefore less of a Damascene conversion and more of a natural progression. Later on when he joined the Labour Party . . .', John Rentoul, *Tony Blair. Prime Minister* (Little Brown & Company, 2001), p.x. Hans Küng offered Blair spiritual guidance, saying that in times of trouble and hours of need, he should seek strength from his deep beliefs. He should pace himself, carry on treading the ethical third way. He should 'stand by his compass . . . In politics we need people with an ethical will'. He recommends to Blair, the hymn written by Cardinal Newman: 'Lead kindly light . . . Give me light for the next step', reported in *Daily Telegraph*, 21 July 2000.

22. Cf. 'he [Gladstone] claimed, and to some extent justified, that religion was more important to him than politics', Roy Jenkins, *Gladstone* (Macmillan, 1995), Preface, p. xvi.

23. Blair's speech to the New Labour Party Conference, 1997.

24. Ibid.

25. Jonathan Sacks named his recent book, *The Dignity of Difference: how to avoid the clash of civilisations* (Continuum, 2002). Cf. Daniel Barenboim, the celebrated Jewish composer and conductor: 'Ariel Sharon is a danger to his homeland', *The Guardian*, 6 Sept. 2002. Cf. his interesting approach to 'pluralism': 'Human beings have not only the possibility, but almost the duty – yes, the duty! – to acquire multiple identities . . . That's what globalisation means at its most positive. That you can feel French when you play Debussy, that you feel German when you play Wagner. You do not have to be one

thing', 'Wake up Israel', Barenboim speaking to interviewer in *The Guardian*, 6 Sept. 2002.

26. Kofi Annan's remark during the Bosnian war. Cf. Francis Cardinal Arinze, *Religions for Peace: a call for solidarity to the religions of the world* (Darton, Longman & Todd, 2001). It would be helpful, perhaps if all religions recognized that God is greater than any religion and is not confined to any idea or institution, even when He is its authentic source. The Spirit of God is free to 'blow where It wills'.

27. See John Bowden, 'The Priest behind the Scene', *The Tablet* Nov. 2002. pp. 10–11. Here Bowden describes the great influence exercised by Küng at the Second Vatican Council. This Vatican Council and the *Evangelii Nuntiandi* of Paul VI required Christians to 'learn to respect and welcome all that is good and holy' in other religions; and of the 'seeds of the Word' and 'ray of Truth which enlightens everyone' to be found in the various religions. All this without denying for a moment the Christian belief in the authentic revelation of God to mankind through the Scriptures and the Church. Cf. 'we may achieve a global civilization in which values from the great traditions are woven together in a glittering net. Perhaps it will turn out like the jewel net of Indra, of which Hus-yen so elequently speaks: each stone reflecting every other'. Ninian Smart, *The World's Religions* (Cambridge Univ. Press, 1995 reprint) p. 561.

28. Blair's Chicago speech before the intervention of the allies in Kosovo against the 'ethnic cleansing' of Muslims. Blair's belief in the need for a strong global ethic to accompany the new global economy, is a major theme in his own speeches. Cf. 'it is time to sacrifice pride, arrogance, lust for power and extremism for the sake of Justice and permanent peace for all of Abraham's grandchildren', Dr. Suheil Aranki, letter to *The Daily Telegraph*, 23 Feb. 2002.

29. Blair's speech to the World Economic Forum in Davos, Switzerland, 28 Jan. 2000, reported in *The Daily Telegraph*, 29 Jan. 2000.

30. Blair's speech in Germany, 30 June, 2000, reported in *The Daily Telegraph*, 1 July, 2000.

31. Ibid.

32. Reported in *The Daily Telegraph*, 1 July, 2000.

33. Schwäb's comments after Blair's speech in Switzerland, 28 Jan. 2000, reported in *The Daily Telegraph*, 29 Jan. 2000.

34. 'You are, for me, a symbol of value-based leadership, a man who knows the difference between right and wrong and a man who is prepared to stand up for what you believe is right'. Ibid.

35. Blair's speech to the joint meeting of the Nigerian Senate and the House of Representatives, 7 Feb. 2002, reported in *The Daily Telegraph*, 8 Feb. 2002.

36. Ibid.

37. Ibid.

38. Ibid.
39. Ibid.
40. Michael Alridge, 20 June, 2002, *Today Programme*, BBC Radio 4, reporting on position in Afghanistan. The Afghans have also found expression again for their love of music and singing, repressed by the Taliban.
41. Britain had acceeded to the International Covention Against Torture in 1984.
42. See documentation in *The Tablet*, 12 Dec. 1998.
43. See Cherie Blair and Matriz Chambers, 'Human Rights Act' in *The Daily Telegraph*, 7 Aug. 2000.
44. See above p. 114–16.
45. For example, since these rights – including the right to life itself – belong inalienably to all human beings, it is vitally important to make the most informed decisions – in the light of all available knowledge – as to exactly when this life begins and ends.
46. All the 15 countries of the European Union (except Denmark, Sweden and Britain) adopted the single currency in Jan. 2001.
47. Blair's speech in Edinburgh, May, 2001.
48. Ibid.
49. Ibid.
50. Blair's speech to the New Labour Party Conference, Blackpool, October, 2002.
51. Ibid.
52. Cf. 'Europe has no competition as a world shaper', M. Roberts, *History of the World* (Penguin ed. 1997); Cf. 'The impact of the History of the World (Penguin ed. 1997); Cf. 'The impact of the West on the rest of the world is a central theme of world history in the last two centuries', P. Curtin, *The World and the West* (Cambridge Univ. Press, paperback ed. 2002), p. vii.
53. See John Dicks (American staff member of the European Centre for Ethics in the University of Leuven, Belgium). 'Shock to the American soul', *The Tablet*, 13th Oct. 2001, p. 1446. Cf. C. Longley, *Chosen People. Anglo-American Myth and Reality* (Hodder & Staughton, 2002).
54. This, of course, is one of the main themes of the author's *The English Nation: The Great Myth* (Sutton, 3rd ed. 2003).
55. Al Gore's speech, Sept. 2002, reported in the *South Wales Evening Post*, 12 Sept. 2002.
56. Letter of Cardinal Hume to Tony Blair, reported in *The Tablet*, 22 Nov. 1997, p. 5.
57. He is at the moment debarred from being an MP, having been convicted for reading a 'seditious' poem in which he compared minarets with bayonets. He therefore has to rule, initially, through a proxy prime minister.
58. See Rosemary Richter, 'Danger of Theocracies', *The Times*, 30 July

2002. She emphasizes the need for legal, political, economic, social, educational and technological reform, without which 'the Arab countries will not make it'. Cf. Scott Thomas, Bath University lecturer in International Relations, 'Can the West and Islam live together', *The Tablet*, 6 Oct. 2001. He recognizes that 'there may be religious resources . . . for international order . . . the impact of religion and culture in international politics is distorted when religion is invented by social theory as a set of privately held doctrines of beliefs . . . and is applied to societies which have not yet made, or are struggling to make - as part of the clash within civilisations - this kind of social transition'. For the great majority of people in the world: 'Their experience of the moral life is rooted in the virtues, social practices and traditions of their communities, however imperfectly they live this out. This is where general dialogue between civilisations can begin', Ibid.

59. See Ambrose Evans-Pritchard, '"Asiatic"' Turkey is threat to EU, warns Giscard, *The Daily Telegraph*, 9 Nov. 2002, p. 23.

60. Ibid.

61. Ibid.

62. Russia has made progress. Boris Yeltsin became its first ever directly elected leader in 1991 and Russia has become a member of NATO and the human right of religious worship has been partially accepted. It recognizes the need for change and development. In China during the rule of Jiang Zemin, the condemnation of private ownership or control of land or indstury has gone; and that against religion only partly relaxed. They fall badly behind in terms of internationally-accepted human rights and there is a huge problem of corruption. The voluntary retirement of Jiang Zemin in Nov. 2002 and the methodical nature of his replacement by his deputy, the much younger Hu Jintao (59 years old) are clear indications of the way in which China is changing.

63. Robin Cooke, Speech to the Royal Institute for International Affairs in London, reported in *The Daily Telegraph*, 29 Jan. 2000.

64. See above, p. 321. I think Bill Clinton paid Blair a sincere compliment in his Speech to the New Labour Party Conference, October 2002, when he said quite simply: 'Thank you for giving Tony Blair to Britain and to the World'.

65. Cf. 'Mankind is simply going to destroy itself unless it succeeds in growing together into something like a single family', Arnold Toynbee, *A Study of History*; (Oxford Univ. Press and Thames & Hudson Ltd., 1972).

Manuscript Sources

In the history of historical writing, the primary sources will be mainly the works of historians, written during the periods with which we are concerned. Other background books and printed collections of documents are also essential.

I have made extensive use of footnotes which act as a 'running' bibliography, so that a further bibliographical section would be superfluous. It may well be useful for some readers, however, if I include here a list of the main manuscript sources, related to the research behind this study, some of which are referred to in the text.

1. The Bodleian Library Oxford

Add. D. 18 (Burnet's History of My Own Time – Autograph 1)

Ballard 3 (92 Original Letters Wake to Charlett).

Ballard 5 (including letters from Givson to Charlett).

Ballard 15 (Strype to Charlett – letters).

Ballard 18 (Crowne Willis to Charlett – letters).

Ballard 41 (194 Original letters from Thomas Hearne, William Brome and Thomas Rawlinson, to George Ballard).

Eng. Hist. D. 1 (Non-Jurors' Papers – transcripts).

Eng. misc. c. 75 (Thomas Hearne's letters).

Eng. misc. c. 88 (Hearne's letters to Constable &c. transcripts).

Eng. misc. e. 49 (Hearne's Catalogue of his Library).

Eng. Th: c. 22 (Dr. Geo: Hickes: Reply to Vindication of Bishop of St Asaph's Sermons).

Hearne's Diaries (vols 5, 44, 48, 52, 56, 58, 61, 63, 71, 72, 102, 104, 106, 112, 114, 115, 122, 124, 142, 174).

Ms. Musaeo 107 (Sir Henry Spelman's 'Original of the Law Terms'").

Rawlinson B. 180 (Hearne's Prefaces).

Rawlinson B. 263 (Collections given to Hearne by Browne Willis).

Rawlinson B. 264 (Willis's Mitred Abbies, with some correction by Hearne).

Rawlinson D. 1002 (Life of Thomas Hearne).

Rawlinson D. 1166 (Transcripts of Hearne's letters).

Rawlinson J. fol. 8 (Rawlinson's Collections for Cambridge Writers).

Rawlinson Letters 8 (letters to Hearne).

Rawlinson Letters 22 (Thomas Baker to Hearne – 93 letters).

Rawlinson Letters 23 (177 letters. Baker to Hearne).

Rawlinson Letters 26 (including letters from George Hearne to his son, Thomas).

Rawlinson Letters 27A (incl. letters from Browne Willis to Hearne).

Rawlinson Letters 39 (Mostly transcripts of Hearne's letters, including some originals).

Rawlinson Letters 89 (including a letter from Spelman to Ussher).

Rawlinson Letters 107 (including letters from Thomas Baker to Rawlinson).

Rawlinson Letters 110 (Drafts of letters from Hearne).

Smith 5, 9, 14, 16 (including letters exchanged between Dom Jean Mabillon and Edward Bernard).

Smith 47 (including letters from Thomas Baker to Smith).

Smith 127 (Smith's letters to Hearne).

Willis 35 (Miscellaneous Collections For the Province of York).

Willis 37 (Collections for the Cathedral & Diocese of St David's).

Willis 38 (Collections for Cathedrals & Dioceses).

Willis 39 (Collections for the Cathedral & Diocese of Lincoln).

Willis 44 (Collections relating to English Monasteries).

Willis 45 (Collections for the Cathedrals and Dioceses of Ely, Oxford & Peterborough).

Willis 49 (Notes of Leases of Abbey & Crown Lands: Temp. R. Eliz.).

Willis 76 (Collections for the Cathedrals & Dioceses of Ely, Oxford, Bristol, Worcester & Peterborough).

II. Cambridge University Library

(Add. = Additional Manuscripts)

Add. 4022 (Some Remarks upon Bishop Burnet's *History of his own Times* by William Sherwin, 1725).

Add. 4479 (Sir Henry Ellis: Observations upon Saxon Literaure, 1810).

Add. 4481 (Sir Henry Ellis: Notes on Anglo-Saxon Scholars).

Add. 4863 (box full of slips of papers in Lord Acton's own hand).

Baker, Thomas (Marginal notes on his copy of G. Burnet's *History of the Reformation.*

Baker Collection, Vol. 27. Mm. I. 38. Vol. 28. Mm. I. 39; Vol. 29. Mm. I. 40; Vol. 30, Mm. I. 41; Vol. 31. Mm. I. 42; Vol. 32, Mm. I. 43; Vol. 33, Mm. I. 44; Vol. 34, Mm. I. 45; Vol. 35, Mm. I. 46; Vol. 36, Mm. I. 47; Vol. 37, Mm. I. 48; Vol. 38, Mm. I. 49; Vol. 39, Mm. I. 50; Vol. 42, Mm. I. 53. Vols. A, B, C.

Baumgarten papers: 8 (vols of Strype Correspondence). 9 (Strype Correspondence, Baker Papers part I). 10 (Strype Correspondence, Baker Papers, Part II).

Dd. 3. 12 (Original letters of Sir Henry Spelman II).

Dd. 3. 64 (Folio book of Original Letters written during the seventeenth century).

Dd. 8. 52 (Thomas Barlow, Bishop of Lincoln, Queen's College, Oxford, Paper MS. volume of 43 pages on 'The English Historians' dated 30 October 1656).

Mm. 2. 25 (ff. 166–173 – materials on the Dissolution of Religious Houses).

Mm. vi. 49 (Collection of Letters bound in a folio volume: 'The Correspondence of the Rev. John Strype, 1679–1721).

III. St John's College Library, Cambridge

'Life of Baker' – Collections. 54.0.

Letter – Thomas Baker to Hon. John Anstis, Garter Principal King of Armsk, 15 July 1700.

Photograph of a letter – Gilbert Burnet to Thomas Baker, Windsor Castle 23 July, 1700.

(These two letters, in individual envelopes, are among other letters deposited in cardboard boxes. The classmark of the boxes is W.I, and the letters are indexed under authors).

IV. Corpus Christi College Library, Cambridge

MS. 102, f. 271 'Cogitationes Lutheri de sacramento, *Scriptae* manu *propria*' (Thoughts of Luther on the Sacrament – in his own hand).

MANUSCRIPT SOURCES

V. British Museum Library

(Add. = Additional manuscripts)

Add. 5820, 5829, 5832, 5833, 5840, 5841, 5845, 5853, 5860 (Cole Collections).

Add. 6209 (Letters of Learned Men to Professor Ward – ff. 59–60, Baker to Ward).

Add. 22596 (Huddesford's Lives of A. Wood, Hearne and Lister).

Add. 25384 (Letters of Sir Henry Spelman, 1611–1683).

Add. 34599 (Sir Henry Spelman's Correspondence I – 1600–1633).

Add. 34600 (Sir Henry Spelman's Correspondence II – 1634–1640).

Add. 20763, folio 70 (This is a letter of Lingard).

Hargrave 15932 (Autographs Connected with Oxfordshire – f.2, Thomas Tanner to Browne Willis).

Hargrave 15935 (Original letters of Browne Willis to Ducarel).

Harley 3777 (Letters: Baker to H. Wanley).

Harley 3780 (Letter to H. Wanley 1692–1725, vol. iv).

Harley 7048 (Thomas Baker's Collections, vol. xxi).

Lansdowne 1024 (Bishop Kennett's Collections, vol. xxi).

Sloane 1008 (Dr. E. Borlase – Irish Rebellion Papers, 1608–1682, ff. 291, 295, letters of Burnet).

Sloane 1710 (ff. 219, 221, 223 – Burnet's letters).

Sloane 2251 (Letters and Papers of F. Glisson – f. 19, on R. Brady).

Sloane 3299 (Original letters, Warrants etc, – f. 150, Burnet).

Sloane 4042 (Original letters to Sir Hans Sloane, vol. vii).

Sloane 4043 (Original letters to Sir Hans Sloane, vol. ix).

Sloane 4044 (Original letters to Sir Hans Sloane, vol. ix).

Sloane 4045 (Original letters to Sir Hans Sloane, vol. x).

VI. Ushaw College Library (near Durham)

File A.1 is marked: 'Lingard to Canon Walker of Scarborough, April i, 1837–Dec. 28 U841'. These are originals.

File A.2 continues this correspondence from 1 Jan. 1842 to 26 Dec. 1845. These are originals.

Fiel A.3 continues this correspondence from 2 Jan. 1846 to 18 Oct. 1850. These are originals.

File A.4 is a box marked 'Lingard Transcripts and Gradwell Correspondence'. These are transcripts.

File Ab is marked 'Lingard to Newsham, 1837–50' These are originals.

File B.3 is marked 'Lingard to Mawman, 1818–27'. These are originals.

File B.4 is marked 'Lingard to Tate'. These are originals.

File B.10 is marked 'Lingard Transcripts'.

File B.11 is marked 'Lingard Transcripts'. Includes a section of transcripts from the archives of the English Jesuit Province. Also, letters to Husenbeth.

File marked: 'Lingard to Various Others 1815–51'. Originals.

File marked: 'Lingard Correspondence F–M, 1805–48'. Originals.

File marked: 'Lingard Correspondence N–Y, 1806–51'. Originals.

Folder 6 is marked: 'Lingard to Rev. Canon Walker of Scarborough, June 1840–Dec. 1849'. Originals.

Folder 7 is marked: 'Lingard to Walker Jan. 12, 1850–April 25, 1851'. Originals.

Folder 8: contains miscellaneous letters.

Folder marked: 'Wiseman Papers, 772–833'. Originals.

The books of transcripts are kept apart from the files and folders, in a special part of the library. They were presented to the college by Joseph Gillow and are sometimes referred to as the 'Gillow Transcripts'.

Three books are marked: 'Correspondence between the Rev'd Dr. Lingard and The Rev'd G. Oliver – Code letter O.

Other books are marked: 'Lingard's letters and C. Butler's': 'Correspondence of Rev. John J. Lingard – Miscellaneous': 'The Rev. J. Lingard's Journal on a tour to Rome and Naples in the summer of 1817'.

There is also a notebook marked: 'Lingard Notes. W.W. St Peter's Lancaster.

Index

Notes: **Bold** page numbers indicate major entries. Numbers in brackets indicate note numbers.

INDEX